Single Case Research Methodology

The fourth edition of this bestselling text provides a comprehensive discussion of single case research methodology, with updated information throughout the book, including new content on design types, design selection, social validity, fidelity, generality, visual analysis, and writing. Students, researchers, and practitioners can use this detailed reference tool to conduct single case research design studies; interpret findings of single case design studies; and write proposals, manuscripts, or systematic reviews of single case methodology research. The new text features updates relevant to contemporary guidelines about single case research and includes examples of recent and historical studies in education and behavioral sciences.

Jennifer R. Ledford is an Associate Professor in the Department of Special Education at Vanderbilt University.

David L. Gast is Professor Emeritus of Special Education in the Department of Communication Sciences and Special Education at the University of Georgia.

Single Case Research Methodology

Applications in Special Education and
Behavioral Sciences

Fourth Edition

Edited by Jennifer R. Ledford and David L. Gast

NEW YORK AND LONDON

Designed cover Image: Donny DBM/shutterstock

Fourth edition published 2024
by Routledge
605 Third Avenue, New York, NY 10158

and by Routledge
4 Park Square, Milton Park, Abingdon, Oxon, OX14 4RN

Routledge is an imprint of the Taylor & Francis Group, an informa business

© 2024 selection and editorial matter, Jennifer R. Ledford and David L. Gast; individual chapters, the contributors

The right of Jennifer R. Ledford and David L. Gast to be identified as the authors of the editorial material, and of the authors for their individual chapters, has been asserted in accordance with sections 77 and 78 of the Copyright, Designs and Patents Act 1988.

All rights reserved. No part of this book may be reprinted or reproduced or utilised in any form or by any electronic, mechanical, or other means, now known or hereafter invented, including photocopying and recording, or in any information storage or retrieval system, without permission in writing from the publishers.

Trademark notice: Product or corporate names may be trademarks or registered trademarks, and are used only for identification and explanation without intent to infringe.

First edition published by Taylor & Francis 2009
Third edition published by Routledge 2018

Library of Congress Cataloging-in-Publication Data
Names: Ledford, Jennifer R., editor. | Gast, David L., editor.
Title: Single case research methodology : applications in special education and behavioral sciences / edited by Jennifer R. Ledford and David L. Gast.
Description: Fourth edition. | New York, NY : Routledge, 2024. | Includes bibliographical references and index.
Identifiers: LCCN 2023053818 | ISBN 9781032279312 (hardback) | ISBN 9781032265810 (paperback) | ISBN 9781003294726 (ebook)
Subjects: LCSH: Single subject research. | Psychology--Research. | Educational psychology--Research.
Classification: LCC BF76.6.S56 G37 2024 | DDC 300.72/1--dc23/eng/20240109
LC record available at https://lccn.loc.gov/2023053818

ISBN: 978-1-032-27931-2 (hbk)
ISBN: 978-1-032-26581-0 (pbk)
ISBN: 978-1-003-29472-6 (ebk)

DOI: 10.4324/9781003294726

Typeset in Minion
by SPi Technologies India Pvt Ltd (Straive)

Every effort has been made to contact copyright-holders. Please advise the publisher of any errors or omissions, and these will be corrected in subsequent editions.

Contents

Preface ix
Author Bios xi

SECTION 1 INTRODUCTION TO RESEARCH AND MEASUREMENT   1

1 Research Approaches   3
DAVID L. GAST AND JENNIFER R. LEDFORD
   Callout
   1.1 Questions for Scientist-Practitioners   5

2 External Validity and Generalizable Knowledge   15
JOSEPH M. LAMBERT, JENNIFER R. LEDFORD, TARA FAHMIE, AND DAVID L. GAST

3 Establishing Internal Validity via Within-Study Replication   28
JENNIFER R. LEDFORD AND KEVIN M. AYRES
   Callout
   3.1 A Note on Terminology   30

4 Selection, Characterization, and Measurement of Dependent Variables   43
JENNIFER R. LEDFORD, JUSTIN D. LANE, AND BLAIR P. LLOYD
   Callout
   4.1 A Commentary on Why Interval Systems are Used Despite Evidence of Inaccuracy   62

5 Reliability and Validity of Dependent Variables   69
JENNIFER R. LEDFORD AND JUSTIN D. LANE

6 Development and Measurement of Independent Variables   83
ERIN E. BARTON AND JENNIFER R. LEDFORD

7 Measuring Generality and Social Validity in Single Case Research   96
JOSEPH M. LAMBERT, HEDDA MEADAN-KAPLANSKY, AND
JENNIFER R. LEDFORD
    Callout
    7.1   Labeling Generalization and Maintenance Conditions   103

8 Data Representation and Performance Characteristics   118
AMY D. SPRIGGS, JUSTIN D. LANE, AND DAVID L. GAST
    Callouts
    8.1   What are the Basic Components of Graphs?   120
    8.2   Does the X-axis Actually Depict Time?   123
    8.3   When Should I Graph My Data?   127

SECTION 2   SINGLE CASE DESIGNS   135

9 Conducting Studies Using Sequential Introduction and Withdrawal of Conditions   137
JENNIFER R. LEDFORD AND KATHLEEN N. TUCK
    Callouts
    9.1   Baseline, Business-As-Usual, and Treatment Conditions   139
    9.2   Applied Example of Withdrawal Design   143
    9.3   Applied Example of Reversal Design   146
    9.4   Applied Example of Multitreatment Design   149
    9.5   Applied Example of Changing Criterion Design   156

10 Analyzing Data from Studies Using Sequential Introduction and Withdrawal of Conditions   161
JENNIFER R. LEDFORD AND KATIE WOLFE
    Callouts
    10.1   Should I Include Extra Phases to Establish Non-Effects?   164
    10.2   Reliability of Visual Analysis   170
    10.3   Applied Example of Withdrawal Design   173
    10.4   Applied Example of Reversal Design   174
    10.5   Applied Example of Multitreatment Design   175
    10.6   Applied Example of Changing Criterion Design   176

11 Conducting Studies Using Time-Lagged Condition Ordering   179
JENNIFER R. LEDFORD AND KATHLEEN N. TUCK

Callouts
- 11.1 Selecting Intervention Targets — 183
- 11.2 How Rigorous are Nonconcurrent MB Designs? — 185
- 11.3 Applied Example of Multiple Baseline Across Participants Design — 188
- 11.4 Applied Example of Multiple Baseline Across Behaviors Design — 189
- 11.5 Applied Example of a Multiple Probe Across Behaviors Design (Days Variation) — 193
- 11.6 Applied Example of a Multiple Probe Across Participants Design (Days Variation) — 196
- 11.7 How do I Choose Between Multiple Baseline and Multiple Probe Design Variations? — 199

12 Analyzing Data from Studies Using Time-Lagged Conditions — 204
JENNIFER R. LEDFORD AND JOSEPH M. LAMBERT

Callouts
- 12.1 Masked Visual Analysis — 209
- 12.2 Baseline Lengths: How Different is Different Enough? — 210
- 12.3 Inconsistent Inter-Participant Replication in Single Case Design Studies — 212
- 12.4 Applied Example of Multiple Baseline Across Participants Design — 215
- 12.5 Applied Example of Multiple Baseline Across Behaviors Design — 216
- 12.6 Applied Example of a Multiple Probe Across Behaviors Design (Days Variation) — 218
- 12.7 Applied Example of a Multiple Probe Across Participants Design (Days Variation) — 219

13 Conducting Studies Using Rapid Iterative Alternation of Conditions — 223
KATHRYN M. BAILEY, NATALIE S. PAK, AND JENNIFER R. LEDFORD

Callouts
- 13.1 What's in a Name? Multielement versus Alternating Treatments Designs — 226
- 13.2 Applied Example of ME-ATD — 229
- 13.3 Why do You Need Multiple Behavior Sets for AATDs But Not ME-ATDs? — 235
- 13.4 Applied Example of AATD — 237
- 13.5 Applied Example of Repeated Acquisition Design — 238
- 13.6 Applied Example of Simultaneous Treatments Procedure — 243

14 Analyzing Data from Studies Using Rapid Iterative Alternation — 247
JENNIFER R. LEDFORD, KATHRYN M. BAILEY, AND NATALIE S. PAK

Callouts
- 14.1 Applied Example of ME-ATD — 251
- 14.2 Applied Example of AATD — 252
- 14.3 Applied Example of Repeated Acquisition Design — 253

15 Selecting and Combining Single Case Designs — 262
JENNIFER R. LEDFORD AND KATHLEEN N. TUCK

SECTION 3 ETHICS, RIGOR, AND WRITING — 275

16 Ethical Principles and Practices in Research — 277
JENNIFER R. LEDFORD, JUSTIN D. LANE, AND DAVID L. GAST

17 Evaluating Single Case Research — 292
JENNIFER R. LEDFORD, JUSTIN D. LANE, AND ROBYN TATE

18 Writing Research Proposals and Empirical Reports — 307
BLAIR P. LLOYD AND KATHLEEN LYNNE LANE
  Callouts
  18.1 Making Sense of Replications — 310
  18.2 Classifying Research Questions from the Single Case Literature — 313

19 Conducting Systematic Reviews and Syntheses — 328
KATHLEEN LYNNE LANE, ERIC ALAN COMMON, BLAIR P. LLOYD, AND JENNIFER R. LEDFORD
  Callout
  19.1 Literature Review for Informing Proposals and Reports vs. Stand-Alone Studies: What's the Difference? — 329

Index — *352*

Preface

This 4th edition of *Single Case Research Methodology* was edited to include information regarding contemporary developments in single case design, while retaining an emphasis on lessons learned from more than 50 years of work by early single case research scholars, including the work of Dr. David Gast, the driving force behind this text (first published in 2010) and its predecessor, *Single Subject Research in Special Education* (along with Dr. James Tawney, 1984). His work began at the University of Kansas Department of Human Development and Family Life, where he worked among some of the preeminent early behavioral researchers, including Drs. Joseph Spradlin, Sebastian Striefel, James Sherman, Donald Baer, and Montrose Wolf. He continued the mentorship model, in which professors worked closely alongside graduate students to conduct meaningful applied research, at the University of Kentucky (1975–1989) and then the University of Georgia (1990–2016), where we met and I conducted my first research synthesis and single case experimental design study. It was here first, and then at Vanderbilt University, where I worked with Dr. Mark Wolery, where I was taught the intricacies and importance of single case research design for researchers and practitioners. I continue to be humbled and excited to work with and in the shadow of so many great single case methodology researchers and to help share what I've learned with the next generation of single case scholars.

Our goal in editing this edition, as with the previous editions, is to present a thorough, technically sound, user-friendly, and comprehensive discussion of single case research methodology. We intend for this book to serve as a detailed reference tool for students, researchers, and practitioners who intend to conduct single case studies; interpret findings of these studies; or write proposals, manuscripts, or reviews of single case research. We expect readers will come from a variety of disciplines in social, educational, and behavioral science including special and general education; school, child, clinical, and neuropsychology; speech, occupational, recreation, and physical therapy; and social work. In the book, we present a variety of single case research studies with a wide range of participants, for a range of purposes, in various settings. As in previous editions, much of the work originates in the fields of special education and behavior analysis, although, increasingly, other fields are also represented (e.g., school psychology, speech language pathology).

The organization of this edition is somewhat different from previous editions, with 19 chapters instead of the traditional 14. The biggest organizational departure from previous editions is that we discuss research designs according to three primary condition ordering types (sequential introduction and withdrawal, time lagged, and rapid iterative alternation) and have one chapter dedicated to the analysis of each primary type. We added content about generality, validity, fidelity, and choosing design types. We expanded content related to writing about single case design, including one chapter on writing proposals and reports and a second dedicated to writing systematic reviews. The guidelines presented in this text are intended to assist you in the design, analysis, implementation, and dissemination of meaningful and rigorous single case research. We hope this text helps you to conduct work that matters to you and provides meaningful information to move your field forward—good luck!

Jennifer R. Ledford

Author Bios

Jennifer R. Ledford is Assistant Professor at Vanderbilt University. She was introduced to single case design by Dr. David Gast at the University of Georgia and was further mentored by Dr. Mark Wolery during her doctoral program at Vanderbilt University. Her research interests include improving the use and synthesis of single case design research and instructional practices for young children with disabilities in classroom settings. She urges single case researchers to remember that you cannot answer all the interesting questions in a single study—ask and answer one question well and you'll have done a service to the field.

David L. Gast is Professor Emeritus at the University of Georgia. He earned his doctorate from the University of Kansas in 1975. Prior to joining the faculty at the University of Georgia he collaborated extensively with Dr. Mark Wolery at the University of Kentucky (1975–1989). His research interests include use of errorless instructional strategies and use of single case experimental designs to evaluate clinical and educational practices. Most of his studies used multiple probe designs across behaviors because of their practicality when conducting research in applied settings. With this and other single case experimental designs, the effectiveness of an intervention can be determined early in the study by monitoring data trends and, if necessary, making modifications to the independent variable to achieve the educational or clinical objective.

Kevin M. Ayres is Professor at the University of Georgia where he also received his doctoral degree. He was introduced to single case design by Dr. David Gast at the University of Georgia. Dr. Ayres's current research interests primarily include focus on evaluations of behavior analytic practices in classroom contexts as well as evaluating parameters of reinforcement as they relate to response allocation. He likes to remind his students that experiments require careful and thoughtful choices that are steered by a mix of experience and a risk reward calculus. In the end, even if the experiment does not "work," a good scientist still learns something.

Kathryn M. Bailey is a doctoral student in Special Education at Vanderbilt University. She was mentored in single case design by her advisors, Joseph Lambert and Ann Kaiser, during her master's and doctoral program. Kathryn's research interests include the relations between language and behavioral development, language intervention for children with disabilities, and caregiver-mediated interventions. Her favorite part of single case design is the ongoing process of blending scientific rigor with practical considerations for children with disabilities and their caregivers.

Erin E. Barton is the owner and Lead Consultant at Barton Consulting, LLC. She received her doctoral degree from Vanderbilt University. Mark Wolery was her advisor and introduced her to single case design. Her research interests include identifying practices that support young children's full participation in the settings in which they live and play. Her favorite aspect of conducting single case research is the dynamic nature of the designs.

Eric Alan Common is Associate Professor at the University of Michigan-Flint. He received his doctoral degree from the University of Kansas. His research focuses on social-emotional and behavior preventive and intervention in educational settings delivered through Comprehensive, Integrated, Three-Tiered (Ci3T) Models of Prevention and school-based applied behavior analysis. His favorite single case design is the changing criterion design because he finds the research questions and procedures innovative, inherently humanistic, and socially just.

Tara Fahmie is Associate Professor at the University of Nebraska Medical Center. She received her doctoral degree from the University of Florida and became passionate about single case design under the teachings and mentorship of Drs. Hank Pennypacker, Gregory Hanley, and Brian Iwata, among others. Her research interests include the prevention, assessment, and treatment of severe problem behavior in individuals with intellectual and developmental disabilities. Her two favorite things about single case design are that it promotes an understanding of individual variation and allows moment-to-moment decision making in service of personalized goals.

Joseph M. Lambert is Assistant Professor in the Department of Special Education at Vanderbilt University. He received his doctoral degree from Utah State University and was introduced to single case design by Drs. Bill Ahearn and Sarah Bloom. His research interests include practitioner training, functional analysis, function-based interventions, and environmental factors that influence the maintenance of these interventions. His favorite single case design is the multielement-alternating treatments design (ME-ATD) because of its efficiency. His favorite part of conducting single case design is the curiosity it requires. Specifically, the process of contemplating why people do what they do.

Justin D. Lane is Associate Professor of Special Education at the University of Kentucky. Mark Wolery introduced him to single case design at Vanderbilt University and later David Gast at the University of Georgia. His research interests include evaluating and refining interventions for young children with complex communication needs and coaching parents and educators to embed naturalistic language interventions in play. His advice for students planning a single case design study is to remember the saying, "Clear is kind." That is, students should focus on clearly describing their amazing ideas so others can learn from and replicate their work with precision.

Kathleen Lynne Lane is a Roy A. Roberts Distinguished Professor in the Department of Special Education at the University of Kansas and Associate Vice Chancellor for Research. She earned her doctoral degree from University of California, Riverside. Her research interests focus on designing, implementing, and evaluating Comprehensive, Integrated, Three-tiered (Ci3T) models of prevention to (a) prevent the development of learning, behavior, and social and emotional well-being challenges and (b) respond to existing instances, with an emphasis on systematic screening. She appreciates the beauty of single case research design: The rigor, flexibility, and transparency.

Blair P. Lloyd is Associate Professor of Special Education at Peabody College, Vanderbilt University (where she also received her doctoral degree). Her research interests include school-based behavioral assessment and intervention methods for students with emotional/behavioral disorders; the intersection of Applied Behavior Analysis and School Mental Health; and issues in observational measurement. Blair's favorite part of single case research is its emphasis on transparent visual data display—and how one well-constructed graph can tell the story of an experiment from beginning to end.

Hedda Meadan-Kaplansky is the Margaret Valpey Professor in the Department of Special Education and Health Innovation Professor in the Carle Illinois College of Medicine at the University of Illinois Urbana Champaign. She received her doctoral degree from the University of Illinois. Her research and scholarship address the social communication behavior of young children with disabilities, including design and testing of interventions to enhance children's communicative functioning and caregivers' and professionals' use of recommended practices. A word of advice she would give students planning single case design study is to give special attention to and assess, through multiple methods and sources, the social validity of their intervention.

Natalie S. Pak is an Assistant Professor in the Department of Communication Sciences and Disorders at the University of South Florida. She received her doctoral degree from Vanderbilt University. Her research interests include family-centered early language interventions for children who are dual language learners and/or who use augmentative and alternative communication. Her favorite part of single case design research is the ability to see the data over time for every participant.

Amy D. Spriggs is Associate Professor at the University of Kentucky. She received her doctoral degree from University of Georgia where she was introduced to single case design by David Gast. Her research interests include using everyday technology to increase independence in individuals with significant support needs, promoting generalization, empirically evaluating generalization, and evaluating the rigor of single case research. A word of advice she would give to students planning a single case design study is to ask questions. This is a collaborative field and two heads are always better than one!

Robyn Tate is Emeritus Professor at the University of Sydney, Australia. She received her doctoral degree from the University of Newcastle, Australia. Her research interests include the methodology of single case designs and evidence-based clinical practice in people with neurological conditions. Her favorite single case design is probably the concurrent multiple-baseline design across behaviors/settings because it is appropriate for both withdrawable and non-withdrawable interventions and more feasible in the clinical setting than concurrent designs. A word of advice she would give to students planning a single case design is to use field notes at the implementation stage to document unforeseen events that might influence outcomes.

Kathleen N. Tuck is Assistant Professor of Special Education at the University of Kansas. She received her doctoral degree from Vanderbilt University. Her research interests include supporting educator implementation of evidence-based instructional practices to promote the engagement of children with language and behavioral support needs in inclusive classrooms and enhancing the methods and measurement of single case research design studies and syntheses. Her favorite part of conducting single case design research is the ability to rigorously and flexibly adapt interventions and designs based on child or educator preferences and experiences.

Katie Wolfe is Associate Professor at University of South Carolina. She received her doctoral degree from Utah State University. Her research interests include data-based decision making, visual analysis, and parent training. A word of advice she would give to students planning a single case design study is to be flexible—things probably won't go according to plan!

Section 1

Introduction to Research and Measurement

Before conducting a single case design study, you must understand the purposes and foundations of research in general, and the importance of reliable, accurate, and valid measurement. The first section of the book focuses on these topics.

In this section, we begin with a broad introduction to research in general in Chapter 1. We briefly discuss different research paradigms (qualitative, between-groups, single-case) and different approaches to conducting single case research (inductive/deductive, dynamic/static, process/procedure). The overarching questions answered in this chapter are: (1) What is research? (2) What are the different approaches to doing it?

Then, in Chapter 2, we discuss replication and how we draw conclusions across multiple experiments. Questions relevant for this chapter are: (1) What is external validity, and how is it different than ecological and construct validity? (2) What are the different types of replication, and how do they relate to internal versus external validity? (3) What factors should you consider when you are conducting an experimental replication?

In Chapter 3, we focus in on single case research specifically, by identifying confounding factors (i.e., threats to internal validity) whose impacts we must attempt to mitigate when we conduct single case research studies. Questions critical for this content include: (1) What is internal validity, and how is that related to identifying functional relations? (2) What are several major threats to internal validity, and how do we control for and/or detect them?

Chapter 4 focuses on the "why" and "how" of measuring behavior. We discuss continuous and discontinuous methods, how to choose a system appropriate for the dimension of interest, and the strengths and weaknesses of major systems. Questions you should be able to answer after reading this chapter include: (1) What are some examples of reversible versus non-reversible behaviors, long- versus short-duration behaviors, and free operant versus trial-based behaviors? (2) What are the major dimensions of interest, and how can you (a) measure them with continuous systems and (b) estimate them with discontinuous systems?

Next, we focus on the validity, accuracy, and reliability of data collection in Chapter 5. Much of the chapter is dedicated to interobserver agreement, the primary method by which single case researchers evaluate reliability. Questions relevant for this chapter include: (1) What are some steps for ensuring data reliability, before, during, and after measurement? (2) What are the differences between point-by-point and gross agreement? (3) Why do we collect interobserver agreement (IOA) data?

DOI: 10.4324/9781003294726-1

In Chapter 6, we focus on planning and ensuring reliability of experimental procedures. We discuss using the theory of change to identify active ingredients and likely impacts of your intervention, ways to conceptualize independent variables in complex experiments, and the importance of measuring independent variable implementation. Critical questions from this chapter include: (1) Why do you need to understand your theory of change? (2) What is the difference between procedural fidelity and treatment fidelity, which is superior, and why? (3) What is the difference in purpose for formative and summative analysis of fidelity?

The content in Chapter 7 is focused on generality of behavior change. We discuss generality and social validity and explain the importance of using multiple sources of data for evaluating outcomes of single case research. We discuss the complexity of the typical use of terms "generalization" and "maintenance." Questions you should be able to answer after reading this chapter are: (1) What are generality and social validity, and why are they important? (2) What are some relevant ways to measure generalization? (3) What are the different ways in which the term "maintenance" is used? (4) How should you know if maintenance and generalization would be expected in your study?

1
Research Approaches

David L. Gast and Jennifer R. Ledford

Important Terms

basic research, applied research, independent variables, dependent variables, participants, participatory action research, experimental research, non-experimental research, evidence-based practice, nomothetic, idiographic, dynamic research, static research, baseline, intervention

---

Table of Contents

Applied Research
    Integrating Science into Educational and Clinical Practice
    Participatory Action Research
Evidence-Based Practice
Characterizing Designs
    Attributions of Causality
    Assumptions about Generalizability
    Process versus Procedure Questions
    Research Approach
        Qualitative Research
        Descriptive and Correlational Research
        Between-Groups Research
        Single Case Research
        Mixed Methods Approaches
Conclusion
References

Callout

1.1 Questions for Scientist-Practitioners

DOI: 10.4324/9781003294726-2

The goal of science is to advance knowledge. One process by which we advance knowledge is via research—the systematic investigation and manipulation of variables to identify associations and understand processes. The effectiveness of educational and behavioral interventions is dependent on the use of evidence derived from research, but this process is not straightforward. This complexity results in a "research to practice gap" problem that suggests that research outcomes are not necessarily directly applicable to problems of practice. For example, outcomes of research studies have been reported to be non-replicable (Open Science Collaboration, 2015); to be dependent on counterfactual conditions (Lemons et al., 2014); to fail to generalize to outside of research contexts, in applied or authentic settings (Spriggs et al., 2016); and to be largely inapplicable to "real" problems faced by practitioners (Snow, 2014). How then does research contribute to the advancement of knowledge, and does it do so in a useful manner? In this chapter, we introduce the concepts of applied research and evidence-based practice, describe different ways to characterize research, and explain several research approaches and their corresponding rationales and assumptions.

Applied Research

Basic research is concerned with the advancement of knowledge that may or may not have immediate and specific application to practical concerns. **Applied research** involves systematic investigation related to the pursuit of knowledge in practical realms or to solve real-world problems. For example, a great deal of basic research has demonstrated that "resurgence" (i.e., the return of previously eliminated behavior when reinforcement conditions for current behavior worsen) consistently occurs across species, including humans (Kimball et al., 2023). The findings of this body of basic research guided translational researchers to demonstrate how the phenomenon could manifest following effective intervention; for example, when challenging behavior resurges after communicative responses are not reinforced (e.g., Volkert et al., 2009). Because translational research paradigms demonstrated the phenomenon's relevance to socially important situations (i.e., the assessment and treatment of challenging behavior), applied researchers have now begun to develop procedures intended to "inoculate" treatment outcomes against the environmental determinants of resurgence (Banerjee et al., 2022; Bloom & Lambert, 2015; Fuhrman et al., 2021; Neely et al., 2020).

In applied research evaluated with single case designs, we are most interested in determining the relation between **independent variables**—the variables manipulated by researchers (i.e., intervention) and **dependent variables**—the variables we expect to change given the manipulation (e.g., percentage of time engaged in challenging behavior), to solve problems of practice. For example, we might evaluate the impact of a specific coaching model (the independent variable) on the percentage of correct implementation of a naturalistic intervention (the dependent variable; Quinn et al., 2021) or the impact of using a differential reinforcement intervention package (the independent variable) for increasing time spent in a nonpreferred environment to reduce elopement (the dependent variable; Lambert et al., 2017). This book is primarily focused on the use of single case design in applied research, although single case designs can also be used to evaluate basic and translational questions. In applied research, we refer to the people who choose to participate in the study as **participants**, although historically they were referred to as subjects—because we assume that participants *willingly volunteer* rather than being *subjects* of the studies (Boynton, 1998).

Integrating Science into Educational and Clinical Practice

The purpose of a research project is to produce generalizable knowledge about relations between variables that can be used by others to expand understanding of a given phenomenon.

Applied research also has this goal, although some difficulties may arise when attempting to balance this goal with the additional goal of improving outcomes for participants. That is, the goal to establish confidence in relations is sometimes at odds with providing the best services for a given participant. One example is that we may need to collect a significant amount of data in non-intervention contexts to increase experimental rigor and confidence in the relation between the independent and dependent variables. However, increasing the amount of time a participant spends in counter therapeutic environments is generally objectionable when considering only the participant's best interests. We will discuss the ethical ramifications of decisions like this in Chapter 16. We refer to practitioners who engage in research as scientist-practitioners (a label coined by Barlow and colleagues in 1984 to describe interventionists who make data-based decisions an integral part of their practice).

When research is conducted under highly controlled conditions, as is often the case in studies using single case designs, the ability of those working in "typical" or "authentic" community settings to replicate conditions may be unclear. That is, interventions found to be effective in resource-rich controlled settings may not be able to be carried out at the same level of fidelity, thus affecting the outcome of the intervention. Snow (2014) suggested educational research should include more collaboration with practitioners, to address applied problems and enhance the pertinence of research. This position is not new, and that single case designs are particularly well suited to answer these applied problems has been acknowledged for decades (Barlow et al., 1984; Borg, 1981; Odom, 1988; Tawney & Gast, 1984). We suggest that there are important similarities between practice and research, and provide guidance for practitioners interested in conducting research in applied settings in Callout 1.1.

Callout 1.1 Questions for Scientist-Practitioners

Successful practitioners must demonstrate that they can bring about positive behavior change in their clients. Practitioners who collect data on client or student behavior in response to the treatments they implement can show behavior change that occurs over time. However, sometimes behavior change may be the result of other factors, rather than the treatment itself (e.g., other treatments or experiences). The utilization of single case designs allows practitioners to go one step further than showing behavior change—to establish a causal link between his or her practices and the child's behavior change. That is, single case designs can help practitioners increase the confidence that the treatment they implemented *and only that treatment* caused behavior to change. Given the potential for single case design to enhance conclusions drawn by practitioners, and the guidelines suggesting practitioners use scientific evidence and data-based decision making, the use of the scientist-practitioner model is valuable. Given the potential difficulties, and to ensure that a planned applied project has not only scientific value, but also practical value for participants, Eiserman and Behl (1992) suggested considerations for special educators conducting research, which we have summarized and adapted below:

1. Is the dependent variable meaningfully related to educational or therapeutic goals?
2. Does available research suggest that the participant is likely to benefit?
3. Are procedures and goals in line with the policies of the institution and with objectives of the clients (e.g., school, clinic, family)?
4. Is the answer to the question of interest to all relevant stakeholders?
5. Can the research be completed given the participants' other scheduled activities, or is there an acceptable modification of these activities that allows for completion?

> 6. How does the research interact with ongoing therapeutic, educational, or leisure activities?
> 7. How much time is required for participation, and is that amount of time justifiable, given participant needs?
> 8. Do participants agree to participate, and are they given opportunities to continue to agree (assent) or to withdraw their agreement (dissent)?
> 9. Do other important stakeholders support participation?
> 10. Are personnel and materials resources sufficient for the project?
> 11. Are there any ethical concerns that should be addressed prior to initiation of the project?

Participatory Action Research

One framework that might be particularly helpful for considering the relationship between applied research and real-world contexts is **participatory action research**. This framework explicitly acknowledges the critical importance of the experiential knowledge and values of people who are to be impacted by any research. While the primary motivation for direct stakeholders (e.g., parents, teachers, children) is to solve a problem that directly impacts them, the primary motivation for researchers is the pursuit of knowledge for the greater good. These differing contingencies are sometimes at odds with one another (Pritchett et al., 2022).

When using this framework, researchers (1) build relationships with those potentially impacted by their research (e.g., teachers and students in schools), (2) generate a common understanding of any problems that exist, (3) generate data about the problem and analyze those data, (4) plan solutions, and (5) take action (Cornish et al., 2023). These steps align quite well with single case research, given the ability of single case research to be dynamic and individualized (thus allowing for steps 1, 2, and 4), the need to collect baseline and intervention data (steps 3 and 5), and the ability to modify action steps (i.e., procedures) as needed (steps 4 and 5).

It is important to note that single case design does not necessarily follow this framework; participatory action research requires that people who are affected by a particular issue take a leading role in the trajectory described above (Kindon et al., 2007). Researchers serve as methodology experts but acknowledge the content and experiential expertise of other stakeholders. A project that is designed by researchers to answer a question that they are interested in may include important steps during which they get stakeholder feedback but would not be considered participatory action research. There is a large continuum of research approaches that range from entirely researcher-driven and with little participant input to entirely practice-driven with researchers serving only as methodological experts. Many structures (e.g., funding agencies) uphold a more researcher-driven research process, which requires that questions and processes are well-described and justified prior to beginning a project. Although there is no "wrong way" to do research, it is important to understand that the extent to which research matters in the real world may be considerably impacted by decisions about the ways in which non-researcher stakeholders are included in the process.

Evidence-Based Practice

Guidelines in the Individuals with Disabilities Education Improvement Act (IDEIA) and Every Student Succeeds Act (ESSA) mandate the use of evidence-based practice (alternately, "scientific, research-based intervention"; IDEIA; or "empirically supported practice"; Ayres et al., 2011). Similarly, professional organizations like the American Psychological Association (APA), American Speech-Language Hearing Association (ASHA), and the Behavior Analysis Certification Board (BACB) have standards requiring the use of evidence-based interventions. Though the term is relatively new, the idea that research should guide practice is not, particularly in the field of applied behavior analysis (cf., Baer et al., 1968). A narrow view of **evidence-based practice** (Spencer et al., 2012) refers to intervention procedures that have been scientifically verified as being effective for changing a specific behavior of interest, under given conditions, and for particular participants (Horner et al., 2005; Steinbrenner et al., 2020). The APA (2005) adds to its definition of evidence-based practice the integration of research evidence with clinical expertise and context (e.g., the preferences and values of stakeholders). Similarly, ASHA adds both clinical expertise and evidence—which can refer to both external evidence (e.g., published research) and internal evidence (e.g., data gathered from a particular case). Even reviews that have focused on identified practices as evidence-based due to scientific support have acknowledged that the identification of effective practices must take into consideration context and the expertise of practitioners (e.g., Steinbrenner et al., 2020).

In behavioral sciences, "trustworthiness" or credibility of research findings is based on the rigor of the scientific method employed and the extent to which the research design controls for alternative explanations. The scientific method requires investigator objectivity, reliability of measurement, and independent replication of findings. Given the components described above, quantitative research, including single case research (as well as other types of scientific inquiry) is *necessary but not sufficient* for identifying evidence-based practices. Moreover, different research questions or objectives require different research approaches—no one research method or design is appropriate for answering all research questions, and research evidence must be synthesized with clinical expertise and client values to improve implementation of evidence-based practice in typical contexts.

Characterizing Designs

Research designs can be categorized according to a range of features, including attributions of causality, assumptions about generalizability, and flexibility of procedural rules (e.g., ability to change based on response to intervention). Designs can also be grouped by general approach, including several quantitative approaches as well as qualitative methods. We briefly describe these categorizations below.

Attributions of Causality

The act of intentionally manipulating an environmental variable to see if there is a measurable change in some outcome while controlling for other probable reasons for change differentiates **experimental research** from **non-experimental research**. Appropriately utilized single case designs can be categorized as experimental, in addition to group comparison approaches, such as randomized controlled trials (Horner et al., 2005; Ledford et al., 2023). Experimental studies include (1) descriptions of the target behavior(s), (2) predictions regarding what impact the independent variable will have on the dependent variable(s), and (3) appropriate tests to see if the prediction is correct. One characteristic that differentiates an experimental design study from a non-experimental design study is the extent to which the design controls for threats to internal validity—variables other than the planned independent variable that could result in changes in the dependent variable. Correlational, descriptive, and qualitative research designs are non-experimental. Only single case designs that adequately control for likely threats to internal validity can be considered to be experimental.

Assumptions about Generalizability

Nomothetic research approaches are generally based in the natural sciences and are characterized by attempting to explain associations that can be generalized to a population with certain characteristics. **Idiographic research approaches**, common in the humanities, attempt to specify associations that vary based on certain characteristics or contingencies present for the participant or case of interest. Both nomothetic and idiographic approaches are valid, depending on the research question of interest (Ottenbacher, 1984). Traditional group design approaches generally apply assumptions applicable to nomothetic research while traditional qualitative approaches generally apply assumptions applicable to idiographic approaches. Single case design was historically considered to be idiographic in nature, but increasingly has been used to draw conclusions using nomothetic approaches (e.g., hypothesis-testing versus hypothesis-generating data). These terms are not quite synonymous with, but are related to inductive research approaches versus deductive research approaches. When using an **inductive approach**, researchers collect data, analyze patterns, and establish theory. When using a **deductive approach**, researchers begin with a hypothesis, collect data, and analyze those data with an emphasis on whether their hypothesis was correct.

Relatedly, single case often uses a **dynamic research** approach. That is, researchers might alter a planned independent variable based on response to intervention. Other research approaches, including group designs like randomized controlled trials, are generally considered static research approaches. **Static research** approaches generally test a pre-determined hypothesis, and no changes are made to the approach based on data. In some cases, single case research can also be static—that is, researchers can choose to evaluate an intervention without making data-based changes. The lines between static and dynamic approaches exist in both single case research (e.g., when a researcher sets out to answer a specific question in a static design but makes dynamic changes when the study progresses) and also in group design studies (e.g., SMART designs; Chow & Hampton, 2019). It is important for researchers to determine whether they are using a dynamic or static approach prior to initiation of their study.

Process versus Procedure Questions

Researchers, especially single case researchers, might also consider whether they are interested in evaluating a **process** or a **procedure** when they develop a research study. Differentiating these two types of questions and research approaches is in its infancy but may be likely to inform future work. Evaluating a procedure via single case design tends to be associated with a more static approach, wherein researchers answer the question of "Does procedure A result in changes in behavior B?" Evaluating a process is more associated with a dynamic approach and might answer a question like "How do we use process A to get a desirable change in behavior B?" The latter type of research often involves clinical judgment and modifications based on ongoing data analysis but these decisions can be built into a static research approach (i.e., the decisions are built into the intervention approach). Both types of research are valuable—procedure research may be most easily translated into conclusions about evidence-based practice while process research may contribute to knowledge about underlying processes, variations in implementation required across contexts and participants, and complex interventions requiring practitioner decision making. In later chapters, we will discuss complexities of conducting and evaluating each of these types of research.

Research Approach

As the book title connotes, the focus of this text is on single case design research methodology and its use by applied researchers in behavioral sciences. Despite this focus on a single type of research design, it is important to be able to compare and contrast research approaches on the basis of their research logic, strategies for controlling for threats to internal validity, and generalization of findings to individual cases. Understanding variability in research approaches will allow you to choose the appropriate type for answering your research questions. As we mentioned previously, no single research approach or design is appropriate for answering all research questions. In the sections that follow, common research approaches and designs are briefly overviewed. More detailed design descriptions and analyses are found elsewhere in such general research methodology texts as Creswell and Clark (2017), deMarrais and Lapan (2004), Farmer et al. (2022), Fraenkel and Wallen (2006) as well as recent methodological guidelines (e.g., Leko et al., 2023; Toste et al., 2023).

Qualitative Research

Qualitative research is generally considered to be ideographic and non-experimental. It does not involve manipulation of an independent variable, but instead is focused on observation of naturally occurring events. Qualitative research approaches provide a detailed, in-depth description of the case under study. The term qualitative research is an "umbrella" term that refers to several approaches with a focus on description rather than quantification of events. Three approaches have particular prominence among educational and clinical researchers who conduct qualitative research studies: Case study, ethnography, and phenomenology. The case study approach entails an in-depth and detailed description of one or more cases, while ethnography refers to the study of a specific cultural group. Both are conducted in a natural setting without an attempt to influence a specific target behavior—thus, although the names are similar, a qualitative *case study* is not the same as an experimental *single case study*. Sometimes confused with ethnography, phenomenology is the study of perceptions of a particular event or situation. Common activities for qualitative research studies include observations, interviews, surveys, and focus groups. For a more in-depth discussion of these and other qualitative research approaches see Glasser and Strauss (1967), Lincoln and Guba (1985), Patton (2014), and a recent article in *Exceptional Children* by the QR Collective (2023).

Descriptive and Correlational Research

Descriptive and correlational research methods are both focused on the quantitative characterization of phenomenon, without any efforts to impact their occurrence. Descriptive research includes quantification of a variable or variables of interest (e.g., To what extent are children with disabilities included in general education classrooms?), while correlational research describes relations between variables (e.g., Does socio-economic status predict the extent to which children with disabilities are included in general education classrooms?). Correlational research is different from both between-group and single case research because the relations are descriptive rather than causal—that is, correlational research allows you to determine that a relation exists between two or more variables but does not allow you to determine whether the relation is *caused* by one of the variables.

Between-Groups Research
Group research approaches are generally considered nomothetic and static. They can be experimental or non-experimental. The basic logic underlying group research is that a large number of individuals are divided and assigned to one of two or more study conditions. In the simplest version, the study includes a control condition, in which participants are not exposed to the independent variable, and treatment condition, in which participants are exposed to the independent variable. Participants could also be equally divided between two treatment groups (e.g., Treatment A and Treatment B). In some group studies more than two conditions may be compared, in which case an equal number of participants would be assigned to each of the conditions (e.g., 30 assigned to control, 30 assigned to Treatment A, 30 assigned to Treatment B). A critical variable to consider when evaluating a group design study is how participants are assigned to study conditions. The optimal method is random assignment of participants (experimental study), but this is not always possible.

The group research approach is the most common research methodology used in some areas of behavioral science and education. Group research designs are well suited for large-scale efficacy studies or clinical trials in which a researcher's interest is in describing whether a practice or policy, on average, will be effective for a specific population. With such research questions a group design methodology is recommended. Numerous designs and statistical analysis procedures are available for your consideration if you choose to study group behavior. Despite its usefulness for detecting average group effects, group comparison designs cannot be generalized to the individual. To paraphrase Barlow et al. (1984), generalization of group research findings to individuals requires a "leap of faith," the extent to which depends on the similarity of the individual to study participants for whom the intervention was effective. You must never lose sight when attempting to generalize a practice supported by group research to an individual, that some participants performed better, while others performed worse than the average participant. Contemporary guidelines for group design studies were recently published in *Exceptional Children* (Toste et al., 2023).

Single Case Research
Single case research can be experimental or non-experimental, ideographic or nomothetic, inductive or deductive, and static or dynamic. Single case design methodology has a long tradition in the behavioral sciences and is commonly used in behavioral sciences, special education, and school psychology (King et al., 2023; Radley et al., 2020; Shepley et al., 2023). Historically, studies using single case designs were referred to as "single subject research," but over time, the term participant replaced subject when humans involved in a study provided informed consent (Pyrczak, 2016); throughout the book we will use the contemporary term participant, although some historical references may include the term subject.

Sidman (1960) described the single case research approach in the authoritative book, *Tactics of Scientific Research*, which exemplified its application within the context of basic experimental psychology research. In 1968, Baer and colleagues elaborated on single case research methodology and how it could be used in applied research to evaluate intervention effectiveness with individuals. Since that time numerous articles, chapters, and books have been written describing single case design methodology and its use in a number of disciplines, including psychology (Bailey & Burch, 2002; Barlow & Hersen, 1984; Johnston & Pennypacker, 1993, 2009; Kazdin, 1998, 2020; Kratochwill & Levin, 1992, 2014; Skinner, 2004), special education (Gast, 2005; Kennedy, 2005; Richards et al., 1999; Tawney & Gast, 1984), occupational therapy (Lane et al., 2017), literacy education (Neuman & McCormick, 1995), communication sciences (McReynolds & Kearns, 1983; Schlosser et al., 2018), and therapeutic recreation (Dattilo et al., 2000).

Single case research is a quantitative experimental approach in which study participants serve as their own control, a principle known as baseline logic (Sidman, 1960). In the simplest single case study, each participant is exposed to both a "control" condition, generally referred to as the baseline condition, and an intervention condition. In a **baseline condition**, participants experience environmental arrangements that are not expected to result in improvements in targeted outcomes; these can be conditions without any intervention (e.g., assessment of whether a child can complete a task with no help) or conditions that represent business-as-usual (e.g., the environment remains unchanged from its typical state, such as measuring engagement during a typical math activity in a classroom). Each participant also usually participates in an **intervention condition** in which they are exposed to environmental arrangements (e.g., contingencies, materials, teaching) that are expected to result in desirable behavior change. There are some variations on this typical set-up, such as when participants are exposed only to assessment conditions in a design (e.g., as in the case of a functional analysis) or when they are exposed to only intervention conditions (e.g., the two conditions being compared are both treatments, rather than one being a treatment and one being a non-treatment condition).

Baseline logic is different from group design logic in which similar or matched participants are assigned to one of two or more study conditions (control *or* intervention). In studies using single case designs, each participant participates in *both* conditions of interest (e.g., baseline and intervention). In group design, posttest data are collected at an a priori specified time point (e.g., after three weeks of intervention), and are analyzed using statistical methods comparing the average performance of participants assigned to one condition to the average performance of participants assigned to other conditions. In single case research, data are collected regularly *while the intervention is occurring*, and intervention conditions are generally continued until a performance criterion is met or until progress is apparent via visual analysis of graphed data (although there are instances where a set time period is used instead). The use of visual analysis of graphic data for individual participants make single case design studies ideal for applied researchers and practitioners who are interested in answering research questions and/or evaluating interventions designed to change the behavior of individuals.

Mixed Methods Approaches
Mixed methods approaches to answering research questions are increasingly popular although their use in special education and behavioral sciences is relatively uncommon (Corr et al., 2021). When using mixed methods, researchers combine multiple quantitative and/or qualitative methods. Several types of mixed methods research have been identified, and include explanatory sequential designs, exploratory sequential designs, and convergent designs (Creswell & Clark, 2017). Explanatory sequential designs begin with a quantitative analysis and are followed by qualitative analyses that provide insight into the "why" and "how" for the quantitative outcomes. One example would be using single case methods to measure whether teachers implemented certain procedures more accurately during intervention conditions as compared to baseline conditions (quantitative) followed by qualitative methods for explaining why the procedures were not implemented as expected. Exploratory sequential analyses follow the opposite sequence—they begin with a qualitative component, which informs a later quantitative component. For example, a researcher might conduct focus groups with teachers, which informs the development of an intervention (qualitative) whose effects are measured with a single case design (quantitative). Convergent designs are used to compare the results of quantitative and qualitative analyses to allow for a more complete picture for a given question. For example, researchers could measure social networks in classrooms via quantitative measurement of interactions during free play, while also using interviews with children where they

are asked to explain who they play with and why. As discussed in Chapter 7, the use of qualitative research methods alongside quantitative single case methods aligns particularly well with social validity questions related to single case research outcomes (Snodgrass et al., 2022). That is, when designed well, mixed methods studies can answer questions that go beyond "Did this intervention work?" (a traditional quantitative single case question) to include "Why did this intervention work?"; "How did participants feel about this intervention?"; and "How can we improve this intervention for current participants and in the future?"

Conclusion

In this chapter, we introduced various ways of categorizing research and described the basis of single case research. We defined a number of important terms that will continue to be used throughout the text, including *dependent variables*, *independent variables*, *baseline logic*, *baseline conditions*, and *intervention conditions*. In later chapters, we will focus on single case research methods, including further expansion on the different types of single case designs that can be used to answer a wide variety of questions across many different contexts.

References

American Psychological Association. (2005). Report of the 2005 presidential task force on evidence-based practice. Washington, DC: Author.
Ayres, K. M., Lowrey, A., Douglas, K. H., & Sievers, C. (2011). I can identify Saturn but I can't brush my teeth: What happens with the curricular focus for students with severe disabilities shifts. *Education and Training in Autism and Developmental Disabilities*, 46, 11–21.
Baer, D. M., Wolf, M. M., & Risley, T. R. (1968). Some current dimensions of applied behavior analysis. *Journal of Applied Behavior Analysis*, 1, 91–97.
Bailey, J. S., & Burch, M. R. (2002). *Research methods in applied behavior analysis*. Thousand Oaks, CA: Sage.
Banerjee, I., Lambert, J. M., Copeland, B. A., Paranczak, J. L., Bailey, K. M., & Standish, C. M. (2022). Extending functional communication training to multiple language contexts in bilingual learners with challenging behavior. *Journal of Applied Behavior Analysis*, 55(1), 80–100.
Barlow, D. H., Hayes, S. C., & Nelson, R. O. (1984). *The scientist practitioner: Research accountability in clinical and educational settings*. New York: Pergamon Press.
Barlow, D. H., & Hersen, M. (1984). *Single case experimental designs: Strategies for studying behavior change* (2nd ed.). New York: Pergamon Press.
Bloom, S. E., & Lambert, J. M. (2015). Implications for practice: Resurgence and differential reinforcement of alternative responding. *Journal of Applied Behavior Analysis*, 48(4), 781–784.
Borg, W. R. (1981). *Applying educational research: A practical guide for teachers*. New York: Longman.
Boynton, P. M. (1998). People should participate in, not be subjects of, research. *British Medical Journal (BMJ)*, 317(7171), 1521.
Chow, J. C., & Hampton, L. H. (2019). Sequential multiple-assignment randomized trials: Developing and evaluating adaptive interventions in special education. *Remedial and Special Education*, 40(5), 267–276.
Corr, C., Snodgrass, M. R., Love, H., Scott, I. M., Kim, J., & Andrews, L. (2021). Exploring the landscape of published mixed methods research in special education: A systematic review. *Remedial and Special Education*, 42(5), 317–328.
Cornish, F., Breton, N., Moreno-Tabarez, U., Delgado, J., Rua, M., de-Graft Aikins, A., & Hodgetts, D. (2023). Participatory action research. *Nature Reviews Methods Primers*, 3(1), 34.
Creswell, J. W., & Clark, V. L. P. (2017). *Designing and conducting mixed methods research*. Los Angeles: Sage Publications.
Dattilo, J., Gast, D. L., Loy, D. P., & Malley, S. (2000). Use of single-subject research designs in therapeutic recreation. *Therapeutic Recreation Journal*, 34, 253–270.
deMarrais, K., & Lapan, S. D. (Eds.) (2004). *Foundations for research: Methods of inquiry in education and the social sciences*. Mahwah, NJ: Lawrence Erlbaum Associates.

Eiserman, W. D., & Behl, D. (1992). Research participation: Benefits and considerations for the special educator. *Teaching Exceptional Children*, 24, 12–15.

Farmer, T. W., Talbott, E., McMaster, K., Lee, D., & Aceves, T. (Eds.). (2022). *Handbook of Special Education Research, Volume I*. New York: Routledge.

Fraenkel, J. R., & Wallen, N. E. (2006). *How to design and evaluate research in education* (6th ed.). New York: McGraw-Hill.

Fuhrman, A. M., Lambert, J. M., & Greer, B. D. (2021). A brief review of expanded-operant treatments for mitigating resurgence. *The Psychological Record*, 1–5.

Gast, D. L. (2005). Single-subject research design. In M. Hersen, G. Sugai, & R. Horner (Eds.), *Encyclopedia of behavior modification and cognitive behavior therapy* (pp. 1520–1526). Thousand Oaks, CA: Sage.

Glasser, B. G., & Strauss, A. L. (1967). *The discovery of grounded theory: Strategies for qualitative research*. Chicago, IL: Aldine.

Horner, R. H., Carr, E. G., Halle, J., McGee, G., Odom, S., & Wolery, M. (2005). The use of single-subject research to identify evidence-based practice in special education. *Exceptional Children*, 71, 165–179.

Johnston, J. M., & Pennypacker, H. S. (1993). *Readings for strategies and tactics of behavioral research*. Lawrence Erlbaum Associates, Inc.

Johnston, J. M., & Pennypacker, H. S. (2009). *Strategies and tactics of behavioral research* (3rd ed.). New York: Routledge.

Kazdin, A. E. (1998). *Methodological issues and strategies in clinical research*. Washington, DC: American Psychological Association.

Kazdin, A. E. (2020). *Single-case research designs* (3rd ed). New York: Oxford University Press.

Kennedy, C. H. (2005). *Single-case designs for educational research*. Boston, MA: Pearson/Allyn and Bacon.

Kimball, R. T., Greer, B. D., Fuhrman, A. M., & Lambert, J. M. (2023). Relapse and its mitigation: Toward behavioral inoculation. *Journal of Applied Behavior Analysis*, 56(2), 259–493.

Kindon, S., Pain, R., & Kesby, M. (2007). *Participatory action research approaches and methods: connecting people, participation and place*. Routledge. Retrieved from: https://eprints.icstudies.org.uk/id/eprint/293/1/LT-19-06-Participatory-Action-Research-Toolkit.pdf

King, S., Wang, L., Nylen, B., & Enders, O. (2023). Prevalence of research design in special education: A survey of peer-reviewed journals. *Remedial and Special Education*, 44(6), 443–505.

Kratochwill, T. R., & Levin, J. R. (1992). *Single-case research design and analysis: New direction for psychology and education*. Hillsdale, NJ: Lawrence Erlbaum.

Kratochwill, T. R., & Levin, J. R. (Eds.). (2014). *Single-case intervention research: Methodological and statistical advances*. Washington, DC: American Psychological Association.

Lambert, J. M., Finley, C. I., & Caruthers, C. E. (2017). Trial-based functional analyses as basis for elopement intervention. *Behavior Analysis: Research and Practice*, 17(2), 166.

Lane, J. D., Ledford, J. R., & Gast, D. L. (2017). Current standards in single case design and applications in occupational therapy. *American Journal of Occupational Therapy*, 71, 1–9.

Ledford, J. R., Lambert, J. M., Pustejovsky, J. E., Zimmerman, K. N., Hollins, N., & Barton, E. E. (2023). Single-case-design research in special education: Next-generation guidelines and considerations. *Exceptional Children*, 89(4), 379–396.

Leko, M. M., Hitchcock, J. H., Love, H. R., Houchins, D. E., & Conroy, M. A. (2023). Quality indicators for mixed-methods research in special education. *Exceptional Children*, 89(4), 432–448.

Lemons, C. J., Fuchs, D., Gilbert, J. K., & Fuchs, L. S. (2014). Evidence-based practices in a changing world: Reconsidering the counterfactual in education research. *Educational Researcher*, 43, 242–252.

Lincoln, Y. S., & Guba, E. G. (1985). *Naturalistic inquiry*. Newbury Park, CA: Sage.

McReynolds, L. V., & Kearns, K. P. (1983). *Single-subject experimental designs in communicative disorders*. Baltimore, MD: University Park Press.

Neely, L., Graber, J., Kunnavatana, S., & Cantrell, K. (2020). Impact of language on behavior treatment outcomes. *Journal of Applied Behavior Analysis*, 53(2), 796–810.

Neuman, S. B., & McCormick, S. (Eds.) (1995). *Single subject experimental research: Applications for literacy*. Newark, DE: International Reading Association.

Odom, S. L. (1988). Research in early childhood special education: Methodologies and paradigm. In S. L. Odom & M. B. Karnes (Eds.), *Early intervention for infants and children with handicaps* (pp. 1–22). Baltimore, MD: Paul H. Brookes.

Open Science Collaboration. (2015). Estimating the reproducibility of psychological science. *Science*, 349, aac4716-1–aac4716-8.

Ottenbacher, K. (1984). Nomothetic and idiographic strategies for clinical research: In apposition or opposition? *The Occupational Therapy Journal of Research*, 4, 198–212.

Patton, M. Q. (2014). *Qualitative research & evaluation methods: Integrating theory and practice*. Los Angeles: Sage Publications.

Pritchett, M., Ala'i-Rosales, S., Cruz, A. R., & Cihon, T. M. (2022). Social justice is the spirit and aim of an applied science of human behavior: Moving from colonial to participatory research practices. *Behavior Analysis in Practice*, 15(4), 1074–1092.

Pyrczak, F. (2016). *Making sense of statistics: A conceptual overview*. London: Routledge.

QR Collective. (2023). Reflexive quality criteria: Questions and indicators for purpose-driven special education qualitative research. *Exceptional Children*, 89(4), 449–466.

Quinn, E. D., Kaiser, A. P., & Ledford, J. (2021). Hybrid telepractice delivery of enhanced milieu teaching: Effects on caregiver implementation and child communication. *Journal of Speech, Language, and Hearing Research*, 64(8), 3074–3099.

Radley, K. C., Dart, E. H., Fischer, A. J., & Collins, T. A. (2020). Publication trends for single-case methodology in school psychology: A systematic review. *Psychology in the Schools*, 57(5), 683–698.

Richards, S. B., Taylor, R. L., Ramasamy, R., & Richards, R. (1999). *Single subject research: Applications in educational and clinical settings*. San Diego, CA: Singular Publishing Group.

Schlosser, R. W., Belfiore, P. J., Sigafoos, J., Briesch, A. M., & Wendt, O. (2018). Appraisal of comparative single-case experimental designs for instructional interventions with non-reversible target behaviors: Introducing the CSCEDARS ("Cedars"). *Research in Developmental Disabilities*, 79, 33–52.

Shepley, C., Shepley, S. B., & Spriggs, A. D. (2023). On the history of single-case methodology: A data-based analysis. *Journal of Behavioral Education*. Advanced online publication.

Sidman, M. (1960). *Tactics of scientific research—evaluating experimental data in psychology*. New York: Basic Books.

Skinner, C. H. (2004). Single-subject designs for school psychologists. *Journal of Applied School Psychology*, 20, 2.

Snodgrass, M. R., Chung, M. Y., Kretzer, J. M., & Biggs, E. E. (2022). Rigorous assessment of social validity: A scoping review of a 40-year conversation. *Remedial and Special Education*, 43(2), 114–130.

Snow, C. E. (2014). Rigor and realism: Doing educational science in the real world. *Educational Researcher*, 44, 460–466.

Spencer, T. D., Detrich, R., & Slocum, T. A. (2012). Evidence-based practice: A framework for making effective decisions. *Education and Treatment of Children*, 35(2), 127–151.

Spriggs, A. D., Gast, D. L., & Knight, V. F. (2016). Video modeling and observational learning to teach gaming access to students with ASD. *Journal of Autism and Developmental Disorders*, 46, 2845–2858.

Steinbrenner, J. R., Hume, K., Odom, S. L., Morin, K. L., Nowell, S. W., Tomaszewski, B., ... & Savage, M. N. (2020). Evidence-based practices for children, youth, and young adults with autism. *FPG child development institute*.

Tawney, J. W., & Gast, D. L. (1984). *Single subject research in special education*. Columbus, OH: Charles E. Merrill.

Toste, J. R., Logan, J. A., Shogren, K. A., & Boyd, B. A. (2023). The next generation of quality indicators for group design research in special education. *Exceptional Children*, 89(4), 359–378.

Volkert, V. M., Lerman, D. C., Call, N. A., & Trosclair-Lasserre, N. (2009). An evaluation of resurgence during treatment with functional communication training. *Journal of Applied Behavior Analysis*, 42(1), 145–160.

2
External Validity and Generalizable Knowledge

Joseph M. Lambert, Jennifer R. Ledford, Tara Fahmie, and David L. Gast

Important Terms

external validity, within-study replication, across-study replication, status variables, functional characteristics, endogenous implementers, ecological validity, construct validity

Table of Contents

External Validity
Replication
    Parsing Critical from Non-Critical Features via Across-Study Replication
    Tactics for Maximizing the Impact of a Across-Study Replication
    Considerations Relevant to External Validity
        Participant Characteristics
        Context Characteristics
        Dependent Variables
        Intervention Features
    Related Constructs
        Ecological Validity
        Construct Validity
Recommendations for Across-Study Replications
Conclusion
References

In the previous chapter, we discussed purposes of research and the various paradigms and assumptions associated with different types of research. In this chapter, we specifically focus on single case research design and the importance of replication *across* studies. In the next chapter, we will focus again on replication, but with a focus on replication *within* studies.

External Validity

<u>External validity</u> refers to the extent to which a relation demonstrated in a specific context holds in other contexts (Shadish et al., 2001). For example, can the relation identified in one or more studies be expected to hold in other settings (e.g., classrooms versus clinics), for other types of participants (e.g., with different characteristics or skills, of different ages, who have different histories of intervention), or with different interventionists (e.g., with researchers who did not develop the intervention, with researchers from a different institution who were trained by different people, with non-researchers such as teachers or other service providers). It can also refer to applicability to other measured behaviors and with different treatment features (e.g., dosage, frequency, components). It is worth noting explicitly that external validity is applied to *relations*. That is, a given intervention or study cannot be deemed externally valid.

A common criticism directed at single case research methodology is that findings cannot generalize beyond the individual—there simply are too few participants in studies that employ single case designs. By contrast, group research methodology, in which a researcher randomly assigns many participants to two or more groups, is thought to more directly establish external validity. Few would argue that findings generated by large group research—compared to those generated by single case research—generalize better to other large unstudied groups. Of course, this is only true if individuals in the unstudied group are "similar" to participants in the studied group. Wolery and Ezell (1993) point out, "The more similar the two populations, the greater the likelihood of accurate generalizations, and thus the greater the likelihood that findings will be replicated" (p. 644).

These positions regarding research methodology are reasonable. However—what if your interest is in generalizing findings to a specific individual, rather than a group of individuals? Remember, in large group research the data reported are measures of central tendency; thus, there are always individuals within the group who perform better and worse than the average participant. Seldom do these studies provide detailed descriptions of individual participants nor do they often report how individual participants responded to the independent variable. Their focus is on the group, not the individual. It might be reasonable then, to expect that findings of group design research generalize more readily to groups of people, while findings of single case design research generalize more readily to individuals.

Replication

Before we discuss strategies for establishing external validity through single case research, it is likely worth exploring the concept of replication. Johnston and Pennypacker (2009) defined a *replication* as a repetition of any parts of an experiment and a *reproduction* as a repetition of results, usually as an outcome of repetition of procedures (p. 241). When replication yields reproduction, it is possible to accumulate at least one of two types of evidence. First, replication that yields reproduction allows scientists to establish the reliability, or reproducibility, of a finding. It also allows them to rule out incidental contact with extraneous confounds and/or experimental artifacts as alternative explanations for observed effects. That is, replications that yield reproduction contribute to a study's believability because it offers confidence that changes in an independent variable are responsible for changes in a dependent variable (see Chapter 3). The strategies for producing this type of evidence include within-session, within-phase, and within-experiment replication (see Table 2.1) and entails repeating a procedure exactly as it was previously implemented to answer the question: "When I repeat this procedure, will I get the same outcome?" (Johnston & Pennypacker, 2009). This type of replication has been referred to as a *direct replication* by both Sidman (1960) and Kazdin (2010) and is the focus of Chapter 3.

Table 2.1 Contributions of Various Types of Replications

Contribution		Replication Types		Classification		
		Johnston & Pennypacker (2009)		Sidman (1960)	Kazdin (2009)	This text
Reliability of Effect	Internal Validity	Within-session replication	Repetition of a basic element of a procedure throughout each session (e.g., multiple opportunities to respond presented in a discrete trial format).	Direct Replication	Direct Replication	Within-Study Replication
		Within-phase replication	Repetition of the same condition many times in succession throughout a phase.			
		Within-experiment replication	Repetition of an entire phase over the course of an experiment.			
Generality of Effect	External Validity	Within-literature replication	Repetition of an earlier experiment, usually by other researchers, in which all known critical features are held constant.	Systematic Replication		Across-Study Replication
			Repetition of an earlier experiment, usually by other researchers, in which some elements of the previous experiment are held constant and others are intentionally altered.		Systematic Replication	
		Across-literature replication	Repetition of phenomena under different conditions across different fields of science.			

Note: The gray-filled cell represents ambiguity, given that replication across multiple participants in a single study could contribute to generality, but within-study replications do not necessarily include multiple participants. Black-filled cells represent no contribution to generality of effect.

A second function of replication allows scientists to establish the generality of a given effect. That is, replication can help scientists determine whether a specified relation is constrained to a single individual or circumstance, or if it represents a generalizable principle which might contribute to scientific knowledge. The strategies for producing this type of evidence include *within-literature* and *across-literature replications* (see Table 2.1) and entail repeating some elements of a previously implemented procedure while intentionally modifying others to answer the question: "If I change the procedure, will I get the same outcome?" (Johnston & Pennypacker, 2009). This second function has been referred to as a *systematic replication* by both Sidman (1960) and Kazdin (2010).

However, Kazdin (2010) distinguished two types of *within-literature* replication and classified each differently. First, when researchers are only interested in reproducing a previously established outcome and do not seek to explore which elements of the original procedure were critical to producing the original outcome, or how a parametric manipulation of the independent variable might alter the outcome, then they replicate as many elements of the original procedure as possible. By contrast, when researchers are uncertain about the status (i.e., critical vs. non-critical) of procedural details present in a previous experiment, or when they seek to expand understanding of *how* an independent variable controls a dependent variable through parametric manipulation, they will replicate some elements of the original procedure while intentionally changing other elements. Kazdin referred to the former as a direct replication and the latter as an indirect replication. Although somewhat inconsistent with earlier conceptualizations of a direct replication (e.g., Sidman, 1960), this newer framing can be useful for communicating a study's intended contribution and is often adopted by scientists who employ, and journals that publish, single case design. Despite subtle differences in terminological nuance, all *within-literature* and *across-literature* replications serve the dual function of establishing the reliability of a phenomenon while simultaneously probing its generality (Sidman, 1960).

Given disagreement on exact terminology that has persisted across years, we elect to use the terms **within-study replication** to refer to replication that occurs in the context of a single case design study and primarily impacts internal validity and **across-study replication** to refer to replication across more than one study that impacts external validity.

Parsing Critical from Non-Critical Features via Across-Study Replication

Importantly, external validity can be evaluated for a group of studies, but not for an individual single case design study (Birnbrauer, 1981). That is, variability across attempts (e.g., number and types of differences between studies) determines the range of generality established through single case design. Sidman (1960, p. 111) noted that "replication demonstrates that the finding ... can be observed under conditions different from those prevailing in the original experiment." As mentioned above, across-study replication can: (1) demonstrate the reliability of an effect, and (2) extend the generality of a finding. They are also useful for identifying exceptions to such generality. Perhaps one of the best examples of systematic across-study replication via single case design is a long series of studies conducted by David Gast and Mark Wolery (and colleagues) related to the effectiveness and efficiency of time delay prompting procedures. Over years, they conducted many studies, systematically expanding evidence of generality, including variation in participants, instructional arrangements (i.e., individual, group), and target behaviors (e.g., discrete academic behaviors, chained self-help skills), as well as less commonly studied parameters like fidelity errors. They published many studies—here we cite a representative but small subset that exemplifies the overall findings that this procedure was effective for teaching a variety of behaviors to individuals with disabilities, in a variety of contexts (Doyle et al., 1990; Gast et al., 1990, 1991; Holcombe et al., 1994; Schuster et al., 1988; Wolery et al., 1997, 2002). Another smaller-scale example is a series of studies conducted by Vanderbilt students under the direction of M. L. Hemmeter and Jennifer Ledford, providing more limited evidence of the generality of peer-mediated intervention *Stay-Play-Talk* for establishing proximal play between children in early childhood classrooms (Milam et al., 2021; Osborne et al., 2019; Severini et al., 2019; Soemarjono, 2022; Tang, 2023; Taylor, 2023). This group of studies, along with studies done by unaffiliated researchers, suggests that *Stay-Play-Talk* will result in changes in proximal play behaviors (for a review, see Ledford & Pustejovsky, 2023) but the across-study replications were less comprehensive than the previous series by Gast and Wolery because most implementers were researchers, rather than a mix of researchers and various endogenous implementers.

When conducting across-study replications, it is important to identify potential critical and non-critical features of the intervention, implementers, participants, and settings. These can be established using your theory of change (see Chapter 6) and will guide the direction of your replication attempt. For example, if you identify a specific intervention component as a critical feature, you would include that feature in all replication attempts. If it is potentially non-critical, it may be worthwhile to vary the feature to answer the question about criticalness.

We agree with previous researchers (Cronbach et al., 1980; Cronbach & Shapiro, 1982) who have argued that scientists should not be responsible for answering questions that other researchers or practitioners have about a topic and that no one context is more important than another. While applicability across multiple contexts is useful for understanding the boundaries of generality, there is no "appropriate" amount of external validity that can be established for a given relation. The external validity of relations is viewed along a continuum in which the number of variables that change between studies will determine the extent of generality established. A relation that only holds in limited contexts for a specific *type* of participant is quite important to a practitioner when that context and participant type matches their context and client.

Tactics for Maximizing the Impact of an Across-Study Replication

There are no universally accepted guidelines indicating how many variables a researcher should modify during an across-study replication, nor how such experiments should be arranged. Sidman (1960) called systematic replication a gamble, one that if successful, would "buy reliability, generality, and additional information" (p. 112). On the one hand, large changes that yield a reproduction of previous outcomes can speak volumes about the generality of a previously established effect. On the other, when there are a substantial number of changes to a protocol and the new procedure fails to reproduce the original effect, it can be challenging to determine which of the modified or omitted variables was critical to a procedure's original success(es).

If designed properly, whatever the outcome of an across-study replication attempt, our understanding of the phenomenon being studied can be enhanced. The key to success may be to remain conservative in scope and to modify only a few variables at a time (Johnston & Pennypacker, 2009; Kazdin, 2010). In so doing, even failures to replicate can be instructional because it is easier to determine how the omission of a previously unknown critical variable impacts the overall outcome of an intervention; thus, leading to the discovery of limitations of current interventions and the discovery of new interventions.

Relatedly, Sidman (1960) recommended that researchers initiate across-study replications including extensions by first replicating the original experiment in question, with the intent of reproducing the original outcome. When a direct replication fails to reproduce the original effect, information about the generality of said effect is offered. By contrast, when a direct replication reproduces the original effect, this outcome can serve as a baseline condition which can then be used to extend our understanding of *how* controlling variables alter participant performance.

For example, consider a researcher who wants to explore the durability of treatment effects following functional communication training (FCT; Carr & Durand, 1985)—which most often includes reinforcer available for 100% of opportunities—to situations in which reinforcement for a communicative response is reduced to 10% of opportunities. Following Sidman's recommendation, they would first directly replicate the original FCT procedure (i.e., reinforce communicative responses across 100% of opportunities) and reproduce the original outcome (i.e., a precipitous decrease in challenging behavior and an increase in independently emitted communicative responses). Then, they would explore how (if at all) a 90% decrease in reinforcer availability might impact baseline performance. In so doing, the baseline demonstration (1) serves as a direct replication and offers additional evidence of the reliability of the original effect, and (2) offers the research team a degree of credibility which allows them to more convincingly draw conclusions about the interpretability of both positive and/or null effects resultant from their subsequent manipulation. For example, if the above-mentioned researcher found that FCT was ineffective when reinforcement was only available 10% of the time, the baseline demonstration would allow them to assert that the degradation in treatment outcome was due to the corresponding decrease in reinforcer availability, rather than a lack of talent. That is, because the researcher first demonstrated that they could produce the original effect, critics could not claim that the lack of effect was attributable to the researcher's incompetence. Of course, this strategy does not always align with the intended research questions—for example, if a researcher was interested in whether FCT was effective when reinforcers were provided for 80% of opportunities *from the beginning of intervention*, the authors could not first replicate traditional FCT. Nonetheless, when procedures consistently produce stable outcomes, systematic lines of inquiry that employ this "baseline" strategy can amass a considerable amount of evidence supporting the reliability of the original relation while simultaneously exploring the parameters and boundary conditions that establish such relations.

Failures to replicate should "spur further research rather than lead to a single rejection of the original data" (Sidman, 1960, p. 74). "Science progresses by integrating, and not by throwing out, seemingly discrepant data" (Sidman, 1960, p. 83). In this regard, as an applied researcher, your responsibility is to identify modifications to the original intervention, or identify an alternative intervention, that will be beneficial to the participant. It is not generally acceptable to simply note that there was a failure to replicate and move on; this is partially because identifying and evaluating an alternative *effective* behavior change procedure will provide information about *why* the original procedure was ineffective and provides evidence that the behavior was amenable to change and that data collection procedures were sufficiently sensitive and valid.

Considerations Relevant to External Validity

Below we discuss the four features that are commonly discussed in relation to the external and ecological validity of relations (Shadish, Cook, & Campbell, 2001)—participants, contexts (settings), dependent variables, and intervention features.

Participant Characteristics

When an educator or practitioner considers using an intervention with a student or client based on one or more single case studies, they may ask: "What individual characteristics or variables should I consider in determining the likelihood that the intervention under consideration will be successful with my students or clients?" There are several variables that they might consider, including status variables and functional characteristics. **Status variables** are participant descriptors including gender, age, race, ethnicity, disability, academic achievement, grade level, educational placement, and geographic location (Research Committee of the Council for Learning Disabilities; Rosenberg et al., 1992). This type of descriptive information is common and expected in research reports, but is it sufficient for determining whether an intervention will generalize to an individual with similar status variable descriptors? Wolery and Ezell (1993) assert that status variables are only "part of the picture" for determining external validity, and "that failure to replicate in subsequent research or in clinical and educational settings is undoubtedly related to many other variables than the precise description of subject characteristics" (p. 643). In a brief review of constant time delay (CTD) research they found that despite consistent findings across several studies, procedural modifications were necessary even though participants "were nearly identical on status variables." They concluded that status variables were, if not unimportant, at least not *the most important* considerations for intervention success.

But if status variables are not the best predictors of generalization, what variables are? We suggest that functional characteristics are likely better predictors. **Functional characteristics** are features that are particularly relevant to the relation being studied; that is, they are functionally related to the independent and dependent variables. For example, when studying naturalistic developmental behavioral interventions (NDBIs) for young children, the extent to which children initiate communication, engage in conventional play behaviors, and actively avoid proximity with others may be functional characteristics that impact intervention success more so than age, disability status, or race/ethnicity. In a study designed to increase conversation for young children with autism, Bateman et al. (2023) reported important demographic/status variables (e.g., age, diagnosis, home language spoken) but also reported each participant's typical expressive and receptive language levels ("vocally labeled a wide variety of two-dimensional and three-dimensional stimuli and receptively identified many common items ... imitated adult actions, followed many 1-step directions, and was beginning to respond appropriately and correctly when asked personal information questions," p. 167). This information is likely critical for determining the characteristics of autistic children likely to benefit from the intervention. (We note here that we use both person-first and identify-first language in this text, given the variability in preferences for the subset of the population who have had the opportunity to share their opinions (e.g., Bury et al., 2023; Kenny et al., 2016).)

One way to assess functional characteristics is to describe the characteristics of participants' pre-intervention environments (e.g., response contingencies, number of opportunities to respond) and their behavior patterns. For example, during a large group activity in a classroom, with multiple opportunities for choral responding and social praise for correct answers, assume two young children (JD and Kenton) respond often and correctly and two young children (Kyson and Myles) respond rarely. In this case, all are 4-year-old males but baseline responding is consistently different for Kyson and Myles, perhaps indicating that intervention is required. This, however, is not enough to confirm that the *same* intervention is likely to result in behavior change. For example, during teacher interviews you might learn that Kyson's academic skills are advanced, but his motivation is low (indicating potential need for a reinforcement-based intervention), while Myles has more difficulty with acquiring the academic skills targeted during the large group activity (indicating a potential need for a focused academic intervention). Thus, information about the baseline performance of participants can, and should, be gleaned from multiple sources and used to determine the extent to which participants are similar on critical variables potentially impacting intervention success. Another example of this critical concept is that high rates of challenging behavior in a baseline condition for two individuals do not necessarily implicate that the same intervention would be successful for reducing those behaviors—instead the function of the behavior (along with other contextual information) is more likely to lead to appropriate intervention selection. To determine what variables are critical, you must gain expertise in the relation being studied, including specifying a theory of change for your independent variable (see Chapter 6).

Context Characteristics

Experiments, including single case experiments, are often performed in atypical settings or activities. For example, even work described as *naturalistic* often takes place in research clinics (e.g., NDBIs, Windsor & Ledford, 2023) and work conducted in inclusive settings often takes place during activities carefully designed and controlled by researchers (e.g., pull-out instructional sessions with a researcher; Eyler & Ledford, 2023; Chazin & Ledford, 2021). We will refer to settings, activities, materials, and social partners as "context characteristics."

Not all experiments include questions about applicability in typical settings, and some researchers have pointed out that findings in a "typical" setting are no more generalizable (i.e., to other, different settings) than those in laboratory contexts (Birnbrauer, 1981). However, variability in context characteristics across multiple studies does provide evidence that the relations identified in one or more studies are robust to context differences. Thus, it is critical to describe the important, functional characteristics of contexts and activities so that others understand the evidence of generality that is present in a given body of work. For example, in the study by Bateman et al. (2023) discussed above, researchers describe the type of classroom, number of children present and their disability status, the activity type and seating arrangement, and procedures for redirecting non-participants—all of this information is important for replicability and understanding the context in which the relation can be expected.

Dependent Variables

Relations between dependent and independent variables can also vary by measurement and features of the dependent variable. For example, the relation between Intervention A and the rate of challenging behavior may vary based on the sensitivity of the measurement system and the topographical characteristics of the measured behavior (e.g., whether the behaviors are defined to include aggression, disruption, self-injury, etc.). Similarly, the relation between Intervention B and academic performance may be different based on the similarity of teaching targets to measurement, the breadth and number of targets, and the domain of behaviors (e.g., math, reading). The more variable the dependent variable features are across studies, the greater the evidence for generality of the relation with the larger construct of interest.

Intervention Features

The relation between an independent variable and dependent variable can also vary based on differences in implementation of the independent variable present across studies. Common ways interventions may vary include:

- **Frequency and dosage of intervention implementation.** The frequency and dosage of intervention implementation may impact relations between the intervention and dependent variables. The relation between frequency/dosage and outcomes is rarely experimentally established, but a body of work that shows relations are consistent even when variability in dosage exists provides evidence of external validity in this domain.
- **Variations in procedures.** Generally, interventions conducted across studies are not implemented in identical ways. For example, one researcher may use poker chips as tokens for correct responding during an instructional session, while another may provide brief

access to a preferred toy. Generality across differences in implementation provide evidence that the relation is robust to variations in procedures. Sometimes, a general framework is used to establish a relation between a given dependent variable (e.g., rate of challenging behavior) and a *process of intervention selection and implementation* rather than a specific procedure. This type of research provides evidence that *decisions* made using a framework, which vary by participant, can lead to similar outcomes. These studies may provide *within-study* evidence of external validity in relation to procedural variations.

- **Implementer role, training, and qualifications**. Evidence that a given relation holds with a variety of implementers may be valuable in predicting its utility outside the research context. For example, enhanced milieu teaching, an NDBI, has been implemented by teachers, parents, and graduate students (increasing evidence of external validity in relation to implementer status), but only after considerable training and coaching from skilled researchers (providing limited evidence of external validity in relation to variations in intensity of implementer training; Quinn, Kaiser & Ledford, 2021; Roberts et al., 2014; Wright & Kaiser, 2017).
- **Fidelity of intervention implementation**. Relations that hold even when the intervention is not implemented as planned are highly valuable, since it may be difficult for **endogenous implementers** (i.e., individuals normally present in an individual's typical environment) to consistently implement some interventions with high fidelity. Some relations may be durable in the presence of fidelity failures while others could require high-fidelity implementation. Data regarding the extent to which intervention implementation occurred as planned is critical for identifying relations between fidelity and outcomes (see Chapter 6).

Related Constructs

Ecological Validity

Ecological validity refers to the extent to which study features relate to *real-world* contexts, and as such, is considered an important aspect of external validity. Studies with a high degree of ecological validity (e.g., studies conducted in a typical setting with endogenous implementers) provide greater confidence that discovered relations will hold in those relevant contexts; by contrast, studies with a low degree of ecological validity (e.g., studies conducted in an austere research space with unfamiliar researchers as implementers) do not establish the generality of relations to other non-research contexts. When single case research is conducted to improve the everyday life of human participants, it is paramount to establish that demonstrated relations hold under typical and relevant conditions. As such, ecologically valid research is commonly desired among behavioral researchers. However, it is not accurate to assume that relations demonstrated under highly contrived conditions cannot contribute to robust and generalized phenomena; rather, across-study replication along the continuum of ecological validity (from basic, to translational, to applied research) has proven a successful strategy for the discovery of phenomena with high degrees of generality and has formed the foundation of the science of human behavior (Fahmie et al., 2023).

Construct Validity

Another concept somewhat related to generality and external validity is that of **construct validity**, which refers to the extent that features of a study are representative of the actual concepts of interest. Generally, construct validity has been conceptualized as pertaining primarily

Table 2.2 Examples of Threats to Construct Validity

Domain	Threats to Construct Validity		
	Inadequate Explication of Constructs	*Inaccurate or Non-Conventional Explication of Constructs*	*Construct Confounding*
Participants	Authors describe participants as being "at risk" but do not describe characteristics leading to this designation.	Authors describe participants with autism but include infant siblings without official autism diagnoses.	Authors describe children as having challenging behavior, but they are identified by teacher report, which is confounded with race and culture.
Settings	Authors report their study is conducted in a "school" but fail to describe that it is a private program with 1:1 staffing and highly-trained, research-involved implementers.	Authors describe the setting as "free play in the classroom" but provide only one toy and no peers are present.	Authors describe two settings for measurement as *segregated* and *inclusive* but do not specify supports and structure in each setting likely to be related to intervention success variation (e.g., one-to-one support in one setting but not the other).
Treatment Variables	Authors report the use of *visual supports* but provide no information about topographical or functional characteristics of these visuals.	Authors describe the use of response interruption and redirection (RIRD) but only use interruption rather than providing redirection to a meaningful activity.	Authors describe the use of a reinforcement-based intervention but fail to describe that one active ingredient of the intervention was more consistent use of response cost (a punishment-based procedure).
Measurement Variables	Authors measure *challenging behavior* but do not provide operational definitions of the behaviors included.	Authors use *challenging behavior* to refer to a variety of behaviors, including "precursor behaviors" which would not conventionally be considered to be problematic.	Authors measure stereotypy across conditions, but in one condition, they do not include stereotypy occurring during active intervention segments.

to dependent variables. However, as with external validity, Shadish et al. (2001) describe four areas in which construct validity issues can occur: Participants, settings, dependent variables, and intervention features. One way to think about construct validity is to ask: Are the labels used in my study representative of the ideas I'm attempting to convey, or are they misaligned, incomplete, or not sufficiently specific? Construct validity is not necessarily tied to the relation identified, although difficulties with construct validity can impact conclusions drawn about the relation. Here, we identify two threats to construct validity most applicable to single case design, using terms suggested by Shadish et al. (2001); and describe one additional problem not identified by Shadish (inaccurate or non-conventional explication of constructs). In Table 2.2, we describe examples of how these problems can occur across the four types of study features.

- **Inadequate explication of constructs**: This problem refers to the insufficient description of a study feature. Insufficient descriptions of participants, settings, dependent variables, and intervention characteristics limits correct interpretation of the concepts that authors intended to convey in their studies. For example, an author who describes participants simply as *children with autism* prevents readers from understanding functional characteristics of participants likely to benefit from the intervention given the heterogeneity associated with autistic individuals.
- **Inaccurate or non-conventional explication of constructs**: This problem, not described by Shadish et al. (2001), refers to the use of a term that is applied non-conventionally

rather than non-adequately. For example, authors might use different terms for the same intervention, or the same term for interventions that are quite different. This problem has been identified as a serious impediment to synthesizing relations across studies (cf. Ledford et al., 2021). Relatedly, authors can use terms such as *challenging behavior* to refer to a variety of behaviors, including "precursor behaviors" which would not conventionally be considered to be problematic.

- **Construct confounding**: This problem occurs when a described feature of a study is confounded with an unconsidered feature. For example, authors of a study may suggest that Intervention A is effective for changing the behavior of children with challenging behaviors. However, the components of the described intervention (one construct) co-occurred with an uncontrolled additional feature—positive and responsive adult interactions (a separate construct). Thus, it is possible that the second construct, rather than the intended one, could be partly or wholly responsible for the intervention effect.

We note that some items described by Shadish as related to *construct validity* are conceptualized as being threats to *internal validity* and described in Chapter 3 (experimenter expectancies and treatment diffusion, as related to procedural infidelity; novelty and disruption effects as related to adaptation; reactivity to experimental situation as Hawthorne effects). The differences are subtle—there is a construct validity issue when there is a concern about the extent to which study features match constructs of interest, but an internal validity issue when something about the study features impede our ability to draw causal conclusions. Construct validity has not been explicitly discussed in previous versions of this textbook (Ledford & Gast, 2018) or other well-regarded single case texts. Thus, we provide considerations for construct validity as preliminary guidance for the field. We acknowledge that additional work in this area, including specific guidance for avoiding these threats, would be beneficial for the field.

Recommendations for Across-Study Replications

If you wish to initiate an across-study replication attempt, we suggest you proceed using the following general steps. More information is provided about reviewing and summarizing literature in Chapters 18 and 19.

1. Identify studies that relate to your research interest(s) or question(s) via electronic search, author search, or ancestral search (see Chapter 19). It may be helpful to review recently published literature reviews and meta-analyses on your topic for a comprehensive reference list of empirical investigations that addressed the same or similar research question(s).
2. Organize information about the studies, including ways they are similar and different across domains (e.g., participants, settings, dependent variables, intervention features).
3. Read and list researchers' suggestions for future research on the topic. These are commonly found in the discussion section of research reports.
4. Write your research question(s), if you haven't already, considering previous research, your own clinical or educational expertise, and practical resource constraints (e.g., access to participants, daily schedule, availability of materials, control of contingencies).
5. Identify potential critical and non-critical features of the intervention, critical functional characteristics of participants, setting features that might impact replication, and measurement issues that have not been addressed in previous work.
6. Determine which features will remain the same as in previous work and which feature(s) will vary, using your theory of change (Chapter 6).

7. Write and revise a research proposal, explicitly stating that the study is a replication attempt, and report the specific differences between your proposed study and those that have preceded it.
8. Conduct the study according to your written protocols and note whether relations identified in previous studies hold given your specific variations. In cases of "failure to replicate," your ability to implement a successful variation of, or alternative to the original intervention, will advance understanding of the reliability, generality, and limitations of the relation of interest.

Conclusion

Careful consideration of the constructs of interest and replication of previously identified relations are essential for evaluating generality. Across-study replication is ongoing, never over, as a failure to replicate may be just around the corner. When outcomes are not reproduced as expected, a limitation to the external validity of the relation is revealed. Applied behavioral researchers approach such failures as a challenge and attempt to identify their cause, as well as to identify modifications to the original intervention that will bring about the desired behavior change. Through the replication process, the science of human behavior is advanced and our ability to design effective and efficient instructional and treatment programs enhanced.

References

Bateman, K. J., Wilson, S. E., Gauvreau, A., Matthews, K., Gucwa, M., Therrien, W., ... & Mazurek, M. (2023). Visual supports to increase conversation engagement for preschoolers with autism spectrum disorder during mealtimes: An initial investigation. *Journal of Early Intervention*, 45(2), 163–184.

Birnbrauer, J. S. (1981). External validity and experimental investigation of individual behavior. *Analysis and Intervention in Developmental Disabilities*, 1, 117–132.

Bury, S. M., Jellett, R., Spoor, J. R., & Hedley, D. (2023). "It defines who I am" or "It's something I have": What language do [autistic] Australian adults [on the autism spectrum] prefer?. *Journal of Autism and Developmental Disorders*, 53(2), 677–687.

Carr, E. G., & Durand, V. M. (1985). Reducing behavior problems through functional communication training. *Journal of Applied Behavior Analysis*, 18(2), 111–126.

Chazin, K. T., & Ledford, J. R. (2021). Constant time delay and system of least prompts: Efficiency and child preference. *Journal of Behavioral Education*, 30(4), 684–707.

Cronbach, L. J., & Shapiro, K. (1982). *Designing evaluations of educational and social programs*. San Francisco: Jossey-Bass.

Cronbach, L. J., Ambron, S. R., Dornbusch, S. M., Hess, R. D., Hornik, R. C., Phillips, D. C., ... & Weiner, S. S. (1980). *Toward reform of program evaluation* (p. 3). San Francisco: Jossey-Bass.

Doyle, P. M., Gast, D. L., Wolery, M., Ault, M. J., & Farmer, J. A. (1990). Use of constant time delay in small group instruction: A study of observational and incidental learning. *The Journal of Special Education*, 23(4), 369–385.

Eyler, P. B., & Ledford, J. R. (2023). Efficiency and child preference for specific prompting procedures. https://osf.io/dpq5w/

Fahmie, T. A., Rodriguez, N. M., Luczynski, K. C., Rahaman, J. A., Charles, B. M., & Zangrillo, A. N. (2023). Toward an explicit technology of ecological validity. *Journal of Applied Behavior Analysis*, 56(2), 302–322.

Gast, D. L., Doyle, P. M., Wolery, M., Ault, M. J., & Baklarz, J. L. (1991). Acquisition of incidental information during small group instruction. *Education and Treatment of Children*, 14(1), 1–18.

Gast, D. L., Wolery, M., Morris, L. L., Doyle, P. M., & Meyer, S. (1990). Teaching sight word reading in a group instructional arrangement using constant time delay. *Exceptionality: A Special Education Journal*, 1(2), 81–96.

Holcombe, A., Wolery, M., & Snyder, E. (1994). Effects of two levels of procedural fidelity with constant time delay on children's learning. *Journal of Behavioral Education*, 4, 49–73.

Johnston, J. M., & Pennypacker, H. S. (2009). *Strategies and tactics of behavioral research* (3rd ed.). New York: Routledge.

Kazdin, A. (2010). *Single-case research designs: Methods for clinical and applied settings*. New York: Oxford University Press.

Kenny, L., Hattersley, C., Molins, B., Buckley, C., Povey, C., & Pellicano, E. (2016). Which terms should be used to describe autism? Perspectives from the UK autism community. *Autism*, 20(4), 442–462. https://doi.org/10.1177/1362361315588200

Ledford, J. R., Lambert, J. M., Barton, E. E., & Ayres, K. M. (2021). The evidence base for interventions for individuals with ASD: A call to improve practice conceptualization and synthesis. *Focus on Autism and Other Developmental Disabilities*, 36(3), 135–147.

Ledford, J. R., & Gast, D. L. (2018). *Single case research methodology*, 3rd ed. New York: Routledge.

Ledford, J. R., & Pustejovsky, J. E. (2023). Systematic review and meta-analysis of stay-play-talk interventions for improving social behaviors of young children. *Journal of Positive Behavior Interventions*, 25(1), 65–77.

Milam, M. E., Hemmeter, M. L., & Barton, E. E. (2021). The effects of systematic instruction on preschoolers' use of Stay-Play-Talk with their peers with social delays. *Journal of Early Intervention*, 43(1), 80–96.

Osborne, K., Ledford, J. R., Martin, J., & Thorne, K. (2019). Component analysis of stay, play, talk interventions with and without self-monitored group contingencies and recorded reminders. *Topics in Early Childhood Special Education*, 39(1), 5–18.

Quinn, E. D., Kaiser, A. P., & Ledford, J. (2021). Hybrid telepractice delivery of enhanced milieu teaching: Effects on caregiver implementation and child communication. *Journal of Speech, Language, and Hearing Research*, 64(8), 3074–3099.

Roberts, M. Y., Kaiser, A. P., Wolfe, C. E., Bryant, J. D., & Spidalieri, A. M. (2014). Effects of the teach-model-coach-review instructional approach on caregiver use of language support strategies and children's expressive language skills. *Journal of Speech, Language, and Hearing Research*, 57(5), 1851–1869.

Rosenberg, M. S., Bott, D., Majsterek, D., Chiang, B., Bartland, D., Wesson, C., Graham, S., et al. (1992). Minimum standards for the description of participants in learning disabilities research. *Learning Disabilities Quarterly*, 15, 65–70.

Schuster, J. W., Gast, D. L., Wolery, M., & Guiltinan, S. (1988). The effectiveness of a constant time-delay procedure to teach chained responses to adolescents with mental retardation. *Journal of Applied Behavior Analysis*, 21(2), 169–178.

Severini, K. E., Ledford, J. R., Barton, E. E., & Osborne, K. C. (2019). Implementing stay-play-talk with children who use AAC. *Topics in Early Childhood Special Education*, 38(4), 220–233.

Shadish, W. R., Cook, T. D., & Campbell, D. T. (2001). *Experimental and quasi-experimental designs for generalized causal inference*. Boston, MA: Cengage Learning.

Sidman, M. (1960). *Tactics of scientific research—Evaluating experimental data in psychology*. New York: Basic Books.

Soemarjono, F. (2022). Comparing stay play talk with or without reinforcement versus business-as-usual on children's duration of play and talk (Unpublished Master's thesis). Vanderbilt University.

Tang, L. (2023). *Using stay-play-talk to increase levels of initiations and responses for children with social delays* (Master's thesis). http://hdl.handle.net/1803/18085

Taylor, A. L. (2023). *An adaptation of stay-play-talk for young children with internalizing behaviors.* (Doctoral dissertation, Vanderbilt University).

Windsor, S. A., & Ledford, J. R. (2023). Naturalistic developmental behavioral interventions: A systematic review of procedures, participants, and outcomes. *Under review*.

Wolery, M., Anthony, L., Caldwell, N. K., Snyder, E. D., & Morgante, J. D. (2002). Embedding and distributing constant time delay in circle time and transitions. *Topics in Early Childhood Special Education*, 22(1), 14–25.

Wolery, M., Anthony, L., Snyder, E. D., Werts, M. G., & Katzenmeyer, J. (1997). Training elementary teachers to embed instruction during classroom activities. *Education and Treatment of Children*, 20(1), 40–58.

Wolery, M. & Ezell, H. (1993). Participant descriptions and single participant research. *Journal of Learning Disabilities*, 26, 642–647.

Wright, C. A., & Kaiser, A. P. (2017). Teaching parents enhanced milieu teaching with words and signs using the teach-model-coach-review model. *Topics in Early Childhood Special Education*, 36(4), 192–204.

3
Establishing Internal Validity via Within-Study Replication

Jennifer R. Ledford and Kevin M. Ayres

Important Terms

intra-participant replication, inter-participant replication, internal validity, history effects, history threats, maturation effects, maturation threats, facilitative testing effects, inhibitive testing effects, testing threats, instrumentation, procedural infidelity, attrition, attrition bias, sampling bias, data instability, cyclical variability, multi-treatment interference, regression to the mean, adaptation, Hawthorne Effect

Table of Contents

Within-Study Replication
Internal Validity
   Threats to Internal Validity
      History
      Maturation
      Testing
      Instrumentation
      Procedural Infidelity
      Selection Bias
      Multiple-Treatment Interference
      Data Instability
      Adaptation
      Design-Related Confounds
Conclusions
References

Callout

3.1 A Note on Terminology

DOI: 10.4324/9781003294726-4

As described in Chapter 2, replication refers to repeating attempts to establish a functional relation between a specific independent variable on a dependent variable. Replication is important in all research paradigms, and, in fact, the failure to replicate has been referred to as a "crisis" in psychology, behavioral science, education, and related literatures (Coyne et al., 2016; Locey, 2020; Shrout & Rodgers, 2018). The replication rate in published single case design research is higher than that of between-groups research (Lemons et al., 2014), although failures to replicate are difficult to locate because of the "file drawer effect" which describes the reluctance or inability of researchers to publish findings that show that an intervention *does not work* under some conditions (Gage et al., 2017; Tincani & Travers, 2019). As described in Chapter 2, there is some inconsistency in terminology used across time within in the field. We will refer to replication that occurs in a single study as *within-study replication*, and that is the focus of this chapter.

Within-Study Replication

What we refer to as within-study replication was defined as *direct replication* by Sidman (1960) as "the repetition of a given experiment by the same experimenter … accomplished either by performing the experiment again with new subjects or by making repeated observations on the same subject under each of several conditions" (p. 73). He describes two relevant classes of these replications: Intra-participant direct replication and inter-participant direct replication (historically, "intra-subject" and "inter-subject"—see Chapters 1 and 16 for a discussion of the use of the term "participant" rather than "subject"). Contemporary guidelines (e.g., Ledford et al., 2023) call for every single case study to include multiple attempts at replication (see Chapters 9, 11, and 13 for more information about the various ways in which replications are built into common single case designs).

Both intra-participant and inter-participant replications refer to an investigator's attempts to repeat an experimental effect. Repeated attempts for the same participant are referred to as **intra-participant replication**. For example, researchers have evaluated whether parent training improved the extent to which parents of young children with disabilities used *matched turns* (first demonstration), *target talk* (replication), and *expansions* (another replication) with their children (Peredo, Zelaya, & Kaiser, 2018) when intervention was applied to each behavior sequentially. Thus, for each participant, there were three opportunities for demonstration of the relation between the intervention and targeted interaction skills. Repeated attempts for different participants in the same study are referred to as **inter-participant replication**. For example, researchers have evaluated whether children learn better with and prefer time delay prompting procedures or the system of least prompt strategy, and included replication of the comparison for 6–10 children in a single study (e.g., Eyler & Ledford, 2023; Chazin & Ledford, 2021). Single case design studies with more than one participant can include both intra- and inter-participant replication. See Figures 3.1 and 3.2 for examples of a replicated relation for a single participant (intra-participant replication) and multiple participants (inter-participant replication). In Figure 3.1, the comparison between baseline and intervention conditions is repeated over time with the same participant by alternating between phases (an A-B-A-B design, discussed in detail in Chapters 9 and 10). In Figure 3.2, the comparison between baseline and intervention conditions is repeated with three different participants (a multiple baseline across participants design, discussed in detail in Chapters 11 and 12).

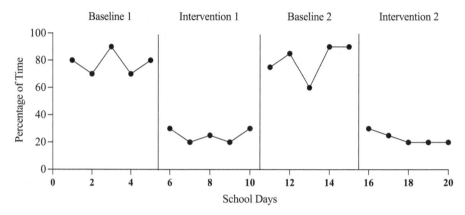

Figure 3.1 Intra-Participant Replication.

Note: This figure depicts within-participant replication of effects (i.e., intra-participant replication), with high levels of behavior in the first baseline condition (School Days 1–5), followed by a decrease in levels in the first intervention condition (School Days 6–10). This effect is then replicated with the same participant (School Days 11–20).

Callout 3.1   A Note on Terminology

Given we have already used the term *condition* multiples times, it seems important to define the term and to compare it with the similar term *phase*, since these terms are often used interchangeably and were not consistently used in the previous version of this text. We will use the term **condition** to refer to a collection of **measurement occasions** (e.g., each time point at which you measure behaviors, often divided into segments such as days, dates, or sessions) during which identical procedures are used. For example, a **baseline condition** refers to a collection of sessions during which the same non-intervention conditions are applied while an **intervention condition** refers to a collection of sessions during which the same treatment procedures are applied. These sessions need not be consecutive or adjacent; they are referred to as a single condition because of their procedural identicalness. To confuse matters, the plural of the term is sometimes used to refer to the procedures themselves (e.g., *baseline conditions* can be used interchangeably with *baseline procedures*). We will use the term **phase** to refer to a collection of sessions that occur during a given period of time. In some designs, conditions can be implemented in two different phases (e.g., baseline conditions can occur in two temporally separate phases, one before intervention implementation and one after intervention withdrawal), and in some phases, multiple conditions can be implemented (you can read more about this in Chapters 13 and 14 on rapid iterative alternation designs). In summary, a *condition* refers to a collection of sessions that are procedurally connected, while a *phase* refers to a collection of sessions that are temporally connected.

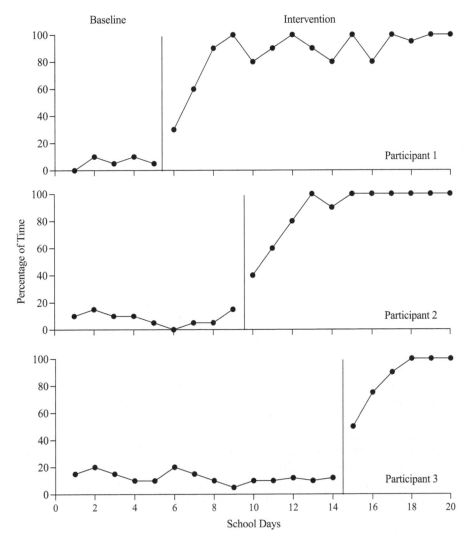

Figure 3.2 Intra-Participant Replication.

Note: This figure depicts across-participant replication of effects (i.e., inter-participant replication), with low levels of behavior in the baseline condition for Participant 1, followed by an increasing trend and high levels in the intervention condition (top panel). This effect is then replicated with two additional participants (Participant 2, middle panel; Participant 3, bottom panel).

Internal Validity

The purpose of both intra- and inter-participant replication is to provide confirmatory evidence that the relation that was initially observed is the result of a researcher's planned manipulations rather than any other cause that is external to the study. That is, within-study replication is necessary for establishing **internal validity**—the extent to which the relations observed in the study can be confidently attributed to the planned changes between conditions *and only to those changes*. For example, a researcher might collect data in a classroom across five days during a school week and observe high rates of off-task behavior for a particular child. That researcher might devise and implement an intervention the next school week and observe reduced rates of off-task behavior. However, many alternative explanations are possible for the change in behavior—perhaps the child was ill during the first week of observations and felt well the second week. Or they may have been distracted by the researcher during the first week but acclimated to his presence the second week. Many possible and plausible explanations could exist for the difference. However, if the researcher attempted to replicate the relation by observing *without the intervention* during a third week, and again *with the intervention* during a fourth week, and the relations held (e.g., higher off-task behavior during no-intervention weeks and lower off-task behavior during intervention weeks), we would be more confident that differences in condition procedures were the cause of behavior change. Of course, even this is not foolproof—for example, the child may have been with a parent who enforced an early bedtime in weeks 2 and 4 but with a parent who had a later bedtime rule during weeks 1 and 3. This is why contemporary guidelines require specific ways of ordering the replications to ensure probable alternative explanations are ruled out (see Chapters 9, 11, and 13).

Threats to Internal Validity

Internal validity of a study depends on how well the researcher has controlled or mitigated other plausible explanations for behavior change beyond those planned experimental changes. Two concepts are important for understanding the pragmatics of internal validity. First, it is impossible to control for every possible alternative explanation. Second, a possible alternative explanation may not be an actual threat. Each possible alternative explanation should be considered in the design of your study and the analysis of other researchers' studies. The extent to which threats to validity are evaluated and controlled for, along with the presence of a sufficient number of within-study replications, will determine the level of confidence you have in the findings. You should not be disheartened to learn that just as there is no free lunch, there is no perfect experiment. Instead, there are carefully designed experiments, experiments that are executed as carefully as they were planned and that provide "adequate and proper data" (Campbell & Stanley, 1963, p. 2) for analysis. Your task is to describe what happened during the experiment and to be able to account for planned and unplanned outcomes. Below is a non-exhaustive list of threats to internal validity that may be likely in studies using single case design; many are also applicable for other experimental studies (e.g., group comparison studies). Table 3.1 lists these threats in relation to threats listed by Shadish et al. (2002, a book primarily concerned with between-groups research). We note that he identifies some threats as related to internal validity and some to statistical conclusion validity (the extent to which changes occur, without regard to causality) or construct validity (discussed in Chapter 2). We consider all to be relevant to internal validity, as they relate to single case design. Also in Table 3.1 is how the threats identified by Shadish and colleagues were categorized by Petursdottir and Carr (2018), in relation to single case design.

It is important to minimize the likelihood of threats to internal validity so that you can draw confident conclusions about the relation between the independent variable (e.g., intervention) and dependent variable in a single case study. A <u>functional relation</u> is established when consistent behavior change occurs, in the expected direction, when and only when condition changes occur, *and* when likely threats to internal validity have been mitigated. Specific requirements for functional relations and how to establish them via visual analysis will be discussed more in Chapters 10, 12, and 14.

History
History effects refer to events that occur during an experiment, but that are not related to planned procedural changes, that may influence the outcome. These effects, and their potential influence on conclusions about internal validity, are detected via visual inspection of graphs and (when applicable) careful session notes (e.g., describing the occurrence of events that could

Table 3.1 Threats to Internal Validity, as Categorized by Other Researchers

Threats	Terminology Used by Shadish et al. (2002)	Type (Shadish et al., 2002)	Relevance to Single Case (Petursdottir & Carr, 2018)
History	History	Internal	Relevant
Maturation	Maturation	Internal	Relevant
Testing	Testing	Internal	Relevant
Attrition	Attrition	Internal	Not Relevant
Selection	Selection	Internal	Not Relevant
Regression to the Mean	Regression Artifacts	Internal	Not Relevant
Instrumentation	Unreliability of Measures	SC	Relevant
	Instrumentation	Internal	Relevant
Procedural Infidelity	Unreliability of Implementation	SC	Relevant
	Experimenter Expectancies	Construct	Relevant
	Treatment Diffusion	Construct	Relevant
Adaptation	Novelty and Disruption Effects	Construct	Relevant
Hawthorne Effect	Reactivity to Experimental Situation	Construct	Relevant
Multi-treatment Interference	Not Addressed	–	Relevant
Data Instability	Extraneous Variance in Experimental Setting	Statistical Conclusion	Relevant
Design-related Confounds	Not Addressed	–	–

Note: Shadish defines some threats as related to construct or statistical conclusion rather than internal validity. Petursdottir & Carr (2018) identify some as relevant to single case design. We consider all potentially relevant for at least some studies. SC = Statistical Conclusion Validity.

be related to participant behavior). Generally speaking, the longer the study (both in terms of the number of experimental sessions and number of calendar days), the greater the threat due to history. Potential sources of history effects, when a study is conducted in community settings, are the actions of others (parents, siblings, peers, childcare providers) or by study participants themselves (independent online research, observational learning, serendipitous exposure via social media). For behaviors that demand immediate attention in the eyes of a significant other, there may be an attempt to intervene prior to the scheduled intervention time. For example, while a researcher is implementing a token economy to reduce problem behaviors, a parent might introduce a separate (and unplanned) punishment procedure while the study is ongoing. While the parent may intend for the additional procedures to enhance your planned intervention (and while they may do this), this unplanned "history" effect will render your results less interpretable. Also, participants may learn target content through television or learn target social behaviors through observing the consequences delivered to others; the change in behavior resulting from this learning is a history effect. Other individual-specific unplanned events (e.g., seizure the night before, fight on the school bus, medication change) or community-wide events (e.g., school-wide policy change, widespread social unrest) may temporarily alter the occurrence of the target behavior.

A history effect that has a minimal impact on confidence in outcomes is depicted in the top panel of Figure 3.3. In this hypothetical example, a participant engaged in much lower levels of challenging behavior on a school day when he was ill. Because levels of challenging behavior

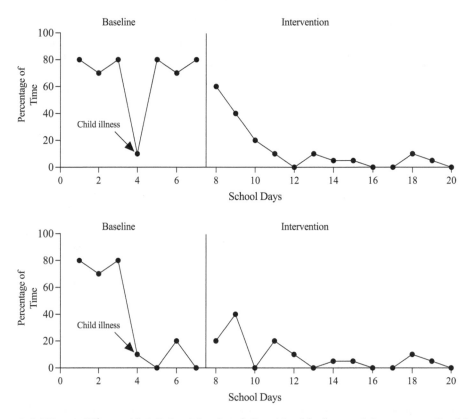

Figure 3.3 History Effects with Minimal (top) and Considerable (bottom) Impacts on Confidence in Relation between Independent and Dependent Variables.

Note: In the top panel, a potential history effect is depicted in the baseline condition. On School Day 4, a child was ill, which corresponded with unusually low levels of challenging behavior compared with the other six measurement occasions during baseline. Because levels were similar before and after the day that event occurred, our confidence in the relation between the independent and dependent levels is minimally impacted. In the bottom panel, the same decrease in level occurred when a child was ill, but levels remained low in the baseline condition following the illness. Thus, we cannot be reasonably certain that the intervention was responsible for any change in challenging behavior.

were consistently high on other days (before and after the illness), that one event has little impact on our interpretation of the effectiveness of the intervention. However, in the bottom panel of Figure 3.3, a **history threat**—an instance of a history effect that decreases internal validity and interpretability of results—is depicted. In this hypothetical example, the participant's challenging behavior does not increase in the school days following the illness. This prevents us from drawing conclusions about the effectiveness of the intervention. History threats generally cannot be prevented, although in some cases, it might be appropriate to ask participants to not engage in related outside activities that increase risk of history threats (e.g., beginning new related therapies, doing an Internet search about the intervention procedures prior to training); when these types of instructions are given to participants, they should be reported in written descriptions of the study.

It is important to note that history, as well as maturation and testing effects, may be unclear or indistinguishable from other threats via visual analysis. That is, we can hypothesize that a given event occurred (history threat) but we often cannot be certain that the hypothesized event is responsible for behavior change. Similarly, it may not be clear from graphs whether a history event outside of the study resulted in behavior change, or whether behavior change is due to testing procedures during baseline (described below), or some other factor.

Maturation

Maturation effects refer to changes in behavior due to the passage of time and are also detected via visual inspection of graphs. In a "short" duration study maturation is not likely to influence the analysis of the effectiveness of a powerful independent variable that focuses on improving language or motor skills of a child who has a history of slow development. If the study is carried out over several months or longer with the same young child, especially if an intervention is used during which slow and gradual improvements in skills are expected, there is a greater likelihood that maturation effects result in decreased interpretability. The top panel of Figure 3.4 shows a data pattern in baseline that might indicate a *maturation effect* (i.e., a child's behavior is changing due to the passage of time), but one that does not significantly impact conclusions drawn about change that occurs when the intervention is implemented. The bottom panel shows an instance of a **maturation threat**—an instance of a maturation effect that threatens the internal validity of the study, making interpretation of intervention effects difficult. Maturation threats are primarily prevented by avoiding long-duration studies (e.g.,

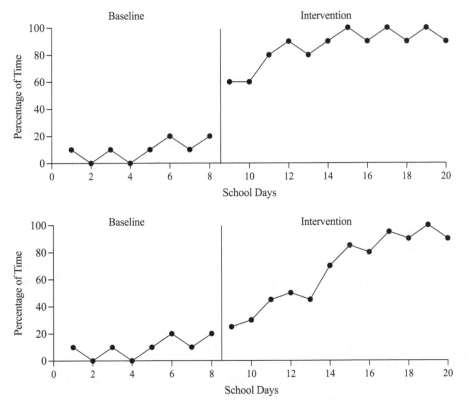

Figure 3.4 Maturation Effects with Minimal (top) and Considerable (bottom) Impacts on Confidence in Relation between Independent and Dependent Variables.

Note: In the top panel, the maturation effect is not worrisome because there is a clear and large change in behavior when the intervention condition begins. In the bottom panel, the maturation effect threatens internal validity because it is difficult to tell whether behavior gets to high levels because of maturation, the intervention, or an interaction of these factors.

scheduling sessions multiple times per week rather than one time per week, to reduce total time spent in each phase) and by assessing interventions that are likely to result in substantial and immediate improvements relative to baseline. Between-groups designs (see Chapter 1) are better suited for behaviors that are likely to change slowly over time during baseline *and* relatively slowly or with a delay during intervention.

Testing
Testing is a potential threat in any study that requires participants to respond to the same test repeatedly, especially during a baseline or probe condition; **testing effects** occur when repeated assessment tasks result in participant behavior change. Like history and maturation effects, testing effects can be detected via visual analysis of graphs.

Repeated testing may have a facilitative effect (improvement in performance over successive baseline or probe testing or observation sessions) or an inhibitive effect (deterioration in performance over successive baseline or probe testing or observation sessions) depending on how the "test" condition is designed. A test condition that repeatedly presents the same academic task, prompts correct responses through a correction procedure, or delivers reinforcement contingent upon a correct response, may result in a **facilitative testing effect**. This is, of course, beneficial for participants, but renders conclusions about subsequent intervention effects difficult to draw. Detecting facilitative testing effects in baseline often results in a decreased need for intervention; if researchers continue to intervene despite these effects, they produce a **testing threat**—which occurs when a history effect results in decreased internal validity and difficulty drawing conclusions about outcomes (see top panel of Figure 3.5). Test sessions of long duration, requiring substantial participant effort, with minimal or no reinforcement for attention and active participation may result in an **inhibitive testing effect**. If potential inhibitive effects are identified, baseline procedures can be modified to mitigate the effects to avoid a testing threat to internal validity that reduces internal validity. For example, the bottom panel of Figure 3.5 shows initial levels of behavior that ranged from 20–30% correct then decreased to 0% correct responding. This might happen, for example, if you failed to reinforce attempts or accurate responding during baseline conditions. A modified baseline (perhaps with additional instructions and opportunities for reinforcement) resulted in levels of behavior that was similar to that in initial sessions, perhaps representing a participant's "best effort."

Testing effects can be prevented by designing conditions so that they yield participants' best effort so that you neither overestimate nor underestimate the impact of the independent variable on the behavior. Facilitative effects of testing can be avoided by not reinforcing correct responses, particularly on receptive tasks; not correcting incorrect responses; and not prompting (intentionally or unintentionally) correct responses. Of course, these procedures (e.g., failing to reinforce correct responses) might be ethically or practically objectionable, and may impede later learning. Thus, you may decide that some level of facilitative procedures in baseline are acceptable. Procedural reliability checks will help with detecting procedural errors that could influence participant performance. Inhibitive effects of testing can be avoided by conducting sessions of an appropriate length and difficulty level (i.e., avoid session fatigue; intersperse known stimuli with unknown stimuli and reinforce correct responses to known stimuli; and reinforce correct responses on expressive, comprehension, and response chain tasks).

Instrumentation
Instrumentation threats refer to concerns with the measurement system that reduce confidence in outcomes (i.e., threaten internal validity); they are of particular concern in single case design studies because of repeated measurement by human observers who may make

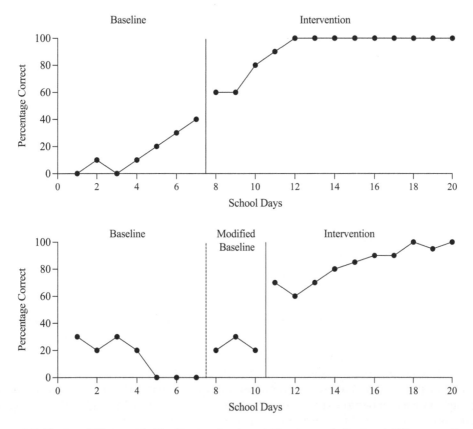

Figure 3.5 Testing Effects with Facilitative (top) and Detrimental (bottom) Effects on Baseline Performance.

Note. In the top panel, the participant could be learning the targeted behaviors due to simple repeated exposure or reinforcement for guessing in baseline, threatening internal validity because it isn't clear the extent to which changes in behavior are due to testing effects, the intervention, or a combination of those factors. In the bottom panel, failing to reinforce correct responding could have led to decreased effort for the participant and zero correct responding. Thus, a modification was required to get accurate baseline performance before initiating the intervention condition.

systematic errors. In studies using single case logic, the percentage agreement between two independent observers is the most common strategy for determining whether there is a threat to internal validity due to instrumentation (see more in Chapter 5). That is, two people observe the same event and record their decisions about how to characterize the event according to a specific set of rules. Afterward, they check to see the extent to which their decisions agree. Instrumentation threats are detected via analysis of these interobserver agreement (IOA) data. If agreement is low or changes over time, it may suggest that the data were not measured in a way consistent with the intent of researchers. You can avoid common problems by carefully defining behaviors of interest, using appropriate recording procedures, frequently checking for reliability by using a secondary observer, and visually analyzing data from both observers on the same graph (Artman et al., 2012; Ledford et al., 2012; Ledford & Wolery, 2013). Analyzing these data is covered in depth in Chapter 5.

Procedural Infidelity
Procedural infidelity refers to the lack of adherence to condition protocols by study implementers. It is detected via collection and analysis of *procedural fidelity data*—data that describe the extent to which implementers are implementing procedures as intended. Procedural infidelity might occur once (e.g., when a new research assistant has a misunderstanding about the situations under which she should reinforce a specific behavior and conducts one session using the wrong rules) or consistently (e.g., if teachers implementing your intervention consistently cannot engage in all of the planned behaviors in the complex setting of their classrooms). If the procedures of an experimental condition (baseline, probe, intervention, maintenance, generalization) are *consistently* not implemented as described in the Methods section of the research proposal or report, confidence that outcomes are related to the intervention is considerably reduced, resulting in a **procedural fidelity threat**. Further, even some momentary procedural fidelity lapses may result in uninterpretable data (e.g., Lambert et al., 2023). Procedural infidelity threats to internal validity can be avoided by defining clear rules for implementation, adequate implementer training and supports, and consistent collection and analysis of fidelity data, with modifications to training and supports provided as needed.

Selection Bias
Generally, participants are selected according to rules called *inclusion criteria*. **Selection bias** involves choosing participants using rules that are different than reported inclusion criteria and that are not apparent to non-researchers, and this is a threat when these rules are used in a way that differentially impacts the inclusion or retention of participants in a study, when compared to the population of interest. Several resources are available which discuss selection bias in group comparison designs (Pyrczak, 2016; Shadish et al., 2002). In single case research, the population refers to individuals who meet the inclusion criteria for the study and have similar functional characteristics to the participants (Lane et al., 2007; Wolery, Dunlap, & Ledford, 2011). For example, Ledford et al. (2017) included 12 children in a study to assess preference for massed versus embedded instruction, and named the following inclusion criteria: (1) ability to play developmentally appropriate games with turn-taking, (2) ability to make choices given line drawings, and (3) verbal imitation. Assume that Ledford and colleagues had 14 potential participants but decided to request consent from 12 due to resource constraints. Thus, she excluded two boys who had a history of not following directions during teacher-led activities (e.g., massed instruction) to reduce the risk of attrition. This decision leads to the potential for inaccurately identifying differential outcomes because of the purposeful exclusion of participants unlikely to perform well in one of the two conditions. As a side note, this particular hypothetical situation did not occur, but participants were chosen from a larger set of eligible students based on convenience, so sampling bias is still possible (e.g., we may have chosen students who had relatively high academic skills because students with higher support needs received more therapy and were thus available less frequently).

Attrition is the loss of participants during the course of a study, which can limit the generality of the findings, particularly if participants with certain characteristics are likely to drop out (e.g., participants who are not benefitting from the intervention). **Attrition threats** occur when participant loss (attrition) impacts the outcome of the study. Thus, when *any participant consents to participate in your study and does not complete the study*, you should always (1) explicitly report it, along with relevant information about why it occurred, and (2) include any data collected for that participant in your research report. This ensures that data from "non-responders" are not systematically excluded from published research, resulting in bias regarding evidence of intervention effectiveness. Preventing attrition may be difficult, but attrition may be less likely to occur when (1) baseline durations are effectively managed, (2) you choose participants likely to benefit from the intervention, and (3) you are forthcoming about any difficulties that could be associated with research participation (e.g., uncomfortable baseline sessions, difficult-to-implement intervention components). All participants who are included in a study, even those who drop out and especially those who have unexpected response to intervention, should be included in all reports.

Multiple-Treatment Interference
Multiple-treatment interference (also called **multi-treatment interference**) can occur when a study participant's behavior is influenced by more than one planned intervention during the course of a study. These effects can be detected via visual analysis when appropriate designs are selected and suitable condition ordering is used (see Chapters 9 and 13). One type is sequential confounding (sequence effects), which refers to the influence of a participant's behavior that is due specifically to the order in which interventions are introduced. Another is a carryover effect, which occurs when a procedure used in one intervention condition influences behavior in an adjacent condition. It is important to note that multi-treatment interference refers to interference between *planned treatment conditions*, not from uncontrolled outside treatments (e.g., participant begins taking medication on the same day that you start your intervention condition); the latter is a history effect. You can prevent or detect multi-treatment interference by selecting appropriate designs, counterbalancing conditions (see Chapter 9), having sufficient phase lengths for reaching stability, and (when possible) providing participants with sufficient information about differences between conditions.

Data Instability
Instability refers to the amount of session-to-session change in the values of data (dependent variable); when you have variable data, it is difficult to predict the approximate value of the next data point. When you have stable data, it is relatively easy to predict a small range in which the next data would fall given no changes in condition. A **data instability threat** to internal validity occurs when the instability of data in one or more conditions makes it more difficult to draw conclusions about differences in outcomes across phases (i.e., decreased internal validity). Generally, instability threats are detected via visual analysis and prevented by changing conditions only when data are stable or when variability does not exceed expectations. When very large changes in outcomes between conditions are expected, more tolerance of variable data is allowable. When small, delayed, or variable changes in outcomes are expected, instability will result in a threat to internal validity. Thus, conservative researchers will wait until baseline data are stable, regardless of behavior change expectations, to ensure data instability threats will not materialize. The top panel in Figure 3.6 shows instability in a baseline phase with minimal influence on conclusions about behavior change (i.e., even though data are variable in baseline, the change in outcomes between phases is apparent). The bottom panel in Figure 3.6 shows instability in the baseline that makes it difficult to confidently conclude that outcome changes between phases are due to planned differences between conditions alone (i.e., a threat to internal validity).

Data instability (also referred to as variability) can result in a specific threat, referred to as **regression to the mean**. Regression to the mean refers to the likelihood that following an outlying data point, data are likely to revert to levels closer to the average value. For example, suppose you are hoping to intervene to increase behavior occurrence, and data are somewhat low (e.g., 30%) for the first three data points. For the fourth data point, values drop all the way to 0%. Some would say that this is a clear indication that intervention is needed; however, even without intervention, data are likely to improve after this outlying value. Changing conditions at this point can decrease confidence that your intervention, rather than typical variability, is

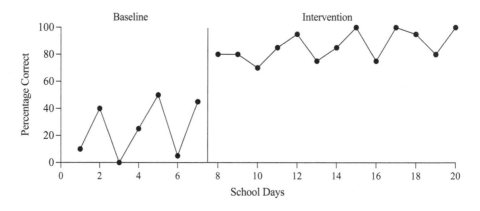

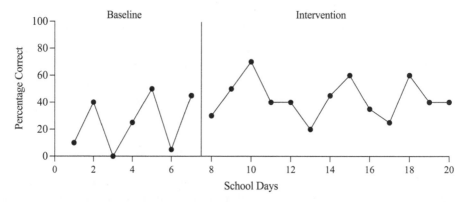

Figure 3.6 Data Instability Effects with Minimal (top) and Considerable (bottom) Impacts on Confidence in Relation between Independent and Dependent Variables.

Note: Data instability is depicted in both panels, with especially large variability in baseline conditions. Although instability (variability) is identical in both panels, confidence is less impaired in the top panel due to large changes between conditions. In the bottom panel, variability makes confidence in relations between behavior change and the intervention low.

the cause. You can avoid threats associated with regression to the mean, continue collecting data until stability is established. **Cyclical variability** is a specific type of data instability that refers to a repeated and predictable pattern in the data series over time. When phases are of equal length (e.g., five days in each condition) it is possible that your observations coincide with some unidentified natural source that may account for the variability. For example, if your experimental schedule coincides with a parent's work schedule (away from home for five days, at home for five days) you may incorrectly conclude that the independent variable is responsible for changes in behavior when in fact it may be due to the presence or absence of the parent at home. To avoid confounding due to cyclical variability it is recommended that you vary phase lengths across time.

Adaptation
Adaptation refers to a period of time at the start of an investigation in which participants' recorded behavior may differ from their natural behavior due to the novel conditions under which data are collected. **Adaptation threats** occur when adequate measures are not taken to ameliorate these effects prior to data collection beginning; this results in changes in baseline data that make changes between phases more difficult to interpret. The **Hawthorne Effect**,

which refers to participants' observed behavior not being representative of their natural behavior as a result of their knowledge that they are participants in an experiment (Kratochwill, 1978; Portney & Watkins, 2000), is a specific type of adaptation threat to validity. We recommend study participants be exposed to unfamiliar adults, settings, formats, and data collection procedures (e.g., video recording) prior to the start of a study (sometimes referred to as history training), to increase the likelihood that data collected on the first day of a baseline phase is representative of participants' "true" behavior. You can also avoid adaptation effects by reducing the obtrusiveness of your measurement procedures and using endogenous implementers rather than researchers when that is feasible.

Design-Related Confounds

One important internal validity consideration, undiscussed in previous versions of this text, and to our knowledge, generally unconsidered in single case design, is the impact of design on outcomes. That is, the changes in behavior that occur in your experiment may be due—in whole or part—to the design used to assess the outcomes, rather than the condition procedures themselves. Although this threat has not been widely discussed, some authors have noted that design-specific effects might have influenced findings. For example, Chazin and Ledford (2021) made the following point about their findings regarding efficiency differences between two prompting procedures:

> Because conditions alternated rapidly, children in the SLP superior group may have been unable to discriminate when incorrect responding would result in error correction (CTD) versus an additional learning opportunity (SLP)…researchers in future studies should pre-teach use of waiting versus responding incorrectly; they could then indicate during alternating instructional sessions that responding incorrectly is acceptable for SLP while it is not for CTD. This would ensure that only children who have appropriate prerequisite skills for both the procedures themselves <u>and those required due to the study design (e.g., alternation of procedures)</u> are included in the study.
>
> (underlined emphasis ours)

Thus, authors of that study acknowledged that the apparent differences between conditions in the study could have either been due to intervention effects or due to *design* effects. This is different from multi-treatment interference because it is unrelated to the interventions being implemented and instead is due to the ordering of conditions (in this case, the rapid alternation, which is required given the design type used in the study). Preventing and detecting these threats require a comprehensive understanding of the theory and processes driving behavior change in a given experiment (see discussions about Logic Models in Chapter 6) and the logic and use of different types of single case designs. We will discuss specific considerations for preventing and detecting these threats for different design types in Chapters 9, 11, and 13.

Conclusions

In this chapter, we discussed a cornerstone in all research—replication. Single case research relies on replication to increase confidence that changes in the *dependent variable* between conditions are due to changes in the *independent variable* between conditions, and only to those changes. We also introduced some potential threats to internal validity, which reduce confidence in conclusions that we can draw from an individual single case study. In subsequent chapters, we will address many of these threats more thoroughly, and provide detailed guidelines for avoiding, detecting, and minimizing these threats.

References

Artman, K., Wolery, M., & Yoder, P. (2012). Embracing our visual inspection and analysis tradition: Graphing interobserver agreement data. *Remedial and Special Education, 33*(2), 71–77.

Campbell, D. T., & Stanley, J. C. (1963). *Experimental and quasi-experimental designs for research*. Chicago, IL: Rand McNally.

Chazin, K. T., & Ledford, J. R. (2021). Constant time delay and system of least prompts: Efficiency and child preference. *Journal of Behavioral Education, 30*, 684–707.

Coyne, M. D., Cook, B. G., & Therrien, W. J. (2016). Recommendations for replication research in special education: A framework of systematic, conceptual replications. *Remedial and Special Education, 37*(4), 244–253.

Eyler, P. B., & Ledford, J. R. (2023). Systematic review of time delay instruction for teaching young children. *Journal of Early Intervention*, 10538151231179121

Gage, N. A., Cook, B. G., & Reichow, B. (2017). Publication bias in special education meta-analyses. *Exceptional Children, 83*(4), 428–445.

Kratochwill, T. R. (Ed.) (1978). *Single subject research—Strategies for evaluating change*. New York: Academic Press.

Lambert, J. M., Copeland, B. A., & Alexandrova, M. (2023). Reinforcer value moderates response magnitude and persistence during extinction: A randomized trial. *Journal of Applied Behavior Analysis*.

Lane, K., Wolery, M., Reichow, B., & Rogers, L. (2007). Describing baseline conditions: Suggestions for study reports. *Journal of Behavioral Education, 16*, 224–234.

Ledford, J. R., Chazin, K. T., Harbin, E. R., & Ward, S. E. (2017). Massed trials versus trials embedded into game play: Child outcomes and preference. *Topics in Early Childhood Special Education, 37*, 107–120.

Ledford, J. R., Lambert, J. M., Pustejovsky, J. E., Zimmerman, K. N., Hollins, N., & Barton, E. E. (2023). Single-case-design research in special education: Next-generation guidelines and considerations. *Exceptional Children, 89*(4), 379–396.

Ledford, J. R., & Wolery, M. (2013). Effects of plotting a second observer's data on ABAB graphs when observer disagreement is present. *Journal of Behavioral Education, 22*, 312–324.

Ledford, J. R., Wolery, M., Meeker, K. A., & Wehby, J. H. (2012). The effects of graphing a second observer's data on judgments of functional relations in A-B-A-B graphs. *Journal of Behavioral Education, 21*, 350–364.

Lemons, C. J., Fuchs, D., Gilbert, J. K., & Fuchs, L. S. (2014). Evidence-based practices in a changing world: Reconsidering the counterfactual in education research. *Educational Researcher, 43*, 242–252.

Locey, M. L. (2020). The evolution of behavior analysis: Toward a replication crisis?. *Perspectives on Behavior Science, 43*, 655–675.

Peredo, T., Zelaya, M., & Kaiser, A. (2018). Teaching low-income Spanish-speaking caregivers to implement EMT en Español with their young children with language impairment: A pilot study. *American Journal of Speech-Language Pathology, 27*(1), 136–153.

Petursdottir, A. I., & Carr, J. E. (2018). Applying the taxonomy of validity threats from mainstream research design to single case experiments in applied behavior analysis. *Behavior Analysis in Practice, 11*, 228–240.

Portney, L., & Watkins, M. P. (2000). *Foundations of clinical research: Applications to practice*. Upper Saddle River, NJ: Prentice Hall.

Pyrczak, F. (2016). *Making sense of statistics: A conceptual overview*. London: Routledge.

Shadish, W. R., Cook, T. D., & Campbell, D. T. (2002). *Experimental and quasi-experimental designs for generalized causal inference*. Belmont, CA: Wadsworth.

Shrout, P. E., & Rodgers, J. L. (2018). Psychology, science, and knowledge construction: Broadening perspectives from the replication crisis. *Annual Review of Psychology, 69*, 487–510.

Sidman, M. (1960). *Tactics of scientific research—Evaluating experimental data in psychology*. New York: Basic Books.

Tincani, M., & Travers, J. (2019). Replication research, publication bias, and applied behavior analysis. *Perspectives on Behavior Science, 42*, 59–75.

Wolery, M., Dunlap, G., & Ledford, J. R. (2011). Single case experimental methods: Suggestions for reporting. *Journal of Early Intervention, 33*, 103–109.

4

Selection, Characterization, and Measurement of Dependent Variables

Jennifer R. Ledford, Justin D. Lane, and Blair P. Lloyd

Important Terms

reversible, non-reversible, continuous recording, non-continuous recording, onset, offset, count, duration, latency, inter-response time, event recording, timed event recording, free-operant, trial-based, partial interval recording, whole interval recording, momentary time sampling, construct validity

Table of Contents

Choosing and Defining Behaviors
Characterizing Behaviors
   Reversible versus Non-Reversible Behaviors
   Behaviors of Long and Short Duration
   Trial-Based versus Free-Operant Behaviors
Selecting a Data Recording Procedure
Continuous Recording Systems
   Event and Timed Event Recording to Measure Count
      Transforming Count
   Duration and Latency Recording to Measure Time
      Time per Occurrence
      Total Time
      Transforming Duration
   Estimating Count and Duration with Interval-Based Systems
   Partial Interval Recording
      Benefits and Weaknesses
      Steps for Use of PIR
   Whole Interval Recording
      Benefits and Weaknesses
      Steps for Use of WIR

DOI: 10.4324/9781003294726-5

Momentary Time Sampling
    Benefits and Weaknesses
    Steps for Use of MTS
Variations in Use of Interval Systems
    Onset Variation of PIR
    Majority Variation of PIR
    PLA-CHECK Variation of MTS
    Interval Systems with Rotating Observations
    Interval Systems with Interspersed "Record" Intervals
Comparisons Among Interval-Based Systems
Illustration of Accuracy for Behaviors with Non-Trivial Durations
Illustration of Accuracy for Behaviors with Trivial Durations
Reporting Use of Interval Systems
Data Collection
    Planning and Conducting Data Collection
    Using Technology
    Collecting Data on More than One Behavior
Conclusions
References

Callout

4.1 A Commentary on Why Interval Systems are Used Despite Evidence of Inaccuracy

Applied research is generally conducted because of a desire to change participant performance (behavior) in some way. Thus, the careful and appropriate selection, characterization, and measurement of **target behaviors** is of critical importance for reducing the likelihood of threats to internal, external, and construct validity. **Dependent variables** are the targeted behaviors that are measured in a given study, along with the relevant measurement parameters. That is, you might select a target behavior of *engagement* and your dependent variable might be the *percentage of time a child is engaged*.

Choosing and Defining Behaviors

As an applied researcher, what you decide to measure will depend directly on your research question and objective. Several sources are available to help you determine what to measure. In addition to using personal observations, you can consult with direct and indirect stakeholders (e.g., participants, parents, practitioners, members of the community), and examine previous assessments. You can also consult a current individual education program (IEP), individual family service plan (IFSP), or treatment plan. Often in applied research, there is an apparent problem that needs to be solved for an individual (e.g., a scientist-practitioner has a client who has reported a specific need) or a population of individuals (e.g., a review of the extant research shows inadequate research support for the use of social narrative interventions for young children without autism (Zimmerman & Ledford, 2017).

After choosing a target behavior, you must determine what dimension of the behavior is of interest (Barlow & Hersen, 1984). There are two primary dimensions: Time and number. For example, you may be interested in reducing the number of tantrums a child engages in during each school day, or you may be interested in reducing the amount of time in which a child engages in tantrums. Similarly, for the child who displays tantrums, you may want to increase the number of prosocial interactions with peers and simultaneously increase the duration of appropriate play during the school day. Often, but not always, a change in time or count results in a corresponding change in the other dimension. The procedures, difficulties, and benefits of measuring and estimating each are different; thus, it is important to carefully select the dimension of interest before defining behavior occurrence and choosing measurement procedures.

You should define target behaviors in observable and measurable terms (Barlow & Hersen, 1984). For example, if a teacher frequently has observed a student leaving his desk without permission, talking with classmates during class presentations, and dropping pencils and books, you would have a much clearer idea as to what the teacher considers disruptive behavior. When writing operational definitions for behaviors, you should also provide examples and non-examples to ensure that all relevant behaviors are coded and that all non-relevant behaviors are not. Examples and non-examples should include *close examples* and *close non-examples* (what Barlow & Hersen called "questionable instances," p. 112). For example, disruption might include *being more than 1 meter away from desk for at least 3 seconds* and a close non-example of the behavior would be *leaving the desk area within 10 seconds of a teacher instruction or permission to do so*. Examples and non-examples should be written and used to clarify, rather than as exhaustive lists. See Table 4.1 for several examples of definitions, examples, and non-examples used in a study designed to assess the effects of a playground-based intervention on physical activity behaviors (Ledford et al., 2016).

Table 4.1 Example Coding Definitions, Examples, and Non-Examples

Code	Definition	Examples	Non-examples
Social Interaction	Verbal or non-verbal initiations or responses that are directed toward a peer and that are neutral or positive in nature	Calling a peer's name Responding to a peer initiation by looking Responding to a peer request to give an item Calling multiple peers at once (e.g., Hey everyone!)	Any interactions directed to an adult Any negative interaction (aggression, threats, and other actions or words considered "not nice" by classroom staff such as "shut up" or "I hate you")
Engagement	Appropriately playing with materials or peers or engaging in purposeful physical activity	Playing chase Playing with a bat to hit a ball Running toward the slide	Wandering Walking in a repetitive sequence Sitting at the top of the slide for more than 2 s
Proximal Play	(1) Being within 5 ft of another child while playing with the same materials or activities *and* (2) either oriented to the same object/action/direction or oriented toward each other	Standing next to a peer, both watching bubbles Rolling a ball to a peer Playing on the same structure (if within 5 ft)	Any behavior while swinging Playing on opposite sides of the same structure Running more than 5 ft apart

Source: Ledford, J. R., Lane, J. D., Shepley, C., & Kroll, S. (2016). Using teacher-implemented playground interventions to increase engagement, social behaviors, and physical activity for young children with autism. *Focus on Autism and Other Developmental Disabilities*, 31, 163–173.

Characterizing Behaviors

In addition to selecting and defining behaviors, it is important to consider how to characterize these behaviors. These characterizations have important implications for the specific single case design you will select and the measurement procedures that you will choose.

Reversible and Non-Reversible Behaviors

For the purposes of measuring dependent variables in the context of a single case design study, you will need to decide whether the behaviors of interest are reversible or non-reversible (not readily reversible). **Reversible** behaviors are those behaviors that are likely to revert to baseline levels if an intervention is removed, meaning the target behavior will be sensitive to or shift based on researcher-planned environmental changes across conditions of a study. Examples may include challenging behaviors like aggression, on-task behavior, active student responding, and social interactions. Changes in **non-reversible** behaviors are not truly permanent, but these changes may be likely to maintain in the absence of an intervention condition. Examples may include most academic behaviors (e.g., sight word reading, picture-naming), some functional behaviors (e.g., learning how to use an iPad to access games), and motor behaviors (e.g., learning how to ride a bike). Some similar behaviors could be conceptualized as reversible in some studies, and non-reversible in others. For example, you might include visual supports to improve engagement in a large group circle time activity, and conceptualize that behavior as reversible—that is, when the child doesn't have access to those visual supports, their engagement decreases (e.g., Zimmerman et al., 2020). In another context, a child may have low engagement with circle time because they do not have the skills required to engage; once taught those skills, the child might have improved engagement even when the intervention is removed. Instructional practices, such as constant time delay or a dialogic reading intervention, designed to improve cognitive skills or academic performance (e.g., naming specific stimuli), will likely lead to the dependent variable functioning contextually as a non-reversible behavior. In contrast, supports, such as visual schedules or peer modeling, designed to improve social and communication skills (which typically fluctuate by context), will likely be characterized as reversible. This will not always be the case, but such considerations will help narrow the behavior of interest by category. The type of design you select will depend partly on whether the behavior of interest is better characterized as reversible or non-reversible (see Chapter 9).

Behaviors of Long and Short Duration

In addition to characterizing behaviors according to reversibility, it is important to know whether your behaviors of interest occur briefly or for at least a few seconds at a time. Some behaviors last a very brief (trivial) amount of time, such as hitting or scratching peers, cursing, imitating a child's utterance, choosing a response from a field of four by pointing, or responding to a multiple choice question. That is, they occur for less than a second, and the time it takes for them to occur is generally not of interest. We will refer to these behaviors as *short duration* behaviors or *behaviors of trivial duration* (Yoder et al., 2018a). Other behaviors tend to last for at least a few seconds at a time. Examples of these *long duration* behaviors include off-task behavior, tantrum behavior, engagement, parallel play, and physical activity. Some behaviors may be short duration or long duration depending on the context—for example, measuring conversational turns for a 3-year-old with autism and limited verbal skills (short duration) versus measuring conversational turns for typically developing teenage participants (long duration) or measuring correct responses to sight words (short duration) versus measuring how long it takes a child to read a given passage (long duration). Once you have determined the type of behavior you are interested in measuring, you can select a data recording procedure.

Trial-Based versus Free-Operant Behaviors

A third way to categorize behaviors is according to whether they occur freely or in response to some environmental cue. Some behaviors can occur at any time during a measurement occasion (e.g., number of social initiations during free play), while others are dependent on specific antecedent events (e.g., number of correct responses on a word-reading task). Events that are free to occur at any time are referred to as **free-operant** events (Ferster, 1953); we will refer to events that have specific antecedent conditions (e.g., task direction, peer initiation) as **trial-based** events. Knowing whether your behaviors of interest are free-operant or trial-based will be important when considering interobserver agreement data (Chapter 5).

Selecting a Data Recording Procedure

After identifying and defining the behavior of interest, you must decide on a method for quantifying the behavior. There are a variety of recording procedures available to single case design researchers, each with its own advantages and disadvantages. You must decide the behavior characteristic that deserves attention (e.g., how often it occurs, how long it lasts, or percentage of opportunities for which it is done correctly) and then select a recording procedure that will capture the characteristic of interest, is feasible for use, and can be used accurately. Variables that require consideration include the (1) target behavior, (2) objective of the intervention program, (3) practical constraints of the setting(s) in which the behavior is to be measured, and (4) sensitivity to document behavior change.

The most common type of behavior measurement in single case design research is direct, systematic observation and recording (DSOR). That is, humans watch their participants and measure what they do, in a rule-bound and systematic fashion (Wolery & Ledford, 2013). Specifically, DSOR requires indicating occurrence of a behavior *whenever it occurs, throughout the observation*, as opposed to noting whether it occurred during the observation at the end of the session (Yoder et al., 2018b). We will spend the remainder of the chapter focusing on DSOR, but two additional methods for measuring behavior are worth noting. First, the use of automated recording devices, including bio-behavioral records like electroencephalography (EEG; cf. Au et al., 2014) and physical activity trackers (Ledford et al., 2016), may become more common as these measures become pervasive in practice and feasible for use. Additional research is needed to determine to what extent these measures correlate with observed behavior, but the decreased resource needs for human data collection make automated measurement appealing. Second, permanent products are sometimes used to measure behaviors, particularly related to acquisition of academic skills (Tawney & Gast, 1984). For example, without watching a child perform the task, you could assign an accuracy score to a math test. This permanent product is typical in educational and clinical settings, but is less common in single case research (SCR), in part because of the risk of testing effects (see Chapter 3).

When using DSOR, you can use continuous recording or non-continuous recording (Johnston & Pennypacker, 2009). Continuous recording *quantifies* the occurrence of behavior within a specific time frame; and non-continuous recording *estimates* the occurrence within a specific time frame. **Continuous recording** requires counting or timing each behavior occurrence. For example, you might tally the number of words a child correctly reads (count) or time how long it takes her to read a passage of a given length (time). **Non-continuous recording** involves *sampling* behavior occurrence to estimate the actual count or time. Generally, non-continuous recording involves selecting an interval length and using specific rules to code whether or not a behavior occurrence is scored for the interval. Continuous recording is generally superior to non-continuous recording, since it does not rely on behavior sampling, which can introduce systematic or random error. However, continuous recording may prove to be infeasible, prohibitively resource-intensive, or too difficult (e.g., it may be difficult to define on-task behavior in a way in which observers can accurately identify the **onset** and **offset** of the behavior—that is, the moment a behavior begins, and the moment it stops).

Before choosing a procedure, you should identify the dimension of the target behavior that is of interest. The two most commonly measured dimensions are *time* and *number*. If the primary interest is number, the measurement system will be based on **count** (the number of times a behavior occurs). Time-related measures include **duration** (amount of time for which the behavior occurs, or the time between the onset and the offset; Johnston & Pennypacker, 2009; Wolery & Ledford, 2013), **latency** (amount of time between a signal or cue and the onset of the target behavior; Johnston & Pennypacker, 2009; Wolery & Ledford, 2013), and **inter-response time** (amount of time that passes between the offset of a behavior and the onset of the next behavior occurrence; Johnston & Pennypacker, 2009). Latency is a continuous variable that offers many of the same advantages as rate (when count is of interest) and can be ideal for practitioners who don't have the resources to collect rate-based data (e.g., Boyle et al., 2020; Caruthers et al., 2015; Lambert et al., 2019; LeJeune et al., 2019) and/or don't want to expose participants to environmental conditions which repeatedly occasion challenging behavior (e.g., Thomason-Sassi et al., 2011). Thus, latency is sometimes used when the interest is reducing the *number* of occurrences of behavior, because it does not require that participants engage in very high numbers of behaviors in non-treatment conditions.

See Table 4.2 for examples of the use of count, duration, and latency measures in applied research. Inter-response time is rarely used, although it is sometimes used in behavioral definitions (e.g., a new occurrence is counted if the onset of the behavior is more than 2 seconds from the offset of a previous occurrence).

Continuous Recording Systems

Event and Timed Event Recording to Measure Count

Perhaps the simplest option for measuring behavior is to count the number of times it happens; this is an intuitive metric and one often used in typical non-research settings (e.g., counting the number of correct responses on a test, number of social interactions, or number of discipline referrals for a child). When using count, you must attend to (1) carefully defining a behavior in such a way that two independent observers can agree whether a potential instance of a behavior should be recorded, and (2) under what conditions a new occurrence happens. As previously described, careful consideration of examples and non-examples will assist with the first task of defining the behavior. The conditions for a new occurrence may be simple (e.g., each successive hit counts as an occurrence of self-injurious behavior; each item correctly answered on a worksheet), but are sometimes more complicated (e.g., two statements count as two separate social interactions if they are separated by at least 2 seconds in time *or* if they are separated by a related peer response).

The simplest way to measure events is by denoting how many occur (i.e., a tally); this is referred to as **event recording** (Tawney & Gast, 1984). A more precise measure, **timed event recording**, involves denoting that an event has occurred *and* noting the time of the event (Yoder et al., 2018b). Electronic data collection applications have made this type of recording, which was historically rare, more common. Specifically, the ease of video recording and/or the

Table 4.2 Examples of Use of Count, Duration, and Latency Measures in Applied Research

Citation	Behavior	Recording System	DV
Measuring Count			
Kang & Kim 2023	Target word approximations	Free-operant event recording	Number per session
Shepley et al., 2016	Correctly labeling actions	Trial-based event recording	Percentage correct
Chazin et al., 2017	Correctly completing steps for cooking task	Trial-based event recording	Percentage of steps
Sutherland et al., 2003	Opportunities to respond, correct responses, disruptive behaviors	Free-operant event recording	Number (rate) per minute
Measuring Time			
Leatherby et al., 1992	Switch activation for toy access	Duration per occurrence	Number of seconds + Number of occurrences
Majeika et al., 2022	Engagement	Total duration	Percentage of session
Drew et al., 2022	Time with toothbrush in mouth	Total duration	Number of seconds
Wehby & Hollahan, 2000	Compliance with low-probability demand	Latency per occurrence	Seconds to compliance
Estimating Count			
Zimmerman & Ledford, 2017	Challenging behaviors	Partial interval recording (10 s)	Estimated number per session
Estimating Time			
Reichow et al., 2009	Engagement, challenging behavior	Momentary time sampling (10 s)	Percentage of intervals
Luke et al., 2014	On-task behavior	Momentary time sampling (15 s)	Percentage of intervals

use of electronic data collection applications make timed event recording feasible for use in many research studies. There are two main benefits of timed event recording. First, information about the timing of behaviors may be important. For example, if a child engages in challenging behavior near the beginning of each session but not late in the session, this may indicate that the child might benefit from a contingency review prior to the session. Second, timed event recording allows more precise agreement calculations (Yoder et al., 2018b; see Chapter 5).

Another variation of event recording can be used when timed event recording is not possible, which could be referred to as *tally-by-interval* recording. In this case, you can use event recording, but can "group" events based on time. To do this, you (1) determine the smallest period of time that is feasible for measurement (e.g., 1-minute intervals); (2) set a timer or other device to alert the data collector at regular intervals; and (3) count the number of occurrences between alerts (e.g., from timer start to 1 min, from 1:01 to 2 min, etc.). This data collection allows for more precision than using event recording alone, but less precision than using timed event recording. Using intervals to divide counts *does not constitute using non-continuous, interval-based recording*. It is simply a strategy used to improve the precision of event recording. For example, similar to timed event recording, using event recording within intervals allows you to identify the temporal characteristics of the behavior (i.e., at approximately when they occur) and offers superior evaluation of agreement between raters (see Chapter 5). When this variation is used, the total number of occurrences is reported (cf. Barton et al., 2013).

Generally, event recording can be used when trial-based events are of interest because there is an anchor for each event. For each opportunity, an occurrence or non-occurrence is usually recorded. Free-operant events can be more difficult to measure because there is no specification regarding when a behavior should occur. When using event recording for free-operant behaviors, only responses (not non-responses) are recorded. Because free-operant responses can be more difficult to measure using event recording, especially if resources are limited, researchers often use interval-based systems to estimate behavior occurrence.

Transforming Count
When count is used to measure behavior occurrence, it can be transformed for data presentation for ease of comparison between measurement occasions. Specifically, it is often transformed into a percentage or a rate.

Percentage. Trial-based counts are often transformed to a percentage of opportunities. For example, authors might report a percentage of trials during which a student correctly responded to a query related to multiplication facts or a percentage of words read correctly in a reading passage. When differences among measurement occasions exist (e.g., the number of words in passages vary), using percentages allow for fair comparisons between sessions. In addition, percentage is often used and well understood outside of research contexts. Using a percentage also facilitates comprehension because there is less need to understand context (Cooper, 1981; Gentry & Haring, 1976). For example, if the number of correct responses were reported on a graph as 10 (count), the reader would need to determine the maximum number of correct responses (e.g., scores of 10/10 and 10/20 are quite different). Percentage is calculated as the number of behaviors (or number of correct behaviors) divided by the total number of opportunities or trials, multiplied by 100. Free-operant behaviors cannot be transformed into percentages. Thus, if you are interested in how much challenging behavior occurs overall in a typical activity, you would not be able to transform that into a percentage of opportunities. However, if you are interested in how often challenging behavior occurs following a specific event (e.g., when an adult gives a demand), a percentage is appropriate.

Rate. Free-operant behaviors can be reported as a simple count, but if the measurement occasions differ in length, they are often converted to rate. Rate refers to the number of occurrences measured within a specific period of time. For example, you might report number of words read per minute or number of challenging behaviors per hour. As with percentage, even when the measurement occasion is consistent in duration, rate facilitates quick understanding regardless of session length (Gentry & Haring, 1976). Rate is calculated as number of occurrences divided by duration of the measurement occasion (e.g., session); if 11 challenging behaviors occurred during a 5-minute session, the reported rate would be 2.2 challenging behaviors per minute. Rate would also be appropriate if your research question and subsequent dependent variable relates to fluency (displaying the behavior at an age-expected frequency within a given time during academic probes or sessions). Trial-based behaviors should not be reported using rates because a non-participant (i.e., researcher, implementer, peer) controls the rate of trial presentation, which constrains the rate of responding.

Duration and Latency Recording to Measure Time

Sometimes, the number of times a particular behavior occurs is less important than the amount of time for which it occurs. For example, suppose two children, Lauren and Andrew, were both on-task three times during a math activity. Without knowing the *duration* of the on-task behavior, knowing the number is relatively unhelpful (e.g., Lauren may have been on-task for three 1-minute intervals; Andrew may have been on-task for three 5-minute intervals). When the interest is duration, there are two options for measuring time: Time per occurrence and total time. For latency measurement, researchers are typically only interested in time per occurrence.

Time per Occurrence
Time per occurrence is measured by using a timing device to count the number of seconds of occurrence for each instance of the behavior. Historically, time per occurrence was unwieldy because for each behavior occurrence, researchers needed to start a timer at the onset of the behavior, stop the timer at the offset of the behavior, and record the time. However, the increasing availability of free or low-cost data collection applications makes time per occurrence relatively simple to record. For example, some applications allow toggling a code "on" at the behavior onset and toggling it "off" when the behavior is discontinued; the program itself calculates the number of seconds per occurrence (e.g., Countee application for iPhone). Whether collected by hand or via an electronic device, time per occurrence data yields a number of potentially useful statistics: Number of occurrences, average duration per occurrence, and total duration. Latency measurement is similar, but when measuring latency, the "occurrence" is the amount of time that occurs between one environmental event (e.g., a task direction) and another (e.g., a child initiating the task).

Total Time
Total time recording involves starting a timing device at each behavior onset and stopping the timing device at each behavior offset, without recording the time for each occurrence. At the end of a measurement occasion (e.g., session, class period), the total time is recorded. Unlike time per occurrence, no information is available regarding the number of occurrences or mean time per occurrence. However, especially if electronic recording devices are not feasible or available, this method is sufficient for determining the overall amount of time for which a behavior occurs.

Transforming Duration
As with count, duration measures can be, and often are, transformed into percentage statistics. You can calculate percentage by dividing the number of seconds of behavior occurrence by the total number of seconds in a measurement occasion (e.g., 600 seconds in a 10-minute session) and multiplying by 100. Thus, if 60 seconds of off-task behavior occurred in a 10-minute session, you could report that it occurred for 10% of the session ([60/600]×100).

Estimating Count and Duration with Interval-Based Systems

Although it is often possible to directly measure number and time variables, it is sometimes difficult or infeasible, especially in applied contexts. Thus, researchers often choose to *estimate* behavior occurrence using interval-based systems with the assumption that estimation systems parallel a continuous measure of behavior, representing an approximation of the true value of a given behavior in context. These non-continuous recording systems all involve use of pre-determined intervals and systematic rules for counting occurrences within intervals (Powell et al., 1975). In research, intervals tend to be between 5 and 30 seconds in length (Lane & Ledford, 2014). When using these systems, an interval timer (i.e., timing device that provides a notification on a regular schedule) is needed; many are available for electronic devices. Physical interval timers are also available (e.g., GymBoss®).

We caution researchers to only use these non-continuous systems if continuous measurement is not possible or feasible, since all non-continuous systems are associated with estimation error (i.e., estimating time or number using these systems results in reliably *inaccurate* measurement). If you must use one of these systems, follow the recommendations below to ensure you choose the best system for estimating the dimension of interest, choose reasonable parameters, and make necessary corrections to improve estimations. For all interval systems, an estimated *count* should be reported when *number* is the dimension of interest (e.g., number of intervals in which the behavior occurred estimates number of occurrences) and *percentage of intervals* should be reported when *duration* is the dimension of interest (e.g., percentage of intervals in which the behavior occurred estimates percentage of time the behavior occurred). We note that authors almost exclusively report percentage of intervals, even when behaviors of interest are of trivial duration (and thus, researchers are unlikely to be interested in duration). Below, we describe procedures, weaknesses, and recommendations for each of the three interval-based systems; following, we describe problems associated with the use of interval-based systems. Figure 4.1 is a visual depiction of three 10-second intervals, along with the questions asked to determine occurrence for three systems.

Partial Interval Recording

Partial interval recording (PIR) is the most widely used interval-based system (Lane & Ledford, 2014; Lloyd et al., 2016; Mudford et al., 2009). When PIR is used, the observer (data collector) records an occurrence if the target behavior occurs at any time during the interval. Thus, a behavior is recorded as occurring in the interval regardless of whether it occurred for the whole interval or for a very small part of the interval and whether the behavior occurs once or many times during the interval. Functionally, PIR requires continuous observation across a session or observation, especially with a relatively small interval size (e.g., 5 seconds), but not a continuous count of behaviors within an interval.

Benefits and Weaknesses
The primary benefit of PIR is ease of use because once a behavior has occurred for an interval, additional observation is extraneous because behavior is only recorded once per interval regardless of the number of occurrences. Weaknesses of PIR include inaccurate estimates of both count and duration and the need for very small interval lengths and statistical corrections to minimize these shortcomings.

Steps for Use of PIR
If you use PIR to estimate count or duration, we advise you to follow these guidelines:

1. Operationally define behavior occurrence.
2. Choose an interval length that is as short as is feasible given measurement and resource constraints (e.g., 5 seconds).
3. Set up a data collection system that allows for coding of a behavior occurrence or non-occurrence during each interval.
4. Set an interval timer to alert you via alarm or vibration at the end of each interval.
5. Record occurrences and non-occurrences:
   a. Record a behavior occurrence if the behavior occurs *at any time during the interval*. Only record one occurrence per interval, regardless of the number of times the behavior occurs.
   b. Record a behavior non-occurrence if the behavior does not occur at all during the interval.

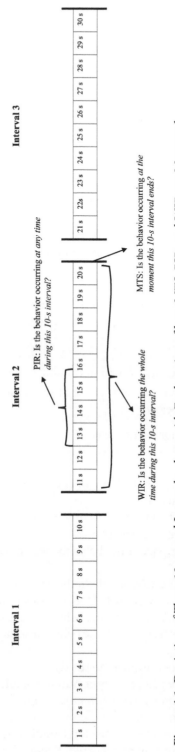

Figure 4.1 Depiction of Three 10-second Intervals, along with Explanation of how MTS, PIR, and WIR are Measured.

Note: PIR = partial interval recording. WIR = whole interval recording. MTS = momentary time sampling.

6. Following session completion, summarize the data:
   a. If you are interested in *number*, count the number of intervals in which the behavior occurred. Use the Poisson correction to reduce error (see below). Report this number as an *estimated count*.
   b. We do not recommend PIR as an estimate of time, but if you use it as such, count the number of intervals in which the behavior occurred and divide that number by the total number of intervals to get a percentage of intervals in which the behavior occurred. Report this percentage as an *estimated duration*.

Whole Interval Recording

Whole interval recording (WIR) is the least widely used interval-based recording system (Lane & Ledford, 2014; Lloyd et al., 2016; Mudford et al., 2009), perhaps given the common acknowledgment that it performs poorly under most conditions (Ledford et al., 2015). When WIR is used, the observer (data collector) records an occurrence if the target behavior occurs for the entire duration of the interval. Thus, a behavior is *only* recorded as occurring if the behavior begins at or before the interval onset and continues until the interval is complete.

Benefits and Weaknesses
WIR has no notable benefits, since it is more resource-intensive than simple timing or counting and is largely inappropriate for estimating count and duration.

Steps for Use of WIR
Although we do not recommend the use of WIR, it is important to understand the procedures used to better interpret the data from studies that used this measurement system. For this reason, we have outlined procedures below:

1. Operationally define behavior occurrence.
2. Choose an interval length that is as short as is feasible given measurement and resource constraints (e.g., 5 seconds).
3. Set up a data collection system that allows for coding of a behavior occurrence (or non-occurrence) during each interval.
4. Set an interval timer to alert you via alarm or vibration at the end of each interval.
5. Record occurrences and non-occurrences:
   a. Record a behavior occurrence if the behavior occurs *for the entire duration of the interval*.
   b. Record a behavior non-occurrence if the behavior does not occur for the entire interval; non-occurrences are recorded for intervals in which the behavior does not occur at all *and* for intervals in which the behavior occurs for some but not the entire interval (including intervals in which the behavior occurs for most but not all of the interval).
6. Following session completion, summarize the data:
   a. If you are interested in *number*, count the number of intervals in which the behavior occurred. Report this number as an *estimated count*.
   b. If you are interested in *time*, count the number of intervals in which the behavior occurred and divide that number by the total number of intervals to get a percentage of intervals in which the behavior occurred. Report this percentage as an *estimated duration*.

Momentary Time Sampling

Momentary time sampling (MTS), like PIR, is widely used in single case research (Lane & Ledford, 2014; Lloyd et al., 2016; Mudford et al., 2009). When MTS is used, the observer (data collector) records an occurrence if the target behavior is occurring at the moment the interval ends. The occurrence or non-occurrence of the behavior at any other time during the interval is disregarded.

Benefits and Weaknesses
MTS is likely the easiest-to-use interval-based system because it requires attending to the presence or absence of a target behavior at a single point in time for each interval; however, it is most accurate when small intervals are used (e.g., 5 seconds), minimizing this advantage. In addition, for accurate recording, although you only collect data when the interval ends, you often need to watch the entire interval. For example, if you are coding peer interactions, you are unlikely to be able to only watch the moment the interval ends because you may not be able to assess whether what the child is saying at that moment meets your criterion for an occurrence (e.g., is directed at a peer, is neutral or positive in nature). MTS is the most accurate interval-based system for estimating duration (Ledford et al., 2015) but generally should not be used for estimating count.

Steps for Use of MTS
If you use MTS to estimate duration, you should follow the guidelines below:

1. Operationally define behavior occurrence.
2. Choose an interval length that is as short as is feasible given measurement and resource constraints (e.g., 5 seconds).
3. Set up a data collection system that allows for coding of a behavior occurrence (or non-occurrence) at the end of each interval.
4. Set an interval timer to alert you via alarm or vibration at the end of each interval.
5. Record occurrences and non-occurrences:
   a. Record a behavior occurrence if the behavior occurs *at the moment the interval ends*.
   b. Record a behavior non-occurrence if the behavior is not occurring at the moment the interval ends, even if the behavior has occurred at other times during the interval.
6. Following session completion, summarize the data:
   a. If you are interested in *number*, count the number of intervals in which the behavior occurred. Report this number as an *estimated count*.
   b. If you are interested in *time*, count the number of intervals in which the behavior occurred and divide that number by the total number of intervals to get a percentage of intervals in which the behavior occurred. Report this percentage as an *estimated duration*.

Variations in Use of Interval Systems

The basic types of interval systems vary according to whether behavior is assessed as occurring for part of an interval (PIR), the whole interval (WIR), or at a specific moment (MTS), but other variations in systems have been used in applied research. Some of these are relevant to only one type (i.e., PIR, WIR, or MTS), while others can be applied across types. More research is needed to determine the effects of using different interval-based systems (and variations of those systems) on accurate and valid identification of relations.

Onset Variation of PIR
In some instances, researchers have used PIR, but only recorded an occurrence when the *onset* of the behavior occurred during the interval—we refer to this as the *onset variation*. That is, each behavior is only recorded as occurring in one interval, even if the occurrence continues into subsequent intervals. When using PIR, it is important to define whether an onset or any occurrence of behavior within an interval is used to establish occurrence versus non-occurrence. This variation is used to estimate count and is accurate for doing so when a correction is used (see below). For short duration behaviors, this variation of PIR is unlikely to be substantially different from the version which considers any part of the behavior as an occurrence. When used for behaviors of long duration, the differences are likely to be greater, but research is needed to determine whether one variation is superior to the other.

Majority Variation of PIR
In some studies, authors report using a variation of PIR which includes an occurrence of behavior *only if the behavior occurs for the majority of the interval* (e.g., Bessette & Wills, 2007; Blair et al., 2010; Kim et al., 2017). This variation implies that the measured behaviors are of long duration, and that the dimension of interest is duration rather than count. Data are needed to determine the extent to which this variation of PIR results in accurate estimates of duration; in the meantime, when estimates of duration are of interest, we suggest selecting MTS.

PLA-CHECK Variation of MTS
A variation of MTS, dubbed the PLA-CHECK, involves measuring the behavior of a group of participants by counting the number of engaged participants out of the total number of participants at the end of each interval (Doke & Risley, 1972). The data reported for PLA-CHECK systems is the average number of children engaged in each interval, or the average percentage of children engaged in each interval (cf. Ginns & Begeny, 2019). One study demonstrated that in both simulated and classroom data, a 1-minute PLA-CHECK system resulted in data that were acceptably aligned with 5-second MTS data from individual participants (Dart et al., 2016); thus, when group data are relevant, PLA-CHECK may be a reasonable measurement system aligned with more resource-intensive systems.

Interval Systems with Rotating Observations
When more than one participant is of interest, some researchers have used interval systems with rotating observations. When these are used, the researcher divides the observation into intervals, but observes different participants across intervals (cf. Austin & Soeda, 2008; Massar et al., 2023; Stremel et al., 2022). For example, if there are three participants of interest, the researcher might observe Participant #1 during every third interval (e.g., Interval 1, 4, 7, 10, 13 …) and Participant #2 during every third interval starting with the second one (e.g., Interval 2, 5, 8, 11, 14 …), with observations of Participant #3 in the remaining third of intervals (e.g., Interval 3, 6, 9, 12, 15 …). If there are 30 intervals per session (e.g., 10-second intervals in a 5-minute observation), each participant is observed for 10 intervals (essentially making each observation per participant only 100 seconds in duration). The benefit is the ability to collect data on multiple participants at once; the primary drawback is less data per participant.

Interval Systems with Interspersed "Record" Intervals
We have described the PIR and WIR systems without including a separate "record" interval (Barlow & Hersen, 1984). When used in this (most common) way, you record behaviors as occurring for one interval as the next interval starts, without taking a break. Separate record intervals can also be used such that, for example, you record an occurrence or non-occurrence

Table 4.3 Behavior Data Resulting from Interval Systems With and Without Distinct Record Intervals

Interval & Time	1 (0–10 s)	2 (11–20 s)	21–30 s	31–40 s	41–50 s	51–60 s
Typical Interval System						
Observer Behavior	Watch & Record	Watch & Record	Watch & Record	Watch & Record	Watch & Record	Watch & Record
Data Recorded	Occurrence in Interval 1	Occurrence in Interval 2	Occurrence in Interval 3	Occurrence in Interval 4	Occurrence in Interval 5	Occurrence in Interval 6
Interval Systems with Interspersed Record Intervals						
Observer Behavior	Watch	Record	Watch	Record	Watch	Record
Data Recorded	N/A	Occurrence in Interval 1	N/A	Occurrence in Interval 3	N/A	Occurrence in Interval 5

at the end of the first interval during a 5-second break, before you begin the second interval. Other researchers have referred to this variation as *intermittent sampling* and to the more common version without record intervals as *continuous sampling* (Yoder et al., 2018b). These record intervals have been used somewhat often and may be most useful when recording complex or several different behaviors in-situ (e.g., Biggs et al., 2017). Table 4.3 shows the use of 10-second intervals with and without distinct record intervals. When using this variation, less data are available than when using interval-based systems with no record interval; of course, *less data* is preferable to *inaccurate recording*, so these intervals should be used when they are necessary for accuracy. Note that the interspersed record interval variation is relevant for PIR and WIR systems, given that MTS requires only momentary watch and record behaviors from the observer.

Comparisons Among Interval-Based Systems

Of course, given that the rules are different based on which system you use, the same behavior occurrence would be scored differently based on which interval system is used. Three different occurrences (in a single 10-second interval) are depicted in Figure 4.2 via shaded cells. As

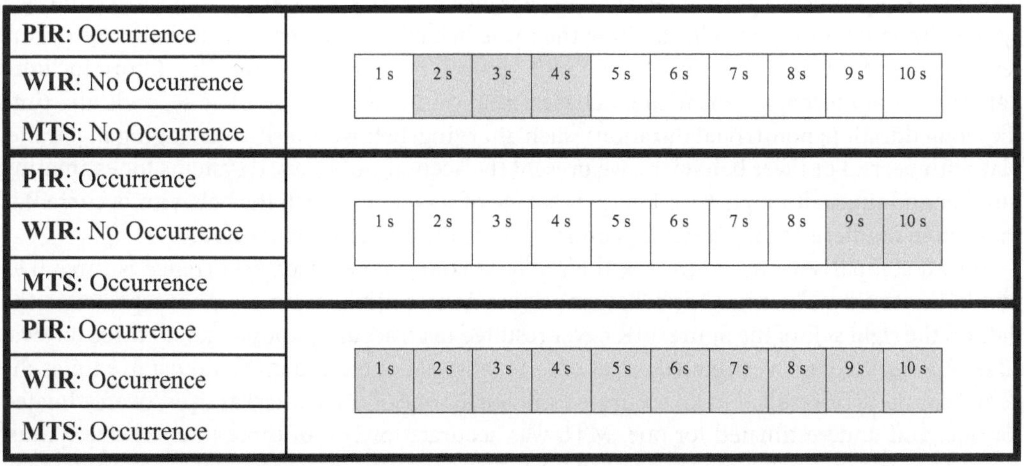

Figure 4.2 Depiction of Three 10-second intervals, with Behavior Occurrence Indicated with Shading and the Determination of Occurrence by System Shown on the Left.

Note: PIR = Partial interval recording. WIR = whole interval recording. MTS = momentary time sampling.

you can see in the figure, PIR is the procedure most likely to capture any occurrence since a short occurrence at any time during the interval gets scored as an occurrence while even long occurrences are not coded with WIR (unless it covers the whole interval) or MTS (unless it is occurring at the end of the interval).

There are numerous research studies demonstrating the inaccuracies of interval-based systems (Ary & Suen, 1983; Harrop & Daniels, 1986; Ledford et al., 2015; Powell et al., 1975; Prykanowski et al., 2018; Rapp et al., 2007; Yoder et al., 2018a). Despite these studies, interval-based recording procedures continue to be used in the applied behavioral literature, especially for measuring prosocial behaviors, communicative responses, or challenging behaviors. Recommendations have been provided, including the use of intervals that are approximately the same length as or smaller than the average behavior duration per occurrence (Kazdin, 2010; Cooper et al., 2007), although these recommendations do not always result in accurate measurement. It is also commonly reported that PIR overestimates behavior occurrence and may result in erroneous, stable ceiling effects, especially when larger intervals are used. WIR underestimates behavior occurrence, and MTS both overestimates and underestimates behavior occurrence across different sessions. However, the behavior of all interval-based systems is more complicated than simple under or overestimation. For example, the extent to which each under or overestimates behavior is reliant on (1) whether it is an estimation of count or duration, (2) size of interval relative to the average duration per occurrence, (3) whether the estimate is for a short duration or long duration behavior, and (4) number of occurrences per session.

Illustration of Accuracy for Behaviors with Non-Trivial Durations

Figure 4.3 depicts a 1-minute "session"; this is not a typical session length but results from this brief illustration hold for session lengths common in single case research (Ledford et al., 2015; Yoder et al., 2018a). Each cell in the top row corresponds to 1 of 60 seconds in that minute; shaded cells represent a behavior "occurring" during that portion of the session. Thus, you can see that the minute-long session included three behavior occurrences, totaling 24 seconds (40% of the session). The second through fourth rows depict the time period divided into thirty 2-second intervals. In each of these cells is a "+", denoting that a behavior occurrence was coded, or a "−", indicating that a behavior occurrence was not coded, according to each interval system. The remaining two charts show the same behavior occurrence, with behavior occurrences marked for 5-second (middle) and 10-second (bottom) intervals. This figure includes data that would be consistent with a behavior that occurs for at least a few seconds at a time (i.e., long duration; non-trivial duration), such as crying, being on-task, or engaging in parallel play with peers. For these behaviors, we present the accuracy of interval systems for estimating number and time, although duration (percentage of session in which the behavior occurred) is most often of interest when behaviors of non-trivial durations are measured.

For all comparisons in Figure 4.3, the accurate count of behavior occurrence is three (i.e., within the 1-minute interval, the behavior occurred three different times). As is reported in the data on the right side of the figure, PIR never resulted in an accurate count—for all three interval sizes, PIR resulted in an estimated count of 6–14, at least double and up to almost five times the actual count. WIR resulted in an accurate estimate for one of three interval sizes, overestimated for one, and underestimated for one. MTS was accurate for two of three interval sizes. Thus, when 2-second intervals were used, all three systems resulted in overestimates of count; when 5-second intervals were used, PIR resulted in overestimates; and when 10-second intervals were used, PIR resulted in overestimates and WIR resulted in underestimates of behavior counts.

Selection and Measurement of Dependent Variables • 59

Time in Seconds	5 s	3 s	16 s		Count	Duration (Percent)
				Continuous	3	24 s (40%)
PIR (2 s intervals)	− − + +	+ − − − − − − − −	+ + + + + + + + − − − − − − −	PIR	14	47%
WIR (2 s intervals)	− − + +	− − − − − − − −	− + + + + + + − − − − − − − −	WIR	10	33%
MTS (2 s intervals)	− − + +	− − + + − − − −	− + + + + + + + − − − − − − −	MTS	12	40%
				Continuous	3	24 s (40%)
PIR (5 s intervals)	− +	+ − −	+ + + − − −	PIR	7	58%
WIR (5 s intervals)	− −	− − −	+ + + − − −	WIR	3	25%
MTS (5 s intervals)	− +	− − −	+ + − − − −	MTS	3	25%
				Continuous	3	24 s (40%)
PIR (10 s intervals)	+	+	+ + −	PIR	6	100%
WIR (10 s intervals)	−	−	+ − −	WIR	1	12%
MTS (10 s intervals)	−	−	+ − −	MTS	3	50%

Figure 4.3 Sample Data Depicting Three Occurrences of a Long-Duration Behavior and Estimates of Count and Duration When Using Three Different Recording Systems.

Note: Behavior occurrence is depicted with filled cells. PIR = partial interval recording. WIR = whole interval recording. MTS = momentary time sampling. The estimated count and duration are calculated when each system is used with 2 (top), 5 (middle), or 10 second (bottom) intervals.

For all comparisons in Figure 4.3, the accurate duration of behavior occurrence is 24 seconds, or 40% of the session. As is reported in the data on the right side of the figure, all three interval systems resulted in somewhat accurate estimates with very small intervals (33–47%), but with larger intervals, PIR overestimated and WIR underestimated duration of behavior occurrence and MTS under-(5 seconds) *or* overestimated (10 seconds) occurrence. These patterns occur because WIR will "miss" occurrences that do not span an entire interval (e.g., any occurrence less than 10 seconds in duration, if intervals are 10 seconds), while PIR will overcount any occurrence that lasts for longer than an interval length (e.g., a 3-second occurrence will always be estimated as two 2-second occurrences when 2-second intervals are used). MTS, on the other hand, includes random error—that is, behavior occurrence is likely to be somewhat accurate, with increased accuracy when the interval size is shorter.

Illustration of Accuracy for Behaviors with Trivial Durations

Figure 4.4 depicts a 1-minute "session," with cells depicting occurrences and interval system data similar to Figure 4.3. However, in Figure 4.4, behavior occurrences are depicted that are trivial in duration (1/3 of a second, for the purposes of this illustration). These types of behaviors are often measured in single case research—for example, utterances made by a toddler, hits to the head by a child with autism and self-injurious behavior, and number of times an adult imitates a child's play behavior. Count is most often of interest when behaviors of trivial duration are measured (e.g., a child can hit himself 50 times during a 10-minute session, and still a relatively short duration of total hits would be measured).

For all comparisons in Figure 4.4 the accurate count of behavior occurrence is 12. As is shown in the data on the left side of the figure, none of the interval-based systems resulted in accurate counts; all were underestimates. For behaviors with trivial durations, neither MTS nor WIR is appropriate, even when very small intervals are used. PIR resulted in underestimates, with greater underestimates for bigger intervals and when more behaviors occur (e.g., are closer in time to each other). This predictable and lawful behavior by PIR allows us to use a statistical Poisson correction to improve the accuracy for estimating counts (Yoder et al., 2018a). The formula involves a natural log transformation of the quotient of the number of "non-occurrence" intervals divided by the total number of intervals; that number is multiplied by the quotient of session duration divided by interval duration (in seconds) to obtain the final, corrected count estimate. A spreadsheet that performs the necessary calculations is available at: http://vkc.vumc.org/tapp/Poisson-Correction.zip (Yoder et al., 2018a); the formula is:

$$-\ln\left(\frac{\#\,non\,occurrence\,intervals}{total\,\#\,intervals}\right) \times \left(\frac{session\,duration}{interval\,duration}\right)$$

Use of the Poisson transformation considerably increases accuracy of count estimations of behaviors of trivial duration (Yoder et al., 2018a); thus, we suggest its use when count of these behaviors is of interest. Even when the correction is used, more accurate results are obtained by using small intervals (Yoder et al., 2018a).

We also present duration data for Figure 4.4; it is almost never of interest to estimate duration of these types of behaviors. No interval-based systems allow us to do so accurately, although MTS with *very small intervals* results in somewhat accurate estimates. We suggest interval-based systems not be used to estimate duration of behaviors with trivial durations; suggestions for the use of measurement systems by dimension (count, time) and type (continuous, non-continuous) are shown in Table 4.4.

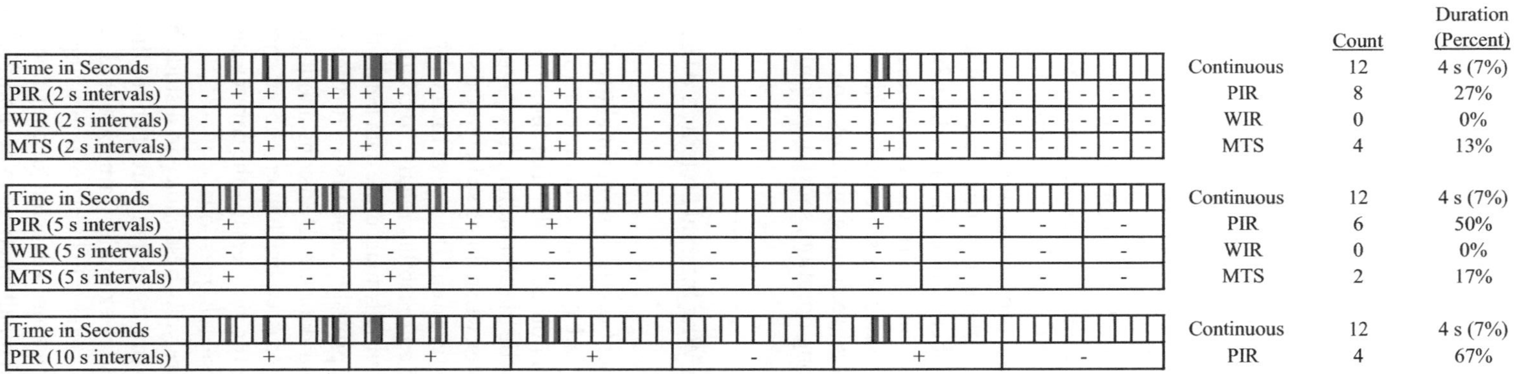

	Count	Duration (Percent)
Continuous	12	4 s (7%)
PIR	8	27%
WIR	0	0%
MTS	4	13%
Continuous	12	4 s (7%)
PIR	6	50%
WIR	0	0%
MTS	2	17%
Continuous	12	4 s (7%)
PIR	4	67%

Figure 4.4 Sample Data Depicting 12 Occurrences of a Short-Duration Behavior and Estimates of Count and Duration Using Three Different Recording Systems.

Note: Behavior occurrence is depicted with filled cells. PIR = partial interval recording. WIR = whole interval recording. MTS = momentary time sampling. The estimated count and duration is calculated when each system is used with 2 (top), 5 (middle), or 10 second (bottom) intervals.

Table 4.4 Suggestions for Measurement Based on Dimension of Interest and Type

	Number	Time
Continuous	Event recording Timed event recording	Total duration recording Duration per occurrence recording
Non-Continuous	PIR, using a Poisson Correction, for behaviors of trivial duration (e.g., hits, imitation, utterances). Report **number** of intervals as **count** estimate.	MTS, using small intervals, for behaviors of non-trivial duration (e.g., engagement, parallel play, tantrum behavior). Report **percentage** of intervals as **duration** estimate.

Note: We do not suggest the use of PIR for estimating time, MTS for estimating count, or WIR for estimating either.

Reporting Use of Interval Systems

When interval-based systems are used, researchers should take care to report all parameters (system type, duration of intervals, number of intervals per session), explicitly identify the system as an *estimate* of behavior occurrence, name what dimension of behavior is being estimated (e.g., number, time), and discuss the likelihood of error. If time is being estimated (i.e., duration, latency, inter-response time), provide results as a percentage of intervals in which the behavior occurred as an estimated percentage of duration of the session. If number is the dimension of interest, report the number of intervals in which behavior occurred as an estimated count, using the Poisson correction for PIR previously described. In Figure 4.5, we provide a flow chart that can be used for selecting a measurement system based on whether you will use continuous or non-continuous recording systems, the dimension of interest (time, number), and the type of behavior (long duration, short duration).

Callout 4.1 A Commentary on Why Interval Systems are Used Despite Evidence of Inaccuracy

Throughout the chapter, we comment on the non-optimal use and reporting of interval-based systems, and report that they are quite inaccurate under many circumstances. Why then do they continue to be used so ubiquitously? The short answer is that despite their shortcomings, they may sometimes be the best option. It is quite difficult to measure many behaviors, and it is especially complex when doing so in typical settings common in behavioral and educational intervention research. The use of interval-based systems, especially PIR and WIR, likely lead to improved reliability relative to continuous recording of count or duration. But is reliable, but potentially inaccurate data better than unreliable, accurate data? The answer to that question probably depends on further information—including *how* inaccurate and *how* unreliable data are. Decisions about prioritizing reliability or validity mirror those and will be discussed in Chapter 7 about choices that increase internal validity but decrease generality (or vice versa)—the correct answer depends on study-specific characteristics and your research questions.

When interval-based systems are your best choice in a study because of reliability or feasibility concerns, we encourage you to be transparent about this, and to interpret your data with appropriate caution (see, for example, Campbell et al., 2023). We've developed guidelines for using interval-based systems in hopes of improving accuracy and maintaining the likelihood of reliability, but we also advocate for continued research on the performance of interval systems and even on alternatives to or modifications of current systems to improve accuracy of measurement.

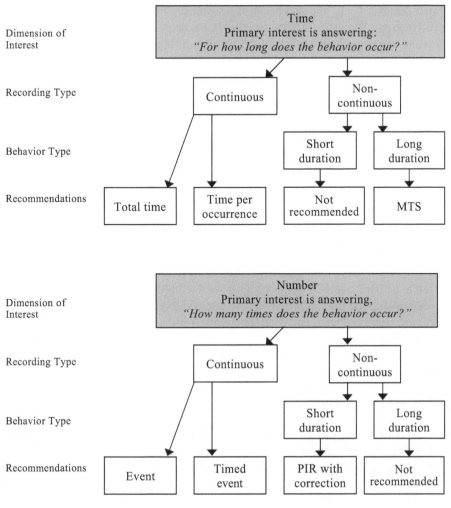

Figure 4.5 Flow Charts for Determining which Measurement System to Use When Time is the Dimension of Interest (top) or Number is the Dimension of Interest (bottom).

Data Collection

DSOR is a hallmark of single case research. This aligns well with the type of data collection that occurs (or should occur) in practice. Generally, single researchers use measures that align with proximal and context-bound outcomes (e.g., directly measure change in the behavior we targeted in the context in which it was taught; Yoder et al., 2018b; see Chapter 7). This is in contrast to measures that are distal and generalized. For example, teaching a child to name math facts in a small group in his classroom and measuring his progress in acquiring those facts during the small group session involves measuring a proximal and context-bound outcome. Teaching a child to name math facts and then measuring growth on a standardized measure of math achievement in a clinical setting is a distal and generalized outcome. These concepts are not truly dichotomous and single case research includes dependent variables that are more or less proximal and more or less context-bound. In any case, almost all SCR data are collected via researcher-developed measures, in part due to the lack of appropriate standardized measures for repeated use over time, but also because researcher-developed measures can be designed to be sensitive to small but meaningful changes in participant behavior. Designing and testing these measures requires considerable thought and planning prior to study initiation.

Planning and Conducting Data Collection

Developing data collection forms and procedures likely to result in accurate, reliable data collection is critically important given that analysis of these data via graphs facilitates high-stakes experimental decisions throughout the study and allows for interpretation of the results of the study once it is complete. Data collection not only involves gathering information about the specific behavior of interest (performance information), but also other information critical to interpretation and organization (situational data; i.e., participant identification numbers, implementer initials, date, time; McCormack & Chalmers, 1978). Sample data forms are available online (cf. Lane & Ledford, 2023; Ledford, 2016). In addition, study-specific information such as instructional phase or modifications should be recorded so that you have a historical record of decisions made during the study and to ensure accurate transmission of data to graphs. Finally, when using pencil-and-paper forms, you might include a section for summary information (e.g., percentage of correct responses during the session, total number of behaviors recorded during the session) and whether interobserver agreement (IOA) and procedural fidelity (PF) data were collected and if so, the scores. If you use the exact same form for primary and secondary (IOA) data collection, it is important to have a section on the form to designate whether you are the primary or secondary observer to facilitate accurate graphing and facilitate formative reliability checks.

Using Technology

Although the critical nature of data collection and essential components of measurement have remained more or less unchanged over time, technological advances have resulted in changes in the processes of data collection. Most of these changes are beneficial (e.g., increased feasibility, improved analysis, automatic calculations). Some potentially troublesome issues with technology include increased risk for confidentiality violations due to information stored on electronic devices and increased risk for data loss due to electronics failure. However, overall, the use of technology for data collection has moved the field forward and increased the feasibility of measuring increasingly complex behaviors. Although technology changes at a rate faster than book publication changes, two important technological advances seem relevant to discuss: Use of video recording and use of electronic applications.

Video recording experimental sessions is not a new idea; however, the relative ease and widespread social use of recording via portable electronics devices has increased the feasibility and social acceptability of using these devices in applied settings. Video recording sessions have several notable benefits; they allow for: (1) a researcher to implement a condition as intended, while collecting data at a later time; (2) researchers to have more detailed discrepancy discussions (see below); and (3) naïve observers (i.e., for someone who is unaware of condition assignment to collect data). Despite these considerable positive attributes, video recording may pose additional concerns for participants, including those related to privacy and confidentiality.

The use of electronic applications for data collection fall into two primary categories: Computer-based programs that can be used to code data from video (e.g., ProCoderDV, Tapp & Walden, 1993) and mobile applications on phones or other portable electronic devices. When codes are used for participant information (e.g., pseudonyms or participant numbers rather than names), use of these products does not necessarily increase the likelihood of privacy or confidentiality concerns. Moreover, they allow for more precise measurement (e.g., timed event recording) and often perform basic calculations (e.g., percentage of intervals). These applications are often free or low-cost; some high-cost options are available and widely used in practice. When determining whether an electronic application is the right fit for a single case design study, you should consider whether: (1) use of the device is permitted and feasible, and whether connectivity is required and likely to be an issue; (2) the device provides or allows you to input all of the relevant information needed; (3) all data collectors have easy access to a device compatible with the data collection software or application; and (4) you can adequately manage, analyze, and store data given the constraints of the product.

Collecting Data on More than One Behavior

As single case design researchers, we are often interested in changes in more than one behavior. For purposes of experimental decisions, you must always specify a primary dependent variable. It is the analysis of this behavior that will drive decisions about condition changes (read more about condition changes for specific designs in Chapters 9–11). However, additional behaviors are often measured in the context of single case design research. For example, you might measure both duration of engagement and number of social interactions for child participants (Ledford et al., 2015) or measure adult fidelity to procedures (percentage correct) for adult participants as well as duration of engagement for a child participant (Ledford et al., 2017). Whether the variables are for the same or different participants, one should be named explicitly as the primary variable.

Sometimes, we are interested in coding a group of variables that are related to each other. For example, in a study designed to assess the effects of an intervention on engagement for a young child, we might be interested in coding whether he or she was conventionally engaged with materials or people, unengaged, engaged in stereotypy, or appropriately waiting. Given video records, we could separately code for each behavior using duration per occurrence or MTS recording. However, especially in the case of MTS, we could also code all behaviors simultaneously if they are *exhaustive* (i.e., inclusive of all potential behaviors) and *mutually exclusive* (i.e., cannot occur at the same time). That is, at the end of each interval, rather than recording "occurrence" or "non-occurrence," we would record *engaged, unengaged, stereotypy,* or *waiting*. Although these behaviors will co-vary (e.g., if engagement improves, one of the other behaviors must decrease), a single behavior should still be named as the primary behavior of interest and that behavior should be used to make experimental decisions. Use of an exhaustive and mutually exclusive code (including simple occurrence/non-occurrence codes) allows for more flexibility in the analysis of reliability data, which we discuss in the next chapter.

Conclusions

Selecting, defining, and considering how targeted behaviors should be measured is one of the most important parts of conducting a single case experiment. In Chapter 5, we will discuss how to ensure that you select and measure behaviors that are valid and reliable; in Chapter 6, we will consider match between dependent and independent variables, and in Chapter 7, we will discuss social validity and generalization considerations for dependent variables. The attention paid to dependent variables across chapters in this text is an indication of the critical nature of selection and measurement of target behaviors to effective single case research.

References

Ary, D., & Suen, H. K. (1983). The use of momentary time sampling to assess both frequency and duration of behavior. *Journal of Behavioral Assessment*, 5, 143–150.

Au, A., Ho, G. S., Choi, E. W., Leung, P., Waye, M., Kang, K., & Au, K. (2014). Does it help to train attention in dyslexic children: Pilot case studies with a ten-session neurofeedback program. *International Journal on Disability and Human Development*, 13, 45–54.

Austin, J. L., & Soeda, J. M. (2008). Fixed-time teacher attention to decrease off-task behaviors of typically developing third graders. *Journal of Applied Behavior Analysis*, 41(2), 279–283.

Barlow, D. H., & Hersen, M. (1984). *Single case experimental designs: Strategies for studying behavior change* (2nd ed.). New York: Pergamon Press.

Barton, E. E., Pribble, L., & Chen, C. (2013). The use of e-mail to deliver performance-based feedback to early childhood practitioners. *Journal of Early Intervention*, 35, 270–297.

Bessette, K. K., & Wills, H. P. (2007). An example of an elementary school paraprofessional-implemented functional analysis and intervention. *Behavioral Disorders*, 32(3), 192–210.

Biggs, E. E., Carter, E. W., & Gustafson, J. (2017). Efficacy of peer support arrangements to increase peer interaction and AAC use. *American Journal on Intellectual and Developmental Disabilities*, 122(1), 25–48.

Blair, K. S. C., Fox, L., & Lentini, R. (2010). Use of positive behavior support to address the challenging behavior of young children within a community early childhood program. *Topics in Early Childhood Special Education*, 30(2), 68–79.

Boyle, M. A., Bacon, M. T., Brewer, E. M., Carton, S. M., & Gaskill, L. A. (2020). Evaluating a treatment without extinction for elopement maintained by access to stereotypy. *Journal of Applied Behavior Analysis*, 53(3), 1531–1541.

Campbell, A. R., Sallese, M. R., Thompson, J. L., Burke, M. D., & Allen, M. L. (2023). Social-emotional and behavioral support for first- and second-grade Black learners at risk for emotional and behavioral problems. *Journal of Positive Behavior Interventions*, 25(3), 147–158.

Caruthers, C. E., Lambert, J. M., Chazin, K. M., Harbin, E. R., & Houchins-Juarez, N. J. (2015). Latency-based FA as baseline for subsequent treatment evaluation. *Behavior Analysis in Practice*, 8, 48–51.

Chazin, K. T., Bartelmay, D. N., Lambert, J. M., & Houchins-Juarez, N. (2017). Brief report: Clustered forward chaining with embedded mastery probes to teach recipe following. *Journal of Autism and Developmental Disorders*, 47, 1249–1255.

Cooper, J. O. (1981). *Measuring behavior* (2nd ed.). Columbus, OH: Charles E. Merrill.

Cooper, J. O., Heron, T., & Heward, W. (2007). *Applied behavior analysis*. New York: Pearson.

Dart, E. H., Radley, K. C., Briesch, A. M., Furlow, C. M., & Cavell, H. J. (2016). Assessing the accuracy of classwide direct observation methods: Two analyses using simulated and naturalistic data. *Behavioral Disorders*, 41(3), 148–160.

Doke, L. A. & Risley, T. R. (1972). The organization of day-care environments: Required vs. optional activities. *Journal of Applied Behavior Analysis*, 5, 405–420.

Drew, C. M., Machalicek, W., Crowe, B., Glugatch, L., Wei, Q., & Erturk, B. (2022). Parent-implemented behavior interventions via telehealth for older children and adolescents. *Journal of Behavioral Education*, 1–20.

Ferster, C. B. (1953). The use of the free operant in the analysis of behavior. *Psychological Bulletin*, 50(4), 263.

Gentry, D., & Haring, N. (1976). Essentials of performance measurement. In N. G. Haring & L. Brown (Eds.), *Teaching the severely handicapped Volume 1*. New York: Grune and Stratton.

Ginns, D. S., & Begeny, J. C. (2019). Effects of performance feedback on treatment integrity of a class-wide level system for secondary students with emotional disturbance. *Behavioral Disorders*, 44(3), 174–389.

Harrop, A., & Daniels, M. (1986). Methods of time sampling: A reappraisal of momentary time sampling and partial interval recording. *Journal of Applied Behavior Analysis*, 19, 73–77.

Johnston, J. M., & Pennypacker, H. S. (2009). *Strategies and tactics of behavioral research* (3rd ed.). New York: Routledge.

Kang, V. Y., & Kim, S. (2023). Effects of enhanced milieu teaching and book reading on the target word approximations of young children with language delay. *Journal of Early Intervention*, 45(2), 122–144.

Kazdin, A. E. (2010). *Single-case research designs. Methods for clinical and applied settings* (2nd ed.). New York: Oxford University Press.

Kim, S., Koegel, R. L., & Koegel, L. K. (2017). Training paraprofessionals to target socialization in students with ASD: Fidelity of implementation and social validity. *Journal of Positive Behavior Interventions*, 19(2), 102–114.

Lambert, J. M., Parikh, N., Stankiewicz, K. C., Houchins-Juarez, N. J., Morales, V. A., Sweeney, E. M., & Milam, M. E. (2019). Decreasing food stealing of child with Prader-Willi syndrome through function-based differential reinforcement. *Journal of Autism and Developmental Disorders*, 49, 721–728.

Lane, J. D., & Ledford, J. R. (2014). Using interval-based systems to measure behavior in early childhood special education and early intervention. *Topics in Early Childhood Special Education*, 34, 83–93.

Lane, J. D., & Ledford, J. R. (2023). Data collection forms. Available from: https://osf.io/b28yf/

Leatherby, J. G., Gast, D. L., Wolery, M., & Collins, B. C. (1992). Assessment of reinforcer preferences in multi-handicapped students. *Journal of Developmental and Physical Disabilities*, 4, 15–36.

Ledford, J. R. (2016). Data collection sheets. Available from: https://ebip.vkcsites.org/data-sheets/

Ledford, J. R., Ayres, K. A., Lane, J. D., & Lam, M. F. (2015). Accuracy of interval-based measurement systems in single case research. *Journal of Special Education*, 49, 104–117.

Ledford, J. R., Lane, J. D., Shepley, C., & Kroll, S. (2016). Using teacher-implemented playground interventions to increase engagement, social behaviors, and physical activity for young children with autism. *Focus on Autism and Other Developmental Disabilities*, 31, 163–173.

Ledford, J. R., Zimmerman, K. N., Chazin, K. T., Patel, N. M., Morales, V. A., & Bennett, B. P. (2017). Coaching paraprofessionals to promote engagement and social interactions during small group activities. *Journal of Behavioral Education*, 26, 410–432.

LeJeune, L. M., Lambert, J. M., Lemons, C. J., Mottern, R. E., & Wisniewski, B. T. (2019). Teacher-conducted trial-based functional analysis and treatment of multiply controlled challenging behavior. *Behavior Analysis: Research and Practice*, 19(3), 241.

Lloyd, B., Weaver, E., & Staubitz, J. (2016). A review of functional analysis methods conducted in public school classroom settings. *Journal of Behavioral Education*, 25, 324–356.

Luke, S., Vail, C. O., & Ayres, K. M. (2014). Using antecedent physical activity to increase on-task behavior in young children. *Exceptional Children*, 80, 489–503.

Majeika, C. E., Wehby, J. H., & Hancock, E. M. (2022). Are breaks better? A comparison of Breaks Are Better to Check-In Check-Out. *Behavioral Disorders*, 47(2), 118–133.

Massar, M. M., Horner, R. H., Kittelman, A., & Conley, K. M. (2023). Mechanisms of effective coaching: Using prompting and performance feedback to improve teacher and student outcomes. *Journal of Positive Behavior Interventions*, 25(3), 169–184.

McCormack, J. E., & Chalmers, A. J. (1978). *Early cognitive instruction for the moderately and severely handicapped: Program guide* (Vol. 1). Champaign, IL: Research Press.

Mudford, O. C., Taylor, S. A., & Martin, N. T. (2009). Continuous recording and interobserver agreement algorithms reported in the *Journal of Applied Behavior Analysis* (1994–2005). *Journal of Applied Behavior Analysis*, 42, 164–369.

Powell, J., Martindale, A., & Kulp, S. (1975). An evaluation of time-sample measures of behavior. *Journal of Applied Behavior Analysis*, 8, 463–469.

Prykanowski, D. A., Martinez, J. R., Reichow, B., Conroy, M. A., & Huang, K. (2018). Brief report: Measurement of young children's engagement and problem behavior in early childhood settings. *Behavioral Disorders*, 44(1), 53–62.

Rapp, J. T., Colby, A. M., Vollmer, T. R., Roane, H. S., Lomas, J., & Britton, L. (2007). Interval recording for duration events: A re-evaluation. *Behavioral Interventions*, 22, 319–345.

Reichow, B., Barton, E. E., Good, L., & Wolery, M. (2009). Brief report: Effects of pressure vest usage on engagement and problem behaviors of a young child with developmental delays. *Journal of Autism and Developmental Disorders*, 39, 1218–1221.

Shepley, C., Lane, J. D., & Shepley, S. B. (2016). Teaching young children with social-communication delays to label actions using videos and language expansion models. *Focus on Autism and Other Developmental Disabilities*, 31, 243–253.

Stremel, J. M., Hawkins, R. O., Collins, T. A., & Nabors, L. (2022). Positive behavior change: Effects of an intervention package for disruptive behavior in a specialized school setting. *Psychology in the Schools*, 59(3), 607–627.

Sutherland, K. S., Alder, N., & Gunter, P. L. (2003). The effect of varying rates of opportunities to respond to academic requests on the classroom behavior of students with EBD. *Journal of Emotional and Behavioral Disorders*, 11, 240–248.

Tapp, J., & Walden, T. (1993). PROCODER: A professional tape control, coding, and analysis system for behavioral research using videotape. *Behavior Research Methods, Instruments, & Computers*, 25(1), 53–56.

Tawney, J. W., & Gast, D. L. (1984). *Single subject research in special education*. Columbus, OH: Charles E. Merrill.

Thomason-Sassi, J. L., Iwata, B. A., Neidert, P. A., & Roscoe, E. M. (2011). Response latency as an index of response strength during functional analyses of problem behavior. *Journal of Applied Behavior Analysis*, 44, 51–67.

Wehby, J. H., & Hollahan, M. S. (2000). Effects of high-probability requests on the latency to initiate academic tasks. *Journal of Applied Behavior Analysis*, 33, 259–262.

Wolery, M., & Ledford, J. R. (2013). Monitoring child progress. In M. E. McLean, M. L. Hemmeter, & P. Snyder (Eds.) *Essential elements for assessing infants and preschoolers with special needs*. Boston, MA: Pearson.

Yoder, P. J., Ledford, J. R., Harbison, A. L., & Tapp, J. T. (2018a). Partial-interval estimation of count: Uncorrected and Poisson-corrected error levels. *Journal of Early Intervention*, 40(1), 39–51.

Yoder, P., Lloyd, B., & Symons, F. (2018b). *Observational measurement of behavior* (2nd ed.). Baltimore: Brookes.
Zimmerman, K. N., & Ledford, J. R. (2017). Beyond ASD: Evidence for the effectiveness of social narratives. *Journal of Early Intervention*, 39(3), 199–217.
Zimmerman, K. N., Ledford, J. R., Gagnon, K. L., & Martin, J. L. (2020). Social stories and visual supports interventions for students at risk for emotional and behavioral disorders. *Behavioral Disorders*, 45(4), 207–222.

5
Reliability and Validity of Dependent Variables

Jennifer R. Ledford and Justin D. Lane

Important Terms

observer drift, observer bias, naïve observer, interobserver agreement, discrepancy discussion, occurrence agreement, non-occurrence agreement, gross agreement

Table of Contents

Validity
Accuracy
Reliability
Ensuring Reliability and Validity of Data Collection
    Operationalize Behaviors
    Pilot Data Collection Procedures
    Train Observers
    Use Naïve Observers
    Collect IOA Data
    Analyze IOA Data and Conduct Discrepancy Discussions
    Calculate Agreement
    Report Agreement
Calculating Interobserver Agreement
    Percentage Agreement
        Point-By-Point Agreement (Trial-Based Behaviors and Interval-Based Systems)
        Occurrence and Non-occurrence Agreement
        Point-by-Point Agreement (Timed Event Recording)
        Point-by-Point Agreement (Event Recording within Intervals)
        Percentage Agreement (Event Recording for Free Operant Behaviors and Total Duration)
    Kappa
Conclusions
References

DOI: 10.4324/9781003294726-6

Carefully considering definitions and measurement of your dependent variables is critical. However, even carefully considered dependent variable measurement is not foolproof. Thus, you should properly plan for and monitor data collection throughout your study to increase the likelihood that your dependent variable data are valid, accurate, and reliable. As discussed in the previous chapter, data collection within the context of a single case design occurs repeatedly over time, and almost always via observational recording. Humans observe and record behavior (usually based on researcher-devised systems) and, in turn, make decisions based on those observations. Mark Wolery, a single case researcher who considerably influenced the field of early childhood special education, has said, "humans are the worst data collectors but are often superior to all other options" (2011). Although difficulties are not specific to single case design or repeated observational measurement, the nature of measurement in single case design does pose some different problems than those generally faced by group design researchers. We describe potential issues and discuss the ways that single case researchers can prevent these problems and detect and minimize the effects when they do occur.

Validity

As discussed in Chapters 2 and 3, the concept most closely aligned with validity of dependent variables is *construct validity* (whether your measurement procedures accurately reflect the concept you are interested in measuring; Crano & Brewer, 2002). Although we measure specific, observable behaviors in single case design research, we do so because they represent an important construct such as social or academic competence (Shadish, Cook, & Campbell, 2002). However, the match between well-defined and reliably measured behaviors and broadly-defined, socially important constructs can be difficult to achieve. For example, assume your definitions for problem behavior include touching others without permission. Given that definition, pats on the back, and inadvertent touching in line count as problem behavior—thus, your construct validity might be low if those behaviors are not problematic. While specific and observable operational definitions might result in high reliability, it does not necessarily ensure that the definitions are sufficient for allowing the measurement of the behavior you are interested in. Especially when measuring broader social constructs like "interactions" or "engagement," you should ensure that your specific and observable defined behaviors are well aligned with the concepts from which they were derived (Barlow & Hersen, 1984).

Accuracy

Inaccuracy refers to the failure of the measurement system to perfectly reflect behaviors that actually occurred: (1) behaviors that occurred were not coded or (2) behaviors that did not occur were coded. Reasons for inaccuracy include human error (e.g., missed opportunities or misinterpretation by human observers) as well as nonspecific definitions that omit or provide limited information regarding examples and non-examples in context. Unfortunately, accuracy is not a construct that is easily measured; that is, a "true" value of behaviors is dependent on a human observer (or sometimes computerized or other mechanized counts), but these transformations can never be considered "true" values. Instead, we increase confidence in the *accuracy* of measurement via assessment of reliability (Kazdin, 2010).

Reliability

To increase the likelihood of accurate measurement, we rely on measuring the *reliability* of measurement. In single case, we usually assess reliability as the extent to which two observers record a behavior occurrence in the same way. When two people disagree, we cannot say for sure which (if either) is *accurate*, but we can say that the measurement was not *reliable*. When observers disagree on behavioral occurrences, one of three common problems may be present: Bias, drift, or error.

Observer bias refers to the likelihood that a data collector has conscious or unconscious beliefs that impact their data collection in a predictable direction. Bias generally occurs when a researcher believes his or her intervention will "work" to change behavior (cf. Chazin et al., 2018), although it can also occur such that a researcher believes the intervention is unlikely to work. For example, if a behavioral researcher compares a behavioral intervention to a sensory-based intervention, he or she may likely be biased *against* the sensory intervention and be biased *in favor of* the behavioral intervention. It is important to note that bias does not necessarily include conscious decision making or malevolent or unethical intent. Including *positionality statements* in research may also allow consumers of research to evaluate the likelihood of bias in a general way (cf. Cumming et al., 2023; Leko et al., 2023), but bias specific to data collection can be detected and prevented by collecting interobserver agreement data, frequently graphing and analyzing data, and using naïve observers.

Observer drift refers to the tendency of a data collector to depart from accurate use of definitions over time. As with bias, this is generally not a product of conscious decision making or unethical intent. It is especially problematic in single case research because of the repeated and extended nature of data collection for a single participant. For example, researchers might initially fail to count an unconventional communication attempt by a child (e.g., a vocalization that is not readily understandable) but as they observe the child over time, they may come to recognize the behavior as communicative and count it as such. This is problematic because it means that initial observations (usually under baseline conditions) will underestimate the true occurrence of the behavior compared to later observations. Observer drift can be detected and prevented by collecting interobserver agreement data, frequently graphing and analyzing data, encouraging consistent referencing of coding definitions, and having discrepancy discussions.

Bias and drift are specific inaccuracies that lead to predictable errors. However, some mistakes are simply unsystematic inaccuracies that result from observers incorrectly applying definitions. These can include (1) observer inattention, generally leading to underestimates of low-frequency behavior occurrence or overestimates of high-frequency behavior occurrence; (2) difficulty adjusting coding given new conditions (e.g., onset of a new phase dramatically changes number of behaviors that occur, increasing complexity of data collection), (3) misinterpretation of definitions, and (4) unexpected ambiguous occurrences. Error can be reduced by training observers to a set criterion before beginning data collection, and training in a range of contexts (e.g., situations likely to be contacted during the study, across experimental phases); limiting the amount of data collection done in a short period of time; being familiar with your research participants and their likely behaviors; and having discrepancy discussions.

Ensuring Reliability and Validity of Data Collection

When planning and conducting single case design research, it is of paramount importance to ensure that you collect valid and reliable data on your dependent variables of interest. Doing so improves the internal validity of your study by improving the confidence that any changes between conditions indicated by your data are indicative of actual changes in participant behavior and not unplanned or unrelated factors.

Operationalize Behaviors

As discussed in Chapter 4, operationalizing behaviors is of critical importance for increasing construct validity. It is also important for improving reliability; that is, for ensuring that two observers can apply the definitions identically. Definitions should be specific enough that two individuals can read them and apply them to the same behaviors in the same way. Examples and non-examples, in addition to carefully written definitions, are helpful. When writing non-examples, clearly exemplify behaviors that are similar to those of interest, but do not represent the construct of interest (e.g., if you are interested in vocal social interactions between peers, ensure that non-socially directed labeling of items is *not* counted as an occurrence) to minimize the likelihood of ambiguous occurrences. Non-examples should not simply be a list of opposites of the examples provided; rather they should serve to identify behaviors that represent questionable instances of the target behavior. If possible, individualize operational definitions for each participant prior to study onset.

Pilot Data Collection Procedures

When conducting research, it is important to ensure that definitions and measurement procedures are accurate and appropriate for gathering information about the dependent variable of interest. It is prudent to ensure this is the case *prior* to beginning data collection for the study. Thus, when possible, researchers should consider piloting their data collection systems before beginning the first phase of a study. This pilot can be conducted with the intended participants, individuals who are similar to the intended participants, or confederates. Benefits and drawbacks of piloting with each group are shown in Table 5.1. Note that these data will *not* be reported in research reports and generally do not require Institutional Review Board (IRB) approval; however, you generally do need client or parent/guardian permission to collect data, especially if individuals are identifiable (e.g., via video). During the pilot data collection period (using your definitions), ask yourself whether all observers (1) captured all relevant behaviors that matched your construct of interest, and (b) did not capture similar behaviors that did not match your construct. Following piloting procedures, you should assess reliability and validity, and revise definitions, examples, and non-examples accordingly. For example, in a recent project in which data collectors were coding play behaviors of young children, our research team piloted data collection procedures with two non-study videos. Following this practice data collection, we realized that there was confusion about how to code *cleaning-up* behaviors. We then clarified definitions in relation to this behavior, which was not considered in initial definitions.

Train Observers

To train data collectors, we suggest (1) providing definitions, examples, non-examples, and procedures in writing; (2) practicing coding alongside the data collector, answering questions and resolving conflicts; (3) discussing any discrepancies and revising written guidelines as appropriate; (4) independently coding a separate session (e.g., at the same time or from the same video) and calculating the extent to which you agree; (5) discussing any discrepancies and revising written guidelines as appropriate; and (6) repeating until the trainee reaches your criterion level. Generally, an acceptable criterion level for training is 90% agreement between the primary investigator and all other observers, but this varies by the complexity of the code and contexts. See below for specifics regarding calculating agreement.

Table 5.1 Benefits, Weaknesses, and Examples of Use of Varying Participants in Pilot Activities

	Benefit	Weakness	Example
Intended participants	If participants are easily accessible, identify idiosyncratic behaviors not considered in initial development.	Participants may display similar levels of behavior during practice and later baseline sessions, but the data system may not work well when the behavior changes during intervention phases.	While planning a study intended to improve toy engagement, Jen practiced using her data collection system by observing the young child she intended to recruit for study participation in her typical classroom activities.
Individuals similar to intended participants	If participants are difficult to access, similar individuals can result in identification of likely issues during data collection such as potentially ambiguous behaviors.	Same as above; choosing several different individuals with different levels of behavior can help to remediate this problem.	While planning a study designed to improve reading rates in a public school, David practices his data collection system with several young children in a lab school he visits frequently.
Confederates	Confederates can devise a variety of situations with multiple levels and types of behavior occurrence.	Confederates may not engage in behaviors that are similar to participants.	While planning a study designed to improve social interactions among peers, Justin recruits several undergraduate students to set up pretend play scenarios among themselves, with some sessions including high rates of interactions and some including low rates.

Use Naïve Observers

Naïve observers (also referred to as blind observers) are data collectors who do not know the condition in effect for the data they are collecting. Using naïve observers can be costly and logistically difficult because on many research teams, all members are aware of study procedures (Wolery & Garfinkle, 2002) or available resources limit the number of people who can be on the team. However, in some cases and for some designs, it might be possible to have coders who can observe sessions without knowing whether the session represents a specific condition. For example, Chazin et al. (2018) conducted three different types of sessions to determine whether physical activity had an impact on subsequent behavior during large group activities—seated activities, activities designed to evoke moderate-to-vigorous physical activity, and typical classroom activities. Following implementation of one of three conditions each day, the classroom large group activity was recorded. In the video recording, there was no indication of which condition had preceded the large group activity, so observers could code data without being potentially biased regarding outcome measurement (Chazin et al., 2018). Although naïve observers are rarely used in single case research (Tate et al., 2016), they can be helpful by reducing the possibility of observer bias in instances where condition type is not apparent (an assumption that has received recent attention but was acknowledged years ago; cf. Bushell et al., 1968). For some research questions, naïve observers are less feasible (e.g., in a study regarding the use of visual supports, it will be apparent to observers whether these supports are present or absent). However, observers can be recruited who are naïve to study purpose and hypotheses (e.g., observers are trained on dependent variable data collection but are given no information about changes between condition and how that may impact measurement). Using naïve observers may be more feasible when collecting data that are not context-bound (for more information about this concept, see Chapter 7).

Collect IOA Data

Single case researchers most often assess reliability between two observers who have observed and recorded behavior simultaneously but independently and reported the extent to which they agree as a percentage; this is often referred to as **interobserver agreement** (IOA) but can also be called inter-rater reliability or inter-assessor agreement. To collect IOA data, two independent data collectors observe and record behavior during a single measurement occasion on identical but separate data collection forms. When data are collected in situ, rather than via video, observers should take care to truly be independent; this may require consideration of physical positions and data collection forms. For example, the two observers may need to position themselves on opposite sides of the room so that they are less likely to view each other's data collection forms or devices. In addition, when interval-based systems or trial-based event recording is used, observers should collect data for occurrences and non-occurrences so decisions are not apparent (i.e., one observer will not be able to ascertain whether the other observer is marking an occurrence or a non-occurrence). When interval-based recording is used, take care to synchronize your recording devices so that uncoordinated timing does not result in discrepant outcome measurement.

Analyze IOA Data and Conduct Discrepancy Discussions

Following data collection, researchers should analyze IOA data. Immediate analysis should be formative in nature and should occur following each IOA measurement occasion. Formative analysis should be used to inform the extent to which definitions and procedures are adequate and to alert researchers when additional training is needed. That is, frequent and systematic analysis of agreement data allow researchers to immediately identify data collection problems and attempt to remediate them before these problems render data uninterpretable.

For formative analysis purposes, researchers should graph data from both observers on a single graph (Artman, Wolery, & Yoder, 2010; Chazin et al., 2018; Ledford et al., 2012; Ledford & Wolery, 2013). This allows for the visual analysis of differences between observers and allows researchers to identify potential observer drift or bias. Graphing both observer's data can identify some of the problems described in earlier sections. For example, the top panel of Figure 5.1 shows generally high agreement between observers, with differences potentially due to *observer error*. You can see that the naïve observer sometimes counted more occurrences than the primary observer, and sometimes counted fewer occurrences. This suggests that systematic bias is *not* present, and drift is unlikely.

The middle panel of Figure 5.1 shows data with similar agreement as the top panel, but it shows an example of what *observer bias* might look like on a graph. All errors in baseline were such that the naïve observer identified more positive outcomes (a greater number of initiations) in baseline and fewer positive outcomes during intervention (fewer initiations). That is, one reason for the differences could be that the primary observer who is aware of condition changes is biased (e.g., believes the intervention is working) and is influenced by this, while the naïve observer is unaware and thus potentially a more neutral observer. Of course, we cannot know for sure that this is happening; it is also possible that the secondary observer was simply less attentive during some sessions compared to others. However, the consistency of differences in the middle panel compared to the top panel suggests that this explanation is less likely.

A depiction of *observer drift* is shown in the bottom panel of Figure 5.1. In these hypothetical data, you can see that the naïve observer's data slowly drifts farther from the primary observer's data. This might suggest that drift is present, although it is not possible to determine which observer (if not both) is becoming less accurate in applying definitions.

Reliability and Validity of Dependent Variables • 75

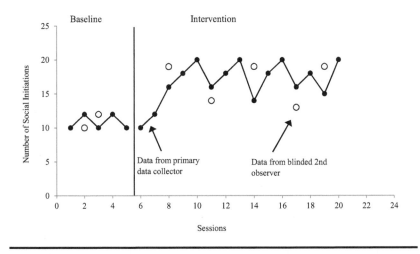

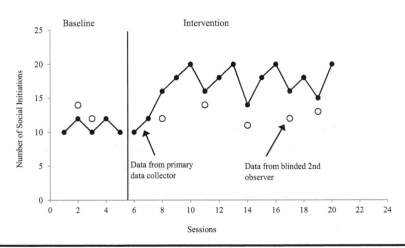

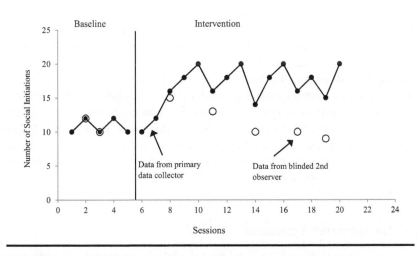

Figure 5.1 Graphs Depicting Data from a Primary Observer Alongside Data from a Secondary Observer.

Note: The top panel depicts adequate agreement with disagreements occurring in both directions. The middle panel depicts adequate agreement with potential observer bias. The bottom panel depicts adequate agreement with evidence of observer drift.

When video recording, it is possible to discuss disagreements following each session and reach a consensus in each instance (e.g., What is the correct response?); this is referred to above as a **discrepancy discussion**. Following consensus coding, primary data can be altered to more accurately match coding definitions and reduce errors. However, original calculations should be reported (i.e., data can be re-plotted so that error is not shared with eventual consumers, but *recorded IOA percentages should never be altered*; see below). If bias is likely, use of a naïve observer should be considered. If drift or error is likely, observers should be re-trained. When recording in situ, discussing differences immediately after a session might lead to similar results as discrepancy discussions; researchers should take careful notes given either type of discussion. For example, a novel occurrence of a close non-example in one session might result in disagreements between observers. Given a discussion following the session, researchers can agree that this non-example should be added to the official documentation of the target behavior, and thus, future disagreements can be avoided. However, we clarify that *changing* definitions during the course of the study is not acceptable. That is, if you count something as an occurrence in initial sessions, you should not revise definitions such that it is counted as a non-occurrence in later sessions (and vice versa). Any clarifications made to definitions throughout the study should be transparently described in research reports.

Calculate Agreement

In addition to plotting IOA data for formative analysis, researchers should calculate agreement using either percentage agreement or the Kappa coefficient for the purposes of formative and summative evaluation. Formatively, researchers should analyze disagreements and determine whether additional training is needed. Summatively, researchers should report agreement to allow consumers to draw conclusions about the reliability of data collection.

Report Agreement

In written reports, single case researchers typically report agreement with summary statistics. When percentage agreement is used, average agreement of 80% or better has been considered acceptable (Kazdin, 2010) and it is a common threshold for determining sufficiency (What Works Clearinghouse, 2020). The extent to which this is true depends on several factors, including the complexity of the behavior and context and the degree of behavior change between conditions (Ledford et al., 2023). For example, 80% average agreement regarding whether a child named sight words correctly is likely to be viewed as too low because coding correct and incorrect responding to a simple task is generally quite straightforward; 80% average agreement for social interactions in a typical classroom free play context is more reasonable due to the complexity of the code and the context. Also, as illustrated in Figure 5.1, 80% agreement when changes between phases are small results in decreased confidence that the change was due to the intervention rather than bias. Any sessions in which IOA was lower than 80% should be explained in text or in supplemental materials.

Calculating Interobserver Agreement

Below, we describe several procedures used for calculating agreement, with percentage agreement being used in the overwhelming majority of single case research studies.

Percentage Agreement

Percentage agreement is a simple calculation that is intuitive and widely used. When percentage agreement is used, you simply report the extent to which two observers agree using percentages (e.g., observer 1 agreed with observer 2 for 90% of opportunities). Although percentage agreement is almost always used to report the extent to which data collection is reliable, it is not perfect because it is influenced by chance agreement, behavior rates, and measurement system used (cf., Kratochwill & Wetzel, 1977). Percentage agreement is calculated and interpreted differently depending on the measurement system used.

Point-By-Point Agreement (Trial-Based Behaviors and Interval-Based Systems)
When trial-based or interval-based measurement is used, agreement can be calculated using trial-by-trial (interval-by-interval) comparisons (**point-by-point agreement**). To conduct agreement in this way, compare the code for each interval (or trial) for one observer with the code for the corresponding interval (or trial) for the second observer. Note whether the codes are the same (agreement) or different (disagreement). After determining the number of intervals coded as agreement or disagreement, calculate percent agreement (Tawney & Gast, 1984):

$$\left(\frac{\# \text{ of agreements}}{\# \text{ of agreements} + \# \text{ of disagreements}} \right) \times 100$$

Occurrence and Non-occurrence Agreement
When chance agreement is likely when rates of behaviors are low (e.g., if almost all trials or intervals are non-occurrences), some researchers have suggested the use of **occurrence agreement** (Tawney & Gast, 1984). To calculate occurrence agreement, you code agreements and disagreements (as described above) *only for intervals in which at least one observer noted an occurrence* (which we have abbreviated as "occurrence trials" or OT). The calculation is:

$$\left(\frac{\# \text{ of agreements for occurrence trials}}{\# \text{ of agreements for OT} + \# \text{ of disagreements for OT}} \right) \times 100$$

Similarly, **non-occurrence agreement** can be calculated when change agreement is likely due to very high behavior rates, using only trials in which at least one observer noted that a behavior did not occur (which we have abbreviated as "non-occurrence trials," or "NOT").

$$\left(\frac{\# \text{ of agreements for non-occurrence trials}}{\# \text{ of agreements for NOT} + \# \text{ of disagreements for NOT}} \right) \times 100$$

Non-occurrence agreement and occurrence agreement may be greater than or less than total agreement, depending on the types of disagreements that occurred in the session. We recommend calculating occurrence and non-occurrence agreements when behavior rates are low or high for formative decision making. High occurrence and non-occurrence agreement increases confidence in reliability and are similar to point-by-point agreement for free operant behaviors; this level of agreement is rarely reported in published studies.

Point-by-Point Agreement (Timed Event Recording)

Before collecting data for behaviors measured with timed event recording, you should establish a time frame within which you will record an agreement if both observers mark an occurrence. For example, in Figure 5.2, the middle panel depicts that Observer #1 marked an occurrence at 1:28 and Observer #2 marked an occurrence at 1:26. Although the time stamp is not exactly the same, it seems unlikely that Observer #1 would count a true occurrence and miss another true occurrence, and vice versa for Observer #2. What is more likely is that one observer had a slightly quicker response time. Generally, a window of a few seconds (e.g., a maximum of 2–5 seconds, depending on the complexity of the code and context) is acceptable. With timed event recording, there are no non-occurrences, so total agreement is calculated similarly to occurrence agreement for trial-based behaviors or interval-based measurement. First, you will line up occurrences to determine how many agreements you have within your given time window. Then you will count disagreements that occurred *outside* the time window (e.g., if your time window was 2 seconds, and one observer marked an occurrence at 3:32 and the other marked an occurrence at 3:36) and the instances in which one observer marked an occurrence and the other observer marked nothing. Thus, agreements include instances where both observers marked an occurrence at exactly the same time and instances where both observers noted an occurrence within the given time window. Disagreements include instances in which both

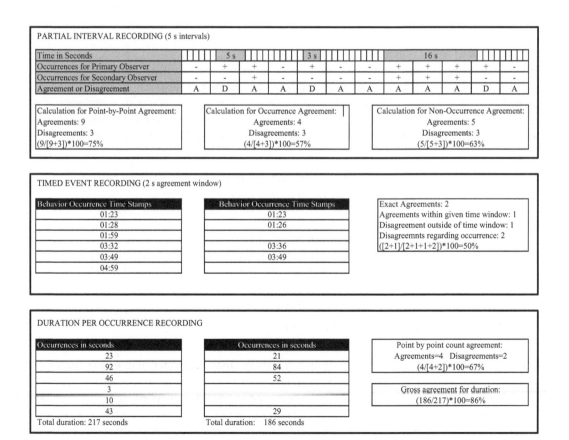

Figure 5.2 Sample Agreement Calculations.

Note: Agreement for trial or interval-based data (top panel), timed event recording (middle panel), and duration recording (bottom panel).

observers marked an occurrence outside of the time window and occurrences that were only marked by one observer. Then, agreement is calculated as:

$$\left(\frac{\#\ of\ agreements\ within\ given\ time\ window}{\#\ of\ agreements + \#\ disagreements}\right) \times 100$$

When the number of occurrences is very low (which is often true in either baseline phases or intervention phases, depending on intervention goals), even one disagreement can result in very low agreement. In these cases, the reason for low disagreement should be reported and additional IOA data should be collected (above and beyond the usual minimum levels). *The threshold for acceptable agreement with this type of agreement calculation should be lower than the threshold for total agreement with trial-based or interval-based recording.*

Point-by-Point Agreement (Event Recording within Intervals)
When timed event recording is not possible, event recording within intervals is recommended. Prior to beginning data collection, the observation is divided into equal intervals (e.g., 10 s); the same interval length is used for the duration of the study. During each interval, you count each occurrence of the behavior (e.g., target behavior occurred once during the first interval, none during the second, twice during the third, etc.). There are two options for calculating agreement. First, you can measure exact agreement. For example, if Observer 1 counted two occurrences of the behavior and Observer 2, one occurrence, that would count as a disagreement for that interval. Given the chance that a single behavior could occur at the end of one interval and continue into the next, you could calculate agreement within a numerical window. For example, add a rule where agreement for an interval is recorded when both observers are within ±1 count of the behavior, given that both observers counted the behavior at least once during the interval. The numerical window of agreement will likely be dependent on the extent to which a behavior occurs during a session, with higher rate behaviors likely necessitating +2 instances to count as an agreement.

$$\left(\frac{\#\ of\ agreements\ within\ given\ numerical\ window}{\#\ of\ agreements + \#\ disagreements}\right) \times 100$$

Percentage Agreement (Event Recording for Free Operant Behaviors and Total Duration)
Unlike the previous examples above, it is not possible to measure point-by-point when using event or total duration recording. Instead, **gross agreement** (total agreement) is calculated.

$$\left(\frac{smaller\ measurement}{larger\ measurement}\right) \times 100$$

For example, if one observer recorded a total duration of 220 seconds and the second observer recorded a total duration of 242, the agreement would be 90.9% ([220/242]×100). This type of agreement is inferior because it prevents identifying discrepancies (e.g., no information is available about at what point the disagreements occurred) and because no evidence is available that all of the "agreement" (e.g., 220 seconds in the example above) actually referred to time in which both observers marked the same code. Thus, this is the least conservative and least preferred agreement method. When duration per occurrence is measured, point-by-point agreement can be measured based on onset (e.g., agreement on number of events) and gross agreement can be measured based on duration (e.g., agreement on duration), as shown in the bottom panel of Figure 5.2.

An alternative when using duration per occurrence is measuring point-by-point agreement based on the onset *and* offset of each occurrence of the behavior. In this scenario, a window of agreement is selected for the onset and offset of a behavior; for feasibility and reliability purposes, we recommend keeping that window consistent within and across sessions for the duration of the study. For example, in a study we may decide to measure functional engagement with toys using a duration per occurrence measurement system. Prior to beginning the study, we select a 2 s window of agreement. During the fourth session, Observer 1 times each occurrence of the behavior and Observer 2 does the same during the session. When we assess agreement, we notice that both observers said the behavior happened four times. Both observers agreed about the onset of the behavior (within 2 s of one another) but disagreed based on offset, with Observer 2 consistently recording that each behavior happened for 5 to 6 s longer than Observer 1. This yields more precise information than a gross measure of agreement, as well as important information that requires immediate attention before the next session. Relatedly, given that duration per occurrence yields time-related data *and* count, point-by-point agreement for onsets allows us to assess agreement for how many times a behavior occurs during a session, which was described earlier in this chapter.

$$\left(\frac{\text{\# of agreements within the onset and offset window of time}}{\text{\# of agreements} + \text{\# disagreements}} \right) \times 100$$

Kappa

As mentioned previously, chance agreement is likely when rates of behavior are very low and very high (i.e., a non-observer could score all intervals as occurrences or non-occurrences and have adequate agreement with an accurate observer). Although we don't expect many data collectors to purposefully falsify data, this chance agreement is still somewhat troubling, since it indicates that high agreement may not be highly associated with accuracy. The Kappa coefficient is superior relative to percentage agreement, because it mathematically corrects for chance agreement (Cohen, 1960); over time many researchers have argued that Kappa should be used instead of the more common percent agreement (Hartmann, 1977; Kratochwill & Wetzel, 1977; Watkins & Pacheco, 2000), despite different methodological issues related to base rates (for a more comprehensive review, see Yoder et al., 2018). Kappa can be calculated when interval-based systems or duration recording is used, but cannot be calculated for event recording or timed event recording because to use Kappa, you must have information on occurrence *and* non-occurrences. To calculate Kappa, you divide percentage agreement minus chance agreement by one minus chance agreement; this leaves the proportion of agreement that is not related to chance. The calculation for chance agreement is:

$$\frac{\left(\text{\# of OT for O1}\right) \times \left(\text{\# of OT for O2}\right)}{\left(\text{Total \# of trials}\right)^2} + \frac{\left(\text{\# of NOT for O1}\right) \times \left(\text{\# of NOT for O2}\right)}{\left(\text{Total \# of trials}\right)^2}$$

Note: O1=observer 1. O2=observer 2. OT=occurrence trials. NOT=non-occurrence trials.

Note we use "trials" for the example, but it could also refer to intervals (for interval-based systems) or time (for duration measures). Several online calculators are available for the calculation of Kappa since the calculations are somewhat complex. Because Kappa removes the portion of agreement attributable to chance, acceptable Kappa values are somewhat lower than percentage agreement values (generally, 0.60 rather than 0.80 as the minimum acceptable value).

Conclusions

After choosing a behavior of interest, researchers follow systematic steps to ensure meaningful assessment of the outcome of a single case design study. These steps include: Carefully defining the behavior and identifying examples and non-examples, characterizing the behavior based on reversibility and duration type, determining the dimension of interest, choosing a measurement system, piloting use of the system, training observers, and making modifications if needed. Following the initiation of data collection, additional steps are needed to ensure the reliability of data collection, including collection and formative and summative assessment of interobserver agreement data. Following the steps outlined in this chapter will ensure that the dependent variable assessment in your study results in meaningful conclusions about actual behavior occurrence and change.

References

Artman, K., Wolery, M., & Yoder, P. (2010). Embracing our visual inspection and analysis tradition: Graphing interobserver agreement data. *Remedial and Special Education*, 33, 71–77.
Barlow, D. H., & Hersen, M. (1984). *Single case experimental designs: Strategies for studying behavior change* (2nd ed.). New York: Pergamon Press.
Bushell, D., Wrobel, P. A., & Michaelis, M. L. (1968). Applying "group" contingencies to the classroom study behavior of preschool children. *Journal of Applied Behavior Analysis*, 1, 55–61.
Chazin, K. T., Ledford, J. R., Barton, E. E., & Osborne, K. C. (2018). The effects of antecedent exercise on engagement during large group activities for young children. *Remedial and Special Education*, 39(3), 158–170.
Cohen, J. (1960). A coefficient of agreement for nominal scales. *Educational and Psychological Measurement*, 20, 37–46.
Cumming, M. M., Bettini, E., & Chow, J. C. (2023). High-quality systematic literature reviews in special education: Promoting coherence, contextualization, generativity, and transparency. *Exceptional Children*, 89(4), 412–431.
Crano, W. D., & Brewer, M. B. (2002). *Principles and methods of social research* (2nd ed.). Mahwah, NJ: Lawrence Erlbaum.
Hartmann, D. P. (1977). Considerations in the choice of interobserver reliability estimates. *Journal of Applied Behavior Analysis*, 10, 103–116.
Kazdin, A. E. (2010). *Single-case research designs. Methods for clinical and applied settings* (2nd ed). New York: Oxford University Press.
Kratochwill, T. R., & Wetzel, R. J. (1977). Interobserver agreement, credibility, and judgment: Some considerations in presenting observer agreement data. *Journal of Applied Behavior Analysis*, 10, 133–139.
Ledford, J. R., Artman, K., Wolery, M., & Wehby, J. (2012). The effects of graphing a second observer's data on judgments of functional relations for A-B-A-B graphs. *Journal of Behavioral Education*, 21, 350–364.
Ledford, J. R., Lambert, J. M., Pustejovsky, J. E., Zimmerman, K. N., Hollins, N., & Barton, E. E. (2023). Single-case-design research in special education: Next-generation guidelines and considerations. *Exceptional Children*, 89(4), 379–396.
Ledford, J. R., & Wolery, M. (2013). The effects of graphing a second observer's data on judgments of functional relations when observer bias may be present. *Journal of Behavioral Education*, 22, 312–324.
Leko, M. M., Hitchcock, J. H., Love, H. R., Houchins, D. E., & Conroy, M. A. (2023). Quality indicators for mixed-methods research in special education. *Exceptional Children*, 89(4), 432–448.
Shadish. W. R., Cook, T. D., & Campbell, D. T. (2002). *Experimental and quasi-experimental designs for generalized causal inference*. Belmont, CA: Wadsworth Cengage Learning.

Tate, R. L., Rosenkoetter, U., Vohra, S., Horner, R., Kratochwill, T., Sampson, M., … Wilson, B. (2016). Single case reporting guidelines in behavioral interventions (SCRIBE) 2016 statement. *Archives of Scientific Psychology*, 4, 1–9. doi:10.1037/arc0000026

Tawney, J. W., & Gast, D. L. (1984). *Single subject research in special education*. Columbus, OH: Charles E. Merrill.

Watkins, M. W., & Pacheco, M. (2000). Interobserver agreement in behavioral research: Importance and calculation. *Journal of Behavioral Education*, 10, 205–212.

What Works Clearinghouse (2020). Procedures and standards handbook. (Version 4.1). Retrieved from https://ies.ed.gov/ncee/wwc/Docs/referenceresources/WWC-Standards-Handbook-v4-1-508.pdf

Wolery, M., & Garfinkle, A. N. (2002). Measures in intervention research with young children who have autism. *Journal of Autism and Developmental Disorders*, 32, 463–478.

Yoder, P., Lloyd, B., & Symons, F. (2018). *Observational measurement of behavior*, (2nd ed.). Baltimore: Brookes.

6
Development and Measurement of Independent Variables

Erin E. Barton and Jennifer R. Ledford

Important Terms

theory of change, procedural fidelity, dosage, control variables, independent variables, implementation fidelity, treatment integrity, direct systematic observation, checklists, self-reports

Table of Contents

Planning Study Conditions Using a Theory of Change
Different Ways to Approach Condition Design
   Evaluation of Procedures versus Evaluation of Processes
   Static versus Dynamic Condition Design
Cascading Logic Models
Measurement of Fidelity
   Defining Experimental Conditions
   Types of Fidelity
Formative Analysis
Summative Analysis
Reporting Fidelity
Conclusions
References

Planning Study Conditions Using a Theory of Change

Single case design research allows for assessment of causal relations between one or more researcher-manipulated independent variables (intervention or treatment) and one or more dependent variables (behaviors). Identifying causal relations in single case studies includes careful planning and measurement of the dependent variables, as discussed in the previous two chapters, and careful planning and measurement of *independent variables*, the focus of this chapter. Once you have identified behaviors of interest and have defined your dependent variables with precision, the independent variable can be planned and designed to produce the hypothesized change (Kennedy, 2005).

You can develop independent variables given a myriad of scenarios. For example, you might develop a single case design study using a specific "bottom-up" approach common in practice. That is, you have a relationship with specific individual(s) and an identified challenge that you are actively attempting to solve. Alternatively, you might begin with an interest in solving a particular type of problem (e.g., challenging behavior) for a specific population (e.g., adolescents with autism who require significant supports), but without a specific case in mind. In either case, you should use your clinical judgment, practical knowledge of the problem and/or the context and participants, relevant theory, and existing experimental research to drive the planning of independent variables. Development of the independent variable should be based on a well-informed theory of change. A **theory of change** is a model based on theoretical assumptions about how a proposed intervention "works." To develop a theory of change, you begin with the desired outcome and establish what changes need to occur for this desired outcome to be achieved (Mayne, 2017).

A simple theory of change model is shown in Figure 6.1. On the left side of the model is a description of the problem and on the right side is the *impact* (the final desired outcomes—usually distal and generalized behavior change). The middle of the theory change includes the intervention and intermediate outcomes (proximal, context-bound changes) that contribute to the overall impact. For this model, it is important to note that three theories are implicated in the treatment process—reinforcement, social learning, and intergroup contact (Bandura, 1969; Davies et al., 2011; Skinner, 1965). In this model, increased peer interactions is an intermediate outcome that is prerequisite to this impact. Thus, an important output of an intervention designed with a final goal in mind is increased opportunities and support for prosocial interactions among these groups of children. A peer-mediated intervention model that prompts and supports positive interactions, such as stay-play-talk (Goldstein et al., 1997), is a reasonable intervention model. Generally, after identifying a problem and the desired impacts, it is advisable to work backwards to an intervention approach, explicating theoretical and empirical assumptions.

After you explicate expected relations between interventions and outcomes using a theory of change model, you can use that model to formulate research questions and clarify the goals of the study. Then, you can use your research questions to select an appropriate single case design and operationalize, plan, order, and implement all conditions such that a relation can be detected, if one exists (Kennedy, 2005; see Chapter 15 for design selection).

Different Ways to Approach Condition Design

The process/procedure and static/dynamic frameworks discussed in Chapter 1 might be a helpful structure as you consider your research questions.

Evaluation of Procedures versus Evaluation of Processes

Most group design intervention research is designed to evaluate specific procedures—usually a pre-determined intervention or treatment with specified components and dosages. The groups of studies discussed in Chapter 2, designed to evaluate time delay and stay-play-talk interventions, are examples of this type of research. That is, the authors described research questions that were focused on evaluating whether a specific set of procedures, operationalized in a particular way, would result in changes in the behaviors of interest. However, single case logic can

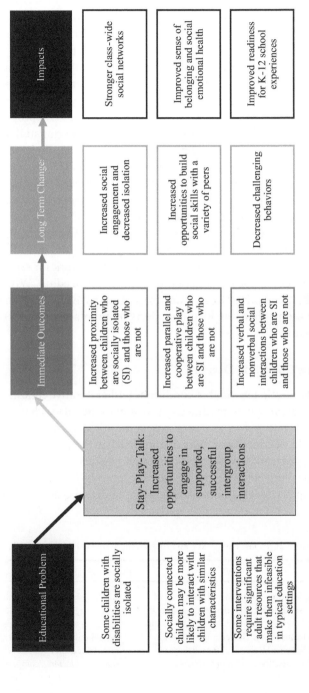

Figure 6.1 Theory of Change for an Intervention Model Assessed in a Single Case Design.

also be used to evaluate the effectiveness of *processes* or *frameworks* for changing behaviors of interest. That is, rather than specifying exact topographies of implementer behaviors (e.g., using Stay-Play-Talk strategies), researchers may specify rules used to identify topographies within a study (e.g., if X and Y conditions are true, choose B intervention variation).

The difference between these two approaches can be illustrated via consideration of common intervention approaches for challenging behavior. These interventions are often based on functional features of the behavior (e.g., Why does the behavior occur?), topographical features of the behavior (e.g., What does the behavior look like?), and other contextual characteristics (e.g., Where is the behavior occurring? What resources are available?). Because these characteristics are likely to impact the appropriateness and effectiveness of a specific intervention approach, authors have taken them into account in different ways. For example, using a *procedures* approach, authors might identify a specific intervention that is appropriate given specific factors (e.g., Does a *specific procedure* reduce challenging behavior for students identified with behavioral disorders who engage in challenging behaviors to escape demands, in public school settings; Staubitz et al., 2022). Using a *process* approach, authors include a wider range of contexts and they evaluate a *process* or *framework* that specifies procedures based on features that could impact intervention effectiveness (e.g., Does a *general framework* [function-informed, mechanisms-based treatment] reduce challenging behavior for participants with a range of disabilities; with any hypothesized behavioral function; in clinics, schools, or homes; with behavior of any problematic topography? Lambert et al., 2022). Similar studies exist evaluating processes/frameworks versus specific procedures (e.g., a framework for selecting and prompting procedures, Cowan et al., 2023; evaluation of a specific procedure, Winstead et al., 2019). Note that studies evaluating both processes and procedures have *pre-specified* and *specific* rules that drive implementation—there are just more decision points when processes are evaluated compared with procedures.

Static versus Dynamic Condition Design

A related, but distinct, question is whether conditions (either iterative conditions designated via a process or set procedures) will be modified contingent on behavior change (or lack thereof). This has typically been referred to as a static/dynamic dichotomy and it is associated with whether researchers take a deductive or inductive approach to their science (see Chapter 1). Static research questions are generally yes/no questions about whether a specific process or procedure was effective for establishing behavior change (see the top cells in Table 6.1). However, as mentioned in previous chapters, single case researchers also tend to use data-based decision making

Table 6.1 Examples of Research Questions Associated with Process/Procedure Paradigms and Static/Dynamic Paradigms

	Process	Procedure
Static	Does using the function-informed and mechanisms-based (FIMB) framework (*an iterative framework delineating a decision-making process*) to select and implement treatment for challenging behavior (CB) result in lower levels of CB for participants compared to a baseline condition with countertherapeutic contingencies?	Does using skills-based treatment (*a specific procedure*) result in lower levels of CB and/or precursor behavior for participants with behavioral disorders who engage in escape-maintained CB in public school settings (*specific contextual factors*), compared to a baseline condition with countertherapeutic contingencies?
Dynamic	*Addition*: And what modifications are required when the use of the framework does not result in behavior change?	*Addition*: And what modifications are required when the procedure does not result in behavior change?

to change conditions (above and beyond decision making that is pre-specified in process research). That is, when expected behavior change does not occur, single case researchers often either modify intervention conditions (e.g., change, add, or remove specific components) or implement entirely different conditions. This type of dynamic question is inductive rather than deductive in nature—that is, rather than asking "Does *process/procedure* work?" the question is "What changes can I make to process/procedure to result in desired behavior change?" Notably, these are not falsifiable, generalizable research questions—however, they are critical for informing theory and practice via descriptive analysis. We argue that authors who intend to engage in the evaluation of dynamic intervention conditions should specify both their static questions and questions about modifications made. It is especially helpful when authors report whether the modifications made during the experiment were pre-planned or made when the intervention did not work as planned (cf. Osborne et al., 2019). Considering whether your questions are related to processes or procedures and static or dynamic intervention conditions will assist you in planning and describing your independent variables.

Cascading Logic Models

Thus far, we have primarily discussed interventions with a single "level" of implementation. That is, our questions have been concerned with how Intervention X impacts Behavior Y. However, in applied research, there is often an additional level of directly manipulated variables. For example, researchers might train teachers to use a specific strategy for improving student behavior. In this situation, there is the direct treatment received by the children (teacher-implemented strategy), but there is also an "upstream" component of the independent variable, which is the training implemented by researchers. The support for implementation of an intervention does not necessarily need to come from a researcher—for example, you may be interested in the extent to which behavior analysts can train registered behavior technicians to engage in naturalistic teaching strategies to increase child initiations or the extent to which teachers can support parents to implement behavior intervention plans. In models like these, which are common in behavioral and education sciences, conceptualizing and measuring intervention is more complex. Let's use the scenario in which researchers provide training for teacher implementation as an example. As shown in Model #1 in Figure 6.2, you could conceptualize the intervention as the initial training, and ask a research question about the impact of researcher training (independent variable) on teacher outcomes (dependent variable). Or, you could ask about the impact of the teacher-implemented strategy (independent variable) on child outcomes (dependent variable). Or, you could ask about the impact of researcher training (independent variable) on child outcomes (dependent variable). But each of these research questions fails to describe the complete set of relations (see Figure 6.2 for example questions and explanation of incompleteness).

A more complete way to conceptualize this situation is shown in Figure 6.3. There are *two* related research questions: (1) Does researcher training result in changes in teacher behavior? and (2) Does teacher implementation result in changes in child behavior? In this model, the teacher behavior is both a *dependent variable* which changes as the result of researcher training, and an *independent variable*, which drives the change in child behavior.

Measurement of Fidelity

Given that study conditions are manipulated and implemented by humans, are implemented repeatedly over time, and might change rapidly, appropriately documenting that study

88 • Erin E. Barton and Jennifer R. Ledford

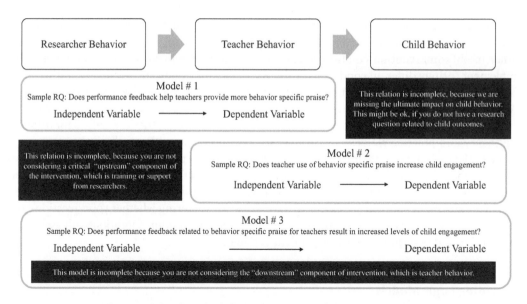

Figure 6.2 Incomplete Models of Study Effects when a Cascading Logic Model is Relevant.

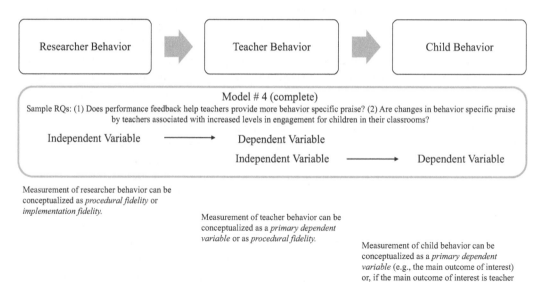

Figure 6.3 Complete Model of Study Effects when a Cascading Logic Model is Relevant.

conditions and all experimental procedures were implemented as planned and operationalized is required—this is referred to as **fidelity measurement** (Billingsley et al., 1980; Kaiser & Hemmeter, 2013; Ledford & Wolery, 2013; Wolery, 2011). When these data are carefully collected and reported, it is possible to use these data to (1) make decisions regarding the likelihood of adequate implementation in regular environments, (2) determine sufficiency of interventions implemented with low fidelity (e.g., If a practitioner implements an intervention correctly only 70% of the time, will it still be effective?), and (3) explain variability in results when this variability is related to inconsistency in intervention implementation (Fettig et al., 2015; Wood et al., 2011; Wood et al., 2007). Conversely, the absence of these data limits conclusions regarding whether experimental procedures were implemented properly and at sufficient dosage levels (i.e., Were procedures implemented each time they should have been implemented, for as long as they should have been implemented?). Adequate measurement and documentation that procedures were implemented as intended across conditions is required to document causal relations. As discussed in Chapter 3, procedural *in*fidelity can threaten internal validity of a study.

Defining Experimental Conditions

All experimental procedures—defined by specific study conditions—should be operationalized to allow for valid interpretations of results and facilitate future replications. That is, you should carefully plan, conduct, and measure implementation of, all procedures in a study, which might include (1) pre-baseline or other initial assessment phase (e.g., inclusion criteria assessment, preference assessment); (2) baseline or control conditions, (3) one or more intervention or training conditions, (4) any other study-specific conditions such as a post-intervention social validity assessment or phases during which maintenance of behavior change is assessed (see Chapter 7).

Some procedures are the same across baseline and intervention conditions (**control variables**); others are differentially implemented across conditions (**independent variable**). Independent and control variables have to be planned, measured, and reported with replicable precision. Reliability of independent and control variables should be measured and documented in all experimental conditions (Ledford & Wolery, 2013). Clear documentation that control variables *did not change* and independent variables *did change*, and corresponded to changes in dependent variables is required to establish a functional relation. You should conduct ongoing measurement of control and independent variables to ensure that changes across conditions occurred for the planned independent variable and *only* for the independent variable. See Table 6.2 for a list of independent and control variables for two common interventions.

Fidelity data are usually collected based on whether implementers are engaging in "correct" behaviors as planned for the study condition and reported as a percentage correct. Thus, 90% fidelity suggests that the implementer performed about 90% of the required steps correctly. This may or may not be sufficient, and likely depends on whether the missing or incorrect steps are critical components or non-critical components of the intervention. Historically, single

Table 6.2 Control and Independent Variables for Two Common Interventions

Planned Step	Variable Type	Condition in which Behavior Occurs
Time delay procedures		
Present stimulus	Control	Baseline, Intervention
Give task direction	Control	Baseline, Intervention
Provide prompt	Independent	Intervention
Wait interval	Control	Baseline, Intervention
Reinforce correct response	Control	Baseline, Intervention
Differential reinforcement for other behaviors		
Provide preferred materials	Control	Baseline, Intervention
Provide five equally spaced task demands	Control	Baseline, Intervention
Provide reinforcement for engaging in behaviors other than aggression	Independent	Intervention

case researchers have not explicitly identified critical and non-critical steps, or prioritized which steps are most important for the intervention to work as hypothesized in the theory of change, although this would likely be helpful.

In addition to percentage correct, it is often helpful to characterize at least some parts of independent variables using other metrics. For example, when measuring naturalistic intervention implementation, it could be reasonable to measure how many times the implementer engaged in certain behaviors (e.g., expansions and time delays; Quinn et al., 2020). It may also be important to separately report a single, critical variable individually. For example, when assessing an intervention with a single component, such as a child wearing a weighted vest, it is critical to report the extent to which a vest was worn for intervention sessions and *not* worn during baseline sessions. The other important part of fidelity for this type of intervention would be *control variables* that would likely impact engagement—for example, the number of opportunities to respond provided by the teacher. If this varied across conditions, any change in child behavior could be attributed to this change in teacher behavior. In sum, the measurement of fidelity requires that you identify key variables that should change across conditions, and key variables that should remain the same across conditions and should report those behaviors in a way that allows readers to accurately interpret the extent to which procedures occurred as intended.

Types of Fidelity

There are at least three relevant conceptualizations of fidelity that warrant discussion. First **procedural fidelity** includes measuring both the extent to which intervention conditions are implemented as intended *and* the extent to which the relevant comparison condition is implemented as intended (e.g., baseline condition). In single case research, procedural fidelity provides evidence that the independent variable was implemented as intended *and* not present (or present at low levels) during baseline or control conditions. Procedural fidelity should provide two types of evidence: *Adherence* (you implemented the intervention as planned) and *differentiation* (you implemented different steps in each condition; Ledford & Wolery, 2013; Sutherland et al., 2013). Adherence to the protocol provides evidence that the intervention was delivered as planned and refers to how closely implementer behavior mirrored prescribed procedures. Differentiation refers to differences between experimental conditions (typically baseline and intervention) and provides evidence that procedures between conditions were implemented differently from one another. Measurement of variables across all experimental conditions is necessary to determine both that independent variables were used correctly during intervention *and* that no other changes occurred between baseline and intervention conditions. Both conclusions are essential for increased confidence that results are due to planned and controlled changes between conditions.

A second type of fidelity measurement is **treatment fidelity**, which refers to the extent to which *intervention conditions* are implemented correctly. To fully control for infidelity threats to internal validity, this type of measurement is insufficient because while it includes documentation of the extent to which the *intervention condition* is implemented as intended, it does not include documentation of the extent to which a relevant *baseline condition* is also implemented as intended. This prevents us from being sure that the intended variables *and only the intended variables* changed between baseline and intervention conditions. That is, we can measure adherence to treatment procedures but cannot measure differentiation between baseline and treatment conditions. However, measurement of this type of fidelity is superior to total lack of fidelity measurement.

When there are multiple "levels" of fidelity in a cascading logic model, measurement of the training or support provided to the implementer can be conceptualized as **implementation fidelity** rather than procedural fidelity (Dunst et al., 2013). The terms used by authors (i.e., implementation fidelity, procedural fidelity) often vary by whether there is a relevant comparison condition. The two examples shown in Table 6.3 may help to clarify this difference.

In Example A, teachers implement baseline and intervention conditions and a two-hour training intended to improve the use of positive comments and praise for desirable behavior is conducted by researchers for teachers. In this situation, we would want to measure whether the training was implemented as described. There is no relevant baseline condition for this one-time training, so researchers generally refer to this measurement as *implementation* fidelity. It would also be important to measure the extent to which teachers provide positive comments in baseline and intervention conditions—this is *procedural* fidelity. In this example, no researchers are present to support teacher in baseline and intervention conditions, so their behaviors during baseline and intervention sessions are not relevant.

In Example B, the same training is provided, and thus, the same implementation and procedural fidelity measures described above are relevant. However, in this example, the researchers are present during study sessions, so we also need to ensure that they are behaving as planned during baseline (*not* providing coaching and feedback to teachers) and intervention (providing coaching and feedback). This could be referred to as *procedural fidelity* given it is related to the fidelity with which planned conditions are implemented but could also be conceptualized as *implementation fidelity* because it is assistance to help the implementer. Similarly,

Table 6.3 Fidelity Measurement for Three Studies with Different Implementation Supports

	Example A	Example B	Example C
Baseline	Typical classroom routines (i.e., business as usual) with no researcher support	Typical classroom routines (i.e., business as usual) with no researcher support	Typical classroom routines (i.e., business as usual) with no researcher support
Training	Two-hour training on importance of positive attention	2-hour training on importance of positive attention	None
Intervention	Typical classroom routines (i.e., business as usual) with no researcher support	Coaching and performance feedback from researchers during typical classroom routines	Coaching and performance feedback from researchers during typical classroom routines
Relevant Fidelity Measures	• To what extent did researchers complete the training as planned? (*implementation fidelity*) • To what extent did teachers use positive attention strategies in baseline and intervention conditions? (*procedural fidelity*)	• To what extent did researchers complete the training as planned? (*implementation fidelity*) • To what extent did researchers follow support plans in baseline and intervention conditions? (*procedural fidelity*) • To what extent did teachers use positive attention strategies in baseline and intervention conditions? (*primary dependent variable*)	• To what extent did researchers follow support plans in baseline and intervention conditions? (*procedural fidelity*) • To what extent did teachers use positive attention strategies in baseline and intervention conditions? (*primary dependent variable*)
Child Outcomes	• Child behaviors (*primary dependent variable*)	• Child behaviors (*secondary dependent variable*)	• Child behaviors (*secondary dependent variable*)

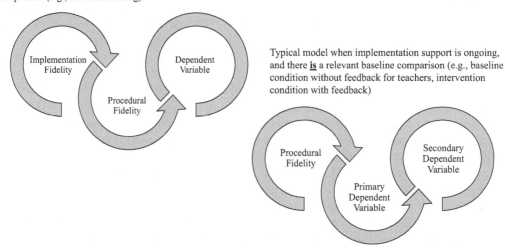

Figure 6.4 Suggestions for Conceptualizing Measurement of Fidelity-Related Variables.

in Example C, there is the need to measure both researcher and teacher behavior in baseline and intervention conditions. However, in this example, there is no separate training.

As shown in Figure 6.4, we suggest the following conventions when a cascading logic model is used in a given study:

1. When a short-term training occurs, and there is no relevant baseline comparison, measure and report the behaviors of the implementer of that condition as *implementation fidelity*.
2. When ongoing intervention is relevant (e.g., coaching, feedback), and there is a relevant baseline comparison, measure and report the behaviors of the implementation supporter as *procedural fidelity* and report the behaviors of the direct implementer as the *primary dependent variable*. Behaviors of the individuals receiving the intervention (e.g., students) can be measured as a secondary dependent variable, given change in these variables is theoretically dependent on change in the implementer's behavior.

Formative Analysis

Formative analysis of procedural fidelity can be used to evaluate ongoing needs and identify when to provide additional training to the implementer. Formative analysis also allows you to detect and minimize threats to internal validity resulting from inaccurate or inconsistent implementation. Common types of fidelity measurement include direct systematic observation, checklists, and self-reports. Although they are often used, **checklists** (i.e., dichotomous yes/no measurement for behaviors that may occur multiple times per session) may not be sensitive to intermittent errors made by implementers. Therefore, the use of checklists should be limited to binary variables or procedures/behaviors that are expected to occur once per session. For example, in the situations described in Table 6.3, a checklist that asked whether a researcher provided positive feedback to a teacher (yes/no) during a session would provide imprecise information about how much support was provided (e.g., Was the feedback frequent or did it happen only once, was the content aligned with the intervention, were there instances of the feedback given correctly *and* incorrectly?). **Self-reports** (i.e., implementers measuring their own implementation) are similar to checklists in that they usually do not include direct measures but ratings of overall occurrence. They have been shown to have low validity for measuring fidelity because implementers typically overestimate the accuracy of their own behaviors (Lane et al., 2008; Martino et al., 2009). Thus, *direct systematic observation of implementer behaviors* is preferable and recommended (i.e., counting whether an implementer used the behavior in the manner in which it was intended, as often as intended). Checklists, self-reports, and direct systematic observation also can be used in combination. In a review of procedural fidelity features, Ledford and Wolery (2013) found that only 40% of studies used direct observation of implementer behavior and that use of direct counts has actually decreased over time. Regardless of which measurement system is used, you should carefully consider which variables should be measured using your theory of change (e.g., Which independent variables will differ across conditions, which other variables with potential to influence dependent variables should remain constant across conditions). Further, if procedural infidelity occurs, you should systematically re-train implementers and closely monitor fidelity.

Summative Analysis

Summative analysis of procedural fidelity increases internal validity (reduces risk of bias) of the study and can be used to describe variability in the dependent variable (Wood et al., 2011). Summative analysis of procedural fidelity should occur for each participant in a study to confirm implementation accuracy did not vary among participants (Moncher & Prinz, 1991) or to determine whether child outcomes are related to differential implementation (e.g., Was implementation more accurate for a child with optimal outcomes when compared with a child with more variable or less accurate implementation?). Summative analysis allows you to document that the intervention was implemented as planned and precisely describe conditions under which it was effective. This provides a foundation for recommendations about circumstances under which an independent variable is likely to work and promotes experimental replications. For example, procedural fidelity measurement might form the basis for parametric comparisons (i.e., studies examining high and low procedural fidelity), component analyses (e.g., to construct and deconstruct multicomponent interventions), or feasibility studies (e.g., identifying behaviors indigenous implementers are most likely to use with accuracy).

Reporting Fidelity

Even when all experimental procedures and variables are adequately assessed, researchers might not report sufficient information to allow readers to analyze data. You should separately report each procedural step (implementer behavior) for which data are collected. These data can be presented in a table, or, in the case of consistently high fidelity, you can identify each behavior and report that each behavior was implemented with adequate fidelity. In addition, you should explicitly report during which conditions and for which participants' fidelity data were collected and to what extent (e.g., during how many sessions) data were collected during each condition and for each participant. Implementer behaviors designed to change (independent variables) should be measured, as well as behaviors designed to remain constant across conditions (control variables; Ledford & Wolery, 2013). Authors should also measure and report physical and social conditions in each experimental condition. At minimum, condition descriptions should include procedural steps and rules, length and frequency of measurement occasions, and environmental characteristics (location, physical size and arrangement, social context). Description of implementers should include role (classroom teacher, researcher), education and experience, specific intervention training, and demographic data. When manuscript length prohibits careful reporting of all relevant fidelity data, we suggest the use of supplemental materials—this is discussed more thoroughly in Chapters 18 and 19.

Conclusions

When it comes to fidelity measurement, we recommend the following: (1) measuring all experimental variables, conditions, participants, and levels of implementation (i.e., procedural fidelity); (2) using direct systematic observations (counts derived from direct observation); and (3) reporting explicitly (e.g., naming variables, conditions, and participants for which data were collected).

References

Bandura, A. (1969). Social learning theory of identificatory processes (pp. 213–262). In *Handbook of socialization theory and research* (D. A. Goslin, Ed). Chicago: Rand McNally.

Billingsley, F. F., White, O. R., & Munson, R. (1980). Procedural reliability: A rationale and an example. *Behavioral Assessment*, 2, 229–241.

Cowan, L. S., Lerman, D. C., Berdeaux, K. L., Prell, A. H., & Chen, N. (2023). A decision-making tool for evaluating and selecting prompting strategies. *Behavior Analysis in Practice*, 16(2), 459–474.

Davies, K., Wright, S. C., Aron, A., & Comeau, J. (2011). Intergroup contact through friendship: Intimacy and norms. In *Advances in intergroup contact* (pp. 214–244). London: Psychology Press.

Dunst, C. J., Trivette, C. M., & Raab, M. (2013). An implementation science framework for conceptualizing and operationalizing fidelity in early childhood intervention studies. *Journal of Early Intervention*, 35, 85–101.

Fettig, A., Schultz, T. R., & Sreckovic, M. A. (2015). Effects of coaching on the implementation of functional assessment-based parent intervention in reducing challenging behaviors. *Journal of Positive Behavior Interventions*, 17, 170–180.

Goldstein, H., English, K., Shafer, K., & Kaczmarek, L. (1997). Interaction among preschoolers with and without disabilities: Effects of across-the-day peer intervention. *Journal of Speech, Language, and Hearing Research*, 40(1), 33–48.

Kaiser, A. P., & Hemmeter, M. L. (2013). Treatment fidelity in early childhood special education research: Introduction to the special issue. *Journal of Early Intervention*, 35, 79–84.

Kennedy, C. H. (2005). *Single case designs for educational research*. Boston, MA: Allyn & Bacon.

Lambert, J. M., Copeland, B. A., Paranczak, J. L., Macdonald, M. J., Torelli, J. N., & Houchins-Juarez, N. J. (2022). Description and evaluation of a function-informed and mechanisms-based framework for treating challenging behavior. *Journal of Applied Behavior Analysis*, 55(4), 1193–1219.

Lane, K. L., Kalberg, J. R., Bruhn, A. L., Mahoney, M. E., & Driscoll, S. A. (2008). Primary prevention programs at the elementary level: Issues of treatment integrity, systematic screening, and reinforcement. *Education and Treatment of Children*, 31, 465–494.

Ledford, J. R., & Wolery, M. (2013). Procedural fidelity: An analysis of measurement and reporting practices. *Journal of Early Intervention*, 35, 173–193.

Martino, S., Ball, S., Nich, C., Frankforter, T. L., & Carroll, K. M. (2009). Correspondence of motivational enhancement treatment integrity ratings among therapists, supervisors, and observers. *Psychotherapy Research*, 19, 181–193.

Mayne, J. (2017). Theory of change analysis: Building robust theories of change. *Canadian Journal of Program Evaluation*, 32(2), 155–173.

Moncher, F. J., & Prinz, R. J. (1991). Treatment fidelity in outcome studies. *Clinical Psychology Review*, 11, 247–266.

Osborne, K., Ledford, J. R., Martin, J., & Thorne, K. (2019). Component analysis of stay, play, talk interventions with and without self-monitored group contingencies and recorded reminders. *Topics in Early Childhood Special Education*, 39(1), 5–18.

Quinn, E. D., Kaiser, A. P., & Ledford, J. R. (2020). Teaching preschoolers with Down syndrome using augmentative and alternative communication modeling during small group dialogic reading. *American Journal of Speech-Language Pathology*, 29(1), 80–100.

Skinner, B. F. (1965). *Science and human behavior*. New York: Simon and Schuster.
Staubitz, J. L., Staubitz, J. E., Pollack, M. S., Haws, R. A., & Hopton, M. (2022). Effects of an enhanced choice model of skill-based treatment for students with emotional/behavioral disorders. *Journal of Applied Behavior Analysis*, 55(4), 1306–1341.
Sutherland, K. S., McLeod, B. D., Conroy, M. A., & Cox, J. R. (2013). Measuring implementation of evidence-based programs targeting young children at risk for emotional/behavioral disorders: Conceptual issues and recommendations. *Journal of Early Intervention*, 35, 129–149.
Winstead, O., Lane, J. D., Spriggs, A. D., & Allday, R. A. (2019). Providing small group instruction to children with disabilities and same-age peers. *Journal of Early Intervention*, 41(3), 202–219.
Wolery, M. (2011). Intervention research: The importance of fidelity measurement. *Topics in Early Childhood Special Education*, 31, 155–157.
Wolery, M. (2013). A commentary: Single-case design technical document of the What Works Clearinghouse. *Remedial and Special Education*, 34, 39–43.
Wood, B. K., Ferro, J. B., Umbreit, J., & Liaupsin, C. J. (2011). Addressing the challenging behavior of young children through systematic function-based intervention. *Topics in Early Childhood Special Education*, 30, 221–222.
Wood, B. K., Umbreit, J., Liaupsin, C. J., & Gresham, F. M. (2007). A treatment integrity analysis of function-based intervention. *Education and Treatment of Children*, 30, 105–120.

7
Measuring Generality and Social Validity in Single Case Research

Joseph M. Lambert, Hedda Meadan-Kaplansky, and Jennifer R. Ledford

Important Terms

generality, context-bound, context-dependent, discrimination, generalization across contexts, stimulus generalization, generalization to non-targeted behaviors, response generalization, generalization to non-targeted individuals, social validity, direct consumers, indirect consumers, immediate community, extended community, identity community, normative comparison

Table of Contents

Generality
   Domains of Performance Relevant to Generality
   Measurement of Generalized Behavior Change
   Terminology, Mechanisms, and Theory of Change
Social Validity
   Social Validity Stakeholders
   Measurement Strategies and Recommendations
      Interviews and Questionnaires
      Direct Observation Measures
Generality and Social Validity: The State of the Field
A Case for Mixed Methods Research
Conclusions
References

Callout

7.1 Labeling Generalization and Maintenance Conditions

In their seminal paper, Baer et al. (1968) described seven dimensions of behavioral research. Two important qualities were (1) outcomes of such work should possess *generality*—behavior change which persists following treatment termination, at the times and in the locations in which such change is needed; and should be (2) *applied*—dependent variables targeted for change should be socially important. Soon after, the concept of social validity, or "the extent to which all the consumers of an intervention like it" (p. 322; Baer et al., 1987), was identified as being important for single case research in the behavioral sciences (e.g., Baer et al., 1987; Kazdin, 1977; Wolf, 1978). The purpose of this chapter is to: (1) introduce each of these concepts, (2) describe how they have historically been measured and studied, (3) highlight challenges to their valid assessment, and (4) propose methods through which they might be studied, in the service of a technology of generality and social validity.

Generality

Generality, as discussed in this chapter, refers to broad behavior change. We provide this very general definition because there are many conceptualizations of generalized behavior change, with multiple potential mechanisms, only some of which are applicable for a given study. Moreover, there are many related and overlapping conceptualizations of generality within and across fields (see Table 7.1). In this chapter, we constrain our discussion of generality to refer to within-participant generality—that is, generality of behavior change that is specific to a single

Table 7.1 Terms Associated with Generality and Social Validity

Term	Definition (Source)
Arbitrarily Applicable Relational Responding	• Forming new stimulus classes without reinforcement (Cooper et al., 2020) • Relational responding that comes under the control of contextual cues that are applied in novel contexts, even without previous exposure to relevant stimulus properties (Stewart et al., 2013)
Behavioral Cusp	• Behavior with extending consequences due to its impact on increased exposures to new environments, continencies, etc. (Cooper et al., 2020) • Behavior change that allows a person to contact new contingencies with far-reaching consequences (Rosales-Ruiz & Baer, 1997)
Discrimination	• Difference in responding in the presence of different stimuli (more restricted usage: resulting from differential consequences in presence of said stimuli) (Catania, 2013)
Distal Behaviors	• Behavior representing broader change in the developmental domain targeted by the intervention or in other domains (Sandbank et al., 2021) (Opposition term: Proximal) • Behaviors that reflect "downstream consequences" of a target behavior (Vivanti & Stahmer, 2021) (Opposition term: Proximal)
Generalized Behavior (generalized tendency)	• Behavior that occurs in contexts different from training, with different implementer/social partners, and with different materials (Sandbank et al., 2021) (Opposition term: Context-Bound) • What people usually do (Yoder et al., 2018) (Opposition term: Context-Dependent)
Maintenance	• Continued responding after complete or partial intervention removal (Cooper et al., 2020; Pennington, 2019) • Continuing to perform learned skills over time (Collins, 2013)
Pivotal behavior	• A behavior that produces corresponding change in other behaviors (Cooper et al., 2020) • Behaviors central to wide areas of functioning that have widespread impact, producing generalized change (e.g., motivation, responsivity to multiple cues) (Koegel & Koegel, 1988)

(Continued)

Table 7.1 Continued

Term	Definition (Source)
Response generalization	• Spread of effects of reinforcement to response outside the operant class (Catania, 2013) • Behavior change in response forms not directly targeted (Pennington, 2019) • Untrained responses emitted that are functionally equivalent to trained responses (Cooper et al., 2020)
Stimulus generalization	• Spread of effects of reinforcement (or other operations) from one stimulus to another (Catania, 2013) • Behavior change observed in presence of novel stimuli (Pennington, 2019) • When stimuli with similar physical properties to trained stimuli evoke behavior associated with the trained stimuli (Cooper et al., 2020)

case and the people and things in their environments (i.e., unrelated to across-participant generality of a relation, discussed in Chapter 2).

Some of the most common recommendations for generalization programming in special education and behavioral sciences (e.g., Cooper et al., 2020) are based on decades-old logic which suggests that the best way to produce socially valid outcomes is to ensure that generalization is not needed by teaching in contexts in which the skills are needed, with social partners with whom the skill is likely to be reinforced in typical daily life (i.e., Bronfenbrenner, 1979; Stokes & Baer, 1977). The evidence base behind this approach is robust (e.g., Halle, 1982; Sandbank et al., 2021; Schreibman et al., 2015). However, the assumption that decontextualized learning will not apply in socially valid contexts is erroneous in at least some situations (e.g., Paranczak et al., 2024).

Of course, it would be unreasonable to expect that all treatment outcomes display unmitigated generality—that is, that behavior change occurring in the context of study sessions or relations identified in the context of an experiment would apply in all situations, would last indefinitely, and would impact all aspects of a participant's life (i.e., a "cure"; Allen et al., 1991; Jacobson, 1989). As discussed in Chapter 4, many behavior changes would not be expected to occur in the absence of certain environmental conditions (i.e., they are reversible). Thus, in many cases, we have theoretically, empirically, and practically supported expectations that treatment outcomes will be very constrained to the treatment context (or contexts with shared critical features; that is, they are **context-bound** or **context-dependent**). In a similar vein, generality is not a desirable outcome in many circumstances. For example, there are clear social limits to the circumstances under which lessons learned from a sex-education curriculum should generalize (Stokes & Baer, 1977). That is, strategies for making a sexual advance should not extend beyond a very constrained set of social contexts (i.e., with another consenting adult who has both implicitly and explicitly offered evidence that such an advance would be welcome). To generalize beyond these bounds is not only inappropriate, but dangerous. Thus, some level of **discrimination** (i.e., the bounds of generality; engaging in a behavior in relevant contexts and not engaging in it in other contexts) is desirable, making generalized behavior change important, but only within certain limits that vary based on the behavior of interest.

As we reference above, some researchers have framed broad behavior change (e.g., that which occurs across contexts and over long periods of time) as a "cure" (Allen et al., 1991; Jacobson, 1989). We consider framing interventions that facilitate contextual control over behavior that can be disruptive in some contexts but harmless in others (e.g., as is sometimes the case with stereotypy; Joyce et al., 2017) in this way risks pathologizing behavioral traits valued by the communities which possess them (e.g., Manor-Binyamini & Schreiber-Divon, 2019). However, rather than a cure, many interventions could be considered an inoculation—they are specific (i.e., is not broad prevention for all illnesses) and somewhat limited (e.g., effects may diminish over time, and may not result in perfect protection). To anticipate broader changes would be to expect too much from the intervention in question (Jacobson, 1989; Kazdin, 1987; Quay & Werry, 1986).

Given all of these considerations, we propose that the extent to which generality is desirable varies by study—there is no perfect "amount" of generality. You should use your theory of change, empirical evidence, and practical information to identify what types of generality are likely to occur and not occur. Then, you should identify whether those broad behavioral changes are important (i.e., socially valid, empirically interesting) and identify measurement systems that are likely to capture these broad changes if they occur.

Domains of Performance Relevant to Generality

Commonly accepted conceptualizations of a generalized outcome have included untrained behavior changes which occur across four general domains: time, setting, behaviors, and non-focal individuals in the participant's environment (Cooper et al., 2020; Drabman et al., 1979; Stokes & Baer, 1977). Response **maintenance** has sometimes been referred to as *performance that persists across time* (Kazdin, 1975). However, most conceptualizations of maintenance also include some aspect of *intervention removal*. For example, if *time* were the only criterion for maintenance, should behavior that begins on Day 1 of an intervention condition be considered to be "maintained" on Day 2 of intervention? What about on Day 20 of intervention? In most cases, researchers have used the term "maintenance" to describe ongoing evaluation of a participant's response status after some period of time, but also following cessation of formal intervention or treatment. Despite this, the term *maintenance* is used for a wide variety of conditions, some including direct intervention provision (see, for example, results of a review by Ledford et al., 2023). In Table 7.2, we propose four categories of *intervention removal* that are relevant when defining maintenance conditions for single case design studies. Thus, we consider maintenance to have two relevant features: (1) length of time for which behavior continues (i.e., short-term change or long-term change, although we recognize that time is a continuous rather than dichotomous variable), and (2) the extent to which intervention is in place.

In addition to *time* and *intervention removal*, there are at least three additional domains of interest. One is *performance that occurs in contexts that differ from the formal treatment context(s)*—**generalization across contexts**. Notably, there is a wide range of variation that can occur in this category, and it can be difficult to distinguish relevant from irrelevant features of a context which might qualify it as a novel context. For example, behaviors learned at school that transfer to home settings are a change in context that is easy to identify and is likely meaningful. For contrast, changes in teacher, therapist, or parent may or may not be as easily identified or clearly meaningful (depending on the prevalence and importance of such transitions to an intervention outcome). Generalization across contexts is loosely equivalent to **stimulus generalization** (see definitions in Table 7.1). Examples include generalization across *implementers or social partners* (engaging in targeted behaviors with untrained people), generalization across *settings* (engaging in targeted behaviors in untrained locations), generalization across *materials* (engaging in targeted behaviors with different physical materials than those used in intervention), and generalization across *activities* or *interaction styles* (engaging in targeted behaviors in contexts in which social interactions are different, such as generalizing behaviors learned in free play to a small group instruction context or generalizing behaviors learned during massed trials to a child-directed portion of an instructional session). Importantly, if intervention is occurring in multiple contexts, measurement across contexts should not be considered to be a measure of generalization. That is, although programming intervention across multiple contexts is advisable for *promoting* generalized use, it is different from evaluating whether generalization has occurred. Once treatment occurs in a second

Table 7.2 Intervention Removal Classes Relevant to Maintenance

	Description	Example
1: Intervention in Place	Planned treatment conditions are being actively implemented.	Data are collected across the school year, evaluating effects of peer-mediated intervention that continues to be implemented across the whole school year.
2: Intervention Partially Removed	Some aspect of the treatment is still in place. Implementers may be fading or systematically removing some components.	One week after concluding a functional communication training condition, researchers withdraw prompting procedures but continue to measure communication responses in the presence of picture cards that were introduced during intervention sessions.
3: Intervention Removed	Planned treatment conditions are not being actively implemented and condition protocols call for complete removal of intervention. If the baseline condition called for absence of intervention procedures, this is a return to baseline condition.	One month after an instructional intervention condition concludes, researchers conduct probe sessions that do not include any intervention components (prompting, reinforcement).
4: Prevailing Contingency	Data are collected under business-as-usual conditions or with endogenous implementers. If the baseline condition called for typical procedures, this is a return to baseline condition (but it typically involves implementers who have been trained, with some expectation that they will continue to engage in at least some intervention procedures).	Data are collected one month after researcher implementation of a peer-mediated intervention in a classroom. Teachers in the classroom were trained in the intervention, and had all available materials, but they were not instructed to use or avoid any specific procedures when measurement occurred.

context, that context becomes a treatment context rather than a generalization context. As is the case with time, it is likely most productive to consider performances that occur in untrained settings to occur along a spectrum.

Another category is *changes in behavior(s) that were not the specific target(s) of intervention*—**generalization to non-targeted behaviors**, which may sometimes be the result of **response generalization**. For example, if an intervention that targets one response (e.g., decreases in out-of-seat behavior) has an untrained collateral impact on another response (e.g., fighting), it would be appropriate to attribute some degree of generality to intervention outcomes in the domain of behavior. However, when an intervention targets a broad class of behavior (e.g., disruptive behavior) and effectively reduces multiple component members of that class (e.g., talking out, out-of-seat behavior, swearing), the generality of treatment outcomes is less apparent. There are likely multiple mechanisms that result in generalization to non-targeted behaviors, including (1) changes in the target behavior directly led to changes in the non-targeted behavior (e.g., a child engaged in less fighting *because* they were in their seat) and (2) the intervention directly impacted the non-target behavior (e.g., a child engaged in less fighting because the intervention increased social skills and this reduced fighting without relation to the reduction in in-seat behavior).

The final category refers to *changes in the behavior(s) of individuals who were not the focus of treatment*—**generalization to non-targeted individuals** (e.g., social partners such as peers, siblings, parents, and teachers). Although it might be difficult to understand why this category would be included in a discussion of generality, consideration for the cascading effects of an effective intervention may add clarity. Specifically, this phenomenon might occur when changes in a target child's responding fundamentally alters a family dynamic in the home setting or when an intervention designed to decrease challenging behavior of one child in a classroom also improves engagement of other children. As the behavior of non-targeted individuals (e.g., parents, peers) changes in response to changes to the ecology of the home or school, these changes, in turn, establish conditions under which generality in the "time" domain become more probable. Thus, an acknowledgment of the interdependent and interlocking nature of most social contingencies responsible for desirable behavior patterns have guided researchers to consider the generality of an intervention across non-focal individuals in the social environment in addition to time, behavior, and context.

Measurement of Generalized Behavior Change

Importantly, it is possible for an intervention to promote generality across more than one domain, and it is not always critical to assess generality in all domains—the domains that are of interest and/or in which change is expected should be related to your theory of change. In acknowledgment of this fact and assuming each domain could be simplified to a dichotomous yes/no code, Drabman et al. (1979) developed a 16-item matrix, referred to as a "generalization map," which specified combinations of generalized outcomes in an attempt to articulate a range of possibilities (and complexity) across which generality might occur. Although we propose that it could be most useful to consider a spectrum of possibilities within each of the four primary domains (as opposed to a dichotomous classification system), the general framework proposed by Drabman et al. (1979) has clear practical utility for conceptualizing potentially relevant phenomena associated with generality. In Table 7.3, we present an adaptation of Drabman et al.' (1979) generalization map. Importantly, this map describes generalization measurement that occurs *when intervention is being actively implemented*. A map that included all four variations of intervention removal (in place, partially in place, removed, prevailing contingencies) would include 64 potential variations of generalization measurement (e.g., all 16 of the options in Table 7.3 could be applied when intervention has been partially removed, removed, or when prevailing contingencies are in place).

Table 7.3 Generalization Map for an Intervention for Engagement, Implemented During Large Group Instruction

Generalization Class	Definition	Example
Targeted Change (1) (no generalization)	Targeted behavior changes in the short term while treatment is in place, in the treatment context.	Child engages in higher levels of engagement during whole group, while treatment is implemented (i.e., short term).
Time (2)	Targeted behavior persists when time passes, while treatment is in place, in the treatment context.	Child continues to engage in high levels of engagement during whole group, as treatment continues to be implemented (i.e., **long term**).
Context (3)	Targeted behavior changes in the short term while treatment is in place, in a non-treatment context.	Child engages in higher levels of engagement during **small group**, while treatment is implemented (i.e., short term) in **large group**.
Time + Context (4)	Targeted behavior persists when time passes, while treatment is in place, in a non-treatment context.	Child continues to engage in high levels of engagement during **small group**, as treatment continues to be implemented (i.e., **long term**) in large group.
Non-Targeted Behavior (5)	An untargeted behavior changes in the short term while treatment is in place, in the treatment context.	Child engages in lower levels of **disruption** during whole group, while treatment is implemented for engagement (i.e., short term).

(Continued)

Table 7.3 Continued

Generalization Class	Definition	Example
Time + Non-Targeted Behavior (6)	An untargeted behavior persists when time passes, while treatment is in place, in the treatment context.	Child continues to engage in lower levels of **disruption** during whole group, as treatment continues to be implemented for engagement (i.e., **long term**).
Context + Non-Targeted Behavior (7)	An untargeted behavior changes in the short term, while treatment is in place, in a non-treatment context.	Child engages in lower levels of **disruption** during **small group**, while treatment is implemented (i.e., short term) for engagement in large group.
Time + Context + Non-Targeted Behavior (8)	An untargeted behavior persists when time passes, while treatment is in place, in a non-treatment context.	Child continues to engage in lower levels of **disruption** during **small group**, as treatment continues to be implemented (i.e., **long term**) for engagement in large group.
Non-Targeted Individual (9)	A non-target individual exhibits changes in a targeted behavior, in the short term, while treatment is in place, in the treatment context.	A **peer** engages in higher levels of engagement during whole group, while treatment is implemented (i.e., short term) for the targeted child.
Time + Non-Targeted Individual (10)	A non-target individual exhibits changes in a targeted behavior, when time passes, while treatment is in place.	A **peer** continues to engage in higher levels of engagement during whole group, as treatment continues to be implemented (i.e., **long term**) for the targeted child.
Context + Non-Targeted Individual (11)	A non-target individual exhibits changes in a targeted behavior, in the short term, in a non-treatment context.	A **peer** engages in higher levels of engagement during **small group**, while treatment is implemented (i.e., short term) for the targeted child in whole group.
Non-Targeted Behavior + Non-Targeted Individual (12)	A non-target individual exhibits changes in an untargeted behavior, in the short term.	A **peer** engages in lower levels of **disruption** during whole group, while treatment is implemented (i.e., short term) for engagement for the targeted child.
Time + Context + Non-Targeted Individual (13)	A non-target individual exhibits changes in a targeted behavior, when time passes, while treatment is in place, in a non-treatment context.	A **peer** continues to engage in high levels of engagement during **small group**, as treatment continues to be implemented (i.e., **long term**) for the targeted child in whole group.
Time + Non-Targeted Behavior + Non-Targeted Individual (14)	A non-target individual exhibits changes in an untargeted behavior, when time passes, while treatment is in place, in the treatment context.	A **peer** continues to engage in lower levels of **disruption** during whole group, as treatment continues to be implemented (i.e., **long term**) for engagement for the targeted child.
Context + Non-Targeted Behavior + Non-Targeted Individual (15)	A non-target individual exhibits changes in an untargeted behavior, in the short term, when treatment is in place, in a non-treatment context.	A **peer** engages in lower levels of **disruption** during **small group**, while treatment is implemented (i.e., short term) for engagement during whole group for the targeted child.
Time + Context + Non-Targeted Behavior + Non-Targeted Individual (16)	A non-target individual exhibits changes in an untargeted behavior, when time passes, when treatment is in place, in a non-treatment context.	A **peer** continues to engage in in lower levels of **disruption** during **small group**, as treatment continues to be implemented (i.e., **long term**) for engagement during whole group for the targeted child.

(Adapted from Allen et al., 1991; Drabman et al., 1979).

Note: This table includes variations of generalization that can be measured when the intervention is in place. These variations are also possible when intervention is removed, partially removed, or when prevailing contingencies are in place after intervention removal.

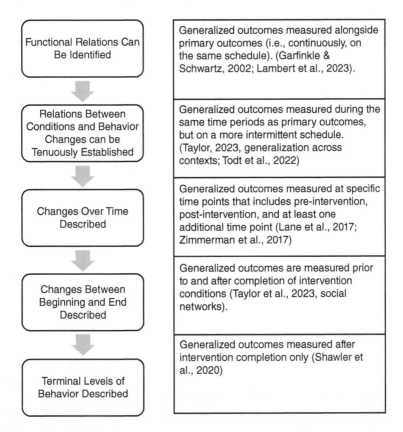

Figure 7.1 Generalization Measurement.

Whichever type of generalization you decide to measure (e.g., across people, contexts, non-target behaviors, non-target individuals, or some combination of those things), we suggest that generalization measurement be conducted prior to, during, and following intervention; this allows researchers to identify whether functional relations exist for the generalized outcome(s). Figure 7.1 depicts the typical temporal arrangements associated with generalization measurement, ordered from least to most rigorous (i.e., provides increasingly compelling evidence of relations). We also suggest explicitly reporting the type of generalized and maintained outcomes that are assessed, both in text and via graphical representations of results (see Callout 7.1). We also acknowledge that generalized behavior change can be assessed in ways that do not involve direct measurement; we address this later in the chapter, following discussion of social validity.

Callout 7.1 Labeling Generalization and Maintenance Conditions

As illustrated in Tables 7.2 and 7.3, there are many ways to conceptualize measurement of whether an intervention results in generalized or maintained behavior change. Despite the conceptual and procedural variability that characterizes these very broad terms, measurement occasions that occur in an attempt to capture *any* of these (at least 64) variations are often simply labeled "maintenance" or "generalization." More concerning is that, in the name of identifying "evidence-based" or "research-supported" practices,

> syntheses of a body of research often make broad statements about the extent to which generalized outcomes are evident in a body of research—without regard to the domains measured and the extent to which the theory of change guiding the intervention would predict that a given type would occur. We suggest that authors of single case research should descriptively label any conditions designed to evaluate whether generalized or maintained outcomes are established by specifically reporting the extent to which intervention remains in place (i.e., in place, partially removed, removed, or prevailing contingencies in place) and the type of generality assessed (e.g., across social partners or materials). In systematic reviews, we suggest that the types of generalization that might be expected to occur should be identified a priori, and that authors of these reviews report variability in types of generalized and maintained behavior change that was measured. Moreover, when conducting systematic reviews, it may be helpful to remember that not all researchers may have attempted to answer questions that *you* find compelling or relevant. Thus, lack of evidence for generalized outcomes may suggest the need for additional research, but it is not necessarily a cause for concern.

Terminology, Mechanisms, and Theory of Change

As mentioned in Callout 7.1, broad behavior change is often referred to as *generalization* and *maintenance* (e.g., Stokes & Baer, 1977; see Table 7.1). However, these terms have technical definitions in basic behavioral science (e.g., Catania, 2013) that are not always relevant to outcomes that fall under the umbrella term of "generality." Certainly, there are circumstances under which newly acquired skills will occur in novel contexts that share common properties with a training context; thus rendering the label of "stimulus generalization" appropriate. Likewise, there are circumstances in which a training context through which reinforcement has historically been delivered will occasion novel responses; rendering the characterization of "response generalization" appropriate. However, generality can also be the product of learning mechanisms that extend beyond the differential reinforcement paradigms that establish formal opportunities for generalization and/or discriminated responding. For example, humans have the generative ability to extend past experiences to effective action given novel circumstances (i.e., to engage in arbitrarily applicable relational responding, AARRing; Barnes-Holmes et al., 2021; Hayes et al., 2001). AARRing is a term that describes a class of behavior unique to verbally proficient humans that is controlled by special contextual variables that alter the functions of other stimuli without a direct history of conditioning; bypassing typical operant-learning processes (e.g., Sidman, 1971). This phenomenon has important explanatory power for behavior-analytic accounts of language, cognition, problem-solving, intelligent behavior, and emotional pain (Hayes et al., 2001; Snyder et al., 2011). The circumstances under which AARRing is likely to occur are considerably different than the circumstances under which response and stimulus generalizations are likely to occur. This fact has direct implications for instructional technology; as there are contexts under which an interventionist would want to leverage the collateral effects of the reinforcement process (i.e., stimulus or response generalization) to promote a non-cognitive, "instinctual," form of generality. Likewise, there are other contexts in which interventionists might seek to leverage the learning mechanisms responsible for AARRing to facilitate a form of generality mediated through problem solving, and/or other distal outcomes. This calls for researchers to carefully consider their theory of change and to understand proposed mechanisms that are likely to control broad behavior change.

For decades, applied scientists have called for the development of a technology capable of consistently and precisely promoting socially valid and generalized outcomes (e.g., Stokes & Baer, 1977). However, more than 50 years later, the techniques available to use for this purpose are based more on logic and convention than on evidence (Lambert, Sandstrom et al., 2022), and it is often unclear *why* they work when they work. As a result, when they don't work, there is little in the way of theoretically driven applied research paradigms capable of guiding diagnostic and corrective action. That is, aspirations of an effective technology of behavior change based in the principles of applied behavior analysis remain largely unmet. Many questions remain pertaining to the circumstances under which generalized outcomes do and should occur, the underlying mechanisms responsible, the techniques and strategies capable for producing it, and the dosage requirements and ceiling effects of particular interventions purported to promote it (Jacobson, 1989; Kazdin, 1987).

To rectify this problem, researchers invested in studying generality should: (1) be familiar with a comprehensive taxonomy of generalized outcomes which can guide the selection of appropriate dependent variables and the development of measurement systems capable of capturing their occurrence, (2) be familiar with known natural learning mechanisms (NLM) responsible for mediating generalized outcomes (e.g., AARRing, differential reinforcement, respondent conditioning), (3) be familiar with intervention techniques that promote generality under at least some circumstances (e.g., sequential modification, multiple exemplar training, matrix training), as well as the NLMs which are purportedly leveraged by these techniques, (4) understand the types of generalized outcome that each type of NLM is, and is not, likely to promote, (5) select as dependent variables from the taxonomy of generalized outcomes forms of generalization predicted by the relevant NLM, as well as forms of generalization not predicted by the relevant NLM but predicted by a competing hypothesis, (6) be familiar with single case design and capable of matching experimental designs to the proposed research question, and (7) be familiar with common threats to generality (e.g., behavioral contrast [Boyle et al., 2018], relapse [Fuhrman et al., 2021; Kimball et al., 2023], counter control [Delprato, 2002], unconsidered and uncontrolled contingencies at molar and/or molecular planes of analysis [Perone, 2003; Staats, 2006], AARRing/rule governance [Hayes et al., 1989]) and account for them either by controlling them, or by making their mitigation the topic of investigation (e.g., Banerjee et al., 2022). That is, researchers need to understand *how* and *why* their interventions may or may not be likely to lead to broad behavior change and must use appropriate strategies for evaluating the extent to which it occurs. Figure 7.2 illustrates the relations between generality, known NLMs that support generalized behavior change, instructional procedures that produce generalized behavior change, and evidence (collected via single case design). To produce believable evidence of generality, you must understand your theory of change and the mechanisms involved, use strategies aligned with those mechanisms to promote generalized behavior change, and apply single case logic and valid measurement systems to assess it.

Social Validity

One way to assess the broad impact of intervention success is via direct measurement of broad behavior change, as described in the previous section. You can also establish the importance of the impact via measurement of social validity. **Social validity** is the extent to a study is of practical significance. Of course, social validity is closely tied to generality because the extent to which a study results in generalized behavior change is likely to impact how important it is, although this relation does not necessarily exist for all studies. Social validity is distinguished

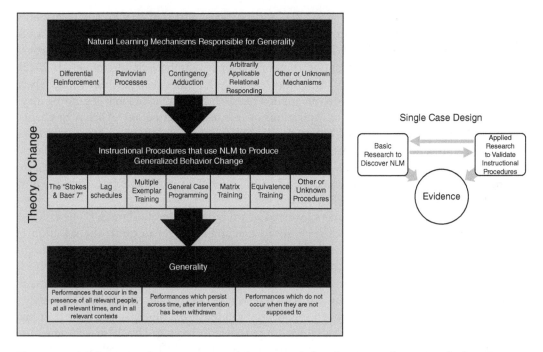

Figure 7.2 Mechanisms, Interventions, and Outcomes Related to Generality in Single Case Design.

Note: NLM = natural learning mechanisms. Stokes & Baer 7 refers to 7 strategies identified by Stokes & Baer (1977): (1) Train and Hope, (2) Sequential Modification, (3) Introduce to Natural Maintaining Contingencies, (4) Train Sufficient Exemplars, (5) Train Loosely, (6) Use Indiscriminable Contingencies, (7) Program Common Stimuli.

from *ecological validity*, which refers to the extent to which a study represents typical contexts (Fahmie et al., 2023; see Chapter 2). Commonly, social validity is concerned with questions such as these:

- *Are the* **goals** *socially important?* (Are we addressing a problem that stakeholders value?)
- *Are the* **intervention** *procedures socially acceptable?* (Are we using an intervention that is likely to be valued and adopted outside the research study?)
- *Are the* **outcomes** *socially significant?* (Did we adequately address the problem we set out to solve?)

Two things are important to note in relation to these questions. First, studies that do not meet one or more of these benchmarks are not without value. For example, if researchers are interested in answering a question about which instructional strategy works best (e.g., Eyler & Ledford, 2024) or the extent to which a strategy works as purported (Paranczak et al., 2024), the content taught to participants may necessarily be socially *invalid* because if socially important targets were taught (e.g., stimuli likely to be taught outside of the study, in typical contexts), important questions about how the interventions worked could not be answered. Second, even if the answer to one of the questions is "yes" for a specific participant or group of stakeholders, no assessment of social validity will hold for all contexts. For example, acceptability for a given intervention may vary widely within and across stakeholder groups, and often depends on context (e.g., a more intrusive intervention may be perceived as acceptable for self-injury but not for vocal stereotypy). Likewise, a teacher might find outcomes of an intervention designed to increase on-task behavior for students to be acceptable, but students might find it too burdensome to be helpful, or too stigmatizing.

Social validity is important because if procedures are not feasible for use in the intended context, require too much time, or are perceived as unethical, they may be unlikely to be used outside of the study. Further, some have argued that socially accepted procedures are more likely to be correctly implemented by endogenous implementers (e.g., Baer et al., 1987). Likewise, if goals are not valued, changes demonstrated in experimental contexts are unlikely to be important in participants' daily lives. Thus, although social validity may not be directly related to identification of a functional relation, it can be valuable when considering likely overall impact of the study, especially for applied work intended to influence the participant's successful participation in typical contexts.

Social Validity Stakeholders

The evaluation of social significance should be based on the perspectives, opinions, and experiences of a variety of stakeholders. Schwartz and Baer (1991) described four groups of stakeholders that could be involved in evaluation of the social validity of an intervention or program. These groups were: (1) **direct consumers**—recipients of the intervention (e.g., children, teachers, parents, administrators); (2) **indirect consumers**—people who could be affected by the intervention, but are not direct recipients (e.g., parents and peers of direct participants); (3) members of the **immediate community**—people who interact regularly with direct and indirect consumers (e.g., neighbors of participants); and (4) members of the **extended community**—people who may not know direct recipients but live in the same community (e.g., librarian at the local library). We propose the addition of a fifth group: *People who are members of the same* **identity community**. For example, if you are assessing an intervention for young children who are deaf, adults who are otherwise unaffiliated with your participants but who are part of the Deaf community are potentially important stakeholders. Similarly, if you are proposing an intervention to improve the problem-solving of ABA practitioners, behavior analysts who are not affiliated with your study are potentially important stakeholders, as they are part of the larger community of potentially impacted consumers.

Consideration of all three elements of social validity (goals, procedures, outcomes) is likely warranted because social objection to any one of them has direct and immediate implications for the overarching project. For example, a caregiver may agree with the goal of reducing severe challenging behavior (e.g., the frequent and highly damaging self-injury of their child). They may also approve of the procedures employed by the targeted intervention package (e.g., antecedent-based interventions paired with differential reinforcement). However, if the desirable intervention fails to reduce self-injurious behavior (SIB) to a meaningful degree, the intervention lacks social validity. Similarly, if the initial treatment package is replaced with contingent electric shock and is successful at reducing SIB, the intervention remains socially invalid despite palatable goals and outcomes, because the procedure (i.e., electric shock) has been condemned by society, prominent researchers, and professional credentialing boards (e.g., Perone et al., 2023). Finally, if an intervention package (e.g., antecedent-based intervention paired with differential reinforcement) is both appropriate and effective, it remains socially invalid if it is used to reduce behavior that should not be reduced (e.g., behavior associated with an individual's sexual identity).

Readers should take care to separate an assessment of whether a study's goals, procedures, and outcomes are socially valid from an assessment of whether those things were measured. For example, if researchers conduct a study with a child engaging in frequent, severe challenging behaviors, they may well have collaborated with the child's family and the child themselves to identify the most important behaviors on which to focus (i.e., they selected socially valid behaviors). However, they may not *measure* or *report* the extent to which this occurred. That is, *having* social validity and *having evidence of* social validity are different.

Navigating the demands of socially valid research paradigms can be complicated and challenging. There are many ways for a research project to either fail to meet the rigorous empirical standards of evidence established in this book, or to fail to meet the standards of significance and acceptability established by stakeholders. Because social standards are culturally established, context-specific, and dynamic, best practices in the assessment of socially validity call for researchers to obtain ongoing samples of key stakeholders' perspectives and experiences with the goals, methods, and outcomes of research; ideally prior to, during, and after the project has been completed. If you have research questions related to generality or social validity, it is important to consider the extent to which you can obtain evidence that generalized and maintained effects occurred, which may require additional data outside of those collected in the context of your primary single case design.

Measurement Strategies and Recommendations

We recommend use of more than one method or tool when evaluating social validity of an intervention; Table 7.4 provides information about what types of questions can be answered given use of different methods.

Table 7.4 Sample Social Validity Questions and Methods Appropriate for Answering Them

Question	Potential Method
How acceptable is this intervention?	When conducting a classroom-based intervention ask (1) teachers to rate acceptability of the proposed interventions and reasonable alternatives, before and after intervention implementation (2) children to choose whether to receive the intervention or not (after they've had exposures to the intervention).
	When using a naturalistic teaching strategy to improve vocalizations by young autistic children, use naïve raters to evaluate the extent to which interactions seem indicative of a responsive, low-pressure relationship with the adult.
	When using an intervention to increase tolerance to engaging with various sensory stimuli for blind youth, ask adults who are blind to make suggestions for any needed intervention modifications.
How feasible and likely to be used is this intervention?	When conducting a classroom-based intervention (1) ask teachers to rate usability of the proposed interventions and reasonable alternatives, before and after intervention implementation and (2) conduct covert observations or self-report data about continued use after intervention cessation.
	When using a naturalistic teaching strategy to improve vocalizations by young autistic children, show videos of the strategy to parents prior to intervention implementation and ask them to suggest modifications that would increase the likelihood that they would use it.
Are goals socially valued?	When using a naturalistic teaching strategy to improve vocalizations by young autistic children, share proposed goals with autistic adults and ask them whether the goals are appropriate.
	When conducting a classroom-based intervention, recruit assistance before the study begins to have teachers in participating classrooms define targeted behaviors and set criterion levels.
Are the outcomes of this procedure important?	When conducting a classroom-based intervention, collect data on a child reported as not having the same presenting problem as the participants, to ensure mastery criteria are set at an appropriate level (e.g., if the class on-task average is 70%, researchers should not set mastery criteria at 80% for target participants).
	When using a naturalistic teaching strategy to improve vocalizations by young autistic children, ask parents to rate the extent to which changes in behaviors learned during sessions resulted in changes in family quality of life.

Interviews and Questionnaires

Often, interviews or questionnaires are used to quantify consumer perception about the social importance of goals, procedures, and outcomes of an intervention. When these assessments are used, standardized instruments are desirable because they can facilitate interpretation and extrapolation of principle (Kazdin, 1977) and are more easily compared across intervention types and studies. However, because they are designed to be broadly applicable and not intervention specific, they may lead to appraisals of acceptability and feasibility which are not reflective of actual perceptions (Halle, 2019) nor protective against eventual intervention abandonment (Schwartz & Baer, 1991). By contrast, individualized assessments can be far more specific to a program's goals and objectives but also often produce data that is difficult to interpret or compare (Kazdin, 1977).

Reasons for satisfaction and dissatisfaction are likely to vary across individual stakeholders (Schwartz & Baer, 1991). This may be why individualized assessments of social validity are both valued and prevalent in single case design research (D'Agostino et al., 2019). Importantly, researchers can expand the impact of individualized assessments by ensuring validity when designing their tool. For example, Schwartz & Baer (1991) recommended that individualized surveys developed by a research team possess important properties associated with psychometric rigor—such as (1) considering at what time points respondent feedback should be collected, (2) including specific and direct questions, (3) using scales with sufficiently wide ranges, and (4) requiring that stakeholders use the entire range of the scale. An example of item 4 would be including the questions "This intervention was difficult for me to implement" and "The outcomes of the intervention were positive" with response options ranging from 1 (strongly disagree) to 7 (strongly agree) (i.e., for some questions, high values represent positive experiences, while for other questions, high values represent negative experiences).

If social desirability bias is a potential concern, we recommend a person who is not directly engaged in the implementation of the intervention collect interview or questionnaire measures (e.g., conduct interviews) and, when appropriate, that individual responses are not shared with the implementing researcher. Of course, this type of data collection may result in a different problem, which is that consumers may be less likely to report positive or negative impacts to an assessor with whom they have not developed a relationship. In either case, researchers should be aware that reports are subject to the typical contingencies present during social interactions.

Direct Observation Measures

There are at least four types of social validity measurement that are conducted via direct observation: (1) normative comparisons (Rapoff, 2010; Van Houten, 1979), (2) blind ratings (Meadan et al., 2014), (3) measurement of maintenance or sustained use (Kennedy, 2005), and (4) participant preference measurement (Hanley, 2010).

When **normative comparisons** are used, the participants' targeted behavior (i.e., dependent variable) is compared to a normative or "typical" group that does not have the same needs as your participants (e.g., if you are conducting an intervention to improve high-frequency challenging behavior, your comparisons would include children who have average levels of challenging behavior). Data for both the target participants and the normative group are collected and compared. Normative comparisons can be helpful to determine: (1) what intervention goals are socially important and (2) whether participants reached typical or acceptable levels of the target behavior following intervention. For example, Dueñas et al. (2021) assessed the effects of a peer-mediated intervention on social interactions between young autistic children and peers without disabilities. They measured social interactions that occurred under baseline conditions for pairs of children without autism to allow for an evaluation of outcomes for the focal pair (one autistic child, one non-autistic child) compared to typical rates for non-focal pairs (two non-autistic children).

Maintenance or sustained use data are measures used to evaluate if procedures and outcomes of an intervention continue after the research is completed (Kennedy, 2002). Although rarely used, this important measure is related to likelihood of maintained and generalized behaviors, especially when indigenous implementers were trained to use intervention procedures. If an intervention is effective in changing participant behavior, but indigenous implementers do not continue its use once a study is completed, likelihood of maintained behavior change may be low. Thus, measurement of continued use by practitioners and caregivers in typical environments is an important measure of social validity that answers the question of how acceptable (and feasible) stakeholders find procedures. Although measures of treatment acceptability (e.g., rating scales) are often used in place of direct measurement, at least one study has shown that these two measures do not necessarily agree (Farmer et al., 1988). True measures of sustained use can also be difficult to obtain because researcher presence may change the likelihood of use; in rare situations, covert observations are possible and provide better evidence of typical use (e.g., Barton et al., 2020).

Naïve ratings can be used to less subjectively determine whether participants' behavior is rated as "different" before and after intervention or during baseline versus intervention conditions (socially important outcomes) by people who are unaware of the condition in effect for the session(s) they watch (e.g., pre- or post-intervention, baseline or treatment conditions) and/or the purpose of the study. These ratings can also be used to determine whether procedures in one condition are more acceptable than those in another (socially acceptable procedures). In one study, music and no-music conditions were compared when used to teach signed vocabulary words to toddlers with disabilities. Graduate students who were blind to condition type rated muted videos of both types of sessions (ones with and without music) regarding whether participants appeared happy. Although acquisition results were similar, one participant appeared happier during music conditions; this finding may suggest that musical interventions may be both equally effective and more socially acceptable for some young children (Koutsavalis, 2011). Naïve ratings typically report broader or supplementary measures—that is, if you directly measure social interactions between children as your primary direct observation dependent variable, you might collect ratings from naïve individuals about the extent to which interactions or the climate were positive or that teachers were appropriately supporting children. It would likely be less helpful to have raters report the extent to which the number of interactions was different, given your primary data answer this question. Instead, these data are supplemental—to answer the question about whether the change is *important*.

Participant preference for interventions has typically been measured using rating scales or post-intervention questionnaires. Objective measurement of participant preference during intervention implementation is both possible and preferable, even for young children or those who have significant language or cognitive impairments (Hanley, 2010). This is perhaps the most important measure of whether intervention procedures are acceptable to the primary consumer (i.e., the recipient of the intervention). Although participant ratings of acceptability as a social validity measure are far less common than other stakeholders' ratings (e.g., parents, teachers; Hurley, 2012), when intervention strategies are similarly effective for a participant, preference for intervention is crucial information for interventionists (Ledford et al., 2017; State & Kern, 2012). For example, Heal and Hanley (2011) measured participant preference for three play-based interventions by allowing participants to choose which intervention they wanted to receive for each session: (1) instruction embedded in play, (2) pre-session modeling then play, or (3) pre-session direct instruction then play. Pre-session direct instruction not only led to greater acquisition of targeted information, but also was chosen most often by participants as the most highly preferred intervention. Similarly, Ledford and colleagues have measured the extent to which participants preferred massed trial versus embedded instruction and time delay versus system of least prompts instruction (Eyler & Ledford, 2024; Chazin & Ledford, 2021; Ledford et al., 2017). Objective preference procedures such as this one may result in more valid results, especially for participants who are young or those who have cognitive or language abilities that impede other types of assessment.

Generality and Social Validity: The State of the Field

Despite their purported importance to the identity of intervention research, measurement of generality and social validity are relatively rare in single case studies (D'Agostino et al., 2019; Ghaemmaghami et al., 2021; Ledford et al.; 2016; Park & Blair, 2019; Snodgrass et al., 2018). Contemporary approaches to measurement in single case design make it difficult to produce compelling demonstrations of generality and social validity. That is, internal validity is often at odds with social validity and generality, in that strictly controlling for potential threats to internal validity often leads to decisions about implementation and measurement that make it difficult for studies to *have* social validity and generality or to *provide rigorous evidence* that they have it. This is an important distinction—a study which does not formally measure social validity or generality is not necessarily devoid of these things.

Studies often fail to generate evidence that can be used to assess social validity and generalized behavior change. For example, response patterns occurring during short sessions in the research context (e.g., 5-min sessions) are not necessarily characteristic of patterns under similar conditions for longer periods of time (e.g., 2-hr sessions; Lindberg et al., 2003) and variables that control responding in contrived settings may not be present in typical ones (Ledford et al., 2016). Although single case design often includes reliable and objective measures of behavior change, there are documented instances in which behavior change under experimental conditions did not predict stakeholder accounts of improvement and satisfaction. For example, Lambert and colleagues demonstrated behavior change during clinical appointments with a wide range of individuals presenting with challenging behavior. They distributed surveys several years later, designed to evaluate social validity from teachers' and parents' perspectives (i.e., indirect stakeholders; Lambert, Copeland et al., 2022; Lambert, Paranczak et al., 2022). In some cases, behavior changes that occurred in the clinical setting were reported to be generalized and socially significant, whereas in other cases, similar behavior changes measured experimentally were reported to have negligible impacts outside of the study.

Importantly, the potential for asymmetry in outcomes across measurement contexts (i.e., relatively narrow behavior change represented in some single case design studies and those that sample the perspectives of stakeholders or that represent broader behavior change) can justify challenges to the social validity of any context-bound demonstration for which generality and social validity are not assessed (e.g., Ghaemmaghami et al., 2021; Sandbank et al., 2021). That is, when generality and social validity are not explicitly evaluated, the extent to which changes are meaningful and applicable outside constrained contexts is not known. Failure to evaluate social validity and generality have rendered summative evaluations of evidence less impactful than ideal (Ledford et al., 2022, 2023), and a cohesive behaviorally based instructional technology capable for ensuring socially valid and generalized outcomes has proven somewhat elusive (e.g., Lambert, Sandstrom et al., 2022). One apparent repercussion of this fact is backlash from members of populations (e.g., the neurodiverse community) who have been exposed to socially invalid methods or objectives (e.g., electric shock, reductions in stereotypy; Ne'eman, 2021; Perone et al., 2023). Perhaps as a result, there have been recent calls for applied researchers to explicitly consider and evaluate the extent to which outcomes produced in experiments are generalizable and socially valid (e.g., Schwartz & Kelly, 2021; Veneziano & Shea, 2023).

A Case for Mixed Methods Research

Demands of practice can be at odds with the need for internally valid procedures in single case design studies. However, it is not impossible to design studies that are internally valid and which provide evidence (for or against) socially valid and generalized behavior change. To ensure the validity and relevance of intervention research, and to protect against misapplications of research evidence, it is important to acknowledge that graphs are two-dimensional depictions of a three-dimensional world. Certainly, and as established by the need to assess observer reliability in Chapter 5, subjective reports of past events can be unreliable and are subject to a slew of confounding influences (e.g., Capitani et al., 1992; Kelly & Risko, 2021; Skinner, 1957). Further, assessments of social validity often overestimate consumer satisfaction and may not be reliable indicators of effective programming (Bornstein & Rychtarik, 1983; Fuqua & Schwade, 1986; Lebow, 1982; McMahon & Forehand, 1983). Despite their limitations, previous research suggests that subjective reports of program efficacy *can* remain fairly consistent across time (e.g., Dillenburger et al., 2004; Hood & Eyberg, 2003; Johnson & Christensen, 1975). Further, the strengths and limitations of subjective reporting serve as complements to the limitations and strengths of objective reporting methods under stringently controlled conditions. Toward this end, recent calls for dynamic evaluative criteria in single case design (i.e., Ledford et al., 2022) suggest researchers should protect against the mostly likely threats to internal validity while de-emphasizing the importance of unlikely threats that impede a project's ability to meaningfully assess difficult-to-study phenomena, such as generality and social validity. That is, there are situations in which minor degradation of internal validity can allow for meaningful contributions to social validity and generality.

One option that has gained traction in single case research and intervention research more generally is mixed methods approaches (Corr et al., 2020; D'Agostino et al., 2019; Kramer, 2011; Leko, 2014; Onghena et al., 2019; Snodgrass et al., 2018). These approaches call for triangulation of data from multiple sources (e.g., parent report, direct observation, child choice) to draw conclusions (Chung et al., 2016). This is different from the traditional approach taken with single case design, which prioritizes experimental observation data and considers social validity and generality as of secondary importance, generally only at the end of the study. Integrating multiple sources of data can assist researchers to identify the extent to which behavior change in tightly controlled experimental conditions translate into socially valid and generalized behavior change. These data can be used to temper and/or corroborate the internally valid results established in experimental conditions (Akemoglu et al., 2019; Halle, 2019; Kazdin, 1977; Schwartz & Baer, 1991).

One major goal of mixed methods approaches is to overcome the limitations intrinsic to any single methodological approach (Creswell & Clark, 2017). That is, even when we have reliable and accurate observational data, these data still provide only part of the picture. Collecting more data—for example, information about perceived feasibility from teachers, behavioral data from outside of sessions reported by parents, use of behaviors in typical contexts, and preference for certain intervention components from participants—provides more comprehensive evidence. When outcomes from all these methods converge (i.e., suggest intervention success or suggest intervention failure), researchers can be more confident in the importance and generality of the identified relation. When the outcomes of these methods diverge in some way, a more complete understanding of the limitations of the research is possible. For example, researchers might find that although behavioral data from sessions and parent report suggested the intervention was effective and resulted in generalized behavior change, and that teachers found the intervention successful, the direct recipients of the intervention (students) did not like it. Collecting and triangulating data in this way allows for nuanced discussions of outcomes *and* suggests future avenues for improving validity and generality (i.e., the need for improving student buy-in).

In one example of the use of a mixed methods approach including single case design data, Lambert and colleagues (2023) described a form of triangulation in which researchers collected both objective and subjective data from a caregiver, on an ongoing basis, about the social validity and generality of intervention programming provided for a child who engaged in high rates of aggression in the home setting. In this study, the authors not only documented caregiver perspectives, but also reacted to them in conjunction with the objective time-series data that they obtained during formal intervention sessions and allowed outcomes from all data sources to determine next steps in intervention design. Due to the role that each data source played in data-based decision making, they referred to their process as "formative triangulation," paying homage to the concept of *formative assessment* in education research in which informal academic assessments are conducted on an ongoing basis for the purpose of guiding future lesson planning and intervention efforts. The intent of that study was to acknowledge the limitations of their primary analytic strategy (i.e., visual analysis of objective data obtained in a formal intervention context), and then to mitigate noted constraints via data triangulation and problem solving (e.g., Lindberg et al., 2003). Additional research that includes ongoing data in the context of single case design *alongside* additional sources of data is needed.

Conclusions

When you have questions related to broad behavior change and social relevance outside the research context, we recommend that you collect data from multiple stakeholders to understand the social validity of the intervention from different perspectives and collect data related to the generality of behavior change as relevant to your theory of change and research goals.

References

Akemoglu, Y., Garcia-Grau, P., & Meadan, H. (2019). Using masked raters to evaluate social validity of a parent-implemented communication intervention. *Topics in Early Childhood Special Education*, 39(3), 144–155. https://doi.org/10.1177/0271121419865945

Allen Jr, J. S., Tarnowski, K. J., Simonian, S. J., Elliott, D., & Drabman, R. S. (1991). The generalization map revisited: Assessment of generalized treatment effects in child and adolescent behavior therapy. *Behavior Therapy*, 22(3), 393–405.

Baer, D. M., Wolf, M. M., & Risley, T. R. (1968). Some current dimensions of applied behavior analysis. *Journal of Applied Behavior Analysis*, 1, 91–97.

Baer, D. M., Wolf, M. M., & Risley, T. R. (1987). Some still-current dimensions of applied behavior analysis. *Journal of Applied Behavior Analysis*, 4, 313–327.

Banerjee, I., Lambert, J. M., Copeland, B. A., Paranczak, J. L., Bailey, K. M., & Standish, C. M. (2022). Extending functional communication training to multiple language contexts in bilingual learners with challenging behavior. *Journal of Applied Behavior Analysis*, 55(1), 80–100.

Barnes-Holmes, D., Barnes-Holmes, Y., McEnteggart, C., & Harte, C. (2021). Back to the future with an updated version of RFT: More field than frame?. *Perspectivas em Análise do Comportamento*, 12(1), 033–051.

Barton, E. E., Velez, M., Pokorski, E. A., & Domingo, M. (2020). The effects of email performance-based feedback delivered to teaching teams: A systematic replication. *Journal of Early Intervention*, 42(2), 143–162.

Bornstein, P. H., & Rychtarik, R. G. (1983). Consumer satisfaction in adult behavior therapy: Procedures, problems, and future perspectives. *Behavior Therapy*, 14(2), 191–208.

Boyle, M. A., Hoffmann, A. N., & Lambert, J. M. (2018). Behavioral contrast: Research and areas for investigation. *Journal of Applied Behavior Analysis*, 51(3), 702–718.

Bronfenbrenner, U. (1979). *The ecology of human development: Experiments by nature and design*. Harvard University Press.

Capitani, E., Della Sala, S., Logie, R. H., & Spinnler, H. (1992). Recency, primacy, and memory: Reappraising and standardising the serial position curve. *Cortex*, 28(3), 315–342. https://doi.org/10.1016/s0010-9452(13)80143-8

Catania, A. C. (2013). *Learning* (5th edn). Cornwall-on-Hudson: Sloan.

Chazin, K. T., & Ledford, J. R. (2021). Constant time delay and system of least prompts: Efficiency and child preference. *Journal of Behavioral Education*, 30, 684–707.

Chung, M. Y., Snodgrass, M. R., Meadan, H., Akamoglu, Y., & Halle, J. W. (2016). Understanding communication intervention for young children with autism and their parents: Exploring measurement decisions and confirmation bias. *Journal of Developmental and Physical Disabilities*, 28, 113–134.

Collins, B. (2013). *Systematic instruction for students with moderate and severe disabilities*. Baltimore: Brookes.

Cooper, J. O., Heron, T. E., & Heward, W. L. (2020). *Applied behavior analysis*. Pearson UK.

Corr, C., Snodgrass, M. R., Greene, J. C., Meadan, H., & Santos, R. M. (2020). Mixed methods in early childhood special education research: Purposes, challenges, and guidance. *Journal of Early Intervention*, 42(1), 20–30.

Creswell, J. W., & Clark, V. L. P. (2017). *Designing and conducting mixed methods research*. Sage Publication.

D'Agostino, S. R., Douglas, S. N., & Dueñas, A. D. (2019). Practitioner-implemented naturalistic developmental behavioral interventions: Systematic review of social validity practices. *Topics in Early Childhood Special Education*, 39(3), 170–182. https://doi.org/10.1177/0271121419854803

Delprato, D. J. (2002). Countercontrol in behavior analysis. *The Behavior Analyst*, 25(2), 191–200. https://doi.org/10.1007/BF03392057

Dillenburger, K., Keenan, M., Gallagher, S., & Mcelhinney, M. (2004). Parent education and home-based behaviour analytic intervention: An examination of parents' perceptions of outcome. *Journal of Intellectual and Developmental Disability*, 29 (2), 119–130. https://doi.org/10.1080/13668250410001709476

Drabman, R. S., Hammer, D., & Rosenbaum, M. S. (1979). Assessing the generalization in behavior modification with children: The generalization map. *Behavioral Assessment*, 1, 203–219.

Dueñas, A. D., Plavnick, J. B., & Goldstein, H. (2021). Effects of a multicomponent peer mediated intervention on social communication of preschoolers with autism spectrum disorder. *Exceptional Children*, 87(2), 236–257.

Eyler, P. B., & Ledford, J. R. (2024). Efficiency and child preference for specific prompting procedures. *Journal of Behavioral Education*.

Fahmie, T. A., Rodriguez, N. M., Luczynski, K. C., Rahaman, J. A., Charles, B. M., & Zangrillo, A. N. (2023). Toward an explicit technology of ecological validity. *Journal of Applied Behavior Analysis*, 56(2), 302–322.

Farmer, R., Wolery, M., Gast, D. L., & Page, J. L. (1988). Individual staff training to increase the frequency of data collection in an integrated preschool program. *Education and Treatment of Children*, 11, 127–142.

Fuhrman, A. M., Lambert, J. M., & Greer, B. D. (2021). A brief review of expanded-operant treatments for mitigating resurgence. *The Psychological Record*, 72(2), 319–323.

Fuqua, R. W., & Schwade, J. (1986). Social validation of applied behavioral research: A selective review and critique. In A. Poling, & R. W. Fuqua (Eds.), *Research methods in applied behavior analysis: Issues and advances* (pp. 265–292). New York: Plenum.

Garfinkle, A. N., & Schwartz, I. S. (2002). Peer imitation: Increasing social interactions in children with autism and other developmental disabilities in inclusive preschool classrooms. *Topics in Early Childhood Special Education*, 22, 26–39.

Ghaemmaghami, M., Hanley, G. P., & Jessel, J. (2021). Functional communication training: From efficacy to effectiveness. *Journal of Applied Behavior Analysis*, 54(1), 122–143. https://doi.org/10.1002/jaba.762

Halle, J. (2019). Avoiding the humdrum: Recommendations for improving how we conceptualize and assess social validity in ECSE. *Topics in Early Childhood Special Education*, 39(3), 139–143. https://doi.org/10.1177/0271121419873525

Halle, J. W. (1982). Teaching functional language to the handicapped. An integrative model of natural environment teaching techniques. *Journal of the Association for the Severely Handicapped*, 7(4), 29–37.

Hanley, G. P. (2010). Toward effective and preferred programming: A case of the objective measurement of social validity with the recipients of behavior-change programs. *Behavior Analysis in Practice*, 3, 13–21.

Hayes, S. C. (1989). *Rule-governed behavior. Cognition, contingencies, and instructional control*. New York: Plenum.

Hayes, S. C., Barnes-Holmes, D., & Roche, B. (Eds.). (2001). *Relational frame theory: A post-Skinnerian account of human language and cognition*. Springer Science & Business Media.

Heal, N. A., & Hanley, G. P. (2011). Embedded prompting may function as embedded punishment: Detection of unexplained behavioral process within a typical preschool teaching strategy. *Journal of Applied Behavior Analysis*, 44, 127–131.

Hood, K., & Eyberg, S. (2003). Outcomes of parent-child interaction therapy: Mothers' reports of maintenance three to six years after treatment. *Journal of Clinical Child & Adolescent Psychology*, 32(3), 419–429. https://doi.org/10.1207/S15374424JCCP3203_10

Hurley, J. J. (2012). Social validity assessment in social competence interventions for preschool children: A review. *Topics in Early Childhood Special Education*, 32, 164–174.

Jacobson, N. S. (1989). The maintenance of treatment gains following social learning-based marital therapy. *Behavior Therapy*, 20, 325–336.

Johnson, S. M., & Christensen, A. (1975). Multiple criteria follow-up of behavior modification with families. *Journal of Abnormal Child Psychology*, 3(1), 135–154. https://doi.org/10.1007/BF00919807

Joyce, C., Honey, E., Leekam, S. R., Barrett, S. L., & Rodgers, J. (2017). Anxiety, intolerance of uncertainty and restricted and repetitive behaviour: Insights directly from young people with ASD. *Journal of Autism and Developmental Disorders*, 47, 3789–3802.

Kazdin, A. E. (1975). *Behavior modification in applied settings*. Homewood, IL: Dorsey Press.

Kazdin, A. E. (1977). Assessing the clinic or applied importance of behavior change through social validation. *Behavior Modification*, 1, 427–452.

Kazdin, A. E. (1987). Treatment of antisocial behavior in children: Current status and future direction. *Psychological Bulletin*, 102, 187–203.

Kelly, M. O., & Risko, E. F. (2021). Revisiting the influence of offloading memory on free recall. *Memory & Cognition*, 50(7), 710–721. https://doi.org/10.3758/s13421-021-01237-3

Kennedy, C. H. (2002). The maintenance of behavior change as an indicator of social validity. *Behavior Modification*, 26, 594–604.

Kennedy, C. H. (2005). *Single case designs for educational research*. Boston, MA: Allyn & Bacon.

Kimball, R. T., Greer, B. D., Fuhrman, A. M., & Lambert, J. M. (2023). Relapse and its mitigation: Toward behavioral inoculation. *Journal of Applied Behavior Analysis*, 56(2), 282–301.

Koegel, R. L., & Koegel, L. K. (1988). Generalized responsivity and pivotal behaviors. Available from: https://files.eric.ed.gov/fulltext/ED336901.pdf

Koutsavalis, M. A. (2011). The effects of sung versus spoken word on the sign acquisition and generalization of preschool children. Unpublished thesis. Vanderbilt University, Nashville, TN.

Kramer, J. M. (2011). Using mixed methods to establish the social validity of a self-report assessment: An illustration using the Child Occupational Self-Assessment (COSA). *Journal of Mixed Methods Research*, 5(1), 52–76.

Lambert, J. M., Copeland, B. A., Paranczak, J. L., Macdonald, M. J., Torelli, J. T., Houchins-Juarez, N. J. (2022). Description and evaluation of a function informed and mechanisms-based framework for treating challenging behavior. *Journal of Applied Behavior Analysis* 55(4), 1193–1219.

Lambert, J. M., Paranczak, J. L., Copeland, B. A., Houchins-Juarez N. J., & Macdonald, M. J. (2022). Exploring the validity of university-based practicum tailored to develop expertise in addressing challenging behavior. *Journal of Applied Behavior Analysis*, 55(4), 1172–1192.

Lambert, J. M., Sandstrom, A., Hodapp, R., Copeland, B. A., Paranczak, J. L., Macdonald, M. J., & Houchins-Juarez, N. (2022). Revisiting the social validity of services rendered through a university-based practicum addressing challenging behavior. *Journal of Applied Behavior Analysis*, 55(4), 1220–1238.

Lambert, J. M., Morgan, A. C., Banerjee, I., Houchins-Juarez, N., & Copeland, B. (2023). Improving the process and product of intensive intervention through formative triangulation: A mixed methods report. https://osf.io/ct93a/

Lane, J. D., Gast, D. L., Ledford, J. R., & Shepley, C. (2017). Increasing social behaviors in young children with social-communication delays in a group arrangement in preschool. *Education and Treatment of Children*, 115–144.

Lebow, J. (1982). Consumer satisfaction with mental health treatment. *Psychological Bulletin*, 91(2), 244–259. https://doi.org/10.1037/0033-2909.91.2.244

Ledford, J. R., Chazin, K. T., Harbin, E. R., & Ward, S. E. (2017). Massed trials versus trials embedded into game play: Child outcomes and preference. *Topics in Early Childhood Special Education*, 37(2), 107–120.

Ledford, J. R., Hall, E., Conder, E., & Lane, J. D. (2016). Research for young children with autism spectrum disorders: Evidence of social and ecological validity. *Topics in Early Childhood Special Education*, 35(4), 223–233. doi: 10.1177/0271121415585956

Ledford, J. R., Lambert, J. M., Pustejovsky, J., Zimmerman, K. N., Hollins, N., & Barton, E. E. (2022). Single case design research in special education: Next generation standards and considerations. *Exceptional Children*. https://doi.org/10.1177/00144029221137656

Ledford, J. R., Trump, C., Chazin, K. T., Windsor, S. A., Eyler, P. B., & Wunderlich, K. (2023). Systematic review of interruption and redirection procedures for autistic individuals. *Behavioral Interventions*, 38(1), 198–218.

Leko, M. M. (2014). The value of qualitative methods in social validity research. *Remedial and Special Education*, 35(5), 275–286. https://doi.org/10.1177/0741932514524002

Lindberg, J. S., Iwata, B. A., Roscoe, E. M., Worsdell, A.S., Hanley, G. P. (2003). Treatment efficacy of noncontingent reinforcement during brief and extended application. *Journal of Applied Behavior Analysis*, 36, 1–19. doi: 10.1901/jaba.2003.36-1

Manor-Binyamini, I., & Schreiber-Divon, M. (2019). Repetitive behaviors: Listening to the voice of people with high-functioning autism spectrum disorder. *Research in Autism Spectrum Disorders*, 64, 23–30.

McMahon, R. J., & Forehand, R. L. (1983). Consumer satisfaction in behavioral treatment of children: Types, issues, and recommendations. *Behavior Therapy*, 14(2), 209–225.

Meadan, H., Stoner, J. B., Angell, M. E., Daczewitz, M. E., Cheema, J., & Rugutt, J. K. (2014). Do you see a difference? Evaluating outcomes of a parent-implemented intervention. *Journal of Developmental and Physical Disabilities*, 26, 415–430.

Ne'eman, A. (2021). When disability is defined by behavior, outcome measures should not promote "passing". *AMA Journal of Ethics*, 23(7), E569.

Onghena, P., Maes, B., & Heyvaert, M. (2019). Mixed methods single case research: State of the art and future directions. *Journal of Mixed Methods Research*, 13(4), 461–480.

Paranczak, J. L., Lambert, J. M., Ledford, J. R., Copeland, B., & MacDonald, J. M. (2024). Deriving relations at multiple levels of complexity following minimal instruction: A demonstration. *Journal of Applied Behavior Analysis*.

Park, E. Y., & Blair, K. S. C. (2019). Social validity assessment in behavior interventions for young children: A systematic review. *Topics in Early Childhood Special Education*, 39(3), 156–169. https://doi.org/10.1177/0271121419860195

Pennington, R. (2019). *Applied behavior analysis for everyone: Principles and practices explained by applied researchers who use them*. Salt Lake City: AAPC.

Perone, M. (2003). Negative effects of positive reinforcement. *The Behavior Analyst*, 26(1), 1–14. https://doi.org/10.1007/BF03392064

Perone, M., Lerman, D. C., Peterson, S. M., & Williams, D. C. (2023). Report of the ABAI Task Force on Contingent Electric Skin Shock. *Perspectives on Behavior Science*, 46(2), 261–304.

Quay, H. C., & Werry, J. S. (1986). *Psychopathological disorders of childhood* (3rd ed.). New York: Wiley.

Rapoff, M. A. (2010). Editorial: Assessing and enhancing clinical significance/social validity of intervention research in pediatric psychology. *Journal of Pediatric Psychology*, 35, 114–119.

Rosales-Ruiz, J., & Baer, D. M. (1997). Behavioral cusps: A developmental and pragmatic concept for behavior analysis. *Journal of Applied Behavior Analysis*, 30(3), 533–544.

Sandbank, M., Chow, J., Bottema-Beutel, K., & Woynaroski, T. (2021). Evaluating evidence-based practice in light of the boundedness and proximity of outcomes: Capturing the scope of change. *Autism Research*, 14(8), 1536–1542. https://doi.org/10.1002/aur.2527

Schreibman, L., Dawson, G., Stahmer, A. C., Landa, R., Rogers, S. J., McGee, G. G., ... & Halladay, A. (2015). Naturalistic developmental behavioral interventions: Empirically validated treatments for autism spectrum disorder. *Journal of autism and developmental disorders*, 45, 2411–2428. https://doi.org/10.1007/s10803-015-2407-8

Schwartz, I. S., & Baer, D. M. (1991). Social validity assessments: Is current practice state of the art? *Journal of Applied Behavior Analysis*, 24, 189–204.

Schwartz, I. S., & Kelly, E. M. (2021). Quality of life for people with disabilities: Why applied behavior analysts should consider this a primary dependent variable. *Research and Practice for Persons with Severe Disabilities*, 46(3), 159–172.

Shawler, L. A., Dianda, M., & Miguel, C. F. (2020). A comparison of response interruption and redirection and competing items on vocal stereotypy and appropriate vocalizations. *Journal of Applied Behavior Analysis*, 53(1), 355–365.

Sidman, M. (1971). Reading and auditory-visual equivalences. *Journal of Speech and Hearing Research*, 14(1), 5–13. https://doi.org/10.1044/jshr.1401.05

Skinner, B. F. (1957). *Verbal behavior*. New York: Appleton-Century-Crofts.

Snodgrass, M. R., Chung, M. Y., Meadan, H., & Halle, J. W. (2018). Social validity in single-case research: A systematic literature review of prevalence and application. *Research in Developmental Disabilities*, 74, 160–170.

Snyder, K., Lambert, J. M., & Twohig, M. P. (2011). Defusion: a behavior-analytic strategy for addressing private events. *Behavior Analysis in Practice*, 4, 4–13.

Staats, A. W. (2006). Positive and negative reinforcers: How about the second and third functions?. *The Behavior Analyst*, 29(2), 271.

State, T. M., & Kern, L. (2012). A comparison of video feedback and in vivo self-monitoring on the social skills of an adolescent with Asperger Syndrome. *Journal of Behavioral Education*, 21, 18–33.

Stewart, I., Barrett, K., McHugh, L., Barnes-Holmes, D., & O'Hora, D. (2013). Multiple contextual control over non-arbitrary relational responding and a preliminary model of pragmatic verbal analysis. *Journal of the Experimental Analysis of Behavior*, 100(2), 174–186.

Stokes, T. F., & Baer, D. M. (1977). An implicit technology of generalization 1. *Journal of Applied Behavior Analysis*, 10(2), 349–367. https://doi.org/10.1901/jaba.1977.10-349

Taylor, A. G. (2003). An Adaptation of Stay Play Talk for Children with Internalizing Behaviors. Dissertation. Vanderbilt University. https://ir.vanderbilt.edu/handle/1803/9598

Todt, M. J., Barton, E. E., Ledford, J. R., Robinson, G. N., & Skiba, E. B. (2023). Teaching and promoting generalization of peer imitation with preschoolers with disabilities. *Journal of Early Intervention*, 45(1), 63–82.

Van Houten, R. (1979). Social validation: The evolution of standards of competency for target behaviors. *Journal of Applied Behavior Analysis*, 12, 581–591.

Veneziano, J., & Shea, S. (2023). They have a Voice; are we listening?. *Behavior Analysis in Practice*, 16(1), 127–144.

Vivanti, G., & Stahmer, A. C. (2021). Can the early start Denver model be considered ABA practice?. *Behavior Analysis in Practice*, 14, 230–239.

Wolf, M. M. (1978). Social validity: The case for subjective measurement or how applied behavior analysis is finding its heart. *Journal of Applied Behavior Analysis*, 11, 203–214.

Yoder, P., Lloyd, B., & Symons, F. (2018). *Observational measurement of behavior* (2nd ed.). Baltimore: Brookes.

Zimmerman, K. N., & Ledford, J. R. (2017). Beyond ASD: Evidence for the effectiveness of social narratives. *Journal of Early Intervention*, 39(3), 199–217.

8

Data Representation and Performance Characteristics

Amy D. Spriggs, Justin D. Lane, and David L. Gast

Important Terms

graphic displays, x-axis/abscissa, y-axis/ordinate, tic marks, quantification of tic marks/axis labels, descriptive/axis titles, phase, condition, phase change line, condition modification line, condition labels, figure number, title, figure note, line graphs, cumulative record, standard celebration chart, level, trend, trend direction, variability, stability, immediacy of change, overlap, consistency

---

Table of Contents

Data Representation
    Figures in Single Case Design Studies
        Types of Figures
        Guidelines for Constructing Figures
    Tables in Single Case Design Studies
Describing Participant Performance
    Level
    Trend
    Variability
    Immediacy
    Overlap
    Consistency
Conclusions
References

Callouts

8.1 What are the Basic Components of Graphs?
8.2 Does the X-axis Actually Depict Time?
8.3 When Should I Graph My Data?

DOI: 10.4324/9781003294726-9

If the purpose of single case designs is to evaluate the impact of an independent variable on a behavior of interest, it is critical that single case researchers accurately represent and report data on the behaviors. In this chapter, we first describe graphing conventions in single case research, and then discuss performance characteristics that can be evaluated via these graphic representations.

Data Representation

Recently, there has been a renewed emphasis on transparency in research (Cook et al., 2018, 2022). Single case researchers are not immune to the need to more transparently present method, findings, and implications of research studies, but we do have an advantage in transparently reporting outcomes compared to researchers in other paradigms. This is because single case data are typically reported on a session-by-session basis via graphical display. Researchers using other paradigms (e.g., qualitative, between-group) rely on representative examples selected by researchers and/or synthesis of data across multiple people and/or measurement occasions. Thus, because we report session-by-session data, the typical method of analysis is transparent in single case design (e.g., readers of a study can analyze the data for themselves, via the graphic display). **Graphic displays**, or representation of quantitative data via figures, also enable you to make formative decisions throughout the process of the study. Tables, well-organized numerical summaries of data, are also helpful, especially for secondary data (e.g., fidelity, social validity, secondary variables). Thus, well-designed figures and tables are essential in good single case research.

Graphs and tables serve two basic purposes. First, they assist in organizing data during the data collection process, which facilitates formative evaluation. Second, they provide a detailed summary and description of behavior over time, which allows readers to analyze the relation between independent and dependent variables. The underlying purpose or function of the graphic display is communication. For the person collecting data, the graph is a vehicle for efficiently organizing and summarizing a participant's behavior over time. It allows the researcher to analyze, point by point, the effect a particular event has on a participant's behavior. In single case design research, visual analysis is the primary method of data evaluation; thus, appropriate graphing is critical. In addition to reliance on graphically displayed data for communication and analysis, practitioners may find graphing economical in terms of time saved by not having to review daily data forms prior to making program decisions and by not maintaining ineffective intervention programs.

Figures in Single Case Design Studies

Graphic representation of data provides researchers and consumers with an efficient, compact, and detailed summary of participant performance. A well-constructed graph communicates to readers (1) the sequence of experimental conditions and phases, (2) time spent in each condition and phase, (3) independent and dependent variables, (4) experimental design, and (5) relations between variables. Therefore, it is not surprising that applied researchers rely heavily on graphic displays.

Four basic principles help graphs communicate information to readers: clarity, simplicity, explicitness, and good design (Parsonson & Baer, 1978). Moreover, graphs should allow the consumer to get "the greatest number of ideas in the shortest time with the least ink in the smallest space" (Tufte, 2001). A well-constructed graph will (1) use easily discriminable data points and data paths, (2) clearly separate experimental conditions, (3) avoid clutter by keeping the number of behaviors plotted on one graph to a minimum, (4) provide brief descriptive labels, and (5) use appropriate proportions. Callout 8.1 describes the major components of graphic displays, and Figure 8.1 depicts those components, using APA-style graphing conventions.

Callout 8.1 What are the Basic Components of Graphs? (See Figure 8.1)

- **X-axis (Abscissa)**: Horizontal line that typically identifies the time variable (e.g., sessions, days, dates).
- **Y-axis (Ordinate)**: Vertical line that typically identifies how much of a behavior occurs for each session (e.g., percentage, number, duration, responses per minute).
- **Tic Marks**: Points along both the abscissa and ordinate representing values (e.g., 0%, 10%, 20%; Sessions 1, 2, 3).
- **Axis Labels (Quantification of Tic Marks)**: Numeric value corresponding to a tic mark.
- **Axis Titles**: Descriptive information about the x-values and y-values found on the graph (e.g., Do x-axis labels refer to days or sessions?).
- **Phase**: A collection of sessions that occur during a given time period. Phases can include a single condition or multiple conditions (e.g., when using rapid iterative designs, multiple condition types are alternated in a single phase, see Chapter 13).
- **Condition**: Procedurally similar sessions (e.g., Baseline, Intervention). A condition may occur multiple times per study (e.g., in sequential introduction and withdrawal designs, baseline conditions are repeated, see Chapter 9).
- **Phase Change Line**: Solid vertical lines that represent a change in phase. Data paths should not cross this line.
- **Condition Modification Line**: Dotted vertical lines that represent a minor condition change (e.g., a change in reinforcement schedule, a modification implemented due to non-response). Data paths should not cross this line.
- **Condition Labels**: One or two descriptive words or common abbreviations that identify each experimental conditions (e.g., Baseline, Prompting). When multiple conditions occur in a single phase, the *phase* is labeled, and conditions are identified via text with arrows pointing to relevant data paths (see Chapter 13).
- **Figure Number** and **Title**: The figure number is used in the narrative to direct a reader's attention to the appropriate graph, and the title provides a brief and explicit description.
- **Figure Note**: Explanations about the content of the figure that are too long for the title and explanation of any abbreviations or ambiguous graph components should be included in the figure note.

Types of Figures

Line graphs represent the most commonly used graphic display, both in single case design research and more broadly (Tufte, 2001); they represent how much of a behavior occurs (y-axis) over time (x-axis). When using a line graph, the left-most data point represents how much of a given behavior occurs for the first measurement occasion, and each subsequent data point represents how much behavior occurs in the following session. Figure 8.1 shows a line graph, during which challenging behavior occurred 10–15 times per measurement occasion for the first

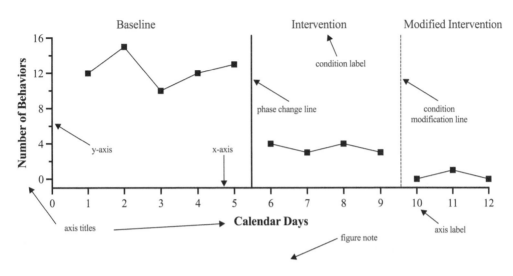

Figure 8.1 Sample Line Graph with Basic Components Labeled.

Note: Modified intervention refers to a change in the frequency with which reinforcement was provided, from an initial once per day to a modified twice per day (once before lunch, and one before dismissal)

five days (baseline), and 3–4 times per measurement occasion for the next four days (intervention), and 0–1 times per measurement occasion for the final three days (modified intervention).

A variation of the typical linear line graph is the **cumulative record**. It is sometimes used to present time series data in single case research. Cumulative records have a long history of use in basic science (e.g., Skinner, 1965). Applied research teams sometimes use cumulative graphs to display data regarding participant preference (cf. Heal & Hanley, 2007; Ledford et al., 2017) and learning (Chazin & Ledford, 2021). Cumulative records are often used for secondary measures when a participant has one opportunity to respond during each measurement occasion or session (e.g., when a participant can choose which intervention condition is in effect for the day; Ledford et al., 2017).

When using a cumulative record, the left-most data point represents how much of a given behavior occurs for the first measurement occasion. Each subsequent data points represents how much occurred in that measurement occasion, *plus all behavior that occurred in previous occasions*. Thus, a flat line in a cumulative record indicates no responding occurring across sessions and an increasing data path represents some level of responding. Because responses are cumulative, or additive, it is not possible to have decreases over time on a cumulative graph. Figure 8.2 shows a cumulative record wherein a child correctly named 0 targets on the first two days, one target on Day 3, and no additional targets on days 4 and 5. On days 6–10, they correctly named 2–3 additional targets per day, for a total of 18 targets learned by the final measurement occasion. Even though no targets were named on days 4 and 5, note that the graph shows one correct, given data represent a cumulative number.

Standard celeration chart is a standardized semi-logarithmic chart and is a line graph variation that is less commonly used but is typical when precision teaching is the independent variable (see Evans et al., 2021; Gist & Bulla, 2022). They represent time continuously (e.g., as days) on an equal-interval scale and represent behavior on a logarithmic scale, which allows for visual analysis of changes in rate over time. They are helpful when absolute changes in

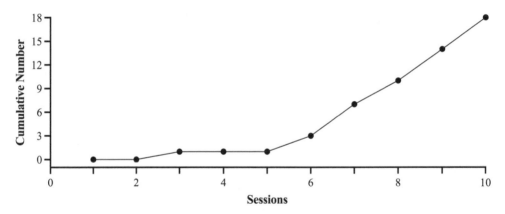

Figure 8.2 Cumulative Record.

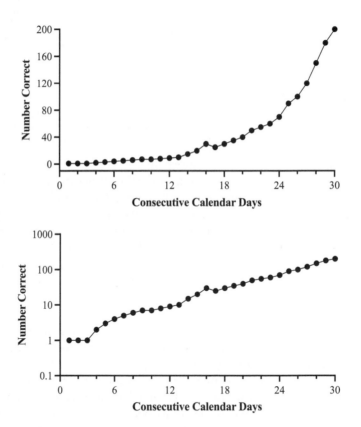

Figure 8.3 Equal-Interval (top) and Logarithmic (bottom) Data Display.

Note: The difference in maximum y-value between graphs is very large.

behavior (which are what we have discussed to this point) are not the focus of research. Absolute behavior changes are documented using equal-interval recording, where amounts are "equal" between tic marks on the graph. In contrast, relative behavior changes can be captured when the distance between tic marks are proportionally equal. "For example, a doubling of response rate from 4 to 8 per minute would appear on a semi-logarithmic chart as the same amount of change as a doubling of 50 to 100 responses per min" (Cooper et al., 2007, p. 139). Figure 8.3

shows the same data depicted on graphs with an equal-interval (typical y-axis; top panel) and a semi-logarithmic axis (bottom panel). Note the differences in the maximum values for these graphs. When published, data are generally depicted on traditional standard celeration charts (for examples, see Bulla et al., 2021; Junaid et al., 2021). Graphing responses on semi-log charts is similar to transforming outcome data using natural log, a common practice in between-groups research.

Callout 8.2   Does the X-axis Actually Depict Time?

Broadly, researchers often consider the x-axis as a depiction of time. However, this is generally true only in an ordinal sense—that is, when you consider one data point, you can be sure that all data points that are depicted to the right of that data point occurred *after* that point in time. Thus, in an ordinal sense, the axis does depict time. However, graphs (excepting standard celeration charts) rarely accurately depict calendar time. Instead, the most common conceptualization of each measurement occasion is the "session," which does not often align with calendar days. For example, most studies depict "sessions" that occur fewer than once per calendar day, but there is no indication of calendar time on the figure (Peredo et al., 2018). However, there are examples where authors use dates (Wright & Kaiser 2017) or use sessions but also indicate progression of calendar time (e.g., weeks; Muttiah et al., 2022). Other sessions might occur multiple times per day in a bout, with many days between bouts of sessions (e.g., Lane et al., 2016; Paranczek et al., 2024). Calendar time is rarely depicted in these scenarios (although see Figure 8.4 for an example of a graph that depicts each session via a data point, and each bout/calendar day with shading). Depicting calendar time on graphs is complicated, because it might often lead to substantial white space and complicate visual analysis. Thus, in narrative descriptions of procedures and graphs, authors should carefully describe their measurement occasions and the relation to calendar dates. Using supplemental materials to provide graphs depicting calendar time is likely a good practice.

Guidelines for Constructing Figures

The primary function of a graph is to communicate without assistance from the accompanying text. This requires that you (1) select the appropriate graphic display and (1) present the data as clearly, completely, and concisely as possible. How data are presented and how figures are constructed directly influences a reader's ability to evaluate functional relations between independent and dependent variables. Though there are few hard and fast rules that govern figure selection, graph construction, or data presentation, there are recommended guidelines for preparing graphic displays (APA, 2009; Parsonson & Baer, 1978; Sanders, 1978). Following these guidelines should facilitate objective evaluations of graphically displayed data.

Graph Proportions. The historically preferred proportion of ordinate (y-axis) to abscissa (x-axis) has been reported to be a ratio of 2:3, 3:5, or 3:4 (Kubina et al., 2017). This has been viewed by researchers as limiting the degree of perceptual distortion. The same data are graphed in Figure 8.5 using different ratios. It is clear that data appear drastically different based on the ratio of height to width; however, it is unclear in what situations the historically-suggested ratios are appropriate. For example, studies suggest that the density of data (e.g., the number of data points *per cm* on the x-axis) impacts data analysis decisions (Shah & Hoeffner, 2002). This outcome is not specific to single case design graphs; additional research is needed to guide the construction of graphs with time series data. A recent review suggests the average

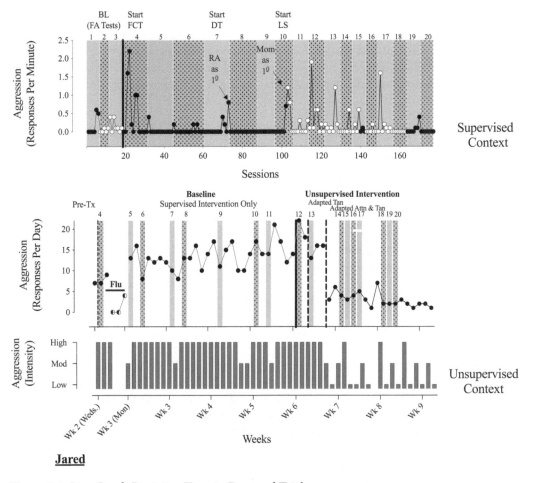

Figure 8.4 Line Graph Depicting Time in Days and Trials.

Note: The data in the top panel represent data occurring in in a clinic, with multiple sessions (data points connected by lines) occurring on each day (represented via different colors of shading). These data represent about 180 sessions occurring across 20 days. The data in the second panel represent about 60 daily reports from the participant's mother, some of which occurred on clinic days (shaded), and some of which occurred on non-clinic days (unshaded).

Source: Lambert, J. M., Morgan, A. C., Banerjee, I., Houchins-Juarez, N. J., & Copeland, B. A. (2023). Improving the process and product of intensive intervention through formative triangulation: A mixed methods report.

ratio for most design types is approximately 4/10 (e.g., 4 cm tall and 10 cm wide), although wide variation exists and expert preference does not align with reported "optimal" ratios (Ledford et al., 2017). We suggest that you use a ratio that does not distort data and allows for discrimination between data points (e.g., 2/3 ratio for graphs with relatively few data points, 1/3 for graphs with a large number of data points).

Font size and Type. Use a font consistent with the font used in your narrative text (usually Times New Roman) for all text on the graph, including figure titles, phase and condition labels, and descriptive titles, and figure notes. Although you may generally use smaller text on figures and tables (e.g., 10 point), it should be easily readable.

Axes. Ensure that numbers associated with both axes are easy to read and that tic marks between axis labels are used to assist the reader in identifying midpoints. For example, if you label every other session (e.g., 2, 4, 6) you should put a tic mark at each session; if you label

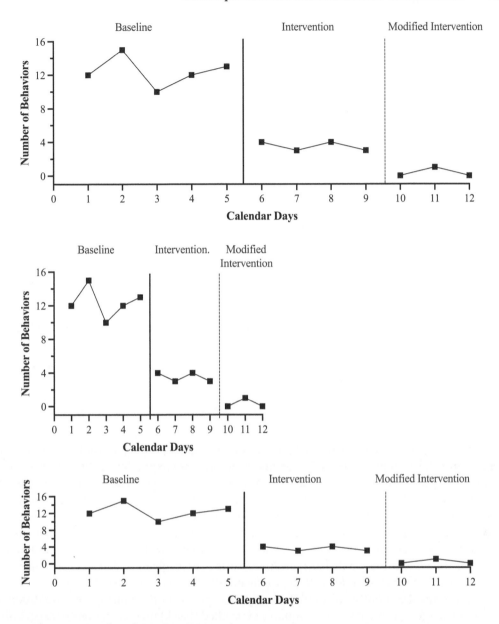

Figure 8.5 Line Graph with Varying Dimensions.

Note: Dimension of the top panel are 1:3. Dimensions of the middle panel are 2:3. Dimensions of the bottom panel are 1:6. Data are identical across panels.

every 10th session (e.g., 10, 20, 30) on a graph with many sessions, you might use tic marks at every 5th session. Use the same ordinate size and maximum y-value on all graphs reporting the same measurement units in the same research report (Kennedy, 1989), or explicitly describe in narrative and figure text that different values are used and explain why. The zero-origin tic mark along the ordinate ideally should be placed slightly above the abscissa when any data point value is zero (referred to as "floating" the zero). Floating the zero is important because it is important not to mistake a zero level for the absence of plotted data. If there are no zero level data points to be plotted on a line graph, the zero-origin tic mark need not be raised above the

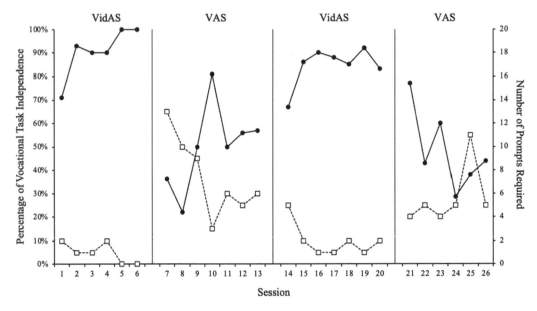

Figure 8.6 Figure using the left and right ordinate to graph two different measures on the same graphic display.

Note: Solid circles represent the percentage of independently completed vocational task steps. Open squares represent the number of adult prompts required.

abscissa. When more than one dependent measure is graphed, the right ordinate may also be used. Figure 8.6 exemplifies using the left and right ordinate to graph two different measures on the same graphic display; percentage of vocational task independence is shown on the left ordinate and number of prompts required is shown on the right ordinate. Abbreviations and symbols (e.g., %, #) are discouraged in favor of descriptive labels.

Axis Labels. On the x-axis label, clearly explicate to what extent the axis corresponds to calendar time or another metric (e.g., school days, sessions, which occurred approximately every third day). On the y-axis label, clearly describe the dependent variable (behavior and unit, e.g., percentage of intervals with engagement, number of correct responses).

Markers and Data Paths. If multiple data paths appear on the same graph, use different marker shapes (e.g., triangles, circles, squares). Use filled (black) markers for one data path and unfilled (white) markers for the second. If a third data path is used, you can use gray fill, but ensure that the markers are big enough for these to be discriminated from black-filled markers. Use thin lines for data paths so as not to obscure marker position (e.g., 1.0 point lines) and markers that are large enough to be differentiated from each other but small enough so that readers can accurately detect the y-value. Label data paths using text boxes and arrows. Do not connect data paths across phase change lines.

Scale Breaks. A scale break is sometimes used when the entire abscissa or ordinate scale is not presented. The abscissa scale should be divided into equal intervals. When data are not collected continuously, a scale break can be inserted on the abscissa between the two non-consecutive data points (see Mayfield & Vollmer, 2007 for examples). You can also use a scale break on the ordinate (cf. Maglieri et al., 2000) if a single outlying data point exists and the absence of a break makes visual analysis difficult. You should ensure that use of a break does not inadvertently distort data (Dart & Radley, 2017). Breaks are particularly helpful when there are extreme outliers (e.g., when nearly all data are between 0–2 occurrences, but there is one instance of approximately 50 occurrences; Hoffmann et al., 2020).

Consistency. When graphing similar behaviors on multiple graphs, we suggest maintaining the same maximum value for the y-axis (Dart & Radley, 2017; Kennedy, 1989). This is especially true for time-lagged designs, to allow for across-tier comparisons (see Chapter 11). If using similar maximum values reduces the ability to accurately visually analyze results, additional graphs can be presented via supplemental materials (see Chapter 18).

Blocking Data. When logistically feasible, single case researchers present all data. On occasion, however, when data have been collected over an extended period of time, it may be necessary to condense data in order to present it on a single graph. A procedure for condensing data, referred to as *blocking*, is infrequently used to reduce the number of data points plotted on a graph. This procedure entails calculating mean or median performance level of two or more adjacent days' data, thereby reducing the length of the abscissa and the number of data points presented on the graph. When data points are blocked, you should (1) note that the data have been blocked, (2) specify how many adjacent data points have been blocked within each condition (the number of data points blocked across conditions should be the same), (3) provide a rationale, and (4) present a minimum of three blocked data points for each condition or phase. As a rule, blocking is done post hoc; during the course of research all data are plotted. It is only after the study has been completed, and all data collected, that you can evaluate the appropriateness of the blocking procedure. The general rule regarding blocking is: Don't; if you must, proceed with caution and assure your reader that blocked data trends parallel and accurately represent unblocked data.

Visual Supports. Some researchers add trend, median, and mean lines to their graphs to supplement point-by-point data plotted on a line graph; they should never be drawn as an alternative to plotting actual data points and data paths. These summative lines should be used sparingly, and as a general rule, we do not recommend their use. These lines may distract readers from potential trends and variability present in a data path within and between conditions and make graphs needlessly complex. Again, these lines could be included on graphs in supplemental materials.

Callout 8.3   When Should I Graph My Data?

Generally, single case data are graphed, automatically or manually, after each measurement occasion. This allows single case researchers to make formative decisions about phase changes and condition modifications. When interobserver agreement data are collected during a session, it also allows for consideration of data from both the primary and secondary observer before making these decisions. In some cases, response-guided decision making is not relevant to a specific design or phase (see, for example, a discussion about randomizing order in alternating treatments designs in Chapter 13 and determining baseline length a priori in nonconcurrent multiple baseline designs in Chapter 11). Even when this is true, it is good practice to graph data after each measurement occasion because visual analysis is the primary data analysis method for single case researchers.

One exception to the graph-every-session rule of thumb is when naïve coders are responsible for coding data and coding is conducted non-sequentially (i.e., out of temporal order) in an attempt to reduce bias associated with experimenter expectations of growth over time. In these situations, either (1) use a second coder that is not naïve to condition and graph daily, or (2) explicate a priori rules about condition changes before data collection begins, and use those rules, rather than collected data, to make decisions.

Tables in Single Case Design Studies

An alternative format for reporting data is the table. Data often reported in tables include participant demographics, condition variables, response definitions with examples and non-examples, and secondary data (e.g., reliability statistics, social validity data, generalization outcomes, number of trials or errors to criterion). Using a table to report supplemental or summative data can accomplish several things. Given the limited space of journal articles, presenting lengthy information in tabular form can condense it considerably. Although tables allow researchers to efficiently highlight and summarize information, seldom are they used to present primary single case data; rather, they are primarily used for reporting supplemental or secondary data. In general, text should supplement rather than duplicate information in tables.

Based on APA guidelines, we suggest that: (1) tables should be numbered in numerical order in the order they are mentioned in your text; (2) table titles should be succinct; (3) headings should be used to concisely organize the information you are sharing; (4) subheadings may also be used under each heading, when necessary; (5) all headings should aide readers in finding pertinent information; (6) lines within tables should be limited to separating parts of the table to aide clarity for readers (e.g. around headings but not within the body); and (7) vertical lines should not be used.

Describing Participant Performance

Observational measures are transformed into quantified representations of dependent variables and graphed. Graphic displays of data allow us to analyze the relation between independent and dependent variables. Performance is commonly described using six components of visual analysis: Level, trend, variability, immediacy of change, overlap, and consistency. We look at level, trend, and variability within each phase and for each condition. We look for differences in level, trend, and variability as well as immediacy of change, overlap, and consistency that are associated with changes between conditions.

Level

The term **level** refers to the amount of behavior that occurs, as indicated by the ordinate scale value (Kennedy, 2005). Level is often the characteristic of highest interest for behavior change, and is generally described as low, moderate, or high. You can also characterize level by describing the range of dependent variable values in a phase or condition (e.g., 10% or fewer of intervals; 90–100% accuracy). Less often, it has been described as a median value. Despite the typical use of means/averages (e.g., in between-group research and outside of research contexts), we do not recommend their use for summarizing level because the relatively small number of data points make the mean susceptible to outliers (i.e., results in the mean being a poor representation of level). The top panel of Figure 8.7 shows a low level of behavior in the first phase and a high level of behavior in the second phase.

Trend

Trend is the slope and direction of a data series, or the direction data are moving over time (increasing, decreasing, or remaining the same; Kennedy, 2005). When visually analyzing data, three characteristics can be described: trend direction, trend magnitude, and trend stability. **Trend direction** is referred to as **accelerating** (increasing in ordinate value over time), **decelerating** (decreasing in ordinate value over time), or **zero celerating** (data series is parallel to the abscissa). Trend can further be characterized by magnitude and is often described as **steep** or **gradual** and paired with direction (e.g., steep accelerating trend or gradual decelerating trend). You should also describe whether the direction of a trend is improving (therapeutic) or deteriorating (countertherapeutic) based on the behavior of interest (e.g., a steep accelerating trend during intervention is desirable [therapeutic] for acquisition of target behaviors, but the same trend is undesirable [contra-therapeutic] if the goal is to decrease problem behaviors). To increase confidence in functional relations, trend direction and stability should align with hypothesized data patterns. The middle panel of Figure 8.7 shows a gradual accelerating trend during the first phase and a steep decelerating trend in the second phase.

The countertherapeutic trend represents a common data pattern in single case design data that might occur within a phase and particularly prior to the introduction of the independent variable. Countertherapeutic trends refer to trends that are in the opposite direction of the hypothesized direction of improvement and can establish need for the intervention. Though contra-therapeutic trends occurring in baseline might seem to provide evidence that immediate intervention is needed, it is optimal to collect data until stability is established, due to the possibility of regression to the mean (i.e., that data are likely to improve even without intervention based on random fluctuations; Kazdin, 2011).

Variability

Variability is fluctuation from one data point to the next and is the opposite of **stability**; in data with no trend (i.e., zero celerating), variability can be summarized as the range of data values within a phase or condition or as the percentage of data points falling within a given stability envelope (Franklin et al., 1996; see Tools section below). In data with trends, it can be calculated via a stability envelope around a split middle trend line (Lane & Gast, 2014). However, in general, data are described as stable or variable without numerical quantification (Kennedy, 2005). Variability might be a function of extraneous events (e.g., health issues, sporadic sleep patterns, caregiver changes) which can be temporary or permanent. Data are generally reported as either highly variable, somewhat variable, or stable; there are no guidelines for quantifying the magnitude of variability. The bottom panel of Figure 8.7 shows an initial phase with highly variable data, followed by a second phase with stable data.

It is generally recommended that phases be extended when data patterns are highly or somewhat variable. However, highly variable data might establish need for an intervention that produces stable levels of responding. That is, variability might be the predicted pattern of the dependent variable under baseline conditions, in which case condition changes might proceed if the expected pattern of behavior change is a decrease in variability. In general, even when expected, variability indicates the need for additional data in a phase (e.g., more than the minimal three data points; Kennedy, 2005; Parsonson & Baer, 1978); additional data establish that variability is likely to continue in the absence of intervention.

Immediacy

Immediacy of change across adjacent phases is the degree to which behavior change occurs as soon as the intervention is introduced (Horner et al., 2005). When a large change in level occurs immediately after introduction of a new phase, it is referred to as an *abrupt* change in level, which is indicative of an immediately "powerful" or immediately effective intervention (Parsonson & Baer, 1978). Generally, immediate and abrupt change in the dependent variable that coincides with a phase change provides a clear indication of behavior change. The more rapid (or immediate) the effect, the more convincing the inference that change in outcome

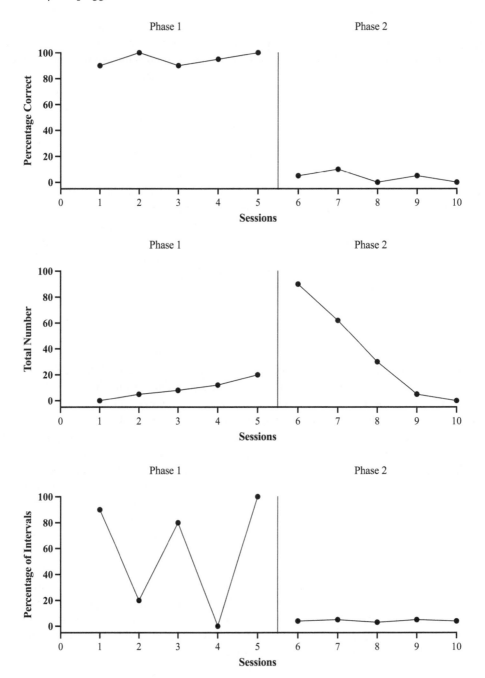

Figure 8.7 Depiction of Level, Trend, and Variability.

Note: The top panel shows high versus low level; the middle panel shows shallow versus steep trends, and the bottom panel shows highly variable versus stable data.

measures was due to manipulation of the independent variable. However, delayed changes might occur and do not necessarily preclude identification of functional relations; in these cases, confidence in functional relations is increased when (1) delay is predicted a priori (e.g., as might be the case with some academic skills), (2) latency to change (number of data points prior to change) is consistent across phases or tiers, and (3) magnitude of change in level or

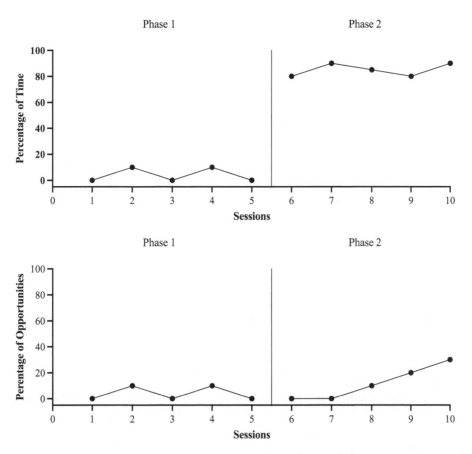

Figure 8.8 Depiction of Overlap.

Note: Top panel has no overlap; bottom panel has moderate overlap (60% of data points in Phase 2 overlap with data in Phase 1).

trend is consistent across phases or tiers (Lieberman et al., 2010; Parsonson & Baer, 1978). The top panel of Figure 8.8 shows an abrupt, immediate change between the first and second phases while the bottom panel shows a delayed and gradual change.

Overlap

Overlap refers to values of data in one phase that are in the same range of values of data in the subsequent, adjacent phase (Kennedy, 2005). Overlap can be reported as the proportion of data from one phase that is of the same level as data from an adjacent phase (e.g., percentage of overlapping data). Confidence in behavior change and the presence of a functional relation is inversely related to the proportion of overlapping data across adjacent phases (Parsonson & Baer, 1978). Larger separation and smaller proportion of overlap are generally associated with more compelling demonstrations. In Figure 8.8, the top panel shows a graph with no overlap while the bottom depicts a graph with considerable overlap.

Consistency

Consistency refers to the extent to which data patterns in one phase are similar to data patterns in other phases (Parsonson & Baer, 1978). Confident determination that a functional relation exists requires consistency in data patterns between iterations of the same condition (e.g., Baseline 1 and Baseline 2) and inconsistency in data patterns between adjacent phases representing different conditions (e.g., Baseline 1 and Intervention 1). Consistency also applies to behavior change across phases. For example, the immediacy and magnitude of behavior change should be consistent each time similar condition changes occur.

Conclusions

In this chapter, we discussed graphical display of data and analyzing those data. As a single case researcher, it is imperative that you understand how to accurately measure, display, and describe participant performance within and across study conditions to formatively and summatively analyze outcomes. In Chapters 10, 12, and 14 we will discuss these performance characteristics in relation to visual analysis of graphic displays for specific design types to establish whether a functional relation exists between dependent variables.

References

American Psychological Association. (2009). *Publication manual of the American Psychological Association* (6th ed.). Washington, DC: American Psychological Association.
Barton, E. E., & Reichow, B. (2012). Guidelines for graphing data with Microsoft Office 2007, Office 2010, and Office for Mac 2008 and 2011. *Journal of Early Intervention*, 34, 129–150.
Barton, E. E., Reichow, B., & Wolery, M. (2007). Guidelines for graphing data with Microsoft® PowerPoint™. *Journal of Early Intervention*, 29, 320–336.
Birkan, B. (2005). Using simultaneous prompting for teaching various discrete tasks to students with mental retardation. *Education and Training in Developmental Disabilities*, 40, 68–79.
Bulla, A. J., Wertalik, J. L., & Crafton, D. (2021). A preliminary investigation of question type used during response card activities on establishing concept formation in an introductory college class. *European Journal of Behavior Analysis*, 22(1), 133–150.
Carnine, D. W. (1976). Effects of two teacher presentation rates on off-task behavior, answering correctly, and participation. *Journal of Applied Behavior Analysis*, 9, 199–206.
Carr, J. E., & Burkholder, E. D. (1998). Creating single-subject design graphs with Microsoft Excel™. *Journal of Applied Behavior Analysis*, 31, 245–251.
Chazin, K. T., & Ledford, J. R. (2021). Constant time delay and system of least prompts: Efficiency and child preference. *Journal of Behavioral Education*, 30, 684–707.
Cook, B. G., Fleming, J. I., Hart, S. A., Lane, K. L., Therrien, W. J., van Dijk, W., & Wilson, S. E. (2022). A how-to guide for open-science practices in special education research. *Remedial and Special Education*, 43(4), 270–280.
Cook, B. G., Lloyd, J. W., Mellor, D., Nosek, B. A., & Therrien, W. J. (2018). Promoting open science to increase the trustworthiness of evidence in special education. *Exceptional Children*, 85(1), 104–118.
Cooper, J. O., Heron, T. E., & Heward, W. L. (2007). *Applied behavior analysis* (2nd ed.). Columbus, OH: Pearson.
Dart, E. H., & Radley, K. C. (2017). The impact of ordinate scaling on the visual analysis of single-case data. *Journal of School Psychology*, 63, 105–118.
Evans, A. L., Bulla, A. J., & Kieta, A. R. (2021). The precision teaching system: A synthesized definition, concept analysis, and process. *Behavior Analysis in Practice*, 14(3), 559–576.
Franklin, R. D., Gorman, B. S., Beasley, T. M., & Allison, D. B. (1996). Graphical display and visual analysis. In R. D. Franklin & D. B. Allison (Eds.), *Design and analysis of single-case research* (pp. 119–158). Mahwah, NJ: Lawrence Erlbaum.
Gist, C., & Bulla, A. J. (2022). A systematic review of frequency building and precision teaching with school-aged children. *Journal of Behavioral Education*, 31(1), 43–68.
Grehan, P., & Moran, D. J. (2005). Constructing single-subject reversal design graphs using Microsoft Word™: A comprehensive tutorial. *The Behavior Analyst Today*, 6, 235–256.
Hammond, D. L., Whatley, A. D., Ayres, K. M., & Gast, D. L. (2010). Effectiveness of video modeling to teach iPod use to students with moderate intellectual disabilities. *Education and Training in Autism and Developmental Disabilities*, 45(2), 525–538.
Heal, N. A., & Hanley, G. P. (2007). Evaluating preschool children's preference for motivational systems during instruction. *Journal of Applied Behavior Analysis*, 40, 249–261.

Hillman, H. L., & Miller, L. K. (2004). Designing multiple baseline graphs using Microsoft Excel™. *The Behavior Analyst Today*, 5, 372–424.

Hoch, H., McComas, J. J., Thompson, A. L., & Paone, D. (2002). Concurrent reinforcement schedules: Behavior change and maintenance without extinction. *Journal of Applied Behavior Analysis*, 35, 155–169.

Hoffmann, A. N., Bogoev, B. K., & Sellers, T. P. (2020). An evaluation of a published intervention selection model for escape-maintained problem behavior. *Journal of Behavioral Education*, 31(2), 388–403.

Horner, R. H., Carr, E. G., Halle, J., McGee, G., Odom, S., & Wolery, M. (2005). The use of single-subject research to identify evidence-based practice in special education. *Exceptional Children*, 71(2), 165–179.

Johnston, S., Nelson, C., Evans, J., & Palazolo, K. (2003). The use of visual supports in teaching young children with autism spectrum disorder to initiate interactions. *Augmentative and Alternative Communication*, 19, 86–103.

Junaid, H., Bulla, A. J., Benjamin, M., Wind, T., & Nazaruk, D. (2021). Using self-management and social media to increase steps in sedentary college students. *Behavior Analysis in Practice*, 14, 734–744.

Kazdin, A. E. (2011). *Single-case research designs: Methods for clinical and applied settings*. (2nd ed.). London: Oxford University Press.

Kennedy, C. H. (1989). Selecting consistent vertical axis scales. *Journal of Applied Behavior Analysis*, 22, 338–339.

Kennedy, C. H. (2005). *Single-case designs for educational research*. Upper Saddle River, NJ: Pearson.

Kennedy, C. H., & Souza, G. (1995). Functional analysis and treatment of eye poking. *Journal of Applied Behavior Analysis*, 28, 27–37.

Kubina, R. M., Kostewicz, D. E., Brennan, K. M., & King, S. A. (2017). A critical review of line graphs in behavior analytic journals. *Educational Psychology Review*, 29(3), 583–598.

Kubina, R. M., Morrison, R., & Lee, D. L. (2002). Benefits of adding precision teaching to behavioral interventions for students with autism. *Behavioral Interventions*, 17, 233–246.

Lambert, J. M., Morgan, A. C., Banerjee, I., Houchins-Juarez, N., & Copeland, B. (2023). Improving the process and product of intensive intervention through formative triangulation: A mixed methods report.

Lane, J. D., & Gast, D. L. (2014). Visual analysis in single case experimental design studies: Brief review and guidelines. *Neuropsychological Rehabilitation*, 24(3–4), 445–463.

Lane, J. D., Ledford, J. R., Shepley, C., Mataras, T. K., Ayres, K. M., & Davis, A. B. (2016). A brief coaching intervention for teaching naturalistic strategies to parents. *Journal of Early Intervention*, 38(3), 135–150. https://doi.org/10.1177/1053815116663178

Ledford, J. R., Chazin, K. T., Harbin, E. R., & Ward, S. E. (2017). Massed trials versus trials embedded into game play: Child outcomes and preference. *Topics in Early Childhood Special Education*, 37(2), 107–120.

Ledford, J. R., Lane, J. D., Shepley, C., & Kroll, S. M. (2016). Using teacher-implemented playground interventions to increase engagement, social behaviors, and physical activity for young children with autism. *Focus on Autism and Other Developmental Disabilities*, 31, 163–173.

Ledford, J. R., Barton, E. E., Severini, K. E., Zimmerman, K. N., & Pokorski, E. A. (2019a). Visual display of graphic data in single case design studies. *Education and Training in Autism and Developmental Disabilities*, 54(4), 315–327.

Lieberman, R. G., Yoder, P. J., Reichow, B., & Wolery, M. (2010). Visual analysis of multiple baseline across participants graphs when change is delayed. *School Psychology Quarterly*, 25(1), 28.

Lindsley, O. R. (1992). Precision teaching: Discoveries and effects. *Journal of Applied Behavior Analysis*, 25, 51–57.

Lo, Y., & Konrad, M. (2007). A field-tested task analysis for creating single-subject graphs using Microsoft® Office Excel. *Journal of Behavioral Education*, 16, 155–189.

Maglieri, K. A., DeLeon, I. G., Rodriguez-Catter, V., & Sevin, B. M. (2000). Treatment of covert food stealing in an individual with Prader-Willi syndrome. *Journal of Applied Behavior Analysis*, 33, 615–618.

Mayfield, K. H., & Vollmer, T. R. (2007). Teaching math skills to at-risk students using home-based peer tutoring. *Journal of Applied Behavior Analysis*, 40, 223–237.

Muttiah, N., Drager, K. D., Beale, B., Bongo, H., & Riley, L. (2022). The effects of an intervention using low-tech visual scene displays and aided modeling with young children with complex communication needs. *Topics in Early Childhood Special Education*, 42(1), 91–104.

Paranczek, J., Lambert, J. M., Ledford, J. R., Copeland, B. A., & MacDonald, M. (2024). Deriving relations and multiple levels of complexity following minimal instruction: A demonstration. *Journal of Applied Behavior Analysis*.

Parsonson, B. S., & Baer, D. M. (1978). The analysis and presentation of graphic data. In T. Kratchwill (Ed.) *Single subject research: Strategies for evaluating change*. New York: Academic Press.

Peredo, T. N., Zelaya, M. I., & Kaiser, A. P. (2018). Teaching low-income Spanish-speaking caregivers to implement EMT en Español with their young children with language impairment: A pilot study. *American Journal of Speech-Language Pathology*, 27(1), 136–153.

Sanders, R. M. (1978). *How to plot data*. Lawrence, KS: H & H Enterprises.

Shah, P., & Hoeffner, J. (2002). Review of graph comprehension research: Implications for instruction. *Educational Psychology Review*, 14, 47–69.

Shepley, S. B., Spriggs, A. D., Samudre, M., & Elliot, M. (2017). Increasing daily living independence using video activity schedules in middle school students with intellectual disability. *Journal of Special Education Technology*, 33(2), 71–82.

Skinner, B. F. (1965). *Science and human behavior* (No. 92904). New York: Simon and Schuster.

Tufte, E. R. (2001). *The visual display of quantitative information* (2nd ed.). Cheshire, CN: Graphics Press.

Vanselow, N. R., & Bourret, J. C. (2012). Online interactive tutorials for creating graphs with Excel 2007 or 2010. *Behavior Analysis in Practice*, 5, 40–46.

Wall, M. E., & Gast, D. L. (1999). Acquisition of incidental information during instruction for a response-chain skill. *Research in Developmental Disabilities*, 20, 31–50.

Wilder, D. A., Atwell, J., & Wine, B. (2006). The effects of varying levels of treatment integrity on child compliance during treatment with a three-step prompting procedure. *Journal of Applied Behavior Analysis*, 39, 369–373.

Williams, G., Perez-Gonzalez, L. A., & Queiroz, A. B. (2005). Using a combined blocking procedure to teach color discrimination to a child with autism. *Journal of Applied Behavior Analysis*, 38, 555–558.

Wolery, M., Anthony, L., Caldwell, N. K., Snyder, E. D., & Morgante, J. D. (2002). Embedding and distributing constant time delay in circle time and transitions. *Topics in Early Childhood Special Education*, 22, 14–25.

Wright, C. A., & Kaiser, A. P. (2017). Teaching parents enhanced milieu teaching with words and signs using the teach-model-coach-review model. *Topics in Early Childhood Special Education*, 36(4), 192–204.

Section 2
Single Case Designs

The second section of the text focuses on the three major condition-ordering systems that are used for single case research: sequential introduction and withdrawal, time-lagged introduction, and rapid iterative alternation. The appropriate use of these ordering systems allows researchers to control for or detect some threats to internal validity, allowing for conclusions to be drawn about whether functional relations exist.

We begin with an introduction to sequential introduction and withdrawal (SIW) designs in Chapter 9, describe time-lagged designs in Chapter 11, and present rapid iterative alternation (RIA) designs in Chapter 13. In Chapter 9, we discuss similarities among withdrawal, reversal, and multitreatment designs and describe a special case—the changing criterion design. In Chapter 11, we discuss the differences between multiple probe and multiple baseline designs and the variations designated by intervention target type (e.g., multiple baseline across participants versus across behaviors). We answer questions such as *are concurrent and nonconcurrent designs both acceptable*? In Chapter 13, we differentiate RIA designs for reversible and non-reversible behaviors and discuss special considerations, including design naming conventions and the assignment of behavior sets for the AATD. The overarching questions to answered in these chapter are: (1) What are features of designs using this ordering type, and how are the major designs different from one another? (2) When should you use and avoid each ordering system? (3) What threats to internal validity may be of particular concern when these designs are used?

In Chapters 10, 12, and 14, we discuss analysis of data from SIW, time-lagged, and RIA designs (respectively). For each chapter, we discuss formative analysis, summative analysis, and supplemental analyses. We also discuss issues such as non-effects (Chapter 10), masked analysis (Chapter 12), inconsistent effects across participants (Chapter 12) and differentiation (Chapter 14). Questions relevant for these chapter are: (1) What are designs using this condition-ordering type that are sufficient and insufficient for confidently determining whether functional relations exist? (2) What visual analysis considerations are specific to this design? (3) What do consistent effects, non-effects, and inconsistent effects look like in these designs, and how do you interpret them?

Chapter 15 focuses on *selecting* the best design for your question and *combining* designs when needed. Questions you should be able to answer after reading this chapter include: (1) What are some examples of when multiple designs can be used, but one is better than the other? (2) What are some examples of combined designs, and what questions would they answer?

DOI: 10.4324/9781003294726-10

9

Conducting Studies Using Sequential Introduction and Withdrawal of Conditions

Jennifer R. Ledford and Kathleen N. Tuck

Important Terms

withdrawal design, multitreatment design, reversal design, changing criterion design

---

Table of Contents

Features of Sequential Introduction and Withdrawal Designs
When to Use Sequential Introduction and Withdrawal Designs
    Strengths and Benefits
    Weaknesses and Drawbacks of SIW Designs
A-B-A-B Designs
    Reversal Variation
    Procedural Steps
Multitreatment Design
    Procedural Steps
Threats to Internal Validity
Special Case: Changing Criterion Design
    Procedural Steps
    Internal Validity for Changing Criterion Designs
Conclusions
References

Callouts

9.1 *Baseline, Business-As-Usual, and Treatment Conditions*
9.2 *Applied Example of Withdrawal Design*
9.3 *Applied Example of Reversal Design*
9.4 *Applied Example of Multitreatment Design*
9.5 *Applied Example of Changing Criterion Design*

DOI: 10.4324/9781003294726-11

In this chapter, we will begin discussing different groups of single case designs. The designs in this chapter, which use sequential introduction and withdrawal (SIW) condition ordering are perhaps the most well-known designs, with a long history of use, especially in the behavioral sciences.

Features of Sequential Introduction and Withdrawal Designs

SIW designs involve slow alternation of two conditions across four adjacent phases. When these designs are used, researchers conduct (1) at least three comparisons; (2) with the same participant, context, and behavior; (3) by introducing and withdrawing two different conditions in four adjacent phases. In other words, in the most basic form, two conditions are compared across adjacent phases in which conditions are introduced, removed, then re-introduced to see changes in a behavior for a single participant in the same context. Thus, all SIW designs include *intraparticipant replication* (see Chapter 3). To get *interparticipant replication*, you would repeat the same evaluation (e.g., use a second SIW design with a second participant).

These designs can be labeled according to conditions included in the design. For example, let's consider three potential conditions: "A," which usually refers to a baseline condition, "B," which usually refers to an intervention condition, and "C," which refers to a second intervention condition. The most common and simplest SIW design involves a comparison between baseline (A) and one intervention condition (B). That design could be called an A-B-A-B design, and the measurement occasions would be arranged in four phases, as shown below and in Figure 9.1. Note that the number of sessions per phase varies between 4 and 6 in this example; generally speaking, each phase should include at least 3 data points, with some contemporary sources suggesting the need for at least 5 data points per phase (e.g., WWC, 2020). The number of data points should ultimately also be influenced by data stability, as discussed in Chapter 10.

Phase 1	Phase 2	Phase 3	Phase 4
A A A A A	B B B B B B	A A A A	B B B B B B

The basic A-B-A-B design, most commonly referred to as a **withdrawal design** (Leitenberg, 1973), has also been referred to as the "reversal design" (Baer et al., 1968), "operant design" (Glass et al., 1975), and "equivalent time series design" (Birnbrauer et al., 1974; Campbell & Stanley, 1966). The same design, used to evaluate differences between two treatments, is generally referred to as a **multitreatment design** (Birnbrauer et al., 1974). We reiterate—these designs are identical, using the same condition ordering procedures—the only difference is that the comparison is between one baseline and one intervention condition (withdrawal) or between two intervention conditions (multitreatment). See Callout 9.1 for a discussion about differences among and between baseline and intervention conditions. An illustration of phases in the basic multitreatment design is depicted below.

Phase 1	Phase 2	Phase 3	Phase 4
B B B B B	C C C C C	B B B B	C C C C C

In addition to differentiating whether the comparison involves a baseline condition, some authors (including ourselves, in previous versions of the text) have differentiated the *type* of baseline condition. When a baseline involves business-as-usual conditions or no-treatment

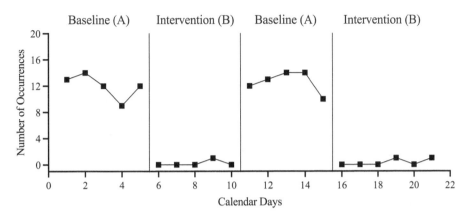

Figure 9.1 Depiction of A-B-A-B Design.

Callout 9.1 Baseline, Business-As-Usual, and Treatment Conditions

Given that the SIW designs are mostly differentiated based on whether a baseline condition is one of the primary comparisons, or what type of baseline is the primary comparison, it might be worthwhile to establish what the term *baseline* means.

No-treatment versus countertherapeutic contingency baselines. Typically, baseline refers to conditions that are absent of treatment for behaviors of interest. Two types of contrived baselines are typical—those in which there are no treatments in place and those in which the contingencies in place are countertherapeutic. For example, in many instruction studies, a baseline condition is one in which an instructor simply requests a response from a participant, with no teaching (e.g., the implementer presents a stimulus, such as a printed letter, and asks the participant to attempt to give a correct answer, such as "What letter is this?"). In some situations, a countertherapeutic contingency is used (see the "Reversal Variation" section later in this chapter). For example, in a baseline condition that occurs prior to implementing a treatment for challenging behavior, researchers might initially remove non-preferred work contingent on challenging behavior (i.e., they reinforce challenging behavior rather than a preferred alternative behavior). This is often done to confirm that the challenging behavior occurs in the expected context (e.g., that a participant consistently engages in challenging behavior when they are presented with work).

Contrived baseline conditions versus business-as-usual conditions. In addition to contriving consistent conditions with no treatment, baseline conditions can, and often do, include typically occurring activities. These types of baseline conditions are typically referred to as "business-as-usual" conditions, and they represent a different type of comparison. Rather than a true absence of any intervention, they represent prevailing conditions in typical contexts. These conditions often are not influenced by the researcher and are present prior to the research study occurring. Although they may not exert control over procedures, the researcher should document the relevant features of the conditions (e.g., presence of strategies, supports, or environmental variables that may likely influence the behavior of interest; see Chapter 6). These relevant features often become control variables held constant across all conditions of the study. This comparison allows for researchers to answer the question about what happens when a contingency is consistently applied (intervention) when compared with what typically happens in the environment. This question might be of interest from a social validity standpoint, but it could be

> more difficult to identify exactly what variables changed between baseline and intervention (i.e., the independent variable), potentially reducing confidence in conclusions that can be drawn.
>
> **Baseline versus treatment.** What is considered baseline versus treatment may seem like an easier distinction than the various types of baselines, but it can also be confusing. For example, later in this chapter we identify a study design reported by Steinhauser et al. (2021) as an A-B-A-B design, including a baseline condition (as authors themselves reported it). However, in the baseline condition, researchers reinforced appropriate vocalizations, which could be considered a treatment strategy for reducing vocal stereotypy (the target behavior of interest). Many baselines, including business-as-usual baseline conditions, likely include low-effort strategies that could theoretically positively impact the behavior of interest. Even contrived baselines could potentially include therapeutic components—for example, in one study, Chazin and colleagues included noncontingent positive attention as a baseline comparison (Chazin et al., 2018), which is often considered a treatment for challenging behavior (cf., Carr et al., 2009).
>
> The bottom line is that the terms we use to describe baseline conditions are established somewhat loosely and may be used idiosyncratically. Regardless of the designation used, you should always carefully consider the independent variables *and* the control variables most likely to impact the behavior of interest, in each condition (see Chapter 6).

conditions, the term withdrawal design has been used. When the baseline condition involves a countertherapeutic contingency, it has been referred to as a **reversal design**. Differences among these designs are listed in Table 9.1 and we discuss the distinction between withdrawal and reversal designs further in the "Withdrawal and Reversal Designs" section.

SIW designs should include at least three potential demonstrations of effect. That is, there are three points in time in which we can evaluate the relation between changes in condition procedures and changes in behavior. In the most basic design, shown in Figure 9.1, the first opportunity for comparison is between Phase 1 and Phase 2, the second is between Phase 2 and Phase 3, and the third is between Phase 3 and Phase 4. It is important to note that each of the three potential demonstrations should be adjacent (e.g., you cannot compare Phase 1 to Phase 3 or 4) and between identical conditions (e.g., every potential demonstration is a switch between the same two conditions). So, while an A-B-A-B design has three potential demonstrations of effect for the relation of interest (i.e., the relation between the dependent variable and

Table 9.1 Conventional Design Names Associated with SIW Condition Ordering

Design	Description
Prototype: Withdrawal	Multiple replications of A-B comparisons with the B condition being introduced, withdrawn, and re-introduced after an initial baseline condition (A-B-A-B)
Multitreatment	Multiple replications of **B-C** comparisons with **both conditions** being introduced, withdrawn, and re-introduced (B-C-B-C)
Reversal	Multiple replications of A-B comparisons with the B condition being introduced, withdrawn, and re-introduced after an initial baseline condition **and with one or more of the A conditions serving as a reversal of the B condition rather than simply a withdrawal (e.g., instead of withdrawing a specific contingency, an "opposite" contingency is applied).** *This <u>design</u> is functionally identical to the withdrawal variation, with <u>condition</u> procedures being different, and terms are often used interchangeably.*

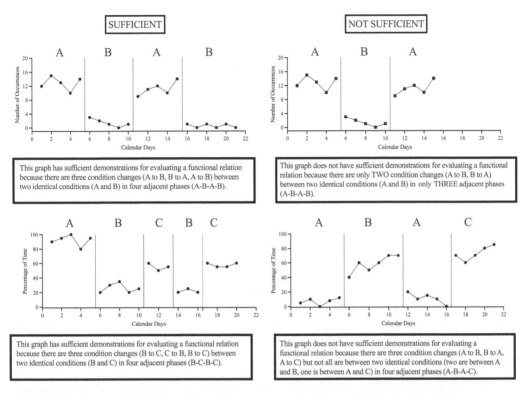

Figure 9.2 Depiction of Designs using Sequential Introduction and Withdrawal Condition Ordering that are Sufficient or Insufficient for Establishing Functional Relations.

implementation of the B condition in comparison to the A condition), an A-B-A-C design does not include three demonstrations *for the same relation*. The A-B-A-C design would have two potential demonstrations of effect for the A-B relation (comparison between Phases 1 and 2 and between Phases 2 and 3) and only one for the A-C relation (comparison between Phases 3 and 4). For this reason, an A-B-A-C design does not have sufficient potential demonstrations of effect for establishing a causal relation (see Chapter 10 for more information). Thus, even designs with four phases do not always allow for functional relations to be established—two conditions alternated across four adjacent phases must be present. See Figure 9.2 for examples of designs that do not include sufficient potential demonstrations of effect for drawing causal relations.

When to Use Sequential Introduction and Withdrawal Designs

Conditions that should result in the selection of a SIW design include:

1. A research question about the impact of two conditions on one or more behaviors.
2. Interest in behaviors that are readily reversible and likely to co-vary with condition changes with no lag or a brief lag in behavior change (e.g., behavior will change immediately or within a few sessions when conditions change).
3. Inclusion of two distinct conditions that can be practically implemented over several sequential sessions and then withdrawn for several sequential sessions.
4. Confidence withdrawal or reversal of intervention will not result in negative impacts on potential participants, resulting in an ethical concern (e.g., increases in self-injurious or dangerous behavior).

Strengths and Benefits

SIW designs provide convincing, repeated demonstrations of a relation for a single participant. It doesn't require identifying multiple participants, behaviors, or contexts for interventions like the common time-lagged designs described in Chapter 11 do (although replicating an SIW design with multiple participants will extend the evidence for external validity, see Chapter 2). Another benefit of SIW designs is that it is relatively easy to extend these designs when the expected relation is not established (e.g., an original plan for an A-B-A-B design can be extended to an A-B-C-B-C design, see "Multitreatment Design" section below). Finally, the total number of measurement occasions is generally fewer for SIW designs in comparison to the common time-lagged designs (see Chapter 11).

Weaknesses and Drawbacks of SIW Designs

One commonly cited drawback of SIW designs, particularly the withdrawal and reversal variations, is that you must remove a potentially effective intervention once you have instated it. You might question whether this is an ethical practice, especially when the targeted behaviors are socially valid and require intervention. However, the cumulative number of data points in baseline conditions in these designs (e.g., as few as three initial baseline data points and three additional baseline data points in the second baseline phase, for a total of 6) is often many fewer than those required in baseline phases in multiple baseline designs, and the calendar time duration of baseline conditions may be shorter than those required for both multiple baseline and multiple probe designs. Because adequate baseline comparisons are required to draw valid conclusions, the way in which they are implemented (e.g., long initial baseline in time-lagged designs, return to baseline in SIW designs, rapidly alternating baselines in rapid iterative alternation designs) can be viewed as a choice akin to "pick your poison." Cavell et al. (1986) demonstrated that withdrawals are viewed as generally acceptable by practitioners, although more contemporary research is needed to assess acceptability. We discuss more about weighing the pros and cons of various design choices in Chapter 15.

A-B-A-B Designs

The withdrawal (A-B-A-B) design has been considered the most convincing single case design (Tawney & Gast, 1984). Despite the strength of the design, it is used relatively infrequently compared to designs using other condition ordering (e.g., time-lagged designs, rapid iterative alternation, Chapters 11 and 13; Ledford et al., 2019). This design allows for a rigorous evaluation of repeated effects of condition changes for a single participant for one or more readily reversible behaviors. A narrative description of the use of this design is depicted in Callout 9.2, in which Joseph and colleagues evaluated the effects of an intervention designed to decrease challenging behavior of preschool children (prevent-teach-reinforce for families).

Most often, two conditions (one baseline condition and one intervention condition) are alternated across four phases in a withdrawal design. In general, a final maintenance condition is not expected when these designs are used, because a necessary condition of choosing this design is that the behavior is readily reversible and likely to revert to previous levels when a condition is withdrawn. It would not be reasonable to expect that behavior would revert to baseline levels when the B condition is withdrawn the first time, but would "maintain" when it was withdrawn a second time. Given the readily reversible nature of behaviors investigated in this design, response generalization to conditions in which the intervention is not present is also not expected. Nonetheless, authors may include conditions that incorporate components likely to facilitate maintenance. For example, if authors introduce a "B" condition in which behaviors are reinforced every time they occur (i.e., FR-1 reinforcement schedule), they might conduct a condition at the end of the study where they systematically change the availability of reinforcement (e.g., move from an FR-1 schedule to an FR-2 schedule to a VR-3 schedule) to increase the likelihood that behaviors maintain over time. Characteristics of some representative studies using withdrawal designs are shown in Table 9.2. Note that none include maintenance conditions, although Simmons and colleagues (2022) include a final condition designated as maintenance by the researchers (designated as C in the table). This condition was conducted with parents implementing B conditions, simply following a break in time and without researcher support (see Chapter 7 for a discussion of maintenance conditions).

Callout 9.2 Applied Example of Withdrawal Design

In a study described by Joseph et al. (2021), three 3-year-old children with challenging behavior and their families were nominated by a childcare center to participate in a study evaluating the effectiveness of prevent-teach-reinforce for families (PTR-F). Challenging behavior included escape-related behaviors (e.g., refusal, running away), and was individually defined for each child and measured using a partial interval recording system. When baseline conditions were in effect, families engaged in business-as-usual routine completion. When intervention conditions were in effect, families followed a behavior support plan (BSP) that was developed with the researcher using the PTR-F framework. The BSPs were individualized, but included components that facilitated predictability (e.g., social narrative, visual schedule) and included planned reinforcement opportunities (e.g., praise, access to preferred items). It is noteworthy that in the second baseline phase, researchers included only two sessions, which is fewer than contemporary standards suggest. This is likely justifiable given the expected increases in challenging behavior in these conditions.

(See related figure in Chapter 10 for analysis of outcomes.)

Reversal Variation

Leitenberg (1973) restricts the use of the term *reversal design* to those single case designs where the independent variable is truly reversed in the third phase (the second A phase), *not* simply withdrawn. Operationalized, the reversal design usually entails concurrently monitoring two behaviors during the first baseline phase (e.g., hands on desk and hands in lap; typically behaviors are incompatible). After a stable baseline level and trend are established with both behaviors, the independent variable is applied to one of the behaviors (e.g., hands on desk) during the initial B phase. If the intervention has the intended effect on this behavior, then the intervention is applied to the concurrently monitored behavior (hands in lap) in the third phase (commonly referred to as A'). It is at this juncture that the reversal design is distinguished from the withdrawal design. Not only is the intervention withdrawn from the target behavior in the reversal design, but it is also applied to a concurrently monitored behavior during the third (A') phase. If there is a decrease in the one behavior (hands on desk) and a concomitant increase in the incompatible behavior (hands in lap), then a functional relation between the independent and two dependent variables is demonstrated. When the independent variable is re-introduced to the first behavior (hands on desk) evidence of effect is further strengthened by reversing data trends of the two behaviors in B_2.

Table 9.2 Studies Using Withdrawal Designs

Reference	Design	Condition 1	Condition 2	Dependent Variable
Collins, T. A., Hawkins, R. O., Flowers, E. M., Kalra, H. D., Richard, J., & Haas, L. E. (2018). Behavior bingo: The effects of a culturally relevant group contingency intervention for students with EBD. *Psychology in the Schools*, 55(1), 63–75.	A-B-A-B	Business as usual classroom procedures (A)	Behavior bingo (B)	(1) On-task behavior, (2) Off-task behavior, (3) Disruptive behavior (all estimated via 10-s MTS)
Dillon, M. B. M., Radley, K. C., Tingstrom, D. H., Dart, E. H., & Barry, C. T. (2019). The effects of tootling via ClassDojo on student behavior in elementary classrooms. *School Psychology Review*, 48(1), 18–30.	A-B-A-B	Business as usual classroom procedures (A)	Tootling via Class Dojo (peer report of positive behavior) (B)	(1) Class-wide disruptive behavior, (2) Class-wide engagement (both estimated via 10-s MTS)
Gibson, J., Pennington, R. C., Stenhoff, D., & Hopper, J. (2009). Using desktop videoconferencing to deliver interventions to a preschool student with autism. *Topics in Early Childhood Special Education*, 29(4), 214–225.	A-B-A-B	Contrived baseline with no consequences for elopement (A)	FCT followed by continuous access to items and redirection contingent on elopement (B)	Elopement, estimated via 20-s partial interval recording
Harbin, S. G., Davis, C. A., Sandall, S., & Fettig, A. (2022). The effects of physical activity on engagement in young children with autism spectrum disorder. *Early Childhood Education Journal*, 50(8), 1461–1473.	A-B-A-B	Business as usual baseline with "sit down" song prior to large group	Intervention with "stand up" (exercise) song prior to large group	Engagement, estimated via 10-s MTS
Schilling, D. L., & Schwartz, I. S. (2004). Alternative seating for young children with autism spectrum disorder: Effects on classroom behavior. *Journal of Autism and Developmental Disorders*, 34(4), 423–432.	A-B-A-B	Typical seating (A)	Alternative seating (therapy ball) (B)	(1) Engagement and (2) Sitting (both estimated via 10-s MTS)
Simmons, C. A., Ardoin, S. P., Ayres, K. M., & Powell, L. E. (2022). Parent-implemented self-management intervention on the on-task behavior of students with autism. *School Psychology*, 37(3), 273.	A-B-A-B-A-C	Business as usual baseline for work completion with parents	Self-monitoring in home with parents + remote researcher coaching	On-task behavior, estimated via 10-s MTS
Steinhauser, H. M., Ahearn, W. H., Foster, R. A., Jacobs, M., Doggett, C. G., & Goad, M. S. (2021). Examining stereotypy in naturalistic contexts: Differential reinforcement and context-specific redirection. *Journal of Applied Behavior Analysis*, 54(4), 1420–1436.	A-B-A-B	Contrived baseline (A) with no consequences for stereotypy	Context-specific redirection contingent on vocal stereotypy	Vocal stereotypy, measured via duration recording
Wright, S., Skinner, C. H., Kirkpatrick, B. A., Daniels, S., Moore, T., & Crewdson, M. (2021). Using tootling to enhance first-grade students' use of a social skill: Evaluating the catching compliments game. *Education and Treatment of Children*, 44(2), 101–113.	A-B-A-B	Business as usual classroom procedures (A)	Catching compliments game (B)	Complimenting, estimated via 20-s partial interval recording

Note: MTS = *momentary time sampling*.

The key distinction between reversal and withdrawal designs is that when the reversal design is used, researchers (1) withdraw or remove the intervention from one behavior and (2) simultaneously apply it to an incompatible behavior. The withdrawal design, on the other hand, involves simply removing the intervention during the third phase. A reversal design is a powerful demonstration of an experimental relation because it includes three potential opportunities for demonstrating the effect of the independent variable on two incompatible behaviors. One early use of a reversal design was one whose purpose was to evaluate an intervention for a child described as withdrawn, who rarely interacted with peers (Allen et al., 1964). During the intervention condition, she received positive attention from adults when she was near peers. During the reversal, positive attention was provided when she was *not* proximal to peers. In a second example, Goetz and Baer (1973) measured the number of different block forms built by children, and then reinforced "new" form building (B). During the reversal, they instead reinforced "old" forms (previously built within the session). In both examples, the initial baseline condition (A) was not identical to the reversal condition (A'), and so you might refer to them as A-B-A'-B (with the second condition referred to as "A prime").

One common contemporary use of true reversals occurs when both A conditions represent opposite contingencies from the intervention condition. This often occurs when challenging behavior is reinforced during an initial functional analysis (FA), which serves as a baseline condition. Then, during intervention conditions, an alternative behavior is taught and reinforced (e.g., a functional communication response). The reversal is a return to initial FA conditions (e.g., reinforcing challenging behaviors instead of the communication response). Just like with the multitreatment design, we emphasize that the reversal design is methodologically identical to the withdrawal design; its name suggests procedurally different conditions rather than a truly different methodology. A review of published studies using A-B-A-B designs found authors did not label SIWs in accordance with rules identified by Leitenberg (1973) (Wine et al., 2015). See Figure 9.3 for graphical examples of designs typically referred to as *withdrawal* and *reversal*, and note that from a methodology perspective, the only difference is in the condition procedures, not the design. Callout 9.3 describes an example of a reversal design, with an FA serving as the initial baseline condition with countertherapeutic contingencies. Table 9.3 provides a list of published examples of reversal designs.

Procedural Steps

When using an A-B-A-B design, adhere to the guidelines and recommendations outlined below.

Before

1. Create your falsifiable research question(s) for a readily reversible behavior.
2. Select an appropriate (sensitive, reliable, valid, feasible) measurement system, test it, and modify as needed.
3. If you have more than one dependent variable, identify which will serve as the *primary dependent variable*, on which condition change decisions will be made.
4. Determine your comparison of interest (e.g., which two conditions will be alternated across four experimental phases) and identify what type of baseline comparison answers your research question.
5. Review previous research and your theory of change for evidence that the intervention can be slowly alternated, with carryover effects being unlikely or likely to diminish quickly.

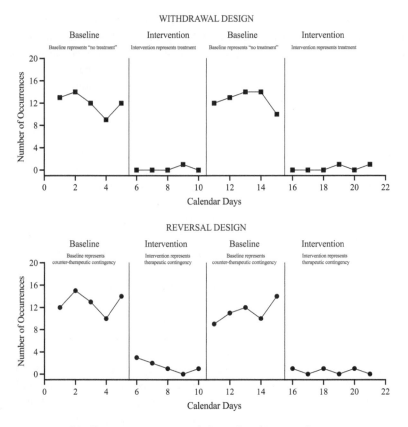

Figure 9.3 Depiction of Difference Between Withdrawal and Reversal Variations.

Callout 9.3 Applied Example of Reversal Design

In a single case design study described by Lambert and colleagues (2017), functional analyses (FAs) were conducted to establish the maintaining variables for elopement (i.e., running away) for a 10-year-old boy with autism who was referred to a university-based clinic for aggression, non-compliance, and elopement. Researchers measured the number of seconds elapsed from trial initiation in a less preferred environment until elopement occurred (i.e., latency to elopement), and reported the metric as time spent in the less preferred environment in seconds (see Chapter 4 for a brief discussion of why latency may be used as an alternative measure for count when the interest is reducing challenging behavior). Researchers also measured the occurrence (yes/no) of elopement for each trial. The baseline condition (in both phases) consisted of guiding the participant to the less preferred environment and allowing **access to the preferred environment contingent on elopement.** The intervention condition (in both phases) consisted of (1) guiding the participant to the less preferred environment, (2) presenting a contingency review of a differential reinforcement of alternative behavior (DRA) procedure wherein the participant earned tokens for engaging in alternative behaviors, and (3) allowed **access to the preferred environment contingent on token exchange.**

Table 9.3 Studies Using Reversal Designs

Reference	Design	Condition 1	Condition 2	Dependent Variable
Allen, K. E., Hart, B., Buell, J. S., Harris, F. R., & Wolf, M. M. (1964). Effects of social reinforcement on isolate behavior of a nursery school child. *Child Development*, 35(2), 511–518.	A-B-A'-B	A: Business as usual A': Reversal (reinforcement for solitary play)	B: Reinforcement for play with peers	Percentage of time spent with peers and adults, estimated via an unclear interval-based system
Davis, T. N., Gerow, S., Wicker, M., Cosottile, D., Exline, E., Swensson, R., & Lively, P. (2022). Utilizing telehealth to coach parents to implement trial-based functional analysis and treatment. *Journal of Behavioral Education*, 32(4), 703–725.	A-B-A-B	A: Access to reinforcer contingent on challenging behavior	B: Access to reinforcer contingent on mand	Occurrence of challenging behavior and mands during a trial, measured via event recording, reported as a percentage of trials with occurrence
Goetz, E. M., & Baer, D. M. (1973). Social control of form diversity and the emergence of new forms in children's blockbuilding. *Journal of Applied Behavior Analysis*, 6(2), 209–217.	A-B-A'-B	A: No reinforcement A': Reversal (reinforcement for sameness)	B: Reinforcement for novel block forms	Number of different block forms, measured via event recording
Lambert, J. M., Parikh, N., Stankiewicz, K. C., Houchins-Juarez, N. J., Morales, V. A., Sweeney, E. M., & Milam, M. E. (2019). Decreasing food stealing of child with Prader-Willi syndrome through function-based differential reinforcement. *Journal of Autism and Developmental Disorders*, 49, 721–728.	A-B-A-B	A: Access to edibles contingent on stealing	B: Intervention, access to edibles contingent on token exchange	Food stealing, measured as a latency to occurrence
Lopez, K., Dewey, A., Barton, E. E., & Hemmeter, M. L. (2017). The use of descriptive praise to increase diversity during easel painting. *Infants & Young Children*, 30(2), 133–146.	A-B-A'-B (Study 1)	A: No reinforcement A': Reversal (reinforce sameness)	B: Instruction on and reinforcement of diversity	Diversity (number of forms, brushes, and colors used), measured via event recording

6. Operationalize all condition procedures, including a baseline condition and a treatment condition. Determine if you are withdrawing an intervention or reversing a contingency between the A and B conditions.
7. Determine how and how often interobserver agreement and procedural fidelity data will be collected (i.e., develop procedural fidelity forms and procedures).
8. If possible, practice (i.e., pilot) procedures with non-participants and assess fidelity to procedures, interobserver agreement, and any changes needed in implementation or fidelity measurement.
9. Given the selected behaviors and planned conditions, are the following conditions met? If not, consider a different design.
    a. A research question about the impact of one treatment condition on one or more behaviors, relative to a baseline comparison.
    b. Behaviors that are readily reversible and likely to co-vary with condition changes with no lag or a brief lag in behavior change.
    c. Two distinct conditions that can be practically implemented over several sequential sessions and then withdrawn for several sequential sessions, without ethical concerns related to the withdrawal.
10. Identify whether you will use a priori or response-guided phase changes. Regardless, define rules for changing conditions (e.g., after five sessions, when there is a clear change in level with no data overlapping with the previous condition for at least three consecutive days), modifying conditions, and discontinuing the evaluation.
11. Identify expected data patterns and describe the conditions that will result in a functional relation determination.
12. Determine whether you will modify one or more conditions if performance is unexpected, and what the criterion for those changes will be (e.g., no change in level between conditions, assessed via visual analysis).
13. Identify participants, and, if applicable, refine definitions of target behaviors (e.g., specify exact topography of challenging behavior for a functional communication intervention).

During/After
14. Initiate the first phase and continue collecting data under those conditions until your phase change, modification, or discontinuation criteria have been met. Continue with remaining conditions until the study is completed.
15. Use visual analysis to determine whether a functional relation exists, does not exist, or whether additional data are needed (see Chapter 10).
16. Collect the specified amount of reliability and procedural fidelity data across all phases, conditions, and participants.
17. If possible, replicate with similar participants.

Multitreatment Design

The multitreatment design refers to the use of the SIW condition ordering paradigm when two intervention conditions are alternated. Often, researchers plan the use of a multitreatment design to compare two interventions. Sometimes, however, researchers use a multitreatment design when their originally planned intervention does not have the expected effects (see Callout 9.4). The most common variations are the B-C-B-C design, A-B-C-B-C design, and A-B-BC-B-BC designs (see depictions in Figure 9.4).

Multitreatment designs can be used to conduct component analyses. When these are conducted, multiple letters together connote a package, while single letters connote a simpler intervention. For example, McDaniel and Bruhn (2019) evaluated an intervention called *Coping Power* (CP) in comparison with the same intervention plus an added component (*Check-In, Check-Out,* CICO). In this example, CP represents a "B" condition, while CP+CICO represents a "BC" condition. The label "BC" is used rather than simple "C" because of the additive nature of the comparison—that is, the second condition represents the same intervention found in the first, plus an additional component.

When comparing two or more interventions in a multitreatment design, the order of conditions should be counterbalanced across participants to control for sequence effects. For example, if all participants had the same order of experimental conditions (e.g., A-B-C-B-C) you could not claim intervention C would be effective without following intervention B. A stronger arrangement is to have half of the participants follow the A-B-C-B-C sequence and half of the participants follow an A-C-B-C-B sequence. If this is done, and C is clearly superior to B across all intra- and interparticipant replications, then you could conclude C is superior regardless of its sequence with B. Note that in both cases, the functional relation is demonstrated for B and C in relation to the other; not for either in relation to baseline (A), though a description of baseline levels is helpful in describing the extent to which behavior of all participants was similar prior to intervention implementation (Birnbrauer, 1981). Table 9.4 includes a description of multitreatment designs used in published studies.

Callout 9.4 Applied Example of Multitreatment Design

Van Camp et al. (2021) describe the original purpose of their study was to evaluate the impact of MoBeGo, a Tier 2 intervention, on a participant's engagement and disruptive behavior. However, given that behavior in the original treatment condition (B) was highly variable, the researchers elected to use an A-B-BC-B-BC design rather than the originally planned A-B-A-B design. After the initial A (business-as-usual baseline condition) and B (MoBeGo) phases, the researchers introduced a BC phase, in which MoBeGo was combined with a Tier 1 intervention, CW-FIT (class-wide function-related intervention teams). Researchers used timed event recording to measure disruptive behavior and duration recording to measure academic engagement. Given their design, they were able to answer a research question about the relative effectiveness of MoBeGo versus MoBeGo combined with CW-FIT (for a graphic representation of results and an analysis of outcomes, see Chapter 10).

Procedural Steps

The basic procedural steps for conducting a multitreatment design are listed below. The steps that are distinct from the A-B-A-B steps listed above are in italic font.

Before
1. Create your falsifiable research question(s) for a readily reversible behavior.
2. Select an appropriate (sensitive, reliable, valid, feasible) measurement system, test it, and modify as needed.
3. If you have more than one dependent variable, identify which will serve as the *primary dependent variable*, on which condition change decisions will be made.

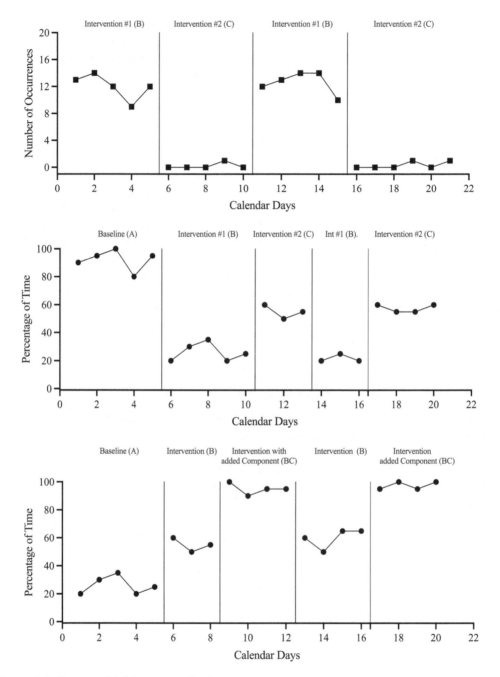

Figure 9.4 Common Multitreatment Designs.

4. Determine your comparison of interest (e.g., which two conditions will be alternated across four experimental phases) *and whether any additional conditions are necessary for providing descriptive information. Specifically consider whether an initial baseline phase is reasonable.*
5. Review previous research and your theory of change for evidence that the intervention can be slowly alternated, with carryover effects being unlikely or likely to diminish quickly.

Table 9.4 Studies Using Multitreatment Designs

Reference	Design	Experimental Analysis	Other Conditions	Dependent Variable
Addison, L. R., Piazza, C. C., Patel, M. R., Bachmeyer, M. H., Rivas, K. M., Milnes, S. M., & Oddo, J. (2012). A comparison of sensory integrative and behavioral therapies as treatment for pediatric feeding disorders. *Journal of Applied Behavior Analysis*, 4(3), 455–471.	A-B-C-B-C	Sensory integration therapy and escape (B) versus escape extinction and non–contingent reinforcement (C)	A: Descriptive information about baseline performance	(1) Bites accepted, and (2) CB per minute, both measured via event recording
Campbell, A., & Anderson, C. M. (2008). Enhancing effects of check-in/check-out with function-based support. *Behavioral Disorders*, 33(4), 233–245.	A-B-BC-B-BC	B versus BC: CICO versus CICO + opportunity to earn time with preferred peer	A: Descriptive information about baseline performance	CB, estimated with 10-s partial interval recording
LeGray, M. W., Dufrene, B. A., Mercer, S., Olmi, D. J., & Sterling, H. (2013). Differential reinforcement of alternative behavior in center-based classrooms: Evaluation of pre-teaching the alternative behavior. *Journal of Behavioral Education*, 22(1), 85–102.	B-BC-B-BC	B versus BC: Differential reinforcement of alternative behavior versus DRA + pre-teaching	None	(1) Appropriate and (2) Inappropriate vocalizations (both estimated with 10-s partial interval recording)
Majeika, C. E., Wehby, J. H., & Hancock, E. M. (2022). Are Breaks Better? A Comparison of Breaks Are Better to Check-In Check-Out. *Behavioral Disorders*, 47(2), 118–133.	B-C-B-C	B versus C: CICO intervention versus Breaks are Better intervention	None	(1) Number of disruptions, measured via timed event recording, and (2) percentage of time engaged, measured via duration recording
Winchester, C., Barton, E. E., Trimlett, G., & Ledford, J. R. (2023). Preventing challenging behavior using physical activity with young children. *Topics in Early Childhood Special Education*, 42(4), 357–369.	A-B-BC-B-BC-C (Max only)	B versus BC: Antecedent exercise (AE) versus AE plus visual supports	A: Descriptive information about baseline performance C: Descriptive information about removal of AE from treatment package	(1) CB, measured via event recording, (2) out of seat, measured via duration recording, and (3) engagement, estimated via 10-s MTS

Note: CICO = Check-in, Check-out. CB = Challenging behavior.

6. Operationalize all condition procedures, including *both treatment conditions and any additional conditions included for descriptive purposes* (e.g., an initial baseline condition).
7. Determine how and how often interobserver agreement and procedural fidelity data will be collected (i.e., develop procedural fidelity forms and procedures).
8. If possible, practice (i.e., pilot) procedures with non-participants and assess fidelity to procedures, interobserver agreement, and any changes needed in implementation or fidelity measurement.
9. Given the selected behaviors and planned conditions, are the following conditions met? If not, consider a different design.
    a. A research question about the *relative impact of two treatment conditions* on one or more behaviors.
    b. Behaviors that are readily reversible and likely to co-vary with condition changes with no lag or a brief lag in behavior change.
    c. *Two distinct treatment conditions* that can be practically implemented over several sequential sessions and then withdrawn for several sequential sessions.
10. Identify whether you will use a priori or response-guided phase changes. Regardless, define rules for changing conditions (e.g., after five sessions, when there is a clear change in level with no data overlapping with the previous condition for at least three consecutive days), modifying conditions, and discontinuing the evaluation.
11. Identify expected data patterns and describe the conditions that will result in a functional relation determination.
12. Determine whether you will modify one or more conditions if performance is unexpected, and what the criterion for those changes will be (e.g., no change in level between conditions, assessed via visual analysis).
13. Identify participants, and, if applicable, refine definitions or target behaviors (e.g., specify the exact topography of challenging behavior for a functional communication intervention).

During/After
14. Initiate the first phase and continue collecting data under those conditions until your phase change, modification, or discontinuation criteria have been met. Continue with the remaining conditions until the study is completed.
15. Use visual analysis to determine whether a functional relation exists, does not exist, or whether additional data are needed (see Chapter 10).
16. Collect the specified amount of reliability and procedural fidelity data across all phases, conditions, and participants.
17. If possible, replicate with similar participants.

Threats to Internal Validity

SIW designs are generally of relatively short duration, so *history* and *maturation* threats are potentially less likely than in the longer designs that are more typical when time-lagged condition ordering is used (see Chapter 11). Maturation threats are generally considered controlled for when performance varies consistently in the expected direction when conditions changes occur (e.g., when performance reverts back to initial baseline levels when the second baseline phase is instituted). There are no specific concerns with *testing, instrumentation, procedural infidelity, selection,* or *adaptation* threats in SIW designs. *Attrition* may be a concern, especially related to the withdrawal of a potentially effective intervention during the third phase. You can mitigate these issues by minimizing duration of that phase and informing participants of the withdrawal component of the study prior to initiation of the study. Multitreatment interference can also occur, when changes between conditions are unclear for participants or when it takes time for these condition changes to impact participant behavior. You can mitigate these issues by prolonging conditions until performance is stable and by counterbalancing conditions when reasonable, to detect any effects related to sequencing. In terms of *data instability*, you should plan to vary the number of sessions in each phase, to avoid cyclical variability coinciding with condition changes. The specific *design-related confound* that is associated with SIW designs is that repeated exposure to treatment comparisons may alter the relation between independent and dependent variables. That is, an initial demonstration of effect between A and B conditions that is "real" (i.e., accurate, naturally occurring) may not be replicated simply due to the fact that conditions are repeated as part of this design. If this confound is likely, you should consider using a different design. See Table 9.5 for a list of potential threats to internal validity, including considerations specific to SIW designs as well as general procedures for preventing or reducing the impact of these threats across design types.

Table 9.5 General Internal Validity Information and SIW-Specific Considerations (In Bold)

Threat	Preventing or Reducing Impact
History: events that occur during an experiment, unrelated to planned procedures	Control outside sources of influence, continue phase until data are stable; describe likely history events in narrative.
Maturation: changes in behavior due to the passage of time	Design a short duration study, include an intervention with effects above and beyond maturation.
Testing: repeated assessment	Design conditions that do not over or underestimate participant performance; choose treatment with effects above and beyond testing effects; if inhibitive effects are noted, modify baseline so accurate performance is measured.
Instrumentation: Problems with measurement	Operationally define behaviors; use appropriate measurement procedures; collect precise reliability data; regularly conduct discrepancy discussions; visually analyze data from both observers to identify bias or drift; when possible, use naïve observers.
Procedural Infidelity: Lack of adherence to condition protocols	Operationally define all procedures; train implementers to a criterion level before the study begins; support implementation, collect and formatively analyze data, especially early in a phase, with modifications to training and supports provided as needed.
Selection: Including certain participants and not others	Describe all rules used to select participants (i.e., inclusion criteria); describe procedures used to choose participants when more participants met inclusion criteria than could participate, and randomly select from this pool if possible.
Attrition: When participants withdraw from the study prior to completion	Manage baseline durations; choose participants likely to benefit from the intervention; be forthcoming about difficulties that associated with research participation; include all data from all participants, even ones who withdraw, in final research reports. **Minimize time in second baseline condition, inform participants of withdrawal component prior to study initiation**
Multitreatment Interference: When behavior is influenced by procedures in conditions not currently being experienced	Provide cues that allow participants to understand differences between conditions. **Increase condition duration to allow effects to diminish; counterbalance condition order to detect sequence effects**

(Continued)

Table 9.5 Continued

Threat	Preventing or Reducing Impact
Data Instability: Large differences in data from session-to-session within a single condition	Control for variables contributing to variability, continue conditions until data are stable or do not exceed expectations for variability, use interventions likely to impact behavior above and beyond variability seen in baseline; do not intervene following an outlying data point *in either therapeutic or countertherapeutic directions.* **Vary phase length to avoid cyclical variability concerns**
Adaptation: Time at beginning of study when participants behavior may not represent typical performance	Allow for an adaptation period before data collection begins; continue baseline conditions until data are stable; use measurement procedures that are not intrusive.
Design-related Confounds: When condition ordering influences identification of relations	Understand the theory of change relevant to your study; choose an appropriate design type.

Special Case: Changing Criterion Designs

Sidman (1960) described a research design that Hall (1971) named the **changing criterion design**. This design has traditionally been considered to be a variation of the time-lagged multiple baseline design and has features in common with that design, but it also has characteristics in common with the SIW family. We discuss it here because our procedural steps for using this design are most similar to those for designs using SIW condition ordering and it may sometimes be a viable alternative to other SIW designs when withdrawal or reversals are not ethically viable.

The changing criterion may be appropriate for practitioners and applied researchers who wish to evaluate instructional or therapy programs that require gradual, stepwise changes in behavior. This design can be used to increase or decrease behaviors already in a participants' repertoire. Hartmann and Hall (1976) describe the changing criterion design as follows:

> The design requires initial baseline observations on a single target behavior. This baseline phase is followed by implementation of a treatment program in each of a series of treatment phases. Each treatment phase is associated with a stepwise change in criterion rate for the target behavior. Thus, each phase of the design provides a baseline for the following phase. When the rate of the target behavior changes with each stepwise change in the criterion, therapeutic change is replicated and experimental control is demonstrated.
>
> (p. 527)

A prototypical changing criterion design is shown in Figure 9.5. In this example, a child engages in 10–15% of assigned math problems in the initial baseline phase. During the first phase of intervention, the criterion is set at 15%, which the child meets. During the next three phases, the required amount increases systematically to 25, 40, and 65%. Then, the requirement moves in a countertherapeutic direction to 35%. Finally, criteria are increased to 60%, 80%, and 95% (the terminal criterion).

Though the changing criterion design has not been widely cited in the applied research literature (e.g., only used in just over 100 articles; Klein et al., 2017), Hartmann and Hall (1976) have suggested it may be useful to monitor a wide range of programs (e.g., systematically increasing correct homework completion, decreasing number of cigarettes smoked per day). Researchers interested in assessing intervention programs that employ differential reinforcement procedures may find the changing criterion design helpful. For example, if a child completed 20–25% of math problems assigned during an independent work period during an initial baseline phase, a changing criterion design could be used such that each subsequent phase

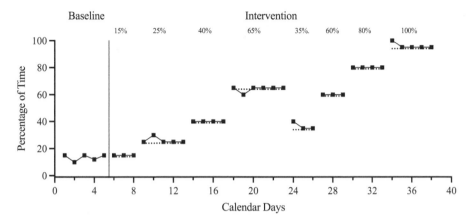

Figure 9.5 Changing Criterion Design.

required an increasing percentage of completion (e.g., criterion 1=30%, criterion 2=50%, criterion 3=80%, criterion 4=65%, criterion 5=100%) to receive reinforcement.

Two variations of changing criterion designs are noteworthy. The first is a changing criterion design with behavior measurement across response topographies. In the typical changing criterion design, behavior is shaped within a response class (e.g., the amount of behavior is changed; the topography is not). A variation of the design may be used such that progressively difficult behaviors or similar behaviors under different environmental conditions are required. For example, Koegel et al. (2004) required changes behavior topography to decrease problem behavior related to noise sensitivity. Changes in criterion for one participant included: Walking by closed bathroom door without toilet flushing, standing 75 feet from open bathroom door while toilet is flushed; standing inside closed stall while toilet is flushed. A similar modified changing criterion design was used by Birkan et al. (2011) to teach children with autism to cooperate with medically necessary injections.

The second variation of the changing criterion design is the distributed criterion design (McDougall, 2006). This design is appropriate when varying amounts of time should be allotted for engaging in multiple, mutually exclusive tasks. McDougall provides an applied example related to research productivity and work towards three writing tasks. This design might also be appropriate for shaping appropriate social behavior (e.g., reinforcing a certain amount of time spent on responding to peers, listening to peers, and engaging in solitary behavior) or independent after school behaviors (e.g., completing chores, engaging in physical activity, doing homework, and playing video games) that may vary over time. This design has not been widely used but may be advantageous when several mutually exclusive behaviors are of interest.

Although it is not frequently used in this way, it is possible that changing criterion designs may provide an alternative to true withdrawals of intervention, which may be ethically preferable in some circumstances. For example, if a child engages in tantrum behaviors any time a task direction is given in baseline, and you are interested in increasing functional responses (requesting an extra minute, complying with the direction, asking for help), you might use a changing criterion design to gradually increase the number of functional responses required prior to access to reinforcement. If you include at least one countertherapeutic change during the intervention condition (e.g., require 3 functional responses and then 2 functional responses), you can evaluate the extent to which the intervention contingencies control behavior, without needing to revert to a true baseline condition, which could be aversive and erode trust between the researcher and participant. Table 9.6 includes a list of changing criterion designs found in published studies.

Table 9.6 Studies Using Changing Criterion Designs

Reference	Intervention	Dependent Variable	Criterion Levels	Include Reversal?
Flood, W. A. & Wilder, D. A. (2004). The use of differential reinforcement and fading to increase time away from a caregiver in a child with separation anxiety disorder. *Education and Treatment of Children*, 27, 1–8.	Reinforcement	Exercise, measured via event recording with automatic counters and reported as number of RPMs	Varied by participant (ex: 80, 115, 130, RPMs)	Yes
Grey, I., Healy, O., Leader, G., & Hayes, D. (2009). Using a Time Timer™ to increase appropriate waiting behavior in a child with developmental disabilities. *Research in Developmental Disabilities*, 30(2), 359–366.	Direction to "wait," visual support, reinforcement	Waiting, measured via duration recording and reported as seconds per session	Many	Yes
Lambert, J. M., Parikh, N., Stankiewicz, K. C., Houchins-Juarez, N. J., Morales, V. A., Sweeney, E. M., & Milam, M. E. (2019). Decreasing food stealing of child with Prader-Willi syndrome through function-based differential reinforcement. *Journal of Autism and Developmental Disorders*, 49, 721–728.	Response blocking, DRO, DRA	Food stealing, measured via latency recording and reported in seconds	3s, 5s, 7s, 11s, 16s, 24s, 36s	No
Luiselli, J. K. (2000). Cueing, demand fading, and positive reinforcement to establish self-feeding and oral consumption in a child with chronic food refusal. *Behavior Modification*, 24(3), 348–358.	Reinforcement	Self-feeding, measured with event recording and reported as number per meal	1, 2, 3, 4, 8, 10	No

Note: DRO = differential reinforcement of other behaviors. DRA = differential reinforcement of alternative behaviors. * = Changing criterion element was part of a combination design.

Callout 9.5 Applied Example of Changing Criterion Design

Wheatley et al. (2020) used a changing criterion design to evaluate an intervention designed to increase compliance with wearing an "anti-strip" suit to prevent inappropriate fecal behavior. The participant was a 12-year-old autistic boy who received educational services in a self-contained classroom with one-to-one support. Throughout, the behaviors of compliance, suit-related disruptive behavior, and inappropriate fecal behavior were measured. The primary variable, compliance, was measured via the number of seconds, minutes, or hours of compliance with suit-related demands. Initially, these demands were increasingly complex (e.g., variation in response topographies variation described above). Once Jacob was wearing the suit, the time increased from 20 seconds to 6 hours. Maintenance probes and generalization to a new high school classroom were measured; it is unclear the extent to which intervention procedures were still in place during these probes but given the variable of "compliance" it seems likely that these were trials conducted under intervention conditions. See Chapter 10 for a graphical depiction of data and analysis of the outcomes of this study.

Procedural Steps

The basic procedural steps for conducting a changing criterion design are listed below. The steps that are distinct from the SIW steps listed earlier in the chapter are in italic font.

1. Create a research question about the impact of intervention on *gradual, stepwise changes on the dependent variable of interest*.
2. Select an appropriate (sensitive, reliable, valid, feasible) measurement system, test it, and modify as needed.
3. If you have more than one dependent variable, identify which will serve as the *primary dependent variable*, on which condition change decisions will be made.
4. Determine your comparison of interest, including a baseline condition and a treatment condition *that can include various criterion levels*.
5. Operationalize all condition procedures, including a baseline condition and a treatment condition *and identify rules for how you will change criteria across the intervention condition*.
6. Determine how and how often interobserver agreement and procedural fidelity data will be collected (i.e., develop procedural fidelity forms and procedures).
7. If possible, practice (i.e., pilot) procedures with non-participants and assess fidelity to procedures, interobserver agreement, and any changes needed in implementation or fidelity measurement.
8. Given the selected behaviors and planned conditions, are the following conditions met? If not, consider a different design.
    a. A research question about the impact of *an intervention condition relative to a baseline condition*.
    b. Interest in behavior that is *readily reversible and likely to correspond to criterion levels set by the researcher*.
    c. *The intervention condition can be modified to include multiple criterion levels*.
9. Specify how and when a reversal of contingencies will be included (i.e., reverting back to a less-optimal criterion at least once during the study).
10. Identify whether you will use a priori or response-guided phase changes.
    a. Define rules for changing conditions (e.g., after five sessions, when there is a clear change in level with no data overlapping with the previous condition for at least three consecutive days), modifying conditions, and discontinuing the evaluation.
    b. *Include decisions about how closely the behavior must align with set criterion levels*.
11. Identify expected data patterns and describe the conditions that will result in a functional relation determination.
12. Determine whether you will modify one or more conditions if performance is unexpected, and what the criterion for those changes will be (e.g., no change in level between conditions, assessed via visual analysis).

13. Identify participants, and, if applicable, refine definitions, target behaviors, *and criterion levels*.
14. Initiate the first phase and continue collecting data under those conditions until your phase change, modification, or discontinuation criteria have been met. Continue with remaining phases until the study is completed.

Internal Validity for Changing Criterion Designs

Two threats specific to the internal validity of changing criterion designs are worth mentioning. The first is maturation. The gradual, stepwise changes in behavior that are expected in changing criterion designs look somewhat similar to growth over time. For this reason, it is <u>critical</u> to include at least one criterion change that is countertherapeutic. That is, you revert to a previous criterion level. If the behavior also reverts to previous levels, you have convincing evidence that your intervention, rather than maturation, is responsible for behavior change. Without this reversal, conclusions drawn from this design are much less credible. The second likely threat to internal validity in changing criterion designs is an instrumentation threat that is easily avoided. It is the failure to allow for the full range of responses during every opportunity. For example, if your criterion for reinforcement is that a child must eat five bites of food, you must not restrict the child's consumption to *only* allow him to eat this much. This artificially restricts the range of the data and prevents a true assessment of whether behavior levels matched criterion levels.

Conclusions

Designs using SIW condition ordering require a reversible behavior (i.e., one that will revert to baseline levels when intervention is removed) and require at least one independent variable that can be introduced and withdrawn. They provide convincing demonstrations, with intraparticipant replications for each design. The changing criterion design is applicable in fewer situation (i.e., when behavior change corresponding to a set criterion is likely), but may be especially helpful for avoiding full withdrawals when there are ethical concerns with doing so.

References

Addison, L. R., Piazza, C. C., Patel, M. R., Bachmeyer, M. H., Rivas, K. M., Milnes, S. M., & Oddo, J. (2012). A comparison of sensory integrative and behavioral therapies as treatment for pediatric feeding disorders. *Journal of Applied Behavior Analysis*, 45(3), 455–471.

Allen, K. E., Hart, B., Buell, J. S., Harris, F. R., & Wolf, M. M. (1964). Effects of social reinforcement on isolate behavior of a nursery school child. *Child Development*, 35(2), 511–518.

Baer, D. M., Wolf, M. M., & Risley, T. R. (1968). Some current dimensions of applied behavior analysis. *Journal of Applied Behavior Analysis*, 1(1), 91–97.

Birkan, B., Krantz, P. J., & McClannahan, L. E. (2011). Teaching children with autism spectrum disorders to cooperate with injections. *Research in Autism Spectrum Disorders*, 5(2), 941–948.

Birnbrauer, J. S. (1981). External validity and experimental investigation of individual behavior. *Analysis and Intervention in Developmental Disabilities*, 1(2), 117–132.

Birnbrauer, J. S., Peterson, C. R., & Solnick, J. V. (1974). Design and interpretation of studies of single subjects. *American Journal of Mental Deficiency*, 79(2), 191–203.

Campbell, A., & Anderson, C. M. (2008). Enhancing effects of check-in/check-out with function-based support. *Behavioral Disorders*, 33(4), 233–245.

Campbell, D. T., & Stanley, J. C. (1966). *Experimental and quasi-experimental designs for research*. Chicago, IL: Rand McNally.

Carr, J. E., Severtson, J. M., & Lepper, T. L. (2009). Noncontingent reinforcement is an empirically supported treatment for problem behavior exhibited by individuals with developmental disabilities. *Research in Developmental Disabilities*, 30(1), 44–57.

Cavell, T. A., Frentz, C. E., & Kelley, M. L. (1986). Consumer acceptability of the single case withdrawal design: Penalty for early withdrawal?. *Behavior Therapy*, 17(1), 82–87.

Chazin, K. T., Ledford, J. R., Barton, E. E., & Osborne, K. C. (2018). The effects of antecedent exercise on engagement during large group activities for young children. *Remedial and Special Education*, 39(3), 158–170.

Collins, T. A., Hawkins, R. O., Flowers, E. M., Kalra, H. D., Richard, J., & Haas, L. E. (2018). Behavior bingo: The effects of a culturally relevant group contingency intervention for students with EBD. *Psychology in the Schools*, 55(1), 63–75.

Davis, T. N., Gerow, S., Wicker, M., Cosottile, D., Exline, E., Swensson, R., & Lively, P. (2022). Utilizing telehealth to coach parents to implement trial-based functional analysis and treatment. *Journal of Behavioral Education*, 32(4), 703–725.

Dillon, M. B. M., Radley, K. C., Tingstrom, D. H., Dart, E. H., & Barry, C. T. (2019). The effects of tootling via ClassDojo on student behavior in elementary classrooms. *School Psychology Review*, 48(1), 18–30.

Gibson, J., Pennington, R. C., Stenhoff, D., & Hopper, J. (2009). Using desktop videoconferencing to deliver interventions to a preschool student with autism. *Topics in Early Childhood Special Education*, 29(4), 214–225.

Glass, G. V., Willson, V. L., & Gottman, L. J. (1975). *Design and analysis of time-series experiments*. Boulder, CO: Colorado Associated University Press.

Goetz, E. M., & Baer, D. M. (1973). Social control of form diversity and the emergence of new forms in children's blockbuilding. *Journal of Applied Behavior Analysis*, 6(2), 209–217.

Hall, R. V. (1971). *Managing behavior: Behavior modificacation, the measurement of behavior*. Lawrence, Kansas: H & H Enterprises.

Harbin, S. G., Davis, C. A., Sandall, S., & Fettig, A. (2022). The effects of physical activity on engagement in young children with autism spectrum disorder. *Early Childhood Education Journal*, 50(8), 1461–1473.

Hartmann, D. P., & Hall, R. V. (1976). The changing criterion design. *Journal of Applied Behavior Analysis*, 9(4), 527–532.

Joseph, J. D., Strain, P. S., & Dunlap, G. (2021). An experimental analysis of Prevent-Teach-Reinforce for Families (PTR-F). *Topics in Early Childhood Special Education*, 41(2), 115–128.

Klein, L. A., Houlihan, D., Vincent, J. L., & Panahon, C. J. (2017). Best practices in utilizing the changing criterion design. *Behavior Analysis in Practice*, 10(1), 52–61.

Koegel, R. L., Openden, D., & Koegel, L. K. (2004). A systematic desensitization paradigm to treat hypersensitivity to auditory stimuli in children with autism in family contexts. *Research & Practice for Persons with Severe Disabilities*, 29(2), 122–134.

Lambert, J. M., Finley, C. I., & Caruthers, C. E. (2017). Trial-based functional analyses as basis for elopement intervention. *Behavior Analysis: Research and Practice*, 17(2), 166.

Lambert, J. M., Parikh, N., Stankiewicz, K. C., Houchins-Juarez, N. J., Morales, V. A., Sweeney, E. M., & Milam, M. E. (2019). Decreasing food stealing of child with Prader-Willi syndrome through function-based differential reinforcement. *Journal of Autism and Developmental Disorders*, 49(2), 721–728.

Ledford, J. R., Barton, E. E., Severini, K. E., Zimmerman, K. N., & Pokorski, E. A. (2019). Visual display of graphic data in single case design studies. *Education and Training in Autism and Developmental Disabilities*, 54(4), 315–327.

LeGray, M. W., Dufrene, B. A., Mercer, S., Olmi, D. J., & Sterling, H. (2013). Differential reinforcement of alternative behavior in center-based classrooms: Evaluation of pre-teaching the alternative behavior. *Journal of Behavioral Education*, 22(2), 85–102.

Leitenberg, H. (1973). The use of single-case methodology in psychotherapy research. *Journal of Abnormal Psychology*, 82(1), 87–101.

Lopez, K., Dewey, A., Barton, E. E., & Hemmeter, M. L. (2017). The use of descriptive praise to increase diversity during easel painting. *Infants & Young Children*, 30(2), 133–146.

Majeika, C. E., Wehby, J. H., & Hancock, E. M. (2022). Are Breaks Better? A Comparison of Breaks Are Better to Check-In Check-Out. *Behavioral Disorders*, 47(2), 118–133.

McDaniel, S. C., & Bruhn, A. L. (2019). Examining the additive effects of check-in/check-out to coping power. *The Elementary School Journal*, 119(4), 580–600.

McDougall, D. (2006). The distributed criterion design. *Journal of Behavioral Education*, 15(4), 237–247.

Schilling, D. L., & Schwartz, I. S. (2004). Alternative seating for young children with autism spectrum disorder: Effects on classroom behavior. *Journal of Autism and Developmental Disorders*, 34(4), 423–432.

Sidman, M. (1960). *Tactics of scientific research*. New York: Basic books.

Simmons, C. A., Ardoin, S. P., Ayres, K. M., & Powell, L. E. (2022). Parent-implemented self-management intervention on the on-task behavior of students with autism. *School Psychology*, 37(3), 273.

Steinhauser, H. M., Ahearn, W. H., Foster, R. A., Jacobs, M., Doggett, C. G., & Goad, M. S. (2021). Examining stereotypy in naturalistic contexts: Differential reinforcement and context-specific redirection. *Journal of Applied Behavior Analysis*, 54(4), 1420–1436.

Tawney, J. W., & Gast, D. L. (1984). *Single subject research in special education*. Columbus, OH: Merrill.

Van Camp, A. M., Wehby, J. H., Copeland, B. A., & Bruhn, A. L. (2021). Building from the bottom up: The importance of Tier 1 supports in the context of Tier 2 interventions. *Journal of Positive Behavior Interventions*, 23(1), 53–64.

What Works Clearinghouse (2020). *Procedures and standards handbook* (v. 4.1). https://ies.ed.gov/ncee/wwc/Docs/referenceresources/WWC-Standards-Handbook-v4-1-508.pdf

Wheatley, T. L., Goulet, M., Mann, K., & Lanovaz, M. J. (2020). Differential negative reinforcement of other behavior to increase compliance with wearing an anti-strip suit. *Journal of Applied Behavior Analysis*, 53(2), 1153–1161.

Winchester, C., Barton, E. E., Trimlett, G., & Ledford, J. R. (2023). Preventing challenging behavior using physical activity with young children. *Topics in Early Childhood Special Education*, 42(4), 357–369.

Wine, B., Freeman, T. R., & King, A. (2015). Withdrawal versus reversal: A necessary distinction?. *Behavioral Interventions*, 30(1), 87–93.

Wright, S., Skinner, C. H., Kirkpatrick, B. A., Daniels, S., Moore, T., & Crewdson, M. (2021). Using tootling to enhance first-grade students' use of a social skill: Evaluating the catching compliments game. *Education and Treatment of Children*, 44(2), 101–113.

10
Analyzing Data from Studies Using Sequential Introduction and Withdrawal of Conditions

Jennifer R. Ledford and Katie Wolfe

Important Terms

formative analysis, response-guided decision making, summative analysis, functional relation

Table of Contents
Formative Analysis and Phase Change Decisions
Summative Analysis and Functional Relation Determination
   Design Adequacy
   Data Adequacy
   Control for Likely Threats to Internal Validity
   Outcome Evaluation
Supplemental Analyses
   Magnitude Estimates
   Overlap Estimates
Describing Visual Analysis
   Visual Analysis Procedures
   Visual Analysis Results
Conclusions
References

Callouts

10.1 *Should I Include Extra Phases to Establish Non-Effects?*
10.2 *Reliability of Visual Analysis*
10.3 *Applied Example of Withdrawal Design*
10.4 *Applied Example of Reversal Design*
10.5 *Applied Example of Multitreatment Design*
10.6 *Applied Example of Changing Criterion Design*

DOI: 10.4324/9781003294726-12

162 • Jennifer R. Ledford and Katie Wolfe

As discussed in Chapter 8, the primary method of analysis for data from single case design studies is visual analysis (Hersen & Barlow, 1976; Gast, 2010, Kazdin, 2020; Tawney & Gast, 1984), for both formative and summative decision making. In this chapter, we will discuss analysis of data from studies using sequential introduction and withdrawal (SIW) designs, including the necessary conditions for analyzing data, formative and summative data analysis and decision-making, and supplemental analyses. We use terminology introduced in Chapter 8, including data characteristics assessed within a given phase (*level, trend, variability/stability*), between two phases (*immediacy, overlap*), and across multiple comparisons in the same design (*consistency*).

As discussed in Chapter 9, designs using SIW condition ordering can be used when you have a question about a relation between a readily reversible behavior and one treatment condition relative to baseline (A-B-A-B design) or the relation between a readily reversible behavior and two treatment conditions (multitreatment design). These designs are not appropriate when non-reversible behaviors are of interest (see Chapters 11 and 13), or when simultaneous comparisons between more than two conditions are of interest (see Chapter 13).

Formative Analysis and Phase Change Decisions

In this chapter, and in Chapters 12 and 14, we discuss both formative and summative evaluation of data in the context of single case design studies. Although summative evaluation is expected across types of research, formative analysis is somewhat unique to single case studies. Ultimately, the purpose of formative analysis is to answer the question "What should I do at this point in the experiment?" and the purpose of summative analysis is to answer the question "What evidence do I have that the relation of interest exists?" Both of these questions are of considerable importance, not only in research, but also for practitioners of the fields that commonly use single case research (e.g., teachers, behavior analysts, occupational therapists, speech-language pathologists). For example, practitioners might use data-based decision making to determine whether adequate progress is being made, and if not, what modifications should be made to improve progress (Kipfmiller et al., 2019; Wolfe et al., 2023).

Formative analysis refers to evaluating data collected during a study *while the study is ongoing* and is generally followed with making decisions in relation to these data. For example, following each measurement occasion, researchers plot their data on a graph (see Chapter 8). Then, they use those graphed data to engage in **response-guided decision making** to determine whether to continue, modify, or discontinue a particular phase. As shown in Figure 10.1,

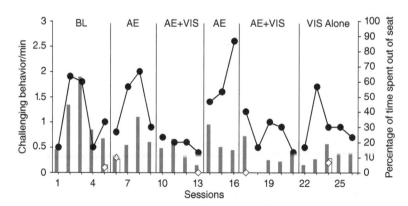

Figure 10.1 Example Graph with Evidence of Formative Visual Analysis used to Determine Discontinuation of Ineffective Intervention (AE) and Initiation of a New Intervention (AE+VIS).

Source: Winchester, C., Barton, E. E., Trimlett, G., & Ledford, J. R. (2023). Preventing challenging behavior using physical activity with young children. *Topics in Early Childhood Special Education*, 42(4), 357–369.

Winchester and colleagues (2023) used formative analysis to *discontinue* a phase. They initially implemented an antecedent exercise intervention (AE) with a participant. Because the data in this phase were not improved relative to the baseline phase, they discontinued the AE phase and implemented the next phase, which included a condition in which AE was combined with visual supports (VIS). This type of formative decision is relatively straightforward in studies that use SIW condition ordering, as a withdrawal design (e.g., A-B-A-B) can be transformed into a multitreatment design (e.g., A-B-C-B-C) if the initial intervention does not improve the behavior relative to baseline.

Figure 10.2 includes hypothetical data from an A-B-A-B design with decisions about continuation, modification, and withdrawal. In this example, we briefly describe the data characteristics that led us to decisions to continue or discontinue phases, although we acknowledge that different decisions could have reasonably been made at some points. For example, after the first, second, and third measurement occasions, we decided to continue the phase because more data were necessary to establish a stable pattern. We determined that a sufficiently stable

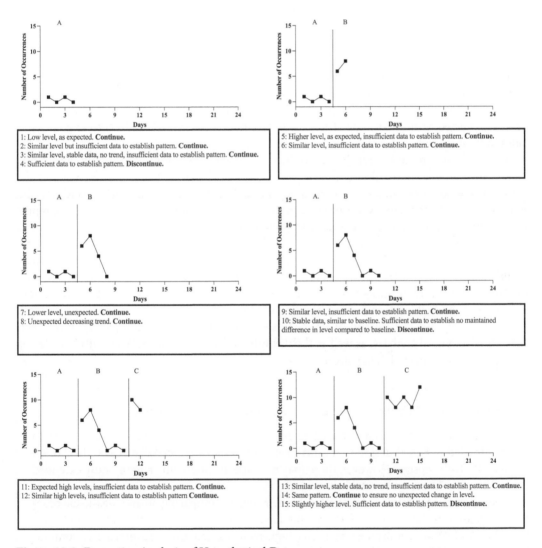

Figure 10.2 Formative Analysis of Hypothetical Data.

Note: Each number represents the data point after which the corresponding formative decision was made, followed by the analysis of the data pattern and the formative decision to continue or discontinue the phase.

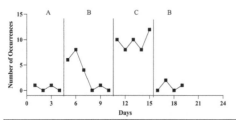
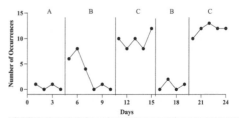

16: Expected low levels, insufficient data to establish pattern. **Continue.**
17: Similar level, insufficient data to establish pattern. **Continue.**
18: Similar level, stable data, no trend, insufficient data to establish pattern. **Continue.**
19: Sufficient data to establish pattern. **Discontinue.**

20: Expected high levels, insufficient data to establish pattern. **Continue.**
21: Similar level, insufficient data to establish pattern. **Continue.**
22: Slightly increasing trend, expected high levels. **Continue.**
23: Stable data, high levels, insufficient data to establish pattern. **Continue.**
24: Same pattern. Sufficient data to establish oattern. **Discontinue.**

Figure 10.2 (Continued)

data pattern had been established in baseline after four measurement occasions. It might be reasonable to have made that decision after three measurement occasions (a less conservative decision) or to confirm the patterns after five measurement occasions (a more conservative decision). As described in Chapter 9, some contemporary guidelines suggest including at least five data points for each phase in SIW designs, so you might elect to collect a fifth data point even if you believe a sufficient pattern has been established, to meet certain standards, although it is generally not recommended from an ethical standpoint (see Chapter 16). It is important to (1) establish any rules you will use prior to data collection (e.g., discontinue after pattern has been established or must include at least five data points per phase), and (2) to explain your rules in final reports.

It is also worth pointing out that in addition to different decisions made about continuing or discontinuing a phase, different decisions could have been made about the course of the study in general. For example, if you wanted to establish definitively that the B condition did not result in differences in level compared to the A condition, you might discontinue B, repeat both A and B phases, and then conduct additional comparisons between A and C or B and C with additional phases. For example, you could have conducted an A-B-A-B-C-B-C design, which would have allowed you to establish relations between A and B as well as those between B and C (see Callout 10.1). Or, you could have added a component to the B condition and conducted an A-B-BC-B-BC design. Moreover, if B was a resource-intensive condition, you might elect to first conduct another A condition and then compare A to C (rather than comparing B to C), in an A-B-A-C-A-C design. We hope this example illustrates the complexity in conducting formative visual analysis, as well as the flexibility of studies using SIW condition ordering to respond to unexpected data patterns.

Callout 10.1 Should I Include Extra Phases to Establish Non-Effects?

In Chapters 9 and 10, we have described decision making which led authors to pivot from an intended A-B-A-B design to a multitreatment design—typically an A-B-C-B-C or an A-B-BC-B-BC design. However, there may be value in conducting a temporally extended multitreatment design to establish non-effects.

For example, Severini et al. (2019) were interested in comparing business-as-usual baseline conditions (A) to a low-effort peer-mediated intervention (stay-play-talk, SPT) (B) for a child with Down syndrome who used a high-tech augmentative and alternative communication (AAC) device. They added two conditions that were originally unplanned: (C) SPT with modified reinforcement, and (D) SPT with modified arrangements.

During the initial A-B-A-B comparison (baseline versus stay-play-talk), only small and inconsistent changes in social interactions were identified and only for one of three children during the first B (SPT) phase. Instead of immediately pivoting to a different intervention or variation, the continued the intervention completed the planned A-B-A-B comparison. If they had used an A-B-C-D-C-D design instead of the A-B-A-B-C-D-C-D design that they used, they would have only been able to answer an experimental question about the impacts of C relative to D. Because they used the more complicated design, they were able to answer two questions: (1) The impact of B conditions compared to A conditions, and (2) the impact of C conditions relative to D conditions. Of course, the drawback is that it took additional resources to conduct the 11 additional sessions and resulted in a delay in access to the most successful variation (Condition D).

In addition to providing more information generally, it is especially important for single case design researchers to identify *non-effects* (Barton, 2019; Tincani & Travers, 2018). That is, in addition to determining what practices and procedures are likely to work under certain condition, for changing specific behaviors, for identified participants, it is also important to identify which procedures are <u>unlikely</u> to result in behavior change and to disseminate those findings.

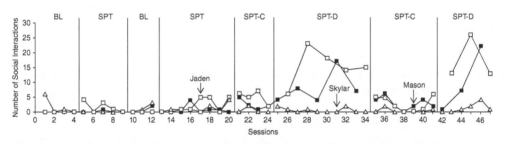

Source: Severini, K. E., Ledford, J. R., Barton, E. E., & Osborne, K. C. (2019). Implementing stay-play-talk with children who use AAC. *Topics in Early Childhood Special Education*, 38(4), 220–233.

Summative Analysis and Functional Relation Determination

<u>**Summative analysis**</u> also generally occurs via visual analysis of graphic data, and it involves evaluating data for the purposes of drawing conclusions about your research questions. When research questions are evaluated in the context of a design using SIW condition ordering, with two conditions alternated across four adjacent phases, decisions can be made about whether a **functional relation** exists between independent and dependent variables (i.e., a causal relation established via consistent change in targeted behaviors when and only when condition changes occurred, given likely threats to internal validity are controlled). Before confident conclusions can be drawn about study outcomes, researchers should evaluate whether the study design was appropriate, whether a sufficient amount of data were collected and whether those data indicated a phase change was needed, and whether there were appropriate controls for other common threats to internal validity.

Summative analyses are generally conducted by researchers who are implementing or directing the study, although it is possible to have analysts who are unaware of conditions under which data are collected (e.g., whether a data point represents measurement in a baseline or a treatment condition). Because this procedure, called *masked analysis*, is typically associated with multiple baseline designs, we discuss it in Chapter 12. However, at least two studies exists where it was used in a design using SIW condition ordering (Fallon et al., 2020; Simmons et al., 2022).

Design Adequacy

To answer the question regarding whether a functional relation exists between a given dependent variable and an independent variable, you should first assess whether the design is sufficient for making the determination. For designs using SIW condition ordering, this includes measurement of a dependent variable that is readily reversible and *at least three potential demonstrations of effect* (although this convention is not universally applied [Wolfe & McCammon, 2022], we continue to advocate for it to be standard). As discussed in Chapter 9, this cannot be just any three phase changes. It must be three phase changes between two identical conditions, in four adjacent phases. For example, A-B-A-B and A-B-C-B-C both meet these criteria, but A-B-C-A-C does not. If the design meets these minimum standards, it is possible that you can assess for whether a functional relation exists. If it does *not* meet this standard, you should conclude that it is not possible to determine whether a functional relation exists (which is quite different from determining that a functional relation *does not* exist).

Data Adequacy

In addition to having a sufficient number of potential demonstrations of effect, you should also assess for whether there is adequate data for drawing conclusions in each phase. Generally, at least three data points are necessary for establishing level, trend, and variability within a phase. Some contemporary guidelines suggest a minimum of five or more (e.g., What Works Clearinghouse, 2020). For some behaviors in some contexts (e.g., dangerous challenging behavior), fewer than three data points have historically been considered acceptable. Data are adequate when you could accurately predict approximately where the next data point would fall if the condition did not change, and when that range is outside the value you would predict in the next phase. In Figure 10.3, we show a variety of data patterns, including those in which three data points in the first baseline phase are sufficient (top), five data points in the first baseline phase are *not* sufficient (middle), and when five but not three data points is sufficient in the first baseline phase. In Chapter 16, we discuss the ethical ramifications of having fewer and more data collection opportunities, especially in baseline conditions.

In addition to predictability, data in the first phase should be adequate for establishing that initiating the second phase is warranted. When data are at or near optimal levels (e.g., floor levels for challenging behavior, ceiling levels for engagement), continuing to the next phase (if it is likely to be therapeutic) is not helpful, because no functional relation can be established, regardless of data. For example, in a study designed to assess the effects of choice (versus a no-choice baseline condition) on non-compliance and engagement (Kautz et al., 2018), the percentage of intervals of engagement for one participant in the initial phase was 100% for the final four sessions (see Figure 10.4). Given this ceiling level performance, there was no opportunity for a functional relation to be identified (unless authors expected choice to reduce engagement, which was not the case). Thus, in this situation, we would say that we were unable to determine whether a functional relation exists. You might also argue that a therapeutic trend in baseline could indicate that intervention was not needed; generally you would need to continue to baseline data collection until the trend "leveled out" below therapeutic levels (at which point you could initiate intervention) or until it reached therapeutic levels (at which point, you would decide not to intervene).

Insufficient data in designs using SIW condition ordering often occurs for one of two reasons. One is that researchers select a *primary dependent variable*, and they make phase change decisions based on this variable. *Secondary dependent variables* may not have similar data patterns, and so the decisions that can be made about these variables are often limited. For this reason, authors should always identify which dependent variables are primary versus secondary. Second, authors may mis-identify inclusion criteria for participation, and include

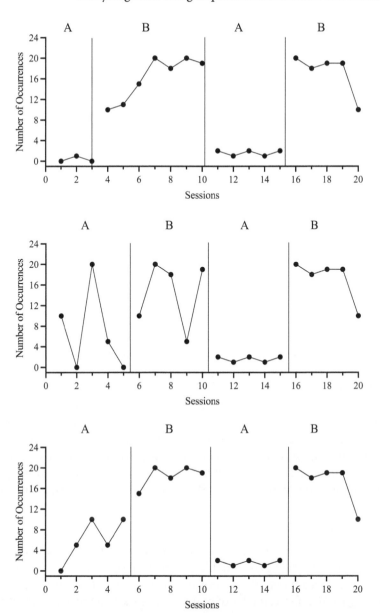

Figure 10.3 Illustration of Data Adequacy in the Initial Baseline Condition.

Note: Visual analysis suggests there are a sufficient number of data points (n = 3) in the initial baseline condition in the top panel, with low and stable levels of data. In the middle panel, more data are needed, despite already having five data points, to determine whether considerable variability is likely or whether the third data point is an outlier. In the bottom panel, a formative decision after the third data point would lead to the decision that more data were needed due to a possible increasing trend—additional data suggests that trend was an artifact.

participants for whom an intervention is not needed. If this is the case, we recommend discontinuing data collection rather than implementing an unnecessary intervention.

Control for Likely Threats to Internal Validity

If a study includes an appropriate design with sufficient potential demonstrations of effect, and adequate data in each phase, the next step is to determine whether any other significant

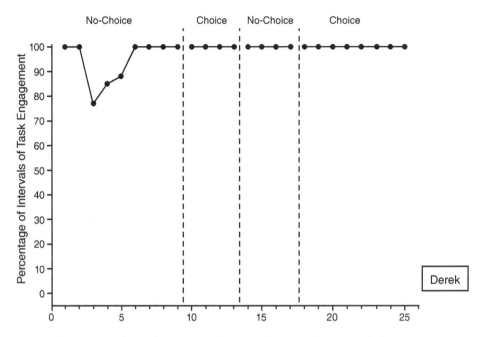

Figure 10.4 Illustration of Insufficient Data due to Ceiling Levels in Initial Phase.

Source: Kautz, M. E., DeBar, R. M., Vladescu, J. C., & Graff, R. B. (2018). A further evaluation of choice of task sequence. *The Journal of Special Education*, 52(1), 16–28.

threats to internal validity decrease confidence that the differences between conditions (and only those differences) are responsible for any behavior changes that occurred (see Chapter 9). For example, you should assess whether a given study provides adequate evidence of reliability of independent and dependent variables. If likely threats are controlled for, you can move forward to summatively evaluating data for the purposes of establishing a functional relation.

Outcome Evaluation

Summative analysis of data in single case designs should result in a determination of whether a functional relation can be identified, and this is historically considered to be a yes/no determination (i.e., evidence that a functional relation exists or evidence that a functional relation does not exist). See Figure 10.5 for examples of graphs where data support identification of a functional relation and ones in which a functional relation is not identified. A functional relation is identified when there are three demonstrations of effect—that is, three changes in level, trend, or variability between the two conditions that are consistent across phase changes and that are in line with the theory of change and expected data patterns. It is important to note that while variability and trend often impact visual analysis, most studies are designed to change the level of behavior, rather than the variability or trend, although there are times when an increasing trend leads to desired level changes and when it is important to reduce variability (especially relative to baseline conditions) to reach a consistently high or low level of behavior.

For A-B-A-B and multitreatment designs, evidence for functional relations is strongest when there are three demonstrations of effect such that:

1. Behavior patterns for the first and third phases in the experimental comparison portion of the design (e.g., both A phases in an A-B-A-B design, both B phases in an A-B-BC-B-BC design) are similar in regard to level, trend, and variability.

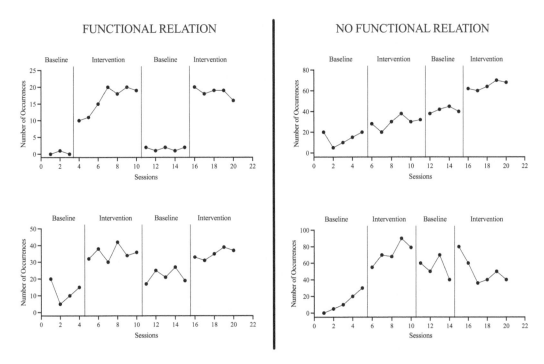

Figure 10.5 Illustration of Summative Functional Analysis Conclusions Regarding Functional Relations.

Note: The panels on the left both depict functional relations, with the magnitude of the behavior change on the top left being larger than the magnitude of the change on the bottom left. The top right panel does not depict a functional relation, despite similar increases in level from the A phases to the subsequent B phase. The reason for the determination of no functional relation here is the lack of countertherapeutic change when the first B phase is discontinued. The bottom right panel has similar levels between the second A and B phases, and you could argue that the increasing trend in baseline makes it impossible to determine whether a functional relation exists.

2. Behavior patterns for the second and fourth phases in the experimental comparison portion of the design (e.g., both B phases in an A-B-A-B design, both BC phases in an A-B-BC-B-BC design) are similar in regard to level, trend, and variability.
3. Changes in data that occur on introduction of second and fourth phases are consistent (e.g., the initiation of <u>both</u> B phases in an A-B-A-B design results in large <u>increases</u> in level of engagement).
4. Changes in data that occur on introduction of the third phase is consistent <u>but in the opposite direction</u> of those that occur on introduction of the second and fourth phases (e.g., the initiation of B phases in an A-B-A-B design results in large <u>increases</u> in level of engagement while the introduction of the second A phase results in large <u>decreases</u> in level of engagement).
5. All changes between phases are immediate or near immediate.
6. Data between adjacent phases are non-overlapping.
7. Variability and trends in any phase do not preclude ability to identify between-phase changes (e.g., therapeutic trend in baseline).

To demonstrate a functional relation using the changing criterion design you must show that each time the criterion level is changed (increased or decreased), there is concomitant change in the dependent variable. This change should be immediate and should follow a stable level and trend in the data at the preceding criterion level; this close alignment with criterion levels is required to rule out maturation effects. In addition, these effects can be detected by reverting to an earlier criterion at some point during the study. If the data move in a countertherapeutic direction, maturation is unlikely. Although this reversal is imperative for demonstrating maturation is unlikely to be a threat, it has been done relatively rarely (e.g., less than 40% of published changing criterion studies; Klein et al., 2017).

Drawing conclusions about functional relations using visual analysis can be relatively straightforward or more complex and nuanced, depending on the data pattern. Graphs with stable data patterns and large changes between adjacent phases that are replicated multiple times are easier to analyze than those with fewer data points, more variability, smaller level changes, and possible trends. More complex data patterns are also more likely to result in different conclusions across different analysts (Wolfe & Seaman, 2023; see Callout 10.2 for more information on reliability among visual analysts). One way to increase consistency in visual analysis is through the use of visual analysis protocols. Protocols to guide conclusions about functional relations for A-B-A-B designs have been published (Wolfe et al., 2019a) and are available online (https://sites.google.com/site/scrvaprotocols/). These protocols are helpful for standardizing evaluations of data across studies and for use in systematic reviews. They provide helpful examples and non-examples of data characteristics such as immediacy and consistency.

In addition to making functional relation decisions, researchers also use visual analysis to assess for the size or strength of effect. That is, you can assess whether the effects are *strong* (i.e., consistent, unequivocal) or *weak* (i.e., less consistent, with more overlap or less immediacy). You can also assess whether effects are *large* (i.e., a big absolute change in level between phases) or *small* (i.e., less level change between phases). These determinations are somewhat subjective, and certainly are dependent on content expertise (i.e., a "large" change in a specific study is not necessarily a "large" change for other types of participants, dependent variables, or contexts). You might consider the strength of effect (strong, weak) as a judgment about the certainty of conclusions (i.e., related to internal validity) while the size of effect might be more related to the value or importance of the outcome (i.e., related to social validity).

Callout 10.2   Reliability of Visual Analysis

It is important to recognize that visual analysis has been criticized as being subjective (Dowdy et al., 2022) and that research on reliability among visual analysts has largely found that agreement is poor under many circumstances (Ninci et al., 2015). Research examining disagreement among visual analysts suggest that raters disagree both about what is considered a change between phases and how many changes between phases are needed for evidence of a functional relation (Wolfe et al., 2016). Further, axis scaling can impact agreement (Dart & Radley, 2017), and graphs that include an apparent trend are more likely to produce disagreement (Wolfe & Seaman, 2023).

However, there are ways to increase consistency across visual analysts and mitigate potential bias in conclusions. Systematic training (Wolfe & Slocum, 2015), visual aids (Fisher et al., 2003; see Chapter 14) and standardized protocols (Wolfe et al., 2019a) can increase the accuracy and reliability of visual analysis. Masked visual analysis (Ferron & Jones, 2006; see Chapter 12), and transparent reporting of visual analysis procedures and conclusions can reduce potential bias in the conduct of response-guided single case designs and interpretation of results.

Supplementary Analyses

Magnitude Estimates

In addition to using visual analysis, researchers can estimate the *magnitude* (i.e., size) of the change in level between two adjacent phases using an appropriate effect size metric. Because data in single case designs are repeatedly collected from a single participant, the effect sizes commonly used in group design research are not appropriate for single case data (Pustejovsky & Ferron, 2017). Fortunately, years of methodological work has been done to develop and refine effect sizes appropriate for single case design data (Shadish, 2014). We do not include detailed information about effect size estimation in this text because the field is rapidly changing, but we suggest that, if you use an effect size metric, you consider the extent to which the metric (1) can be well understood by consumers of your reports, (2) is a reasonable estimate for the type of data you have, (3) has assumptions met by your data, and (4) is appropriately described as a magnitude estimate separate from your visual analysis determination.

As of 2022, the What Works Clearinghouse recommends the between-case standardized mean difference (BC-SMD), also referred to as a design-comparable effect size (D-CES) due to its conceptual similarity to the SMD used in group design studies (What Works Clearinghouse, 2020). Weaknesses of this metric include that it is not useful for all designs, that it requires three participants or more in a single study, and that its premise (i.e., between participant comparisons) is somewhat discrepant from single case logic (Maggin et al., 2022). A similar metric, the within-case SMD (WC-SMD) is a more widely applicable metric for estimating mean differences across phases and may be a better option for estimating magnitude in many single case studies, when the goal is not to combine data from single case design studies and group design studies. The third effect size metric we will mention is the log response ratio (LRR, Pustejovsky, 2018), which is widely applicable to single case studies, and which estimates relative, rather than absolute, changes in mean level across phases. One benefit of LRR is that it can be transformed into a percentage change, a metric easily understood by consumers, and it is less sensitive to procedural variations (e.g., session length, recording system) than SMD (Pustejovsky, 2019).

You should select a magnitude estimate prior to data collection and should report all estimates completed in your written reports rather than "shopping around" to find an estimate that aligns with your interpretations about your data. We suggest collaborating with people with statistical and methodological expertise when selecting, calculating, and reporting effect sizes. It is worth noting that although some effect sizes align more closely with visual analysis decisions (Wolfe et al., 2019b; Zimmerman et al., 2018), *effect size metrics should not always come to the same conclusions as visual analysis.* Visual analysis answers whether a relation is observed between the independent and dependent variables, while effect sizes answers how big differences between conditions are. There are cases where the estimated effect size can be not significantly different than 0, but in which a functional relation exists. Likewise, there can be a large estimated effect size without evidence of a functional relation. For this reason, we suggest always interpreting effect size estimates separate from, and as supplemental to, your primary visual analysis conclusions.

Overlap Estimates

Sometimes, researchers use metrics that quantify the degree to which data overlaps between phases, referred to as non-overlap metrics. The rationale behind these metrics is that a higher proportion of non-overlapping data suggests a stronger effect than a lower proportion. While this is likely usually true, non-overlap metrics do not quantify the *magnitude* of behavior change, simply the degree of overlap. As such, they should not be referred to as effect sizes. Some common non-overlap metrics are Percentage of Non-Overlapping Data (PND), Percentage Exceeding the Median (PEM), Non-Overlap of All Pairs (NAP), Tau-U, and Improvement Rate Difference (IRD). Like SMD, these metrics tend to be sensitive to session length, interval size, and recording system (Pustejovsky, 2019). In addition, some non-overlap metrics do not account for trend and are overly influenced by outliers (Wolery et al., 2010). It is worth repeating: these metrics *do not* appropriately estimate magnitude (Wolery, 2013). When interpreted correctly, as estimates of overlap in secondary analyses, they may be helpful in some cases.

Describing Visual Analysis

Now that we've described the procedures for engaging in visual analysis, we briefly explain the processes for planning and reporting these analyses. More information about writing is provided in Chapter 17.

Visual Analysis Procedures

Prior to data collection, you should plan your visual analysis. You can start by explicating what data patterns you expect within and between phases. For example, you might expect low but variable responding when baseline conditions (A) are in effect and high and stable responding when intervention conditions (B) are in effect, with no notable trends expected in any phase. Or, you may expect variable responding with trend in baseline phases (A) and an increasing trend to high, stable levels during intervention phases (B).

In addition to identifying expected data patterns before you begin your study, you should plan how often you will engage in formative analysis (for SIW designs, usually following each session), and what rules you will follow for discontinuing or modifying a condition. For example, you might decide that you will collect data in the first intervention phase until you (1) have at least three consecutive data points that are higher in level than the initial baseline phase (at which point you would withdraw intervention and conduct the second baseline phase) *or* (2) have at least five consecutive data points without a visually apparent change a level (at which point you would modify the intervention or implement a new intervention to facilitate behavior change).

Finally, you should explicate in writing *a priori* (before data collection) what data patterns you expect that will lead you to conclude that a functional relation exists.

Visual Analysis Results

After planning and conducting your formative and summative analyses, you will describe them to others, usually via written reports (i.e., published articles, thesis or dissertation documents). It is critical to explain your (1) data analysis plan (i.e., the protocol you used to analyze your data), (2) any noteworthy formative decisions that were made (i.e., modifications, phase changes), (3) your summative analysis, and (4) your conclusions about the presence or absence of a functional relation. We recommend that you provide sufficient detail in your summative analysis, describing your data with key visual analysis terms as appropriate, to justify your conclusions regarding the functional relation. Callouts 10.3, 10.4, 10.5, and 10.6 at the end of the chapter show examples of summative visual analysis for three published studies using designs with SIW condition ordering. More information about describing visual analysis results is available in Chapter 16.

Callout 10.3 Applied Example of Withdrawal Design

In the study described in Callout 9.2 in Chapter 9 (Joseph et al., 2021), we describe an A-B-A-B design used to evaluate the effectiveness of prevent-teach-reinforce for families (PTR-F) on challenging behavior of young children.

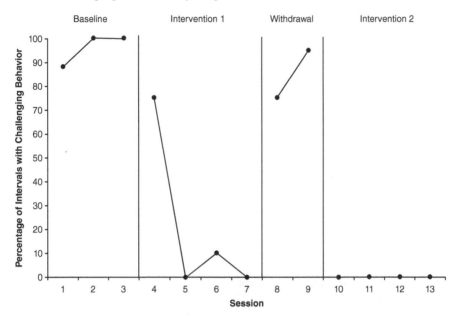

Source: Joseph, J. D., Strain, P. S., & Dunlap, G. (2021). An experimental analysis of Prevent-Teach-Reinforce for Families (PTR-F). *Topics in Early Childhood Special Education*, 41(2), 115–128.

Design Adequacy: This A-B-A-B design includes three potential demonstrations of effect, so is adequate for making a functional relation determination.

Data Adequacy: In three phases (baseline, intervention 1, and intervention 2), there are at least three data points and stable patterns are established before the phase is discontinued. In one phase (withdrawal), there are only two data points. Because authors are measuring challenging behavior in an uncontrolled setting (children's homes), this type of brief withdrawal has historically been considered acceptable.

Control for Common Threats: Visual analysis suggests low likelihood of history and maturation threats. Procedural fidelity and interobserver agreement data are appropriate, suggesting confidence in reliability of the independent and dependent variables.

Visual Analysis: The *level* of data in both the baseline and withdrawal phases (A condition) is high and somewhat *stable*. Analysis of *trend* is impeded by insufficient data points in the withdrawal phase and because data are at ceiling levels in the final two sessions of the baseline phase. Changes between phases lead to *immediate* changes in level, with little to no *overlap*.

Functional Relation Decision: A functional relation is evident between parent-implemented prevent-teach-reinforce and reductions in challenging behavior.

Magnitude Estimate: Log response ratio (decreasing) for the first A-B comparison is 2.50 (95% confidence interval: 0.49, 4.52; Pustejovsky et al., 2023). LRRd cannot be calculated when the mean of a phase is 0, and thus no estimate can be calculated for the second A-B comparison.

Callout 10.4 Applied Example of Reversal Design

In the study described in Callout 9.3 in Chapter 9 (Lambert et al., 2017), assessed the effectiveness of a treatment package for elopement, using *latency to elopement* as the dependent variable. Note that two variables are depicted here: One is the latency to elopement in seconds, which corresponds to the vertical placement of the data points. The second is a dichotomous report of whether any elopement occurred, represented as unfilled data points (no elopement) or black/white data points (elopement occurred). Also note that this design could be considered a *combination design* given that changing criterion levels are used in the second intervention phase, consistent with a changing criterion design (see Chapter 15).

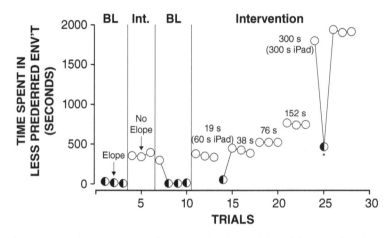

Source: Lambert, J. M., Finley, C. I., & Caruthers, C. E. (2017). Trial-based functional analyses as basis for elopement intervention. *Behavior Analysis: Research and Practice*, 17(2), 166.

Design Adequacy: This A-B-A-B design includes three potential demonstrations of effect, so is adequate for making a functional relation determination.

Data Adequacy: There are at least three data points per phase, with stability established in each phase prior to phase termination.

Control for Common Threats: Visual analysis suggests low likelihood of history and maturation threats. Interobserver agreement and procedural fidelity data are appropriate, suggesting confidence in reliability of the independent and dependent variables.

Visual Analysis: The *level* is low (i.e., elopement occurred soon after the trial started) and *stable* in both baseline phases, with data near floor levels in most trials after a 1-trial delay in level change for the withdrawal phase, and no apparent *trend*. Changes between phases lead to *immediate* or near-immediate changes in level, with stable data in the first intervention phase and an increasing *trend* (consistent with changing intervention criteria) in the second intervention phase, with minimal to no overlap between phases.

Functional Relation Decision: A functional relation is evident between the use of the intervention package and increases in latency to elopement.

Magnitude Estimate: Log response ratio (increasing) for the first A-B comparison is 1.55 (95% confidence interval (CI): 1.30, 1.80) and is 1.46 for the second comparison (95% CI: 0.29-2.64) (Pustejovsky et al., 2023).

Callout 10.5 Applied Example of Multitreatment Design

As explained in Callout 9.4 in Chapter 9, Van Camp et al. (2021) describe the use of a multitreatment design as a modification of a planned A-B-A-B design. They assessed MoBeGo (B) on a participant's engagement and disruptive behavior compared with MoBeGo plus CW-FIT (BC) using an A-B-BC-B-BC design.

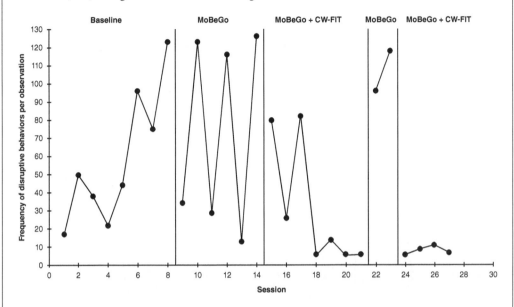

Source: Van Camp, A. M., Wehby, J. H., Copeland, B. A., & Bruhn, A. L. (2021). Building from the bottom up: The importance of Tier 1 supports in the context of Tier 2 interventions. *Journal of Positive Behavior Interventions*, 23(1), 53–64.

Design Adequacy: In this design, there are sufficient potential demonstrations of effect between MoBeGo (B) and MoBeGo + CW-FIT (BC) conditions to evaluate a functional relation. There are not sufficient potential demonstrations to compare either of these conditions with baseline.

Data Adequacy: There are sufficient data in the first B phase to establish variability, and sufficient data in the BC phases to establish stable, low levels. In the second BC phase, there are only two data points. While this is generally insufficient, the large increase in level and potential challenges with ongoing disruptive behavior in classroom settings is a strong rationale for having only two measurement occasions.

Control for Common Threats: Visual analysis suggests low likelihood of history and maturation threats. Interobserver agreement and procedural fidelity data are appropriate, suggesting confidence in reliability of the independent and dependent variables. Graphed data (not shown here) suggest teacher praise and reprimand behaviors co-vary with phase changes, providing precise information about active ingredients. Multitreatment interference may be present during the transition from the first B to the first BC phase; that threat was mitigated by continuing the BC phase until data stabilized.

Visual Analysis: In the first B phase, data are highly *variable*, and data suggest this pattern is likely to continue in the absence of intervention. In the first BC phase, data are initially *variable* but the transition to low, *stable levels*. There is an *immediate* increase in *level* during the second B phase and an *immediate* decrease in *level* during the second BC phase, with *stable* data in both. Following initial variability, data in BC phases are *consistently* low and *stable*, while data in B phases are high (both BC phases) and *variable* (first BC phase).

Functional Relation Decision: A functional relation is evident such that the use of MoBeGo + CW-FIT (BC) results in lower and more stable levels of disruptive behaviors compared with use of MoBeGo alone (B).

Magnitude Estimate: Log response ratio (decreasing) for the first B-BC comparison is 0.81 (95% confidence interval: 0.2-1.82; Pustejovsky et al., 2023). LRR cannot be calculated for the second comparison because there are only two data points in the B condition.

Callout 10.6 Applied Example of Changing Criterion Design

As described in Callout 9.5, Wheatley et al. (2020) used a changing criterion design to evaluate an intervention designed to increase compliance with wearing an "anti-strip" suit to prevent inappropriate fecal behavior.

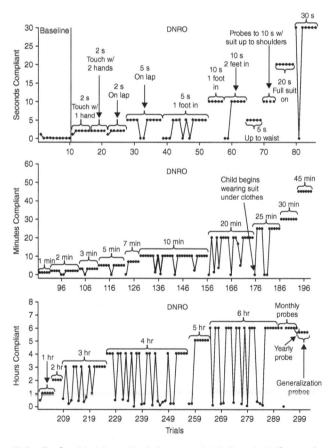

Source: Wheatley, T. L., Goulet, M., Mann, K., & Lanovaz, M. J. (2020). Differential negative reinforcement of other behavior to increase compliance with wearing an anti-strip suit. *Journal of Applied Behavior Analysis*, 53(2), 1153–1161.

Design Adequacy: This changing criterion design includes many more than three potential demonstrations of effect and includes one instance of reverting to a previous criterion, so is adequate for making a functional relation determination.

Data Adequacy: For each criterion, stable patterns are established before the phase is discontinued. Note that a different panel is used based on reporting differences in behavior occurrence (seconds, minutes, hours); this represents a single CC design.

Control for Common Threats: Inclusion of the countertherapeutic criterion change with countertherapeutic changes in behavior suggests history and maturation threats are unlikely.

Visual Analysis: The *level* of data aligns closely with the criterion for most data points in the top and middle panels, with highly variable data in the bottom panel. Changes between phases lead to *immediate* changes in level, with little to no *overlap*.

Functional Relation Decision: A functional relation is evident between differential negative reinforcement of other behaviors and compliance with wearing a strip suit, although certainty of conclusions is greater for shorter durations (seconds, minutes) than longer ones (hours).

Conclusions

Visual analysis is a critical skill for single case researchers. It impacts both the conduct of your study (i.e., formative analysis for phase change decisions) and conclusions that are drawn following study completion (i.e., summative analysis for determining whether a functional relation exists). Planning, executing, and reporting your formative and summative visual analysis in a systematic manner will increase the rigor of your study, reduce the likelihood of drawing incorrect conclusions, and promote clear communication with consumers of the single case literature.

References

Barton, E. E. (2019). A word on contributions of research with noneffects to early childhood special education research. *Topics in Early Childhood Special Education*, 39(1), 4–4.

Dart, E. H., & Radley, K. C. (2017). The impact of ordinate scaling on the visual analysis of single-case data. *Journal of School Psychology*, 63(1), 105–118. https://doi.org/10.1016/j.jsp.2017.03.008

Dowdy, A., Jessel, J., Saini, V., & Peltier, C. (2022). Structured visual analysis of single-case experimental design data: Developments and technological advancements. *Journal of Applied Behavior Analysis*, 55(2), 451–462. https://doi.org/10.1002/jaba.899

Fallon, L. M., Marcotte, A. M., & Ferron, J. M. (2020). Measuring academic output during the good behavior game: A single case design study. *Journal of Positive Behavior Interventions*, 22(4), 246–258. https://doi.org/10.1177/1098300719872778

Ferron, J., & Jones, P. K. (2006). Tests for the visual analysis of response-guided multiple-baseline data. *Journal of Experimental Education*, 75(1), 66–81. https://doi.org/10.3200/JEXE.75.1.66-81

Fisher, W. W., Kelley, M. E., & Lomas, J. E. (2003). Visual aids and structured criteria for improving visual inspection and interpretation of single-case designs. *Journal of Applied Behavior Analysis*, 36(3), 387–406.

Gast, D. L. (2010). *Single subject research methodology in behavioral sciences*. New York: Routledge.

Hersen, M., & Barlow, D. H. (1976). *Single case research designs*. New York: Pergamon Press.

Joseph, J. D., Strain, P. S., & Dunlap, G. (2021). An experimental analysis of Prevent-Teach-Reinforce for Families (PTR-F). *Topics in Early Childhood Special Education*, 41(2), 115–128.

Kautz, M. E., DeBar, R. M., Vladescu, J. C., & Graff, R. B. (2018). A further evaluation of choice of task sequence. *The Journal of Special Education*, 52(1), 16–28.

Kazdin, A. E. (2020). *Single-case experimental research designs: Methods for clinical and applied settings*. Cary, NC: Oxford University Press.

Kipfmiller, K. J., Brodhead, M. T., Wolfe, K., LaLonde, K., Sipila, E. S., Bak, M. S., & Fisher, M. H. (2019). Training front-line employees to conduct visual analysis using a clinical decision-making model. *Journal of Behavioral Education*, 28(3), 301–322.

Klein, L. A., Houlihan, D., Vincent, J. L., & Panahon, C. J. (2017). Best practices in utilizing the changing criterion design. *Behavior Analysis in Practice*, 10(1), 52–61.

Lambert, J. M., Finley, C. I., & Caruthers, C. E. (2017). Trial-based functional analyses as basis for elopement intervention. *Behavior Analysis: Research and Practice*, 17(2), 166.

Maggin, D. M., Barton, E., Reichow, B., Lane, K. L., & Shogren, K. A. (2022). Commentary on the What Works Clearinghouse Standards and Procedures Handbook (v. 4.1) for the review of single-case research. *Remedial and Special Education*, 43(6), 421–433.

Ninci, J., Vannest, K. J., Willson, V., & Zhang, N. (2015). Interrater agreement between visual analysts of single-case data: A meta-analysis. *Behavior Modification*, 39(4), 510–541.

Pustejovsky, J. E. (2018). Using response ratios for meta-analyzing single-case designs with behavioral outcomes. *Journal of School Psychology*, 68(1), 99–112.

Pustejovsky, J. E. (2019). Procedural sensitivities of effect sizes for single-case designs with directly observed behavioral outcome measures. *Psychological Methods*, 24(2), 217.

Pustejovsky, J. E., Chen, M., Grekov, P., & Swan, D. M. (2023). Single-case effect size calculator (Version 0.7.2.9999) [Web application]. https://jepusto.shinyapps.io/SCD-effect-sizes/

Pustejovsky, J. E., & Ferron, J. M. (2017). Research synthesis and meta-analysis of single-case designs. In J. M. Kaufmann, D. P. Hallahan, & P. C. Pullen (Eds.), *Handbook of special education*, 2nd Edition. New York: Routledge.

Severini, K. E., Ledford, J. R., Barton, E. E., & Osborne, K. C. (2019). Implementing stay-play-talk with children who use AAC. *Topics in Early Childhood Special Education*, 38(4), 220–233.

Shadish, W. R. (2014). Analysis and meta-analysis of single-case designs: An introduction. *Journal of School Psychology*, 52(2), 109–122.

Simmons, C. A., Ardoin, S. P., Ayres, K. M., & Powell, L. E. (2022). Parent-implemented self-management intervention on the on-task behavior of students with autism. *School Psychology*, 37(3), 273.

Tawney, J. W., & Gast, D. L. (1984). *Single subject research in special education*. Columbus, OH: Merrill.

Tincani, M., & Travers, J. (2018). Publishing single-case research design studies that do not demonstrate experimental control. *Remedial and Special Education*, 39(2), 118–128.

Van Camp, A. M., Wehby, J. H., Copeland, B. A., & Bruhn, A. L. (2021). Building from the bottom up: The importance of Tier 1 supports in the context of Tier 2 interventions. *Journal of Positive Behavior Interventions*, 23(1), 53–64.

What Works Clearinghouse. (2020). *What Works Clearinghouse standards handbook* (Version 4.1). National Center for Education Evaluation and Regional Assistance, Institute of Education Sciences, U.S. Department of Education. https://ies.ed.gov/ncee/wwc/handbooks

Wheatley, T. L., Goulet, M., Mann, K., & Lanovaz, M. J. (2020). Differential negative reinforcement of other behavior to increase compliance with wearing an anti-strip suit. *Journal of Applied Behavior Analysis*, 53(2), 1153–1161.

Winchester, C., Barton, E. E., Trimlett, G., & Ledford, J. R. (2023). Preventing challenging behavior using physical activity with young children. *Topics in Early Childhood Special Education*, 42(4), 357–369.

Wolery, M. (2013). A commentary: Single-case design technical document of the What Works Clearinghouse. *Remedial and Special Education*, 34(1), 39–43.

Wolery, M., Busick, M., Reichow, B., & Barton, E. E. (2010). Comparison of overlap methods for quantitatively synthesizing single-subject data. *The Journal of Special Education*, 44(1), 18–28. https://doi.org/10.1177/0022466908328009

Wolfe, K., Barton, E. E., & Meadan, H. (2019a). Systematic protocols for the visual analysis of single-case research data. *Behavior Analysis in Practice*, 12, 491–502.

Wolfe, K., Dickenson, T. S., Miller, B., & McGrath, K. V. (2019b). Comparing visual and statistical analysis of multiple baseline design graphs. *Behavior Modification*, 43(3), 361–388.

Wolfe, K., & McCammon, M. N. (2022). The analysis of single-case research data: Current instructional practices. *Journal of Behavioral Education*, 31(1), 28–42.

Wolfe, K., McCammon, M. N., LeJeune, L. M., & Holt, A. K. (2023). Training preservice practitioners to make data-based instructional decisions. *Journal of Behavioral Education*, 32(1), 1–20.

Wolfe, K., & Seaman, M. A. (2023). The influence of data characteristics on interrater agreement among visual analysts. *Journal of Applied Behavior Analysis*, 56(2), 365–376. https://doi.org/10.1002/jaba.980

Wolfe, K., Seaman, M. A., & Drasgow, E. (2016). Interrater agreement on the visual analysis of individual tiers and functional relations in multiple baseline designs. *Behavior Modification*, 40(6), 852–873. https://doi.org/10.1177/0145445516644699

Wolfe, K., & Slocum, T. A. (2015). A comparison of two approaches to training visual analysis of AB graphs. *Journal of Applied Behavior Analysis*, 48(2), 472–477.

Zimmerman, K. N., Pustejovsky, J. E., Ledford, J. R., Barton, E. E., Severini, K. E., & Lloyd, B. P. (2018). Single-case synthesis tools II: Comparing quantitative outcome measures. *Research in Developmental Disabilities*, 79, 65–76.

11
Conducting Studies Using Time-Lagged Condition Ordering

Jennifer R. Ledford and Kathleen N. Tuck

Important Terms

multiple baseline design, multiple probe designs, tiers, functionally independent, functionally similar, concurrent, nonconcurrent, probe session, probe condition, baseline condition, maintenance condition, conditions variation, days variation

Table of Contents

Features of Time-Lagged Designs
    Intervention Targets (Participants, Behaviors, Contexts)
    Concurrence Variations
When To Use Time Time-Lagged Designs
    Strengths and Benefits of Time-Lagged Designs
    Weaknesses and Drawbacks of Time-Lagged Designs
Multiple Baseline Designs
Multiple Probe Designs
    Procedural Steps for MB and MP Designs
Threats to Internal Validity for Time-Lagged Design Family
Conclusions
References

Callouts

11.1 *Selecting Intervention Targets*
11.2 *How Rigorous Are Nonconcurrent MB Designs?*
11.3 *Applied Example of Multiple Baseline Across Participants Design*
11.4 *Applied Example of Multiple Baseline Across Behaviors Design*
11.5 *Applied Example of a Multiple Probe Across Behaviors Design (Days Variation)*

DOI: 10.4324/9781003294726-13

11.6 Applied Example of a Multiple Probe Across Participants Design (Days Variation)
11.7 How Do I Choose Between Multiple Baseline and Multiple Probe Design Variations?

In this chapter, we will describe the most commonly used condition ordering type—time-lagged introduction of conditions, including the multiple baseline design and the multiple probe design. There are many variations of these design types.

Features of Time-Lagged Designs

When time-lagged condition ordering is used, researchers conduct (1) at least three comparisons; (2) each with a *different* intervention target; (3) by introducing two different conditions in two adjacent phases for each intervention target, with at least three data points per phase. In the most basic form, all intervention targets experience one baseline condition that is a different length than the baselines for the other targets, and an intervention condition is introduced after the baseline condition for each target. Time-lagged designs include either *intraparticipant replication* or *interparticipant replication*. These designs are not generally referred to with letter notations like the designs in the SIW family (e.g., A-B-A-B). Nonetheless, it is helpful to show the general design format using the same A (baseline) and B (treatment) notation used to explain SIW designs. You may be able to ascertain from the example below that these designs usually include more measurement occasions (i.e., data points) than SIW designs (an average of about 40 sessions; Ledford et al., 2019), although the precise number of occasions is influenced by the outcome of interest, design variation selected, and data stability. The variation depicted below is the prototypical design is this family—the multiple baseline design (see also Figure 11.1).

	Phase 1	Phase 2
Intervention Target 1	A A A A A	B B B B B B B B B B B B B B B B
	Phase 1	**Phase 2**
Intervention Target 2	A A A A A A A A A	B B B B B B B B B B B B
	Phase 1	**Phase 2**
Intervention Target 3	A A A A A A A A A A A A B	B B B B B B B B B

There are two common designs associated with time-lagged condition ordering: multiple baseline (MB) designs and multiple probe (MP) designs. Baer, Wolf, and Risley (1968) introduced multiple baseline designs to behavioral researchers in their seminal article describing applied behavior analysis. Horner and Baer (1978) described a variation of the multiple baseline design they termed "multiple probe technique" 10 years later. Both designs are based on the same baseline logic for evaluating threats to internal validity and demonstrating functional relations and both are used frequently (Hammond & Gast, 2010; Ledford et al., 2019; Tanious & Onghena, 2021).

Descriptions of the multiple baseline and multiple probe designs listed in Table 11.1. The difference between these designs is the *relative frequency of planned data collection in the initial*

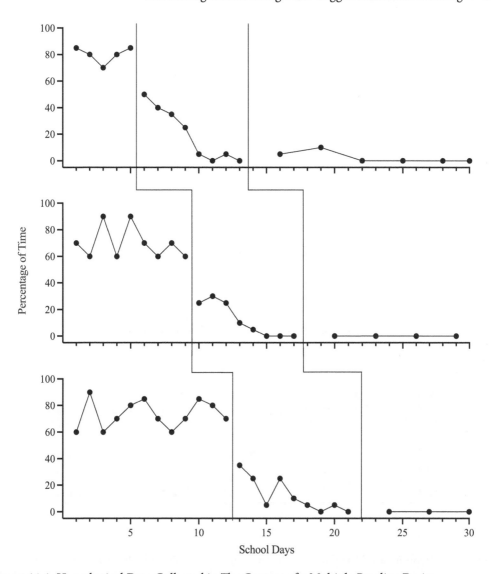

Figure 11.1 Hypothetical Data Collected in The Context of a Multiple Baseline Design.

Table 11.1 Conventional Design Names Associated with Time-Lagged Condition Ordering

Design	Description
Prototype: Multiple Baseline	Multiple replications of A-B comparisons across multiple intervention targets with *time-lagged* introduction of B condition and baselines of different lengths, with continuous measurement during baseline
Multiple Probe	Multiple replications of A-B comparisons across multiple intervention targets with *time-lagged* introduction of B condition and baselines of different lengths, with **intermittent** measurement during baseline

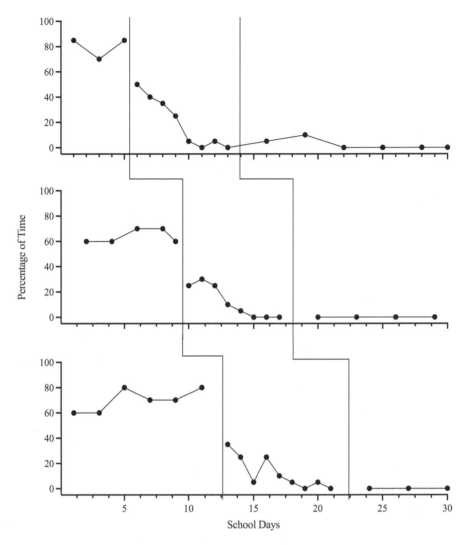

Figure 11.2 Hypothetical Data Collected in The Context of a Multiple Probe Design.

Note: These data are exactly the same as those depicted in Figure 11.1, with approximately half of the baseline data points removed.

baseline phase. In the **multiple baseline design**, data are collected continuously, or at the same frequency at which data are collected in the intervention phase (see Figure 11.1). In the **multiple probe design**, data are collected intermittently, or less frequently than data are collected in the intervention phase (see Figure 11.2). You can see that each intervention target is separately graphed, in a single stacked figure with at least three **tiers**. Across tiers (less often referred to as "legs"), each baseline phase is successively longer in duration—this is true in both multiple baseline and multiple probe designs.

Intervention Targets (Participants, Behaviors, Contexts)

In addition to differentiating whether baseline data are collected continuously or intermittently (i.e., multiple baseline versus multiple probe), a second way to characterize time-lagged designs involves how the intervention target varies (e.g., what the data in each tier represent). There are three primary variations—MB/MP designs across *participants* (MB/MP-Participants), MB/MP designs across *behaviors* (MB/MP-Behaviors), and MB/MP designs across *contexts* (MB/MP-Contexts). When the MB/MP-Participants variation is used, each A-B comparison is applied across the same behavior and contexts for *three or more different participants*. When the MB/MP-Behaviors variation is used, the two conditions are applied across the *three or more different behaviors* for a single participant in the same context. When the MB/MP-Contexts variation is used, the two conditions are applied across the same behavior for a single participant in *three or more different contexts* (e.g., settings, activities, social partners).

The most commonly used time-lagged design is the MB/MP-Participants, followed by the MB/MP-Behaviors. The MB/MP-Contexts is much less frequently used (Ledford et al., 2019). One type of research in which all three have been used is in the evaluation of the peer-mediated stay-play-talk intervention. In most studies, researchers have used an MB/MP-Participants design (Ledford & Pustejovsky, 2019), but there are also examples in which the other two

---

Callout 11.1 Selecting Intervention Targets

The MB/MP designs are flexible, in that you can apply an intervention to three or more *participants*, three or more *behaviors*, or three or more *contexts*. But how do you know which one to choose? You should refer to your research question and consider feasibility. The MB/MP-Contexts design is the least often used. This is because it is not always relevant to apply an intervention in three contexts, and because of difficulties identifying functionally independent contexts for a single participant (see below). The MB/MP-Behaviors variation is quite helpful if your research question is about teaching multiple types of behaviors. For example, if you are interested in whether a specific intervention works well to teach science vocabulary, you can apply the intervention three times to three different sets of vocabulary words (e.g., teach five different words in each tier, for a total of 20 words in a four-tiered MB/MP design) for a single participant. Or, if you are interested in teaching preschool teachers to use three different strategies to support social-emotional learning (e.g., offering choices, providing positive feedback for engagement, encouraging social interactions), you can teach each behavior separately in a three-tiered MB/MP design for a single participant. If multiple behaviors are not of interest, the most practical design is probably the MB/MP-Participants designs (see Chapter 15 for more options, especially if prolonged baseline phases are a problem). Its wide applicability is likely the reason it is the most used variation in the time-lagged family (Ledford et al., 2019). When using MB/MP designs, you should identify intervention targets that are functionally independent and functionally similar. When intervention targets are **functionally independent**, the introduction of the independent variable to one intervention target will not bring about a change in other targets. The intervention targets should also be **functionally similar**, which means that the independent variable is likely to have the same or similar effect on each. See the table below for examples of targets that are more and less likely to be functionally independent and functionally similar.

The terms functionally independent and functionally similar are not necessarily associated with the functions of behavior (e.g., Iwata, 1991). That is, one intervention (e.g., functional communication training) could potentially be used to target multiple functions of challenging behavior (i.e., they are functionally similar) and the changes (i.e., different functional communication responses) could be functionally independent. As described below, the likelihood of generalization across contexts (i.e. different motivations and antecedent events) is difficult to predict, so using these types of intervention targets in a time-lagged design is rare.

Example	Independent?	Similar?	Explanation
Participants: Three children with similar challenging behaviors, expected to be maintained by adult attention in the same classroom.	No	Yes	Because participants are in the same setting, applying intervention for one in the first tier may result in behavioral changes for the other two.
Participants: Three adolescents in different classes, each struggling with math work completion. One has low motivation but advanced mathematics skills, one has an intellectual disability, and one has significant motor delays.	Yes	No	These participants may be unlikely to respond to the same intervention, given that their reason for non-completion of work is different (e.g., the first might need a reinforcement-based intervention, the second might direct academic instruction, and the third modified response requirements).
Contexts: A child has low rates of peer interactions across free play settings (morning centers, afternoon centers, playground).	No	Yes	Teaching a child and their peers to interact more in one of these settings might *generalize* to the other settings because they are so similar.
Behavior: Parents of a preschool child want her to learn to name peers, point to colors, and use single words to request desired toys.	Yes	No	Learning one of these skills is not likely to influence others, but the same intervention is unlikely to be appropriate for academic and requesting tasks.

Table 11.2 Examples of use of Each Type of Intervention Target Variation in the Context of Studies Evaluating Stay-Play-Talk Interventions

Variation (*Author*)	Participant	Behavior	Context
MB/MP-Participants (*Taylor et al., 2023*)	**Different** 4-year-old Black boy, 3-year-old White girl, 3-year-old White boy	**Same** Social Play	**Same** Buddy Time with Peers
MB/MP-Behaviors (*Tang, 2023*)	**Same** 4-year-old White boy	**Different** Proximity, Social Play, Social Interactions	**Same** Buddy Time with Peers
MB/MP-Contexts (*Baldwin, 2013*)	**Same** Boy with ASD (age/race unreported, 1st grade)	**Same** Social Interactions	**Different** Buddy time with Luke, Buddy time with Troy, Buddy time with Karen

variations have been used (see Table 11.2). Taylor and colleagues (in press) taught stay-play-talk strategies to three different children and evaluated effects using a three-tiered nonconcurrent MB-Participants design. Tang (2023) taught each behavior (stay, play, and talk) sequentially, in a time-lagged manner, and measured the impact on each behavior separately, using a three tiered MB-Behaviors design. Baldwin (2013) taught stay-play-talk strategies using three different social partners, time-lagging the intervention introduction with each partner in a three-tiered MB-Contexts (social partners) design. Note that this final design is different from a multiple baseline across participants because one participant's behavior (Brian) was measured throughout—the context in which they were measured varied (i.e., he was with a different peer in each tier). Interestingly, these interventions have also been evaluated using SIW and rapid iterative alternation designs, which is rare given the requirements for using each design family varies (cf. Laushey & Heflin, 2000; Osborne et al., 2019; Severini et al., 2019; Soermajoro et al., 2022).

Concurrence Variations

Given the variations discussed so far, there are six types of designs: MB-Participants, MP-Participants, MB-Behaviors, MP-Behaviors, MB-Contexts, and MP-Contexts. One additional variation type is notable—whether the design is concurrent or nonconcurrent. This variation is generally only applicable to MB, not MP designs (MP designs are concurrent).

Concurrent MB designs are designs in which baseline data collection (i.e., the first measurement occasion) occurs concurrently. The extent to which concurrent means literally *at the same time* varies. For example, in an MB-Behaviors design in which parents are being taught behaviors related to responsivity sequentially, the baseline data for all four behaviors comes from the same session (are all occurring at once; see Golden et al., 2023; Peredo et al., 2018). In an MB-Participants design, a researcher might collect data for one participant at 8:00 each day, and the other two participants at 10:00 and 11:00; here, the concurrence is that they occur on the same day but are not really simultaneous (see Kang & Kim, 2023). Generally, concurrence means that a single measurement occasion or a bout of measurement occasions (see Callout 11.2) occurs for each participant prior subsequent occasions or bouts.

Callout 11.2 How Rigorous are Nonconcurrent MB Designs?

Historically, including in previous editions of this text, *nonconcurrent* multiple baseline designs—that is, designs in which baseline phases did not start concurrently across tiers—were considered to be insufficient for making experimental determinations (i.e., for drawing conclusions about functional relations). The rationale was that these designs offered less control for history and maturation effects. However, they are widely used (Morin et al., 2023) and recent discussions in the field (e.g., Horner & Machalicek, 2022; Kratochwill et al., 2022; Ledford, 2022; Ledford & Zimmerman, 2023; Slocum et al., 2022) have reignited a debate about the place of nonconcurrent designs in single case research. Both Slocum et al. (2022) and Ledford and Zimmerman (2023) argue that the controls for internal validity are just as adequate in nonconcurrent versions of the design, in at least some circumstances. Those conditions include (1) a sufficiently different number of measurement occasions, to control for *testing* threats, (2) a sufficiently different amount of calendar time spent in baseline, to control for *maturation* threats, and (3) a sufficiently different intervention start date, to control for *history* threats. Ledford and Zimmerman (2023) argue the nonconcurrent version of the design should only be used when covariation is unlikely, and thus should only be used in the MB-Participants variation, when all participant behaviors are sufficiently independent (i.e., children are in different classrooms or different school districts, for a classroom-based intervention). We note that to ensure (2) and (3) above, graphing conventions using the ordinal "sessions" is insufficient, and authors should consider using dates instead (or in addition to, via supplemental materials; see Figure 11.3). Regardless of whether you choose a concurrent or nonconcurrent design, you should explicitly report the type chosen and rationalize the extent to which it adequately controls for likely threats to internal validity. Your graph should also clearly reflect your decision through at a minimum a figure caption, although dates or ordinal "sessions" should also reflect this decision through primary or supplementary graphs.

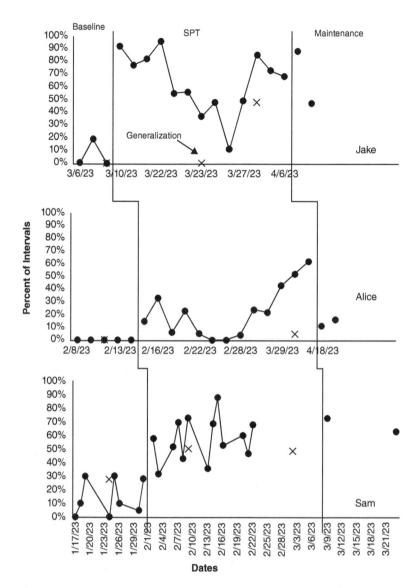

Figure 11.3 Graphed Data from a Nonconcurrent Multiple Baseline Design.

Note: When nonconcurrent designs are used, it is critical to report calendar time. Some authors have suggested this is needed even for concurrent variations (Dart & Radley, 2023).

Source: Taylor, A. G. An adaptation of stay play talk for children with internalizing behaviors. Dissertation. Vanderbilt University. https://ir.vanderbilt.edu/handle/1803/9598

Nonconcurrent MB designs are designs in which baseline data collection (i.e., the first measurement occasion) occurs at different times and sequential data points within a tier are ordinal in relation (see Callout 11.2), but there is no temporal relation across tiers. For example, in an MB across participants design, you might begin data collection with the first participant in January, a second in February, and a third in March (Figure 11.3, Taylor et al., 2023). Some of the data across tiers might overlap (for example, in February when baseline was initiated for the second participant, the intervention phase was ongoing for the first participant). These designs were historically considered to be insufficiently rigorous, or at least considerably less rigorous than the concurrent variation, but recent authors have argued for researchers to reconsider those assumptions. See Callout 11.2 for a discussion about the benefits and drawbacks of nonconcurrent MB designs.

When to Use Time-Lagged Designs

Conditions that should result in the selection of a time-lagged design include:

1. A research question about the impact of two conditions on at least three intervention targets (participants, behaviors, or contexts) that are functionally similar and functionally independent.
2. Interest in behaviors that are either reversible (but for which withdrawing intervention is not desirable), or non-reversible.
3. Ability to conduct baseline phases that have varying lengths across intervention targets, with some intervention targets having relatively few baseline sessions (e.g., 3–6) and some intervention targets having many more (e.g., 10–20 or more).

Time-lagged designs should include at least three potential demonstrations of effect. That is, there are three participants, behaviors, or contexts that experience the same two conditions (baseline and intervention) at three different points in time (see Figure 11.1). The first opportunity for comparison is between Phase 1 and Phase 2 for the first intervention target (participant, behavior, or context); the second is between Phase 1 and Phase 2 for the second intervention target; and the third is between Phase 1 and Phase 2 for the third intervention target. It is important to note that each of the three potential demonstrations should be adjacent (e.g., Phase 2 should always immediately follow Phase 1) and between the same conditions (e.g., not between Baseline and Treatment 1 for the first intervention target and between Baseline and Treatment 2 for the second and third intervention targets). While a two-tiered multiple baseline design is technically still referred to as a multiple baseline design, it does not meet most contemporary definitions of an appropriately rigorous design, and these designs as well as those that include non-identical comparisons result in lower confidence in presence of a functional relation (see Chapter 12).

Strengths and Benefits of Time-Lagged Designs

Time-lagged designs provide repeated demonstrations of a relation for multiple participants, behaviors, or contexts. It does not require the removal of a potentially effective intervention condition, which has historically been considered a substantial benefit. Another benefit of time-lagged designs is that the dependent variable need not be a reversible behavior. MB/MP designs across behaviors often align with the priorities of practitioners, which often include sequentially teaching a number of related behaviors.

Weaknesses and Drawbacks of Time-Lagged Designs

One important drawback of time-lagged designs is that you must identify three participants, behaviors, or contexts that require the same intervention process or procedure. In addition, the number of measurement occasions for these designs is usually substantial, and in the concurrent versions, must be completed during the same period of time across all intervention targets. This can lead to a need for substantial resources related to data collection and implementation. As with the SIW design family, there are also potential concerns with baseline conditions. In the time-lagged design family, this concern is specifically that the time spent in baseline is substantial for intervention targets assigned to later tiers.

Multiple Baseline Designs

The multiple baseline design is the most frequently used single case design (Ledford et al., 2019; Tanious & Onghena, 2021), likely due to its flexibility. It can be used for evaluating change with reversible and non-reversible behaviors and for multiple participants, behaviors, or contexts. When this design is used, you collect continuous data in the baseline condition, and ensure that each baseline phase has sufficiently different baseline lengths (see Callout 11.3).

In the most basic multiple baseline design, you must plan for and implement an initial baseline phase and an intervention phase (although, see Chapter 9 for a discussion about how baseline conditions, especially business-as-usual conditions, might include some characteristics of intervention). Measurement of maintenance and generalization should occur when these conditions align with your research questions and are consistent with your theory of change.

Conclusions drawn about maintenance are generally considered to be answered descriptively rather than experimentally. When multiple levels of intervention are included, you should take care to identify for which level intervention is truly withdrawn (see Chapter 7). For example, when parents are coached to engage in responsive interactions during an intervention condition, and then coaching is withdrawn, the design evaluates parent use of responsive interactions in the absence of coaching (maintenance) but if maintenance of parent behaviors occur, the child is actually still accessing an intervention condition. That is, assessment of parent behaviors occurs when *intervention is absent* and assessment of child behaviors occurs under *prevailing contingencies*.

Generalization conditions are sometimes also included when multiple baseline designs are used; for example, Golden and colleagues (2023) trained teachers to engage in certain behaviors in one context (e.g., center time) and measured whether those same behaviors occurred in untrained contexts (e.g., large group). The extent to which generalization questions are answered descriptively or experimentally is dependent on measurement, with frequent measurement across phases throughout the study leading to more rigorous evaluations of generalization (see Chapter 7). Table 11.3 includes a list of studies using multiple baseline designs, including whether each included generalization and maintenance conditions.

Callout 11.3   Applied Example of Multiple Baseline Across Participants Design

White and colleagues (2023) evaluated modifications to the picture exchange system (PECS) on vocal behavior for three Black children (2 boys, 1 girl) who were eligible for special education services under the categories of autism or significant developmental delay. The study was conducted in a self-contained classroom in a Title 1 School. They measured PECS exchange and vocalizations (imitated, independent before time delay, independent after time delay) using trial-based event recording and reported all dependent variables as a percentage of opportunities. Baseline conditions consisted of typical PECS programming (Phase IV), wherein each participant was prompted and reinforced for combining two icons ("I want" + desired object). Thus, in this case, the baseline condition was an active intervention condition for PECS use but did not contain specific components intended to increase vocalizations. The independent variable (only available during intervention) was a delay to reinforcement (while waiting for a child to vocalize) and differential reinforcement (a larger portion of the requested item) for vocal responding versus PECS exchange alone. In Chapter 12, we share a figure depicting the MB-Participants design and analysis of the outcomes of this study.

Callout 11.4 Applied Example of Multiple Baseline Across Behaviors Design

Capalbo et al. (2022) evaluated the impact of video modeling for improving goalkeeping skills for two 9-year-old boys who played soccer. The intervention targets were three goalkeeping behaviors: High jump, forward smother, and side dive. Data were collected via trial-based event recording for each step in the task analysis and were reported as a percentage correct. During baseline sessions, participants attempted each behavior without modeling or feedback, and the trainer provided general neutral comments if the participants asked questions (e.g., try your best). During the video modeling conditions, the trainer told a participant to watch a video model of the specific behavior and practiced the move three times with no data collected during these attempts. Then the trainer asked the child to engage in the behavior three more times for assessment but did not provide feedback. A third condition, video modeling plus video feedback, consisted of (1) video model presentation, (2) a practice opportunity that was video recorded, (3) viewing of this video alongside the video model, and (4) provision of positive and corrective feedback. After completing this sequence three times, data were collected in a manner similar to the other conditions. During a maintenance phase, the trainer conducted follow-up assessments using procedures identical to baseline. In Chapter 12, we share a figure depicting the MB-Behaviors design and analysis of the outcomes of this study.

Table 11.3 Studies using Multiple Baseline Designs

Reference	Dependent Variable	Conditions	Intervention Targets
Multiple Baseline Across Participants			
Campbell, A. R., Sallese, M. R., Thompson, J. L., Fournier, C. J., & Allen, M. L. (2023). Social-emotional and behavioral support for first- and second-grade black learners at risk for emotional and behavioral problems. *Journal of Positive Behavior Interventions*, 25(3), 147–158.	Externalizing behaviors, estimated via 1-minute partial interval recording	A: Baseline (business-as-usual) *Concurrent* B: Culturally adapted Strong Start + Check-In/Check-Out	Three classrooms
Martinez-Torres, K. A. (2023). Teaching Reciprocal Imitation Training to Puerto Rican Parents of Young Children with Autism Through Tele-Therapy: A Pilot Study (Doctoral dissertation, Vanderbilt University).	Parent use of RIT strategies, estimated using a rating scale	A: Baseline (business-as-usual) *Concurrent* B: Culturally adapted reciprocal imitation training for Spanish-speaking parents in Puerto Rico	Six parent/child pairs in two 3-tiered designs
Salazar, D. M., Ruiz, F. J., Ramírez, E. S., & Cardona-Betancourt, V. (2020). Acceptance and commitment therapy focused on repetitive negative thinking for child depression: A randomized multiple-baseline evaluation. *The Psychological Record*, 70, 373–386.	Psychological inflexibility, repetitive negative thinking, generalized pliance, all measured via Likert-type scale	A: Baseline (no treatment) *Nonconcurrent* B: Acceptance and Commitment Therapy (ACT) C: Maintenance (identical to baseline)	Nine children, three each assigned to 4, 5, or 6 baseline sessions

(Continued)

Table 11.3 Continued

Reference	Dependent Variable	Conditions	Intervention Targets
Sallese, M. R., & Vannest, K. J. (2022). Effects of a manualized teacher-led coaching intervention on paraprofessional use of behavior-specific praise. *Remedial and Special Education*, 43(1), 27–39.	Number of behavior-specific praise statements used by paraprofessionals, measured via event recording	A: Baseline (business-as-usual) *Concurrent* B: Coaching, self-monitoring C: Maintenance (identical to baseline)	Three paraprofessionals

Multiple Baseline Across Behaviors

Reference	Dependent Variable	Conditions	Intervention Targets
Dennis, L., Eldridge, J., Hammons, N. C., Robbins, A., & Wade, T. (2022). The effects of practice-based coaching on paraprofessional implementation of shared book reading strategies. *Preventing School Failure: Alternative Education for Children and Youth*, Advance online publication.	Targeted book reading behaviors used by a paraprofessional, measured via event recording and reported as a percentage of opportunities	A: Baseline (business-as-usual) *Concurrent* B: Practice-based coaching for shared book reading strategies.	Three strategies: Question/evaluate, expansion, repeat
Golden, A. K., Hemmeter, M. L., & Ledford, J. R. (2023). Evaluating the effects of training plus practice-based coaching delivered via text message on teacher use of pyramid model practices. *Journal of Positive Behavior Interventions*, 26(1), 39–51.	Teacher behaviors, measured via timed event recording and presented as a number	A: Baseline (business-as-usual) *Concurrent* B: Training plus practice-based coaching via text C: Fading coaching (reminders) D: Maintenance (identical to baseline)	Four strategies (e.g., providing choices, suggesting interactions)
Quinn, E. D., Kaiser, A. P., & Ledford, J. (2021). Hybrid telepractice delivery of enhanced milieu teaching: Effects on caregiver implementation and child communication. *Journal of Speech, Language, and Hearing Research*, 64(8), 3074–3099.	Correct EMT strategies used by parents, reported as both a number correct and a percentage correct	A: Baseline (business-as-usual) *Concurrent* B: Instruction and coaching for enhanced milieu teaching (EMT) strategy use C: Maintenance (similar to baseline)	Four strategies: Matched turns, target talk and expansions; time delays, and milieu episodes

Multiple Baseline Across Contexts

Reference	Dependent Variable	Conditions	Intervention Targets
Edwards, M. (2022). Efficacy of positive reinforcement to promote glasses wearing for a preschooler who wears glasses and has an intellectual disability (Thesis, The Ohio State University).	Duration of time a preschooler spent wearing glasses, reported as a percentage of session	A: Baseline (no treatment) *Concurrent* B: Prompts, reinforcement	Three classroom settings (motor time, centers, free play)
Huffman, R. W., Sainato, D. M., & Curiel, E. S. (2016). Correspondence training using social interests to increase compliance during transitions: An emerging technology. *Behavior Analysis in Practice*, 9, 25–33	Initiation of transitions, measured via latency to begin, and reported as a number of seconds	A: Baseline B: Correspondence training C: Maintenance (identical to baseline)	Three transitions (clean up, handwashing, table time)

Multiple Probe Designs

The multiple probe design is also frequently used, especially the MP-Behaviors variation, when evaluating acquisition of non-reversible behaviors such as academic skill. It is generally used for evaluating non-reversible, rather than reversible, behaviors because reversible behaviors tend to be more prone to data instability threats (see Internal Validity section below). When this design is used, you collect intermittent data in the baseline condition, and ensure that each baseline phase has sufficiently different baseline lengths (see Callout 11.3). It is important to note that there are no "hard and fast" rules about how often data should be collected in multiple probe designs. See Figure 11.4, which shows the same data presented in Figures 11.1 and 11.2. In this graph, compared with Figure 11.1, we have maintained only about one-third of the data points, rather than the half we included in Figure 11.2. These three graphs show how *sampling* only *some* of the data in baseline conditions may alter conclusions drawn about that condition.

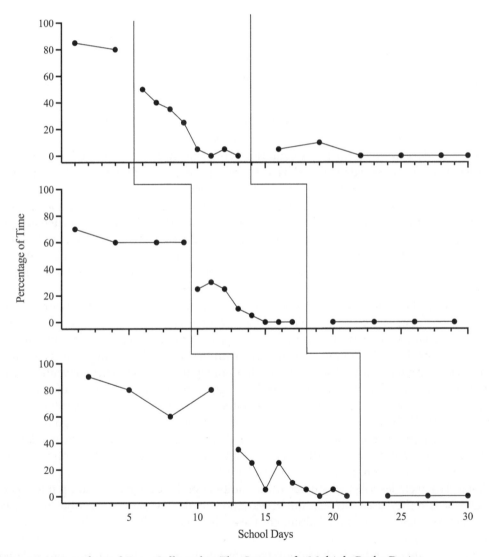

Figure 11.4 Hypothetical Data Collected in The Context of a Multiple Probe Design.

Note: These data are exactly the same as those depicted in Figures 11.1 and 11.2, with approximately one-third as many measurement occasions in baseline phases compared with Figure 11.1.

The phases in multiple probe designs are similar to those in multiple baseline designs (e.g., the primary comparison is between a baseline condition and an intervention condition). Because these designs are often used for non-reversible behaviors, maintenance conditions are often included. There are two different types of naming conventions that may help you interpret other studies and decide what to call the conditions in a study you design. The first convention refers to groups of non-treatment sessions that occur as **probe sessions**. **Probe conditions** are made up of sessions with non-treatment conditions in effect. They are named as such because they do not include intervention (i.e., a researcher is "probing" for behavior occurrence). In multiple probe designs, probe conditions can occur before intervention (i.e., baseline, behavior is expected to be in need of treatment) *and* after intervention (i.e., maintenance, behavior might be expected to remain at intervention levels). To confuse things further, when researchers use the second naming convention, they use the term **baseline phase** when the initial non-treatment condition is in effect and **maintenance phase** for the procedurally identical condition that occurs post-treatment. Neither of these conventions is incorrect (see Figure 11.4)—but it is helpful to be aware that researchers can use different naming conventions that refer to procedurally identical conditions or phases.

In addition to naming differences, there are two different ways to organize baseline/probe sessions in multiple probe designs. One strategy is to *cluster baseline sessions together temporally, with substantial breaks between clusters*. This is referred to as a **conditions variation**, and is most common when using the MP-Behaviors design. This variation is depicted in Figure 11.5, which shows a MP-Behaviors design (condition variation) in which Hardy and Hemmeter (2023) taught math skills to preschoolers. As you can see in the figure, there are clusters of three school days in which the probe condition is implemented for all tiers, followed by intervention in one tier, followed by several days in which the probe condition is implemented in all tiers, and so on. The second strategy for organizing baseline/probe sessions is referred to as the **days variation** and it involves *conducting single sessions in which probe conditions are in effect, followed by several sessions in which no measurement occurs*. This variation is depicted in Figure 11.6, which shows a multiple probe across participants (days variation) in which teachers were coached to provide more and better-quality behavior-specific praise (Gorton et al., 2021). As you can see in the figure, the probe condition is generally implemented for a single measurement occasion rather than in clusters. The exception to this rule in this design is that usually there are several measurement occasions clustered together in the initial sessions for the intervention target assigned to the first tier (i.e., the first three days of the baseline/probe phase are adjacent). You might notice that different graphing conventions are used for the conditions and days variations shown in Figures 11.5 and 11.6, with the "zig zag" lines depicting time lags in Figure 11.5 and a number of straight vertical lines in Figure 11.6. The latter convention can be confusing because it does not highlight the time-lagged introduction of intervention or clearly separate data that are pre-intervention (i.e., baseline) from post-intervention data (i.e., maintenance). Figure 11.7 shows hypothetical data from the same multiple probe design (conditions variation) using each graphing convention. Note that Figure 11.7 also depicts the two different naming conventions discussed earlier in the chapter (e.g., probe and intervention phases versus baseline, intervention, and maintenance phases).

Table 11.4 includes a list of studies using multiple probe designs, including information about whether they used the conditions variation or days variation. We did not include MP-Contexts designs because—although these designs are theoretically viable—almost invariably, possible generalization across contexts (resulting in data instability threats) are considerable threats, and as such multiple baseline designs rather than multiple probe designs should be selected.

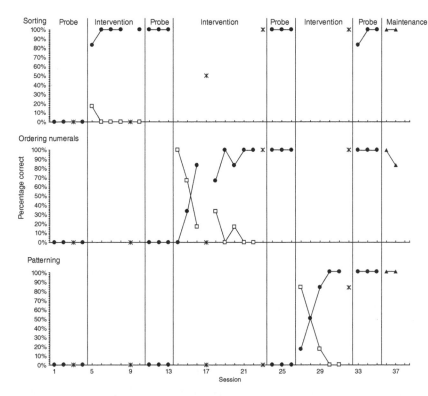

Figure 11.5 Graph Depicting Data in a Multiple Probe Design (Conditions Variation).

Source: Hardy, J. K., & Hemmeter, M. L. (2023). Systematic modeling and prompting to teach math skills to preschoolers with disabilities. *Topics in Early Childhood Special Education*, 43(2), 103–115.

Callout 11.5 Applied Example of a Multiple Probe Across Behaviors Design (Days Variation)

Heider et al. (2019) evaluated the impacts of self-directed video prompting on the correct performance of vocational tasks. Participants were two adults (21-year-olds) with moderate intellectual disability enrolled in a transition program who were proficient readers and who could independently navigate a cell phone. The intervention targets were three different vocational tasks, each consisting of 17–40 steps. Accurate and independent completion of each step of the task was recorded via trial-by-trial event recording, and data were reported as a percentage correct. During baseline conditions, participants were provided with a paper copy of the task analysis and a task direction. They were given the opportunity to correctly perform each step via a multiple opportunity probe, but no error correction was provided. During intervention conditions, students were provided a phone and instructed to use the video clips on the phone to complete the task. Error correction was provided by resetting materials and providing a specific verbal prompt related to the error. If this did not result in a correct response, the researcher provided a model. During maintenance phases, two different procedures were in effect. For the first three sessions, the phone was available, but students were not directly instructed to use it. For the last session, conditions were identical to baseline (i.e., the phone was not available). In Chapter 12, we share a figure depicting the MP-Behaviors design and analysis of the outcomes of this study.

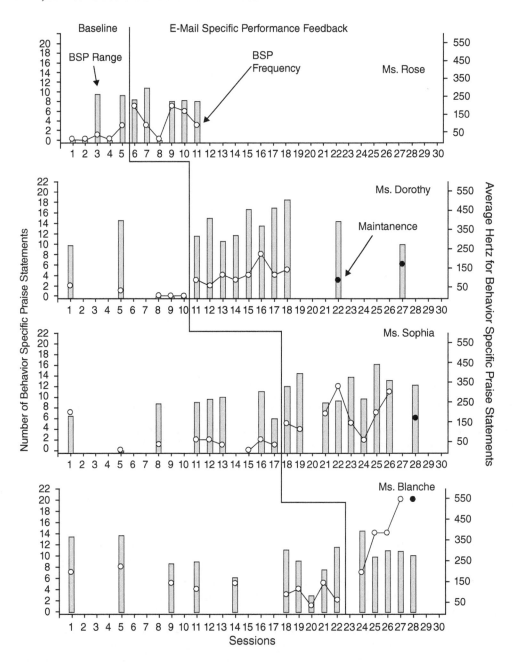

Figure 11.6 Graph Depicting Data in a Multiple Probe Design (Days Variation).

Source: Gorton, K., Allday, R. A., Lane, J. D., & Ault, M. J. (2021). Effects of brief training plus electronic feedback on increasing quantity and intonation of behavior specific praise among preschool teachers. *Journal of Behavioral Education*, 31(4), 731–750.

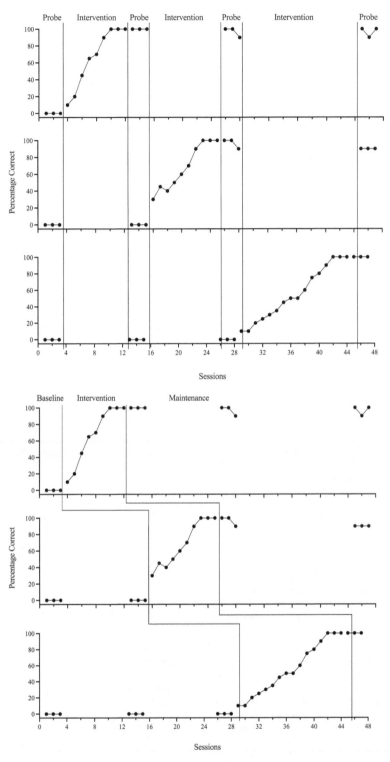

Figure 11.7 Multiple Probe Designs (Condition Variation) Shown with Two Different Graphing Conventions and Two Different Naming Conventions.

> **Callout 11.6** Applied Example of a Multiple Probe Across Participants Design (Days Variation)
>
> D'Agostino et al. (2020) implemented an intervention designed to increase social behaviors during book reading for young children with autism. The participants were 4–5-year-old boys (race and ethnicity not reported) who attended an early intensive behavior intervention (EIBI) program for part of the day and an inclusive preschool for the other part of the day. The primary behavior of interest was social commenting with a point to the book and the secondary behavior was responding to initiations. Both were measured via timed event recording and reported as a total number of independent responses per session. During the baseline condition, the researcher provided an expectant look as an opportunity to comment, and provided social reinforcement if commenting occurred, but did not prompt commenting. During the intervention condition, the researcher used the system of least prompts with token and social reinforcement to teach commenting. An additional procedure was added to the intervention condition for one participant (Elwin), which was a differential reinforcement of low rates of behavior procedure that was typically used by his endogenous service providers. At the conclusion of the session, he was provided access to preferred activities contingent on having fewer than three instances of vocal stereotypy during the session. In Chapter 12, we share a figure depicting the MP-Participants design and analysis of the outcomes of this study.

Table 11.4 Studies Using Multiple Probe Designs

Reference	Dependent Variable	Conditions	Intervention Targets
Multiple Probe across Participants			
Dueñas, A. D., Plavnick, J. B., & Bak, M. S. (2019). Effects of joint video modeling on unscripted play behavior of children with autism spectrum disorder. *Journal of Autism and Developmental Disorders*, 49, 236–247.	1. Unscripted vocalizations and 2. Unscripted play actions, both measured via event recording and reported as a count 3. Scripted pay actions, measured via event recording and reported as a percentage of actions	A: Baseline (Peer-only video modeling) *Days variation* B: Joint video modeling	Participants (3 total)
Kim, S., Kang, V., Kim, H., Wang, J., & Gregori, E. (2022). Online literacy instruction for young Korean dual language learners in general education. *Journal of Behavioral Education*, 32(4), 743–767.	1. Oral fluency, reported as percentage read correctly 2. Target vocabulary, reported as percentage identified correctly 3. Story comprehension, reported as percentage questions answered correctly	A: Baseline (no treatment) *Days variation* B: Read it Again PK C: Maintenance (identical to baseline)	Participants (8 total, 4 each in 2 separate designs)

(Continued)

Table 11.4 Continued

Reference	Dependent Variable	Conditions	Intervention Targets
Paranczak, J. L., Lambert, J. M., Ledford, J. R., Copeland, B., & MacDonald, J. M. (2024). Deriving relations at multiple levels of complexity following minimal instruction: A demonstration. *Journal of Applied Behavior Analysis*.	Correct instructional and game play responses related to derived relations, all measured via event recording and reported as a percentage correct	A: Baseline (no treatment for instruction context; BAU for game play) *Conditions variation* B: Constant time delay (instruction context only, B condition for game play was identical to baseline)	Participants (4 total)

Multiple Probe across Behaviors

Reference	Dependent Variable	Conditions	Intervention Targets
Genc-Tosun, D., Kurt, O., Cevher, Z., & Gregori, E. V. (2022). Teaching children with autism spectrum disorder to answer questions using an iPad-based speech-generating device. *Journal of Autism and Developmental Disorders*, 53(9), 3724–3739.	Independent answers, measured via event recording and reported as a percentage	A: Baseline (no treatment) *Conditions variation* B: Constant time delay C: Maintenance probes (identical to baseline)	Answers to three different questions (what do you want, what is this, personal information)
Mechling, L., Ayres, K. M., Purrazzella, K., & Purrazzella, K. (2012). Evaluation of the performance of fine and gross motor skills within multi-step tasks by adults with moderate intellectual disability when using video models. *Journal of Developmental and Physical Disabilities*, 24, 469–486.	Accuracy, measured using event recording of a single dichotomous response, and reported as a 0 (inaccurate) or 1 (accurate)	A: Baseline (no treatment) *Days variation* B: System of least prompts C: Maintenance (identical to baseline)	Three behaviors: Offering help, responding to feedback, and asking for clarification for unclear instructions
Rogers, L., Hemmeter, M. L., & Wolery, M. (2010). Using a constant time delay procedure to teach foundational swimming skills to children with autism. *Topics in Early Childhood Special Education*, 30(2), 102–111.	Correct swimming responses, measured using event recording and reported as a percentage correct	A: Baseline (no treatment) *Conditions variation* B: Constant time delay C: Maintenance (final probe, identical to baseline)	Three behaviors: Flutter kick, arm strokes, and head turns
Wolery, M., Anthony, L., Caldwell, N. K., Snyder, E. D., & Morgante, J. D. (2002). Embedding and distributing constant time delay in circle time and transitions. *Topics in Early Childhood Education*, 22, 14–25.	Naming academic stimuli, measured using event recording, and reported as percentage correct	A: Baseline (no treatment) *Conditions variation* B: Embedded constant time delay	Four sets of sight words (2 participants) or three sets of multiplication facts (1 participant)

Note: BAU = business-as-usual.

Procedural Steps for MB and MP Designs

When using multiple baseline or multiple probe designs, adhere to the guidelines and recommendations outlined below.

Before
1. Create a falsifiable research question about the impact of two conditions on at least three intervention targets (participants, behaviors, or contexts) that are functionally similar and functionally independent.
2. Select an appropriate (sensitive, reliable, valid, feasible) measurement system, test it, and modify as needed.
3. If you have more than one dependent variable, identify which will serve as the *primary dependent variable*, on which condition change decisions will be made.
4. Determine your comparison of interest (e.g., a baseline condition and an intervention condition) and identify what type of baseline comparison answers your research question.
5. Review previous research and your theory of change for evidence that the intervention can be slowly alternated, with carryover effects being unlikely or likely to diminish quickly.
6. Operationalize all condition procedures, including a baseline condition and a treatment condition (if generalization and maintenance conditions are included, operationalize those, too).
7. Determine how and how often interobserver agreement and fidelity data will be collected (i.e., develop fidelity forms and procedures).
8. If possible, practice (i.e., pilot) procedures with non-participants and assess fidelity to procedures, interobserver agreement, and any changes needed in implementation or fidelity measurement.
9. Given the selected behaviors and planned conditions, are the following conditions met? If not, consider a different design.
    a. A research question about the impact of two conditions on at least three intervention targets (participants, behaviors, or contexts) that are functionally similar and functionally independent.
    b. Interest in behavior that are either reversible (but for which withdrawing intervention is not desirable), or non-reversible.
    c. Ability to conduct baseline phases that have varying lengths across intervention targets, with some intervention targets having relatively few baseline sessions (e.g., 3–6) and some intervention targets having many more (e.g., 10–20 or more).
10. Identify whether a multiple baseline or multiple probe design is most appropriate.
    a. If testing threats are likely, choose a multiple probe design.
    b. If data instability threats are likely, choose a multiple baseline design.
11. Identify whether your design will be implemented *concurrently* or *non-concurrently* and identify how time (e.g., calendar days, session numbers) will be represented on your graph.
12. Identify whether you will use a priori or response-guided phase changes.
    a. Define rules for changing conditions (e.g., after five sessions, when there is a clear change in level with no data overlapping with the previous condition for at least three consecutive days), modifying conditions, and discontinuing the evaluation.
    b. Include decisions about the minimum amount of acceptable lag between tiers based on your substantive knowledge about your independent variable, dependent variable, and participants.

13. Identify expected data patterns and describe the conditions that will result in a functional relation determination.
14. Determine whether you will modify one or more conditions if performance is unexpected, and what the criterion for those changes will be (e.g., no change in level between conditions, assessed via visual analysis).
15. Identify participants, and, if applicable, refine definitions or target behaviors (e.g., specify exact topography of challenging behavior for a functional communication intervention, select unknown sight words for an instructional intervention).

During
16. Initiate the first phase and continue collecting data under those conditions until your phase change, modification, or discontinuation criteria have been met.
17. When criteria have been met, initiate intervention with the second-tier target (for concurrent designs). Continue until all phases are complete for all intervention targets.
18. Use visual analysis to determine whether a functional relation exists, does not exist, or whether additional data are needed (see Chapter 10).
19. Collect the specified amount of reliability and procedural fidelity data across all phases, conditions, and participants.
20. If possible, replicate with similar participants.

Callout 11.7 How Do I Choose Between Multiple Baseline and Multiple Probe Design Variations?

Given the differences between MB and MP designs, why would a researcher choose one instead of the other? MB designs have the benefit of continuous measurement prior to and during intervention, thereby allowing day-to-day data analyses and decisions. Moreover, continuous data collection allows for close visual analysis of potential threats to internal validity such as maturation and instrumentation. As for MP designs, intermittent baseline measurement means data analysis is also intermittent, limiting the ability to identify potential threats. However, some threats are more likely with MB designs than MP designs, including testing threats. In addition, extended baselines with continuous measurement may be less desirable from a practical standpoint (e.g., participants may find these sessions aversive). Sometimes both types of designs are possible given resource constraints and researcher goals. If so, we offer the following guidance for choosing MB or MP designs:

1. When *testing threats* are more likely, choose an MP design. This includes most situations in which baseline conditions consist of researcher-directed trials to complete a specific task.
2. When *data instability* is more likely, choose an MB design. This includes most free operant behaviors, which tend to be more variable than trial-based behaviors and almost always is the case when intervention targets vary by context.
3. If neither threat is likely, choose an MB design because continuous measurement generally allows for closer inspection of potential threats than intermittent measurement.

Threats to Internal Validity for Time-Lagged Design Family

Time-lagged designs are generally of relatively long duration, so history and maturation threats are potentially more likely than in the other design families. *Maturation* threats are generally considered controlled for when performance is stable in baseline conditions for all tiers; to prevent maturation threats, you should not choose behaviors likely to gradually improve over time. *Testing* threats are increased due to the duration of baseline conditions in particular, and can be mitigated by choosing a multiple probe instead of a multiple baseline design. Relatedly, you would choose a multiple baseline design instead of a multiple probe design if *data instability* threats were more likely than testing threats. Several strategies may be employed to overcome testing threats, regardless of design type. First, you can positively reinforce desired behaviors during pre-intervention sessions. You may choose to (1) contingently reinforce target behaviors when performed correctly, assuming you are not interested in studying the influence of contingent reinforcement alone (Wolery et al., 1991); (2) contingently reinforce correct responses to known stimuli interspersed with target behaviors (Gast et al., 1991); (3) intermittently reinforce non-target behaviors emitted between trials or between steps during a response chain task (Wall et al., 1999); or (4) inform study participants prior to the start of a session that a reinforcer menu will be presented immediately after the session from which they will be able choose one activity or item.

Attrition is more likely for studies that are longer in duration, and especially when baseline conditions are extended; thus, this threat can be problematic in MB and MP designs. You can mitigate these issues by informing participants of likely duration of baseline and by making baseline less aversive when possible. You should also randomly assign intervention targets to tier, to avoid attrition differentially impacting intervention targets that were less likely to respond favorably to intervention. *Infidelity threats* are likely when the same control agent implements the intervention *across intervention targets*. For example, a 1:1 aide might be tasked with implementing a token system intervention during math class but asked to withhold the intervention during lunch time and independent work time. Once the paraprofessional has implemented the token system in one tier (particularly if there is a therapeutic behavior change), she might be likely to have low fidelity to baseline conditions (i.e., *not implementing the intervention* in the other two contexts).

The specific *design-related confound* that is associated with the time-lagged design family is that the relation identified between the independent and dependent variables may be partially explained by differing amounts of experience in baseline conditions. For example, spending more time in a non-treatment context could result in slower behavior change once treatment begins. Additional work is needed to determine the extent to which this extent is likely in various applied contexts, but some basic and translational research suggests this phenomenon is potentially likely (Doughty et al., 2010; Winterbauer et al., 2013). This is different than multi-treatment interference because it is an interaction of the history with the previous condition *and specific design ordering requirements*. Similarly, in across participants designs (e.g., MB/MP-Behaviors, MB/MP-Contexts), the previous exposure to intervention (for other behaviors or in other contexts) may change the relation, or the strength of the relation, for later tiers (e.g., a "learning to learn" phenomenon related to total dosage of an intervention across tiers; cf. Ledford & Wolery, 2015).

See Table 11.5 for a list of potential threats to internal validity, including considerations specific to the time-lagged design family as well as general procedures for preventing or reducing the impact of these threats across design types. There are no specific concerns with *instrumentation*, *selection*, or *adaptation* threats in time-lagged designs.

Table 11.5 General Internal Validity Information and Time-Lagged-Specific Considerations (In Bold)

Threat	Preventing or Reducing Impact
History: Events that occur during an experiment, unrelated to planned procedures	Control outside sources of influence, continue phase until data are stable; describe likely history events in narrative; if nonconcurrent, select participants unlikely to have similar experiences in their daily interactions
Maturation: Changes in behavior due to the passage of time	Design a short duration study, include an intervention with effects above and beyond maturation
Testing: Repeated assessment	Design conditions that do not over or underestimate participant performance; choose treatment with effects above and beyond testing effects; if inhibitive effects are noted, modify baseline so accurate performance is measured **Use a multiple probe design instead of a multiple baseline design if testing threats are likely**
Instrumentation: Problems with measurement	Operationally define behaviors; use appropriate measurement procedures; collect precise reliability data; regularly conduct discrepancy discussions; visually analyze data from both observers to identify bias or drift; when possible, use naïve observers
Procedural Infidelity: Lack of adherence to condition protocols	Operationally define all procedures; train implementers to a criterion level before the study begins; support implementation, collect and formatively analyze data, especially early in a phase, with modifications to training and supports provided as needed **Ensure implementers have sufficient training and support to hold one or more participants, contexts, or behaviors in baseline conditions while intervening on one or more different participants, contexts, or behaviors**
Selection: Including certain participants and not others	Describe all rules used to select participants (i.e., inclusion criteria); describe procedures used to choose participants when more participants met inclusion criteria than could participate, and randomly select from this pool if possible
Attrition: When participants withdraw from the study prior to completion	Manage baseline durations; choose participants likely to benefit from the intervention; be forthcoming about difficulties that associated with research participation; include all data from all participants, even ones who withdraw, in final research reports **Randomly assign participants to tiers (multiple baseline or probe across participants variation) to avoid biased attrition; use multiple probe design if baseline conditions are aversive**
Multitreatment Interference: When behavior is influenced by procedures in conditions not currently being experienced	Provide cues that allow participants to understand differences between conditions
Data Instability: Large differences in data from session-to-session within a single condition	Control for variables contributing to variability, continue conditions until data are stable or do not exceed expectations for variability, use interventions likely to impact behavior above and beyond variability seen in baseline; do not intervene following an outlying data point in either therapeutic or countertherapeutic directions **Use multiple baseline instead of multiple probe design if data stability is expected in baseline conditions**
Adaptation: Time at beginning of study when participants behavior may not represent typical performance	Allow for an adaptation period before data collection begins; continue baseline conditions until data are stable; use measurement procedures that are not intrusive
Design-related Confounds: When condition ordering influences identification of relations	Understand the theory of change relevant to your study; choose an appropriate design type **The relation between A and B may be different depending on the duration of time spent in A**

Conclusions

Time-lagged designs rely on time-lagged introduction of an intervention condition and are flexible for assessing the impact of an intervention on reversible and non-reversible behaviors. These designs require the identification of three functionally similar but independent intervention targets (participants, behaviors, or contexts). They are critical and widely used single case designs that are flexible for evaluating many interventions and dependent variables.

References

Baer, D. M., Wolf, M. M., & Risley, T. R. (1968). Some current dimensions of applied behavior analysis. *Journal of Applied Behavior Analysis*, 1(1), 91.

Baldwin, B. (2013). Peer-mediated intervention and technology: Mobile device application use in implementation of peer buddy training (Doctoral dissertation, The Florida State University).

Campbell, A. R., Sallese, M. R., Thompson, J. L., Fournier, C. J., & Allen, M. (2023). Culturally adapted social, emotional, and behavioral support for black male learners. *Remedial and Special Education*, 07419325221143965.

Capalbo, A., Miltenberger, R. G., & Cook, J. L. (2022). Training soccer goalkeeping skills: Is video modeling enough? *Journal of Applied Behavior Analysis*, 55(3), 958–970.

D'Agostino, S. R., Dueñas, A. D., & Plavnick, J. B. (2020). Increasing social initiations during shared book reading: An intervention for preschoolers with autism spectrum disorder. *Topics in Early Childhood Special Education*, 39(4), 213–225.

Dart, E. H., & Radley, K. C. (2023). The effects of x-axis time compression on the visual analysis of single-case data. *Psychology in the Schools*, 60(10), 4029–4038.

Dennis, L., Eldridge, J., Hammons, N. C., Robbins, A., & Wade, T. (2022). The effects of practice-based coaching on paraprofessional implementation of shared book reading strategies. *Preventing School Failure: Alternative Education for Children and Youth*, 1–11.

Doughty, A. H., Cash, J. D., Finch, E. A., Holloway, C., & Wallington, L. K. (2010). Effects of training history on resurgence in humans. *Behavioural Processes*, 83(3), 340–343.

Dueñas, A. D., Plavnick, J. B., & Bak, M. S. (2019). Effects of joint video modeling on unscripted play behavior of children with autism spectrum disorder. *Journal of Autism and Developmental Disorders*, 49, 236–247.

Edwards, M. (2022). Efficacy of positive reinforcement to promote glasses wearing for a preschooler who wears glasses and has an intellectual disability (Thesis, The Ohio State University).

Flood, W. A., & Wilder, D. A. (2004). The use of differential reinforcement and fading to increase time away from a caregiver in a child with separation anxiety disorder. *Education and Treatment of Children*, 27, 1–8.

Gast, D. L., Doyle, P. M., Wolery, M., Ault, M. J., & Baklarz, J. L. (1991). Acquisition of incidental information during small group instruction. *Education and Treatment of Children*, 1–18.

Genc-Tosun, D., Kurt, O., Cevher, Z., & Gregori, E. V. (2022). Teaching children with autism spectrum disorder to answer questions using an iPad-based speech-generating device. *Journal of Autism and Developmental Disorders*, 53(9), 3724–3739.

Golden, A. K., Hemmeter, M. L., & Ledford, J. R. (2023). Evaluating the effects of training plus practice-based coaching delivered via text message on teacher use of pyramid model practices. *Journal of Positive Behavior Interventions*, 26(1), 39–51.

Gorton, K., Allday, R. A., Lane, J. D., & Ault, M. J. (2021). Effects of brief training plus electronic feedback on increasing quantity and intonation of behavior specific praise among preschool teachers. *Journal of Behavioral Education*, 31(4), 731–750.

Grey, I., Healy, O., Leader, G., & Hayes, D. (2009). Using a Time Timer™ to increase appropriate waiting behavior in a child with developmental disabilities. *Research in Developmental Disabilities*, 30(2), 359–366.

Hammond, D., & Gast, D. L. (2010). Descriptive analysis of single subject research designs: 1983–2007. *Education and Training in Autism and Developmental Disabilities*, 45(2), 187–202.

Hardy, J. K., & Hemmeter, M. L. (2023). Systematic modeling and prompting to teach math skills to preschoolers with disabilities. *Topics in Early Childhood Special Education*, 43(2), 103–115.

Heider, A. E., Cannella-Malone, H. I., & Andzik, N. R. (2019). Effects of self-directed video prompting on vocational task acquisition. *Career Development and Transition for Exceptional Individuals*, 42(2), 87–98.

Horner, R. D., & Baer, D. M. (1978). Multiple-probe technique: A variation of the multiple baseline 1. *Journal of Applied Behavior Analysis*, 11(1), 189–196.

Horner, R. H., & Machalicek, W. (2022). Honoring uncontrolled events: Commentary on Slocum et al. *Perspectives on Behavior Science*, 45(3), 639–645.

Huffman, R. W., Sainato, D. M., & Curiel, E. S. (2016). Correspondence training using social interests to increase compliance during transitions: An emerging technology. *Behavior Analysis in Practice*, 9, 25–33.

Iwata, B. A. (1991). Applied behavior analysis as technological science. *Journal of Applied Behavior Analysis*, 24(3), 421.

Kang, V. Y., & Kim, S. (2023). Effects of enhanced milieu teaching and book reading on the target word approximations of young children with language delay. *Journal of Early Intervention*, 45(2), 122–144.

Kim, S., Kang, V., Kim, H., Wang, J., & Gregori, E. (2022). Online literacy instruction for young Korean dual language learners in general education. *Journal of Behavioral Education*, 32(4), 743–767.

Kratochwill, T. R., Levin, J. R., Morin, K. L., & Lindström, E. R. (2022). Examining and enhancing the methodological quality of nonconcurrent multiple-baseline designs. *Perspectives on Behavior Science*, 45(3), 651–660.

Lambert, J. M., Parikh, N., Stankiewicz, K. C., Houchins-Juarez, N. J., Morales, V. A., Sweeney, E. M., & Milam, M. E. (2019). Decreasing food stealing of child with Prader-Willi syndrome through function-based differential reinforcement. *Journal of Autism and Developmental Disorders*, 49, 721–728.

Laushey, K. M., & Heflin, L. J. (2000). Enhancing social skills of kindergarten children with autism through the training of multiple peers as tutors. *Journal of Autism and Developmental Disorders*, 30(3), 183–193.

Ledford, J. R. (2022). Concurrence on nonconcurrence in multiple-baseline designs: A commentary on Slocum et al. (2022). *Perspectives on Behavior Science*, 45(3), 661–666.

Ledford, J. R., Barton, E. E., Severini, K. E., Zimmerman, K. N., & Pokorski, E. A. (2019). Visual display of graphic data in single case design studies. *Education and Training in Autism and Developmental Disabilities*, 54(4), 315–327.

Ledford, J. R., & Pustejovsky, J. E. (2019). Stay-play-talk meta-analysis. https://osf.io/u7cph

Ledford, J. R., & Wolery, M. (2013). Peer modeling of academic and social behaviors during small-group direct instruction. *Exceptional Children*, 79(4), 439–458.

Ledford, J. R., & Wolery, M. (2015). Observational learning of academic and social behaviors during small-group direct instruction. *Exceptional Children*, 81(3), 272–291.

Ledford, J. R., & Zimmerman, K. N. (2023). Rethinking rigor in multiple baseline and multiple probe designs. *Remedial and Special Education*, 44(2), 154–167.

Luiselli, J. K. (2000). Cueing, demand fading, and positive reinforcement to establish self-feeding and oral consumption in a child with chronic food refusal. *Behavior Modification*, 24(3), 348–358.

Martinez-Torres, K. (2023). *Teaching Reciprocal Imitation Training (RIT) to Puerto Rican Parents of Young Children with Autism* (Doctoral dissertation).

Mechling, L., Ayres, K. M., Purrazzella, K., & Purrazzella, K. (2012). Evaluation of the performance of fine and gross motor skills within multi-step tasks by adults with moderate intellectual disability when using video models. *Journal of Developmental and Physical Disabilities*, 24, 469–486.

Morin, K. L., Lindström, E. R., Kratochwill, T. R., Levin, J. R., Blasko, A., Weir, A., ... & Hong, E. R. (2023). Nonconcurrent multiple-baseline and multiple-probe designs in special education: A systematic review of current practice and future directions. *Exceptional Children*, 90(2), 126–147.

Osborne, K., Ledford, J. R., Martin, J., & Thorne, K. (2019). Component analysis of stay, play, talk interventions with and without self-monitored group contingencies and recorded reminders. *Topics in Early Childhood Special Education*, 39(1), 5–18.

Paranczak, J. L., Lambert, J. M., Ledford, J. R., Copeland, B., & MacDonald, J. M. (2024). Deriving relations at multiple levels of complexity following minimal instruction: A demonstration. *Journal of Applied Behavior Analysis*.

Peredo, T. N., Zelaya, M. I., & Kaiser, A. P. (2018). Teaching low-income Spanish-speaking caregivers to implement EMT en Español with their young children with language impairment: A pilot study. *American Journal of Speech-Language Pathology*, 27(1), 136–153.

Quinn, E. D., Kaiser, A. P., & Ledford, J. (2021). Hybrid telepractice delivery of enhanced milieu teaching: Effects on caregiver implementation and child communication. *Journal of Speech, Language, and Hearing Research*, 64(8), 3074–3099.

Rogers, L., Hemmeter, M. L., & Wolery, M. (2010). Using a constant time delay procedure to teach foundational swimming skills to children with autism. *Topics in Early Childhood Special Education*, 30(2), 102–111.

Salazar, D. M., Ruiz, F. J., Ramírez, E. S., & Cardona-Betancourt, V. (2020). Acceptance and commitment therapy focused on repetitive negative thinking for child depression: a randomized multiple-baseline evaluation. *The Psychological Record*, 70, 373–386.

Sallese, M. R., & Vannest, K. J. (2022). Effects of a manualized teacher-led coaching intervention on paraprofessional use of behavior-specific praise. *Remedial and Special Education*, 43(1), 27–39.

Severini, K. E., Ledford, J. R., Barton, E. E., & Osborne, K. C. (2019). Implementing stay-play-talk with children who use AAC. *Topics in Early Childhood Special Education*, 38(4), 220–233.

Slocum, T. A., Pinkelman, S. E., Joslyn, P. R., & Nichols, B. (2022). Threats to internal validity in multiple-baseline design variations. *Perspectives on Behavior Science*, 45(3), 619–638.

Soermajoro, F. (2022). The effects of stay play talk for children who are English language learners. [Unpublished Master's Thesis]. Department of Special Education, Vanderbilt University.

Tang, L. L. (2023). *Using Stay-Play-Talk to Increase Levels of Initiations and Responses for Children with Social Delays* (Thesis, Vanderbilt University).

Tanious, R., & Onghena, P. (2021). A systematic review of applied single-case research published between 2016 and 2018: Study designs, randomization, data aspects, and data analysis. *Behavior Research Methods*, 53, 1371–1384.

Taylor, A. G. n.d. An adaptation of stay play talk for children with internalizing behaviors. (Dissertation, Vanderbilt University). https://ir.vanderbilt.edu/handle/1803/9598

Taylor, A. G., Hemmeter, M. L., Reimers, A., Basler, S., Granger, K., & Ledford, J. R. (2023). An adaptation of stay-play-talk for young children with internalizing behaviors.

Wall, M. E., Gast, D. L., & Royston, P. A. (1999). Leisure skills instruction for adolescents with severe or profound developmental disabilities. *Journal of Developmental and Physical Disabilities*, 11, 193–219.

Wheatley, T. L., Goulet, M., Mann, K., & Lanovaz, M. J. (2020). Differential negative reinforcement of other behavior to increase compliance with wearing an anti-strip suit. *Journal of Applied Behavior Analysis*, 53(2), 1153–1161.

White, E. N., Cagliani, R. R., & Tyson, K. M. (2023). Effects on speech development with modifications to picture exchange communication system. *Focus on Autism and Other Developmental Disabilities*.

Winterbauer, N. E., Lucke, S., & Bouton, M. E. (2013). Some factors modulating the strength of resurgence after extinction of an instrumental behavior. *Learning and Motivation*, 44(1), 60–71.

Wolery, M., Anthony, L., Caldwell, N. K., Snyder, E. D., & Morgante, J. D. (2002). Embedding and distributing constant time delay in circle time and transitions. *Topics in Early Childhood Education*, 22, 14–25.

Wolery, M., Cybriwsky, C. A., Gast, D. L., & Boyle-Gast, K. (1991). Use of constant time delay and attentional responses with adolescents. *Exceptional Children*, 57(5), 462–474.

12
Analyzing Data from Studies Using Time-Lagged Conditions

Jennifer R. Ledford and Joseph M. Lambert

Important Terms

covariation, masked analysis

Table of Contents

Formative Analysis and Phase Change Decisions
Summative Analysis and Functional Relation Determination
    Design Adequacy
    Data Sufficiency
    Control for Threats to Internal Validity
    Outcome Evaluation
Supplemental Analyses
Describing Visual Analysis
    Visual Analysis Procedures
    Visual Analysis Results
Conclusions
References

Callouts

12.1   Masked Visual Analysis
12.2   Baseline Lengths: How Different is Different Enough?
12.3   Inconsistent Inter-Participant Replication in Single Case Design Studies
12.4   Applied Example of Multiple Baseline Across Participants Design
12.5   Applied Example of Multiple Baseline Across Behaviors Design
12.6   Applied Example of a Multiple Probe Across Behaviors Design (Days Variation)
12.7   Applied Example of a Multiple Probe Across Participants Design (Days Variation)

As with sequential introduction and withdrawal (SIW) designs discussed in Chapter 10, analysis of data in designs that use time-lagged condition ordering is conducted using within-phase analysis (level, trend, variability/stability), between-phase analysis (immediacy, overlap), and across multiple comparisons in the same design (consistency). Again, we discuss visual analysis for formative and summative valuation, and briefly discuss the use of quantitative indices of magnitude (effect sizes) as a supplement to visual analysis.

As discussed in Chapter 11, designs using time-lagged condition ordering can be used when you have a question about a relation between one or more behaviors and one treatment condition relative to baseline. They can be used when at least three functionally similar, but independent intervention targets can be identified, and when it is appropriate to have different baseline durations across intervention targets, including extended baseline conditions for targets assigned to "later" tiers. These designs are not appropriate when simultaneous comparisons between more than two conditions are of interest.

Formative Analysis and Phase Change Decisions

As a reminder, the purpose of formative analysis is to answer the question "What should I do at this point in the experiment?" In SIW designs, the determination was generally about whether to continue in the current condition, move to the next planned condition, or discontinue the current procedures in favor of modifications or a new intervention (i.e., when response to a treatment condition is unexpected). In time-lagged designs, formative analysis also includes these decisions, but they are more complicated because decisions are made for at least three intervention targets and (when concurrent designs are used) the decision for each target depends on data patterns across *all* intervention targets. That is, when you conduct formative analysis for concurrent versions of time-lagged designs, you conduct within-tier analyses and across-tier analysis.

Figure 12.1 shows a series of decisions for one concurrent multiple baseline across participants design. Note that the decisions include consideration of data patterns across multiple tiers. That is, when deciding to intervene on the first tier, we first note whether *any* tier has problematic baseline patterns that could inhibit summative decision making later. Then, when deciding whether to intervene on the second tier, we both ask whether data patterns in the first tier are sufficient for concluding whether changes occurred *and* whether data in 2nd baseline are sufficiently stable.

When determining whether data are sufficient across multiple *concurrent* baseline phases, you must answer the question "Do data in the current tier suggest that the intervention condition is needed?" *and* "Do data in any of the tiers include problematic patterns that might inhibit functional relation determination during summative analysis?" Data suggesting intervention is not needed should likely result in a re-assessment of study plans (e.g., Have you set up baseline in a way that changes behavior in an unexpected way? Did you include participants based on inclusion criteria that did not correctly predict need for intervention? Did you include intervention targets that were known behaviors, based on incorrect screening data?).

When determining whether data in one intervention phase are sufficient for initiating intervention in the next tier, you must answer the question: "Do I have sufficient evidence that behavior changed (or sufficient evidence that behavior did *not* change)?" Sometimes, researchers set explicit criteria for this evidence—for example, the participant assigned to Tier 1 must reach a mastery criterion of 100% correct responding across two data collection occasions. Alternatively, researchers might instead set a visual analysis criterion—for example, that data in the intervention condition must be consistently higher in level than data in baseline

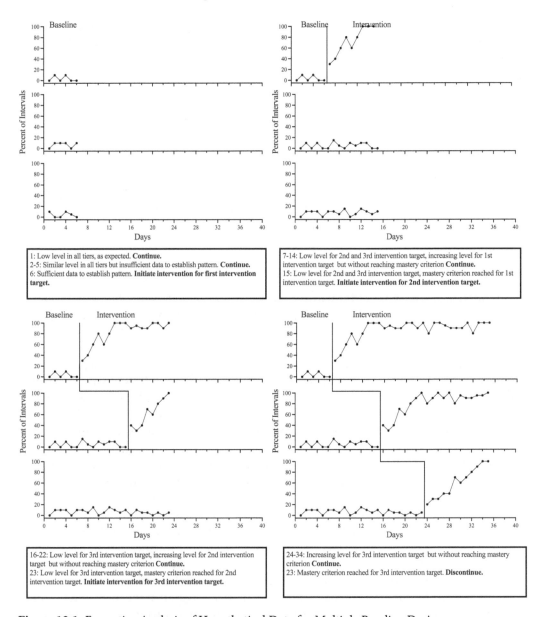

Figure 12.1 Formative Analysis of Hypothetical Data for Multiple Baseline Design.

conditions, for four consecutive sessions, with no overlap between conditions, before intervention can be initiated for the next intervention target/tier. Either of these strategies is acceptable, but you should explicate your rules for phase changes based on expected behavior change (e.g., mastery criteria or visual analysis rules) *and* explicate what would lead to discontinuation in the absence of behavior change (e.g., Will you move to the next intervention target if there is clear evidence that the intervention *does not* result in behavior change for the subsequent target?).

Figure 12.2 shows a second series of decisions for a multiple probe design across behaviors. Importantly, this design includes a condition modification, similar to those discussed in Chapter 10. See the Summative Analysis section to see how the functional relation decisions

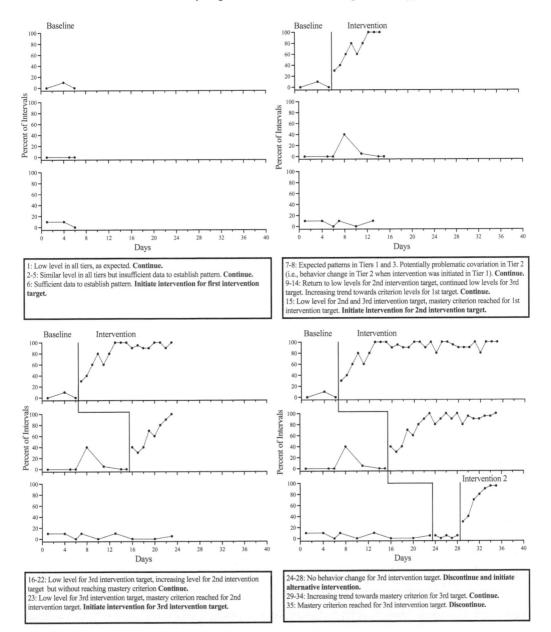

Figure 12.2 Formative Analysis of Hypothetical Data for Multiple Probe Design.

made differ from those possible in SIW designs. Also note here that a potential history effect was noted for the fourth measurement occasion (Day 8) for the second intervention target. Given that data immediately decreased in level after that single data point, the conclusion via visual analysis was that this threat was adequately controlled for, and intervention was initiated. An outlying data point like this can occur for a number of reasons—for example, if these data represent engagement data across three children in a multiple probe across participants design, Day 8 could represent a day in which a special activity occurred that was particularly interesting for one child. Additional data confirmed this increase in engagement that covaried with intervention implementation in the first tier was temporary.

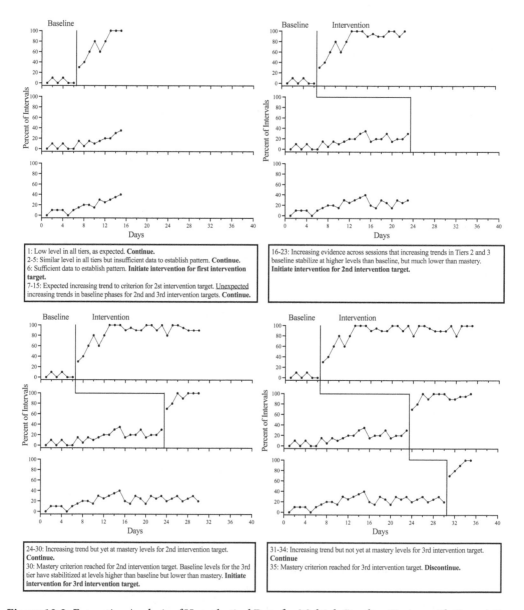

Figure 12.3 Formative Analysis of Hypothetical Data for Multiple Baseline Design with Covariation.

Figure 12.3 demonstrates another instance in which **covariation** occurred and was not temporary (i.e., data for an untreated intervention target changed when another intervention target was intervened on). An increasing trend in the data was noted for both the second and third intervention targets, when intervention was initiated for the first target. This might happen, for example, when an intervention is initiated in one context but not others (e.g., during lunch, but not during playground or after school care), and when the child generalizes behaviors across contexts (see Chapter 7). However, it could also indicate that some outside influence (e.g., a history threat) resulted in changes in all three intervention targets, and that these changes were unrelated to your intervention. In this case, you should continue baseline measurement until (1) data stabilize, at which point you can begin treatment (shown in Figure 12.3), or (2) data reach therapeutic levels during baseline, at which point, you conclude that treatment is not needed (not shown).

As mentioned in Chapter 11, authors sometimes elect to reduce potential for bias in their formative analysis by including masked analysts. See Callout 12.1 for information and an example of masked analysis.

Callout 12.1 Masked Visual Analysis

One protocol for visual analysis involves masked analysts, sometimes called blind analysts (which are different from naïve raters, sometimes called blind raters). **Masked analysts** are members of the research team who do not have explicit information about which measurement occasions correspond with which phase in the study. For example, the masked analyst can direct formative decision making for the study, which allows study teams to rely on response-guided phase change decisions without encountering problems with experimenter bias that are possible when analysts are invested in the outcomes of the study (Byun et al., 2017). Another way masked analysts have been used is that researchers ask them to draw conclusions about graphs after all data have been collected (i.e., summative analysis; e.g., Ottley et al., 2017). They can also engage in both formative and summative analysis (Hua et al., 2018).

In one study, Sallese and Vannest (2022) evaluated whether a functional relation existed between the use of coaching by teachers and increases in behavior-specific praise exhibited by paraprofessionals. In this study, the researchers recruited experts in single case design to assess the presence of a functional relation, without specific knowledge about the study. Although referred to as masked, the experts were not masked to condition changes (e.g., received graphs complete with phase change information). However, decisions by visual analysts who did not make condition change decision and are not involved with other aspects of the research may be helpful for decreasing the potential for bias. We would suggest calling non-masked analysts who are not on the research team *unaffiliated analysts* rather than masked analysts, but encourage expanded use of both masked and unaffiliated analysts in single case research.

Summative Analysis and Functional Relation Determination

As a reminder, as described for SIW designs, the purpose of summative analysis is to answer the question "What evidence do I have that the relation of interest exists?" When research questions are evaluated in the context of a design using time-lagged condition ordering, with at least three intervention targets in at least three tiers, with identical (i.e., A-B) comparisons for each tier (i.e., three potential demonstrations of effect), decisions can be made about whether a functional relation exists between independent and dependent variables. As with SIW designs, prior to drawing conclusions about outcomes, you should first establish whether the study design was appropriate, whether a sufficient amount of data was collected, and whether controls for other common threats to internal validity were appropriately controlled for.

Design Adequacy

To answer the question regarding whether a functional relation exists between a given dependent variable and an independent variable, you should first assess whether the design is sufficient for making the determination. For designs using time-lagged condition ordering, this includes measurement of at least three different intervention targets (i.e., participants, behaviors, or contexts) with different baseline lengths (i.e., *at least three potential demonstrations of effect*). As with SIW designs, the three demonstrations must include three phase changes between *two identical conditions*. For time-lagged designs, it must occur across at least three tiers. If the design meets these minimum standards, it is possible that you can assess for whether a functional relation exists. If it does *not* meet this standard, you should conclude that it is not possible to determine whether a functional relation exists. It's worth repeating that this is a different conclusion than finding that a functional relation does not exist, which occurs when there are sufficient *potential* demonstrations, but data suggest no relation (given sufficient controls for threats to internal validity).

Data Sufficiency

As discussed with formative analysis, determining whether there is a sufficient amount data in time-lagged designs is more complex than the process described for SIW designs. Similar to processes discussed in Chapter 10, you need at least three data points for establishing the data pattern within a phase, and often you need more than that. Data are adequate when you can accurately predict approximately where the next data point would fall if the condition did not change. You also need baseline data that are adequate for establishing that initiating the intervention phase is warranted. When data are at or near optimal levels (e.g., floor levels for challenging behavior, ceiling levels for engagement), continuing to the next phase (if it is likely to be therapeutic) is not helpful, because no functional relation can be established, regardless of data. When data suggest a therapeutic trend in baseline, it is also difficult to establish a functional relation because it is often difficult to parse the cause of eventual behavior change (i.e., what part of behavior change was due to intervention rather than history or maturation).

Insufficient data in designs using time-lagged condition ordering often occurs for one of three reasons. First, authors may mis-identify inclusion criteria for participation, and include participants for whom an intervention is not needed. If this is the case, we recommend discontinuing data collection rather than implementing an unnecessary intervention. Second, intervention targets assigned to extended baseline phases (e.g., third or later tiers) are especially prone to history or maturation effects because of the extended time spent in baseline, and so extra baseline data are often needed to allow for these effects to "level off." Third, sometimes authors do not allow for sufficient "lag" between tiers. See Callout 12.2 for a discussion of "how different" is different enough in terms of baseline lengths.

Callout 12.2 Baseline Lengths: How Different is Different Enough?

Slocum et al. (2022) argued that the nonconcurrent version of the multiple baseline design was sufficiently rigorous under most circumstances. They also suggest that tiers should be sufficiently different across three different measures of length:

1. **Number of sessions**. The number of sessions included in each baseline phase should be different. Generally, this should include a difference of at least a few measurement occasions. This controls for testing threats—that is, it demonstrates that data are not changing once intervention is initiated just based on the number of times the targets were exposed to baseline conditions. For example, if you had baseline lengths of 3, 4, and 5 across three different behaviors, and all changed when intervention was introduced, it is possible that the behaviors changed after 3–5 exposures due to learning that occurred in the testing session. If researchers

instead used 3, 6, and 10 sessions and behavior changed only when intervention was introduced, this potential explanation is minimized because the likelihood that behavior change due to testing varied across tiers *and* aligned with intervention initiation is very low.

2. **Calendar time**. In addition to planning a different number of sessions in baseline phases, each phase should also represent a different amount of calendar time. This will align with a number of sessions if sessions occur at the same frequency for all participants. Having baseline phases occur for a sufficiently different number of days controls for maturation threats.
3. **Intervention start date**. When concurrent designs are used, if the number of sessions and calendar time is sufficiently different, the intervention start date should also be different. However, in nonconcurrent designs this is not given even when the other two are true. Having different start dates for intervention controls for history threats that could impact all tiers.

Because the explicit suggestion to have three different measures for differentiating baseline length is new, most single case design studies do not yet include these data. We encourage researchers to include this information in ongoing and future work.

Control for Likely Threats to Internal Validity

If a study includes an appropriate design with sufficient demonstrations of effect, and adequate data in each phase, the next step is to determine whether any other significant threats to internal validity decrease confidence that the differences between conditions (and only those differences) are responsible for any behavior changes that occurred. For example, you should assess whether a given study provides adequate evidence of reliability of independent and dependent variables. For nonconcurrent multiple baseline designs across participants, it is especially important to identify that data from all participants are included in the analysis (i.e., authors have included all recruited participants, including ones for whom intervention effects were not optimal). This is true of all designs, but anecdotally, is seen as a more commonly occurring problems in nonconcurrent multiple baseline designs. If likely threats are controlled for, you can move forward to summative analysis.

Outcome Evaluation

Summative analysis for single case design data should result in a determination of whether a functional relation can be identified, and, as with other designs, this is historically considered to be a yes/no determination (i.e., evidence that a functional relation exists or evidence that a functional relation does not exist). A functional relation is identified when there are three demonstrations of effect—changes in level, trend, or variability between baseline and intervention conditions that are consistent across tiers and that are in line with the theory of change and expected data patterns. It is important to note that while variability and trends often impact visual analysis, most studies are designed to change the level of behavior. Especially in multiple probe designs, an increase that leads to level changes is expected and desirable (e.g., gradual increases in learning until mastery is reached). Evidence for functional relations is strongest when three demonstrations of effect exist and:

1. Behavior patterns in baseline phases across tiers are similar in regard to level, trend, and variability.

2. Behavior patterns in intervention phases across tiers are similar in regard to level, trend, and variability.
3. Changes in data that occur on introduction of the intervention condition across tiers are consistent.
4. All changes between phases are immediate or near immediate.
5. Data between adjacent phases are non-overlapping.
6. Variability and trends in any condition do not preclude ability to identify between-phase changes.

Drawing conclusions about functional relations using visual analysis is relatively complex for designs using time-lagged condition ordering, as shown in Callouts 12.3 through 12.6 at the end of the chapter. As suggested for SIW designs, researchers might increase consistency in visual analysis via the use of visual analysis protocols. Protocols to guide conclusions about functional relations for multiple baseline designs have been published (Wolfe et al., 2019) and are available online (https://sites.google.com/site/scrvaprotocols/). These protocols are helpful for standardizing evaluations of data across studies and for use in systematic reviews. They provide helpful examples and non-examples of data characteristics such as immediacy and consistency.

In time-lagged designs, you can also use visual analysis to assess whether the effects are *strong* (i.e., consistent, unequivocal) or *weak* (i.e., less consistent, with more overlap or less immediacy) and *large* (i.e., a big absolute change in level between phases) or *small* (i.e., less level change between phases). These determinations are somewhat subjective, and certainly are dependent on content expertise (i.e., a "large" change for a specific study is not necessarily a "large" change for other types of participants, dependent variables, contexts). You might consider the strength of effect (strong, weak) as a judgment about the certainty of conclusions (i.e., related to internal validity) while the size of effect might be more related to the value or importance of the outcome (i.e., related to social validity). In time-lagged designs with multiple participants, inconsistent outcomes in terms of strength and size of effect are common (see, for example, Windsor & Ledford, 2023). The multiple baseline across participants design is the only single case design that relies on inter-participant replication rather than intra-participant replication, and this has implications related to functional relation identification (see Callout 12.3).

Callout 12.3 Inconsistent Inter-Participant Replication in Single Case Design Studies

As mentioned in Chapter 11, the multiple baseline across participants design is the most widely used single case design. However, the primary weakness of this design, from a data analysis standpoint, is that variability across participants leaves the design vulnerable to uninterpretable inconsistent effects.

To explain this phenomenon, we will consider first a study that uses A-B-A-B designs to evaluate Intervention X's effects on Outcome Y for three participants. Assume that Intervention X resulted in consistent improvements in Outcome Y for Participants #1 and #2, and a functional relation was identified. Further assume that Intervention X resulted in no consistent improvements in Outcome Y for Participant #3, and a functional relation was not detected. The resulting conclusions from this study are not equivocal. Importantly, a relation was identified for two participants. This suggests that the intervention is *causally related* to changes in the outcome in at least some instances—it is possible to conclude this given three demonstrations of effect. That is, it is quite unlikely that a cause unrelated to the intervention resulted in behavior change *three times* for Participants #1 and #2, and that those changes co-occurred with condition changes by chance. Instead, the conclusion is that there is an (identified or unidentified) difference in the first two cases and the third, that is related to intervention effectiveness.

However, if similar variability occurs in a multiple baseline across participants design (e.g., expected behavior change for two participants, and lack of change for one participant), *no causal relation can be identified* (i.e., no functional relation). Thus, it is not appropriate to interpret any changes for any participant because we haven't sufficiently demonstrated that these changes are functionally related to the intervention. That is, observed changes could be the result of threats to internal validity such as history or maturation. You might argue that history or maturation threats that co-occurred with condition changes for even two participants is unlikely. You may be correct, but the field has determined that three demonstrations is the standard of evidence that threats have been adequately controlled for. Certainly three demonstrations provides more certainty than two demonstrations, and two more than one. Is two sufficient? Contemporary researchers have argued that it is not. Thus, if you are not certain that you can identify three or more participants who are functionally similar (that is, will respond to your intervention in the same way), the conservative decision would be to select a different design to avoid uninterpretable data.

Supplemental Analyses

We refer you to information presented in Chapter 10 about information regarding effect sizes and overlap metrics. As with SIW designs, you can use effect size metrics to estimate the magnitude of change between baseline and intervention conditions in time-lagged designs. These should be used as an augment to visual analysis. As discussed in Chapter 10, these estimates of magnitude or overlap are not intended to determine whether a functional relation is present but simply are a measure of how large behavior change is from one condition to another (effect sizes) or how much overlap exists between conditions (overlap metrics).

Describing Visual Analysis

Because visual analysis is relatively complicated when time-lagged condition ordering is used, it is especially important to carefully plan and fully describe your visual analysis procedures when you use these designs.

Visual Analysis Procedures

Prior to data collection, you should plan your visual analysis. You can start by explicating what data patterns you expect for baseline and intervention phases. For example, you might expect low but variable responding when baseline conditions are in effect and high and stable responding when intervention conditions are in effect, with immediate changes between phases. Especially when across-participant designs are used, you might consider making explicit a priori predictions about the degree of consistency that is expected across participants (e.g., you might specify that a level change is expected within the first five sessions, with immediate change for some participants and a small delay for others). You should explicate in writing a priori (before data collection) what data patterns you expect that will lead you to conclude that a functional relation exists.

After you make a priori predictions, you should plan how often you will engage in formative analysis (usually following each session), and what rules you will follow for initiating intervention in each tier, including necessary patterns within and across intervention targets. For example, you might decide that you will collect data in the first intervention phase until you (1) have at least three consecutive data points that are higher in level than the baseline phase for that target *and* (2) baseline data for the second intervention target are stable and indicate the need for intervention.

Visual Analysis Results

After planning and conducting your formative and summative analyses, you will describe them to others, usually via written reports (i.e., published articles, thesis, or dissertation documents). It is critical to explain your (1) data analysis plan (i.e., the protocol you used to analyze your data), (2) any noteworthy formative decisions that were made (i.e., modifications, phase changes), (3) your summative analysis, and (4) your conclusions about the presence or absence of a functional relation. We recommend that you provide sufficient detail in your summative analysis, describing your data with key visual analysis terms to justify your conclusions regarding the functional relation.

In the three paragraphs below, we describe summative outcomes for Figures 12.1, 12.2, and 12.3. We vary terminology slightly across descriptions—for example, we say that a functional relation is demonstrated or present and we use "Tier 1" and "first intervention target" when discussing data related to the top panel in each graph. These variations are all acceptable and their use relies on personal preference. The important components of these descriptions are that we use terms to describe data patterns (level, trend, variability) and changes between conditions (immediacy, overlap, consistency) and that we explicitly describe whether a functional relation exists.

In Figure 12.1, there are three potential demonstrations of effect, sufficient data for drawing conclusions about data patterns, and (let's assume) all other likely threats to internal validity are controlled for. In this figure, data in all three baseline phases are low and stable, and when the intervention is initiated, there are immediate changes in level, followed by an increasing trend to mastery levels. There is no overlap between baseline and intervention conditions, and patterns are consistent across tiers. Thus, *data suggest a functional relation is present*.

In Figure 12.2, there are three potential demonstrations of effect, sufficient data for drawing conclusions about data patterns, and (let's assume) all other likely threats to internal validity are controlled for. In this figure, data in all baseline phases are low and stable, with one outlying data point in the second tier (followed by low levels of data). For the first two intervention targets, there is an immediate increase in level, with an increasing trend to mastery following initiation of the intervention. However, there is no change in level, trend, or variability when the intervention is implemented in the third tier. An alternative intervention is initiated on Day 20, resulting in increases in level and trend, with data reaching mastery levels. Because the effect was not consistent across all tiers, *a functional relation was not demonstrated*.

In Figure 12.3, there are three potential demonstrations of effect, sufficient data for drawing conclusions about data patterns, and (let's assume) all other likely threats to internal validity are controlled for. In this figure, data in the second and third tiers have a shallow increasing trend that begins when intervention in the first tier is initiated. However, this trend eventually stabilizes, with data at non-mastery levels. At this point, intervention is initiated with the second and then the third intervention target. At intervention initiation, there are immediate increases in level, with no overlapping data and increasing trends to mastery across all tiers (i.e., consistent changes). Thus, *a functional relation is demonstrated between intervention and the dependent variable*.

Callouts 12.4 through 12.7 at the end of the chapter show examples of summative visual analysis for three studies using designs with time-lagged condition ordering.

Callout 12.4 Applied Example of Multiple Baseline Across Participants Design

As described in Callout 11.3, White and colleagues (2023) evaluated modifications to the picture exchange system (PECS) on vocal behavior for three Black children (two boys, one girl) who were eligible for special education services under the categories of autism or significant developmental delay.

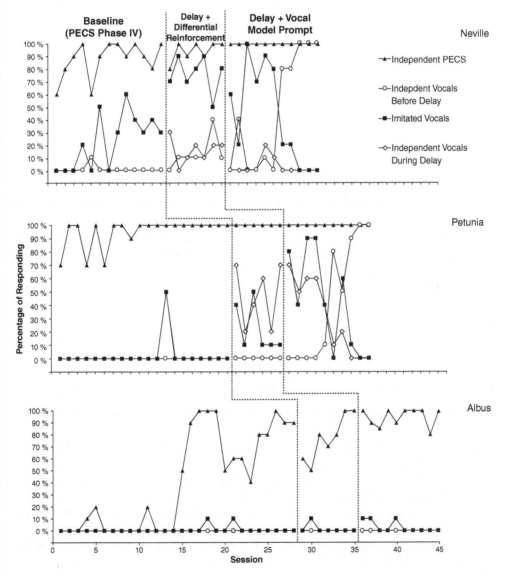

Source: White, E. N., Cagliani, R. R., & Tyson, K. M. (2023). Effects on speech development with modifications to picture exchange communication system. *Focus on Autism and Other Developmental Disabilities*, 10883576231178266.

Design Adequacy: This multiple baseline design across participants includes three potential demonstrations of effect, so it is adequate for making a functional relation determination. We will focus on analyzing independent vocals before delay (open circles) and imitated vocals (filled squares), based on author-reported research questions.

Data Adequacy: In each baseline phase, there more than three data points and stable patterns are established before the phase is discontinued. There are 13, 20, and 28 baseline sessions across tiers. The average number of sessions per day (less than two for each participant) was reported, as was the total number of school days (30 for the first two participants, 44 for the third participant). The exact nature of concurrence (e.g., the extent to which data for session 10 correspond with same/similar date for all participants) is unclear. *It is important to note that the necessity of reporting explicitly the number of sessions, time in baseline, and intervention start dates is a relatively new idea, thus you may be unlikely to find evidence of this in most studies.*

Control for Common Threats: Visual analysis suggests low likelihood of history and maturation threats. Procedural fidelity and interobserver agreement data are appropriate, suggesting confidence in reliability of the independent and dependent variables.

Visual Analysis: For independent vocals, data are *low* and *stable* at or near floor levels for all participants, with no *trend*. On introduction of the intervention, an increasing trend is seen for the first participant only; the other two participants have the same low, stable levels present in baseline. For imitated vocals, the first participant had low baseline levels, followed by a variable increasing trend that leveled off at about 30–40% correct. The second two participants had low, stable levels, with one outlying data point at 50% for the second participant. On introduction of the intervention, there was an *increase in level* for two participants and *no change in level* for the third participant.

Functional Relation Decision: A *functional relation was not identified* for independent vocals before delay or for imitated vocals due to inconsistent change in behaviors across participants (i.e., changes for some participants but not others).

Magnitude Estimate: No magnitude estimates were calculated due to a lack of functional relation (i.e., interpreting magnitude estimates in the absence of a functional relation is not advisable).

Callout 12.5 Applied Example of Multiple Baseline Across Behaviors Design

As described in Callout 11.4, Capalbo et al. (2022) evaluated the impact of video modeling for improving goalkeeping skills for two 9-year-old boys who played soccer. The intervention targets were three goalkeeping behaviors: high jump, forward smother, and side dive.

Design Adequacy: This multiple baseline design across behaviors includes three potential demonstrations of effect, so is adequate for making a functional relation determination.

Data Adequacy: In each baseline phase, there are at least three data points (assessments) and stable patterns are established before the phase is discontinued. There are 6, 10, and 17 baseline assessments across tiers. Authors report that multiple assessments were reported during each 30-minute session, and that sessions occurred twice per week. Readers are not able to determine whether intervention was initiated after a sufficiently different amount of time (days) in baseline or whether the intervention was initiated on sufficiently different days, so data should be interpreted with caution. *It is important to*

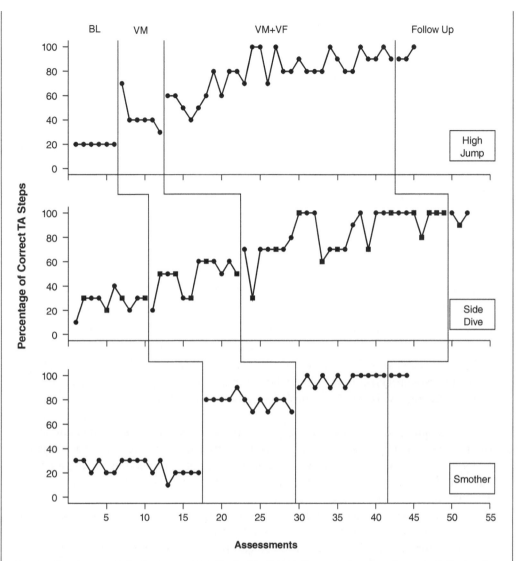

Source: Capalbo, A., Miltenberger, R. G., & Cook, J. L. (2022). Training soccer goalkeeping skills: Is video modeling enough? *Journal of Applied Behavior Analysis*, 55(3), 958–970.

note that the necessity of reporting explicitly the numbers of sessions, time in baseline, and intervention start dates is a relatively new idea, thus you may be unlikely to find evidence of this in most studies.

Control for Common Threats: Visual analysis suggests a low likelihood of history and maturation threats, with no covariation between tiers or unexplained data patterns in any condition. Procedural fidelity and interobserver agreement data are appropriate, suggesting confidence in reliability of the independent and dependent variables.

Visual Analysis: The *level* of data in baseline phases across intervention targets are low and somewhat *stable*. For the final behavior (third tier) there was a slight decreasing trend across the condition, with data stabilizing in the final four sessions. Changes between phases lead to *immediate* changes in level, with little to no *overlap*, with only one exception (the first intervention assessment for the second intervention target). Changes were somewhat *consistent*, with increases in level for all behaviors, although the magnitude of change was larger for the third intervention target.

Functional Relation Decision: A functional relation is evident between video modeling and the correct performance of three soccer behaviors. It is important to note that authors identified these consistent increases in level *not* socially valid, and so they added an intervention component (feedback) to further increase performance. It is difficult to experimentally evaluate the impacts of this BC condition, although you could argue that the comparison between video modeling (2nd phase for each tier) and video modeling plus feedback (3rd condition for each tier) serve as a *nonconcurrent* multiple baseline design with different baseline lengths for each video modeling condition.

Magnitude Estimate: Log response ratio (increasing) for each tier, respectively is 0.78, 0.56, and 1.18 (95% confidence intervals: 0.53, 1.03; 0.31, 0.81; 1.05, 1.31; Pustejovsky et al., 2023).

Callout 12.6 Applied Example of a Multiple Probe Across Behaviors Design (Days Variation)

As described in Callout 11.5, Heider et al. (2019) evaluated the impacts of self-directed video prompting on the correct performance of vocational tasks. Participants were two adults (21-year-olds) with moderate intellectual disability enrolled in a transition program who were proficient readers and who could independently navigate a cell phone.

Design Adequacy: This multiple probe design across behaviors includes three potential demonstrations of effect, so is adequate for making a functional relation determination.

Data Adequacy: In each baseline phase, there are at least five data points and stable patterns are established before the phase is discontinued. There are 5, 7, and 7 baseline sessions across tiers. Thus, there are not a different number of sessions for the final two tiers. Authors do not report concurrence or how many sessions occurred per day, so it is also difficult to know whether the number of days in baseline was different across tiers and whether intervention started on different days. Thus, the outcomes of this study should be interpreted with caution, although zero baseline across all behaviors suggests history and maturation threats are very unlikely even given uncertainty about the degree of time lag. *It is important to note that the necessity of reporting explicitly the number of sessions, time in baseline, and intervention start dates is a relatively new idea, thus you may be unlikely to find evidence of this in most studies.*

Control for Common Threats: Visual analysis suggests low likelihood of history and maturation threats given zero levels in baseline and consistent patterns in intervention. Procedural fidelity and interobserver agreement data are appropriate, suggesting confidence in reliability of the independent and dependent variables.

Visual Analysis: The *level* of data in baseline phases is low and very *stable* with no trend. Data in intervention conditions are high in level and stable at or near 100% correct. Changes between phases were *consistent* with *immediate* changes in level, with no *overlap*.

Functional Relation Decision: A functional relation is evident between self-directed video prompting and the correct performance of vocational tasks.

Magnitude Estimate: Visual analysis suggests the magnitude of change is very large between baseline and intervention conditions. Most effect size estimates do not perform well when all data in a condition are at 0 levels. Given the very clear and consistent changes between conditions, an effect size for estimating magnitude may not be needed.

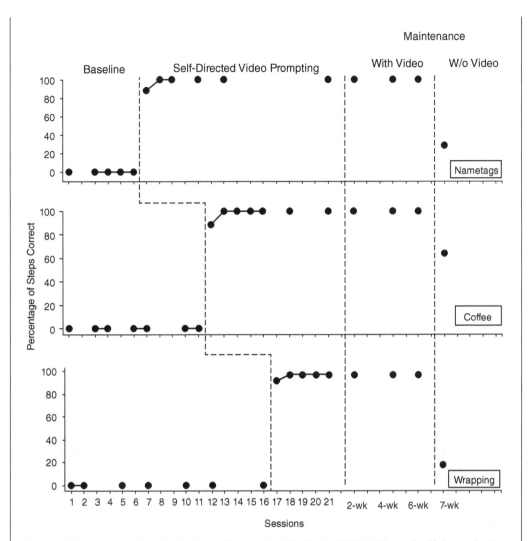

Source: Heider, A. E., Cannella-Malone, H. I., & Andzik, N. R. (2019). Effects of self-directed video prompting on vocational task acquisition. *Career Development and Transition for Exceptional Individuals*, 42(2), 87–98.

Callout 12.7 Applied Example of a Multiple Probe Across Participants Design (Days Variation)

As described in Callout 11.6, D'Agostino et al. (2020) implemented an intervention designed to increase social behaviors during book reading for young children with autism.

Design Adequacy: This multiple probe design across participants includes three potential demonstrations of effect, so is adequate for making a functional relation determination.

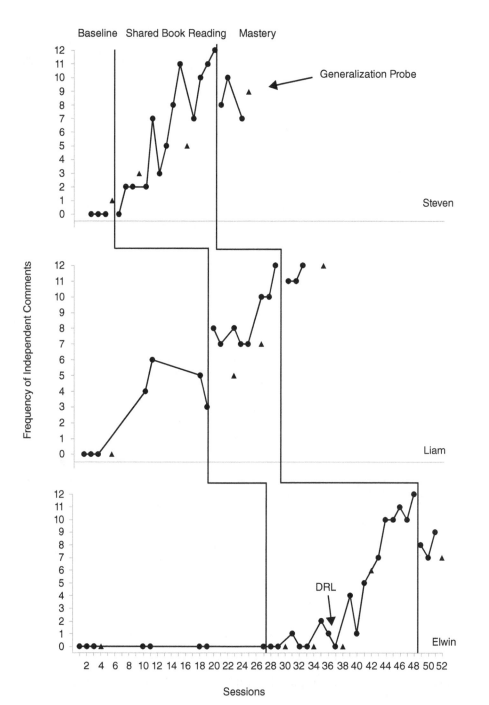

Source: D'Agostino, S. R., Dueñas, A. D., & Plavnick, J. B. (2020). Increasing social initiations during shared book reading: An intervention for preschoolers with autism spectrum disorder. *Topics in Early Childhood Special Education*, 39(4), 213–225.

Data Adequacy: In each baseline phase, there are at least three data points and stable patterns are established before the phase is discontinued in the first and third tiers. Additional data in the second tier would provide confirmation that without intervention, the child would be unlikely to reach mastery levels of independent comments. There are 3, 7, and 8 baseline sessions across tiers, but there isn't direct evidence of the amount of time in baseline or intervention start dates. *It is important to note that the necessity of reporting explicitly the numbers of sessions, time in baseline, and intervention start dates is a relatively new idea, thus you may be unlikely to find evidence of this in most studies.*

Control for Common Threats: A threat to internal validity may be present in that baseline data improved over time during baseline for the second participant. This threat could be related to maturation (the child was learning language over time, unrelated to intervention), history (the child accessed experiences outside of the study that increased responsiveness to shared reading), facilitative testing effects (baseline procedures were sufficient for learning), or infidelity (when the implementer began intervention with one child, she might have inadvertently began including intervention components with the second child). Because fidelity data were adequate, the fourth potential threat is probably the least likely, but the others remain possible.

Visual Analysis: The *level* of data in baseline in the first and third tiers is low and stable, with no trend; on introduction of the intervention, there are changes in *level* with a *delayed* change in level and more overlapping data for third tier (i.e., changes are *consistent* in that there is an increasing trend to mastery, but are not entirely comparable—this pattern is common in across participants designs). The *increasing trend* in the second baseline condition makes it difficult to conclude that the independent variable and only the dependent variable is responsible for behavior change, although the final four data points in that condition are somewhat stable at non-mastery levels.

Functional Relation Decision: Despite the increasing trend in one baseline phase, some analysts might consider the immediate change in level on introduction of intervention and lack of overlap between conditions—thus, they might decide that evidence of a *functional relation exists*. The authors of this study drew that (justifiable) conclusion, and explicitly reported the increasing baseline data as a study limitation. Other analysts might determine that additional data were needed in the baseline phase of the second tier, and thus, that a *functional relation determination cannot be made*. This is also a justifiable conclusion; we use this example to illustrate that visual analysis decisions are sometimes equivocal. In these situations, regardless of conclusion, we urge analysts to use appropriate caution in interpreting outcomes.

Conclusions

Visual analysis of studies using time-lagged condition implementation is complex, requiring within-tier and across-tier analysis. Moreover, it varies based on whether data are collected concurrently or non-concurrently and whether baseline data are collected intermittently or continuously (i.e., multiple probe or multiple baseline designs). Carefully planned and well-described visual analysis procedures are necessary for conducting meaningfully and scientifically valid analyses.

References

Byun, T. M., Hitchcock, E. R., & Ferron, J. (2017). Masked visual analysis: Minimizing type I error in visually guided single-case design for communication disorders. *Journal of Speech, Language, and Hearing Research*, 60(6), 1455–1466.

Capalbo, A., Miltenberger, R. G., & Cook, J. L. (2022). Training soccer goalkeeping skills: Is video modeling enough?. *Journal of Applied Behavior Analysis*, 55(3), 958–970.

D'Agostino, S. R., Dueñas, A. D., & Plavnick, J. B. (2020). Increasing social initiations during shared book reading: An intervention for preschoolers with autism spectrum disorder. *Topics in Early Childhood Special Education*, 39(4), 213–225.

Heider, A. E., Cannella-Malone, H. I., & Andzik, N. R. (2019). Effects of self-directed video prompting on vocational task acquisition. *Career Development and Transition for Exceptional Individuals*, 42(2), 87–98.

Hua, Y., Yuan, C., Monroe, K., Hinzman, M. L., Alqahtani, S., Alwahbi, A. A., & Kern, A. M. (2018). Effects of the Reread-Adapt and Answer-Comprehend and goal setting intervention on decoding and reading comprehension skills of young adults with intellectual disabilities. *Developmental Neurorehabilitation*, 21(5), 279–289.

Ottley, J. R., Grygas Coogle, C., Rahn, N. L., & Spear, C. F. (2017). Impact of bug-in-ear professional development on early childhood co-teachers' use of communication strategies. *Topics in Early Childhood Special Education*, 36(4), 218–229.

Pustejovsky, J. E., Chen, M., Grekov, P., & Swan, D. M. (2023). Single-case effect size calculator (Version 0.7.2.9999) [Web application]. https://jepusto.shinyapps.io/SCD-effect-sizes/

Sallese, M. R., & Vannest, K. J. (2022). Effects of a manualized teacher-led coaching intervention on paraprofessional use of behavior-specific praise. *Remedial and Special Education*, 43(1), 27–39.

Slocum, T. A., Pinkelman, S. E., Joslyn, P. R., & Nichols, B. (2022). Threats to internal validity in multiple-baseline design variations. *Perspectives on Behavior Science*, 45(3), 619–638.

Windsor, S. A., & Ledford, J. R. (2023). Systematic review of naturalistic developmental behavioral interventions for young children on the autism spectrum.

White, E. N., Cagliani, R. R., & Tyson, K. M. (2023). Effects on speech development with modifications to picture exchange communication system. *Focus on Autism and Other Developmental Disabilities*, 10883576231178266

Wolfe, K., Barton, E. E., & Meadan, H. (2019). Systematic protocols for the visual analysis of single-case research data. *Behavior Analysis in Practice*, 12, 491–502.

13
Conducting Studies Using Rapid Iterative Alternation of Conditions

Kathryn M. Bailey, Natalie S. Pak, and Jennifer R. Ledford

Important Terms

rapid iterative alternation (RIA), Multielement-alternating treatments design (ME-ATD), adapted alternating treatments design (AATD), repeated acquisition design, simultaneous treatments procedures

Table of Contents

Features of Designs Using Rapid Iterative Alternation
When to Use Designs with Rapid Iterative Alternation
    Strengths and Benefits
    Weaknesses and Drawbacks
Multielement-Alternating Treatments Design
    Procedural Steps
Adapted Alternating Treatments Design
    Selecting and Assigning Sets
    Procedural Steps
Repeated Acquisition Design
Threats to Internal Validity
Assessing Social Validity Using Simultaneous Treatments
Conclusions
References

Callouts

13.1 What's in a Name? Multielement versus Alternating Treatments Designs
13.2 Applied Example of ME-ATD
13.3 Why Do You Need Multiple Behavior Sets for AATDs But Not ME-ATDs?
13.4 Applied Example of AATD
13.5 Applied Example of a Repeated Acquisition Design
13.6 Applied Example of Simultaneous Treatments Procedure

DOI: 10.4324/9781003294726-15

In this chapter, we introduce the final condition ordering type: rapid iterative alternation of conditions. These designs are flexible and useful, especially for conducting multiple simultaneous comparisons. The rapid alternation used requires different considerations compared to designs with fewer condition transitions (i.e., time-lagged and sequential introduction and withdrawal [SIW] designs).

Features of Designs Using Rapid Iterative Alternation

The final basic condition ordering type is **rapid iterative alternation (RIA)** of conditions. Studies using this ordering type differ from studies that use SIW and time-lagged introduction condition ordering because multiple *conditions* are implemented in a single *phase*. That is, SIW and time-lagged designs are typically implemented such that multiple measurement occasions occur for one condition type (e.g., baseline) and then multiple measurement occasions occur for another condition type (e.g., intervention) in two distinct phases. Thus, the basic comparison in SIW and time-lagged designs might look something like this:

Phase 1/Condition 1	Phase 2/Condition 2
A A A A A	B B B B B

In RIA designs, the basic comparison includes two conditions that are alternated within *a single phase*. It looks something like this:

	Phase I				
Condition 1	A-	A-	A-	A-	A-
Condition 2	B-	B-	B-	B-	B-

In both of these scenarios, data from the first condition (denoted by "A") are compared to data collected in the second condition (denoted by "B"). In SIW and time-lagged designs, each condition is implemented for at least a few temporally adjacent measurement occasions, and only one condition occurs per phase. In RIA designs, two or more conditions are repeatedly and rapidly alternated within a single phase. These differences are graphically depicted in Figure 13.1, with the ordering associated with SIW and time-lagged designs depicted in the top panel and ordering associated with RIA designs depicted in the bottom panel.

The prototypical RIA design is what we will refer to in this text as the **multielement-alternating treatments design** (ME-ATD; see Table 13.1). This design features rapid alternation of two or more experimental conditions in a single phase and is appropriate for evaluation of readily reversible behaviors. When RIA condition ordering procedures are used to evaluate the impact of two or more conditions on *non-reversible* behaviors, we will refer to it as an adapted alternating treatments design (AATD; see Callout 13.1 for a rationale for not calling this design the AME-ATD). We will describe two infrequently used special cases related to RIA ordering later in the chapter: (1) a design in which many comparisons are conducted in quick succession with the same participant, referred to as repeated acquisition design and (2) an application in which both conditions are simultaneously available and condition implementation is dependent on participant choice, often referred to as the *simultaneous treatments design* (but which we will refer to as the use of simultaneous treatments procedures).

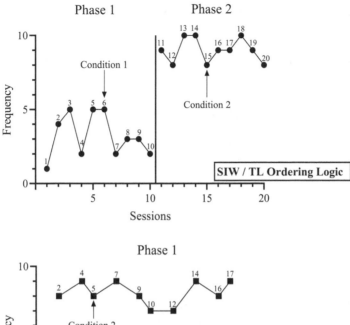

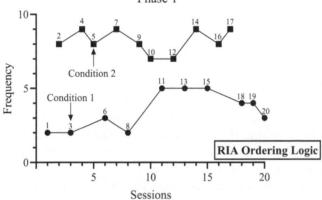

Figure 13.1 Comparison of Condition Ordering Logic Across SIW, TL, and RIA Designs.

Note: Numbers 1–20 represent the order that individual sessions are conducted. SIW and time-lagged designs contain multiple phases, and each phase corresponds to one condition. RIA designs only require a single phase in which multiple conditions are alternated.

Table 13.1 Conventional Design Names Associated with RIA Condition Ordering

Prototypical Design: ME-ATD	Rapid alternation of two or more conditions during a single phase for a single reversible behavior
Adapted Alternating Treatments	Rapid alternation of two or more conditions during a single phase for a single **non-reversible behavior set for each condition** (i.e., there are as many sets as conditions)
Repeated Acquisition	Rapid alternation of two or more conditions during a single phase for **several non-reversible behavior sets for each condition** (i.e., there more sets than there are conditions)
Simultaneous Treatments	**Sequential availability** of two or more conditions during a single phase for a single reversible behavior **(the behavior of interest is generally selection/preference)**

Note: Although we have historically considered the ST design a separate design type in the RIA family, we refrain from referring to it as an RIA design type in this edition, discussed at length later in the chapter.

When to Use Designs with Rapid Iterative Alternation

The conditions that should result in the selection of an RIA design include:

1. A research question about the impact of two or more conditions on one or more behaviors
2. Interest in dependent variables that include either:
   a. Behaviors that are readily reversible and likely to co-vary with condition changes with no lag in behavior change (e.g., behavior will change immediately when conditions change) (ME-ATD)
   b. At least two sets of behaviors that are non-reversible and which are *functionally similar* and *functionally independent* (AATD and repeated acquisition design)
3. Inclusion of two or more distinct conditions that can be alternated rapidly, from both a practical standpoint and an experimentally viable one.

Callout 13.1   What's in a Name? Multielement versus Alternating Treatments Designs

The *ME-ATD* term to describe the prototypical RIA design is discrepant from terms used in past versions of the text, in which we differentiated multielement designs (M-ED) and alternating treatments designs (ATD) based on the kinds of conditions that were alternated. We described conditions varying in relation to *contextual variables* (environmental conditions that are not necessarily designed to be treatments) as being evaluated in the M-ED variation and conditions representing different *interventions* as being evaluated in the ATD variation. For example, researchers might alternate different environmental conditions to determine which of them is associated with the occurrence of challenging behaviors (i.e., a functional analysis, previously referred to as the M-ED variation). In contrast, researchers might alternate two different intervention conditions (i.e., differential reinforcement of other behaviors versus differential reinforcement of alternative behaviors; an intervention analysis, previously referred to as the ATD variation). Barlow and Hayes (1979) describe a historical accounting of the use of both designs.

Interestingly, both design names have been used for both variations (i.e., using the conventions described, but also using the M-ED variation to refer to intervention analyses and ATD variation to refer to contextual analyses). Much of the variation may be related to the field from which a researcher was trained. As shown in the figure below, nearly three-quarters of designs using RIA condition ordering are described as M-EDs in the *Journal of Applied Behavior Analysis [JABA]*, the flagship journal associated with behavior analysis, while only about 5% of RIA designs are described as ME-Ds in *Exceptional Children [EC]*, the flagship journal of Special Education (with an intermediate number, about 25%, in a journal focusing on education and applied behavior analysis, *Journal of Behavioral Education [JOBE]*). This difference cannot only be attributed to more functional analysis studies published in *JABA* (although this is certainly the case) because even when that term is used to exclude studies, the ME-D term remains prevalent in *JABA* and almost non-existent in *EC*. <u>Given the discrepancies by field, and given that from a design perspective, previously described variations are actually methodologically identical, we have elected to refer to the designs as the ME-ATD.</u>

We continue to refer to the variation including measurement of non-reversible behaviors as AATD, given that the term "adapted multielement" design has not been adopted by either field, and that important differences exist between versions of the RIA design that include measurement of reversible and non-reversible behaviors (i.e., there is a need to differentiate ME-ATDs and AATDs).

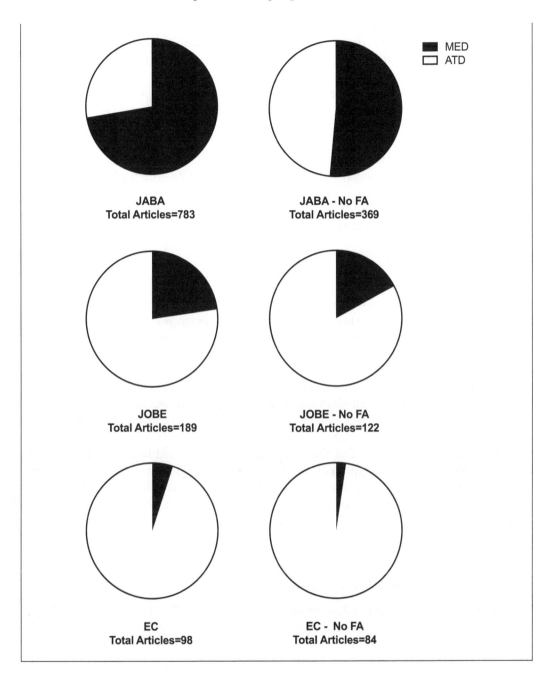

Strengths and Benefits

There are two primary benefits to the use of RIA designs. The first is the rapidity of evaluation. Contemporary standards suggest that there should typically be at least five data points per condition (Kratochwill et al., 2010), which means that the minimum number of sessions required before drawing conclusions about a functional relation is only ten (more are required for the repeated acquisition design). This is fewer than the minimum number required for other design types. The second primary benefit is that three or more conditions can be experimentally compared at the same time (e.g., in the same comparison phase); this is the only condition ordering type for which this is true (i.e., this is not possible when conditions are ordered using SIW and time-lagged paradigms). This benefit is why the ME-ATD is often used to assess multiple variables that could be maintaining challenging behavior (i.e., for functional analyses).

Historically, RIA designs have been considered comparative designs because they allow researchers to compare two or more independent variables (e.g., interventions) to determine which is more effective or efficient at changing target behaviors. However, these designs can be used for both comparison and demonstration purposes. That is, when a baseline or control condition is included *and* the baseline sessions are rapidly alternated with one or more intervention sessions during the comparison phase, then RIA condition ordering logic may be used to demonstrate that a condition is effective for changing a behavior of interest relative to a baseline or control condition. Research question(s) and feasibility of rapid alternation should drive which conditions are included within RIA experimental comparisons.

Weaknesses and Drawbacks

RIA designs are only appropriate when conditions can be rapidly alternated; this is not always practical. For example, if you were interested in comparing *desks in rows* to *desks in groups* for on-task behavior in an elementary classroom, an RIA design would require re-arranging desks daily which is practically infeasible. Additionally, it may be difficult for implementers of study procedures to rapidly alternate between conditions while maintaining high procedural integrity. Moreover, given the theory of change associated with the conditions of interest, it may be that rapid alternation interferes with identification of the relation of interest (e.g., some interventions may only work well when implemented consistently over time).

Relative to SIW and time-lagged designs, there are additional considerations researchers must make when controlling for threats to internal validity within RIA designs. In particular, it can be challenging to ensure that the unique target sets required in AATD and repeated acquisition designs are truly equivalent. Several procedures have been used for this purpose, but it is impossible to perfectly control for all possible idiosyncratic differences that may make target sets non-equivalent. RIA designs currently do not have a widely accepted design-comparable effect size (Maggin et al., 2022). Analysis of data from RIA designs will be discussed in Chapter 14.

Multielement-Alternating Treatments Design

The ME-ATD is the prototypical RIA design. When the ME-ATD is used, two or more conditions are rapidly alternated. Depending on your research question, each condition may be evaluated relative to a single control condition (which is often the case when a functional analysis is conducted), or each can be evaluated relative to all other conditions (which is often the case when multiple treatments are evaluated; more information about evaluating data from RIA designs is discussed in Chapter 14). The design requires a single readily reversible behavior (e.g., engagement, challenging behavior) that is measured across all conditions. The simplest ME-ATD includes a single phase and only two conditions. An example of this design is depicted in Callout 13.2 in which Holyfield et al. (2019) evaluated the effects of augmentative and alternative technology (AAC) mode on children's engagement and communication.

Although experimental logic dictates that only one phase is required (see top panel of Figure 13.2), it is often prudent to include additional phases when ME-ATDs are used. As shown in the second panel, you can also include an initial baseline phase when this may be

> **Callout 13.2** Applied Example of ME-ATD
>
> Holyfield et al. (2019) used an ME-ATD to assess the effects of availability of different augmentative and alternative communication (AAC) modes on the engagement and communication of three school-aged children with multiple disabilities. The children primarily used prelinguistic behaviors (e.g., vocalizing, reaching) to communicate with others at school. Sessions occurred in therapy rooms at the participants' school, and their school speech-language pathologists implemented the intervention procedures. The ME-ATD involved five sessions per condition in a single comparison phase. One of two AAC modes was available in each condition: (1) a high-tech AAC mode using a visual scene display on a tablet or (2) a set of low-tech picture symbols. The activities used in the therapy sessions were individualized, as were the photos and picture symbols for each AAC system. To help ensure high procedural fidelity, the implementers were given fidelity checklists for each condition that they could have available during each session. For each participant, the same speech-language pathologist implemented both conditions. Each session included five trials with each AAC system. During each trial, the implementer engaged in an enjoyable activity with the child for several seconds, presented an AAC mode, waited 5 seconds, modeled or prompted use of the device, waited another 5 seconds, and responded to child communication. The order of conditions was selected randomly for each session. The dependent variables were two measures of engagement and one measure of communication. The first variable was engagement with the AAC system, measured by the time the child spent looking at the system during each trial. The second variable was engagement with the communication partner (the implementer), also measured as time looking at the partner. The communication variable was the number of times in a session the child selected a symbol. In Chapter 14, we share a figure depicting the ME-ATD design and analysis of the outcomes of this study.

important for contextualizing the need for intervention or differences among conditions in the comparison phase. Although no experimental comparison between baseline and either intervention is possible (because there are no replications of effect), establishing the initial baseline level helps to contextualize the results from the comparison phase. If you are interested in experimental comparisons between a baseline condition and one or more assessment or intervention conditions, you can include an ongoing control condition as part of the comparison phase (see third panel in Figure 13.2). For example, ME-ATD are often used in the assessment of motivating operations that maintain challenging behaviors (i.e., functional analyses) and include several conditions (e.g., contingent attention, escape from demands). A control condition in which no challenging behavior is expected is often included. Analysis of these data differs slightly from RIA designs with no ongoing control condition (see Chapter 14). We note here that the term *control condition* is often used when RIA designs are implemented, but the same types of baseline condition variations used in other designs can be used in these designs (e.g., business-as-usual, no-treatment; see Chapter 9) and they can be referred to with a variety of names (e.g., control, probe, baseline; see Chapter 11).

To evaluate the extent to which multitreatment interference might have impacted behavior during the comparison, researchers can include a post-comparison phase (referred to as *best alone*) in which only the optimal condition from the comparison is implemented (see bottom panel in Figure 13.2). Table 13.2 lists several studies that use a ME-ATD.

230 • Kathryn M. Bailey et al.

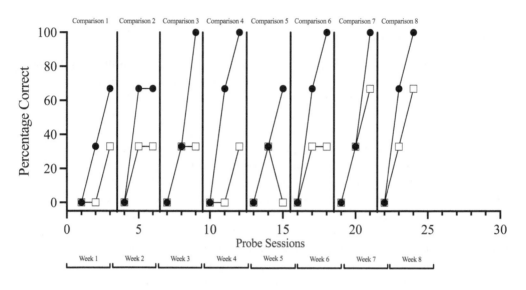

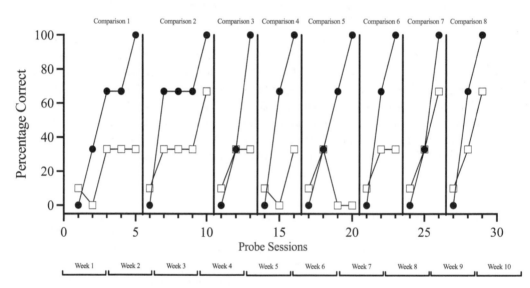

Figure 13.2 ME-ATD Phase Variations.

Table 13.2 Studies using Multielement-Alternating Treatment Designs (ME-ATD)

Reference	Design	Conditions included in Comparison	Dependent Variable
Chazin, K. T., Ledford, J. R., Barton, E. E., & Osborne, K. (2017). The effects of antecedent exercise on engagement during large group activities for young children. *Remedial and Special Education*, 39(3), 158–170.	ME-ATD with initial baseline, comparison, and best alone phases	Typical classroom (control) Seated activities (control) Exercise activities (treatment)	Percentage of intervals with on-task and out-of-seat behaviors measured via MTS; rate of challenging behavior measured via event recording

(*Continued*)

Table 13.2 Continued

Reference	Design	Conditions included in Comparison	Dependent Variable
Hammond, J. L., & Hall, S. S. (2011). Functional analysis and treatment of aggressive behavior following resection of a craniopharyngioma. *Developmental Medicine and Child Neurology*, 53, 369–374.	ME-ATD with comparison phase only	Escape (test) Ignoring (test) Attention (test) Tangible (test) Play (control)	Aggressive behaviors per minute, measured via timed event recording
Ingersoll, B. (2011). The differential effect of three naturalistic language interventions on language use in children with autism. *Journal of Positive Behavior Interventions*, 13, 109–118.	ME-ATD with comparison phase only	Responsive interactions (treatment) Milieu teaching (treatment) Combined interventions (treatment)	Percentage of intervals of total language use (prompted or spontaneous requests or comments), measured via interval system (type unclear)
Kodak, T., Northup, J., & Kelley, M. E. (2007). An evaluation of the types of attention that maintain problem behavior. *Journal of Applied Behavior Analysis*, 40, 167–171.	ME-ATD with comparison phase only	Attention (test) Demand (test) Alone (test) Toy Play (control) (Participant *Johnny*)	Rate of problem behavior per minute measured via timed event recording
Ledford, J. R., Zimmerman, K. N., Severini, K. E., Gast, H. A., Osborne, K., & Harbin, E. R. (2020). Brief report: Evaluation of the noncontingent provision of fidget toys during group activities. *Focus on Autism and Other Developmental Disabilities*, 35(2), 101–107.	ME-ATD with comparison phase only	Baseline (control) Fidget Toys (treatment) Token system (treatment)	Percentage of intervals engaged in activity, measured via MTS
Lynch, A., Theodore, L. A., Bray, M. W., & Kehle, T. J. (2009). A comparison of group-oriented contingencies and randomized reinforcers to improve homework completion and accuracy for students with disabilities. *School Psychology Review*, 38, 307–324.	ME-ATD with initial baseline, comparison, and best alone phases	Dependent contingency (treatment) Interdependent contingency (treatment) Independent contingency (treatment)	Percentage of homework completed, measured via permanent product review
Staubitz, J. L., Staubitz, J. E., Pollack, M. S., Haws, R. A., & Hopton, M. (2022). Effects of an enhanced choice model of skill-based treatment for students with emotional/behavioral disorders. *Journal of Applied Behavior Analysis*, 55(4), 1306–1341.	ME-ATD with comparison phase only	Synthesized test condition Combined control condition	Rate of precursor behaviors measured via event recording
Taylor, T. (2022). Brief report: Packing treatment comparison and use of a chaser to increase swallowing for a clinical case. *Journal of Autism and Developmental Disorders*, 52(7), 3280–3285.	ME-ATD with comparison and best alone phases	Move-on Liquid chaser Puree chaser Brush redistribution Previous treatment	Frequency of clean mouth (percentage of opportunities) measured via event recording; latency to clean mouth measured via duration recording

Note: MTS = momentary time sampling. When conditions varied by participant, we note relevant participant.

Procedural Steps

When planning a ME-ATD, adhere to the following guidelines and recommendations:

Before

1. Create your falsifiable research question(s) for a readily reversible behavior.
2. Identify the target behavior(s) and identify the dimension of interest (e.g., time, number).
3. Select an appropriate (sensitive, reliable, valid, feasible) measurement system, test it, and modify as needed.
4. If you have more than one dependent variable, identify which will serve as the *primary dependent variable* on which condition change decisions will be made.
5. Review previous research and your theory of change for evidence that conditions can be rapidly alternated, with carryover effects being unlikely.
6. Determine your comparison of interest (e.g., which conditions will be rapidly alternated) and identify whether you will include initial baseline and best alone phases.
7. Operationalize all condition procedures, including those included in initial baseline, comparison, and best alone phases.
8. Determine frequency at which you will collect reliability and fidelity data, what calculations you will use to estimate reliability and fidelity, and acceptable levels of reliability and fidelity.
9. Determine rules for alternating conditions and procedures for minimizing order effects (e.g., counterbalancing, randomization) and carryover effects (e.g., time between sessions).
10. Identify expected data patterns and describe the conditions that will result in a functional relation determination.
11. Establish criterion for discontinuing the comparison.
12. Identify participants, and, if applicable, refine definitions of target behaviors (e.g., specify exact topography of challenging behavior).

During/After

13. Collect and graph data for baseline phase (if appropriate).
14. Begin comparison phase. Conduct and graph at least five sessions per condition according to predetermined rules for alternating conditions.
15. Use visual analysis to determine whether a functional relation exists, does not exist, or whether additional data are needed (see Chapter 14).
16. If a functional relation is identified, collect best alone data in which the superior condition is conducted alone.
17. Collect the specified amount of reliability and procedural fidelity data across all phases, conditions, and participants.
18. If possible, replicate with similar participants.

Adapted Alternating Treatments Design

The **adapted alternating treatments design (AATD)** was developed to compare instructional practices with *non-reversible behaviors* (Sindelar et al., 1985). The AATD is useful when comparing the effects of at least two conditions on acquisition of functional, developmental, or academic behaviors. The most common use of the AATD is to compare the *efficiency* of instructional strategies (i.e., how fast they work). This is because most instructional strategies compared with the AATD have been demonstrated to be *effective* in other studies (i.e., they lead to acquisition of behaviors in certain contexts) and the research question answered via the AATD is which of multiple *effective* strategies is superior. Common dimensions of superiority include (1) rapidity of learning, (2) extent of maintenance and generalization, (3) breadth of learning (e.g., learning two things rather than one), (4) acquisition of untrained relations, and (5) influencing future learning (Wolery et al., 1992). The most commonly measured dimension of efficiency is the rapidity of learning. It often is assessed by comparing the number of minutes, sessions, or trials to criterion or mastery.

The AATD, like the ME-ATD design, can be used to refine an intervention, including component analyses. For example, several studies documented the effectiveness of a procedure called instructive feedback (Werts et al., 1995). It involved presenting extra non-target information in praise statements during direct instruction but not asking students to respond to that information. When this was done, students learned a great deal of the extra information. In initial studies, the extra non-target information always had been related to target behaviors. Werts et al. (1993) used the AATD to compare two conditions: One in which instructive feedback information was related to target behaviors and one in which it was unrelated. The AATD is also commonly used to study parametric variations of an intervention. For example, Laher and Dada (2023) used the AATD to compare two dosage levels of augmented language models (40% versus 70% of spoken models) on children's receptive vocabulary learning. Table 13.3 lists several studies that use an AATD.

Table 13.3 Studies using Adapted Alternating Treatment Designs (AATD)

Reference	Design	Conditions Included in Comparison	Dependent Variable
Ledford, J. R., Chazin, K. T., Harbin, E. R., & Ward, S. E. (2017). Massed trials versus trials embedded into game play: Child outcomes and preference. *Topics in Early Childhood Special Education*, 37(2), 107–120.	AATD with initial baseline and comparison phases	Massed instruction (treatment) Embedded instruction (treatment) Control	Percentage unprompted correct responses, measured via trial-based event recording
Werfel, K. L., Brooks, M. C., & Fitton, L. (2020). The comparative efficiency of speech sound interventions that differ by delivery modality: Flashcards versus tablet. *Communication Disorders Quarterly*, 42(1), 31–39.	AATD with initial baseline, comparison, and maintenance phases	Speech sound intervention (SSI) with a tablet (treatment) SSI with flashcards (treatment)	Number of speech sounds correct, measured via trial-based event recording
O'Neill, S. J., McDowell, C., & Leslie, J. C. (2018). A comparison of prompt delays with trial-and-error instruction in conditional discrimination training. *Behavior Analysis in Practice*, 11(4), 370–380.	AATD with initial baseline, comparison, and maintenance phases	Trial-and-error (treatment) 5-s PPD (treatment) 5-s CPD (treatment) 2-s CPD (treatment)	Number of correct responses, measured via trial-based event recording
Mechling, L. C., & Ayres, K. M. (2012). A comparative study: Completion of fine motor office related tasks by high school students with autism using visual models on large and small screen sizes. *Journal of Autism and Developmental Disorders*, 42, 2364–2373.	AATD with initial baseline, comparison, and best alone conditions	Video modeling (VM) on small screen (treatment) VM on large screen (treatment) Control	Percent of correctly completed tasks, measured via trial-based event recording

(Continued)

Table 13.3 Continued

Reference	Design	Conditions Included in Comparison	Dependent Variable
Reichow, B., & Wolery, M. (2009). Comparison of everyday and every-fourth-day probe sessions with the simultaneous prompting procedure. *Topics in Early Childhood Special Education*, 29, 79–89.	AATD with initial baseline, comparison, and final probe (maintenance) phases (control measured in baseline and final probe)	Simultaneous prompting (SP) with every day probes (treatment) SP with every-fourth-day probes (treatment)	Percentage correct responses, measured via trial-based event recording
Torelli, J. N., Noel, C. R., Gross, T. J., & Morris, K. A. (2023). The potential promise of using adapted alternating treatment designs to assess teachers' use of classroom management practices. *Assessment for Effective Intervention*, Advance online publication.	ATD with initial baseline, 1st comparison (module), 2nd comparison (coaching) phases	1st comparison phase: Control (no module) Module 2nd comparison phase: Control (no coaching) Coaching	Number of uses of target teaching practice measured via event recording

Like the ME-ATD, two or more conditions are rapidly alternated in a single comparison phase. Unlike the ME-ATD, a pre-comparison baseline/non-intervention condition is generally considered necessary, even though it is not part of the experimental evaluation. It provides critical contextual information about the extent to which participants performed similarly across behavior sets prior to intervention, which is necessary (but insufficient) evidence that the behavior sets were of equal difficulty. Especially when interventions may be similarly efficient, it is also advisable to include an ongoing baseline condition, often called a **control condition**. Generally, a behavior set is assigned to this condition, but no intervention is applied.

Selecting and Assigning Sets

When the AATD is used, each condition (e.g., intervention) is applied to different behavior sets (e.g., five math problems, ten science definitions) or behavior chains (e.g., putting on a jacket, making a purchase online, or cooking a meal; see Callout 13.3). Target behaviors in AATD studies must meet five criteria:

1. Behaviors must be non-reversible (i.e., participants are likely to continue to perform the behaviors accurately after instruction has stopped).
2. Behaviors should not be in the participants' repertoire.
3. Behaviors must be independent, meaning one behavior set/chain can be acquired without influencing performance on other sets/chains.
4. Behaviors must be functionally similar, meaning behaviors are likely to be influenced by the same environmental variables (e.g., the instructional strategies being studied).
5. Behavior sets/chains must be of equal difficulty.

The last criterion is challenging but extremely important (Cariveau et al., 2021; Cariveau & Fetzner, 2022; Schlosser et al., 2018; Sindelar et al., 1985). Behavior sets/chains must be of equal difficulty because the instructional strategies are applied to separate behavior sets or response chains. If the behavior set taught with one strategy was easier to learn than the behavior set taught with the other, the test of the two interventions would be unfair. Before the study, you must select behavior sets and ensure they are of equal difficulty for each individual; baseline performance of 0% correct is not sufficient for ensuring behaviors are of equal difficulty. For

> **Callout 13.3** Why Do You Need Multiple Behavior Sets for AATDs But Not ME-ATDs?
>
> The number of behavior sets needed differs for AATDs and ME-ATDs because the type of dependent variable is different. The dependent variable for an ME-ATD is a reversible behavior (i.e., engagement, which changes quickly based on environmental context), and the dependent variable for an AATD is a non-reversible behavior (e.g., academic facts, which tend to maintain even once the context changes or intervention is removed).
>
> For ME-ATDs, the same reversible behavior is measured in all conditions. Reversible behaviors are not expected to occur without the intervention procedures or context in place. Therefore, the occurrence of a behavior in one condition would not necessarily influence the occurrence of a behavior in another condition. For example, a child's engagement during a condition in which they were given a favorite toy would not necessarily influence their engagement in a different session in which they were given a nonpreferred toy. In this case, the same reversible behavior (engagement) could be measured in both conditions and compared.
>
> For AATDs, separate non-reversible behavior sets must be used because the effect of the intervention on the behavior is expected to maintain to some degree even after the intervention procedures end. An example of a non-reversible behavior is reading sight words. In an AATD comparing instructional procedures to teach sight word reading, the participant would be expected to retain their ability to recognize a set of sight words after the session. If this same set of words was subsequently taught with a different instructional procedure and the child recognized many of the sight words, it would be impossible to know which procedures accounted for the child's learning. Thus, when teaching non-reversible behaviors, you must assign separate behaviors to each condition, which allows you to demonstrate the effect of *that condition* on behaviors, without interference from learning happening in other conditions.

example, you might have 0% correct responding for dunking a basketball and folding a fitted sheet. However, for most individuals, learning to fold a fitted sheet is likely much easier to master than dunking a basketball. Methods for selecting behaviors of equal difficulty are likely to vary by study and behavior type, but some common methods are listed in Table 13.4. Using more than one method for equating target sets is generally recommended (Cariveau et al., 2021).

Once you have used one or more procedures for establishing behavior sets of equal difficulty, you should randomly assign sets to conditions. For example, you should randomly assign Set 1 to Intervention A, Intervention B, or the control condition. Then you should randomly assign Set 2 to one of the two remaining conditions. Set 3 would then be assigned to the final condition. Randomly, rather than purposefully, assigning behavior sets to conditions disallows researchers from (consciously or unconsciously) assigning sets perceived as more difficult to a less-favored condition. This is especially important when one or more of the conditions being evaluated has been developed, refined, or promoted by the researchers.

When multiple participants are taught the same behavior sets/chains you should counterbalance behavior sets and conditions. For example, given three participants and three sets of vocabulary words, you might randomly assign Set 1 to Intervention A, Set 2 to Intervention B, and Set 3 to the control condition for the first participant. Then, you purposefully counterbalance that random assignment by assigning Set 1 to Intervention B for the second participant and Set 1 to the control condition for the third participant (with similar counterbalancing for Sets 2 and 3).

Table 13.4 Methods for Ensuring Equal Difficulty

Method	Use	Example
Experimental evaluation	Rarely used, resource-intensive, very precise	If teaching children to point to photos of 30 common objects, evaluate how long it takes to teach correct identification of each item to non-participants, and divide photos into sets based on duration to mastery (e.g., the three photos learned most quickly are each assigned to one set, the next three photos learned most quickly are also each assigned to one set, and so on, until each of the three photos that were learned most slowly are each assigned to one set).
Normed lists	Rarely used, access to norms vary, very imprecise	If teaching sight words, use a list such as the Fry sight word list, which is divided into sets of 100, with the first 100 being the most common words found in children's texts. Selecting words from this list ensures children are approximately equally likely to come across these words outside of the study.
Logical analysis	Commonly used, somewhat precise, easy to apply	If teaching children to identify science-related words when provided with a definition, you might try to ensure words in each set were (1) equally similar to each other in form, (2) equally difficult to say or write, and (3) had definitions that were similar in terms of number and complexity of words.
Expert rating	Somewhat commonly used, somewhat precise, easy to apply	When teaching emotion vocabulary to children, you might have early childhood teachers rate a list of emotion words according to complexity and common use by children.
Performance on related behaviors	Commonly used, precise, easy to apply	When teaching children to say words in a different language (e.g., What is the Spanish word for blue?), you can ensure that the child can repeat the Spanish word correctly and that the child knows the English word for the color (i.e., can answer "What color is this?" correctly with "Blue")

Procedural Steps

When planning an AATD, adhere to the following guidelines and recommendations:

Before

1. Develop research question about the impact of two or more conditions on *non-reversible* behavior(s) of interest.
2. Identify the target behavior(s) and identify the dimension of interest (e.g., time, number).
3. Select an appropriate (sensitive, reliable, valid, feasible) measurement system, test it, and modify as needed.
4. If you have more than one dependent variable, identify which will serve as the *primary dependent variable*, on which condition change decisions will be made.
5. Review previous research and your theory of change for evidence that conditions can be rapidly alternated, with carryover effects being unlikely.
6. Determine your comparison of interest (e.g., which conditions will be rapidly alternated) and the extent to which inclusion of a control (e.g., baseline, no-treatment) condition is needed.
7. Operationalize all condition procedures, including those included in initial baseline, comparison, and maintenance phases.
8. Determine frequency at which you will collect reliability and fidelity data, what calculations you will use to estimate reliability and fidelity, and acceptable levels of reliability and fidelity.

9. Create functionally equivalent and independent behavior sets/chains.
10. Randomly assign one behavior set/chain to each condition. When enrolling multiple participants with the same target behaviors, counterbalance assignment.
11. Determine rules for alternating conditions and procedures for minimizing order effects (e.g., counterbalancing, randomization), and carryover effects (e.g., time between sessions). Ensure that an equal number of sessions are conducted and that they are evenly spaced to permit an analysis of efficiency.
12. Establish criterion for mastery and when to discontinue less-efficient or less-effective conditions.
13. Identify participants, and, if applicable, refine definitions of target behaviors (e.g., specify exact response topographies that are acceptable, such as word approximations).

During/After

14. Collect and graph baseline data, five sessions or until data are stable.
15. Begin comparison phase. Conduct and graph at least five sessions per condition according to predetermined rules for alternating conditions.
16. Use visual analysis to determine whether a functional relation exists, does not exist, or whether additional data are needed (see Chapter 14).
17. If a functional relation is identified, collect best alone data in which the superior condition is conducted alone and/or collect maintenance data for all behavior sets.
18. Collect the specified amount of reliability and procedural fidelity data across all phases, conditions, and participants.

Callout 13.4   Applied Example of AATD

McDaniel et al. (2019) used an AATD to compare the effects of monolingual English intervention and bilingual Spanish-English intervention for three bilingual preschool children with hearing loss. The primary dependent variable was children's ability to label vocabulary items in English; however, McDaniel et al. also measured children's ability to label vocabulary items in Spanish and in either language (conceptual vocabulary). Labeling vocabulary items is a non-reversible behavior appropriate for AATDs because children would be expected to remember the vocabulary words after receiving instruction. There were three phases: Baseline, comparison, and maintenance. The sets of target vocabulary words were equated using multiple methods of logical analysis (e.g., part of speech, number of high frequency speech sounds in the word). Unique target sets were developed for each child and then randomly assigned to conditions. The dependent variable was measured during a vocabulary probe at the beginning of each session. Intervention for a condition ended when the child met the mastery criterion of 75% accuracy across three consecutive sessions. The monolingual and bilingual conditions featured shared storybook reading interventions, which occurred three days a week in a specialized preschool setting for children with hearing loss. The number of exposures to target words was equivalent across intervention conditions, and no intervention occurred with control set words. The order of conditions was the same each day. Procedural fidelity and interobserver agreement were high across conditions and phases. In Chapter 14, we share a figure depicting the AATD design and analysis of the outcomes of this study.

Repeated Acquisition Design

Repeated acquisition designs are similar to the changing criterion designs reported in Chapter 9 in that they are rarely reported in single case design literature, and their utility is constrained to a specific use, although there are recent calls for increased use of repeated acquisition designs in a broader range of circumstances (Kirby et al., 2021). These designs are one of a few single case designs appropriate for comparing interventions for teaching non-reversible behaviors (e.g., for comparing academic interventions), along with AATDs. Repeated acquisition designs are usually used when two interventions are being compared (e.g., errorless prompting versus non-errorless prompting), although there are circumstances in which only one intervention was evaluated (see Table 13.5). Like AATDs, repeated acquisition designs are rigorous for evaluating single interventions when an ongoing control condition is used instead of a second ongoing treatment condition (e.g., demonstration questions; Butler et al., 2014). Use of this design is relatively infrequent but several recent studies using this design are described in Table 13.5, and one study is described in Callout 13.5.

Callout 13.5 Applied Example of Repeated Acquisition Design

LaLonde et al. (2020) used a repeated acquisition design to evaluate two different treatments for improving tacts for three 3-year-old autistic children. Twenty-four stimuli were divided into eight sets (three stimuli per set), for a total of four comparisons. They measured the number of correct, independent tacts using trial-based event recording, reported as a percentage correct. In one treatment condition, children were taught to name stimuli with progressive time delay using only non-verbal cues (e.g., presentation of a photo, expectant pause). In the other treatment condition, researchers used the same procedures but also provided a verbal cue (e.g., "What is it?"). Before comparison phases, authors conducted play-based baseline sessions and these were repeated during a maintenance phase following the comparison phase. In Chapter 14, we share a figure depicting the repeated acquisition design and analysis of the outcomes of this study.

Table 13.5 *Studies using Repeated Acquisition Design*

Reference	Design	Conditions Included in Comparison	Dependent Variable
Dennis, L. R., & Whalon, K. J. (2021). Effects of teacher-versus application-delivered instruction on the expressive vocabulary of at-risk preschool children. *Remedial and Special Education*, 42(4), 195–206.	Repeated acquisition with eight sets of comparisons	Teacher-facilitated instruction (treatment) App-facilitated instruction (treatment)	Percentage of correct responses, measured via trial-based event recording
LaLonde, K. B., Dueñas, A. D., Neil, N., Wawrzonek, A., & Plavnick, J. B. (2020). An evaluation of two tact-training procedures on acquired tacts and tacting during play. *The Analysis of Verbal Behavior*, 36, 180–192.	Repeated acquisition with initial baseline plus four comparisons	Object only instruction (treatment) Object plus question instruction (treatment)	Percent independent correct tacts measured via trial-based event recording

(Continued)

Table 13.5 Continued

Reference	Design	Conditions Included in Comparison	Dependent Variable
Seven, Y., Hull, K., Madsen, K., Ferron, J., Peters-Sanders, L., Soto, X., ... & Goldstein, H. (2020). Classwide extensions of vocabulary intervention improve learning of academic vocabulary by preschoolers. *Journal of Speech, Language, and Hearing Research*, 63(1), 173–189.	Repeated acquisition with four alternating rather than simultaneous comparisons	Vocabulary intervention (treatment) Vocabulary intervention plus review strategies (treatment)	"Mastery monitoring score" (0 = incorrect, 1 = partial correct, 2 = correct)
Spencer, E. J., Goldstein, H., Sherman, A., Noe, S., Tabbah, R., Ziolkowski, R., & Schneider, N. (2012). Effects of an automated vocabulary and comprehension intervention: An early efficacy study. *Journal of Early Intervention*, 34(4), 195–221.	Repeated acquisition with six comparison phases and three demonstration phases (pre-to-post changes)	Vocabulary intervention (treatment) Control (*first three sets only*)	"Mastery monitoring score" (0 = incorrect, 1 = partial correct, 2 = correct)
Yuan, C., Hua, Y., & Zhu, J. (2019). The role of reinforcement in multiple response repetition error correction and treatment preference of Chinese children with autism. *Journal of Autism and Developmental Disorders*, 49, 3704–3715.	Repeated acquisition with initial baseline and three sets of comparisons	Error correction with reinforcement (treatment) Error correction without reinforcement (treatment)	Percentage of correct responses, measured via trial-based event recording

When repeated acquisition designs are used, a large pool of target behaviors is required. For example, you might include 60 vocabulary words when comparing two interventions across ten comparisons. You would randomly assign these words to 20 sets of 3, and randomly assign each set of 3 to a condition and phase. Then, you would conduct each comparison sequentially. The graphic below shows the result of pre-study randomization for 60 vocabulary words (which were randomly generated by ChatGPT and randomly ordered using the random function in Excel). To be clear, we do not advocate for this type of stimulus generation in real studies. Some potential problems with equality between sets can be observed in this example likely due to this organization method—for example, *dog* and *kangaroo* in Set 7 for Treatment A are likely more difficult to discriminate than any of the nouns in Set 7 for Treatment B (*doll, star, rain*). Figure 13.3 shows hypothetical results from this comparison.

	Comparison							
Treatment	1	2	3	4	5	6	7	8
A	Truck	Duck	Toothpaste	Snow	Pig	Chair	Cookie	Shoe
	Flower	Bee	Banana	Ball	Ant	Horse	Kangaroo	Tree
	Cake	Cat	Bath	Teddy bear	Plate	Toothbrush	Dog	Ice cream
B	Moon	Rainbow	Fork	Sun	Giraffe	Pizza	Doll	Soap
	Cloud	Bird	Hat	Bear	Cow	Car	Star	Frog
	Elephant	Fish	Apple	Monkey	Table	Butterfly	Rain	Cup

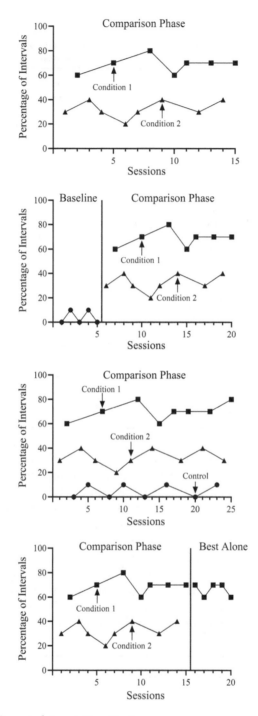

Figure 13.3 Prototype Repeated Acquisition Designs.

There are two primary strategies for comparison phases for repeated acquisition designs. In the first, each comparison phase lasts for a fixed period of time, usually associated with an academic calendar (e.g., a school week). This is represented in the top panel of Figure 13.3, with data representing treatments that are both administered for one school week (with three data collection opportunities during the week). The second strategy is to administer treatments until mastery is reached in one condition, depicted in the bottom panel. Both of these strategies have been used with repeated acquisition designs, but the former (top panel) is more common.

Published repeated acquisition designs include a wide variety of condition types. We recommend that repeated acquisition designs include at minimum five phases, with two alternating conditions occurring in each phase. Data are generally collected in non-intervention probes within the phase. That is, pre-intervention data are collected in a non-treatment context (i.e., a pre-test), and then additional data are collected one or more times after the participant experiences one or more intervention sessions, in the same non-treatment context (i.e., a post-test). For example, on Monday, a child is provided an opportunity to correctly define three vocabulary words from each condition. Then, the child receives instruction on each word on Monday and Tuesday. On Wednesday, the child is provided another testing opportunity to define words. The child receives instruction again on Wednesday and Thursday, and then is afforded one final test on Friday (see Figure 13.3). Researchers have sometimes also included initial baseline conditions; if these are not included, it might be prudent to have screening procedures to ensure meaningful comparisons (i.e., that you are teaching stimuli that are unknown).

Threats to Internal Validity

A few notable threats to internal validity are more likely in RIA designs. These include procedural infidelity, attrition, multitreatment interference, and unequal target sets (in AATDs and repeated acquisition designs). A checklist for evaluating internal validity in AATDs is available (Schlosser et al., 2018), and is helpful given the complexity in dealing with equality of behavior sets and multitreatment interference.

Procedural infidelity threats may be more likely due to the rapid alternation of conditions—that is, implementers are required to frequently change their behaviors, which could result in increased likelihood of errors. Sensitive measures and thorough documentation of procedural integrity in all conditions are important. Using cues and reminders to assist implementers may also be warranted. *Attrition* could be a likely threat if the rapid alternation between conditions results in participant confusion or frustration; this threat could be mitigated by clearly describing and differentiating condition procedures for participants. Attrition as a threat could also be mitigated by the potentially short duration of RIA designs relative to other single case designs for each participant.

Multitreatment interference occurs when the impacts of one condition "bleed over" into another condition. This threat may be more likely for RIA designs because there are typically more conditions than in other single case designs. You can decrease the likelihood of multitreatment interference by maximizing discriminability of conditions (e.g., providing participants with sufficient information about what condition is in effect) and time between sessions. For AATDs specifically, you can also select functionally independent behaviors. Inclusion of a control condition in the comparison phase of an AATD can be used to detect the presence of multitreatment interference between two or more intervention conditions (Cariveau & Fetzner, 2022); however, a control condition would not be expected to prevent this threat.

Another threat to internal validity in AATDs and repeated acquisition designs occurs if behavior sets are assumed to be of equal difficulty but are not. This threat is somewhat unique and does not fall neatly into one of the typical categories of internal validity threats. The likelihood of this threat can be reduced by using one or more of the described methods in Table 13.6 to ensure equality among sets, by randomizing sets to condition, and by counterbalancing across participants when possible. Participant experience may also be a threat to internal

Table 13.6 Threats to Internal Validity in RIA Designs

Threats	Likelihood *Specific to Design*	Prevention and Control *Specific to Design*
History	Potentially decreased due to short duration of evaluation and concurrent nature of comparison	–
Maturation	Potentially decreased due to short duration of evaluation and concurrent nature of comparison	–
Testing	No increased threat	–
Attrition	Potentially decreased due to short duration of evaluation	Clearly describe alternation procedures to reduce participant confusion/frustration
Selection	No increased threat	–
Regression to the Mean	No increased threat	–
Instrumentation	Potentially increased threat for AATD given need for equal sets	**AATD and repeated acquisition**: Use one or more methods to increase likelihood that sets are equally difficulty to learn; randomize sets to conditions; counterbalance across participants when possible
Procedural Infidelity	Potentially increased due to rapid alternation of conditions requiring different procedures	Use cues (e.g., colored materials, verbal reminders) to remind implementers of current condition in place
Adaptation	No increased threat	–
Hawthorne Effect	No increased threat	–
Multitreatment Interference	Potentially increased due to multiple treatments	Maximize discriminability of conditions; extend time between sessions **AATD and repeated acquisition**: Select functionally independent behaviors
Data Instability	No increased threat	–
Design-Related Confounds	Potentially increased due to rapid alternation effects	Use theory of change to predict impact of rapid alternation

validity if not reported. RIA designs are often used to compare the effectiveness and/or efficiency of two or more interventions. Thus, it is important to measure and report whether participants have pre-existing familiarity with one or more of the interventions, as this would be expected to influence the outcomes.

Single case design is predicated on an assumption the behavior is largely determined by environmental circumstances and is context-specific (Robertson et al., 2022). Control is thus established by carefully organizing exposures to different contexts in ways that demonstrates the control that each relevant context has on behavior. Importantly, the manner in which transitions between contexts are arranged exerts its own control over behavior which is independent of the control of either context in isolation (Ferster & Skinner, 1957). In RIA designs, transitions between conditions are nearly constant; thus, the impacts of transitions on behavior, above and beyond any impacts due to the actual conditions in place, are a concern. As with multitreatment interference, this design-specific confound can be detected via a best alone phase.

Assessing Social Validity Using Simultaneous Treatments

Previous editions of this text have described the use of RIA condition ordering logic to assess preference, commonly referred to as the simultaneous treatments design or "concurrent operants" paradigms. **Simultaneous treatments** procedures involve evaluating participant preference or choice-making behavior between two concurrently available conditions. This procedure has a long history, particularly in behavior analytic basic literature (e.g., *Journal of the Experimental Analysis of Behavior*), where it has been used since the 1960s (e.g., Duncan & Silberberg, 1982; Hackenberg & Joker, 1994). These procedures were differentiated from ME-ATDs by Barlow and Hayes (1979), although investigators' use of the distinct terminology has been inconsistent.

In isolation, these procedures are appropriate for research questions concerning participant choice or preference and can be used alongside other single case designs. They are often conducted in combination with RIA designs (e.g., ME-ATD or AATD) to assess which condition among those compared is more effective (RIA design) *and* preferred by participants (simultaneous treatments). That is, instead of randomly ordering conditions, researchers have allowed participants to select which intervention conditions they experience on some occasions; this selection is used as an indication of participant preference for one condition over another. These procedures allow for an ongoing assessment of social validity within single case designs, especially in cases when participants might not be able to verbally communicate their opinions about instructional or assessment procedures.

Importantly, there is not a *planned rapid alternation* when this design is used. The implementation of any condition is dependent on the participant choosing that condition. Thus, while we consider the use of this paradigm critical for social validity purposes, it does not use traditional RIA logic (despite our inclusion in this chapter, and in previous editions). That is, the ways in which RIA designs control for internal validity are not necessarily applicable when assessing participant preference using procedures associated with simultaneous treatments (e.g., Chazin & Ledford, 2021; Ledford et al., 2017). Thus, we will refer to simultaneous treatments *procedures* rather than simultaneous treatments *designs*.

You can use simultaneous treatment procedures when two or more conditions are simultaneously available and when a participant's choice between the options is of interest. You should establish whether participants are able to discriminate between available conditions before making their first selection. Then, rather than determining rules for alternating conditions, identify a method in which participants select the condition they would prefer (e.g., verbal indication of preference, moving to a designated area in a room, pointing to a picture). As in a typical ME-ATD, data on the reversible dependent variable (e.g., the number of times a condition is chosen per session) is collected across all compared conditions.

Callout 13.6   Applied Example of Simultaneous Treatments Procedure

Tönsing (2016) used an AATD to compare different forms of augmentative and alternative communication (AAC) during a storybook intervention for four children with complex communication needs. They evaluated the effects of two AAC modes, a sentence-generating device and a communication board, on children's production of targeted two-symbol combinations.

Three conditions were defined: Sentence-generating device, communication board, and a choice condition. Three sets of target two-symbol combinations were created (i.e., one for each condition). Assignment of sets of target symbol combinations (and their respective stories) to AAC conditions was counterbalanced across participants. The target two-symbol combinations were then taught to children as part of a short story using systematic prompting procedures for each condition. There were four phases: *baseline*, *intervention*, *preference*, and *maintenance*. During the intervention phase, two conditions (sentence-generating device and picture board) were rapidly alternated according to a predetermined session order. Participants met mastery criteria when they produced correct symbol combinations in 83% of opportunities (i.e., 10/12) for two consecutive sessions, or after a maximum of ten intervention sessions per condition.

Following the intervention phase, a simultaneous treatments procedure was conducted to assess participant's preferences for either the speech-generating device or the communication board. In the preference phase, rather than predetermining session order, the researcher asked participants prior to every session: "Which one do you want to use when we read the story?" Sessions were then conducted according to the indicated preferences of each participant. This phase used the "choice" condition target set that was not included in the intervention phase (i.e., this phase only included non-mastered two-symbol combinations). The mastery criterion for the preference phase was the same as the intervention phase, and a minimum of three sessions were required before discontinuing the phase.

Conclusions

Designs using RIA condition ordering require *either* a reversible behavior (for ME-ATDs) or a non-reversible behavior (AATDs, repeated acquisition designs). They typically require two or more independent variables that can be introduced and withdrawn rapidly (e.g., a different intervention for each session). Historically, ME-ATDs have been considered designs appropriate for comparison questions, but they can be used to compare the effects of two or more interventions, compare the effects of two or more contexts for assessment purposes (usually in the form of functional analyses), or compare the effects of a single intervention or assessment condition against a control or baseline condition. Similarly, AATDs and repeated acquisition designs have been historically considered to be most appropriate for comparison questions, but variations have been used that answer demonstration questions (e.g., Peters-Sanders et al., 2020; Torelli et al., 2023). As such, we consider designs using RIA of conditions to be flexible for answering a variety of questions.

References

Barlow, D. H., & Hayes, S. C. (1979). Alternating treatments design: One strategy for comparing the effects of two treatments in a single subject. *Journal of Applied Behavior Analysis*, 12, 199–210.

Butler, C., Brown, J. A., & Woods, J. J. (2014). Teaching at-risk toddlers new vocabulary using interactive digital storybooks. *Contemporary Issues in Communication Science and Disorders*, 41, 155–168.

Cariveau, T., Batchelder, S., Ball, S., & La Cruz Montilla, A. (2021). Review of methods to equate target sets in the adapted alternating treatments design. *Behavior Modification*, 45(5), 695–714.

Cariveau, T., & Fetzner, D. (2022). Experimental control in the adapted alternating treatments design: A review of procedures and outcomes. *Behavioral Interventions*, 37(3), 805–818.

Cariveau, T., Helvey, C. I., Moseley, T. K., & Hester, J. (2022). Equating and assigning targets in the adapted alternating treatments design: Review of special education journals. *Remedial and Special Education*, 43(1), 58–71.

Chazin, K. T., & Ledford, J. R. (2021). Constant time delay and system of least prompts: Efficiency and child preference. *Journal of Behavioral Education*, 30, 684–707.

Chazin, K. T., Ledford, J. R., Barton, E. E., & Osborne, K. (2017). The effects of antecedent exercise on engagement during large group activities for young children. *Remedial and Special Education*, 39(3), 158–170.

Dennis, L. R., & Whalon, K. J. (2021). Effects of teacher-versus application-delivered instruction on the expressive vocabulary of at-risk preschool children. *Remedial and Special Education*, 42(4), 195–206.

Duncan, H. J., & Silberberg, A. (1982). The effects of concurrent responding and reinforcement on behavioral output. *Journal of the Experimental Analysis of Behavior*, 38, 125–132.

Ferster, C. B., & Skinner, B. F. (1957). Mixed schedules. In C. B. Ferster & B. F. Skinner, *Schedules of reinforcement* (pp. 585–662). New York: Appleton-Century-Crofts.

Hackenberg, T. D., & Joker, V. R. (1994). Instructional versus schedule control of humans' choices in situations of diminishing returns. *Journal of the Experimental Analysis of Behavior*, 62, 367–383.

Hammond, J. L., & Hall, S. S. (2011). Functional analysis and treatment of aggressive behavior following resection of a craniopharyngioma. *Developmental Medicine and Child Neurology*, 53, 369–374.

Holyfield, C., Brooks, S., & Schluterman, A. (2019). Comparative effects of high-tech visual scene displays and low-tech isolated picture symbols on engagement from students with multiple disabilities. *Language, Speech, and Hearing Services in Schools*, 50, 693–702.

Ingersoll, B. (2011). The differential effect of three naturalistic language interventions on language use in children with autism. *Journal of Positive Behavior Interventions*, 13, 109–118.

Kirby, M. S., Spencer, T. D., & Ferron, J. (2021). How to be RAD: Repeated acquisition design features that enhance internal and external validity. *Perspectives on Behavior Science*, 44(2–3), 389–416.

Kodak, T., Northup, J., & Kelley, M. E. (2007). An evaluation of the types of attention that maintain problem behavior. *Journal of Applied Behavior Analysis*, 40, 167–171.

Kratochwill, T. R., Hitchcock, J. H., Horner, R. H., Levin, J. R., Odom, S. L., Rindskopf, D. M., & Shadish, W. R. (2010). *Single case designs technical documentation*. https://files.eric.ed.gov/fulltext/ED510743.pdf

Laher, Z., & Dada, S. (2023). The effect of aided language stimulation on the acquisition of receptive vocabulary in children with complex communication needs and severe intellectual disability: A comparison of two dosages. *Augmentative and Alternative Communication*, 39, 96–109.

LaLonde, K. B., Dueñas, A. D., Neil, N., Wawrzonek, A., & Plavnick, J. B. (2020). An evaluation of two tact-training procedures on acquired tacts and tacting during play. *The Analysis of Verbal Behavior*, 36, 180–192.

Ledford, J. R., Chazin, K. T., Harbin, E. R., & Ward, S. E. (2017). Massed trials versus trials embedded into game play: Child outcomes and preference. *Topics in Early Childhood Special Education*, 37(2), 107–120.

Ledford, J. R., Zimmerman, K. N., Severini, K. E., Gast, H. A., Osborne, K., & Harbin, E. R. (2020). Brief report: Evaluation of the noncontingent provision of fidget toys during group activities. *Focus on Autism and Other Developmental Disabilities*, 35(2), 101–107.

Lynch, A., Theodore, L. A., Bray, M. W., & Kehle, T. J. (2009). A comparison of group–oriented contingencies and randomized reinforcers to improve homework completion and accuracy for students with disabilities. *School Psychology Review*, 38, 307–324.

Maggin, D. M., Barton, E., Reichow, B., Lane, K., & Shogren, K. A. (2022). Commentary on the *What Works Clearinghouse Standards and Procedures Handbook* (v. 4.1) for the review of single-case research. *Remedial and Special Education*, 43, 421–433.

McDaniel, J., Benítez-Barrera, C. R., Soares, A. C., Vargas, A., & Camarata, S. (2019). Bilingual versus monolingual vocabulary instruction for bilingual children with hearing loss. *The Journal of Deaf Studies and Deaf Education*, 24(2), 142–160.

Mechling, L. C., & Ayres, K. M. (2012). A comparative study: Completion of fine motor office related tasks by high school students with autism using visual models on large and small screen sizes. *Journal of Autism and Developmental Disorders*, 42, 2364–2373.

O'Neill, S. J., McDowell, C., & Leslie, J. C. (2018). A comparison of prompt delays with trial-and-error instruction in conditional discrimination training. *Behavior Analysis in Practice*, 11(4), 370–380.

Peters-Sanders, L. A., Kelley, E. S., Biel, C. H., Madsen, K., Soto, X., Seven, Y., … & Goldstein, H. (2020). Moving forward four words at a time: Effects of a supplemental preschool vocabulary intervention. *Language, Speech, and Hearing Services in Schools*, 51(1), 165–175.

Reichow, B., & Wolery, M. (2009). Comparison of everyday and every-fourth-day probe sessions with the simultaneous prompting procedure. *Topics in Early Childhood Special Education*, 29, 79–89.

Robertson, R. E., Lambert, J. M., Buonomo, K., & Copeland, B. A. (2022). Theoretical foundations of applied behavior analysis and applications in special education research and practice. In *Handbook of special education research, Volume I* (pp. 10–23). New York: Routledge.

Schlosser, R. W., Belfiore, P. J., Sigafoos, J., Briesch, A. M., & Wendt, O. (2018). Appraisal of comparative single-case experimental designs for instructional interventions with non-reversible target behaviors: Introducing the CSCEDARS ("Cedars"). *Research in Developmental Disabilities*, 79, 33–52.

Seven, Y., Hull, K., Madsen, K., Ferron, J., Peters-Sanders, L., Soto, X., ... & Goldstein, H. (2020). Classwide extensions of vocabulary intervention improve learning of academic vocabulary by preschoolers. *Journal of Speech, Language, and Hearing Research*, 63(1), 173–189.

Sindelar, P. T., Rosenberg, M. S., & Wilson, R. J. (1985). An adapted alternating treatments design for instructional research. *Education and Treatment of Children*, 8, 67–76.

Spencer, E. J., Goldstein, H., Sherman, A., Noe, S., Tabbah, R., Ziolkowski, R., & Schneider, N. (2012). Effects of an automated vocabulary and comprehension intervention: An early efficacy study. *Journal of Early Intervention*, 34(4), 195–221.

Staubitz, J. L., Staubitz, J. E., Pollack, M. S., Haws, R. A., & Hopton, M. (2022). Effects of an enhanced choice model of skill-based treatment for students with emotional/behavioral disorders. *Journal of Applied Behavior Analysis*, 55(4), 1306–1341.

Taylor, T. (2022). Brief report: Packing treatment comparison and use of a chaser to increase swallowing for a clinical case. *Journal of Autism and Developmental Disorders*, 52(7), 3280–3285.

Tönsing, K. M. (2016). Supporting the production of graphic symbol combinations by children with limited speech: A comparison of two AAC systems. *Journal of Developmental and Physical Disabilities*, 28(1), 5–29.

Torelli, J. N., Noel, C. R., Gross, T. J., & Morris, K. A. (2023). *The potential promise of using adapted alternating treatment designs to assess teachers' use of classroom management practices. Assessment for Effective Intervention*. Advance online publication.

Werfel, K. L., Brooks, M. C., & Fitton, L. (2020). The comparative efficiency of speech sound interventions that differ by delivery modality: Flashcards versus tablet. *Communication Disorders Quarterly*, 42(1), 31–39.

Werts, M. G., Wolery, M., Holcombe, A., & Frederick, C. (1993). Effects of instructive feedback related and unrelated to the target behaviors. *Exceptionality*, 4, 81–95.

Werts, M. G., Wolery, M., Holcombe, A., & Gast, D. L. (1995). Instructive feedback: Review of parameters and effects. *Journal of Behavioral Education*, 5, 55–75.

Wolery, M., Ault, M. J., & Doyle, P. M. (1992). *Teaching students with moderate and severe disabilities: Use of response prompting strategies*. White Plains, NY: Longman.

Yuan, C., Hua, Y., & Zhu, J. (2019). The role of reinforcement in multiple response repetition error correction and treatment preference of Chinese children with autism. *Journal of Autism and Developmental Disorders*, 49, 3704–3715.

14
Analyzing Data from Studies Using Rapid Iterative Alternation

Jennifer R. Ledford, Kathryn M. Bailey, and Natalie S. Pak

Important Terms

differentiation, summative analysis

Table of Contents

Formative Analysis and Phase Change Decisions
Summative Analysis and Functional Relation Determination
    Design Adequacy
    Data Adequacy
    Controls for Threats to Internal Validity
    Outcomes Evaluation
Supplemental Analyses
    Supplemental Analyses for ME-ATDs
    Supplemental Analyses for AATDs and Repeated Acquisition Designs
Describing Visual Analysis
    Visual Analysis Procedures
    Visual Analysis Results
Conclusions
References

Callouts

14.1 *Applied Example of ME-ATD*
14.2 *Applied Example of AATD*
14.3 *Applied Example of Repeated Acquisition Design*

Although visual analysis is the primary method of analysis across design types (Hersen & Barlow, 1976; Gast, 2010, Kazdin, 2020; Tawney & Gast, 1984), designs using rapid iterative alternation (RIA) have unique features that make visual analysis considerations somewhat different than other design types. This is true for both formative and summative analyses. In this chapter, we discuss analysis of data from studies using RIA condition ordering, including necessary conditions for analyzing data, formative and summative visual analysis and decision making, and supplemental analyses. We also introduce a new term that is relevant for studies using RIA—**differentiation**. This is the extent to which data from two conditions in the same phase have different levels across time.

As discussed in Chapter 13, designs using RIA condition ordering have traditionally been used when a researcher has a question about the *relative efficiency* or *effectiveness* of one intervention in relation to one or more other interventions. They can also be used to identify a relation between a behavior and one or more treatment conditions relative to baseline, so long as there is an *ongoing* baseline condition as part of the comparison phase (i.e., an initial baseline condition that is not rapidly alternated with another condition is not sufficient; Skinner et al., 2022). They are the only designs that permit simultaneous, direct comparisons between three or more conditions for establishing functional relations. These designs can be used for reversible (ME-ATD) and non-reversible (AATD, repeated acquisition design) behaviors.

Formative Analysis and Phase Change Decisions

Designs using RIA tend to involve fewer formative decisions than other condition ordering paradigms. Because conditions are often ordered randomly within the comparison phase, and because the data are collected for two or more conditions simultaneously across phases, there are fewer opportunities to ask "What should I do at this point in the experiment?" For example, it is common to determine a priori that you need to collect at least five data points per condition before making a functional relation decision. Furthermore, let's say that you will randomly order sessions (with the rule that no more than two sessions in the same condition can occur consecutively). In this case, you will collect data for ten sessions before making any further decisions. Of course, monitoring data is still necessary from a clinical standpoint, but the analysis is limited to assessing for adverse events or unexpected patterns that might indicate a need to change procedures before a determination is made (i.e., prioritizing participant well-being over the ability to make decisions about a functional relation). After ten sessions, you might have evidence of clear differentiation, like that shown in the top left panel Figure 14.1 (Study 1). In this instance, the first opportunity for a formative decision point would be the end of the experiment. By contrast, Study 3 in Figure 14.1 shows a situation in which additional formative analyses are needed even after the first set of data have been collected, indicating the need for more data. However, there are relatively fewer formative analysis decision points when these designs are used, compared to other design types. For example, in an A-B-A-B and multiple baseline designs, if you assume the need for at least three data points per condition, there are generally opportunities for decision making after each data point, excepting those that occur for the first two sessions of each condition.

Generally, formative analysis decision rules lead to decisions to (1) continue the comparison because more data are needed, or (2) discontinue the comparison because data are sufficient to determine whether a functional relation exists. When a functional relation does not exist, sometimes an additional comparison phase is conducted in which one or more conditions is modified. For example, for one participant, Lambert et al. (2022) conducted a functional

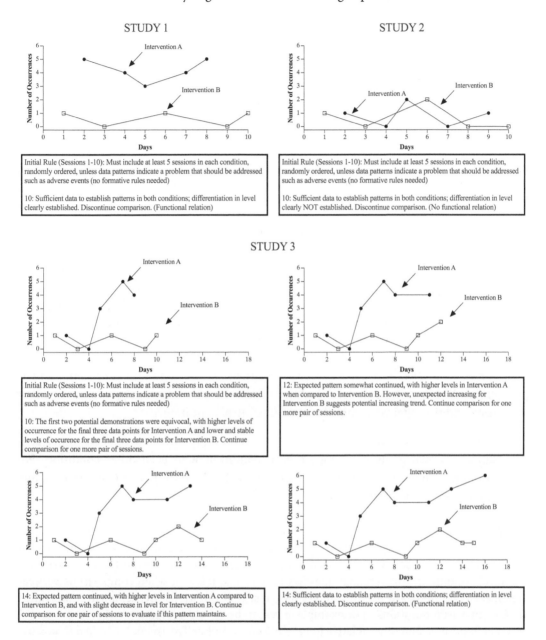

Figure 14.1 Formative Analysis Decisions for Three ME-ATD Studies.

analysis with undifferentiated, low rates of challenging behavior using an ME-ATD (see Figure 14.2). Then, they made a modification and conducted a second comparison phase during which there was clear differentiation, with the attention condition resulting in high levels of behavior. This type of modification can be relatively quickly assessed in the ME-ATD. This type of additional comparison would take many more sessions in a sequential introduction and withdrawal design (e.g., an A-B-A-B-C-D-C-D design).

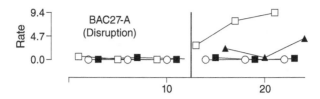

Figure 14.2 Example of an ME-ATD with no Functional Relation Identified During Initial Comparison, followed by a Second Comparison during which a Relation was Identified.

Source: Reprinted from supplemental materials via the Open Science Framework (https://osf.io/wcsuh) (BAC 27). Unfilled squares represent attention conditions, unfilled circles represent control conditions, filled squares represent tangible conditions, and filled triangles represent escape conditions.

Summative Analysis and Functional Relation Determination

Summative analysis of data in designs using RIA of conditions occurs via visual analysis of graphic data for the purposes of drawing conclusions about research questions, as was described for designs using SIW and time-lagged condition ordering. Depending on your research questions, functional relation determinations are usually made using either all available comparisons or using one condition as a control. Examples of these types of research questions that these two different variations answer are shown below.

> **RIA Research Question Type 1**: Is each treatment or test condition consistently differentiated from a single control condition? (Visual analysis: Compare each treatment or test condition against a single baseline or control condition.)
>
> **RIA Research Question Type 2**: Is each condition differentiated from each other condition? (Visual analysis: Compare each condition with each other condition. For example, compare Condition A to Condition B, Condition A to Condition C, and Condition B to Condition C.)

Research question Type 1 commonly applies to summative evaluation of functional analyses (Iwata et al., 1994). In experimental functional analyses, the question is something similar to: Does challenging behavior consistently occur under one or more conditions, compared to a control condition? This research question type is also relevant when comparisons *between* treatment conditions are not of interest (i.e., research questions are demonstration, rather than comparison questions). For example, a researcher could evaluate whether Treatment A resulted in positive outcomes relative to baseline *and* whether Treatment B resulted in positive outcomes relative to baseline. The question in this instance would essentially be "Do either of these treatments work?" rather than "Which of these treatments work better?" Researchers might elect to do this if they have reason to believe that two treatments will work (i.e., their theory of change suggests this is true) but they are interested in evaluating secondary questions about which intervention is preferred by implementers or recipients (see Chapters 7 and Chapter 13 for more information about evaluating participant preference).

Research question Type 2 typically applies to summative analysis of treatment evaluations in which researchers are interested in the relative efficiency of two treatments. When a comparison phase includes two treatment conditions, researchers can identify a functional relation such that they identify that Treatment A results in better/worse outcomes than Treatment B. When a comparison phase includes two treatment conditions *and* an ongoing baseline condition, researchers can identify a functional relation such that they identify that (1) Treatment A results in better/worse outcomes than Treatment B. In addition, they can also answer (2) whether Treatment A results in better/worse outcomes than baseline or control conditions, *and* (3) whether Treatment B results in better/worse outcomes than baseline or control conditions. Callouts 14.1, 14.2, and 14.3 at the end of the chapter show examples of summative visual analysis for three published studies using designs with RIA condition ordering.

Callout 14.1 Applied Example of ME-ATD

In the study described in Callout 13.3 in Chapter 13 (Holyfield et al., 2019), we describe an ME-ATD used to evaluate the effects of the availability of different augmentative and alternative communication (AAC) modes on the eye gaze and independent communication behaviors of three school-aged children with multiple disabilities. The graph below depicts a secondary variable, the number of independent uses of the AAC, which was measured using trial-based recording (five trials per session). The black data path represents the availability of high-tech AAC, while the gray data path represents the availability of low-tech AAC. Sessions are depicted on the horizontal axis and the number of independent communication responses is depicted on the vertical axis.

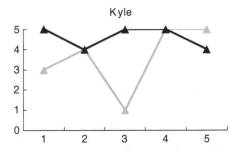

Source: Holyfield, C., Brooks, S., & Schluterman, A. (2019). Comparative effects of high-tech visual scene displays and low-tech isolated picture symbols on engagement from students with multiple disabilities. *Language, Speech, and Hearing Services in Schools, 50*(4), 693–702.

Design Adequacy: This ME-ATD includes data from two conditions, and is adequate for answering a comparison question, but not a demonstration question (e.g., intervention relative to baseline).

Data Adequacy: Because data patterns were not consistent (e.g., data were similar for some comparisons and differentiated for others), additional data collection have been helpful for drawing confident conclusions.

Control for Common Threats: Procedural fidelity and interobserver agreement data are appropriate, suggesting confidence in reliability of the independent and dependent variables. A history threat may have been present during Session 3 for the low-tech device.

Visual Analysis: The *level* of data in the high-tech condition was high and data were *stable*. Data in the low-tech condition were variable and/or depict a potential history threat. An overall increasing trend to ceiling levels may be present in the low-tech condition. In two sessions, high-tech availability resulted in more communication responses, while in one condition, low-tech availability resulted in more communication responses, and in two sessions, the number of responses was equal.

Functional Relation Decision: A functional relation determination cannot be made due to the need for more data.

Callout 14.2 Applied Example of AATD

In the study described in Callout 13.5 in Chapter 13 (McDaniel et al., 2019), compared the effects of monolingual English intervention and bilingual Spanish-English intervention for three bilingual preschool children with hearing loss. The primary dependent variable was the percentage of correctly named items in English. The graph depicts data for one participant, including percentage correct for items assigned to monolingual, bilingual, and control conditions.

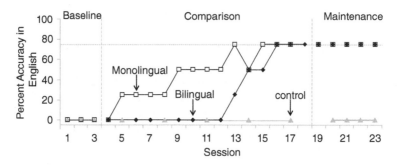

Source: McDaniel, J., Benítez-Barrera, C. R., Soares, A. C., Vargas, A., & Camarata, S. (2019). Bilingual versus monolingual vocabulary instruction for bilingual children with hearing loss. *The Journal of Deaf Studies and Deaf Education*, 24(2), 142–160.

Design Adequacy: This AATD is adequate for answering both demonstration and comparison questions, given that it includes two comparison condition and an ongoing control condition, as well as an initial baseline condition.

Data Adequacy: There are at least three data points per condition and the comparison was conducted until the child reached mastery criteria in both intervention conditions (three sessions at criterion level, which is indicated with a horizontal gray line).

Control for Common Threats: Visual analysis suggests low likelihood of history and maturation threats given continued low levels of correct responding in the control condition. Interobserver agreement and procedural fidelity data are appropriate, suggesting confidence in reliability of the independent and dependent variables. Appropriate steps were taken to increase likelihood that sets were equally difficult to learn (see Chapter 13).

Visual Analysis: The *level* in all 3 conditions is at 0 during baseline. Monolingual instruction resulted in an immediate increasing *trend* and data reached criterion at Session 17. Bilingual instruction resulted in a delayed increasing trend, with data reaching criterion at Session 18.

Functional Relation Decision: A functional relation is evident between the use of either instruction package and acquisition of English vocabulary. No differentiation between intervention conditions and a one-session difference in acquisition suggests a functional relation is not present between language of instruction and rate of acquisition (i.e., monolingual and bilingual instruction were equally efficient, and both were superior to the control condition).

Callout 14.3 Applied Example of Repeated Acquisition Design

As described in Callout 13.6 in Chapter 13, Lalonde et al. (2020) describe the use of a repeated acquisition design to assess two interventions designed to teach tacts to 3-year-old autistic children.

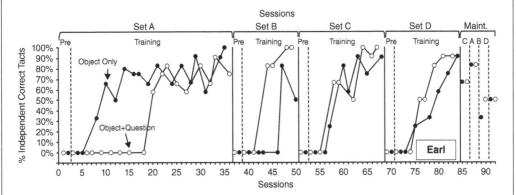

Source: LaLonde, K. B., Dueñas, A. D., Neil, N., Wawrzonek, A., & Plavnick, J. B. (2020). An evaluation of two tact-training procedures on acquired tacts and tacting during play. *The Analysis of Verbal Behavior*, 36, 180–192.

Design Adequacy: In this design, there are four opportunities to establish a superior intervention. Because there is no ongoing control condition, confident conclusions cannot be drawn about the extent to which interventions were superior to a no-intervention condition (i.e., it is possible that repeated exposure alone led to changes in behavior).

Data Adequacy: There are at least three data points per condition and each comparison was conducted until the child reached mastery criteria in at least one intervention condition. Rules used to discontinue instruction were not clear.

Control for Common Threats: Although an ongoing control condition would improve control for history and maturation threats, the consistent low levels of correct tacts during early sessions, followed by mastery in both intervention conditions, may suggest that history threats were unlikely. Interobserver agreement and procedural fidelity data are appropriate, suggesting confidence in reliability of the independent and dependent variables. No information was provided on the development or assignment of stimuli to sets, and thus, no conclusions can be drawn about the extent to which sets were likely to be equal.

Visual Analysis: In the first comparison, there was a near-immediate increasing trend in the object-only condition and a delayed increasing trend in the object + question condition. In both conditions, data were variable between approximately 60–90% correct for the remainder of the condition, with the object-only condition reading mastery criterion after 17 intervention sessions. The other three comparisons were much shorter, with the criterion reached first for the object + question condition in Sets B, C, and D.

Functional Relation Decision: Despite an initial comparison for Set A resulting in more efficient learning in the object-only condition, a functional relation is demonstrated such that the addition of the question was associated with more efficient acquisition of tacts given the superior performance in that condition for Sets B through C.

Design Adequacy

As discussed in Chapters 10 and 12, before answering the question regarding whether a functional relation exists, you should first assess whether the design is sufficient for making the determination. Potential demonstrations include opportunities to assess differences between conditions when condition changes occur, similar to those described in Chapters 10 and 12. However, because conditions change *within phases* for RIA designs, the number of demonstrations of effect is typically approximately equal to the number of data points in the condition. See Figure 14.3 for examples of ME-ATDs with the number of potential demonstrations of effect numbered. If the design does not include *at least three potential demonstrations of effect*, it is not possible to assess for whether a functional relation exists.

It is important to establish *what questions* can be answered if a design is sufficient. For example, an ME-ATD with an initial baseline phase and five data points in each of two intervention conditions during a comparison phase is likely sufficient *only* for answering a comparison question (i.e., which intervention results in higher levels of the targeted behavior) and is *not sufficient* for answering how effective interventions are in relation to baseline. That is, questions about functional relations can only be answered for conditions that are included in a relevant, rapidly-alternated comparison phase; other phases can assist with (1) providing descriptive information (i.e., initial baseline phase, best alone phase, generalization phases), and (2) evaluating likely threats (e.g., best alone phase).

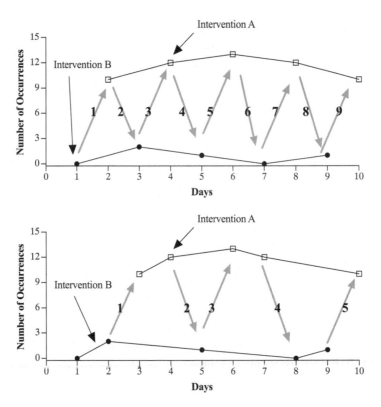

Figure 14.3 ME-ATDs with Potential Demonstrations Labeled.

Note: Top and bottom panels depict designs with five data points per condition. The ordering of the top panel allows for nine demonstrations of effect, while the ordering in the bottom panel allows for five demonstrations. Both variations have sufficient demonstrations for interpreting outcomes.

Data Adequacy

Because each change between conditions *within the phase* is a potential demonstration of effect, three demonstrations of effect can be established with very few data points. However, in addition to having three demonstrations of effect, contemporary guidelines also suggest that at least five data points are included for each condition. Because ME-ATDs are often used with functional analyses, it is important to note that this expectation is tempered when collecting data on behaviors that are dangerous or when it is otherwise problematic to continue to expose participants to one or more conditions. Of course, as with the other types of condition ordering, inclusion of five data points per condition does not ensure sufficient data have been collected. There must be enough data to determine the data pattern for each condition and the extent to which it is different from other conditions.

Control for Common Threats to Internal Validity

If a study includes an appropriate design with sufficient potential demonstrations of effect and adequate data for each condition, the next step is to determine whether any significant threats to internal validity decrease confidence that the differences between conditions (and only those differences) are responsible for observed behaviors. For example, you should assess whether a given study provides adequate evidence of reliability of independent and dependent variables. In AATD and repeated acquisition designs, it is *critical to make a determination regarding whether sets of behaviors are of equal difficulty* (see Chapter 13). If contingencies are different across conditions, it is critical that participants understand which contingencies are operating at a given time. To increase discriminability, researchers often use correlated stimuli (e.g., a blue tablecloth when one response will be reinforced, a red tablecloth when a different response will be reinforced). If likely threats are controlled for, you can move forward to evaluating data for the purposes of establishing a functional relation (i.e., summative evaluation).

Outcomes Evaluation

As with other designs, summative visual analysis should result in an explicit conclusion regarding the presence or absence of a functional relation for each comparison. A functional relation is identified when there are at least three demonstrations of effect—that is, three changes in level, trend, or variability that occur in the expected direction when conditions change within the comparison phase and when there are no or few failed demonstrations of effect (e.g., data patterns that are similar across conditions, or differences that occur in the opposite direction).

Generally, in designs using RIA condition ordering, consistent demonstrations occurring near the end of the phase are weighted more heavily than those in the beginning of the phase. For example, given six data points in each of two conditions, if the final four data points in Intervention A were more therapeutic than those in Intervention B after similar levels for the first two data points, researchers are likely to determine that a functional relation exists. But, if the first four data points are differentiated and the final two data points are similar in level, researchers are less likely to attribute a functional relation. There are no hard and fast rules about these decisions—but there are at least two reasons why this type of decision may be reasonable: (1) it may take participants some experience with each condition to develop typical patterns of responding; and (2) differentiated outcomes that do not persist over time are unlikely to be perceived as important. In AATD and repeated acquisition designs, the "end points" are often meaningful comparison points—that is, the condition resulting in the fastest mastery is likely to be more valuable than a condition that resulted in a fast slope initially but ended up underperforming or equaling the other condition in terms of the final level of behavior.

As discussed in Chapters 10 and 12, expected data patterns should be identified a priori (i.e., before data are collected), including the expected direction and magnitude of change. As with other designs, the strength of effect (strong, weak) can serve as a proxy for the certainty of conclusions (i.e., related to internal validity) while the size of effect might be more related to the value or importance of the outcome (i.e., related to social validity). See Figures 14.4 through 14.6 for example ME-ATD, AATD, and repeated acquisition design graphs that depict scenarios in which a functional relation (1) was demonstrated, (2) was *not* demonstrated, and (3) was demonstrated in some but not all comparisons.

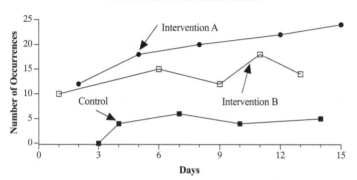

Functional relations identified such that: (1) Intervention A resulted in consistently better outcomes than Intervention B, (2) Intervention A resulted in consistently better outcomes that the control condition, and (3) Intervention B resulted in consistently better outcomes that the control condition.

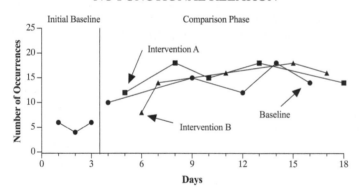

No functional relations identified. Note that the fact that both interventions are consistently higher in level than the *initial baseline phase* does not factor into functional relation decision. Functional relations are determined based on comparison phase only.

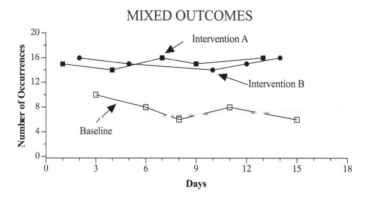

Functional relations identified such that (1) Intervention A resulted in consistently better outcomes compared to baseline, (2) Intervention B resulted in consistently better outcomes compared to baseline. No functional relation identified in relation to outcomes for Intervention A versus Intervention B.

Figure 14.4 Functional Relation Decisions for ME-ATDs.

FUNCTIONAL RELATION

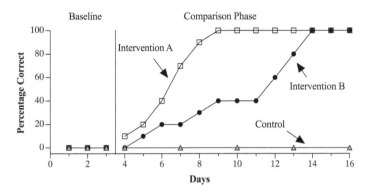

Functional relations identified such that: (1) Intervention A resulted in more efficient acquisition than Intervention B, (2) Intervention A was more effective than the no-treatment control condition, and (3) Intervention B was more effective than the no-treatment control condition.

NO FUNCTIONAL RELATION

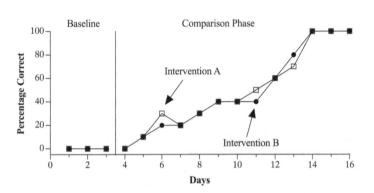

No functional relations identified. Note that the fact that both interventions include similar trends to criterion compared to no responding in the *initial baseline phase* but history and maturation threats are not controlled for. Functional relations are determined based on comparison phase only.

MIXED OUTCOMES

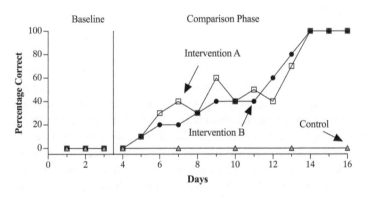

Functional relations identified such that: (1) Intervention A was more effective than the no-treatment control condition, and (2) Intervention B was more effective than the no-treatment control condition. No functional relation was identified for the Intervention A versus Intervention B comparison (neither was determined to be more efficient, although both were determined to be effective in comparison to control).

Figure 14.5 Functional Relation Decisions for AATDs.

258 • Jennifer R. Ledford et al.

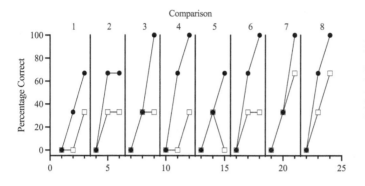

Functional relation identified because Intervention A (data path represented by filled circles) consistently leads to faster acquisition than Intervention B (data path represented by unfilled squares).

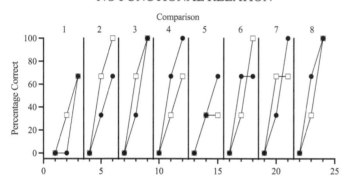

No functional relation identified because results across comparisons are not consistent, with equivocal outcomes in 3 comparisons, faster acquisition in Intervention A in 3 comparisons, and faster acquisition for Intervention B in 2 comparisons.

Figure 14.6 Functional Relation Decisions for Repeated Acquisition Designs.

Supplemental Analyses

Supplemental Analyses for ME-ATDs

A considerable amount of work has been done to establish criteria for conducting supplemental analyses of data in ME-ATDs as they relate to functional analyses of behavior (Hagopian et al., 1997; Roane et al., 2013; Saini et al., 2018). Specifically, structured criteria have been used to establish which, if any, *test* conditions in a functional analysis (e.g., escape, attention, tangible) are different than the *control* condition (e.g., play). Generally, calculations are conducted to establish the mean and standard deviation of the control condition, and differentiation is established when the majority of data in the test condition fall at least one standard deviation above the mean of the control condition. Modifications are established for specific data patterns, such as increasing and decreasing trends. Although researchers have argued for the utility of these objective measures, little more than 1% of recent studies have included them (Dowdy et al., 2022). A spreadsheet to assist with producing these supplemental analyses has been developed and is available online (Walker, 2023; https://osf.io/b28yf/).

Although work is ongoing, there has been relatively little attention paid to RIA condition ordering in terms of development of effect size metrics specifically for these designs. Although somewhat untested, the logic of the log response ratio (LRR, Pustejovsky, 2018) holds for ATDs (see more information about LRR in Chapter 10). As we mentioned in Chapter 10, we suggest collaborating with people with statistical and methodological expertise when selecting, calculating, and reporting effect sizes. It is also worth noting again that although some effect sizes align more closely with visual analysis decisions, *effect size metrics should not always come to the same conclusions as visual analysis.* Visual analysis answers whether a relation is observed between the independent and dependent variables, whereas effect sizes indicate the magnitude of this relation. Thus, we suggest always interpreting effect size estimates separate from, and as supplemental to, your primary visual analysis conclusions.

Supplemental Analyses for AATDs and Repeated Acquisition Designs

AATDs are somewhat different than designs discussed in previous chapters because they almost always include acquisition behaviors that are usually measured at floor levels in baseline conditions (i.e., 0% correct) and that are typically expected to gradually increase to ceiling (or near-ceiling) levels during intervention. Because AATDs usually include two interventions that are both expected to be effective, the relative *efficiency* of each procedure is usually the question of interest. That is, researchers want to know which procedure leads to faster acquisition or mastery. For this reason, authors often augment their visual analysis with quantitative metrics associated with rapidity of learning. Researchers might report the number of trials, number of sessions, amount of instructional time, or rate of errors to describe potential differences between conditions. For example, Cariveau et al. (2023) compared two instructional procedures for teaching first grade students and reported typical line graphs with a percentage of correct responses as well as several supplemental metrics—the number of sessions to mastery, the number of exposures to mastery, and the number of errors to mastery for each procedure (see Figure 14.7). Importantly, available single case effect size metrics do not characterize data patterns that are common in these designs well, and thus, magnitude estimates are typically not calculated for AATDs. Repeated acquisition designs with two alternating conditions can

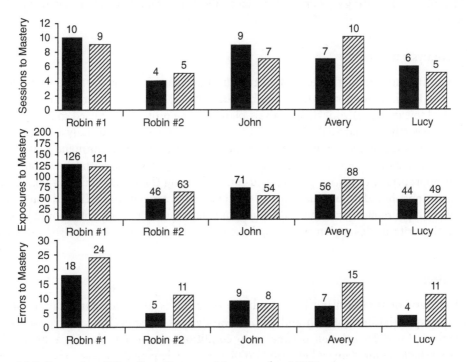

Figure 14.7 Examples of Corollary Outcome Measures for AATD.

Source: Cariveau, T., Ellington, P., Brown, A., & Platt, D. F. (2023). A comparison of prompting by exclusion and delayed prompting during conditional discrimination training. *Education and Treatment of Children*, 46, 107–119.

be analyzed similarly to AATDs; overall conclusions can be drawn about the extent to which one condition resulted in more efficient acquisition of targeted behaviors across comparisons. When only one condition is evaluated in a repeated acquisition design, functional relations are difficult to establish because it is essentially a series of "B" conditions with no comparison conditions (similar to a pre-test/post-test comparison with no control group in a group design).

Describing Visual Analysis

Visual Analysis Procedures

As with design types featured in Chapters 10 and 12, you should plan your visual analysis prior to data collection. You can start by explicating what data patterns you expect within the comparison phase. For example, for an ME-ATD, you might expect that both treatment conditions will result in stable levels of engagement higher than the ongoing baseline condition, but will not be differentiated from each other. For an AATD, you might expect initial low levels followed by an increasing trend to criterion for both intervention conditions, with continued low levels for the ongoing control condition, and with Intervention A reaching criterion prior to Intervention B. After you describe expected patterns, you should delineate what condition ordering rules you will use, and the minimum number of data points per condition. Then, you should explicate how often you will engage in formative analysis, and what rules you will follow for discontinuing the comparison. For example, you might decide that you will collect data in the comparison phase for at least five data points per condition and until differentiation in level is apparent via visual analysis or until it is clear that differentiation is not present. You should explicate in writing *a priori* (before data collection) what data patterns you expect that will lead you to conclude that a functional relation exists.

Visual Analysis Results

After planning and conducting formative and summative analyses, you will describe them to others, usually via written reports (i.e., published articles, thesis or dissertation documents). It is critical to explain (1) your data analysis plan (i.e., the protocol you used to analyze data), (2) any noteworthy formative decisions that were made, (3) summative analysis, and (4) conclusions about the presence or absence of a functional relation. We recommend that you provide sufficient detail in your summative analysis, describing your data with key visual analysis terms as appropriate, to justify your conclusions regarding the functional relation. Analyses and conclusions should be explicated for all participants in a given study. That is, when a study includes multiple replications, the consistency of results across participants should be clearly stated in the write-up. If supplementary analyses were included, those should also be described.

Conclusions

Visual analysis of studies using RIA condition ordering is different than analysis of time-lagged or sequential introduction and withdrawal designs. Specifically, researchers are typically looking for *differentiation* between two conditions that occur during a single phase, rather than looking for *changes* between two phases. Supplemental analyses are often used in both ME-ATDs and AATDs and can be helpful in determining whether a functional relation exists and contextualizing your findings.

References

Cariveau, T., Ellington, P., Brown, A., & Platt, D. F. (2023). A comparison of prompting by exclusion and delayed prompting during conditional discrimination training. *Education and Treatment of Children*, 46, 107–119.

Dowdy, A., Jessel, J., Saini, V., & Peltier, C. (2022). Structured visual analysis of single-case experimental design data: Developments and technological advancements. *Journal of Applied Behavior Analysis*, 55(2), 451–462.

Gast, D. L. (2010). *Single subject research methodology in behavioral sciences*. New York: Routledge.

Hagopian, L. P., Fisher, W. W., Thompson, R. H., Owen-DeSchryver, J., Iwata, B. A., & Wacker, D. P. (1997). Toward the development of structured criteria for interpretation of functional analysis data. *Journal of Applied Behavior Analysis*, 30(2), 313–326.

Hersen, M., & Barlow, D. H. (1976). *Single case experimental designs: Strategies for studying behavior change*. New York: Pergamon Press.

Holyfield, C., Brooks, S., & Schluterman, A. (2019). Comparative effects of high-tech visual scene displays and low-tech isolated picture symbols on engagement from students with multiple disabilities. *Language, Speech, and Hearing Services in Schools*, 50(4), 693–702.

Iwata, B. A., Pace, G. M., Dorsey, M. F., Zarcone, J. R., Vollmer, T. R., Smith, R. G., ... & Willis, K. D. (1994). The functions of self-injurious behavior: An experimental-epidemiological analysis. *Journal of Applied Behavior Analysis*, 27(2), 215–240.

Kazdin, A. E. (2020). *Single-case experimental research designs: Methods for clinical and applied settings*. Cary, NC: Oxford University Press.

LaLonde, K. B., Dueñas, A. D., Neil, N., Wawrzonek, A., & Plavnick, J. B. (2020). An evaluation of two tact-training procedures on acquired tacts and tacting during play. *The Analysis of Verbal Behavior*, 36, 180–192.

Lambert, J. M., Copeland, B. A., Paranczak, J. L., Macdonald, M. J., Torelli, J. T., Houchins-Juarez, N. J. (2022). Description and evaluation of a function informed and mechanisms-based framework for treating challenging behavior. *Journal of Applied Behavior Analysis*, 55(4), 1193–1219.

McDaniel, J., Benítez-Barrera, C. R., Soares, A. C., Vargas, A., & Camarata, S. (2019). Bilingual versus monolingual vocabulary instruction for bilingual children with hearing loss. *The Journal of Deaf Studies and Deaf Education*, 24(2), 142–160.

Pustejovsky, J. E. (2018). Using response ratios for meta-analyzing single-case designs with behavioral outcomes. *Journal of School Psychology*, 68, 99–112.

Pustejovsky, J. E. (2019). Procedural sensitivities of effect sizes for single-case designs with directly observed behavioral outcome measures. *Psychological Methods*, 24(2), 217.

Roane, H. S., Fisher, W. W., Kelley, M. E., Mevers, J. L., & Bouxsein, K. J. (2013). Using modified visual-inspection criteria to interpret functional analysis outcomes. *Journal of Applied Behavior Analysis*, 46(1), 130–146.

Saini, V., Fisher, W. W., & Retzlaff, B. J. (2018). Predictive validity and efficiency of ongoing visual-inspection criteria for interpreting functional analyses. *Journal of Applied Behavior Analysis*, 51(2), 303–320.

Skinner, C. H., McClurg, V., Crewdson, M., Coleman, M. B., Bennett, J., Fowler, K., & Killion, J. B. (2022). Alternating treatments designs: Interpretation challenges and design solutions for validating and comparing interventions. *Psychology in the Schools*, 59(4), 678–697.

Tawney, J. W., & Gast, D. L. (1984). *Single subject research in special education*. Columbus, OH: Merrill.

Walker, S. (2023). Structured visual analysis worksheet for calculating analyses in accordance with rules established by Roane et al., 2013. Excel worksheet available at https://osf.io/b28yf/

15
Selecting and Combining Single Case Designs

Jennifer R. Ledford and Kathleen N. Tuck

Important Terms

combination designs, parallel treatments design, interaction effect

---

Table of Contents

Combination Designs
   Types of Combinations
      Time-Lagged + Time-Lagged Combinations
      SIW + SIW Combinations
      Time-Lagged + SIW Combinations
      Time-Lagged + RIA Combinations
      SIW + RIA Combinations
Summary
Design Selection
   Choosing Between ME-ATD Designs and SIW Design Variations
   Choosing Between SIW/ME-ATD Designs and Time-Lagged Design Variations
   Choosing Among Time-Lagged Variations
   Choosing Between AATD and Repeated Acquisition Designs
Conclusions
References

In previous chapters, we've discussed considerations for planning, conducting, and analyzing single case studies using sequential introduction and withdrawal (SIW) of conditions, time-lagged introduction of conditions, and rapid iterative alternation (RIA) of conditions. These three condition ordering paradigms allow for single case researchers to answer a wide variety of questions. In the preceding chapters, we provided information on situations in which different condition ordering types and specific designs were appropriate. In some cases, more than one design could be selected. When this happens, conclusions about the design that should be used to answer a particular research question may be selected based on practicality or necessity (e.g., which design gives me the answer to my question with the fewest resources?), while other times, there are internal validity considerations that make one design more appropriate than others. Occasionally, the questions of interest cannot be answered using a single condition ordering strategy, and thus researchers elect to combine strategies. In this chapter, we will first discuss **combination designs**, which are single case designs that use two condition ordering strategies. Then we will discuss considerations for design selection.

Combination Designs

Researchers might choose to use a combination design to (1) answer multiple questions (e.g., demonstration and comparison questions), (2) to address the limitations of the primary design type or strengthen internal validity, or (3) to answer an interaction question. Estimates of the prevalence of combination designs vary, with low estimates of less than 10% (Hammond & Gast, 2010; Ledford et al., 2019) and high estimates of more than 25% (Shadish & Sullivan, 2011). Table 15.1 identifies several studies using combination designs, and the related functional relation conclusions that were drawn given each design type. As we discuss at length later in the chapter, the reason for selecting any specific design, including a combination design, is that it is the best option for answering your research question.

Types of Combinations

Hypothetically, there are at least five different types of combination designs, which include combination designs merging multiple instances of the same condition ordering type (e.g., time-lagged + time-lagged, SIW + SIW) and combination designs using multiple condition ordering types (i.e., time-lagged + SIW, time-lagged + RIA, SIW + RIA). We do not discuss RIA + RIA designs because although they might be possible, they would be conducted in much the same way as a typical RIA design (see SIW + SIW combination discussion below). Combined designs with time-lagged plus SIW components are the most common, followed by time-lagged plus RIA components (Shadish & Sullivan, 2011). It is difficult to specifically search for the use of combination designs, as they are often labeled descriptively (e.g., withdrawal design with alternating treatments comparisons) or with varying terms (e.g., combination design, design "embedded" within another design, hybrid designs; Tanious & Onghena, 2022).

Time-Lagged + Time-Lagged Combinations

Time-lagged designs, such as multiple baseline and multiple probe designs, can be combined to answer questions about both inter-participant and intra-participant replication. For example, researchers can combine a multiple baseline across participants design with a multiple baseline across behaviors design. This allows researchers to evaluate whether intervention effects are consistent *within* and *across* participants. It also protects against history effects, including generalization across tiers. For example, Smith and colleagues (2016) conducted a multiple probe across participants design with an embedded multiple probe across contexts design. They taught participants to self-initiate instruction across three contexts. Because it had not been studied before, researchers were not sure whether contexts were functionally independent. That is, they did not know whether instruction in the first context would generalize to other contexts. Using the combination design allowed them to identify a functional relation between instruction and acquisition of skills (using the multiple probe across participants component), and also provided information about likely generalization (using the multiple probe across contexts component).

Table 15.1 Examples of Studies Using Combination Designs

Citation	Dependent Variable	Design Types	Outcomes (Design 1)	Outcomes (Design 2)
Boyle, M. A., Keenan, G., Forck, K. L., & Curtis, K. S. (2015). Treatment of elopement without blocking with a child with autism. *Behavior Modification*, 43(1), 132–145.	Elopement, measured via duration and reported as latency between trial initiation and behavior.	SIW + SIW (A-B-A-B design with changing criteria in B phases)	A functional relation was demonstrated in the A-B-A-B evaluation with consistent increased levels in B compared to A.	A functional relation was demonstrated in the changing criterion evaluation with consistent changes in behavior aligned with changes in criteria.
Campbell, A. R., Sallese, M. R., Thompson, J. L., Fournier, C. J., & Allen, M. (2023). Culturally adapted social, emotional, and behavioral support for black male learners. *Remedial and Special Education*, 44(6), 443–456.	Challenging behavior, measured via partial interval recording and reported as a number of intervals.	Time-lagged + RIA (multiple baseline across classrooms + ME-ATD)	Two functional relations were demonstrated in MB across classrooms designs, with high and stable levels in baseline and a decreasing trend during intervention sessions for both interventions.	Functional relations were identified for each participant such that culturally adapted CICO plus I-Connect was more effective than culturally adapted CICO alone.
Estrapala, S., Bruhn, A. L., & Rila, A. (2022). Behavioral self-regulation: A comparison of goals and self-monitoring for high school students with disabilities. *Journal of Emotional and Behavioral Disorders*, 30(3), 171–184.	Academic engagement, measured via duration recording and reported as a percentage of time.	Time-lagged + RIA (multiple probe across participants + ME-ATD)	No functional relations identified with no consistent differences in level, trend, or variability between baseline and either intervention condition.	No functional relations identified, with no consistent differentiation between ongoing baseline, self-monitoring, and goal reminder conditions.
Shepley, S. B., Spriggs, A. D., Samudre, M. D., & Sartini, E. C. (2019). Initiation and generalization of self-instructed video activity schedules for elementary students with intellectual disability. *The Journal of Special Education*, 53(1), 51–62.	Correctly initiating and navigating technology for self-instruction, measured via trial-based event recording and reported as a percentage correct.	Time-lagged + Time-lagged (multiple baseline across participants + multiple baseline across contexts)	A functional relation was demonstrated in the MB across participants design with consistent increasing trend to mastery levels across four participants.	A functional relation was demonstrated in the MB across contexts design with expected increasing baseline levels in 2nd and 3rd contexts but change in trend/level when intervention was implemented.

Reference	Measurement	Design	Results
Su, P. L., Castle, G., & Camarata, S. (2019). Cross-modal generalization of receptive and expressive vocabulary in children with autism spectrum disorder. *Autism & Developmental Language Impairments*, 4.	Correct responding measured via trial-based event recording, and reported as a percentage correct.	Time-lagged + RIA (Parallel treatments design)	Functional relations were identified for all ten participants such that both expressive and receptive instruction resulted in acquisition of correct responding.	Functional relations were identified for three participants for whom results were consistent across three comparisons, with two participants learning faster during receptive conditions and one learning faster during expressive conditions.
Schulz, T., Cividini-Motta, C., Blair, K. S. C., & MacNaul, H. (2020). A comparison of high-tech and low-tech response modalities to improve student classroom behavior. *Journal of Behavioral Education*, 31(2), 243–264.	Academic responding and disruptive behavior, measured via trial-based event recording and reported as percentage of opportunities.	SIW + RIA (A-B-A-B + ME-ATD)	Functional relations were identified such that both interventions resulted in higher levels of academic responding and lower levels of disruptive behavior than baseline (with some concerning data patterns in second baseline).	For two participants (Nick, Kelly), effects were not differentiated for academic responding (no functional relation). For two participants (Nick, Timmy), effects were not differentiated for disruptive behavior (no functional relation).
Torelli, J. N., Lloyd, B. P., Diekman, C. A., & Wehby, J. H. (2017). Teaching stimulus control via class-wide multiple schedules of reinforcement in public elementary school classrooms. *Journal of Positive Behavior Interventions*, 19(1), 14–25.	Recruitment of attention, measured as a count and reported as a rate per minute.	SIW + RIA (A-B-C-B-C + ME-ATD)	Functional relations were identified between B and C conditions such that recruitments were higher under conditions in which they were reinforced (across days).	Functional relations were identified such that during segments when recruitments were reinforced, levels were higher than during segments when they were extinguished (within days).

SIW + SIW Combinations
Although there is some disagreement about the categorization of changing criterion designs, we have included them as a special case of SIW designs. Thus an SIW-SIW combination design could include conducting a prototypical A-B-A-B design, but including a changing criterion in the B condition. For example, Lambert et al. (2019) conducted an A-B-A-B design to evaluate a treatment for food stealing for an individual with Prader Willi Syndrome. After establishing an effect at a low criterion, researchers gradually increased requirements in a changing criterion design in the second B phase. Similarly, Boyle et al. (2019) evaluated a treatment for elopement; they included a short changing criterion component in the first B phase and a longer changing criterion evaluation in the second B phase. Combining two SIW designs sequentially would result in a multitreatment designs (e.g., A-B-A-B-C-D-C-D, which we discussed in Chapters 9 and 10. Combining two SIW designs simultaneously would result in an A-B-A-B design with ME-ATD comparisons in each condition (i.e., it would functionally result in an SIW + RIA comparison; see related section).

Time-Lagged + SIW Combinations
Time-lagged designs can be combined with A-B-A-B designs and changing criterion designs, which allow for additional potential demonstrations of effect, close monitoring of behavior change that is likely to occur in a slow, stepwise fashion (Time-lagged + changing criterion), and for the inclusion of intra-participant replication (Time-lagged across participants + either A-B-A-B or changing criterion). For example, Sweeney and colleagues (2018) used a multiple probe across participants design to evaluate changes in imitation during instruction relative to a baseline condition and embedded a withdrawal design (A-B-A-B-B') for each participant. Levy et al. (2017) used a multiple baseline across participants design combined with a changing criterion design to evaluate a behavioral treatment package for teaching water safety skills by setting several criterion levels of submersion.

Time-Lagged + RIA Combinations
Some combinations are somewhat difficult to categorize. For example, the **parallel treatments design** (PTD; Gast & Wolery, 1988) was devised to compare instructional practices with non-reversible behaviors (Gast & Wolery, 1988). It can be conceptualized as two concurrently operating multiple probe designs (a time-lagged + time-lagged combination)—one instructional strategy is evaluated with one multiple probe design, and the second is evaluated with another multiple probe design. You can also conceptualize the designs as three time-lagged AATDs (a time-lagged + RIA combination).

The PTD is useful when comparing interventions for teaching functional, developmental, and academic behaviors. As with the AATD the instructional strategies being compared with the PTD are applied to separate behavior sets/chains. When comparing two intervention strategies, three sets are recommended for AATDs (one for each intervention and one as a control) and six are required for PTDs (three for each intervention). No control sets are needed for PTDs because the time lag serves as a control for history and maturation. As originally noted (Gast & Wolery, 1988) and recently acknowledged (Frampton et al., 2021), this design requires a considerable amount of time, which might limit its use relative to the AATD. Figure 15.1 shows a prototypical parallel treatments design. Figure 15.2 shows how the data represented in Figure 15.1 is from two concurrently operating multiple probe designs, and Figure 15.3 highlights the time-lagged AATD components.

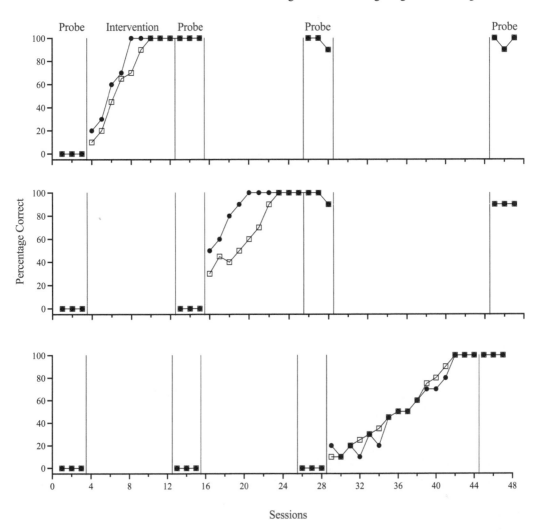

Figure 15.1 Typical Depiction of a Parallel Treatments Design.

SIW + RIA Combinations
Combining an SIW design and an RIA design gives researchers the option to detect an **interaction effect**—a relation that changes in magnitude based on other contextual factors. That is, you might evaluate student engagement when desks are in rows (A phase) versus desks in groups (B phase) with two conditions in each phase—typical response modes and electronic clickers (see Figure 15.4). This allows researchers to answer questions related to (1) relations between desk arrangement and engagement (groups result in consistently higher engagement); (2) relations between response modes and engagement (clickers result in consistently higher engagement); and (3) interactions between desk arrangements and response modes (e.g., the magnitude of differences between *clickers* and *no clickers* conditions is larger when children are in groups). They can also be used to answer simultaneously questions about the effectiveness of two interventions relative to baseline (A-B-A-B design components) and the relative effectiveness of each (ME-ATD components).

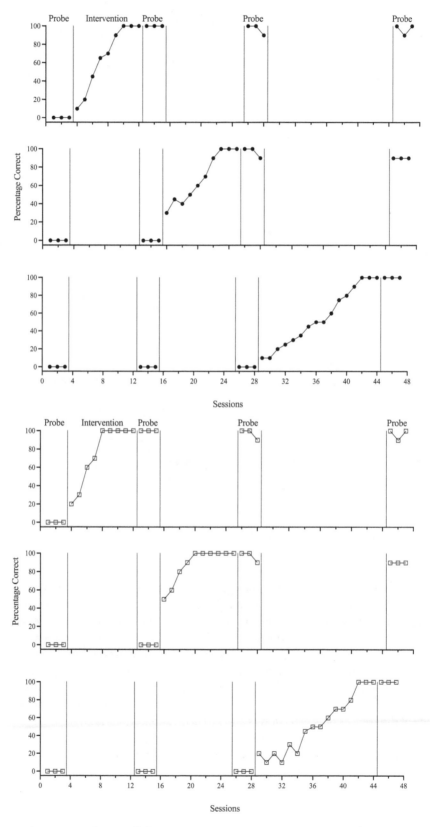

Figure 15.2 Depiction of A Parallel Treatments Design as Two Concurrently Operating Multiple Probe Designs.

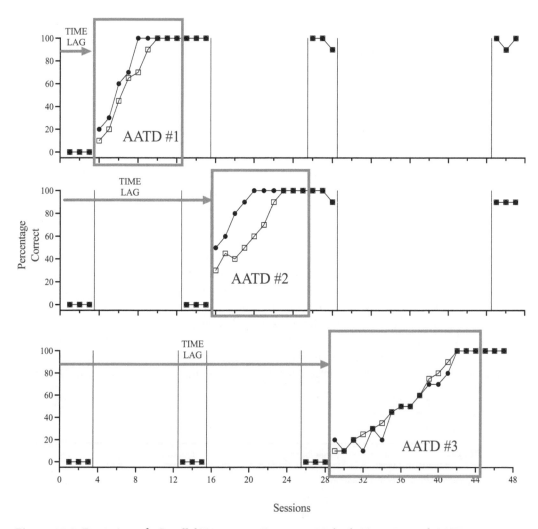

Figure 15.3 Depiction of a Parallel Treatments Design as Multiple Time-Lagged AATDs.

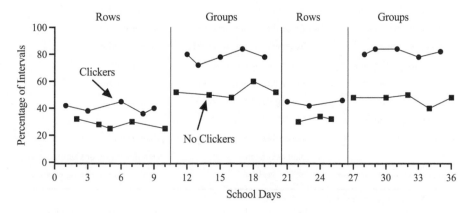

Figure 15.4 Depiction of a SIW-RIA Comparison Design with an Interaction Effect.

Summary

Combination designs can be used to answer multiple research questions and/or to provide more demonstrations of effect than what would be present in a single design. However, these designs are procedurally complex and often longer in duration than other design options. Thus, researchers should consider their use when their utility outweighs their disadvantages.

Design Selection

We have presented a number of design types and condition ordering methods in the preceding chapters. Acknowledging that nuance exists, we have attempted to summarize the conditions under which each type of design might be useful in Table 15.2. You might note that several designs are listed as appropriate for answering the same kinds of questions with the same types of dependent variables. For example, we have the ME-ATD and A-B-A-B design variations listed as appropriate for answering demonstration questions (i.e., How effective is this intervention relative to baseline?) for reversible behaviors. Likewise, we have the AATD and repeated acquisition designs listed as appropriate for evaluating comparison questions (i.e., What is the relative effectiveness of two interventions?) for non-reversible behaviors. Finally, all of the time-lagged variations are appropriate for answering demonstration questions for reversible or non-reversible behaviors. Given that multiple designs might be appropriate for answering your research questions, how should you choose among them? We make some suggestions below, understanding that there are multiple considerations (experimental, practical, ethical) that are

Table 15.2 Design Types and Dependent Variables and Questions for Which They Are Appropriate

Design	Behavior	Question
Sequential Introduction and Withdrawal		
A-B-A-B[1]	Reversible	Demonstration
Multitreatment[1]	Reversible	Comparison
Changing criterion	Reversible[2]	Demonstration
Time-Lagged Implementation		
MB across Participants	Reversible or non-reversible	Demonstration
MB across Behaviors	Reversible or non-reversible	Demonstration
MB across Contexts	Reversible or non-reversible	Demonstration
MP across Participants	Reversible or non-reversible	Demonstration
MP across Behaviors	Reversible or non-reversible	Demonstration
MP across Contexts	Reversible or non-reversible	Demonstration
Rapid Iterative Alternation		
ME-ATD	Reversible	Demonstration or Comparison
AATD	Non-reversible	Demonstration or Comparison
Repeated acquisition	Non-reversible	Demonstration or Comparison

Note: MB = multiple baseline. MP = multiple probe. ME-ATD = multielement-alternating treatments design. AATD = adapted alternating treatments design. 1 = there are no design differences in A-B-A-B and multitreatment designs; the only difference is whether the question answered is a demonstration or comparison question. 2 = additional requirement: likely to change in stepwise fashion in alignment with a criterion.

individual to each study. Flowcharts for selecting designs have also been developed (Ledford & Tuck, 2023), although they provide beginning guidance and points for consideration rather than authoritative decisions.

Choosing Between ME-ATD Designs and SIW Design Variations

As mentioned above, ME-ATD designs can answer demonstration or comparison questions for reversible behaviors. Likewise, the prototypical SIW designs (A-B-A-B, multitreatment) can do the same. Following are some considerations when choosing between design types.

1. Practically, some interventions are amenable to session-to-session implementation and others are not. If it will be difficult to change conditions rapidly, you should choose an A-B-A-B design. This practicality may be determined by the implementers of the study (e.g., endogenous implementers may prefer more consistency in session procedures) or the study procedures (e.g., changing seating in a classroom repeatedly and rapidly across class periods or sessions may not be feasible).
2. Ethically, it may be problematic to consistently change conditions repeatedly. For example, if you are alternating between two different conditions using an ME-ATD paradigm, participants may become frustrated when the less preferred condition is implemented. If changes between conditions are likely to be unwelcome, you can minimize the number of changes by using an A-B-A-B design.
3. As discussed in Chapter 13, transitions between conditions *in and of themselves* may result in behavior change above and beyond the differences that might exist between conditions in isolation. If this is a concern, you can minimize the number of transitions with an A-B-A-B design or use a best alone condition to confirm levels in the absence of alternation. (See also the next section regarding time-lagged design.)
4. If withdrawing an intervention (for an extended period in an A-B-A-B design or frequent, briefer periods in an ME-ATD) is problematic for participant morale and/or establishing trusting relationships between the researcher and participants, researchers might consider using a changing criterion design instead of the other two options. (See also the next section regarding time-lagged design).
5. If you have questions among three or more conditions (e.g., functional analysis) or you want to evaluate two or more interventions in relation to each other *and* to baseline conditions, choose an ME-ATD.
6. If you require efficiency, ME-ATDs typically results in faster comparisons than A-B-A-B designs.
7. If you want to explore an untested intervention or an intervention with mixed results in the previous literature that *may not* result in therapeutic changes in the outcome, you may consider utilizing an ME-ATD with a continuous baseline and comparing the untested/mixed results intervention to a known effective intervention. Choosing an ME-ATD with a continuous baseline may be preferred to an A-B-A-B design for untested or mixed results interventions to allow for confidence in the possible detection of the presence of non-effects through the ME-ATD comparison to both the known effective intervention and the no-intervention baseline conditions, rather than just a no-intervention baseline condition (A-B-A-B design).
8. If the intervention you are testing may require repeated continuous exposure or practice for participants meaningfully access the intervention (e.g., self-monitoring interventions), you may choose an A-B-A-B design rather than an ME-ATD.

Choosing Between SIW/ME-ATD Designs and Time-Lagged Design Variations

As shown in Table 15.2, ME-ATD and SIW designs are appropriate for evaluating questions in relation to reversible behaviors. Assuming you have used the points above to choose either an ME-ATD or A-B-A-B design, when should either be used instead of a multiple baseline design (and vice versa)?

1. When three or more intervention targets (behaviors, participants, contexts) that are functionally independent and functionally similar are not available, an A-B-A-B or ME-ATD design should be selected. For example, when evaluating a challenging behavior intervention designed specifically for one child in their home, time-lagged variations are likely to be unhelpful, unless you think the child will not generalize across contexts (typically a tenuous assumption).
2. When transitions between conditions are likely to be problematic, either due to practical, ethical, or experimental concerns, using a multiple baseline across participants design allows for one transition, from baseline to intervention, for each participant.
3. If withdrawals are ethically problematic due to reasons discussed above, you might consider a multiple baseline design rather than an ME-ATD or A-B-A-B design.
4. The multiple baseline design is resource intensive due to measurement across at least three intervention targets (participants, behaviors, or contexts) and typically requires more sessions than ME-ATD and A-B-A-B design. Thus, you may choose the latter designs due to resource constraints.
5. If the potential for conducting many *sessions* is problematic, but a time-lagged design is otherwise preferred, choose (a) a multiple probe design or (b) a nonconcurrent variation with a priori baseline lengths.
6. If the potential for conducting baseline over a long period of time is problematic, choose a nonconcurrent variation with a priori baseline lengths or an A-B-A-B or ME-ATD design.

Choosing Among Time-Lagged Variations

Time-lagged designs are flexible for answering demonstration questions for either reversible or non-reversible behaviors. Theoretically they can also be used to answer comparison questions if the initial condition is an intervention condition and the time-lagged condition introduced second is a different intervention. Because that variation is rarely used, we will focus on the demonstration question.

1. You should choose the multiple baseline variation if potential threats to internal validity related to *variability* is likely (usually more likely to occur for free operant behaviors and in typical, less-controlled environments).
2. You should choose the multiple probe variation if potential threats to internal validity related to *testing* are likely (usually more likely to occur for trial-based behaviors with floor levels of responding and/or with participants who find baseline aversive).
3. Practically, you can choose the intervention target which is most available or feasible. For example, some interventions are conducive to sequential application across behaviors (Genc-Tosun et al., 2023; Pak, 2023) while others are not. If multiple behaviors can be identified, conducting MB or MP designs across behaviors *and* replicating with multiple participants results in across-participant and within-participant replication.
4. Generally, if you can identify three participants or behaviors, you should avoid using contexts as the intervention target because it is difficult to be certain a priori that generalization across contexts will not occur.

Choosing Between AATD and Repeated Acquisition Designs

As discussed in Chapter 13, both AATD and repeated acquisition designs are primarily used for evaluating relative effects of instructional interventions on acquisition of non-reversible behaviors (although both can also be used to answer demonstration questions with the inclusion of a control set in the comparison condition). There are two situations in which a repeated acquisition design should be chosen—if behaviors will be learned very quickly, and/or if the context is such that each set of behaviors will only be taught for a short time (e.g., in relation to curriculum units that change weekly). Otherwise, AATDs are generally the more rigorous design option, especially if they are replicated across or within participants.

Conclusions

In this chapter, we have attempted to outline some of the decisions that researchers face when selecting a single case design. Considerations of design selection should be driven by the research question and outcome of interest, but may also be impacted by resource constraints, practical considerations, and ethical concerns. The suggestions presented here are often not black and white, and researchers have many competing contingencies, including resources (time, data collectors), ethical responsibility to participants, and internal validity considerations. Thus, selection of a design is often less a question of making the perfect choice, but of making the choice with the fewest drawbacks. Nevertheless, there are a range of designs to choose from, all of which are well-suited to a number of questions and outcomes.

References

Boyle, M. A., Keenan, G., Forck, K. L., & Curtis, K. S. (2019). Treatment of elopement without blocking with a child with autism. *Behavior Modification*, 43(1), 132–145.

Campbell, A. R., Sallese, M. R., Thompson, J. L., Fournier, C. J., & Allen, M. (2023). Culturally adapted social, emotional, and behavioral support for black male learners. *Remedial and Special Education*, 44(6), 443–456.

Estrapala, S., Bruhn, A. L., & Rila, A. (2022). Behavioral self-regulation: A comparison of goals and self-monitoring for high school students with disabilities. *Journal of Emotional and Behavioral Disorders*, 30(3), 171–184.

Frampton, S. E., Guinness, K. E., & Axe, J. B. (2021). The parallel treatments design: A systematic review. *Behavioral Interventions*, 36(4), 941–961.

Gast, D. L., & Wolery, M. (1988). Parallel treatments design: A nested single subject design for comparing instructional procedures. *Education and Treatment of Children*, 11(3), 270–285.

Genc-Tosun, D., Kurt, O., Cevher, Z., & Gregori, E. V. (2023). Teaching children with autism spectrum disorder to answer questions using an iPad-based speech-generating device. *Journal of Autism and Developmental Disorders*, 53(9), 3724–3739.

Hammond, D., & Gast, D. L. (2010). Descriptive analysis of single subject research designs: 1983–2007. *Education and Training in Autism and Developmental Disabilities*, 45(2), 187–202.

Lambert, J. M., Parikh, N., Stankiewicz, K. C., Houchins-Juarez, N. J., Morales, V. A., Sweeney, E. M., & Milam, M. E. (2019). Decreasing food stealing of child with Prader-Willi syndrome through function-based differential reinforcement. *Journal of Autism and Developmental Disorders*, 49, 721–728.

Ledford, J. R., Barton, E. E., Severini, K. E., Zimmerman, K. N., & Pokorski, E. A. (2019). Visual display of graphic data in single case design studies. *Education and Training in Autism and Developmental Disabilities*, 54(4), 315–327.

Ledford, J. R., & Tuck, K. N. (2023). Flowcharts for selecting single case design types. Available at: https://osf.io/b28yf/

Levy, K. M., Ainsleigh, S. A., & Hunsinger-Harris, M. L. (2017). Let's go under! Teaching water safety skills using a behavioral treatment package. *Education and Training in Autism and Developmental Disabilities*, 52(2), 186–193.

Pak, N. S. (2023). *EMT en Español Para Autismo: A Single Case Design Study* (Doctoral dissertation).

Schulz, T., Cividini-Motta, C., Blair, K. S. C., & MacNaul, H. (2020). A comparison of high-tech and low-tech response modalities to improve student classroom behavior. *Journal of Behavioral Education*, 31(2), 243–264.

Shadish, W. R., & Sullivan, K. J. (2011). Characteristics of single-case designs used to assess intervention effects in 2008. *Behavior Research Methods*, 43, 971–980.

Shepley, S. B., Spriggs, A. D., Samudre, M. D., & Sartini, E. C. (2019). Initiation and generalization of self-instructed video activity schedules for elementary students with intellectual disability. *The Journal of Special Education*, 53(1), 51–62.

Smith, K. A., Ayres, K. A., Alexander, J., Ledford, J. R., Shepley, C., & Shepley, S. B. (2016). Initiation and generalization of self-instructional skills in adolescents with autism and intellectual disability. *Journal of Autism and Developmental Disorders*, 46, 1196–1209.

Su, P. L., Castle, G., & Camarata, S. (2019). Cross-modal generalization of receptive and expressive vocabulary in children with autism spectrum disorder. *Autism & Developmental Language Impairments*, 4.

Sweeney, E., Barton, E. E., & Ledford, J. R. (2018). Using progressive time delay to increase levels of peer imitation during sculpting play. *Journal of Autism and Developmental Disorders*, 53(2), 516–552.

Tanious, R., & Onghena, P. (2022). Applied hybrid single-case experiments published between 2016 and 2020: A systematic review. *Methodological Innovations*, 15(1), 73–85.

Section 3

Ethics, Rigor, and Writing

The final section of the text focuses on critical issues related to single case design: ethical decisions made by researchers, evaluating the rigor of single case design studies, and writing proposals, reports, and systematic reviews.

We present these topics last, although we anticipate that, if you are reading this text as part of a class, your instructor could assign different chapters from this section at nearly any time during the semester. You'll notice that some of the ideas in these chapters were previewed in earlier chapters.

In Chapter 16, we discuss ethics, both in terms of ethical considerations for researchers generally (i.e., ethical considerations related to baseline data collection, equity in recruitment) and discuss specific obligations related to human subjects (i.e., institutional review board appraisal). Questions relevant for this chapter include: (1) What are consent and assent, and why are they important? (2) What are major historical markers in the history of ethical research? (3) What ethical dilemmas might you face as you engage in single case research?

In Chapter 17, we discuss evaluating the rigor of single case research, including internal validity and generality/applicability. We introduce a non-exhaustive list of tools and standards that readers might find helpful when evaluating the rigor of studies using single case design. After reading this chapter, you should be able to answer these questions: (1) What are the differences between critical and non-critical features of single case studies, and what are some examples? (2) What are some tools for evaluating single case research?

Finally, we discuss writing in Chapters 18 and 19. In these chapters, we discuss the important considerations for writing proposals before a single case study begins, writing reports of the study once it has concluded, and conducting and writing systematic reviews that encompass summarizing multiple single case design studies. These chapters are designed to help you write scientifically accurate, conventional, and easily understandable documents for the scientific community.

16
Ethical Principles and Practices in Research

Jennifer R. Ledford, Justin D. Lane, and David L. Gast

Important Terms

Institutional Review Board, consent, assent, dissent, conflicts of interests, positionality, confidentiality, anonymity, equity, potential risks, informed consent, reporting results

Table of Contents

History of Ethics in Applied Research
Ethical Considerations When Conducting Research in Applied Settings
    Fully Informed Participants
    Consent and Assent
    Outcomes that Benefit the Participant Versus the Field
    Conflicts of Interest
    Confidentiality
    Equity
    Culturally Responsive Research
Formal Approvals to Conduct Research
    Site-Specific Approval
    University Institutional Review Board
Considerations for IRB Applications
    Special Populations
    Potential Risk
    Defining Methods and Procedures
    Data Storage and Confidentiality
        Data Storage
        Confidentiality
    Informed Consent and Assent Procedures
    Sharing of Information
    Researcher Expertise

DOI: 10.4324/9781003294726-19

> *Ethical Practice*
> **Publication Ethics and Reporting of Results**
>   *Authorship*
>   *Reporting Results*
> **Conclusions**
> **References**

When conducting single case research to evaluate the impacts on certain interventions or environmental arrangements on people's behavior, it is important to attend to ethical issues that could arise, even if you believe that your research is unlikely to cause harm. In this chapter, we will provide a brief history of ethics in applied research with humans (referred to as "human subjects research" in federal regulations); discuss some ethical considerations for researchers, with specific attention to marginalized and vulnerable populations; and describe processes often required to conduct research via the Institutional Review Board (IRB) process. Note that we will sometimes refer to participants as subjects in this chapter, consistent with the terminology associated with ensuring ethical treatment of "human subjects" in the Federal Policy for the Protection of Human Subjects (also known as the "Common Rule").

History of Ethics in Applied Research

Historically, some researchers have violated basic human rights, committing crimes against humanity and attempting to hide unspeakable atrocities under the veil of science (National Institutes of Health [NIH], 2008). Examples include such instances as the Nuremberg War Crime Trials (Nazi medical war crimes) and the Tuskegee Study (untreated syphilis in Black males; Breault, 2006). Such atrocities led to the development of regulations designed to ensure protection for human participants in research studies (e.g., Surgeon General, 1966), including the development of committees responsible for reviewing proposed research studies, known today as the **Institutional Review Board (IRB)**.

A key historical moment in applied research is the passing of the National Research Act (Pub. L. 93–348), which led to the development of the National Commission for the Protection of Human Subjects of Biomedical and Behavioral Research in 1974. In 1978 the commission put forth the Belmont Report, which provided guidelines, and corresponding action points, for those conducting applied research. The Belmont Report focused on three overarching principles to improve protection of human participants in applied research studies: (1) respect for persons, (2) beneficence, and (3) justice. The principle of *respect for persons* highlighted the importance of voluntary involvement in research and explaining the purpose of a study and corresponding procedures (informed consent), as well as protection of vulnerable populations (e.g., children, adults with intellectual disability). The principle of *beneficence* focused on the rules of "do no harm" and "maximize possible benefits and minimize possible harms" (ratio of cost to benefits). Finally, the principle of *justice* highlighted the importance of fairness, especially as it relates to recruitment of participants and treatment of those from vulnerable or marginalized populations. To further assure the protection of human participants, the Common Rule was published in 1991, which further specified the application of the principles of the Belmont Report in applied research. These examples highlight continued efforts to ensure the protection of human participants in research studies.

The following sections describe ethical issues that must be considered in applied research, the steps you must go through to obtain institutional approval to conduct a thesis, dissertation, or independent research project, and then, the ethical guidelines researchers must follow when using single case designs to answer research questions related to the effectiveness of their instructional and treatment programs.

Ethical Considerations When Conducting Research in Applied Settings

Fully Informed Participants

One requirement for human subjects research is that participants are fully informed about the potential risks and benefits associated with the study. This process requires that participants fully understand all procedures. If you are working with children or populations who are unable to provide legal consent for participation, this "fully informed" requirement applies to the participant's parent or legal guardian. Common risks in behavioral research include missing other potentially beneficial activities (e.g., a child may miss academic or social opportunities if they participate in a study during school hours); making a target behavior worse, at least temporarily (e.g., during an intervention designed to reduce challenging behavior); loss of confidentiality (e.g., a video recording of a child is lost and recovered by a non-researcher); and discomfort with procedures (e.g., a teacher who feels uncomfortable with video recording). Most of these risks would be considered "minimal"—that is, they are similar to risks people face in their day-to-day lives. Some behavioral research carries higher risks (referred to as "more than minimal risk" studies; e.g., participants may cause harm to themselves or someone else). In either case, participants (or their parents/guardians) should be informed of risks, benefits, and procedures before they agree to be in the study.

Consent and Assent

Consent to participate in a study is provided by the participant (if they are at least 18 years of age and do not have a legally appointed guardian) or the participant's parent/guardian (for children or adults unable to consent). Except in rare, approved situations, consent must occur via a written (paper or electronic) consent form which explains in detail the purpose of the research, procedures and duration of activities, risks, benefits, information about confidentiality, and contact information for the investigator and the approving review board. Only after recruiting and receiving a signed consent document should you consider any human a participant.

Assent to participate in a study should be provided by participants unable to consent; it refers to agreement to participate. Assent involves providing information about the study that is understandable by the participant. Assent for adolescents without cognitive or learning disabilities can include the provision of information similar to that which is found in a consent form. Assent for younger children (e.g., 7–12 years old) may include a shorter, written form that includes simplified explanations of the content in the consent form. For example, in relation to confidentiality, researchers may say something like "We will not tell anyone else that you are in this study. Only researchers will watch the videos." For younger participants; participants with significant cognitive, intellectual, or learning disabilities; or participants with significant difficulties understanding written language, you can use a simple assent script. For the youngest participants, it can be as simple as assessing at the beginning of each session that the child is willing to interact with the researcher by saying something like "Will you come to the table and play with me today?". For participants with limited language skills, assent does not necessarily need to be vocal—if a child responded to the question above by taking the researcher's hand or walking to the table, that can be considered assenting behavior. Relatedly, some children may use augmentative and alternative communication as their primary mode of communication. Thus, assent may take the form of pointing to a photograph or symbol or using a speech generating device.

Dissent refers to indication that a participant is not (or is no longer) willing to participate in the research and can include verbal refusals ("I don't want to do this") as well as other behaviors (e.g., running away, crying). Thus, you should consider, for all participants, regardless of intellectual and verbal aptitude, what reasonable indicators of assent and dissent are, and you should regularly evaluate the extent to which these behaviors are present.

One ethical dilemma relates to assent for participants who are likely to gain benefit from procedures that are initially aversive. For example, a child who regularly harms themselves or others may stand to have considerable quality of life improvements following successful treatment. However, these treatments are unlikely to be preferred in the early stages and could be quite aversive initially. In these situations, there are no black-and-white rules for when parent consent plus likely benefit should overrule temporary dissent from a participant (although these rules do exist, for example, in medical research when a child might not agree to potentially life-saving experimental treatment for cancer). When initial discomfort is likely, explicitly reporting this to parents and participants, and having a plan for responding to participant dissent is critical, even if that plan is not immediate termination of participation.

Outcomes that Benefit the Participant Versus the Field

Researchers using single case design are generally searching for conclusive evidence of intervention effects, including controlling for possible alternative explanations. That is, we need any behavior change to be convincingly demonstrated to be *the result of* the intervention. This is different than typical practice. For example, when using an intervention for challenging behavior, a practitioner might first collect data to ensure the treatment is needed (i.e., baseline) and then collect data under intervention conditions to evaluate the extent to which the treatment worked. If outcomes are positive, the practitioner is content—the problem has been solved. The researcher, however, must convince the scientific community that the behavior change was not due to history, maturation, or another alternative explanation. Thus, they are likely to remove the treatment and assess the behavior under baseline conditions again, even though it is (at least momentarily) likely to be an aversive experience for both the participant and the researcher. It is important to explicitly consider the requirements of your research design, that improve generalized knowledge **for the greater good** but which could lead to harmful side effects **for the individual themselves** and to try to mitigate those side effects when it is possible.

Similar problems can be identified when determining how much baseline data are required prior to intervening. Some standards suggest more data are required to draw confident conclusions from a study (e.g., a minimum of five or six; What Works Clearinghouse, 2020), and too few measurement occasions certainly inhibit the researcher's ability to conduct some statistical analyses. But, when the relative benefits of such gains are minor and not aligned with your research purposes (i.e., the ability to calculate one type of effect size), you should prioritize the needs of your participants over the standards of the field. That is, you need to control for threats to internal validity in order to make scientific contributions, but it may not be ethically viable to expose participants in need of intervention to non-treatment conditions for any length of time beyond what is necessary to provide convincing evidence.

Conflicts of Interest

Researchers should divulge—to participants and to consumers of their research reports—the extent to which they have any conflicts of interest. **Conflicts of interest** (COIs) occur when a researcher stands to benefit from the research. Bottema-Buetel and colleagues (2021) identify different types of conflicts in autism research (this review did *not* include single case research, but these conflicts are all applicable). They include: (a) assessing an intervention that the researcher developed; (b) affiliation with or employment by a clinical provider that uses the intervention or with an institution that trains others to use the intervention; (c) direct financial benefit (e.g., author receives payments or royalties related to the intervention or the study uses a measure authored by the researchers that is commercially available); and (d) funding of a study by an intervention provider. When these COIs are likely, it is important to report them, although research suggests this occurs infrequently (Bottema-Buetel et al., 2021).

Increasingly, the positionality of authors is seen as another important disclosure (Wahman et al., 2023). **Positionality** refers to characteristics of the researchers that are likely to influence the conduct or interpretation of the research study. Positionality statements are common in qualitative and mixed methods research (e.g., Doubet et al., 2023; Essien & Wood, 2023) and less common in single case research—as a matter of fact, nearly all examples (as of August, 2023) are found in unpublished dissertation studies (e.g., Chazin, 2022). However, increasingly, the field is attending to positionality and suggesting that researchers attend to their own positions throughout the course of research (Boveda & Annamma, 2023, Cumming et al., 2023).

One example of when a positionality statement is critical is when a researcher assesses the effectiveness of one intervention relative to another, when only one of the interventions is aligned with the researcher's expertise and/or beliefs. For example, I (Ledford) have conducted a few studies about the relative impacts of sensory-based interventions and strategies based on the science of applied behavior analysis (Ledford et al., 2020; Pokorski et al., 2019). In these studies, it would have been ideal to share positionality statements explaining that the majority of authors (Pokorski et al., 2019; one author was an occupational therapist) or all authors (Ledford et al., 2020) were board certified behavior analysts (BCBAs). Although rare in single case research at the time of publication, it seems reasonable to add these statements to future research studies, given their potential role in helping consumers interpret findings.

Confidentiality

Confidentiality refers to the protection of the identity of single case research participants. When conducting research, you should generally use codes or pseudonyms to refer to participants, in *all* study documentation—even those documents which are only intended to be seen by researchers. This adds a layer of protection for confidentiality—that is, if you lose a data collection form that only includes a randomly generated participant number, the identity of the participant would not be at risk of being shared with non-researchers. Confidentiality is different than **anonymity**, which is when the identity of a participant *is not known*. This is never the case in single case research, but it could be true of data collected for secondary questions (e.g., you could post a link to an *anonymous* survey on social media. If you do not collect identifying information, those data may be anonymous). To protect confidentiality, take action to protect data. Also be sure your participants understand the ways in which data will not be confidential (e.g., if you will share a child's data with their teachers or therapists, who are not researchers).

Equity

Generally, research participation has been inequitably accessed by populations with more resources. When possible, you should consider modifications that could increase access for underrepresented or marginalized groups. When this is not possible, you should explicitly acknowledge that your outcomes may be limited to populations that are highly resourced (e.g., if participation in your study requires 1-hour visits to a clinic three times per week, you should acknowledge this potential barrier and that findings are limited to families that had the resources for participation). Research in special education and behavioral sciences, like in other areas (e.g., cognitive psychology, Roberts et al., 2020), would benefit from increased diversity both in terms of researchers and participants. Considering ways to make access to research equitable may serve us in achieving this goal.

Culturally Responsive Research

At the outset, we design single case design studies to adequately control for potential threats to internal validity to increase our confidence that the outcome is associated with our intervention instead of alternative explanations (e.g., history effects). Part of this process involves clearly defining our inclusion and exclusion criteria, independent and dependent variables, and identifying appropriate measurement system(s). Because our work involves human subjects, we cannot overlook the importance of identifying overt or covert practices that are culturally insensitive or racist (e.g., evaluating a parent coaching intervention that centers a researcher's own cultural viewpoint instead of considering cultural variables and allowing for adaptations). Thus, we highly recommend educating yourself about culturally responsive research practices (e.g., Crenshaw, 1991; Pope et al., 2019). Part of this process requires that we "recognize the role that oppression, privilege, and power may play in the relationship between the researcher and the participants" (Najdowski et al., 2021, p. 463). In addition, we can continually self-reflect (e.g., our own cultural identity, cultural humility, and biases), expand our knowledge (e.g., learn more about cultures outside of our own), and apply recommended practices in our research (e.g., implement culturally responsive interventions) (Jimenez-Gomez & Beaulieu, 2022).

Formal Approvals to Conduct Research

For the most part, research conducted in the fields of special education and behavioral sciences are conducted by researchers at a university or partnering with a university—thus, our description of procedural issues will primarily focus on this situation. Generally, a research study is planned, and researchers systematically recruit participants who meet certain criteria. On other occasions, a research study may be initiated by researchers after practitioners (e.g., schools, clinics) identify a problem and one or more individuals who would benefit from participation in a research study designed to answer a question about that problem. In either case, it is likely that researchers will need formal approval from both their affiliated university and the setting in which the research will take place. Some settings may require no additional formal approvals beyond a university-approved IRB while others may require several additional steps, including IRB approval from the site, local or state approval agencies, or a Human Rights Committee.

Site-Specific Approval

When conducting research in non-research settings, you must obtain initial permission to conduct research at a particular site. Many agencies have specific and delineated procedures for requesting this permission; some smaller agencies may simply require permission from a director or board of directors. Some organizations have separate processes for practitioners (employees) and outside researchers. It is prudent to attempt to learn as much as possible about the agency and their procedures prior to requesting permission to conduct research. Researchers should take care to maintain good relations with all stakeholders (e.g., participants, parents, practitioners, administrators). Copies of the final report may be requested by the school or agency as a condition for permission to conduct the research; carefully document how much information you will provide to stakeholders prior to beginning the project, especially when the information is sensitive (e.g., diagnostic or evaluative information about children, work performance information for adults). At every stage, the behavior of the researcher is critical to successful completion of the project.

University Institutional Review Board

The process of institutional review varies among agencies and universities. In all cases, your research will either undergo full committee review, expedited review, or exempt review. In nearly all cases, single case studies are *minimal risk* studies (as described earlier in the chapter) and will go through expedited review. This means that IRB committee members review the application (and most often, request modifications), but the full committee does not meet to discuss the study. In any case, the first step of IRB approval is to have a clearly written, well-defined study protocol before beginning the IRB application process. Then, you can complete and submit an application. Preparation of a clearly written application, submitted early, should increase the probability that approval is obtained in sufficient time to conduct the research. A second requisite of early attention is the completion of "training for human subject researchers" which is required prior to IRB reviewing the research application and fulfills the NIHs human subjects training requirement (www.citiprogram.org). This mandatory training is generally provided online and available through university research foundations, sponsored programs or Offices of the Vice President for Research, as well as agencies like the National Cancer Institute. Free, web-based tutorials provide information about the rights and welfare of human participants in research and are based on the all-important Belmont Report (National Commission for the Protection of Human Subjects, 1978). Thus, prior to completing an IRB application, you should become familiar with the rules and regulations of completing human subjects research and should have your own procedures clearly planned and described.

Considerations for IRB Applications

The best recommendation to increase the probability of approval on the first submission of the application is to write clearly and succinctly, elaborating on those points that are likely to be viewed critically, easily misunderstood, or sensitive. The application should use technical (jargon) free language that can be understood by a review board, which may be comprised of people from an array of disciplines. Investigators new to the field of research may also find it helpful to consult other investigators who have recently had successful submissions. You should take special care to describe your procedures in a way such that they can be understood by someone without specialized knowledge in your field; reviewers of your application should be able to understand exactly what will happen to your participants, who will be doing it, for how long they will be doing it, and under what circumstances they will stop.

Special Populations

Researchers should note that special populations receive specific attention in the application and may require full review by the IRB, depending on the nature of the intervention and vulnerability of proposed participants. For example, if you plan to conduct a study with young children with autism spectrum disorder, you might need to justify the need to include these participants in the research; this often involves describing and explaining characteristics of participants that make them likely to benefit from the potential research. Selecting vulnerable populations—such as individuals with disabilities, those who are institutionalized, or people who are imprisoned—due to convenience or availability is not an acceptable justification. Guidelines also require a description of safeguards for the protection of vulnerable populations. For example, you might need to describe what special forms of dissenting behaviors will be accepted for individuals with limited communication repertoires and to explain whether your intervention sessions will interfere with ongoing therapy regimens.

Potential Risk

Researchers will be required to indicate the level of **potential risk** to participants and whether the level constitutes "minimal" or "more than minimal" risk. Minimal risk is considered to be the same risk that a person would encounter in daily life or while performing routine physical or psychological examinations (United States Department of Health and Human Services: Code of Ethics, 2005). At first glance, it might seem that the issue of potential risk is easily dismissed in a classroom-based academic intervention or in a social behavior change project employing positive consequences. However, risk may be interpreted broadly. Suppose that the researcher engages a student in an intervention during a time when the student would otherwise be receiving academic instruction; then suppose that the intervention does not succeed. The student's behavior is unchanged, and he has lost instructional time. If the intervention proceeds for an extended period without positive results, is the researcher responsible for the student's lost instructional time (e.g., the student is now behind her peers in the early literacy curriculum)? Suppose that a traditional and an experimental instructional program are presented alternately to students who perform better under the traditional program. Has the experimental program interfered with more effective instruction and thus disadvantaged the students? Suppose that the intervention involves physical manipulation of the research participants (e.g., using physical prompting of motor responses such as switch activation) with children with cerebral palsy. What is the potential risk of physical injury to a child who resists or responds defensively? What are the risks involved with community-based instruction where research participants will be required to cross streets, ride public transportation, or learn to seek adult assistance when "lost" in the community? Thus, although many researchers might be tentative about suggesting that their planned procedures carry any risk, it may be reasonable to consider the possibility. Even if no other reasonable risks are likely, most studies have the potential risk of loss of confidentiality.

Defining Methods and Procedures

The human subjects review application requires an abbreviated version of the written thesis research proposal (see Chapter 18 for information regarding writing a proposal). We recommend that the human subjects review prospectus be drawn from a fully developed proposal to ensure you begin the task of technical writing early in the research process. The human subjects review process focuses on specific elements of the procedures. The protocol requires a complete but abstracted description of the procedures. Then, special attention is directed to two questions: "What will happen to the participants?" and "What will happen to the data?"

Researchers with a background in education, psychology, and the various therapies (speech, occupational, physical) should be skilled in task analysis and should be adept at writing an explicit description of the steps or sequence of events in the research procedure. You will find it helpful to "walk through" the procedure as you write it and "talk through" the procedures with colleagues. A review committee is less likely to take special interest in antecedent events that are common or easily defined, than in esoteric or potentially aversive procedures. If a procedure involves a series of statements and actions by the researcher, these should be written exactly as they will occur (i.e., a script). If the procedure involves physical prompting, the nature and degree of effort should be described (e.g., the researcher will say, "Ralph, throw me the ball," and if no spontaneous response occurs, she will gently grasp him at the wrist and lift the hand/arm so that it rests on the ball. Physical assistance will be terminated if the child pulls away, cries, or shows other signs of distress).

We suggest that researchers include, in their original IRB application, a "Plan B" for all research studies. Because single case designs are dynamic in nature, you can (and in at least some cases, should) modify or change interventions in the case of non-response. If you need to make substantive changes (e.g., use a different intervention), and you have not specified this in your original IRB, you will need to go through a potentially lengthy amendment process later. Thus, it is prudent for researchers to assume that the planned intervention may not work optimally for all participants, and to explicate a priori conditions under which a modified or different intervention will be used.

Data Storage and Confidentiality

The concern for "What happens to the data?" is based on three factors: (a) Is the information sensitive? (b) Can individual participants be identified? (c) Is there a plan to control access to the data and then to destroy it when it is no longer needed?

Data Storage
Researchers should ensure careful storage of all data collected for research purposes. Data should be stored separately from identifying information (e.g., consent forms with participant names stored in a different location than participant data—which can be identified with an identification number rather than a name). If sensitive tests are conducted as part of research (e.g., tests identifying a child's IQ or achievement levels, which may be considered "high stakes" in schools), researchers should take care to report to participants (or guardians) the manners in which they will and will not be used (i.e., whether you will share individual results with non-researchers). It is most conservative to treat all data collected as potentially sensitive, and to always use identification numbers rather than participant names or other identifiers. Note that participation in single case design studies is generally not anonymous—that is, researchers will be generally able to connect data with a specific participant. Non-anonymous data collection always results in the possibility that participant data could be matched with the corresponding participant by a non-researcher. Examples of anonymous data collection include asking a large group of teachers to fill out questionnaires without asking them to report their names or any identifying information. Generally, single case data are not anonymous; thus, we must take appropriate steps to ensure confidentiality of participants.

Confidentiality
Protecting the confidentiality of participants (i.e., ensuring that only researchers can tie individual responses with a particular participant) is a potential problem in single case design research studies. To minimize the potential for loss of confidentiality, you should (a) describe how participants will be coded (e.g., by fictitious names or initials), (b) verify that the researcher will be the sole holder of the code (or the researcher and academic advisor), and (c) state where the code will be stored (e.g., in a locked file in the advisor's office). When a study is prepared for publication, you may use a fictitious name and so label it, fictitious initials, or the real initials of the participant. The location where the study was conducted may be described in ambiguous terms (e.g., a resource room in an elementary school in a medium-sized city in the Northeast). Participants should be informed about how all data including photographs, audio, and video recordings will be used and stored. You should also be cognizant of the vulnerability of information exchanged electronically through the Internet. Expert advice may be necessary to learn how to protect data and confidential information and participants should be informed of the risks to privacy and limits of confidentiality of information exchanged electronically (Smith, 2003).

A special problem arises when a study is conducted in a small school or community, when a participant is unique (e.g., the only child with cerebral palsy in the school). Under such circumstances, the review committee may question the disposition of the final report and the number of individuals who have access to it. If a study is prepared for publication, the committee may question whether confidentiality can be sufficiently guaranteed, arguing that any person reading the article would recognize the participant.

Confidentiality is a complex issue that requires considerable attention by applied researchers. Accepted confidentiality procedures have been delineated in the Belmont Report (National Commission for the Protection of Human Subjects, 1978) and by the American Psychological Association (APA, 2002, section 5), Behavior Analyst Certification Board (BACB, 2014, section 10), and incorporated into IDEA. At the end of the research project, the researcher should have a file of raw data sheets, coded for confidentiality, and in a separate place, the key to the code. You should delineate specific procedures before your study begins regarding data storage and destroying data following study completion, and should closely follow stated procedures during and after the study.

Informed Consent and Assent Procedures

Written consent must be obtained from the participant or the participant's parent or legal guardian. Below are a few guidelines for the written form:

1. The procedures must be described fully, including purpose and expected duration.
2. Potential risks, as well as benefits should be discussed.
3. Consent can be revoked at any time, and the participant is free to withdraw from participation (or withdraw their child from participation).
4. The consent form and the description of the study must be communicated in simple language, at approximately an 8th grade reading level.
5. Information as to who to contact if questions or concerns arise during the study should be shared.

Assent and **informed consent** must be obtained if working with minors or participants who cannot legally provide informed consent, including some individuals with disabilities. Assent is non-legal permission provided by this participant. For example, you might ask a high-school-aged student to sign a simple form stating they understand the research and want to participate in it. Or, you might read a script to a very young child (e.g., "We're going to do some work every day after circle time. You can say no if you don't want to come with me. Are you ready to do the work now?"), and the researcher may sign the script, attesting that they read the script and the child agreed to participate. Researchers should allow participants to dissent as well—to decide at any time that they do not want to participate, separately from their guardian's rights to withdraw consent.

Sharing of Information

Parents, as well as other persons involved in the research project, are likely to be interested in the outcome of the study. Human subjects review committees require that such information be provided. In order to conduct a study, at a minimum, you may be expected to share information with participants' teachers and therapists, and sometimes an administrator. Other professionals (e.g., speech, occupational, and physical therapists) may benefit from knowing the results of the study as well. You should learn what is typical, or expected, in the school system, clinic, or community business where the study is to be conducted and should list those who will be informed of study outcomes in your IRB protocol and your consent documents. You should decide in advance how detailed an explanation will be given to those who have limited direct involvement with the participant. Parents, teachers, and therapists may request a step-by-step review of the study, focusing on daily sessions where performance was well above or below other data points. Others will be satisfied with a general description of the procedure and the extent to which it was successful. Refer to Table 16.1 examples of ethical scenarios and appropriate responses related to data storage, anonymity, confidentiality, and informed consent and assent.

Table 16.1 Ethical Scenarios Related to Data Storage and Confidentiality

Scenario 1
Jonathan is a third-year doctoral student in special education who is implementing a study with preschool age children with Down syndrome at a local public school. Per guidelines laid out by the university's IRB, Jonathan is to keep data in a locked file cabinet in a locked office on campus. Due to Jonathan's schedule, he does not always adhere to the IRBs guidelines for storing data and keeps data at home and in his car for purposes of convenience. One day, Jonathan's home is burglarized and his backpack, which contained his computer and data, was stolen.

Response 1
Jonathan should adhere to guidelines in place per the IRB and store data in a locked cabinet in a locked room on campus. Data should only be in his car during his commute from the school to campus. In addition, Jonathan is required to report to the IRB that potentially confidential information was stolen by an unknown party and participants' confidentiality and related information is compromised.

Scenario 2
Cora is a first-year professor in psychology and her research interests include training teachers to conduct and implement functional behavior assessments for students with intellectual disability who display aggressive behavior during academic tasks. Cora received a grant to conduct a study on teacher training for decreasing aggressive behavior. One evening, when Cora is purchasing groceries, she meets a teaching assistant who works in a classroom where she is conducting her study. The assistant asks questions about study participants and proceeds to provide personal information, as well things she has heard others say about the participants. While hesitant to discuss participants, Cora does not want to offend the assistant and discusses current classroom issues.

Response 2
Cora should not discuss research participants in a public setting due to a possible breach of confidentiality and potential exposure of personal information to persons who may know participants and/or their families. Cora should also be aware that she should not discuss specific information about participants with someone not directly involved in the study. Cora should have indicated to the paraprofessional that she ethically cannot discuss participants due to confidentiality issues.

Scenario 3
Matthew is a professor who specializes in increasing social interactions for high-school-age students with social delays. He is conducting a study, training students to practice appropriate social interactions with same age peers. During training, an adult provides prompts for participants to engage in appropriate social interactions. During the third week of instruction Jon decides to drop out of the study because intervention sessions make him "uncomfortable" and "anxious." Matthew tells Jon he needs to remain in the study because it will "help him interact with peers." Jon does not agree, but Matthew tells him that he needs social support and this study can assist in improving his social skills. Matthew also informs Jon that the peer involved in the study will want to be his friend once the study is complete.

Response 3
Matthew is attempting to coerce Jon to remain in the study, even though it is Jon's right to leave the study at any time. Prior to implementing the study, Matthew should provide clear guidelines for responding to participant requests to leave a study in the IRB application. Coercion is never an option for persons conducting research studies. In addition, Matthew reported false claims related to the effects of the intervention on friendship, which Matthew was not directly measuring. It is the responsibility of researchers to only provide known information to participants and not do so in an attempt to coerce participants to start or continue participation.

Researcher Expertise

Human subjects review committees require assurance that the researcher knows what she is doing and, if a student, that she is going to be supervised by a knowledgeable faculty member. Researchers who have teaching or clinical experience should list and describe the length and type of the experience. Certification, licensures, and endorsements should be shared. The committee may wish to be assured that practitioners have worked with children, have worked in and/or understand the protocol of working in schools, and have experience with the procedure under study. It is helpful to explicate (and carry out) specific training procedures for implementers—for example, you may set a training criterion of 90% correct and accurate implementation of procedures prior to study onset.

Ethical Practice

A practitioner is likely to use single case designs under two conditions—as part of graduate training or as part of evaluating an evidence-based practice. In the first instance, you will follow the processes described in the first part of this chapter. In the second instance, you have a somewhat different set of responsibilities. When single case design is used as an integral part of the instructional or therapeutic process, you will seldom need to seek approval from the school or clinic administration. However, to the extent that such applied research represents an innovation, you are advised to make public the strategies (e.g., data collection, experimental design, baseline and intervention procedures) that will be employed. The scientist-practitioner's major tasks are to set up data systems, explain the logic for the specific research design, and describe how the design permits certain conclusions (i.e., evaluates threats to internal validity). Since these events go beyond typical practice, little disagreement should be encountered. Refer to Table 16.2 for examples of ethical scenarios and appropriate responses related to methodology, results, and publication of data.

Table 16.2 Ethical Scenarios Related Methodology, Results, and Publication of Data

Scenario 1	Response 1
William is a second-year master's student with interests in reading instruction for middle-school students with dyslexia. William is implementing a study for increasing fluency of reading known passages for students with dyslexia who spend at least 50% of their day in a resource classroom. Two of four participants in William's study display challenges related to attending to materials and require multiple prompts to begin reading. William decides to add a specific attending cue for participants who require multiple prompts to begin the reading intervention. He decides to video record sessions to show colleagues for purposes of obtaining their feedback on changes. William did not include the specific attending cue or video recording permission in his IRB application and consent forms.	It is not necessary for William to report the addition of an attending cue to IRB prior to implementing the methodological change since it does not alter the primary intervention procedures or add any additional risk for participants, but he would report such changes in any final reports or publication of information. It is necessary for William to submit an amendment to his IRB application for purposes of requesting to video record sessions. If the amendment were approved, William would then need to obtain consent for video recording from participants and their legal guardians.
Scenario 2	Response 2
Sheila is an associate professor of communication sciences at a research university and has been employed by the university for the past 10 years. Sheila has focused her work on increasing the number of different words students with autism spectrum disorder use at home and school. She has published multiple articles replicating positive effects of a language intervention for students with autism and has decided to extend her work to students with aphasia. Following completion of her study with students with aphasia, using the language intervention, the results are highly variable with some students making no progress following 12 weeks of intervention. Sheila feels strongly the intervention was successful, even though the data indicates otherwise. She decides to submit an article based on her perceptions of the data and omit or limit information related to participants who made no progress.	It is the responsibility of persons involved in research to be honest when reporting results of a research study. While results may violate expectations of outcomes, personal biases related to expectations of results and related areas cannot impede clear, concise, and honest reports of results. While there are multiple issues with dishonest claims, some key issues to consider are future misuse of monies for persons who attempt to replicate this study and a waste of time and resources for persons who choose to use this intervention in practice with persons with aphasia.

Publication Ethics and Reporting of Results

You will face additional challenges regarding the preparation and submission of a written manuscript for publication consideration after the completion of the formal research procedures.

Authorship

The Ethical Principles of Psychologists and Code of Conduct (American Psychological Association, 2017) and the Ethics Code for Behavior Analysts (Behavior Analyst Certification Board, 2020) have standards regarding publication. The only guideline provided by the BACB, also shared in the APA guidelines, is that authorship should reflect relative contributions (e.g., the second listed author should have greater contributions than the third listed author). In journals associated with single case design, typically the first listed author should have the greatest substantive contributions. The APA guidelines suggest that the thesis and dissertations that are published should include the student as the first author, except in extraordinary circumstances. In general, it is good practice to discuss authorship "early and often." That is, all contributors should be informed about expected authorship status at the beginning of a project, and if authorship status changes over time, additional discussions should be had.

Reporting Results

Researchers will likely be familiar with ethical procedures for preparing manuscripts and professional documents which avoid the issue of plagiarism or the use of other's ideas and work without proper credit being given to the author or originator of the work. They may be unaware, however, that these procedures apply to their work as researchers, even if the work is completed under the direction of faculty advisors. They may be even less familiar with the provision of intellectual credit for non-published material including information shared at meetings, conferences, and through informal conversations with advisors, other students, and professionals. You should be given appropriate acknowledgment for your original ideas, and your work, whether published or unpublished should not be used by others for personal gain (Sales & Folkman, 2000). You should also be aware that your unpublished work is "copyrighted from the moment it is fixed in tangible form—for example, typed on a page" and that this copyright protection is in effect until the author transfers the copyright on a manuscript accepted for publication (*Publication manual of the American Psychological Association*, 2009, pp. 19–20). Finally, you will be required to present a statement with a manuscript submitted for publication consideration that the manuscript is not being simultaneously submitted to any other journal.

Researchers should take care to report all applicable results, including data for all dependent variables and participants. Although it is not uncommon for journal editors to request removal of specific participants (based on our experiences, generally because a participant withdrew or did not respond to the intervention), this increases the likelihood of biased results and is not an ethical practice. When responding to journal reviews, it is appropriate to decline such a request. You should also take care to not overstate your results in the discussion section of any written manuscript, as this is also a problematic practice. For example, you evaluated an intervention to increase the rate of social behaviors for small groups of children during centers. For two of the three groups, half of the children made gains from baseline to intervention and for the other group, no substantial differences were observed. When writing implications for practitioners or researchers, you should carefully state the context-bound limitations of the study and variations observed in the data.

Conclusions

In this chapter we have provided a context for conducting applied research within a set of ethical principles. We have stated our assumptions about the prerequisite behaviors necessary to conduct academic and social behavior change programs within the framework of single case design research methodology. Specific procedures have been listed, designed to help you obtain approval to conduct research in a manner that protects the rights of participants. We acknowledge that some ethical dilemmas are difficult to address in a single chapter and that behaving ethically requires ongoing analysis and action.

References

American Psychological Association. (2002). Ethical principles of psychologists and code of conduct. Washington, DC: Author. Retrieved August 13, 2007, from www.apa.org/science/research/regcodes.html

American Psychological Association. (2009). *Publication manual of the American Psychological Association* (6th ed.). Washington, DC: American Psychological Association.

Behavior Analyst Certification Board. (2020). *Ethics code for behavior analysts.* https://bacb.com/wp-content/ethics-code-for-behavior-analysts/

Bottema-Beutel, K., Crowley, S., Sandbank, M., & Woynaroski, T. G. (2021). Research review: Conflicts of Interest (COIs) in autism early intervention research–a meta-analysis of COI influences on intervention effects. *Journal of Child Psychology and Psychiatry*, 62(1), 5–15.

Boveda, M., & Annamma, S. A. (2023). Beyond making a statement: An intersectional framing of the power and possibilities of positioning. *Educational Researcher*, 0013189X231167149.

Breault, J. L. (2006). Protecting human research subjects: The past defines the future. *The Ochsner Journal*, 6(1), 15–20.

Chazin, K. T. (2022). *Improving social validity of behavioral interventions implemented with young children* (Doctoral dissertation, Vanderbilt University).

Crenshaw, K. (1991). Mapping the margins: Intersectionality, identity politics, and violence against women of color. *Stanford Law Review*, 43(6), 1241–1299. https://doi.org/10.2307/1229039

Cumming, M. M., Bettini, E., & Chow, J. C. (2023). High-quality systematic literature reviews in special education: Promoting coherence, contextualization, generativity, and transparency. *Exceptional Children*, 89(4), 412–431.

Doubet, S., Ostrosky, M. M., & Quesenberry, A. C. (2023). The impact of young children's persistent challenging behavior on child care providers: "It's like floating in a sea with no paddle". *Topics in Early Childhood Special Education*, 02711214231180871.

Essien, I., & Wood, J. L. (2023). "Treat them like human beings": Black children's experiences with racial microaggressions in early childhood education during COVID-19. *Early Childhood Education Journal*. Advance online publication.

General, S. (1966). Surgeon General's directives on human experimentation. Retrieved from https://history.nih.gov/research/downloads/surgeongeneraldirective1966.pdf

Jimenez-Gomez, C., & Beaulieu, L. (2022). Cultural responsiveness in applied behavior analysis: Research and practice. *Journal of Applied Behavior Analysis*, 55(3), 650–673. doi: 10.1002/jaba.920

Ledford, J. R., Zimmerman, K. N., Severini, K. E., Gast, H. A., Osborne, K., & Harbin, E. R. (2020). Brief report: Evaluation of the noncontingent provision of fidget toys during group activities. *Focus on Autism and Other Developmental Disabilities*, 35(2), 101–107.

Najdowski, A. C., Gharapetian, L., & Jewett, V. (2021). Toward the development of antiracist and multicultural graduate training programs in behavior analysis. *Behavior Analysis in Practice*, 14, 462–477. doi: 10.1007/s40617-020-00504-0

National Cancer Institute: U.S. National Institute of Health. (n.d.). Human participants protections education for research teams. Retrieved August 13, 2006, from www.cancer.gov/clinicaltrials/learning/humanparticipant protections

National Commission for the Protection of Human Subjects of Biomedical and Behavioral Research. (1978). The Belmont Report: Ethical principles and guidelines for the protection of human subjects of research. (DHEW Publication No. OS 78–0012). Washington, DC: Government Printing Office. Retrieved August 27, 2007, from http://ohsr.od.nih.gov/guidelines/belmont.html

National Institutes of Health (2008). Protecting human research participants. NIH Office of Extramural Research. Retrieved from: https://phrp.nihtraining.com/users/PHRP.pdf

Pokorski, E. A., Barton, E. E., Ledford, J. R., Taylor, A. L., Johnson, E., & Winters, H. K. (2019). Comparison of antecedent activities for increasing engagement in a preschool child with ASD during a small group activity. *Education and Training in Autism and Developmental Disabilities*, 54(1), 94–103.

Pope, R. L., Reynolds, A. L., & Mueller, J. A. (2019). "A change is gonna come": Paradigm shifts to dismantle oppressive structures. *Journal of College Student Development*, 60(6), 659–673. doi: 10.1353/csd.2019.0061

Roberts, S. O., Bareket-Shavit, C., Dollins, F. A., Goldie, P. D., & Mortenson, E. (2020). Racial inequality in psychological research: Trends of the past and recommendations for the future. *Perspectives on psychological science*, 15(6), 1295–1309.

Sales, D. B., & Folkman, S. (Eds.) (2000). *Ethics in research with human participants*. Washington, DC: American Psychological Association.

Sidman, M. (1960). *Tactics of scientific research—Evaluating experimental data in psychology*. New York: Basic Books.

Smith, D. (2003). What you need to know about the new code. *Monitor*, 34, 62. Retrieved August 13, 2007, from www.apa.org/monitor.jan03/newcode.html

US Department of Health and Human Services. (2005). Code of federal regulations (45 CFR 46). Sub-part D: Additional Protections for Children Involved as Subjects in Research.

Wahman, C. L., Fettig, A., & Zimmerman, K. (2023). Social and emotional intervention research as justice: A case for accountability. *Remedial and Special Education*, 07419325221143761.

What Works Clearinghouse (2020). *Procedures and standards handbook* (v. 4.1). https://ies.ed.gov/ncee/wwc/Docs/referenceresources/WWC-Standards-Handbook-v4-1-508.pdf

Williams, E. P., & Walter, J. K. (2015). When does the amount we pay research participants become "undue influence"? *AMA Journal of Ethics*, 17, 1116–1121.

17
Evaluating Single Case Research

Jennifer R. Ledford, Justin D. Lane, and Robyn Tate

Important Terms

internally valid, rigor, risk of bias, standards, quality indicators, rating frameworks, questionable research practices

---

Table of Contents

Internal Validity, Rigor, and Risk Of Bias
Critical Characteristics of Single Case Studies
    Design Appropriateness
    Potential Demonstrations of Effect
    Reliability
    Fidelity
    Data Sufficient
Potentially Important Characteristics
    Generality and Applicability
    Randomization
Resources for Characterizing Rigor
    CEC-DR Evidence-Based Practice Paper (2005)
    RoBiNT Scale (2013) and Updated Algorithm (2019)
    CEC Standards for Evidence-Based Practice (2014)
    Single Case Reporting Guideline in Behavioral Interventions (2016)
    Risk of Bias Tool (2017)
    Comparative Single Case Experimental Design Rating System (2018)
    WWC Procedures and Standards Handbook (2020)
    CEC-DR Next Generation Guidelines (2023)
    Single Case Analysis and Review Framework v 3.1 (2023)
    QualiCase (2023)

> Examples of Use
> Questionable Research Practices
> Conclusions
> References

To this point, we have primarily discussed the design, implementation, and analysis of single case studies conducted by you as a researcher or practitioner. Of course, researchers and practitioners must also analyze the studies conducted by others to contextualize their own studies and determine the extent to which evidence exists for a given practice in specific contexts (What works, for whom, and under what conditions?). Researchers evaluate rigor for several interrelated reasons, including to determine (1) to what extent an individual study was conducted in a manner to allow confidence in results, (2) to what extent a *group* of studies was conducted in a manner to allow confidence in overarching conclusions regarding outcomes, and (3) ways in which a body of research related to a specific independent or dependent variable should be expanded (e.g., What improvements in rigor are needed in future research? What questions have not been answered yet?). Regardless of whether you are assessing a single study or a group of related studies, it is critical that you assess rigor *before you assess outcomes*. This will allow you to determine whether changes in behavior are believable when compared against the degree of control for and detection of potential alternative explanations for an outcome across studies (i.e., whether you are confident that changes in behavior are due to experimental manipulations *and only* those manipulations).

Internal Validity, Rigor, and Risk of Bias

As stated in earlier chapters, an **internally valid** study includes mechanisms associated with increased confidence that outcomes are related to the intervention and not extraneous factors. Reviewing a study or collection of related studies (e.g., a group of studies in which the same intervention is evaluated) often involves evaluating internal validity at the study or source level (i.e., all designs included in a single article or paper) or design level (i.e., individual rating for each single case design within an article or paper). **Rigor** is commonly conceptualized as a measure of the extent to which a study is internally valid when compared against a set of indicators. In such situations, rigor represents a summative classification of internal validity (e.g., a study is rated as having a "high level of rigor" because of the increased number of indicators). More broadly, rigor can be described as the level of confidence you have that the study outcomes are related to your independent variable manipulation, and only to that. In this chapter, we do not use the term quality when discussing rigor, because quality is a broad term that usually encompasses rigor but also other factors. In relation to single case research, some researchers may refer to a "high-quality study" as one that is rigorous or internally valid, while others may specifically label indicators as "quality indicators" or refer to social and ecological validity, generalization, and maintenance as indicative of the quality of a study.

Regardless of how we evaluate internal validity, it is important to first understand the purpose of a study (preferably captured in the introduction and research questions). An omission of an indicator, or even many indicators, is not necessarily problematic if the purpose and subsequent experimental evaluation of conditions allowed the researcher to definitively answer their questions. Assume, for example, that one research team is interested in demonstrating the effectiveness of an intervention, and another is interested in experimentally evaluating the use of the intervention in typical contexts. Conceptually, both studies are important and they will likely both include some of the same design features that increase internal validity (e.g., construct validity, sufficient potential demonstrations of effect), but each may weight different features as more important, given their discrepant purposes. This is acceptable if the conceptualization and implementation by both teams are rigorous *given their goals*.

Increasingly, systematic reviews and meta-analyses include a measure of bias. **Risk of bias**, a component of rigor, refers to the likelihood that the outcomes of a study are *biased* due to some methodological decision made by the researchers, resulting in potential overestimation of effects (Higgins et al., 2011). For example, observer bias is possible in all studies, including single case research, and is minimized by using naïve observers (blind assessors). Evaluating rigor, including the potential for bias, and making subsequent professional decisions or recommendations to the field requires a nuanced understanding of the purpose (research questions), procedures, and outcome data in a study.

Critical Characteristics of Single Case Studies

We identify five critical elements that are crucial for establishing adequate rigor. These include (1) using an appropriate design to answer your research questions, (2) having adequate opportunities to demonstrate effects, (3) demonstrating adequate reliability of dependent and (4) independent variables, and (5) collecting enough data from which to draw conclusions. These characteristics are widely considered important, but no consensus exists regarding whether each is critical and how sufficiency or adequacy is determined (cf. Hitchcock et al., 2014; Kratochwill et al., 2023; Ledford, Lambert et al., 2023; Wolery, 2013; WWC, 2020). We briefly discuss each characteristic below but note that the relative weight of these characteristics may vary based on the purposes of a given study.

Design Appropriateness

Confident conclusions regarding functional relations can only be drawn when an appropriate design is used to answer your research questions. Basic study characteristics (e.g., behavior reversibility and research question type) should be used to narrow down design options, and additional study-specific considerations should be used to select a final design, as described in Chapter 15. Examples of common inappropriate use of single case designs for answering research questions include: (1) measuring non-reversible behaviors in the context of a design intended to be used with reversible behaviors; (2) drawing conclusions relative to baseline conditions without adequate replications (e.g., in ATD designs without a continuing baseline condition or in A-B-C-B-C designs); and (3) failure to include a control set when using AATD designs, to control for history or maturation threats.

Potential Demonstrations of Effect

If authors chose an appropriate design to answer their research questions, the next step is to determine whether they have included a sufficient number of demonstrations to adequately control for threats to internal validity, allowing for an experimental demonstration of effect. Generally, three potential demonstrations at three different points in time is sufficient (Ledford, Lambert et al., 2023). Common variations that are *insufficient* include multiple baseline or probe designs with two tiers and withdrawal or multitreatment designs with too few *adjacent conditions* (e.g., A-B-A, A-B-C-D-C, A-B-A-C). Note that multiple baseline designs with three or more tiers but fewer than three start points have an insufficient number of potential demonstrations (see Callout in Chapter 11 about sufficient differences in baseline lengths in time-lagged designs). Likewise, multiple baseline designs that have different interventions following a concurrent baseline (e.g., A→B for two tiers, and A→C in the third tier) cannot be considered to have a sufficient number of potential demonstrations, given contemporary recommendations. If at least three potential demonstrations are not possible, the study does not have adequate internal validity. We will note that these guidelines are relatively new in the field; thus, many "older" studies may not meet these and other rigor guidelines. When conducting a systematic review (see Chapter 19), it may be appropriate to include studies without sufficient potential demonstrations if you analyze whether there are consistent differences among studies with sufficient replications and those without. That is, if studies that include two demonstrations have similar outcomes to those that include three or more demonstrations, confidence in outcomes across studies is high.

Reliability

In Chapter 5, we discussed the potential hazards of human observers, including error, bias, and drift. Here, we reiterate that studies should include secondary observers, who are naïve to condition if possible (Chazin et al., 2018; Tate et al., 2013). Secondary observers should be independent (e.g., not influenced by responding of the primary observer) and should collect data alongside the primary observer for at least one-third of all sessions in all conditions for all participants, in most cases (Ledford, Lambert et al., 2023). Determining minimum frequency should vary based on code complexity and ongoing agreement (Kazdin, 2011; e.g., when low agreement occurs in a particular condition, additional agreement data should be collected) as well as study purpose (e.g., less often in contexts where measurement is intrusive or likely to change "typical" behavior of interest, such as in homes). In addition, interobserver agreement should be calculated using the most precise method given the recording system (e.g., point-by-point if possible). Means and ranges across participants and conditions should be reported, and reasons for any low values should be described. Preferably, authors should indicate that they visually analyzed secondary data to assess for potential bias and drift and should report procedures for retraining and discrepancy discussions. Many tools (see below) report that an 80% agreement value is acceptable; as outlined in Chapter 5, this is a somewhat arbitrary criterion. When determining acceptability, you should assess the complexity of the codes and contexts, the relative subjectivity of the dependent variable, and (most importantly) whether low agreement has the potential to alter data patterns (and thus, your decisions regarding functional relations; Barlow & Hersen, 1984; Ledford et al., 2012). If reliability data are not collected and reported at a sufficiently high level for all dependent variables and participants, to permit confidence of changes between conditions, the confidence in any identified relation is decreased.

Fidelity

We also consider reliability of independent variable implementation (i.e., fidelity) to be a critical component of rigorous studies; without confirmation that all conditions were conducted as planned, we cannot be confident that programmed changes between conditions occurred. This, of course, precludes confidence that differences between conditions resulted in changes in participant behavior. As discussed in Chapter 6, researchers should provide evidence that *all* conditions were implemented as intended, not just treatment conditions (Ledford & Gast, 2014; Ledford & Wolery, 2013). There are no consistent criterion levels defined as adequate, but implementation should generally be high unless your research questions are related to fidelity levels (e.g., if you intend to answer the question of whether certain conditions lead to high-fidelity use of interventions). Low procedural fidelity can be mitigated by re-training (see Chapter 6). Reasons for low fidelity should be described and implications of low fidelity should be explicitly stated (e.g., if positive outcomes occurred despite intermittent low fidelity, this might serve as evidence that the intervention is powerful even if practitioners cannot complete it to 100% fidelity all of the time).

Data Sufficiency

The final characteristic we will define as critical is the presence of a sufficient amount of data for determining whether a functional relation is present. Different minimum criteria have been specified and argued about (e.g., three versus five data points; CEC, 2014; Kratochwill et al., 2023; Ledford, Lambert et al., 2023; WWC, 2020). Rather than identifying a specific number, we suggest that analysts answer the question: Does the number of data points in one or more conditions prohibit or seriously impede the ability to identify (1) whether behavior change occurred, and (2) whether these changes were due to changes between conditions *and only* changes between conditions? If the answer to this question is "yes," the study does not have adequate internal validity. Generally, you need few data points if data are at floor or ceiling levels and stable; you need more data points if data are variable. Of course, as mentioned in Chapter 16, there are also ethical ramifications regarding the sufficiency of baseline data in particular. Although ethical issues do not mitigate internal validity concerns, they still justify action in some cases.

Potentially Important Characteristics

While some characteristics are necessary for drawing confident conclusions regarding the relation between independent and dependent variables, others are desirable in some situations—depending on your research questions—but are not necessarily critical for all studies. We have addressed two domains—generality/applicability and randomization—and summarize considerations for these domains below.

Generality and Applicability

Some features of single case studies can increase applicability, importance, or generality of study findings, but do not directly influence your ability to draw confident conclusions about results. Four such factors are ecological validity, social validity, evaluation of generality of outcomes, and evaluation of maintenance of outcomes. These factors are all discussed at length in Chapter 7 in relation to designing and conducting a single case study. When evaluating the studies of others, the important question for you is—to what extent are these factors important for answering *your* question? For example, assume you are a practitioner interested in the extent to which a certain intervention consistently results in behavior change. In this case, it is **not** necessarily important for this intervention to have been evaluated:

- In many relevant contexts (e.g., an elementary school, a clinic that provides early intensive behavioral intervention, an outpatient clinic for challenging behavior, a childcare setting)
- With a range of participants (e.g., young children with autism, young adults with behavioral disorders, typically developing Kindergarteners)
- With evidence of social validity from a range of stakeholders (e.g., parents of young children, elementary school principals, autistic adults)

Instead, you might be most interested in whether this intervention has been successfully used in an elementary school, with ethnically and racially diverse students in general education settings, and whether there is evidence that principals find it appropriate, and teachers maintain use after research support ends. Research that doesn't answer *your* question is not invalid, it's just not relevant to you.

Similarly, if you are a researcher interested in summarizing the state of the field in regard to a specific intervention, it is important to answer questions about what intervention components or modifications were used, under what conditions (i.e., contexts such as settings, implementers), for whom (what participants), and for what behaviors. However, a group of studies that has more narrow impacts (e.g., for minimally verbal children with autism) or in limited settings (e.g., inpatient hospital or clinical settings) is not unimportant. These studies might be worthy of review because practitioners who work in those narrow settings or with that narrow population are likely to find the outcomes very applicable.

Randomization

Some researchers have suggested that randomization should be liberally used in single case research (Kratochwill & Levin, 2010). Randomization is not new in single case research and as many as 30 years ago was discussed and applied in single case studies (e.g., Wolery & Billingsley, 1982; Wolery et al., 1993). Randomization of intervention condition implementation has a long history of use in both rapid iteration designs (e.g., ATD designs; discussed by Barlow & Hayes, 1979 and Holcombe et al., 1994) and multiple probe or baseline designs (Wolery & Billingsley, 1982). As described in Chapters 13 and 14, it is commonly used to order condition implementation in studies using ATD and AATD (cf. Haydon et al., 2010; Ingersoll, 2011; Lynch et al., 2009) and less commonly used to order intervention implementation in multiple probe and baseline designs (cf. Ledford et al., 2008; Wolery et al., 1993).

Additional uses of randomization have been suggested: (1) randomized start times for intervention conditions ("randomized phase start-point designs"; Kratochwill & Levin, 2010, p. 131) and (2) randomization of intervention condition implementation ("randomized phase order designs," p. 131). Randomized phase start-point designs would be used, for example, if a researcher randomly determined the session during which a participant would move between baseline (A) and intervention (B) conditions during an A-B-A-B design without consideration of data patterns (i.e., without response guided decision making). Difficulties would arise when these random start points are selected without consideration for data patterns (e.g., when a therapeutic trend exists during baseline condition, which would usually result in postponement of condition changes). Randomized phase order designs include randomly determining which condition was implemented at a given time for a participant (e.g., beginning with A or B conditions in an A-B-A-B design). Difficulties exist with this method when it is logically important for a baseline condition to be completed prior to an intervention condition.

Despite misgivings about some uses of randomization, we find the following uses of randomization helpful, given other internal validity indicators are also present:

1. *Randomized start times for interventions*: Randomly determining the start date for an intervention can be reasonable, and it could reduce bias that occurs if implementers wait until a data pattern is ideal before implementing. However, this increases the likelihood that unexpected data patterns will result in the inability to identify a functional relation.
2. *Randomized condition implementation*: Randomly ordering conditions is reasonable (and widely used) in designs using rapid iterative alternation (RIA; see Chapter 13).

Blocked randomization is typically used, to avoid situations in which some conditions are conducted more frequently than others (e.g., randomize a block of sessions, such that Interventions 1, 2, and 3 are all conducted once; then randomize a second block of sessions).

3. *Randomized stimuli assignment*: When two interventions are compared in the contexts of designs using RIA for non-reversible behaviors, it is critical to randomly assign stimuli or sets of stimuli to interventions to avoid potential bias (e.g., assigning an "easier" set to a preferred intervention). When multiple participants are assigned the same stimuli, counterbalancing across participants is possible.
4. *Randomized assignment of tiers*: When using MB and MP designs, it is important to randomly assign order of implementation across tiers to minimize the likelihood of bias. This is especially critical when using MB and MP designs across participants. However, this decrease in potential for bias must be balanced with participant need and data-based decision making.

In sum, internal validity does not *depend* on randomization in single case designs. However, the inclusion of randomization may decrease risk of bias and thus increase rigor.

Resources for Characterizing Rigor

A number of resources and tools have been designed to assist researchers in assessing the rigor of single case studies; the purpose, content, guidelines, and use of each is slightly different. As a matter of fact, researchers have found that you may draw different conclusions based on the tool or source you use (Hardy et al., 2022; Zimmerman et al., 2018). Below, we briefly describe some widely used resources that are designed to help researchers assess the rigor of single case research. Other resources and tools are available, and still more are likely to be developed after this text is in press; thus, the information below is not comprehensive. The critical factor when determining which tool to use is to choose one that (1) matches your purpose, and (2) includes valuation of factors that are critical *for your research questions*.

CEC-DR Evidence-Based Practice Paper (2005)

In 2005, *Exceptional Children* printed a special issue on quality indicators across different research paradigms. In the article on single case research, Horner and colleagues (2005) described the use of single case studies to establish evidence-based practices in special education, described "experimental control" in single case designs (a term we have avoided using in this text, given that it conflates high internal validity with positive outcomes), and explicated that rigorously conducted single case research was experimental in nature. They also described 21 quality indicators for single case research, in seven areas: Descriptions of participants and settings, dependent variable measurement, independent variable measurement, baseline, experimental control, external validity, and social validity. This article has been highly cited and numerous reviews of single case research have used these quality indicators to assess rigor in groups of related studies. Suggested indicators are comprehensive but require expertise for analysis because two studies with similar numbers of addressed quality indicators might have very different adequacy in terms of rigor. For example, if two studies each addressed 20 of the 21 indicators, but one had low ecological validity (e.g., used researcher rather than endogenous implementers) and one had low internal validity (e.g., did not include three potential demonstrations of effect), confidence in conclusions from each is considerably different despite the identical quality score. Regardless, this is a highly used and well-regarded tool that includes many critical components for assessing rigor and quality.

RoBiNT Scale (2013) and Updated Algorithm (2019)

A group of researchers from Australia (Tate et al., 2013) developed and updated the SCED Scale (2008), naming the replacement tool the Risk of Bias in N-of-1 Trials (RoBiNT) Scale. The RoBiNT includes 15 items and uses terminology common to medicine (e.g., N-of-1). Unlike many other tools, the items are not rated in a binary fashion, but rather using a three-point scale. It includes many of the same items as described in the 2005 CEC-DR paper. Additional items include replication to improve generality (not including within-design replication) and measurement of generalization in the context of the design. Some items more common in medical research (as compared to typical single case research in education, psychology, or behavioral sciences) are the inclusion of randomization, blinding participants and implementers, and blinding data collectors. Most evaluated single case studies received scores of 0 for all of these items (Tate et al., 2013). Items are divided into two sub-scales allowing the evaluator to calculate separate scores for internal and external validity; the ability to separate rigor and generality is a considerable strength of this tool.

In 2019, Perdices and colleagues published an algorithm that weighted the items in the RoBiNT (internal validity subscale) to address the problems evident in other tools—that all items are not equally important. They weighted most heavily having three potential demonstrations of effect with control for likely threats to internal validity—if this is not met, methodological rigor is rated as "very low" (categories: very high, high, moderate, fair, low, very low). The next step, assessing whether data are sufficient, is also highly impactful, with a score of 0 meaning the highest rigor score possible would be "low." The authors of this algorithm found that it had good agreement with the WWC categorization of studies.

CEC Standards for Evidence-Based Practice (2014)

The Council for Exceptional Children (CEC) published their *Standards for Evidence-Based Practices in Special Education* in 2014. These guidelines, including quality indicators (QIs) applicable to group design, single case designs, and both types of designs, include many of the same indicators the CEC-DR paper. There are eight areas of assessment; the first four (context and setting, participants, intervention agent, and description of practice) are related to adequate reporting of study characteristics. The next three areas (implementation fidelity, internal validity, and outcome measures/dependent variables) are related to both rigor and reporting (e.g., dependent variables should be described well and measured reliably). The final category, data analysis, requires the presentation of data via a single case design line graph. In order to be considered "methodologically sound," studies must meet *all quality indicators*.

Following quality appraisal, outcomes analysis is conducted. There are three potential outcome categories. *Positive effects* are present when a functional relation is established, with three-quarters of participants showing positive and "meaningful" behavior change and no contra-therapeutic effects. Negative effects are present when behavior changes for three-quarters of participants *in the unintended direction*. Neutral or mixed effects are present when neither positive nor negative effects can be established. We should note that outcomes analysis for this tool occurs *at the study level* rather than at the design level. This is incongruent with other tools (e.g., WWC, SCARF) and can lead to discrepant conclusions. To be considered an evidence-based practice based on single case research, the CEC QIs stipulate there must be (1) at least five methodologically sound studies including at least 20 participants with positive effects *and* (2) include 0 methodologically sound studies with negative effects *and* (3) have more methodologically sound studies with positive effects than neutral or mixed effect (at least a 3:1 ratio). Other potential classifications of evidence include *potentially evidence-based practice, mixed evidence, insufficient evidence*, and *negative effects*. Because this tool stipulates that studies should include 100% of quality indicators in order to be designated as methodologically sound, it is likely that most practices would be evaluated as having "insufficient evidence" (i.e., an insufficient number of methodologically sound studies).

Single Case Reporting Guideline in Behavioral Interventions (2016)

To facilitate adequate reporting practices in the literature, guidelines are available to assist authors in creating written reports of single case studies. The **S**ingle-**C**ase **R**eporting guideline **I**n **Be**havioral interventions (SCRIBE; Tate et al., 2016a, 2016b) is a contemporary reporting guide developed specifically for single case studies and was a response to inadequate or uneven reporting practices observed in the literature. For example, Maggin et al. (2011) found that even basic demographic information was often not reported in 24 single case studies evaluating token economies for challenging behaviors in students. Similarly, in 253 single case studies in the neuro-rehabilitation field, Tate et al. (2013) found no information reported on inter-rater agreement of the target behavior (46% of reports) or whether the assessor was independent of the therapist (86%). SCRIBE was developed using procedures recommended by Moher et al. (2010) for the CONSORT (***CON**solidated **S**tandards **O**f **R**eporting **T**rials*) family of reporting guidelines.

The incentive to create SCRIBE derived from an endeavor to develop a reporting guide for N-of-1 Trials in the medical literature (Shamseer et al., 2015; Vohra et al., 2015), although it is intended to be applicable to all fields of the behavioral sciences. Accordingly, a group of world experts was assembled, with representation from content experts in clinical and neuropsychology, educational psychology and special education, medicine, occupational therapy and speech pathology, as well as single-case methodologists and statisticians, journal editors and a medical librarian, and guideline developers. SCRIBE items were evaluated in two rounds of an online Delphi survey, and subsequently finalized during a two-day consensus conference. The methodology and procedures used to develop SCRIBE are described in Tate et al. (2016a). That article was published in ten journals simultaneously, representing a broad range of disciplines, to facilitate widespread dissemination of the work. A more detailed "explanation and elaboration" article (Tate et al., 2016b) provides the rationale for including each of the items of SCRIBE and examples of adequate reporting from the literature.

The main product of SCRIBE is a 26-item checklist, which users can download from the SCRIBE website (www.sydney.edu.au/medicine-health/our-research/sydney-medical-school.html). SCRIBE provides authors with information on <u>what</u> to report in sections, and subsections, commonly included in published literature (Introduction, Method, Results, Discussion). Readers should be aware of the different purposes of a reporting guide versus tools for assessing rigor. The former is a guide for authors writing a report, to instruct on <u>what</u> to report. Such guides are also helpful for journal editors and reviewers to determine whether a written report provides all the necessary information. In contrast, tools for assessing rigor inform the reader of <u>how well</u> a study was conducted. For example, item 14 of SCRIBE (concerned with measures) asks the author to describe "how and when they [the target behaviors] were measured." An author might report, for example, that in an A-B-A-B design study, the target behavior was measured weekly during each two-week baseline (A) and each two-week intervention (B) conditions. This is an example of adequate reporting because the reader knows exactly what was done (measures of the target behavior were collected twice in every baseline and intervention condition). However, such a study would likely not meet contemporary standards for adequate internal validity, as assessed via a tool for assessing rigor.

Risk of Bias Tool (2017)

Reichow and colleagues (2018) developed a specific tool designed to evaluate the risk of bias in single case studies; this tool was modified from the risk of bias tool used in Cochrane Collaboration meta-analyses for group design studies (Higgins & Altman, 2008). The risk of bias tool assesses biases in seven areas, including sequence generation, participant selection, blinding of participants and personnel, procedural fidelity, blinding of outcome assessment, dependent variable reliability, and data sampling. This tool has been used in a few published reviews (e.g., Barton et al., 2017; Biggs & Robison, 2023). The risk of bias tool's primary strength is that it is somewhat easily compared to the risk of bias tool designed for group design studies. Thus, when a review includes both group comparisons and single case studies, this tool might be particularly valuable to allow readers to draw conclusions regarding bias across similar categories.

Comparative Single Case Experimental Design Rating System (2018)

The CSCEDARS was introduced in 2018 by Schlosser and colleagues, for the specific purpose of evaluating two or more interventions' relative effects on non-reversible behaviors (e.g., AATDs). The CSCEDARS is divided into three sections. The first section includes rating considerations for single case designs generally. The second contains items relevant to comparisons, such as randomly assigning stimuli to conditions. The third section is relevant to outcomes. This tool is relevant for only a small portion of single case designs, but when evaluating rigor of AATDs, it is very helpful given inclusion of items that are specifically relevant to those designs.

WWC Procedures and Standards Handbook (2020)

The What Works Clearinghouse (WWC) "pilot" design standards were introduced in 2010 and pilot was removed from the designation with the introduction of version 4.1 in 2020. The current WWC standards include indicators related to: (1) systematic implementation of the intervention; (2) adequate dependent variable reliability; (3) number of potential demonstrations, (4) number of data points; (5) design concurrence; and (6) lack of other confounding factors. One prominent difference in the WWC Standards and most other resources in this list is that the WWC standards do not include an item regarding fidelity measurement (discussed at length in several published articles; Hitchcock et al., 2014; Wolery, 2013). The WWC standard suggesting that 5–6 data points should be the minimum acceptable number in most conditions has drawn considerable ire from single case researchers (Harris et al., 2019). These standards are widely applied in systematic reviews and have arguably impacted single case research and related syntheses more than other contemporary guidelines in recent years, despite controversy.

CEC-DR Next Generation Guidelines (2023)

In 2023, *Exceptional Children* published an issue on contemporary issues in research design, as an update to the 2005 issue mentioned above. In the article devoted to single case, Ledford, Lambert and colleagues (2023) provided three sets of guidelines—one for evaluating *internal validity* of single case studies, one for evaluating *generality* of single case studies, and one for evaluating *reporting* for single case studies. They argued that when considering the overall usefulness of studies, internal and external validity should be evaluated separately and should not be conflated with reporting. They also assert that guidelines for single case designs should be flexible, in opposition to most other tools. For example, they argue that the historically appropriate 80% criterion for interobserver agreement data may be too lax in some situations and too harsh in others. They also include considerations for diversity, equity, and inclusion such as making research participation accessible, and argue for use of open science practices (Cook, Fleming et al., 2021; Cook, Johnson, et al., 2021), such as sharing data and using online supplemental materials to share a variety of information (e.g., protocols, fidelity forms). Authors of these guidelines specify that their suggestions should be taken as recommended practices, rather than used to evaluate whether studies should be included in a systematic review.

Single Case Analysis and Review Framework v 3.1 (2023)

The Single Case Analysis and Review Framework (SCARF) was developed in 2016 and updated in 2019 (v.2.0) and 2023 (v 3.1; Ledford, Chazin, et al., 2023). It is a spreadsheet, accessible online, which is designed to be used to evaluate the rigor of single case studies at the design level; that is, when multiple single case designs are included in one manuscript, each is evaluated separately. It allows for the evaluation of primary outcomes as well as generalized and maintained outcomes using a rating scale based on visual analysis of data. It also allows for separate characterization of internal validity, external validity (when those questions are of interest), and reporting quality. One novel feature of the SCARF tool is that there is a convention for presenting the results of analysis of multiple studies, via a scatterplot, with one axis representing the number of internal validity indicators and the other representing the outcome (countertherapeutic, null, inconsistent, weak functional relation, strong functional relation). This allows researchers interested in evaluating the overall outcomes and rigor in a body of research to visualize the extent to which rigor is high and the proportion of studies for which a functional relation was identified.

QualiCase (2023)

One recently developed tool, the Quality Enhancement for Single Case Proposals (QualiCase), has a somewhat different purpose than the tools listed above. QualiCase was specifically designed to enhance the *planning* of single case design research studies. That is, instead of assessing the extent to which published or completed studies have adequate internal validity, this tool is intended to help researchers develop studies that are internally valid. Due to its recent development, it has not been cited or tested in published works.

Examples of Use

Examples of syntheses of single case research that used tools discussed in this chapter are shown in Table 17.1. Tools first published in 2023 are not included in this table; these recently developed resources lack corresponding published syntheses that applied that tool to a group of studies (outside of potentially providing an example of how to use the tool in the initial description or manual).

Questionable Research Practices

Recently, in addition to discussing the extent to which single case studies are internally valid, researchers have discussed to what extent single case researchers rely on **questionable research practices**. These are practices that *could* be problematic but are not outright wrong or unethical.

Table 17.1 List of Syntheses that Use Various Tools for Assessing Rigor

Citation	Tool
Gulboy, E., Yucesoy-Ozkan, S., & Rakap, S. (2023). Embedded instruction for young children with disabilities: A systematic review and meta-analysis of single-case experimental research studies. *Early Childhood Research Quarterly*, 63, 181–193.	CEC-DR Evidence-Based Practice Paper (2005)
Steel, J., Elbourn, E., & Togher, L. (2021). Narrative discourse intervention after traumatic brain injury: A systematic review of the literature. *Topics in Language Disorders*, 41(1), 47–72.	RoBiNT Scale (2013) and Updated Algorithm (2022)
Beckers, L. W., Stal, R. A., Smeets, R. J., Onghena, P., & Bastiaenen, C. H. (2020). Single-case design studies in children with cerebral palsy: A scoping review. *Developmental Neurorehabilitation*, 23(2), 73–105.	RoBiNT Scale (2013)
Gersib, J. A., & Mason, S. (2023). A meta-analysis of behavior interventions for students with emotional-behavioral disorders in self-contained settings. *Behavioral Disorders*, 01987429231160285.	CEC Standards for Evidence-Based Practice (2014)
Martinez, J. R., Waters, C. L., Conroy, M. A., & Reichow, B. (2021). Peer-mediated interventions to address social competence needs of young children with ASD: Systematic review of single-case research design studies. *Topics in Early Childhood Special Education*, 40(4), 217–228.	Risk of Bias Tool (2017)
Pak, N. S., Bailey, K. M., Ledford, J. R., & Kaiser, A. P. (2023). Comparing interventions with speech-generating devices and other augmentative and alternative communication modes: A meta-analysis. *American Journal of Speech-Language Pathology*, 32(2), 786–802.	Comparative Single Case Experimental Design Rating System (2018)
Samudre, M. D., LeJeune, L. M., Anderson, E. J., Viotto, J. A., Brock, M. E., & Nichols, H. (2023). A meta-analysis on behavioral support training and general education teacher implementation. *Exceptional Children*, 00144029231172175.	WWC Standards (2020)
Ledford, J. R., Trump, C., Chazin, K. T., Windsor, S. A., Eyler, P. B., & Wunderlich, K. (2023a). Systematic review of interruption and redirection procedures for autistic individuals. *Behavioral Interventions*, 38(1), 198–218.	Single Case Analysis and Review Framework (previous version)

For example, it is clearly wrong to falsify data, but it is a questionable research practice to omit data from analysis that were collected under problematic conditions (i.e., a day a child was sick). That is, it would not necessarily be problematic to do this, if it is explicitly reported. But, doing this without clear explication may lead to erroneous conclusions. Questionable research practices may occur because of lack of author knowledge, competing contingencies (e.g., publication), or attempts to convey complex information with limited publication space. Identification of questionable research practices, and broad dissemination of alternative, improved research practices may lead to increased research quality in the field (Slocum, 2023; Tincani & Travers, 2022). Preregistration of single case studies and other open science practices can also reduce the use of questionable research practices (Cook, Johnson et al., 2021). In group research, a considerable amount of work has been done related to questionable research practices (e.g., John et al., 2012; Nosek et al., 2012); work specifically related to single case is emerging.

Conclusions

The impetus of applied research is identifying efficacious, effective, and efficient interventions to establish well-developed technologies for endogenous implementers in typical environments. This process encompasses (1) conducting rigorous single case studies and (2) evaluating the collection of available studies to answer what we already know about a given topic and what is next for the corresponding field of study. Evaluating rigor of single case studies is the critical first step in determining to what extent subsequent analysis of data should occur. Adherence to guidelines, especially transparency in reporting practices, when preparing reports on single case studies will facilitate evaluations of rigor in future reviews; we will discuss these issues in the final two chapters.

References

Barlow, D. H., & Hayes, S. C. (1979). Alternating treatments design: One strategy for comparing the effects of two treatments in a single subject. *Journal of Applied Behavior Analysis*, 12(2), 199–210.

Barlow, D. H. & Hersen, M. (1984). *Single case experimental designs: Strategies for studying behavior change* (2nd ed.). New York: Pergamon Press.

Barton, E. E., Pustejovksy, J. P., Maggin, D. M., & Reichow, B. R. (2017). A meta-analysis of technology aided instruction and intervention for students with ASD. *Remedial and Special Education*, 38(6), 371–386.

Beckers, L. W., Stal, R. A., Smeets, R. J., Onghena, P., & Bastiaenen, C. H. (2020). Single-case design studies in children with cerebral palsy: A scoping review. *Developmental Neurorehabilitation*, 23(2), 73–105.

Biggs, E. E., & Robison, S. E. (2023). Review of the evidence base for peer network interventions for students with intellectual and developmental disabilities. *Remedial and Special Education*, 44(1), 43–59.

Chazin, K. T., Ledford, J. R., Barton, E. E., & Osborne, K. C. (2018). The effects of antecedent exercise on engagement during large group activities for young children. *Remedial and Special Education*, 39(3), 158–170.

Cook, B. G., Fleming, J. I., Hart, S. A., Lane, K. L., Therrien, W. J., van Dijk, W., & Wilson, S. E. (2021). A how-to guide for open-science practices in special education research. *Remedial and Special Education*, 43(4), 270–280.

Cook, B. G., Johnson, A. H., Maggin, D. M., Therrien, W. J., Barton, E. E., Lloyd, J. W., & Travers, J. C. (2021). Open science and single-case design research. *Remedial and Special Education*, 43(5), 359–369.

Council for Exceptional Children (2014). Standards for evidence-based practices in special education. Author: Arlington, VA. Retrieved on May 4, 2017 from: www.cec.sped.org/~/media/Files/Standards/Evidence%20based%20Practices%20and%20Practice/CECs%20Evidence%20Based%20Practice%20Standards.pdf

Gersib, J. A., & Mason, S. (2023). A meta-analysis of behavior interventions for students with emotional-behavioral disorders in self-contained settings. *Behavioral Disorders*, 01987429231160285

Gulboy, E., Yucesoy-Ozkan, S., & Rakap, S. (2023). Embedded instruction for young children with disabilities: A systematic review and meta-analysis of single-case experimental research studies. *Early Childhood Research Quarterly*, 63, 181–193.

Hardy, J. K., McLeod, R. H., Sweigart, C. A., & Landrum, T. (2022). Comparing and contrasting quality frameworks using research on high-probability requests with young children. *Infants & Young Children*, 35(4), 267–284.

Harris, K. R., Stevenson, N. A., & Kauffman, J. M. (2019). CEC Division for Research position statement: Negative effects of minimum requirements for data points in multiple baseline designs and multiple probe designs in the What Works Clearinghouse Standards Handbook, Version 4.0. https://cecdr.org/sites/default/files/2021-01/_DR_Position_Statement_5_data_points_WWC_SCD_final_0.pdf

Haydon, T., Conroy, M., Scott, T. M., Sindelar, P. T., Barber, B. R., & Orlando, A. (2010). A comparison of three types of opportunities to respond on student academic and social behaviors. *Journal of Emotional and Behavioral Disorders*, 18, 27–40.

Higgins, J. P., & Altman, D. G. (2008). Assessing risk of bias in included studies. In *Cochrane handbook for systematic reviews of interventions: Cochrane book series* (pp. 187–241).

Higgins, J. P., Altman, D. G., Gøtzsche, P. C., Jüni, P., Moher, D., Oxman, A. D., … & Sterne, J. A. (2011). The Cochrane Collaboration's tool for assessing risk of bias in randomised trials. *British Medical Journal*, 343, d5928.

Hitchcock, J. H., Horner, R. H., Kratochwill, T. R., Levin, J. R., Odom, S. L., Rindskopf, D. M., & Shadish, W. R. (2014). The What Works Clearinghouse single-case design pilot standards: Who will guard the guards? *Remedial and Special Education*, 35, 145–152.

Holcombe, A., Wolery, M., & Gast, D. L. (1994). Comparative single-subject research: Description of designs and discussion of problems. *Topics in Early Childhood Special Education*, 14, 119–145.

Horner, R. H., Carr, E. G., Halle, J., McGee, G., Odom, S., & Wolery, M. (2005). The use of single-subject research to identify evidence-based practice in special education. *Exceptional Children*, 71, 165–179.

Ingersoll, B. (2011). The differential effect of three naturalistic language interventions on language use in autism. *Journal of Positive Behavior Interventions*, 13, 109–118.

John, L. K., Loewenstein, G., & Prelec, D. (2012). Measuring the prevalence of questionable research practices with incentives for truth telling. *Psychological Science*, 23(5), 524–532.

Kazdin, A. E. (2011). *Single-case research designs*. New York: Oxford University Press.

Kratochwill, T. R., Horner, R. H., Levin, J. R., Machalicek, W., Ferron, J., & Johnson, A. (2023). Single-case intervention research design standards: Additional proposed upgrades and future directions. *Journal of School Psychology*, 97, 192–216.

Kratochwill, T. R., & Levin, J. R. (2010). Enhancing the scientific credibility of single-case intervention research: Randomization to the rescue. *Psychological Methods*, 15, 124–144.

Ledford, J. R., Chazin, K. T., Lane, J. D., Zimmerman, K. N., Bennett, P. B., & Ayres, K. A. (2023, May). Single case analysis and review framework (SCARF). Retrieved from: http://ebip.vkcsites.org/scarfv2

Ledford, J. R., & Gast, D. L. (2014). Measuring procedural fidelity in behavioral research. *Neuropsychological Rehabilitation*, 24, 332–348.

Ledford, J. R., Gast, D. L., Luscre, D., & Ayres, K. M. (2008). Observational and incidental learning by children with autism during small group instruction. *Journal of Autism and Developmental Disorders*, 38, 86–103.

Ledford, J. R., Lambert, J. M., Pustejovsky, J. E., Zimmerman, K. N., Hollins, N., & Barton, E. E. (2023). Single-case-design research in special education: Next-generation guidelines and considerations. *Exceptional Children*, 89(4), 379–396.

Ledford, J. R., Trump, C., Chazin, K. T., Windsor, S. A., Eyler, P. B., & Wunderlich, K. (2023). Systematic review of interruption and redirection procedures for autistic individuals. *Behavioral Interventions*, 38(1), 198–218.

Ledford, J. R., Wolery, M., Meeker, K. A., & Wehby, J. H. (2012). The effects of graphing a second observer's data on judgments of functional relations in A–B–A–B graphs. *Journal of Behavioral Education*, 21, 350–364.

Ledford, J. R., & Wolery, M. (2013). Procedural fidelity: An analysis of measurement and reporting practices. *Journal of Early Intervention*, 35, 173–193.

Lynch, A., Theodore, L. A., Bray, M. A., & Kehle, T. J. (2009). A comparison of group-oriented contingencies and randomized reinforcers to improve homework completion and accuracy for students with disabilities. *School Psychology Review*, 38, 307–324.

Maggin, D. M., Chafouleas, S. M., Goddard, K. M., & Johnson, A. H. (2011). A systematic evaluation of token economies as a classroom management tool for students with challenging behavior. *Journal of School Psychology*, 49, 529–554.

Martinez, J. R., Waters, C. L., Conroy, M. A., & Reichow, B. (2021). Peer-mediated interventions to address social competence needs of young children with ASD: Systematic review of single-case research design studies. *Topics in Early Childhood Special Education*, 40(4), 217–228.

Moher, D., Hopewell, S., Schulz, K. F., Montori, V., Gotzsche, P. C., Devereaux, P. J., … Altman, D. G. (2010). CONSORT 2010 explanation and elaboration: Updated guidelines for reporting parallel group randomised trials. *British Medical Journal*, 340, c869. doi: 10.1136/bmj.c869

Nosek, B. A., Spies, J. R., & Motyl, M. (2012). Scientific utopia: II. Restructuring incentives and practices to promote truth over publishability. *Perspectives on Psychological Science*, 7(6), 615–631.

Pak, N. S., Bailey, K. M., Ledford, J. R., & Kaiser, A. P. (2023). Comparing interventions with speech-generating devices and other augmentative and alternative communication modes: A meta-analysis. *American Journal of Speech-Language Pathology*, 32(2), 786–802.

Reichow, B., Barton, E. E., & Maggin, D. M. (2018). Development and applications of the single-case design risk of bias tool for evaluating single-case design research study reports. *Research in Developmental Disabilities*, 79(1), 53–64.

Samudre, M. D., LeJeune, L. M., Anderson, E. J., Viotto, J. A., Brock, M. E., & Nichols, H. (2023). A meta-analysis on behavioral support training and general education teacher implementation. *Exceptional Children*, 00144029231172175.

Shamseer, L., Sampson, M., Bukutu, C., Schmid, C. H., Nikles, J., Tate, R., … & Vohra, S. (2015). CONSORT extension for reporting N-of-1 trials (CENT) 2015: Explanation and elaboration. *British Medical Journal*, 350, h1738.

Slocum, T. (May, 2023). *Questionable research practices*. Presentation at the Wing Institute Single Case Conference. Vanderbilt University, Nashville, TN.

Steel, J., Elbourn, E., & Togher, L. (2021). Narrative discourse intervention after traumatic brain injury: A systematic review of the literature. *Topics in Language Disorders*, 41(1), 47–72.

Tate, R. L., Perdices, M., Rosenkoetter, U., Wakim, D., Godbee, K., Togher, L., & McDonald, S. (2013). Revision of a method quality rating scale for single-case experimental designs and n-of-1 trials: The 15-item Risk of Bias in N-of-1 Trials (RoBiNT) Scale. *Neuropsychological Rehabilitation*, 23(5), 619–638.

Tate, R. L., Perdices, M., Rosenkoetter, U., Shadish, W., Barlow, D. H., Horner, R., … Wilson, B. (2016a). The **S**ingle-**C**ase **R**eporting guideline **I**n **BE**havioural Interventions (SCRIBE) 2016 Statement. *Archives of Scientific Psychology*, 4, 1–9.

Tate, R. L., Perdices, M., Rosenkoetter, U., McDonald, S., Togher, L., Shadish, W., … Vohra, S., for the SCRIBE Group. (2016b). The **S**ingle-**C**ase **R**eporting guideline **I**n **BE**havioural Interventions (SCRIBE) 2016: Explanation and elaboration. *Archives of Scientific Psychology*, 4, 10–31.

Tincani, M., & Travers, J. (2022). Questionable research practices in single-case experimental designs: Examples and possible solutions. In *Avoiding questionable research practices in applied psychology* (pp. 269–285). Cham: Springer International Publishing.

Vohra, S., Shamseer, L., Sampson, M., Bukutu, C., Schmid, C. H., Tate, R., ... & Moher, D. (2015). CONSORT extension for reporting N-of-1 trials (CENT) 2015 Statement. *British Medical Journal*, 350, h1738.

What Works Clearinghouse (2020). *Procedures and standards handbook* (v. 4.1). https://ies.ed.gov/ncee/wwc/Docs/referenceresources/WWC-Standards-Handbook-v4-1-508.pdf

Wolery, M. (2013). A commentary: Single-case design technical document of the What Works Clearinghouse. *Remedial and Special Education*, 34, 39–43.

Wolery, M., & Billingsley, F. F. (1982). The application of Revusky's Rn test to slope and level changes. *Behavioral Assessment*, 4, 93–103.

Wolery, M., Holcombe, A., Werts, M. G., & Cipolloni, R. M. (1993). Effects of simultaneous prompting and instructive feedback. *Early Education and Development*, 4, 20–31.

Zimmerman, K. N., Ledford, J. R., Severini, K. E., Pustejovsky, J. E., Barton, E. E., & Lloyd, B. P. (2018). Single-case synthesis tools I: Comparing tools to evaluate SCD quality and rigor. *Research in Developmental Disabilities*, 79, 19–32.

18
Writing Research Proposals and Empirical Reports

Blair P. Lloyd and Kathleen Lynne Lane

Important Terms

research proposals, empirical reports, demonstration questions, comparison questions, parametric questions, component analysis questions, introduction, abstract, method, results, discussion, supplemental material

Table of Contents

Scientific Writing
Writing Research Questions
   Finding Research Topics
   Moving from Topics to Questions
   Classifying and Stating Research Questions
      Experimental Research Questions
      Descriptive Research Questions
   Writing Research Proposals
   Why Write Research Proposals?
   Primary Sections
      Introduction
      Method
   Writing Empirical Reports
   Why Write Empirical Reports?
   Primary Sections
      Abstract
      Introduction
      Method
      Results
      Discussion
      Supplemental Material

> *Considerations for Success*
> *Conclusions*
> *References*
>
> **Callouts**
>
> *18.1 Making Sense of Replications*
> *18.2 Classifying Research Questions from the Single Case Literature*

If you have read this far, you know that single case researchers rely heavily on visual displays of data to interpret and communicate their findings. But, like all scientists, single case researchers also rely on the written word. Scientific writing allows researchers to establish a record of their work; exchange ideas within the scientific community; and communicate effectively with broader audiences who care about implications of the research. Learning to write technically for these purposes is no different from learning any other complex skill. It requires purposeful attention, practice, feedback from others, and an ongoing commitment to improve.

Scientific Writing

Standards and styles of scientific writing vary by discipline and research methodology, yet key principles apply. These include strong organization, transparency, precision, economy of expression, and internal consistency. Beyond endorsing these general principles, the purpose of this chapter is to offer specific guidance on writing research proposals and empirical reports featuring single case research. **Research proposals** (e.g., grant proposals, dissertation proposals) are written to communicate a rationale and detailed plan for addressing one or more research questions in a *future* study. **Empirical reports** (e.g., research articles, master's theses, doctoral dissertations) are written *after* the study has been conducted. They include detailed descriptions of actual methods used, as well as presentation, interpretation, and discussion of study results.

Throughout the chapter, we aim to identify and describe the functions, structures, and components of scientific manuscripts. In doing so, our aim is to help clarify and streamline the writing process for the researcher, which ultimately leads to more effective written products for their audiences. We hope to provide students and early career researchers with a strong start on writing single case proposals and reports. Additionally, we hope such guidance might be useful for more seasoned researchers tasked with providing clear and constructive feedback on research proposals, grant applications, and manuscript submissions featuring single case research.

This chapter has three main sections: Writing research questions, writing research proposals, and writing empirical reports. Throughout the chapter, we (1) emphasize the purpose and function each part of the writing process serves; (2) identify their critical components and features; and (3) offer models and examples for illustration.

Writing Research Questions

Every good single case study begins with a research question. Research questions serve as an anchor to which all other study components are tied. Without them, it would not be possible to plan, execute, and interpret results of rigorous single case research. But where do research questions come from? We begin this section by offering guidance on where and how to start for those who may not yet have a research question in mind. Then, we classify common types of research questions in single case design; identify their necessary components; and provide examples of each type.

Finding Research Topics

If identifying a research question feels like an overwhelming task, you might first take a step back and consider more broadly what you want to study. Whether a student, practitioner, or tenured faculty member in the midst of an existential crisis, start with what you know—or what first brought you to your field of study. Was there a problem you struggled to navigate in practice? Was there a specific child, family, or teacher whom you did your best to support with the tools you had, but wished you could have done more? Did you wonder why one support strategy could work so well for one person, and not at all for another? This simple thought exercise will likely lead you to at least one critical component of a single case research question: A group of people with a common need (participants); an outcome you hope to change (dependent variable); or some strategy, support, or intervention you want to refine or better understand (independent variable).

If "starting with what you already know" still leaves you feeling adrift, there are other concrete steps you might take to find meaningful research topics and questions to pursue using single case design. If you have not yet spent much time with the people or in the contexts you hope to impact through your research, seeking out new or continued experiences in the field is a good place to start. You might talk with people (e.g., practicing professionals, caregivers, people with disabilities) whose daily life experience relates to the topics you hope to study. What is the highlight of their day? What are their daily struggles? What types of supports or resources would they benefit from, and how? What questions do they grapple with? If you hope to contribute to an applied science, then actively engaging members of the very communities you seek to learn from and serve through research is vital—including partnering to determine which questions are worth investigating (Fawcett, 1991; Pritchett et al., 2021). Expert researchers, clinicians, or practitioners who are well-connected in your general area of interest can also be helpful resources. They can point out important research-to-practice gaps that have yet to be addressed; share recommendations for how and where to seek more information; and facilitate connections to relevant community leaders or organizations. Finally, reading published single case intervention studies might spark your curiosity with respect to a distinct intervention goal, type, or context. A single study might inspire new questions you hadn't thought to ask before.

Moving from Topics to Questions

Regardless of the origins of your research idea, research questions must be clearly situated in the extant literature. This means you will need to identify the most relevant and recently published single case studies on the topic to get a sense of what is already known and what questions have yet to be addressed. Chapter 19 provides guidance on how to search and navigate the published literature on a topic, including how to conduct comprehensive, systematic literature reviews to learn all that is currently known about your topic of interest.

With respect to using the literature to generate or refine your research question, keep in mind your goal is to propose a study that will contribute to the current evidence base on the topic. In other words, you want to identify a gap in the empirical literature your study will address. Gaps come in all shapes and sizes, and several will likely become apparent after closely reading the studies most relevant to your research idea. In fact, discussion sections often include a description of the study's limitations and potential avenues for future research. Reviewing discussion sections can therefore help you identify potential directions for what study should come next. Important gaps can also be found in other sections of empirical reports, though they might not be mentioned explicitly. Method sections, for example, provide information on what the intervention entailed, where it was done, and who were involved. Results sections present data on whether and how well the intervention worked, and for which behaviors. Regardless of how conclusive a study's outcomes are, the knowledge produced by any single study is always conditional. That is, whether the same results would be found if one or more aspects of the study were varied is a new empirical question that can only be answered by conducting another study. This is good news for the curious at heart, as there are always new questions to ask and answer.

The quantity and quality of prior research on a topic should also inform what types of questions are prioritized as the next step in a line of research. For example, if there are only one or two published studies evaluating the effects of a given intervention, and that intervention shows promise, then the next question to address might be whether the results of those studies can be replicated by a different research team. Or, suppose there are many published studies demonstrating the efficacy of an intervention when implemented by trained therapists in a clinical setting. If the logic model underlying this intervention suggests it would be beneficial to implement in more naturalistic contexts, then an important research question might be whether the same (or adapted) intervention is similarly effective when implemented by teachers in classroom settings, or by caregivers in the home.

Callout 18.1 Making Sense of Replications

Students tasked with proposing new single case studies sometimes struggle with the concept of proposing systematic replications. Some students want to propose something original; they consider replication of others' work less exciting or less important than generating something new. From our perspective, innovation should be encouraged in all scientific research—especially when research questions are guided by strong conceptual frameworks, logic models, or theories of change (see Chapter 6). However, replication in all its variations is critical to building conceptually systematic evidence bases that inform practice (Cook, 2014; Travers et al., 2016). And, for those new to single case research, proposing and implementing systematic replications can be a good starting point for acquiring the necessary skills to conduct single case studies. This is because, relative to other studies, replications require fewer methodological and procedural decisions to be made and defended.

Other students who choose the systematic replication route sometimes have trouble understanding the difference between *replicating* a study's methods and *plagiarizing* parts of a manuscript. For this reason, it is critical to distinguish the two. Purposeful and transparent replication of a research team's methods and procedures requires appropriate levels of citation and clear descriptions of which components were based on prior studies and which ones were not. Replication does not involve presenting words or ideas of another research team or author without giving credit (i.e., plagiarism; American Psychological Association [APA], 2020). Regardless of whether you plan to replicate prior studies, consulting resources on plagiarism (e.g., APA, 2020; university or college library resources such as https://researchguides.library.vanderbilt.edu/plagiarism) will help you credit others' work appropriately and ensure your written words are your own.

Classifying and Stating Research Questions

Research questions are stated explicitly in research proposals and empirical reports, as they serve critical functions for both study investigators and their audience. Research questions focus the investigator on the primary purpose of their study. They provide boundaries for making key decisions on participants, procedures, measures, and designs. Similarly, for readers and consumers of the research, research questions serve to orient them to the purpose and nature of the study, as well as provide them an opportunity to assess whether the study's methods allow the research questions to be addressed.

Experimental Research Questions

All studies using single case design have at least one experimental research question. By experimental research question, we mean the question that will be addressed via the single case design (i.e., will allow a conclusion about a functional relation). Experimental research questions should identify three main components: An independent variable, a dependent variable, and a participant description (Kennedy, 2005).

How research questions are stated can vary depending on whether the researchers are following an inductive or deductive approach to single case research (Johnson & Cook, 2019). Applied Behavior Analysis (ABA) has a long tradition of taking an *inductive* approach. That is, rather than test a falsifiable hypothesis about how an independent variable will impact a dependent variable, they lean on the dynamic nature of single case design to search for and find the environmental variables controlling the dependent variable. For this reason, inductive research questions are often framed as purpose statements (e.g., to identify what social consequences are reinforcing challenging behavior) or in non-directional terms (e.g., what is the effect of noncontingent attention on engagement?). Explicitly labeling your research question as inductive is useful because it has direct implications for how you will approach implementing the single case design (e.g., adapting or creating new experimental conditions mid-experiment, using a response-guided approach to phase change decisions; Ledford et al., 2023).

Over time, and especially as single case studies have become an accepted methodology for contributing to the evidence-based practice literature, *deductive* approaches to single case design have become more prominent. Under this approach, the primary aim is to test a prediction about whether a specific intervention is effective under certain conditions (Johnson & Cook, 2019). For this reason, deductive single case research questions should be stated in a directional and falsifiable form, such that the question can be answered *yes* or *no* (Ledford et al., 2023). For example, *Does self-monitoring increase levels of engagement for elementary students with attention disorders?* In many cases, it can also be useful to include a reference to the condition to which the independent variable is being compared. For example, *Relative to being seated in rows, does a small group seating arrangement increase rates of academic-related peer interaction for middle schoolers who are struggling academically?* Including a reference to the relative comparison helps clarify the difference between experimental conditions, and in doing so, further specifies the independent variable.

Primary experimental questions can also be classified according to how researchers conceptualize their independent variable(s) and what they hope to learn about the intervention(s) under study. This classification includes four main types of experimental research questions: Demonstration questions, comparison questions, parametric questions, and component analysis questions (Kennedy, 2005; see examples in Table 18.1).

Demonstration questions essentially ask: *Does this intervention work?* (deductive) or *What is the impact of this intervention?* (inductive). That is, they evaluate whether and how the presentation of an independent variable impacts one or more participant behaviors. For example:

Table 18.1 Example Research Questions by Type

Experimental	Descriptive
For young children with internalizing behaviors …	
Demonstration: Does the Stay-Play-Talk intervention increase duration of play with peer buddies?	Do the social networks of target children increase from pre-to post-intervention?
Comparison: Is Stay-Play-Talk more effective at increasing durations of peer play than 1:1 social skills practice with an adult?	What are early childhood educators' perceptions of the procedures and outcomes from each intervention?
Parametric: Does the Stay-Play-Talk intervention with two peer buddies lead to longer durations of play than Stay-Play-Talk with one peer buddy?	When given the option, which Stay-Play-Talk variation do participants choose?
Component analysis: Does the Stay-Play-Talk intervention with choice of peer buddy lead to longer durations of play than Stay-Play-Talk with teacher-assigned peer buddies?	Based on 1- and 3-month follow up observations, to what extent do increased durations of play maintain?

Note: These sample research questions were informed and adapted from Severini et al. (2019) and Taylor (2023).

Does the use of a systematic prompting procedure increase percentage of correct responses on math activities for kindergarten students with developmental delays? To address demonstration questions, the independent variable (e.g., prompting procedure) will be present in the intervention condition and absent in the baseline condition. Demonstration questions are not only simple and straightforward; they are critical questions to pursue when building evidence for new interventions, as well as identifying the boundary conditions of intervention effects via systematic replication (Tincani & Travers, 2018).

Comparison questions are applicable when two or more independent variables (i.e., interventions) are being evaluated. These questions essentially ask some form of: *Which one works better?* For example: *Does a most-to-least prompting procedure or a least-to-most prompting procedure lead to more efficient mastery of object identification for children with intellectual disability?* To address comparison questions, each independent variable will be assigned to a different experimental condition. Importantly, comparing effects of different interventions by applying them to the same participants comes with challenges (i.e., distinct threats to internal validity; see Chapter 3). Comparison questions should be reserved for situations in which each intervention already has some evidence to suggest it is effective. Comparison questions might also be appropriate when one or more interventions have a strong theoretical basis or are commonly used in practice. For these reasons, comparison questions are useful to guide recommendations on selecting interventions when multiple evidence-based (or theoretically-supported) options are available and to identify conditions in which one intervention may be more efficient or effective than another.

Parametric questions focus on the amount of the independent variable, essentially asking some form of: *Does more or less of this procedure work better*? Thus, parametric questions are essentially questions about intervention dosage. There are, however, many aspects of dosage that can be studied, depending on which dimensions of intervention are considered most relevant. Parametric questions might focus on the frequency of treatment sessions, duration of treatment sessions, number of opportunities to respond during teaching sessions, rates of reinforcement, percentage of correct implementation, or other quantifiable dimensions of intervention. For example: *Relative to a 20-minute schedule, does self-monitoring with self-reinforcement on a 10-minute schedule produce greater reductions in disruptive behavior for students referred for Tier 2 support?* Parametric questions are useful in helping us understand how much of a procedure or intervention must be present to achieve the desired effects.

Component analysis questions become relevant when the independent variable(s) of interest represent multi-component interventions (i.e., treatment "packages") and the goal is to understand the effects of interventions with or without certain active ingredients. Component analysis questions can be used to build interventions (i.e., *Does adding a component make this intervention more effective?*) or break them down (i.e., *Does the intervention still work if we take away a component?*). For example, to evaluate whether extinction is a necessary component of functional communication training, a component analysis question would be: *Does functional communication training with versus without extinction lead to greater reductions in challenging behavior for children with behavior disorders?*

Descriptive Research Questions
In addition to experimental research questions, single case studies often address one or more descriptive questions. These are still empirical questions, but ones that are not answered directly via the experimental design. Instead, these questions are addressed using descriptive data, often providing context to the primary study results or informing a related aspect of study quality. Because these questions are descriptive, and oftentimes exploratory, there is more flexibility in how they are stated. That is, they need not be stated in directional or falsifiable terms. In single case research, descriptive research questions commonly include questions related to social validity, procedural fidelity, maintenance of intervention effects, or generalization of intervention effects. For example, following an experimental comparison of two distinct teaching procedures, a research team might ask as a descriptive question: *When given the choice between the two teaching procedures, which procedure did participants choose?* Unless a separate experimental design was used to systematically evaluate and replicate choice patterns, results of this social validity question would not offer evidence of a functional relation, but would provide important contextual information about the acceptability of intervention procedures from the participant's perspective. Similarly, questions about the maintenance or generalization of intervention effects are descriptive questions when maintenance or generalization data are collected and interpreted at the end of a study, or collected and compared pre- and post-intervention (as opposed to throughout all experimental phases; see Chapter 6. Example descriptive research questions can be found in Table 18.1.

Callout 18.2 Classifying Research Questions from the Single Case Literature

Golden et al. (2023) stated the following four research questions in a study focused on training early childhood educators to use Pyramid Model practices:

1. Is training + text practice-based coaching effective for increasing teacher use of Pyramid Model practices?
2. Do teachers' use of targeted practices generalize to activities in which coaching was not provided?
3. Do teachers maintain use of Pyramid Model practices when coaching is removed?
4. Do teachers find the remote coaching package feasible, effective, and acceptable?

In this study, Research Question 1 was the primary experimental question (i.e., a deductive, demonstration question). Teacher use of Pyramid Model practices in the coaching context was the primary dependent variable collected throughout all experimental phases. Research Question 2 was a secondary experimental question. Teacher use of targeted practices was also measured intermittently in a separate context in which coaching was not provided. Though the intermittent data collection impacts the rigor with which this question was addressed, it is an experimental question because generalization data were collected in a way that allowed visual analysis of these data within and between experimental conditions. Research Questions 3 and 4 were descriptive questions addressing maintenance and social validity. Because these data were collected at the end of each experimental evaluation, they would not allow conclusions about functional relations. The maintenance and social validity data did, however, address empirical (and important) research questions related to study quality.

Table 18.2 Questions to Consider When Choosing a Research Question

Self-Check	Questions and Considerations
Content Expertise	Do I have the necessary content expertise (or access to content expertise via mentor or advisor) to address the research question?
Design Match	Is my research question a good match for single case design? Consider critical characteristics of single case design (see Chapters 1–3; 15).
Importance	Are one or more audiences outside my research community (e.g., practitioners, children, caregivers) likely to care about this research question? Do I and my colleagues/students/mentors consider this question important enough to invest collective time and resources to answer?
Access	Do I have access to the participants and/or settings needed to address the research question? Or access to colleagues/mentors who are positioned and willing to facilitate access?
Resources	Do I have the resources necessary to carry out the study well? Consider costs related to time, effort, equipment, data collection, training, implementation, and travel.

As a final word of advice on choosing research questions, we suggest consulting the list of questions and considerations in Table 18.2 before committing to a question you plan to address via single case design. If you can answer each question with *yes*, you are well-positioned to move forward with the proposal and study.

Writing Research Proposals

Why Write Research Proposals?

The purpose of writing a research proposal is to communicate a rationale and plan for a future study. Graduate students write proposals before conducting theses or dissertations. University faculty write research proposals when they apply for grants. Proposals are submitted to academic advisors, thesis and dissertation committees, funding agencies, and grant review panels where reviewers evaluate and share feedback on the significance, quality, and rigor of the proposed research. Such feedback provides proposal authors the opportunity to strengthen the proposed study before the research begins (or in the case of grant writing, revise their application to increase the likelihood of securing funding). Yet even before submitting proposals for review, the act of writing them can be of great value. The writing process, after all, is when the deepest thinking happens (Zinsser, 2006). A hole or flaw in your logic model might not become apparent until you draft your study rationale. It might not be until you create a procedural fidelity data collection form that you define—in clear and explicit terms—the critical components of your independent variable. Writing research proposals pushes us to critically engage with our own ideas, rationales, and methods before soliciting feedback from outside reviewers.

Primary Sections

Research proposals for theses and dissertations typically include two main sections: An introduction and method. The introduction sets the stage and presents a rationale for the proposed study; the method section presents a detailed plan for how the study will be carried out. Proposals for research grants often include additional sections (e.g., Personnel, Resources, Dissemination). Because these additional sections are often specific to requirements delineated by the funding agency (e.g., Institute of Education Sciences, National Institutes of Health), we focus our discussion on the introduction and method sections.

Introduction
Introduction sections serve two main functions. First, introductions *educate* the reader on the topic being studied. This is why authors often begin their introductions with facts or statistics informing the status of some challenging issue; definitions of important terms; descriptions of conceptual frameworks; or various other explanations that lay a foundation for the study. Second, introductions *persuade* the reader—not only on why they should care about the topic or issue at hand, but why and how the proposed study will meaningfully contribute to the extant literature.

Many scholars and students alike find introduction sections difficult to write (Silvia, 2015). One reason this is true is because introductions allow authors more freedom in determining the scope, sequence, and structure of content than other sections of a proposal or report. Method and results sections, for example, come with structures and outlines for what to say and where to say it. In contrast, there are many ways to craft one study's background and rationale. If you look closely at strong introductions, however, you will see they do have an internal structure. Recognizing this structure in other studies can be immensely helpful as you craft your own introductions.

Imagine the scope of your introduction as a funnel: Wide at the top and narrow at the bottom (Schimel, 2012; see Figure 18.1). The opening paragraph of your introduction should be broadest in scope—communicating to your audience the general issue or topic of study and why it is important. The last paragraph of your introduction should be narrowest in scope. This is where you state the purpose of your proposed study and list your research questions. The middle of the introduction can be the trickiest part, as this is where you must forge a path from the broader issue to the specific study you are proposing. It is in this middle part that you transition from summarizing what is already known to shining a light on what is unknown. The task, however, is not to provide an exhaustive summary of the literature on the topic (i.e., knowns) or an exhaustive summary of the questions that have yet to be answered (i.e., unknowns). Instead, the goal is to highlight the most relevant knowns and unknowns that build a case for the proposed study. Table 18.3 presents a summary and sequence of recommended introduction components that may serve as a useful guide when writing introductions.

Method
Most research proposal content is provided in the **method section**. This is where you will map out study activities from start to finish. In doing so, you will need to make a host of decisions on how you'll go about addressing each research question, from recruiting participants to visually analyzing graphed data. For readers and reviewers, method sections allow an independent

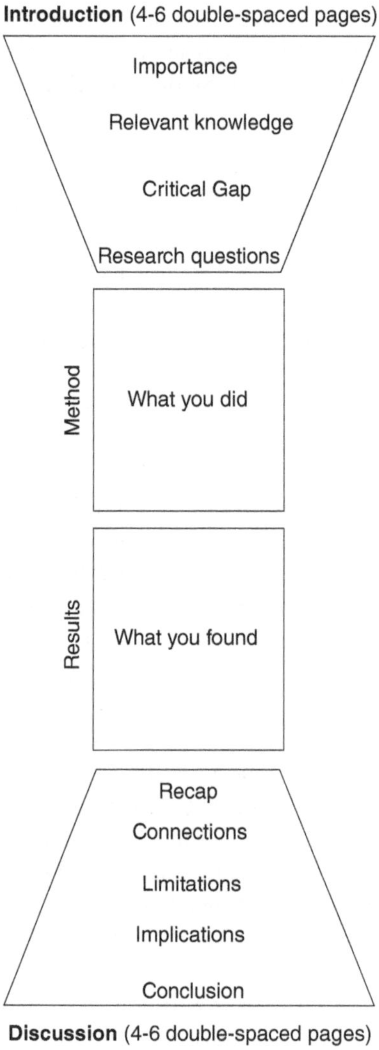

316 • Blair P. Lloyd and Kathleen Lynne Lane

Introduction (4-6 double-spaced pages)
- Importance
- Relevant knowledge
- Critical Gap
- Research questions

Method: What you did

Results: What you found

- Recap
- Connections
- Limitations
- Implications
- Conclusion

Discussion (4-6 double-spaced pages)

Figure 18.1 Visualization of the Scope and Sequence of an Empirical Report.

Source: Schimel, J. (2012). *Writing science: How to write papers that get cited and proposals that get funded.* Oxford University Press.

Table 18.3 Recommended Sequence and Structure for Writing Introductions

Introduction Components	Questions to Address
1. Importance	Briefly (1 paragraph), why is the general topic important?
2. Relevant Knowledge	What do we know from prior empirical research on this topic *that sets the stage for the proposed study*?
3. Critical Gap	What do we still not know *that the proposed study will address*?
4. Summary of rationale	Briefly (1–3 sentences), why is this study needed?
5. Purpose statement and research questions	What is the purpose of the study? What research questions will you address?

assessment of whether the proposed methods and procedures are appropriate given the questions they are designed to address. The more detailed the description of proposed methods and procedures, the more opportunity for meaningful feedback and the better prepared you will be to carry out the study.

With respect to form, method sections of research proposals should be written in active voice (to clarify *who* will do *what*) and in future tense, as these are proposed procedures that have not yet happened. For example, instead of writing "Timed-event count data were collected on student participation" (passive voice, past tense), write "Trained graduate research assistants will collect timed-event count data on student participation" (active voice, future tense). Using first-person pronouns (e.g., "I/We will randomly assign word sets to tiers") is also generally recommended over third person pronouns (e.g., "The first author/research team will randomly assign word sets to tiers") to acknowledge the role of the author in the research (APA, 2020; Silvia, 2015).

As mentioned above—and in contrast to introductions—the method section is defined by an internal structure and outline. Outlines vary by research methodology, but single case research proposals typically include the following components: Participants, Settings, Materials, Dependent Variables, Reliability, Experimental Design, Procedures, Procedural Fidelity, Social Validity, and Data Analysis. These components are typically presented in this (or similar) sequence. However, there may be cases where certain components are combined (e.g., Settings and Materials) or presented in different sequences (e.g., concluding with Experimental Design and Data Analysis) to allow more cogent and streamlined descriptions.

Although method sections of single case research proposals are lengthier than introductions, their built-in structure makes them relatively straightforward to write. There are, however, aspects of writing about *proposed* methods that can be tricky. You might wonder, for example, how to go about writing detailed descriptions of participants for a study that is months away from recruitment? Rather than trying to describe hypothetical participants, participant descriptions should focus on how you plan to recruit participants; what criteria you will set for study inclusion and exclusion; and what sources of information you will rely on to confirm each criterion is met. Inclusion criteria should focus on what critical characteristics, needs, or skills participants must have to benefit from the intervention or independent variable being evaluated. For example, a study evaluating a school-based social-emotional intervention for students with internalizing behaviors might identify a threshold score on the Student Risk Screening Scale for Internalizing and Externalizing (SRSS-IE; Drummond, 1994; Lane & Menzies, 2009) behaviors screening tool as a primary criterion for inclusion. Exclusion criteria typically relate to factors that might preclude the research questions from being answered adequately. For example, if the data collection schedule is set for 1–2 times per week, students with frequent school absences might be excluded based on their attendance records. In sum, your task in writing the *Participants* section is not to try and guess who your participants will be, but to describe the steps you will take to find them and confirm they meet relevant criteria to participate.

Another challenging aspect of writing proposed methods and procedures comes into play when certain study procedures will be individualized to each participant. You might wonder, for example, how to describe study materials in sufficient detail when the selection of those materials will depend on the results of a caregiver interview and preference assessment for each participating child. In cases where a critical aspect of a study will be individualized, it is important to describe the *process* for individualization. Again, rather than trying to describe hypothetical toys or materials, describe what steps the research team will take to select preferred items, perhaps providing a few examples for context. Information on process is what allows researchers to describe their methods with *replicable precision* (i.e., sufficient detail to allow other research teams to replicate their study).

Table 18.4 presents a series of questions that should be addressed for each component of the method section. This table can serve as a useful outline and guide to ensure critical information is included for each aspect of your study method. In addition to addressing these questions, we encourage preparing sample graphic displays that illustrate the proposed experimental design and include hypothetical data that show expected data patterns. Additional description of each method section component is provided in the next section (Writing Empirical Reports).

Table 18.4 Questions to Address for each Component of the Method Section

Method Component	Critical Questions to Address
Participants	How many participants do you plan to include? What steps will you take to recruit participants? What are your inclusion and exclusion criteria, and how will you determine each criterion is/is not met? Aside from measures related to inclusion or exclusion, what additional data will you collect to describe participants?
Setting	In what type of setting will your study take place? What are the critical physical and/or social characteristics of the environment where study procedures will take place? If aspects of the setting will be individualized, what process will you use to select the setting for each participant?
Materials	What materials are needed to implement experimental conditions? What non-experimental (i.e., uncontrolled) materials will likely be available for participants to engage with during sessions? What materials are needed for data collection? If any materials will be selected on an individual basis, what process will you use to select them?
Dependent Variables	What behaviors will you collect data on (include operational definitions, examples, and non-examples)? Do the measured behaviors represent context-bound behavior or generalized skills? How proximal (vs. distal) are they to the intervention (see Chapter 7)? What data collection method will you use, including parameters such as observation duration and context? What data collection tools (e.g., forms, software) will you use? Include templates when possible. If you have multiple dependent variables, which one will be used to make experimental decisions?
Reliability	How will you train observers to collect study data? How will you select sessions for inter-observer agreement checks? How will you define agreements vs. disagreements? What type of agreement index will you calculate, and how will you calculate it?
Experimental Design	What type of single case design will you use, and why? How will you address and/or monitor plausible threats to internal validity most relevant to your study? For aspects of the design that will not depend on study data (e.g., random assignment of participant to tier; block randomization for alternating treatments designs), how will you implement the design?
Procedures	In chronological order and with replicable precision, what research activities and experimental procedures will happen in the study? During each experimental condition, who will do what with whom for how long? When describing baseline procedures, focus on what will happen during baseline sessions (avoid repeating what will be measured). What variables will remain the same across conditions (control variables)? What variables will change between conditions (independent variables)?

(Continued)

Table 18.4 Continued

Method Component	Critical Questions to Address
Procedural Fidelity	How will you measure procedural fidelity? Which planned behaviors or events will you collect data on per condition? Do the planned behaviors or events include both independent and control variables? What method of data collection will you use? Include templates when possible. How often will you collect procedural fidelity data (per condition, participant, implementer)? How will you calculate and summarize fidelity data? If research participants will serve as primary implementers, how will you train them? How will you check their understanding of the implementation procedures? How will you measure the fidelity of your training procedures?
Social Validity	If one or more of your research questions relates to social validity: How will you measure social validity? When will you measure social validity, and using what type of instrument or data collection method? What aspect of the intervention (e.g., goals, procedures, outcomes) is the measure designed to inform?
Data Analysis	How often will you graph data? How will you make decisions for moving to a different phase? What potential modifications will you make if planned criteria are not met? What visual data characteristics will you analyze (or what visual data patterns do you hypothesize)? How will you monitor reliability (inter-observer agreement) throughout the study? What level of agreement will be considered acceptable, and what will you do if the agreement falls below this criterion? How will you monitor procedural fidelity throughout the study? What level of fidelity will be considered acceptable, and what will you do if fidelity falls below this criterion?

Writing Empirical Reports

Why Write Empirical Reports?

Whereas research proposals communicate a rationale and plan for a future study, empirical reports are written once the study has concluded to present and discuss the primary findings. Empirical reports include master's theses, doctoral dissertations, and manuscripts submitted to peer-reviewed journals for publication. Writing and disseminating results of high-quality single case research is essential for building evidence bases that impact practice, policy, and future scientific inquiry.

Primary Sections

Empirical reports include the following main sections: Abstract, introduction, method, results, discussion, and supplemental material. For each of these sections, we describe what content to include and offer guidance on how to make each section most effective in communicating key aspects of single case research.

Abstract

The **abstract** provides a concise and accurate summary of the study. Abstracts include information on the study's primary purpose, key features of the methods (e.g., participants, experimental design), a summary of key findings, and a statement about study implications. Writing abstracts is no simple task, given they often come with strict word limits (e.g., 250 words). Yet it is a critical section, as the abstract is a reader's first impression (and sometimes only impression) of your study. For this reason, the abstract must provide an accurate depiction of the study, without over-stating or over-simplifying outcomes. Given word limits, each statement of the abstract must be specific to the study it summarizes; general statements that could apply to any other study (e.g., "Implications and future directions are discussed") should be avoided or replaced with a specific implication or future direction.

Introduction
The purpose, components, and structure of introductions for research proposals (see *Writing Research Proposals* section) also apply to introductions for empirical reports. In fact, a benefit of writing a well-articulated proposal rationale—especially those including a logic model or theory of change—is that there is typically little to change after the study has concluded. New and relevant research might emerge, however, in the time it takes to complete the study. Such research, as well as any meaningful changes or developments in legislation, practice, or policy, should be incorporated. Additionally, purpose statements and research questions should be revised from future to past tense now that the study has concluded.

In addition to the components highlighted in Table 18.4, it is important that introductions include relevant and recent citations to primary sources (i.e., data-based studies, including single case studies). That is, when making claims about the status of a particular issue in the field, or whether certain interventions are or are not effective, it is important to cite the original, data-based sources that support those claims, rather than citing other articles that summarized those studies. For example, if you state that challenging behavior is a barrier to the delivery of effective instruction in classrooms, you might cite studies that present data from teacher surveys on perceived barriers to teaching effectively. Or, you might cite observational studies showing lower rates of instructional interactions between teachers and students with challenging behavior relative to students without challenging behavior. Either type of data-based citation would be preferred over citing articles in which authors stated a similar point in their introduction. In addition, it is important to always directly consult each source you cite. Avoid citing sources summarized or cited by other authors without consulting those sources yourself. Sometimes studies are cited inaccurately, and you want to steer clear of replicating such errors.

Method
The **method** section of an empirical report provides an accurate and comprehensive description of study activities, promoting both transparency and replicability. That is, readers of a strong method section should come away with a clear enough understanding of what took place to be able to replicate (to a reasonable degree) the study's methods and procedures. All method components and corresponding questions to address for research proposals (see Table 18.4) also apply to method sections of final reports. However, the verb tense should shift from future to past and revisions should be made across all method components to reflect any deviations from planned procedures—making sure to clearly articulate what actually occurred in the study. Below, we provide descriptions of what each component of the method section typically includes, with emphasis on what content will likely be added or revised when shifting from a prior research proposal to an empirical report.

Participants. This section should include a description of all study participants. Study participants include those who received the intervention (e.g., students, children, caregivers, teachers) and those who delivered intervention (e.g., caregivers, teachers) or provided any other source of data for the study (e.g., blind raters for social validity measures, students from whom peer comparison data were collected). When working from a research proposal, make any necessary adjustments to descriptions of the process for recruiting or selecting participants, and if major changes were made (e.g., adjusting inclusion criteria), report what was changed and why. It is also important to report whether participant attrition occurred (e.g., student moved to another school, child stopped assenting to research visits) or if any participants were withdrawn by the research team, and why. When describing participants, include information most relevant to the study's independent and dependent variables (e.g., summary of baseline performance, communication skill repertoire, confirmation of motor imitation skills). Participant characteristics are often summarized in table form to conserve space and facilitate easy reference by readers.

Setting. The setting section should describe the location of all experimental procedures and conditions, including where all types of study data were collected; where assessment procedures were conducted; and where the independent variable was implemented. Relevant physical and social characteristics of the setting should be reported. These might include, for example, physical dimensions of an instructional context or the relative positioning of those implementing and receiving intervention (e.g., the teacher and student were seated across a table from one another). If quality measures (e.g., rating scales) or other descriptive setting indicators are available (e.g., a measure of classroom management practices for a classroom-based intervention; a Title 1 school), these indicators should also be reported.

Materials. This section should include a description of the materials, supplies, and equipment used to carry out the research. Materials include those required for (1) carrying out each experimental condition (e.g., toys, academic worksheets, visual schedules) and (2) collecting study data (e.g., video or audio recorders, observational software, paper-pencil data collection forms, timers). When published curricula or measures are used, their citations should also be included. In cases where the research team created critical study materials related to independent or dependent variables (e.g., generated word sets for reading instruction), a description of how those materials were selected or developed is warranted.

Dependent Variables. This section includes descriptions of the behaviors that were measured (i.e., operational definitions, examples, non-examples); the data collection system (e.g., timed event duration; 5-second momentary time sampling), and other relevant aspects of the measurement system (e.g., session duration, schedule of observations, whether data were collected live or from video recordings). If aspects of measurement procedures were based on prior studies, those studies should be cited. When a variety of behaviors are measured, definitions and examples may be presented in table form for efficiency. Copies of data collection forms, complete coding manuals, or screenshots of observational data collection software may be included as supplemental material (see *Supplemental Material* section).

Some aspects of the measurement procedures may change between writing the proposal and report; others may be individualized once participants and study contexts are known and other forms of data collection (e.g., interviews, observations) completed. When working from a research proposal, make sure operational definitions and all other facts of the measurement system accurately reflect how data were collected in the study.

Reliability. This section is sometimes included as a component of *Dependent Variables* and sometimes as a stand-alone section. The reliability section should include descriptions of how data collectors were trained, including whether they were required to meet a training criterion before collecting study data. Interobserver agreement (IOA) assessment methods should be described, including how often IOA was assessed, what formula was used to calculate the agreement estimates, and what levels of agreement were considered acceptable. Reliability data (e.g., percentages of agreement obtained) also are typically reported in this section, ideally with means and ranges by participant and experimental condition and for each dependent variable. Instances of below-threshold agreement may be pointed out and explained (e.g., 50% agreement in one session reflected a single disagreement for a low-rate behavior). Reliability data may also be summarized in table format (as part of the main manuscript or as supplemental material; see *Supplemental Material* section) for efficiency and easy reference.

Experimental Design. This section identifies and describes the experimental design used to address the primary research question. Often a citation to the design is included. It is important to describe the manner in which the design was implemented in the study. For example, if a multiple baseline design was used, it would be important to identify the number of tiers (i.e., opportunities to demonstrate an effect), whether the tiers represented participants, behaviors, or contexts, and whether data were collected concurrently or nonconcurrently across tiers. We encourage you to also include the rationale for selecting the proposed experimental design as well as how relevant threats to internal validity will be detected and/or addressed (Ledford et al., 2023). If aspects of the experimental design changed from what was planned in the proposal, be sure those changes are reflected in the design description—ideally with explanations for each modification.

Procedures. This section should include a detailed description of study procedures, beginning with how university and district (or other institutional approvals) were secured; how agencies or practitioners were contacted for recruitment; and how informed consent and assent were obtained. When writing this section, it is important to note the organizational structure can vary, but describing procedures chronologically is generally recommended. Keep in mind the level of detail should be sufficient to ensure anyone reading this section has a firm understanding of exactly what took place.

Each experimental condition should be described in its own labeled sub-section (e.g., Baseline, Stay-Play-Talk, Generalization). Sometimes—and especially in studies with three or more experimental conditions—a general procedures section is included that first describes procedures to be used across all experimental conditions (i.e., control variables; see Chapter 6). The description of the baseline condition (or probe condition) should focus on the procedures used, and when possible, the parameters (quantification) of those procedures (Lane et al., 2007). A common mistake in writing baseline condition descriptions—especially when baseline represents a business-as-usual context—is to reiterate what was measured in baseline rather than describing what actually happened during the condition (e.g., What instructions were teachers given prior to baseline sessions? What activities took place? How did teachers respond to disruptive behavior?). The description of intervention conditions should specify and describe the independent variable, including procedures and parameters used to implement the independent variable. Ideally, the only difference between the baseline and intervention conditions is the independent variable or the level at which the independent variable is used. However, if other factors differed across conditions, those too should be specified.

Procedural Fidelity. This section describes how implementation of study procedures were measured (see Chapter 6). This includes how often procedural fidelity data were collected, what data collection tools were used, and how percentages of fidelity were calculated. For studies including natural change agents (e.g., teachers were trained to deliver the intervention), procedures on how intervention agents were trained (including checks for understanding) should also be reported, as well as the degree to which those training procedures were implemented by the research team as planned (implementation fidelity; see Chapter 6). Procedural fidelity data (e.g., percentages of correct implementation) are sometimes reported in the method section and sometimes reported in the results section (often depending on whether one or more research question focuses on fidelity). Regardless of location, procedural fidelity percentages should be reported by participant and condition—and in some cases, by component (i.e., independent and control variables). As a general rule, the more fidelity percentages vary by participant, condition, or component, the more important it becomes to report fidelity at the level that displays such variability. Similar to IOA, procedural fidelity data can be summarized in table format (as part of the main manuscript or as supplemental material; see *Supplemental Material* section) for efficiency and easy reference.

Social Validity. When studies include research questions about social validity, this section should be included to describe how social validity was assessed. Descriptions of social validity measures should include which aspects of social validity were assessed (goals, procedures, effects; see Chapter 7), for whom, and when the assessment(s) occurred. If existing social validity measures were used, they should be cited. If the research team developed their own tool to assess social validity, they should describe the tool and indicate it was developed for the current study. Copies of social validity measures or protocols also can be included as supplemental material (see *Supplemental Material* section).

Data Analysis. For single case studies, the data analysis section includes aspects of both formative evaluation (i.e., analyzing data throughout the study to inform study decisions) and summative evaluation (i.e., analyzing data after the study to draw conclusions about results). With respect to formative evaluation, describe how the research team monitored IOA and procedural fidelity data. For example, how often were IOA and fidelity assessed? What levels were considered acceptable? What actions were taken if/when levels fell below this threshold? Another aspect of formative evaluation relates to how the experimental design was executed. For example, how often were data graphed and visually analyzed? What criteria or decision rules were used to change experimental conditions? With respect to summative analysis, and especially when applying a deductive approach, describe the expected data patterns (within and between conditions) and what patterns would be considered sufficient to demonstrate a functional relation (Ledford et al., 2023). As you review your proposed data analytic procedures, report any changes to the a priori plan, with explanations for why those changes were made.

Results

Whereas the method section explains what research activities took place, the purpose of the **results** section is to answer the research questions. With respect to form and structure, results sections are written in past tense and are often framed and organized by research question. For example, assume a study addressed the following research questions: (1) Does an interdependent group contingency increase levels of classwide engagement in K-2 classrooms? (2) To what degree of fidelity do K-2 teachers implement the interdependent group contingency? And (3) Do teachers continue to use the interdependent group contingency after the conclusion of the study? The results section for that study might be divided into the following three sections: *Impacts of Group Contingencies on Classwide Engagement*; *Teacher Implementation*; and *Social Validity*. In some cases, researchers begin their results section with a summary paragraph reporting results of IOA and procedural fidelity checks. However, most often information on IOA is reported in the method section, and information about procedural fidelity is reported in the results section—particularly when there is a research question related to implementation.

Results sections of experimental single case studies include figures (i.e., graphs) depicting session-by-session data within and across experimental phases. Data patterns depicted in these graphs are also described in the narrative, where the researcher (1) draws conclusions on the presence or absence of a functional relation and (2) defends their conclusions by pointing to the specific patterns in the data that demonstrate the functional relation (or lack thereof). In these descriptions, visual analysis terms and characteristics should be emphasized over condition means and ranges (see Chapter 8). We recommend against adding mean, median, or trend lines to graphed data, as they can interfere with visual analysis of within- and between-condition data patterns. To promote transparency, it is also important to report any unusual events that occurred during the experiment (e.g., extended absences, changes in implementer) that may have impacted data patterns.

When describing results of experimental research questions based on graphed data, the descriptions should be closely aligned to the experimental design and method used to demonstrate control. For example, if the study used a multiple baseline design across four participants and had two dependent variables, then results should be organized by dependent variable rather than by participant. This is because data patterns would need to be analyzed *across* participants (i.e., tiers) to address whether there was a functional relation for each dependent variable. On the other hand, if the study used A-B-A-B withdrawal designs and included four participants and two dependent variables, then results would likely be organized by participant. This is because data patterns would need to be analyzed *within* participant to determine the presence or absence of functional relations for each dependent variable.

Additional tables or figures are sometimes prepared to address descriptive research questions. For example, procedural fidelity data might be presented in a table to document percentages of correct implementation by participant, experimental condition, or component (i.e., independent and control variables). Social validity data might be presented in a table to document ratings by participant or item, or in a figure to depict the number of times each participant selected each intervention condition when given a choice. In such cases, relevant data patterns should also be summarized in text, though at a broader level than what is presented in the table or figure.

Because figures and tables feature prominently in the results sections of single case research, we recommend creating all figures and tables before writing the narrative portion of the results section. Doing so will help guide your data interpretation and inform how you summarize the results. Once you have drafted the results section, check to make sure you have only reported data patterns and answers to research questions, and not waded into explaining or interpreting the findings. Interpretation of study results is saved for the final section of the report: The discussion.

Discussion

The purpose of the **discussion** section is to interpret the study's results, situating findings in relation to the broader context of literature described in the introduction. Whereas the scope of the introduction can be visualized as a funnel (wide at the top, narrow at the bottom), the scope of the discussion section can be visualized as an upside-down funnel (narrow at the top, wide at the bottom; see Figure 18.1). The first paragraph of the discussion is narrowest in scope—often beginning with a brief recap of the study's purpose and answers to each research question. The last paragraph of a discussion (often labeled Conclusion) is the widest in scope. The concluding paragraph reminds the reader of the broader issue at hand (aligned in scope to the opening paragraph of the introduction) and summarizes the current study's contribution to the topic.

The middle part of the discussion should accomplish three main tasks: (1) connecting findings to the extant literature; (2) identifying study limitations; and (3) proposing implications for practice and/or future research. Each of these tasks can be tackled in sequence (as separate sub-sections) or integrated throughout the discussion by addressing all three for each study finding. Whichever method allows a more streamlined, cohesive, and concise presentation of ideas is the better approach.

When connecting study findings to the extant literature, speak to how study outcomes converge or diverge from those of previous related studies, and what might explain the similarities or differences in outcomes. In many cases, relevant studies cited in the introduction will be re-considered in light of the current study's findings.

The discussion of limitations should include an even-handed depiction of factors that impact the degree of confidence in answering the research questions. Every study has limitations, and it is the researcher's responsibility to apply the same degree of skepticism and curiosity to their own work as they do when examining other research. For each stated limitation, it is important to explain why it is a limitation, or how the limitation might impact interpretation of study results. You might also identify how the limitation could be addressed in future research. When writing about study limitations, however, we encourage you to consider the difference between primary limitations of the study and directions for future research. While some limitations may indeed underscore a need for another study addressing that limitation, limitations should be specific to answering the study's research questions. For example, when developing a new intervention, a research team might decide to have trained research staff implement the intervention to ensure the independent variable is delivered as planned. If the research question is whether this intervention—when implemented correctly—leads to some change in behavior, then the decision to have research staff as implementers is not a limitation. Whether the intervention would have shown the same effects when delivered by natural implementers (e.g., teachers, caregivers) is a different research question, and thus better classified as a direction for future research.

The degree to which avenues for future research and implications for practice are discussed depends on where the study falls on the continuum of basic to applied research, as well as how much research has already been done on the topic. For example, directions for future research are often emphasized over practical implications for translational studies that bridge basic and applied research, or studies that contribute to new or emerging areas of scholarship. For highly applied studies, or those building from extensive bodies of literature, practical implications for key audiences (e.g., special educators, behavior analysts, school administrators, families, policy makers) are often warranted. Of course, there are plenty of studies for which implications for research and practice are worthy of equal discussion.

Once you have drafted the discussion, we recommend reviewing it carefully to make sure all primary discussion points tie directly to a study finding, and that the study's outcomes and contribution to the literature have been neither overstated nor understated (Silvia, 2015).

Supplemental Material
Including supplemental material with manuscript submissions is becoming more common as open science practices gain traction in single case research (Cook et al., 2022). **Supplemental material** offers researchers a way to make materials that do not fit within journal article page limits available to readers. The intent behind including supplemental material is to promote both transparency and reproducibility of research. Common types of supplemental material include coding manuals, intervention protocols, data collection forms, or sample intervention materials. Spreadsheets with raw (e.g., session level) data might also be included to facilitate future meta-analyses (i.e., eliminating the need to manually extract data from figures). Fortunately, there are various mechanisms for sharing supplemental material. Some journals host supplemental content on their websites. There are also a number of online data repositories (e.g., Open Science Framework [OSF; https://osf.io]; Inter-University Consortium for Political and Social Research [ICPSR; www.icpsr.umich.edu/web/pages/) for sharing data and other study materials.

Considerations for Success

We conclude this chapter with a few additional considerations for success in writing single case research proposals and empirical reports.

1. *Begin every writing project with an audience and outlet in mind.* If the goal of writing is effective communication, then you'd better know who you're communicating with. For theses and dissertations, your academic advisor or doctoral committee might be

your first audience, but if you write with only those people in mind, they will likely be your only audience. Consider the broader audience you hope to reach (e.g., special education researchers, practicing behavior analysts, educational professionals involved in multi-tiered systems of support), by reviewing journal websites (see aims and scope, editorial board) and requests for applications from funding agencies. With respect to manuscript submissions, we recommend identifying 2–3 target outlets with overlapping audiences.

2. *Carefully attend to technical/formatting requirements.* If you are preparing a master's thesis or doctoral dissertation, read your university's guidelines early in the writing process. If you are preparing a manuscript to submit for publication, review your target journal's full set of editorial guidelines to avoid desk rejections. Attending to technical guidance provided by universities, publishers, and/or funding agencies on the front end will save you a great deal of time in editing and formatting prior to submission.

3. *Make time to read about writing.* Scientific writing may initially be challenging, but it does get easier when you take the time to learn about it. We have found a variety of guiding resources on writing useful over the years, including those focused on writing research proposals (e.g., Schimel, 2012; Walker & Pascoe, 2019), writing empirical reports (e.g., Silvia, 2015), and attending to writing style (e.g., APA, 2020; Baker, 1973; Zinsser, 2006). We also encourage you to review the scientific literature from the lens of a writer—not only to learn about the types of articles featured in various journal outlets, but to recognize models of effective writing strategies used by study authors.

4. *Engage in pre-writing activities.* Various pre-writing activities can facilitate the writing process by helping you separate the tasks of (1) deciding *what* to say and (2) figuring out *how* to say it. For example, drafting outlines of each manuscript section (especially introduction and discussion sections) and sharing them with advisors or co-authors can make sure everyone is on the same page with respect to content before anyone spends a lot of time and effort on drafting full sections. Similarly, creating visuals to organize your thoughts prior to writing can be helpful. These might include logic models or theories of change (see Chapter 6) to prepare before writing an introduction; or sketching out experimental designs, mapping study timelines, or creating data collection templates as you prepare to draft the method section. Especially for those who struggle with facing a blank page, starting with outlines and illustrations can take the pressure off while still allowing you to make progress by putting your ideas on the page.

5. *Review the paper with attention to style, typographical errors, and citations prior to submitting for review.* Once you are satisfied with the content of the paper, review it carefully with an eye towards style and form. Remove any unnecessary words or phrases (i.e., those that do not add meaning); simplify sentence structure for clarity; check for consistent use of active voice and tense throughout (especially for method and results sections); and review for typos, grammatical errors, and APA formatting errors. Additionally, check to make sure all sources referenced in the text, tables, and figures are included in the reference list *and* that all listed references are cited in the text, tables, or figures. These may seem like small or insignificant aspects of writing, but such errors and inconsistencies can distract readers from the content of the writing and are therefore critical to address.

Conclusions

Scientific writing is an essential part of the research enterprise. After all, what is the use of conducting single case experiments if we don't share what we learn with the rest of the field?

Learning to write research proposals and empirical reports requires time, practice, openness to feedback, and perseverance. Our hope is that this chapter's guidance empowers you to tackle these writing projects with confidence. Having a strong sense of the purpose, scope, structure, and content of each manuscript section will no doubt make the writing process easier and the final product stronger.

References

American Psychological Association. (2020). *Publication manual of the American Psychological Association* (7th ed.). https://doi.org/10.1037/0000165-000

Baker, S. (1973). *The practical stylist* (3rd ed.). New York: Thomas Y. Crowell Company.

Cook, B. G. (2014). A call for examining replication and bias in special education research. *Remedial and Special Education*, 35(4), 233–246. https://doi.org/10.1177/0741932514528995

Cook, B. G., Johnson, A. H., Maggin, D. M., Therrien, W. J., Barton, E. E., Lloyd, J. W., Reichow, B., Talbott, E., & Travers, J. C. (2022). Open science and single-case design research. *Remedial and Special Education*, 43(5), 359–369. https://doi.org/10.1177/0741932521996452

Drummond, T. (1994). *The Student Risk Screening Scale (SRSS)*. Grants Pass, OR: Josephine County Mental Health Program.

Fawcett, S. B. (1991). Some values guiding community research and action. *Journal of Applied Behavior Analysis*, 24(4), 621–636. https://doi.org/10.1901/jaba.1991.24-621

Golden, A. K., Hemmeter, M. L., & Ledford, J. R. (2023). Evaluating the effects of training plus practice-based coaching on teacher use of Pyramid Model practices. *Journal of Positive Behavior Interventions*. https://doi.org/10.1177/10983007231172188

Johnson, A. H., & Cook, B. G. (2019). Preregistration in single-case design research. *Exceptional Children*, 86(1), 95–112. https://doi.org/10.1177/0014402919868529

Kennedy, C. H. (2005). *Single-case designs for educational research*. Upper Saddle River, NJ: Pearson.

Lane, K. L., & Menzies, H. M. (2009). *Student Risk Screening Scale for Internalizing and Externalizing Behavior (SRSS-IE)*. Screening scale available at Ci3t.org/screening

Lane, K., Wolery, M., Reichow, B., & Rogers, L. (2007). Describing baseline conditions: Suggestions from research reports. *Journal of Behavioral Education*, 16, 224–234. https://doi.org/10.1007/s10864-006-9036-4

Ledford, J. R., Lambert, J. M., Pustejovsky, J. E., Zimmerman, K. N., Hollins, N., & Barton, E. E. (2023). Single-case-design research in special education: Next-generation guidelines and considerations. *Exceptional Children*, 89(4), 379–396. https://doi.org/10.1177/00144029221137656

Pritchett, M., Ala'i-Rosales, S., Cruz, A. R., & Cihon, T. M. (2021). Social justice is the spirit and aim of an applied science of human behavior: Moving from colonial to participatory research practices. *Behavior Analysis in Practice*, 15, 1074–1092. https://doi.org/10.1007/s40617-021-00591-7

Schimel, J. (2012). *Writing science: How to write papers that get cited and proposals that get funded*. New York: Oxford University Press.

Severini, K. E., Ledford, J. R., Barton, E. E., & Osborne, K. C. (2019). Implementing Stay-Play-Talk with children who use AAC. *Topics in Early Childhood Special Education*, 38(4), 220–233. https://doi.org/10.1177/0271121418776091

Silvia, P. J. (2015). *Write it up: Practical strategies for writing and publishing journal articles*. Washington, DC: American Psychological Association.

Taylor, A. L. (2023). *An adaptation of Stay-Play-Talk for young children with internalizing behaviors*. [Unpublished doctoral dissertation]. Vanderbilt University.

Tincani. M., & Travers, J. (2018). Publishing single-case research design studies that do not demonstrate experimental control. *Remedial and Special Education*, 39(2), 118–128. https://doi.org/10.1177/0741932517697447

Travers, J. C., Cook, B. G., Therrien, W. J., & Coyne, M. D. (2016). Replication research and special education. *Remedial and Special Education*, 37(4), 195–204. https://doi.org/10.1177/0741932516648462

Walker, H. M., & Pascoe, S. M. (2019). *Foundations of grant writing: A systemic approach based on experience*. Eugene: University of Oregon.

Zinsser, W. (2006). *On writing well: The classic guide to writing non-fiction*. New York: HarperCollins Publishers.

19
Conducting Systematic Reviews and Syntheses

Kathleen Lynne Lane, Eric Alan Common, Blair P. Lloyd, and Jennifer R. Ledford

Important Terms

published literature, peer-reviewed, gray literature, electronic search, search terms, Boolean operators, backward searching, forward search

Table of Contents

Literature Reviews
Approaches and Procedures
   Types of Literature Reviews
   Process of Conducting Literature Reviews
      Selecting the Topic
      Focusing the Topic
      Locating Relevant Sources
      Reading and Coding Relevant Reports
   Organizing Findings and Writing the Review
   Using the Literature Review
PRISMA Guidelines
   PRISMA 2020 Statement, Checklist, and Flow Diagram
   PRISMA Protocol
   PRISMA Extensions
Considerations for Success
Conclusions
References

Callout

   19.1   *Literature Review for Informing Proposals and Reports vs. Stand-Alone Studies: What's the Difference?*

DOI: 10.4324/9781003294726-22

People conduct research for several reasons. For example, someone may conduct a study to satisfy their curiosity about how best to increase a students' written expression skills (Little et al., 2010) or the degree to which incorporating instructional choices increases students' engagement (Ennis et al., 2020a). Other studies may be conducted to solve a challenge such as addressing learning loss and helping students manage anxious feelings as their educators navigate the pandemic (Lane, Oakes et al., 2021). Still, other studies may be conducted to inform policy, such as the role of artificial intelligence in supporting student learning. In each case, conducting a single study or programmatic line of inquiry begins with understanding what lessons have been learned to date. This process begins with a comprehensive literature review to understand what the field already knows about your topic and questions of interest.

Literature Reviews

Reviewing the literature on a topic or question of interest is a worthy endeavor. Conducting a comprehensive literature review enables you to not only discover what is known about a particular topic but also learn about *how* it has been studied. For example, what types of research designs have been used? How has a particular intervention been defined and taught to implementers? How have accuracy of implementation and student performance been measured? What are the implications for practice—and policy decisions—based on the overall body of evidence on a strategy, practice, or program? What are the limitations and directions for future research noted by authors who have conducted previous studies? By exploring these types of questions during the review process, the curious researcher or practitioner benefits from lessons learned by those who have explored the topic before them. They can use this information to refine their purposes, research questions, procedures, and outcome measures in the next study advancing this line of inquiry. In short, conducting comprehensive literature reviews allows the benefit of looking back to learn from prior inquiry, build on existing knowledge, and answer new questions (see Chapter 18).

Literature reviews generally serve three main purposes. First, they inform what is known and what is unknown about a given topic. Second, they help build the logical argument or rationale for a study (or line of inquiry). And third, they inform plans for future studies (e.g., such as when writing proposals, see Chapter 18) by noting successes (e.g., designs, measures, and procedures) and areas for refinement (e.g., building on limitations of previous studies). While sometimes literature reviews are conducted for these purposes—to inform research proposals and reports—in other instances, literature reviews *are* the study of interest (see Allen et al., 2020; Buckman et al., 2021; Common et al., 2020; Royer et al., 2017). In Callout 19.1, we provide additional information on distinctions between literature reviews conducted to frame proposals and reports and *systematic* literature reviews as stand-alone studies.

Callout 19.1 Literature Review for Informing Proposals and Reports vs. Stand-Alone Studies: What's the Difference?

Literature reviews can be conducted to (1) inform the framing of research proposals and reports or (2) systematically address one or more research questions about empirical literature (i.e., systematic literature review). While there are similarities in process for both types of reviews (part of a proposal or report vs. stand-alone studies), they differ in how the literature is described, how they are used, as well as how they are featured in final products. For example, introductions to studies (e.g., articles, book chapters, proposals,

> and dissertations) feature less detailed information about how studies were located than do stand-alone reviews, which provide extensive details to enable others to replicate the review in the future. Introductions also typically only use a subset of studies, which best illustrate the need for the relevant study, while stand-alone reviews offer a more comprehensive analysis. This difference also results in differences in manuscript length. Whereas introductions to studies may be four to six pages in length (double spaced), systematic reviews are often approximately 40 pages in length (double spaced inclusive of: Title page, abstract, introduction, method, results, discussion, references, tables, and figures). The primary purpose of a review for an introduction section is to *justify* the need for the single case study. The primary purpose of a stand-alone systematic literature review is to provide new knowledge for the field about a particular topic.

The focus of this chapter is on conducting comprehensive, systematic reviews of single case literature. Systematic literature reviews require detailed and comprehensive plans to identify, select, and evaluate research studies to address one or more research questions related to empirical literature (e.g., treatment-outcome studies). In this way, systematic literature reviews themselves are a form of empirical research—data are collected from the studies included in the review. Specifically, in this chapter we (1) describe approaches and procedures for conducting literature reviews, (2) detail how to conduct systematic reviews using PRISMA (Page et al., 2021), and (3) offer considerations for conducting successful literature reviews.

Approaches and Procedures

We begin this chapter by providing an overview of the various types of literature reviews. Then, we explain the procedures involved in conducting a literature review, including guidance for organizing your findings, writing the actual review, and explaining how to use the information you have learned.

Types of Literature Reviews

There are many types of academic writing: Chapters, manuscripts detailing research studies, masters' theses, doctoral dissertations, monographs, as well as systematic reviews. Each necessitates a comprehensive overview of the literature, including a review of the major theories, concepts, and findings in the field. In fact, across the American Psychological Association (APA, 2020) and their style guide Journal Article Reporting Standards (JARS), emphasis is placed on reviewing relevant scholarship across all types of research (quantitative, qualitative, and mixed methods). Originating from healthcare (Cochrane et al., 1980; Sackett et al., 1977) and education fields (Glass, 1976; Slavin, 1977), two types of evidence synthesis emerged in the 20th century: Systematic reviews and meta-analyses.

While systematic reviews and meta-analyses are the reference standard for synthesizing evidence in health, education, and other related fields for their methodological rigor, there remains a range of stand-alone literature review types disseminated across the behavior sciences. Specific examples include: Narrative review, systematic review, scoping review, rapid review, umbrella review, and meta-analysis (see Table 19.1 for definitions and examples).

Table 19.1 Types of Reviews: Characteristics and Examples

Type of Review	Characteristics	Example
Narrative	Mainly descriptive and focus on a subset of studies selected based on author selection and/or availability. May or may not follow Journal Article Reporting Standards (JARS).	Lerman and Vorndran (2002) reviewed basic and applied findings on punishment and discussed the significance of pursuing additional investigations in this domain.
Systematic	Detailed and comprehensive plan to identify, select, and evaluate research studies on a specific question (or questions). Exhaustive, rigorous, and described with replicable detail while reporting indicators of trustworthiness.	Common et al. (2020) exhaustively identified studies with increasing students' teacher-delivered opportunities to respond while synthesizing the characteristics and methodological quality of included strategies, classifying the evidence base, and reporting the magnitude of effects across methodologically sound studies.
Scoping	Subset of systematic review, purpose is to map the body of literature on a topic area. Exhaustive and rigorous (see systematic).	Buckman et al. (2021) exhaustively identified studies with primary prevention components within tiered systems while synthesizing the extent to which treatment integrity was monitored and reported.
Rapid	Subset of a systematic review, within a predetermined time constraint. May not be exhaustive in nature but maintains rigor and is described with replicable detail while reporting indicators of trustworthiness.	Bell and Foiret (2020) examined the extant literature on assistive technology and education for students with hearing impairment while synthesizing experimental research.
Umbrella	Subset of a narrative or systematic review that focuses on other systematic reviews. Exhaustive and rigorous.	Riden et al. (2022) synthesized systematic reviews or meta-analyses of interventions for students with or at-risk for emotional/behavioral disorders and summarizing the evidence base of all previously reviewed interventions research
Meta-analysis	Subset of systematic review, purpose is to use statistical methods to combine the results of multiple studies (e.g., calculate average effect sizes) to answer research questions. Exhaustive and rigorous.	Ledford and Pustejovsky (2023) evaluated the magnitude of effects of Stay-Play-Talk towards improving social behavior of young children. In addition to synthesizing study and participant characteristics and methodological rigor, they calculated average effect size and determined the distributions of effects.

Across the behavior sciences, systematic reviews can answer a range of questions, but have become a major driver towards identifying and summarizing the evidence base of interventions (i.e., strategies, practices, programs). These systematic reviews often (1) conduct quality appraisals of the methodological strengths and consistency of findings of studies constituting a knowledge base and (2) assess the overall body of literature reviewed to draw meaningful conclusions that inform practice as well as future research (Lane, Common, et al., 2022; Maggin et al., 2017; Manolov et al., 2017). As you might imagine, each type of review listed in Table 19.1 fulfills an important contribution to the field. As time permits, we encourage you to read some of the cited example reviews to familiarize yourself with each type of review.

We also want to point out that while meta-analyses provide important contributions to the field by quantifying the magnitude of the impact of various interventions (e.g., functional assessment-based intervention; Common et al., 2017; Umbreit et al., 2023), procedures and recommendations for conducting meta-analyses are changing rapidly. As such, current guidance may likely become dated soon after this chapter is published. In particular, issues related to computing effect sizes for treatment-outcome studies conducted using single case research design (SCRD) methodology remain in a state of flux with rapidly changing developments, refinements, and critiques in the research community as we write this chapter (e.g., Chen et al., 2023; Maggin et al., 2022). If you are considering conducting a meta-analysis that involves reviewing treatment-outcome studies conducted using SCRD, we encourage you to seek input from scholars with meta-analytic expertise, describe your methods with replicable precision, and justify your decisions theoretically and empirically with the best available evidence.

In this chapter we focus on how systematic reviews can be used broadly, with emphasis on evaluating the methodological rigor of single case literatures. Moreover, we provide explicit guidance on conducting, writing, and disseminating systematic literature reviews as stand-alone studies. Our goal is to facilitate dissemination of your article. When considering preparing a systematic review of the literature as a stand-alone article, consider what the final product will include. Many journals include author guidelines with specifications for original research articles—and sometimes more specifically literature reviews—which include page or word limits (APA, 2020). We will discuss the sections of a manuscript later in this chapter yet wanted to be clear: This is a study requiring substantial time and other resources.

Process of Conducting Literature Reviews

As you might expect, the process of reviewing the literature involves several steps. Steps include: (1) selecting a topic, (2) focusing that topic, (3) locating relevant sources, (4) reading and coding relevant reports, and (5) sorting reports by rigor and quality. In the sections that follow, we provide guidance for carrying out each of these steps. As you learn more about systematic reviews, in addition to resources like this chapter, there are also free-access and commercially available resources to support various stages of the literature review process. Some examples of free-access tools include Abstrackr (Wallace et al., 2012) and citationchaser (Haddaway et al., 2022). These tools support screening abstracts and locating relevant sources through ancestral searches (described subsequently). REDCap and Covidence are examples of commercially available programs. REDCap (Harris et al., 2009) is a web-based application for building and managing online forms and databases, which can be used throughout the systematic search (from article procurement to coding). Covidence is a commercially available cloud-based platform that facilitates various aspects of systematic reviews and meta-analyses (e.g., importing citations, screening titles and abstracts, uploading references, screening full texts, extracting data, analyzing risk of bias). Rayyan (Ouzzani et al., 2016) is a similar web and mobile application with free student and professional memberships. Helpful materials for organizing searching and coding are also available on the website for the Comprehensive Integrated Three-Tiered Model of Prevention (Ci3T; www.ci3t.org/practice). Whichever resources help you plan and organize your coding, once done, you will be ready to organize and write up the outcomes of the review and disseminate the lessons learned.

Selecting the Topic
Selecting a research topic is both exciting and challenging. It is exciting because conducting a high quality, comprehensive, systematic review allows you to satisfy your curiosity about something that interests and inspires you. It is challenging because you are likely interested in a range of topics, or perhaps have multiple questions about a given topic. There will be moments in conducting the literature review when you might ask yourself: Why am I doing this!? The process of searching systematically to make sure you have located all studies on a particular topic, checking the accuracy of your article selection, developing detailed plans for how you will code each article, checking the accuracy of your coding, keeping track of the full set of details for each step, summarizing these steps in a way others could replicate, and then

analyzing, reporting, and interpreting what you learned requires time and effort. At times, it may feel tedious. Therefore, it is important to pick a topic that holds meaning for you and the mission of your work. As you explore the various topics of interest, be certain to determine as soon as possible if someone else was equally inspired and already completed and published a similar review. If so, you may need to ask yourself how your review extends the literature (e.g., different research question, re-analysis, replication, and extension) or you may decide you want to select a novel topic of interest.

If you are not yet certain as to what inspires you: Read! Read journal articles, special issues, and textbooks, as well as listen to podcasts in your field to see what sparks your interest. Sometimes a single article may inspire you to ask the question: "I wonder if …," launching your journey of learning more about what has been done on this topic. In addition to reading, engage! Consider talking with professionals who share similar interests about what led them to focus on specific areas of inquiry. You might look for professional organizations such as the Council for Exceptional Children Division for Research (CEC-DR) to find your intellectual home or professional community. It may be through attending a conference session or informal conversations with colleagues that you might find your topic of interest for your systematic literature review.

Focusing the Topic
Often the selected topic of interest is quite broad (e.g., how to implement reading interventions during remote instruction, how to manage anxious feelings in the pandemic era, or how to support families in teaching self-determined behaviors to their children). Each topic is important and interesting, but volumes have been (or could be) studied and written about them. It is important to focus the scope of the literature review to be manageable. While there is no exact minimum and maximum number of studies to be included in a literature review, Wolery et al. (2018) suggested systematic reviews are more manageable with fewer than 30 sources (e.g., studies, including dissertations), but at least ten to warrant the synthesis. However, it is possible the research questions of interest will lead to systematic reviews examining fewer than 10 (e.g., Allen et al., 2020) or more than 30 sources (e.g., Chow & Ekholm, 2018; Torelli et al., 2022). What matters is whether you have an exhaustive search, can answer the research questions, and have sufficient data for drawing conclusions that will be interesting to the field.

There are a range of approaches to narrowing the topic. One approach is to brainstorm a list of questions to focus the topic. For example, if you are interested in learning more about the role of instructional choice, you might generate questions such as: What types of instructional choice interventions have been evaluated to increase task engagement in elementary classrooms? For what types of students have instructional choice interventions been evaluated? Which type of instructional choices—within or across task activities—are more effective at increasing engagement for students receiving special education services for emotional disturbances? As these questions are generated, one may spark your interest for the review, providing guidance for the refined focus. *Remember, not all questions of interest can be answered with a single review.*

A second approach to focusing the topic is to anchor the review to a specific strategy, practice, or program (i.e., independent variable). Reviews anchored to independent variables can answer important questions about whether and to what degree a given intervention works. For example, Ledford and Pustejovsky (2023) reviewed studies evaluating the effects of peer-mediated (i.e., Stay-Play-Talk) interventions (independent variable) on social behaviors of young children. Similarly, Royer et al. (2017) examined the role of coaching in supporting teachers to use behavior-specific praise in K-12 classrooms.

A third approach to narrowing the topic is to focus on a specific behavior or skill (dependent variable), like student engagement, peer initiations, social interactions, or elopement. For example, Ledford and Gast (2006) conducted a systematic literature review on interventions for feeding problems in children with autism. Lane, Bruhn, and colleagues published a systematic review of functional assessment-based interventions designed using a systematic approach (Umbreit et al., 2007) to support students exhibiting challenging behavior. Chazin et al. (2022) conducted a systematic literature review of interventions designed to address escape-maintained challenging behavior. Across these reviews, the intervention strategies may have varied, but they all targeted the same type of behavior.

As an alternative to focusing on independent or dependent variables, a fourth approach involves focusing on other elements such as methodology. For example, Odom and Strain (2002) conducted a systematic review of studies using SCRD for a specific set of recommended practices. Peltier et al. (2022) conducted a brief systematic review to evaluate graphical displays of data from SCRD in the field of EBD. Snodgrass et al. (2022) conducted a scoping review of recommendations to increase the rigor of social validity assessment in intervention research. Buckman et al. (2021) mapped the literature in a similar scoping review focusing on the use of treatment integrity measurement of primary (Tier 1) prevention efforts within tiered systems.

A fifth approach is to focus the review on a specific time frame. The time frame is not selected for convenience purposes, but instead due to an important marker such as (1) a previously published systematic review (e.g., Common et al., 2017; Lane et al., 2009), (2) publication of a formative paper or advancement (e.g., a review of treatment integrity of Tier 1 practices, building from the date treatment integrity was introduced; Buckman et al., 2021), or (3) a critical event (e.g., litigation, legislation, policy) such as the passage of the Individuals with Disabilities Education Improvement Act (IDEA, 2004; e.g., Lane et al., 2012). To elaborate on time frame considerations, Lane et al. (2012) reviewed studies examining teacher expectations for student behavior and organized their findings from the passage of P.L. 94-142 to IDEA (1997) and studies following the IDEA reauthorization (1997). Across time frames, the rights of students with disabilities shifted from initial access to special education services to prioritizing inclusion and access to the general curriculum. This allowed the authors to reflect on shifts in teacher perceptions around behavior expectations for the classroom.

Finally, some reviews focus on a specific dissemination context, such as specific scientific journals or disciplines within a field. This approach has been used for many years. However, this strategy may be less useful for answering comprehensive questions, but appropriate for answering questions about the state of a particular journal (e.g., To what extent do studies in this journal do X?) as a proxy for changes over time in a given field, or the current state of practice for that field (see, for example, a commentary on ecological validity in the field of behavior analysis; Fahmie et al., 2023).

Collectively, these represent common approaches for identifying and appropriately narrowing the topic of systematic literature reviews. In some instances, you might apply two or more of these approaches. For example, Pérez et al. (2023) conducted a review of professional learning related to the use of behavior-specific praise (anchoring to dependent variable) while also building from prior systematic reviews of behavior-specific praise conducted by Ennis and Royer (e.g., Ennis et al., 2020b; Royer et al., 2019). In other cases, it is not until the review is underway that you realize the scope of studies is too broad. In such cases, it will be important to refine the research question of interest using a second approach or other contextual factors (e.g., age or diagnosis of participants, setting, or implementers). For example, Lloyd et al. (2019) focused their systematic review of function-based interventions on those implemented by school personnel in K-8 general education settings.

You might also apply other distinct approaches to focusing your literature review based on the factors motivating your review and your primary research questions. There are even ways to conduct a systematic review beyond your typical academic dissemination outlets. For example, Briesch et al. (2020) reviewed state department of education websites as their records of interest to understand guidance afforded to local education agencies around the behavioral component of tiered systems. More recently, Fleming and Cook (2022) synthesized special education journal website guidelines as their record of interest to summarize the state of open access polices within their field of study.

Locating Relevant Sources

After the topic is narrowed, the next step is to begin the search procedures to locate all relevant sources (i.e., records)—and do so accurately as measured by reliability of the article selection procedures. This step requires a sound organizational structure and precise record keeping towards ensuring you find all relevant sources, enabling you to describe what is known about a topic and answer the research questions of interest (e.g., To what extent is precorrection an evidence-based practice according to CEC [2014] quality indicator standards?).

Before you start searching, build on the work you did to focus your topic by identifying inclusion and exclusion criteria to determine which sources to keep, and which ones to eliminate. Inclusion criteria refer to the specific characteristics each study must have to be included in the review. Exclusion criteria refer to specific factors or characteristics that, when present, make the study ineligible (i.e., excluded from the review). Each set of criteria vary according to the research question(s) posed. For example, if you are interested in how well an intervention works in inclusive classroom settings, you would exclude studies conducted in self-contained classrooms.

Typical inclusion and exclusion criteria tend to focus on: Type of study (e.g., including experimental studies, excluding descriptive studies), source (e.g., peer-reviewed articles or dissertations included, chapters and conference proceedings excluded), and population (e.g., including students with emotional and behavioral disorders educated in inclusive settings, excluding students who are typically developing). When applying these criteria, keep in mind some articles include more than one study (e.g., Study 1 and Study 2). In some cases only one of two studies featured in an article will meet inclusion criteria. In addition, reviews may only include studies from articles written in English given researchers may not be fluent in other languages. As discussed previously, other reviews may include a specific year to inform inclusion and exclusion criteria, to focus on inquiry conducted before or after a critical point in history, a pivotal article, or a previous systematic review. Each decision needs to be justifiable and may lead to limitations that need to be addressed in the discussion. For example, if grey literature (e.g., dissertations and theses) are excluded, this may lead to risk of publication bias. Or the exclusion of non-English language may diminish the exhaustiveness of the extant record and provide an incomplete picture.

The *data* for a systematic literature review may include unpublished and/or published records aligned to answer your research questions. **Published literature** includes studies that are officially distributed, generally via **peer-reviewed** articles in academic journals. These sources include articles submitted to a journal and reviewed by members of an editorial board (e.g., editor, associate editor, two to three reviewers), usually with a double-blind process, to determine whether the study is sufficiently internally valid and useful to the relevant field to warrant publication. Published, peer-reviewed literature is generally the most highly regarded source of information for systematic reviews. **Grey literature** refers to information not published in a peer-reviewed outlet, with the most common relevant sources for single case reviews being doctoral dissertations and master's theses. The advantage of records focusing on peer-reviewed articles is they have been vetted by the scientific community. Masters' theses and doctoral dissertations are developed with input from committee members, but sometimes evaluations and feedback from well-intended committees may be less rigorous than those specified by rigorous journal outlets (although some data suggest that these unpublished sources are not—on average—less rigorous than their published counterparts; Dowdy et al., 2020). The primary advantage of including gray literature in systematic reviews is to counteract publication bias, which can considerably impede our ability to accurately summarize available data in a given area (Cook, 2016). Other contributions to the literature such as conceptual pieces, other reviews, descriptive or correlational studies, and case studies provide important background information, but are not typically included as part of the *data* evaluated to answer the research questions.

When establishing inclusion and exclusion criteria, remain focused on answering the proposed questions—not convenience. A well-constructed search is the one yielding sufficient data to answer the questions related to the topic of interest. After inclusion and exclusion are established, write a detailed description of each. This information is first detailed in a code book, and then later included in the Method section when the systematic review results are prepared. We recommend being as precise as possible and citing sample articles to illustrate the various criteria. For example, if a study was excluded because the participants included preschool students taught in a self-contained rather than inclusive classroom, you might cite the specific study (see ci3t.org/practice for tools to organize your search procedures).

In general, there are four components constituting a comprehensive, exhaustive search to locate all relevant articles: Electronic searches, ancestral searches, hand searches, and expert nomination (e.g., author searches, editor contacts; Lane et al., 2022). First, begin with an **electronic search** within reputable databases of scientific publications available in many university libraries such as PsycINFO and Education Resources Information Center (ERIC). You might also search Google Scholar, which often offers the complete articles of the identified sources. Yet, this advantage needs to be balanced against the limitations of variability and general lack of replicability of the search process, as Google Scholar algorithms shift regularly and a full accounting of the search is difficult to document. A strength of searching databases affiliated with university library subscriptions is that they tend to remain more consistent over time and the search features can be specified and replicated as a reliability check. Yet, when university budgets shrink, access to databases may also constrict. Be certain to select databases most relevant to your field of interest (see Lucas & Cutspec, 2005; McHugo & Drake, 2003 for additional detail). If including grey literature, target databases that include pre-prints (osf.io/preprints/), theses, and dissertations (ProQuest Dissertations & Theses Global).

Before launching into electronic searches, develop relevant **search terms**. Most databases include detailed guidance on selecting and entering terms to identify the largest number of relevant sources. For example, including the use of **Boolean operators** ensures derivatives of key words are included (e.g., using interven* to detect intervene, intervention, interventions, and intervening). Boolean operators typically allow for combining terms (e.g., terms related to intervention and participants of interest) to search more precisely (see Table 19.2 for an overview). Many databases enable study titles and abstracts to be extracted into Excel spreadsheets, which can be read to inform initial decisions about whether or not to read the article in full for consideration. We suggest searching at least two electronic databases, as the content will likely vary between the two. If you are at an institution with access to library services, many universities have content experts in accessing and exhaustively searching the literature. Some even include guides to support the search process (e.g., University of Michigan Library, 2023).

It is important to create structures and keep detailed records to organize and document each stage of the literature review, including search procedures (e.g., search terms used, full extraction of titles and abstracts). Doing so will prevent the need to repeat tasks unnecessarily, allows for reliability checks, and makes documenting and reporting your processes easier. Reliability checks are done to confirm whether another person who follows the same steps

Table 19.2 Overview of Boolean Operators

Title	Operator	Description	Example
And	AND	Retrieves results that include both search terms	student AND teacher will return results that contain both *student* and *teacher*
Or	OR	Retrieves results that include either search term	emotional disturbance OR emotional behavior disorder will return results that contain either *emotional disturbance* or *emotional behavior disorder*
Not	NOT	Excludes results containing the specified term	public NOT private will return results that do contain *public* and do not contain *private*
Phrase Search	" "	Retrieves results with the exact phrase specified within the quotation marks	"social skills training" will return results that contain *social skills training*
Wildcard	*	Matches any number of characteristics	behav* will return results that contain the word *behav* with any number of additional characters, such as *behavior*, *behaviour*, *behaviors* or *behave*.
Parentheses	()	Puts it all together and groups search terms within parentheses for complex queries	("behav* intervention plan" OR "treatment plan") AND ("functional behav* assessment" OR "functional analysis")?

makes the same (or very similar) decisions about which studies to include. For example, detailed records should be kept on (1) search terms used in each field; (2) how many sources were found on each search, as well as the exact listing of titles and abstracts; and (3) how many located sources (and which ones) met inclusion criteria. Replicate the search as soon as possible, with a different person conducting these same steps, and record what they found to compute reliability of each component.

Screening for eligibility of identified studies to see which studies meet your inclusion criteria typically happens in two stages: Title/abstract *screening* and full text review reading for *eligibility*. Because initial electronic database searches can return thousands of "hits," it is important to determine which criteria can be assessed based on reading titles and abstracts alone, versus which ones will require consulting the article's full text. For example, general information related to participant characteristics (e.g., age range, diagnoses) or settings (e.g., school vs. clinic) is often included in abstracts of single case studies. More nuanced inclusion criteria, such as those related to defining features of interventions, often require reading through the article's method and procedures. Starting with title/abstract screening allows you to screen out any studies that clearly do not meet one or more inclusion criteria based on content in the title and abstract alone. We encourage you to retain any studies that are unclear for full text review as it would be better to over-include rather than accidentally missing a relevant article. Once you have completed the title/abstract screening phase, you can then move on to reviewing full texts of the articles you screened in. Locate the full article for each reference, and conduct *full text reviews* to further determine which articles meet the full set of inclusion criteria, noting any excluded articles.

In addition to detailing search and screening information in your carefully constructed records, this information will be summarized and detailed in the written literature review (e.g., PRISMA flow diagram; described subsequently; see also Figure 19.1). The content

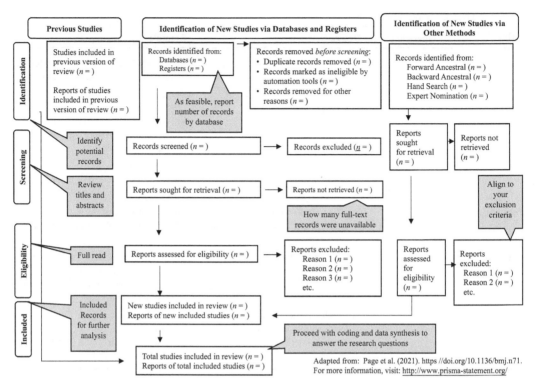

Figure 19.1 Exploring PRISMA 2020 Flow Diagram for Updated Systematic Reviews.

generated will be a master list of studies meeting inclusion criteria. It will also be important to document the reasons why records were excluded following the full-read for eligibility. Write this reference list in APA format, being careful to use the most recent APA guidelines (currently APA 7th edition; 2020).

Once you have identified included articles from the database search, use those articles to conduct an ancestral or bibliographic search. This can involve backward or forward searching. **Backward searching** involves reviewing the full reference list of each article you have previously deemed as eligible, to determine whether any articles that they cite also meet inclusion criteria yet were not identified from the database searches. Such articles may be published in outlets not indexed in the electronic database or may be relevant but may not have been detected during the electronic search due to unforeseen reasons. Reading all the reference lists may also help you locate other useful, non-research reports (e.g., reviews or chapters) to provide additional context. **Forward searching** involves reviewing records that cite each of the studies that you determined were eligible during the database search. Performing this search can be completed using search tools like Google Scholar or Web of Science or using the Shiny App *citationchaser* (an open source R package available for free via a web browser; Haddaway et al., 2022).

After completing ancestral searches, we recommend that you perform a hand search of selected journals. Hand searching refers to manually reviewing journal issues (or conference proceedings) article-by-article to identify potential articles that were missed in the electronic database searches and to confirm articles located in the electronic search. Hand searches historically took place in the stacks of university libraries but are now typically done digitally given the vast electronic collections of articles at most universities. Depending on the intended outlet, you may elect to do hand searches of all journals (e.g., any journal of included record) or a subset of journals (e.g., any journal with two or more included records). You might also search recently published and advanced online copies (i.e., "online first") for articles too new to be indexed by databases, or that were published after you did your database search (you may be several months into the search at this point!). When conducting hand searches, begin with the first year of the oldest article included in the identified study sample. For example, if the first article was published in 2007, then begin hand searching journals starting with 2007. When doing hand searches, begin by reading the table of contents for each issue, followed by a careful read of each title and abstract for articles included. Hand searches are time-intensive, yet important to ensuring an exhaustive search.

Next, from the full references of all reports to be included, read the list to identify expert nominations of researchers and editors, including those who have contributed more than one study. Then, do another electronic search of their names specifically to see if other articles can be detected. You might also contact them directly to see if they have other studies in press (not yet published, but accepted) that might meet inclusion criteria. Similarly, review the reference lists of included articles to identify journal outlets where these studies have been featured. You might even reach out to these journal editors via email to explain your review and see if they have similar studies in press as well.

Now—celebrate what you have accomplished thus far! Collectively, these strategies will likely result in locating all relevant sources to be included. Sometimes a specific strategy will only confirm what has been found, and will not yield new articles to be included. This is good news and suggests you are closer to having located all available studies meeting inclusion criteria. Yet, if each new step yields several new articles that meet inclusion criteria, this might be an indicator that the initial search strategies (i.e., electronic database searches) need to be refined. To avoid "restarts," do not rush the electronic search stage and seek help from trained professionals such as your university librarian (see Considerations for Success). It is also important to conduct reliability checks at each stage along the way (see Lane & Kettler, 2019).

Reading and Coding Relevant Reports
After identifying the relevant records, a thorough reading is necessary alongside your code book to glean or extract all information (e.g., data). Typically, you will want to collect information about (1) descriptive characteristics and (2) quality and rigor of each study. While your research questions will guide the development of your coding protocol, we encourage you to ask the following questions: (1) What is the smallest unit of analysis (microlevel)? (2) What is the largest unit of analysis (macro-level)? And (3) How will dimensions/variables of interest be qualified or quantified (Lane et al., 2022)? You will want to summarize data across studies by coding key information according to specified rules. Coding can include yes/no responses (e.g., Was the intervention implemented by a classroom teacher?), categorical responses (e.g., What was the primary disability of the participant, as defined by IDEA categories?), specific numeric data (e.g., What was the length of intervention sessions, in minutes?), or text (e.g., From whom were social validity data collected?). Generally, coding using very specific questions and responses makes it easier to ensure reliability and reduce subjectivity, as all coders are using the same rules, across all studies. Examples of coded data from systematic reviews can be found online—in one study, Ledford and colleagues reviewed the use of interruption and redirection procedures (https://osf.io/6zpbt/; Ledford et al., 2022). The Excel coding files available via OSF show that they coded data on *source information* (e.g., publication date, journal title), *participant and implementer information* (e.g., participant race, whether implementer was endogenous), and *design-level information* (e.g., dependent variable type, measurement system). The rules for coding within each category are shown on the coding sheet; if you are coding in an online form (e.g., REDCap, Covidence), you may need a separate file for coding rules (see, for example, https://osf.io/bm3c8). Figures 19.2 through 19.6 show sample coding forms for a group of Stay-Play-Talk studies discussed earlier in this chapter. These forms are divided by participant details (Figure 19.2), dependent variable information (Figure 19.3),

Author	Year	Identifier	Gender	Age	Race	Ethnicity/COO	Languages Spoken	Disability
Taylor	2023	Jake	Boy	50	Black	Black	NR	None
Taylor	2023	Alice	Girl	44	White	NR	German, English	None
Taylor	2023	Sam	Boy	44	White	NR	English	None
Severini	2019	Skylar	Girl	38	White	NR	NR	Down syndrome
Severini	2019	Trent	Boy	63	White	NR	NR	Down syndrome
Osborne	2019	Allison	Girl	48	NR	NR	NR	Autism
Osborne	2019	Bryan	Boy	60	NR	NR	NR	Autism
Soemarjono	2023	Aaron	Boy	48	Asian	NR	Korean, English	NR
Soemarjono	2023	Calvin	Boy	37	Asian	NR	Chinese, English	NR
Milam	2020	Faith	Girl	37	White	NR	NR	None
Milam	2020	Garrett	Boy	53	White	NR	NR	None
Milam	2020	Andrew	Boy	42	Black	NR	NR	None

CODING RULES: Author: Last name of first author. **Year:** Four digit of publication or dissertation completion **Identifier**: Report whatever identifier the authors use. **Gender**: Report gender reported by author (_boy_, _girl_, NR [_not reported_]). Gendered pronouns are sufficient evidence. **Age**: Report age in months. If authors report age in years without reporting months, assume the child is X years and 6 months (2 years = 30 months, 3 years = 42 months, 4 years = 54 months, and so on). **Race**: Report race (_Black_, _White_, _American Indian/Pacific Islander_, _Asian_, _Multiracial_). **Ethnicity/Country of Origin**: Report any ethnicity information reported, including Hispanic or Non-Hispanic ethnicity and any country of origin (e.g., Chinese, Iranian). _NR_ (not reported) if neither is reported. **Languages Spoken**: Report languages spoken, if reported. _NR_ (not reported) if no language information is reported. **Disability**: Report disability status using IDEA categories (https://sites.ed.gov/idea/regs/b/a/300.8). Note that "multiple disabilities" has a specific definition and is not simply more than one disability. Report multiple disabilities with a comma, if needed (e.g., Autism, Emotional disturbance). _None_ if no disability. _NR_ (not reported).

Figure 19.2 Coding Form for Participants Included in Studies Evaluating Stay-Play-Talk Procedures.

Author/DV	Design Type	DV Target	DV Type	DV Independence	Measurement System
Severini (Stay)	SIW	Implementer	Buddies	Unclear	MTS
Severini (Play)	SIW	Implementer	Buddies	Unclear	MTS
Severini (Talk)	SIW	Implementer	Buddies	Unclear	MTS
Severini (Interactions)	SIW	Both	Buddies	Unclear	Count
Taylor (Play)	TL	Focal	Buddies	Independent	MTS
Taylor (Talk)	TL	Focal	Buddies	Independent	PIR
Soemarjono (Play)	RIA	Focal	Buddies	Independent	MTS
Soemarjono (Talk)	RIA	Focal	Buddies	Independent	PIR
Osborne (Stay)	SIW	Implementer	Buddies	Unclear	MTS
Osborne (Play)	SIW	Implementer	Buddies	Unclear	MTS
Osborne (Interactions)	SIW	Implementer	Buddies	Unclear	MTS
Milam (strategy use)	TL	Implementer	Buddies	Both	Duration
Milam (social play)	TL	Focal	All	Ind	Duration

CODING RULES: Author: Last name of first author. **Year**: Four digits of publication or dissertation completion. **Source**: Type _unpublished_ for dissertation or thesis and type full journal name for published works. **Design Type**: _SIW_: ABAB or multitreatment. _TL_: Multiple probe or baseline, CC. _RIA_: ATD. _Other_: Combination. **Dependent Variable Target**: _Focal_: Social behavior emitted by target child. _Implementer_: Social behavior emitted by implementing peer. _Both_: Interactive social behavior including multiple children (e.g., interactions between buddies). **Dependent Variable Type**: _Buddies_: The measure of social behaviors is relevant only to interactions between a focal child and identified buddies. _All_: The measure of social behaviors is relevant to interactions between buddies _and_ interactions with non-buddies. _Non-Buddies_: The measure of social behaviors is relevant only to interactions with non-buddies. _Unclear_: Can't tell whether measure includes only interactions between buddies. **Dependent Variable Independence**. _Ind_: DV includes only independent or spontaneous social behavior. _Prompt_: DV includes only prompted social behavior. _Both_: DV includes both prompted and independent behavior. _Unclear_: Cannot tell whether DV includes independent, prompted, or both. **Measurement System**: _Count_ (number of social behaviors were counted and reported as total count or rate). _PIR_ (partial interval recording). _WIR_ (whole interval recording). _MTS_ (momentary time sampling). _Duration_ (length of time child engaged in social interactions, reported as time or percentage of session). _Other or Unclear_ (cannot determine measurement system).

Figure 19.3 Coding Form for Dependent Variables for Studies Evaluating Stay-Play-Talk Procedures.

Author/Comparison	Year	Source	Comparison Condition	Pre-Teaching	Prompting	Reinforcement	Buddies
Severini (BL/SPT)	2019	Topics in Early Childhood Special Education	Contrived	SG	Yes	Yes	Multiple
Severini (SPT-C/SPT-D)	2019	Topics in Early Childhood Special Education	Intervention	SG	Yes	Yes	Multiple
Taylor (BL/SPT)	2023	Unpublished	BAU	WG	Yes	No	Multiple
Soemarjono	2023	Unpublished	BAU	WG	Yes	Yes	Multiple
Osborne (SPT/SPT-GC)	2019	Topics in Early Childhood Special Education	Intervention	SG	No	Yes	Multiple
Osborne (SPT-GC/SPT-RR)	2019	Topics in Early Childhood Special Education	Intervention	SG	No	Yes	Multiple
Milam		Journal of Early Intervention	BAU	SG	Yes	Yes	Multiple

CODING RULES: Author: Last name of first author. **Year**: Four digits of publication or dissertation completion **Source**: Type *unpublished* for dissertation or thesis and type full journal name for published works. **Comparison Condition**: *Baseline (BAU)*: The baseline condition is whatever natural contexts are in place, like a classroom free play. *Baseline (contrived)*: The researchers contrive a baseline condition, that is not typically occurring outside of research. *Intervention*: The comparison is a different intervention condition. **Pre-Teaching**: *1:1*: Teaching SPT behaviors happens in a 1:1 context. *SG*: Happens in a small group context. *WG*: Happens in a whole group context. *Unclear*: Size of pre-teaching group is unclear. **Prompting**: *Yes*: Adults provide prompts to children during measurement occasions. *No*: No prompts are provided during measurement occasions. *Unclear*: It's not possible to tell whether prompts are provided. **Reinforcement**: *Yes*: Adults provide reinforcers to children during measurement occasions. *No*: No reinforcers are provided during measurement occasions. *Unclear*: It's not possible to tell whether reinforcers are provided. **Buddies**: *Single* (one peer implementer is identified for each focal child). *Multiple* (multiple peer implementers are identified for each focal child). *Any* (any child in the class could be the implementing peer, e.g., random selection). *Unclear* (cannot determine how buddies are selected).

Figure 19.4 Coding Form for Independent Variables for Studies Evaluating Stay-Play-Talk Procedures.

independent variable information (Figure 19.4), outcomes for designs including baseline comparisons (Figure 19.5; i.e., studies that answer a question related to "Does SPT work?") and outcomes for designs including intervention comparisons (Figure 19.6; i.e., studies that answer a question related to "Which variation of SPT works better?"). These coding sheets, while not necessarily comprehensive, may give you an idea of how coding is individualized to your context—that is, coding systems for SPT studies may look very different than coding systems for systematic instruction or challenging behavior interventions. These coding sheets are not meant to share with readers, but are designed to assist you in organizing information for analysis and interpretation.

While coding sheets may vary based on the topic, certain essential details need to be captured at the study and participant level, such as the reference, study purpose or research questions, participant characteristics (e.g., age, gender, diagnosis, race, ethnicity), setting, materials, response definitions, measurement procedures, components of the independent variable, research design, and findings. This information allows you to identify potential limitations of the studies included in the review and aid in determining the extent to which findings are applicable to multiple populations of interest. For example, if a study only includes participants from one demographic group (e.g., white male students), findings may not be applicable to other groups.

Author	Design	Comparison	Figure/Design Number	Participant	DV	Functional Relation Determination
Severini	A-B-A-B	Baseline/SPT	1/1	Group 1	Stay	FR
Severini	A-B-A-B	Baseline/SPT	1/2	Group 1	Play	FR
Severini	A-B-A-B	Baseline/SPT	1/3	Group 1	Talk	No FR
Severini	A-B-A-B	Baseline/SPT	1/4	Michael	Interaction	No FR
Severini	A-B-A-B	Baseline/SPT	1/5	Trent	Interaction	No FR
Severini	A-B-A-B	Baseline/SPT	2/6	Jaden	Stay	FR
Severini	A-B-A-B	Baseline/SPT	2/7	Mason	Stay	FR
Severini	A-B-A-B	Baseline/SPT	2/8	Jaden	Play	FR
Severini	A-B-A-B	Baseline/SPT	2/9	Mason	Play	FR
Severini	A-B-A-B	Baseline/SPT	2/10	Jaden	Talk	No FR
Severini	A-B-A-B	Baseline/SPT	2/11	Mason	Talk	No FR
Severini	A-B-A-B	Baseline/SPT	2/12	Jaden	Interaction	FR
Severini	A-B-A-B	Baseline/SPT	2/13	Mason	Interaction	No FR
Severini	A-B-A-B	Baseline/SPT	2/14	Skylar	Interaction	No FR
Taylor	MBP	Baseline/SPT	1/1	All	Social Play	FR
Taylor	MBP	Baseline/SPT	2/2	All	Talk	No FR
Soemarjono	AT/MED	Baseline/SPT	1/1	Aaron	Play	FR
Soemarjono	AT/MED	Baseline/SPT+rewards	1/2	Aaron	Play	FR
Soemarjono	AT/MED	Baseline/SPT	1/3	Calvin	Play	FR
Soemarjono	AT/MED	Baseline/SPT+ rewards	1/4	Calvin	Play	FR
Soemarjono	AT/MED	Baseline/SPT	2/5	Aaron	Talk	FR
Soemarjono	AT/MED	Baseline/SPT+ rewards	2/6	Aaron	Talk	FR
Soemarjono	AT/MED	Baseline/SPT	2/7	Calvin	Talk	FR
Soemarjono	AT/MED	Baseline/SPT+ rewards	2/8	Calvin	Talk	FR
Milam	MBP	Baseline/SPT	1/1	All	Strategy Use	FR
Milam	MBP	Baseline/SPT	2/2	All	Play	FR

CODING RULES: Author: Last name of first author. **Comparison**: Describe comparison, with "baseline" condition listed first and "intervention" listed second. For comparison designs, list first condition or condition with fewer components as baseline. **Design Type**: *A-B-A-B*: SIW design with baseline comparison. *B-C-B-C*: SIW design comparing two interventions. *MBP*: Multiple baseline across participants. *AT/MED*: Alternating treatments/multielement design. **Figure/Design Number**: List the figure number as identified by the author, then consecutively number designs in the study. **Participant**: Participant(s) as named by authors. **DV**: Dependent variable as named by author. **Functional Relation Determination**: *FR*: Functional relation identified (see supplemental visual analysis rules). *No FR*: Functional relation does not exist, changes between conditions are null or inconsistent (see supplemental visual analysis rules). *IV threat/ND*: No functional relation determination can be made due to internal validity threats, for example, behaviors are already at ceiling or floor in baseline conditions (see supplemental visual analysis rules).

Figure 19.5 Coding Form for Outcomes for Studies Evaluating Stay-Play-Talk Procedures in Relation to Baseline Conditions.

Organizing Findings and Writing the Review

Literature reviews typically have the same five sections as single case study reports, described in the previous chapter: Abstract, introduction, method, results, and discussion (APA, 2020). The *abstract* is often a single paragraph that summarizes the main points of the review or article. The *introduction* is the first full section of the literature review and includes a concise rationale for the review and describes relevant scholarship to provide existing context for the current investigation. The introduction concludes with an explicit statement of the aims and research questions the review addresses.

The second section of the literature review report is the *method* and includes a detailed and replicable description of article procurement, data coding, and data analysis. Article procurement begins with a description of the inclusion and exclusion criteria for the review, where information was sourced (e.g., specify all databases or registers used), and what search strategies were used (e.g., electronic, ancestral, hand). If electronic searches were conducted, then

Author	Design	Comparison	Figure/Design Number	Participant	DV	Functional Relation Determination
Severini	B-C-B-C	Multiple/one buddy	2/1	Jaden	Stay	No FR
Severini	B-C-B-C	Multiple/one buddy	2/2	Mason	Stay	IV threat/ND
Severini	B-C-B-C	Multiple/one buddy	2/3	Jaden	Play	FR
Severini	B-C-B-C	Multiple/one buddy	2/4	Mason	Play	FR
Severini	B-C-B-C	Multiple/one buddy	2/5	Jaden	Talk	FR
Severini	B-C-B-C	Multiple/one buddy	2/6	Mason	Talk	FR
Severini	B-C-B-C	Multiple/one buddy	2/7	Jaden	Interaction	FR
Severini	B-C-B-C	Multiple/one buddy	2/8	Mason	Interaction	FR
Severini	B-C-B-C	Multiple/one buddy	2/9	Skylar	Interaction	No FR
Osborne	B-C-B-C	SPT/SPT+GC	2/1	Alex/Allison	Stay	IV threat/ND
Osborne	B-C-B-C	SPT/SPT+GC	2/2	Alex/Allison	Play	IV threat/ND
Osborne	B-C-B-C	SPT/SPT+GC	2/3	Alex/Allison	Interaction	No FR
Osborne	C-D-C-D	SPT+GC/ SPT+GC+RR	2/4	Alex/Allison	Stay	FR
Osborne	C-D-C-D	SPT+GC/ SPT+GC+RR	2/5	Alex/Allison	Play	No FR
Osborne	C-D-C-D	SPT+GC/ SPT+GC+RR	2/6	Alex/Allison	Interaction	No FR
Osborne	B-C-B-C	SPT/SPT+GC	2/7	Anne/Allison	Stay	No FR
Osborne	B-C-B-C	SPT/SPT+GC	2/8	Anne/Allison	Play	No FR
Osborne	B-C-B-C	SPT/SPT+GC	2/9	Anne/Allison	Interaction	No FR
Osborne	C-D-C-D	SPT+GC/ SPT+GC+RR	2/10	Anne/Allison	Stay	FR
Osborne	C-D-C-D	SPT+GC/ SPT+GC+RR	2/11	Anne/Allison	Play	No FR
Osborne	C-D-C-D	SPT+GC/ SPT+GC+RR	2/12	Anne/Allison	Interaction	No FR
Osborne	C-D-C-D	SPT+GC/ SPT+GC+RR	3/13	Ben/Bryan	Stay	No FR
Osborne	C-D-C-D	SPT+GC/ SPT+GC+RR	3/14	Ben/Bryan	Play	No FR
Osborne	C-D-C-D	SPT+GC/ SPT+GC+RR	3/15	Ben/Bryan	Interaction	FR
Soemarjono	AT/MED	SPT/SPT+Reinforcement	1/1	Aaron	Play	FR
Soemarjono	AT/MED	SPT/SPT+Reinforcement	½	Calvin	Play	FR
Soemarjono	AT/MED	SPT/SPT+Reinforcement	2/3	Aaron	Talk	FR
Soemarjono	AT/MED	SPT/SPT+Reinforcement	2/4	Calvin	Talk	FR

CODING RULES: Author: Last name of first author. **Comparison**: Describe comparison, with "baseline" condition listed first and "intervention" listed second. For comparison designs, list first condition or condition with fewer components as baseline. **Design Type**: *A-B-A-B*: SIW design with baseline comparison. *B-C-B-C*: SIW design comparing two interventions. *MBP*: Multiple baselines across participants. *AT/MED*: Alternating treatments/multielement design. **Figure/Design Number**: List the figure number as identified by the author, then consecutively number designs in the study. **Participant**: Participant(s) as named by authors. **DV**: Dependent variable as named by author. **Functional Relation Determination**: *FR*: Functional relation identified (see supplemental visual analysis rules). *No FR*: Functional relation does not exist, changes between conditions are null or inconsistent (see supplemental visual analysis rules). *IV threat/ND*: No functional relation determination can be made due to internal validity threats, for example, behaviors are already at ceiling or floor in baseline conditions (see supplemental visual analysis rules).

Figure 19.6 Coding Form for Outcomes for Studies Evaluating Stay-Play-Talk Procedures in Relation to Baseline Conditions.

the search terms should be listed in full, including Boolean operators. Next, the method section describes the data collection process and defines all data items used and extracted across included records; sharing actual coding manuals via supplemental materials is helpful because it improves replicability. In the method section, the proportion of items screened or coded by two or more persons, the method for calculating reliability, and results of those calculations should be reported at the most granular level. Finally, the method section describes how information was synthesized or analyzed, including any assessment of risk of bias and effect measures as appropriate (see Chapter 17).

The third section of the literature review report is the results section and is the most idiosyncratic section of a literature review; it varies greatly by the content being studied as well as the research questions motivating the review. The results section should closely parallel the objectives or questions of the review as well as the described analysis. Thus, a good outline and organizational strategy is recommended to assist in the writing. In general, we recommend organizing the method section with an initial description of the search and present study and participant characteristics across all included records. Then the results section should present the results of the syntheses by research questions and the reported synthesis plan, including any risk of bias in studies or reporting. This organization focuses the writing on one issue at a time—the "answer" to each question may become a major subsection of the results.

Of course, you are not bound only by the questions generated before actually reading and coding the reports. Sometimes important issues or questions will emerge as the review progresses. These may comprise additional subsections in the results of the document. In some literature reviews, studies may have multiple outcomes or a logical division of the reviewed studies may emerge. When studies have multiple outcome measures, the results section may include separate subsections for each measure. For example, one subsection may be devoted to the initial behavior change, and another subsection may focus on the generalization or the maintenance of those changes. Similarly, when studies have a logical division by timeframe, the results might include separate subsections across the division. For example, subsections may focus on methodological rigor prior to and following the publication of design standards by the What Works Clearinghouse (Shepley et al., 2021).

To assist in synthesizing the results further, a useful method is to put the coded information from each study into tables or figures. Tables are often used in systematic reviews, with each study occupying a row and the variables synthesized occupying the columns. These tables can be long, but they allow for a quick examination of a range of variables across studies. For example, you can scan the table to see who the participants were, what settings were included, what measures were used, and how the independent variables were implemented. These tables can also highlight major differences across studies. For example, you can easily identify the studies that included a generalization measure, the studies that used endogenous implementers, and the types of designs that were used. Similar tables can be constructed to indicate the presence and absence of various rigor and quality indicators by study (e.g., Lloyd et al., 2019). Such tables typically include summary percentages by row and column to represent percentages of indicators met for each study (rows) as well as percentage of studies that met each indicator (columns). These types of summary tables may be included as part of the main manuscript or, depending on manuscript page limits, as supplementary material.

The fourth and final section of the literature review is the *discussion*. This section should reiterate the purpose of the review and summarize the key findings. In addition to pointing out how these key findings extend the current literature, results should be discussed with respect to how they converge or diverge with those from prior studies or reviews on the topic. Implications for future research and practice can be drawn from the findings and the execution of the search. Implications may be particularly important—this is where you can interpret the data for readers to explain the impact of your findings. For example, in their review of interruption and redirection procedures, Ledford and colleagues (2022) emphasize the need for alternative interventions given the findings (presented in their results) that interruption and redirection procedures did not lead to positive generalized or maintained outcomes. Finally, the literature review should include an articulation of the limitations of the review. While limitations might emerge throughout the literature review, they often stem from a priori decisions around article procurement (e.g., inclusion and/or exclusion criteria). For example, limiting the study sample to reports published in peer-reviewed journals could lead to publication bias, as grey literature would not be represented. Additionally, any variables that were difficult to code reliably (i.e., had lower IRA and/or were dropped) should also be discussed. Such limitations should be considered when interpreting the results of the review, and they can also inform future reviews. Another component of the discussion section is to identify areas that require further research. This can be done in the context of discussing each key finding or as a separate section of the discussion. Finally, implications for practice are commonly incorporated in the discussion section.

Using the Literature Review

After conducting a systematic and exhaustive review of the literature, the findings should be disseminated, accessible, and used! As previously highlighted, literature reviews serve multiple functions: (1) providing a comprehensive overview of existing knowledge on a particular topic, (2) establishing a rationale for conducting a study or a series of studies, and (3) identifying research methodologies to enhance the rigor of a study. When the first function (describing what is known) is met, the review will be a useful product for other individuals. The review may be used as a chapter in a monograph, book, thesis, or dissertation. It may also be suitable for submission for review and possible publication in a professional journal—often as an original report or literature review—which are generally considered data-based articles. Many journals accept literature reviews and some even specialize in literature reviews. When looking into outlets for dissemination, authors of any review should consult the submission guidelines published in the journal or on its website. For the latter two functions (building a rationale and identifying procedures), the review is of primary use to the person who conducted the review. Throughout this section we have described how to conduct a systematic review. In the next section we will discuss a minimum set of standards for reporting in systematic reviews.

PRISMA Guidelines

In behavioral science research, systematic reviews play a pivotal role in synthesizing and evaluating existing evidence to inform decision making across research, practice, and policy. In addition to the general guidelines in the previous sections, there are also more formal procedures for conducting systematic literature reviews and meta-analyses. In response to concerns about the suboptimal reporting of meta-analyses in leading health journals (Mulrow, 1987; Sacks et al., 1996), an international group of experts first developed the QUOROM Statement (Quality of Reporting of Meta-analyses; Moher et al., 1999). The QUOROM Statement provided a checklist of items that should be included in meta-analyses of randomized controlled trials. In 2009, the QUOROM Statement was updated and renamed PRISMA (Preferred Reporting Items for Systematic Reviews and Meta-Analyses). Since the release of the PRISMA guidelines in 2009, they have gained widespread recognition and acceptance in the research community. In addition, PRISMA offers a growing body of tools and technology to support researchers conducting systematic reviews (e.g., PRISMA Flow generator, extensions).

We encourage interested readers to read the most current PRISMA statement and related extensions prior to engaging in a rigorous systematic review or meta-analysis (prisma-statement.org). In addition, we encourage you to read examples of recent reviews incorporating these PRISMA features (e.g., Page et al., 2021). Beyond the PRISMA statement, checklist, and flow diagram, PRISMA also includes guidelines for developing protocols and a number of extensions to support nuances within and across systematic reviews (e.g., PRISMA for Diagnostic Test Accuracy, PRISMA Equity, PRISMA Harms [for reviews including Harm outcomes]). Related to single case methodologies, we introduce PRISMA extensions for searching, abstracts, and individual patient data.

PRISMA 2020 Statement, Checklist, and Flow Diagram

Current PRISMA 2020 Guidelines were released in 2021 and include a checklist of reportable items and a flow diagram to help authors report their systematic reviews and meta-analyses in a transparent and comprehensive way (Page et al., 2021). These guidelines aim to enhance the quality, reliability, and reproducibility of published research in the field. The PRISMA 2020 checklist consists of 27 items that cover various aspects of reporting, including the research question, study eligibility criteria, search strategy, data extraction, risk of bias assessment, synthesis methods, interpretation of results, and reporting through dissemination. One of the key changes in the PRISMA 2020 statement was expanding the scope to encompass a broader range of review types beyond traditional systematic reviews (e.g., scoping reviews, rapid reviews, umbrella reviews). The checklist also includes new items related to the title and abstract of the systematic review, emphasizing the importance of clear and concise reporting to facilitate information retrieval and decision making. Other key changes include (1) emphasizing the importance of study protocols and registration to improve transparency; (2) updating guidance on assessing the risk of bias in individual studies included in the systematic review (bias assessment), (3) discussing novel synthesis methods (e.g., network meta-analysis, qualitative synthesis); and (4) offering new guidelines to improve reporting across sections of a review report (Page et al., 2021).

A hallmark characteristic of any literature review guided by PRISMA is the inclusion of a flow diagram to describe the results of the search and selection process (i.e., number of records identified in the search to the number of studies included in review). The PRISMA flow diagram is a graphical representation of the process of selecting studies for inclusion in a systematic review or meta-analysis (see Figure 19.1 for a detailed overview). By providing a visual representation of the review process, the PRISMA flow diagram helps readers understand how the studies were selected and how the data were extracted. This can improve the quality and reliability of the review findings. A template PRISMA flow diagram is available, which can be customized to fit the needs of each systematic review, depending on whether the review is original or updated. The PRISMA flow diagram is divided into three phases of article procurement: Identification, screening, and inclusion. This information should be reported for each step of the process, and ideally, information should be provided on the reliability of the screening process (e.g., interrater agreement).

PRISMA Protocol

A systematic review protocol is a document that outlines the plan for conducting a review. It includes information about research questions, eligibility criteria for studies, search strategy, data extraction methods, risk of bias assessment methods, and planned reporting of results. A protocol ensures that a systematic review is carefully planned and that the planned procedures are explicitly documented before the review begins. This promotes consistency conducted by the review team, including accountability, research integrity, and transparency of the eventually completed review (Moher et al., 2015). Until recently, systematic review protocols were generally available only through select organizations, such as the Cochrane and Campbell Collaborations. Protocols today take many forms, including pre-registration and registered reports that are made publicly available online (e.g., Open Science Framework, Society for Research on Educational Effectiveness). A pre-registration is a detailed plan of your study that is made public before you conduct the research. A registered report is a manuscript that is accepted for publication before the research is conducted, but only if the results are published in the manuscript as part of a two-stage review process. The PRISMA-P checklist is intended primarily for the preparation of protocols of systematic reviews and meta-analyses that summarize aggregate data from studies and can be used across pre-registration and registered reports. The PRISMA-P 2015 checklist contains 17 numbered items (26 including sub-items) categorized into three main sections: Administrative information, introduction, and methods.

PRISMA Extensions

In addition to the PRISMA 2020 Statement, Checklist, and Flow Diagram and PRISMA Protocol, PRISMA offers several extensions. For researchers' procurement, we recommend the PRISMA extension for searching, which was published in 2021. The checklist includes 16 reporting items organized by information sources and methods, search strategies, peer review, and managing records with detailed exemplar reporting and rationales. The PRISMA extension for Abstracts was published within the main PRISMA 2020 paper. This 12-item checklist gives authors a framework for condensing systematic reviews into the essentials for a journal article or conference abstract. Finally, the PRISMA-IPD was published in 2015 and is an extension interested in more detailed information and guidance around the article of PRISMA for how to report individual patient-level data (Stewart et al., 2015). When reporting individual participant data, additional flow of information should be reported to specify availability of and analyses of both individual and group level data (Stewart et al., 2015).

The PRISMA-IPD specifies how data were obtained, became available, and analyzed across individual level outcomes and group level outcomes (e.g., aggregated data). Articles should report data inspection (e.g., consistency and completion) and risk of bias assessment for each outcome in the method section. Authors and peer-reviewers are encouraged to use the checklist to improve reporting of the minimum information needed for a full and transparent individual participant review (Stewart et al., 2015). In the future, PRISMA will release extensions for systematic reviews for research involving children, including protocols and preferred item reporting.

Considerations for Success

As you continue learning about literature reviews—either to (1) frame the introduction of your article, master's thesis, or doctoral dissertation or (2) conduct a comprehensive, systematic review of the literature as a stand-alone study, we encourage you to consider the following suggestions:

1. *Identify target outlets and familiarize yourself with their requirements and guidelines.* Before you begin the review, learn about any relevant requirements for the intended outlet. For example, start by reviewing your university's guidelines (if the review will serve as a chapter in your dissertation) or review editorial guidelines for targeted journals (if the goal is to publish this report in a peer-reviewed journal). Reviewing this information early on will save time and help ensure the final product adheres to their requirements. In addition, read the full set of guidelines for the expected writing style. For example, if APA format is required, you will need to reference the Publication manual of the American Psychological Association (7th edition). Be certain to read the most current version as these manuals are updated regularly.
2. *Get organized before you start searching.* Systematic literature reviews require much planning and organization. Before starting a systematic review, read reputable guidelines such as Journal Article Reporting Standards (APA, 2020), PRISMA (Page et al., 2021), and discussion papers on high quality reviews (Talbott et al., 2018). Reviewing

these resources and recently published systematic reviews in the journal you plan to target for submission can help you understand what systems and structures you will need to accomplish each stage of the review. JARS and PRISMA also offer a variety of resources to help you stay organized throughout this process. There are also available programs designed to support search, screening, and review stages (e.g., Covidence, Mendeley, Rayyan), including free-access resources such as those on www.ci3t.org/ / practice.

3. *Keep detailed records of procedures and decisions.* Systematic literature reviews involve numerous steps and decision points. We strongly recommend keeping detailed records of what you did and why throughout each stage of the review that you can later refer to as needed. In some cases, the search and screening stage alone can take months to complete. Your future self will thank you for documenting each activity and decision point once you start writing the manuscript or crafting responses to reviewer questions during the peer review process. In fact, we recommend drafting the method section as you complete each stage of the review process (though you will still likely need a separate research log to keep an exhaustive list of activities, decision points, and rationales).

4. *Assess reliability early and often.* It is important to collect reliability data early on in each stage of the systematic review (e.g., searches, screening, descriptive coding, and rigor/quality coding). If you move too far ahead at any stage without assessing some form of interrater agreement, you run the risk of having to go back and complete the stage again with a revised set of procedures. When you collect reliability data early on, you can make necessary clarifications or adjustments on the front end, and make sure the time and effort spent at each stage of the review is producing reliable and trustworthy data.

5. *Reach out for help when you need it.* University librarians can be a wonderful resource as you develop your electronic database searches. You might reach out to colleagues, mentors, journal editors, or content experts to ask if they know of additional authors or sources beyond those you identified (including accepted or in-press papers that would likely meet your inclusion criteria). You might contact study authors during the coding process to ask clarifying questions about their methods or measures. The worst that can happen is they do not respond—but many will. When seeking information from study authors, introduce yourself, explain the purpose of the review, ask them your question clearly, and thank them for their time and consideration. If they respond, thank them and offer to share your review when it becomes available (when the article is in press).

Conclusions

Conducting systematic literature reviews takes much time and effort. Yet what a gift to look back and discover all there is to know about a topic or set of questions that inspires you. In this chapter we focused on conducting systematic reviews of single case literature, which involves detailed and comprehensive plans to identify, select, and evaluate research studies to address one or more research question related to an empirical literature. Specifically, we (1) described approaches and procedures for conducting literature reviews, (2) explained how to use PRISMA to conduct systematic reviews, and (3) provided considerations for conducting successful literature reviews. As we have discussed, systematic literature reviews themselves are a form of empirical research, with data collected from the studies included in the review. After reading this chapter, we hope readers will feel equipped to search and navigate the empirical literature on their topic of interest, and, depending on the research questions that emerge, conduct high quality systematic literature reviews worthy of sharing with the field.

References

Allen, G. E., Common, E. A., Germer, K. A., Lane, K. L., Buckman, M. M., Oakes, W. P., & Menzies, H. M. (2020). A systematic review of the evidence base for active supervision in PK-12 settings. *Behavioral Disorders*, 45(3), 167–182. https://doi.org/10.1177/0198742919837646

American Psychological Association (2020). *Publication manual of the American Psychological Association: The official guide to APA style*. (7th ed.). Author.

Bell, D., & Foiret, J. (2020). A rapid review of the effect of assistive technology on the educational performance of students with impaired hearing. *Disability and Rehabilitation: Assistive Technology*, 15(7), 838–843. https://doi.org/10.1080/17483107.2020.1775317

Briesch, A. M., Chafouleas, S. M., Nissen, K., & Long, S. (2020). A review of state-level procedural guidance for implementing multitiered systems of support for behavior (MTSS-B). *Journal of Positive Behavior Interventions*, 22(3), 131–144. https://doi.org/10.1177/1098300719884707

Buckman, M. M., Lane, K. L., Common, E. A., Royer, D. J., Oakes, W. P., Allen, G. E., Lane, K. S., & Brunsting, N. (2021). Treatment integrity of primary (tier 1) prevention efforts in tiered systems: Mapping the literature. *Education and Treatment of Children*, 44(3), 145–168. https://doi.org/10.1007/s43494-021-00044-4

Chazin, K. T., Velez, M. S., & Ledford, J. R. (2022). Reducing escape without escape extinction: A systematic review and meta-analysis of escape-based interventions. *Journal of Behavioral Education*, 31(1), 186–215. https://doi.org/10.1007/s10864-021-09453-2

Chen, M., Pustejovsky, J. E., Klingbeil, D. A., & Van Norman, E. R. (2023). Between-case standardized mean differences: Flexible methods for single-case designs. *Journal of School Psychology*, 98, 16–38. https://doi.org/10.1016/j.jsp.2023.02.002

Chow, J., & Ekholm, E. (2018). Do published studies yield larger effect sizes than unpublished studies in education and special education? *A meta-review. Educational Psychology Review*, 30(3), 727–744. https://doi.org/10.1007/s10648-018-9437-7

Cochrane, S., O'Hara, D., & Leslie, J. (1980). *The effects of education on health*. World Bank. https://unesdoc.unesco.org/ark:/48223/pf0000167953

Cook, B., (2016). Reforms in academic publishing: Should behavioral disorders and special education journals embrace them? *Behavioral Disorders*, 41(3), 161–172. https://doi.org/10.17988/0198-7429-41.3.161

Common, E. A., Lane, K. L., Cantwell, E. D., Brunsting, N., Oakes, W. P., Germer, K. A., & Bross, L. A., (2020). Teacher-delivered strategies to increase students' opportunities to respond: A systematic methodological review. *Behavioral Disorders*, 45(2), 67–84. https://doi.org/10.1177/0198742919828310

Common, E. A., Lane, K. L., Pustejovsky, J. E., Johnson, A. H., & Johl, L. E. (2017). Functional assessment-based interventions for students with or at-risk for high-incidence disabilities: Field-testing single-case synthesis methods. *Remedial and Special Education*, 38(6), 331–352. https://doi.org/10.1177/0741932517693320

Council for Exceptional Children (CEC). (2014). *CEC standards for evidence-based practices in special education*. Arlington, VA: Author.

Dowdy, A., Tincani, M., & Schneider, W. J. (2020). Evaluation of publication bias in response interruption and redirection: A meta-analysis. *Journal of Applied Behavior Analysis*, 53(4), 2151–2171.

Ennis, R. P., Lane, K. L., Oakes, W. P., & Flemming, S. C. (2020a). Empowering teachers with low-intensity strategies to support instruction: Implementing across-activity choices in 3rd grade reading. *Journal of Positive Behavioral Interventions*, 22(2), 78–92. https://doi.org/10.1177/1098300719870438

Ennis, R. P., Royer, D. J., Lane, K. L., & Dunlap, K. D. (2020b). Behavior-specific praise in K-12 settings: Mapping the 50-year knowledge base. *Behavioral Disorders*, 45(3), 131–147. https://doi.org/10.1177/0198742919843075

Ennis, R. P., Royer, D. J., Lane, K. L., & Dunlap, K. D. (2020c). Behavior-specific praise in K-12 settings: Mapping the 50-year knowledge base. *Behavioral Disorders*, 45(3), 131–147.

Fahmie, T. A., Rodriguez, N. M., Luczynski, K. C., Rahaman, J. A., Charles, B. M., & Zangrillo, A. N. (2023). Toward an explicit technology of ecological validity. *Journal of Applied Behavior Analysis*, 56(2), 302–322.

Fleming, J. I., & Cook, B. G. (2022). Open access in special education: A review of journal and publisher policies. *Remedial and Special Education*, 43(1), 3–14. https://doi.org/10.1177/0741932521996461

Glass, G. V. (1976). Primary, secondary, and meta-analysis of research. *Educational Researcher*, 5(10), 3–8. https://doi.org/10.3102/0013189x005010003

Haddaway, N. R., Grainger, M. J., & Gray, C. T. (2022). Citationchaser: A tool for transparent and efficient forward and backward citation chasing in systematic searching. *Research Synthesis Methods*, 13(4), 533–545. https://doi.org/10.1002/jrsm.1563

Harris, P. A., Taylor, R., Thielke, R., Payne, J., Gonzalez, N., & Conde, J. G. (2009). A metadata-driven methodology and workflow process for providing translational research informatics support. *J Biomed Inform*, 42(2), 377–381. https://doi.org/10.1016/j.jbi.2008.08.010

Lane, K. L., Bruhn, A. L., Crnobori, M. L., & Sewell, A. L. (2009). Designing functional assessment-based interventions using a systematic approach: A promising practice for supporting challenging behavior. In T. E. Scruggs & M. A. Mastropieri (Eds.), *Policy and practice: Advances in learning and behavioral disabilities* (Vol. 22, pp. 341–370). Leeds, UK: Emerald.

Lane, K. L., Carter, E. W., Common, E., & Jordan, A. (2012). Teacher expectations for student performance: Lessons learned and implications for research and practice. In B. G. Cook, M. Tankersley, & T. J. Landrum (Eds.), *Classroom behavior, contexts, and interventions: Advances in learning and behavioral disabilities* (Vol. 25, pp. 95–129). Leeds, UK: Emerald.

Lane, K. L., Common, E. A., Royer, D. J., & Muller, K. (2014). Group comparison and single-case research design quality indicator matrix using Council for Exceptional Children 2014 standards. Unpublished tool. Retrieved from https://www.ci3t.org/practice

Lane, K. L., Common, E. A., Royer, D. J., & Oakes, W. P. (2022). Conducting systematic reviews of the literature: Guidance for quality appraisal. In M. Tankersley, B. G. Cook, and T. J. Landrum (Eds). *Advances in learning and behavioral disabilities* (Vol. 32, pp. 109–130). Leeds, UK: Emerald.

Lane, K. L. & Kettler, R. J. (2019). Literature reviews, questions, and hypotheses. In R. J. Kettler, *Research methodologies of school psychology: Critical skills* (pp. 24–41). New York: Routledge.

Lane, K. L., Oakes, W. P., & Menzies, H. M. (2021). Considerations for systematic screening PK-12: Universal screening for internalizing and externalizing behaviors in the COVID-19 era. *Preventing School Failure: Alternative Education for Children and Youth*, 65(3), 275–281. https://doi.org/10.1080/1045988X.2021.1908216

Little, M. A., Lane, K. L., Harris, K., Graham, S., Brindle, M., & Sandmel, K. (2010). Self-regulated strategies development for persuasive writing in tandem with schoolwide positive behavioral support: Effects for second grade students with behavioral and writing difficulties. *Behavioral Disorders*, 35, 157–179.

Ledford, J. R., Chazin, K. T., Lane, J. D., Zimmerman, K. N., Bennett, P. B., & Ayres, K. A. (2022). Single case analysis and review framework (SCARF). http://ebip.vkcsites.org/scarfv2

Ledford, J. R., & Gast, D. L. (2006). Feeding problems in children with autism spectrum disorders: A review. *Focus on Autism and Other Developmental Disabilities*, 21(3), 153–166. https://doi.org/10.1177/10883576060210030401

Ledford, J. R., & Pustejovsky, J. E. (2023). Systematic review and meta-analysis of stay-play-talk interventions for improving social behaviors of young children. *Journal of Positive Behavior Interventions*, 25(1), 65–77. https://doi.org/10.1177/1098300720983521

Lerman, D. C., & Vorndran, C. M. (2002). On the status of knowledge for using punishment: Implications for treating behavior disorders. *Journal of Applied Behavior Analysis*, 35(4), 431–464. https://doi.org/10.1901/jaba.2002.35-431

Lloyd, B. P., Barton, E. E., Ledbetter-Cho, K., Pennington, B., & Pokorski, E. A. (2019). Function-based interventions in K–8 general education settings: A focus on teacher implementation. *The Elementary School Journal*, 119(4), 601–628. https://doi.org/10.1086/703114

Lucas, S. M., & Cutspec, P. A. (2005). The role and process of literature searching in the preparation of a research synthesis. *Centerscope*, 3(3), 1–26.

Maggin, D. M., Barton, E., Reichow, B., Lane, K. L., & Shogren, K. A. (2022). Commentary on the What Works Clearinghouse Standards and Procedures Handbook (v. 4.1) for the review of single-case research. *Remedial and Special Education*, 43(6), 421–433. https://doi.org/10.1177/0741932521105131

Maggin, D. M., Talbott, E., Van Acker, E. Y., & Kumm, S. (2017). Quality indicators for systematic reviews in behavioral disorders. *Behavioral Disorders*, 42(2), 52–64. https://doi.org/10.1177/0198742916688653

Manolov, R., Guilera, G., & Solanas, A. (2017). Issues and advances in the systematic review of single case research: A commentary on the exemplars. *Remedial and Special Education*, 38(6), 387–393. https://doi.org/10.1177/0741932517726143

McHugo, G. J., & Drake, R. E. (2003). Finding and evaluating the evidence: A critical step in evidence-based medicine. *Psychiatric Clinics of North America*, 26(4), 821–831. https://doi.org/10.1016/s0193-953x(03)00075-3

Moher, D., Cook, D. J., Eastwood S., Olkin I., Rennie D., Stroup, D. F for the QUOROM Group (1999). Improving the quality of reporting of meta-analysis of randomized controlled trials: The QUOROM statement. *Lancet*, 354, 1896–1900. https://doi.org/10.1016/s0140-6736(99)04149-5

Moher, D., Shamseer, L., Clarke, M., Ghersi, D., Liberati, A., Petticrew, M., Shekelle, P., Steward, L. A., & PRISMA-P Group (2015). Preferred reporting items for systematic review and meta-analysis protocols (PRISMA-P) 2015 statement. *Systematic Reviews*, 4(1), 1–9. https://doi.org/10.1186/2046-4053-4-1

Mulrow, C. D. (1987). The medical review article: State of the science. *Ann Intern Med*, 106(3), 485–488. https://doi.org/10.7326/0003-4819-106-3-485

Odom, S. L., & Strain, P. S. (2002). Evidence-based practice in early intervention/early childhood special education: Single subject design research. *Journal of Early Intervention*, 25(2), 151–160. https://doi.org/10.1177/105381510202500212

Ouzzani, M., Hammady, H., Fedorowicz, Z., & Elmagarmid, A. (2016). Rayyan—A web and mobile app for systematic reviews. *Systematic Reviews*, 5, 1–10.

Page, M. J., Mckenzie, J. E., Bossuyt, P. M., Boutron, I., ... & Moher, D. (2021). The PRISMA 2020 statement: an updated guideline for reporting systematic reviews. *BMJ*, 71, 1–9. https://doi.org/10.1136/bmj.n71

Peltier, C., McKenna, J. W., Sinclair, T. E., Garwood, J., & Vannest, K. J. (2022). Brief report: ordinate scaling and axis proportions of single-case graphs in two prominent EBD journals from 2010 to 2019. *Behavioral Disorders*, 47(2), 134–148. https://doi.org/10.1177/0198742920982587

Pérez, P., Gil, H., Artola, A., Royer, D. J., & Lane, K. L. (2023). Behavior-specific praise: empowering teachers and families to support students in varied learning contexts. *Preventing School Failure: Alternative Education for Children and Youth*, 67(2), 83–90.

Riden, B. S., Kumm, S., & Maggin, D. M. (2022). Evidence-based behavior management strategies for students with or at risk of EBD: A mega review of the literature. *Remedial and Special Education*, 43(4), 255–269. https://doi.org/10.1177/07419325211047947

Royer, D. J., Lane, K. L., Cantwell, E. D., & Messenger, M. (2017). A systematic review of the evidence base for instructional choice in k-12 settings. *Behavioral Disorders*, 42(3), 89–107. https://doi.org/10.1177/0198742916688655

Royer, D. J., Lane, K. L., Dunlap, K. D., & Ennis, R. P. (2019). A systematic review of teacher-delivered behavior-specific praise on K-12 student performance. *Remedial and Special Education*, 40(2), 112–128. https://doi.org/10.1177/0741932517751054

Sackett, D. L., Chambers, L. W., MacPherson, A. S., Goldsmith, C. H., & McAuley, R. G. (1977). The development and application of indices of health: general methods and a summary of results. *American Journal of Public Health*, 67(5), 423–428. https://doi.org/10.2105/ajph.67.5.423

Sacks, H. S., Reitman, D., Pagano, D., & Kupelnick, B. (1996). Meta-analysis: an update. *The Mount Sinai Journal of Medicine, New York*, 63(3–4), 216–224.

Shepley, C., Zimmerman, K. N., & Ayres, K. M. (2021). Estimating the impact of design standards on the rigor of a subset of single-case research. *Journal of Disability Policy Studies*, 32(2), 108–118.

Slavin, R. E. (1977). Classroom reward structure: An analytical and practical review. *Review of Educational Research*, 47(4), 633–650. https://doi.org/10.3102/00346543047004633

Snodgrass, M. R., Chung, M. Y., Kretzer, J. M., & Biggs, E. E. (2022). Rigorous assessment of social validity: A scoping review of a 40-year conversation. *Remedial and Special Education*, 43(2), 114–130. https://doi.org/10.1177/07419325211017295

Stewart, L. A., Clarke, M., Rovers, M., Riley, R. D., Simmonds, M., Stewart, G., & Tierney, J. F. (2015). Preferred reporting items for a systematic review and meta-analysis of individual participant data. *JAMA*, 313(16), 1657. https://doi.org/10.1001/jama.2015.365

Talbott, B., Maggin, D. M., Van Acker, E. Y., & Kumm, S. (2018). Quality Indicators for Reviews of Research in Special Education. *Exceptionality*, 26(4), 245–265. https://doi.org/10.1080/09362835.2017.1283625

Torelli, J. N., Lloyd, B. P., & Pollack, M. S. (2022). A systematic review of direct assessments to evaluate psychotropic medication effects for children with disabilities. *American Journal on Intellectual and Developmental Disabilities*, 127(2), 103–124. https://doi.org/10.1352/1944-7558-127.2.103

Umbreit, J., Ferro, J., Lane, K. L., & Liaupsin, C. (2023). *Functional assessment-based intervention: A practical, effective, and integrated approach*. New York: Guilford.

Umbreit, J., Ferro, J., Liaupsin, C., & Lane, K. L. (2007). *Functional behavioral assessment and function-based intervention: An effective, practical approach*. Upper Saddle River, NJ: Prentice Hall.

University of Michigan Library (2023). Systematic reviews information on how to conduct systematic reviews in the health sciences. Author. https://guides.lib.umich.edu/sysreviews

Wallace, B. C., Small, K., Brodley, C. E., Lau, J., & Trikalinos, T. A. (2012). Deploying an interactive machine learning system in an evidence-based practice center: abstrackr. *Proc. of the ACM International Health Informatics Symposium (IHI)*, 819–824.

Wolery, M., Lane, K. L., & Common, E. A. (2018). Writing tasks: Literature reviews, research proposals, and final reports. In J. Ledford & D. L. Gast (Ed.). *Single case research methodology: Applications in special education and behavioral sciences* (3rd Ed.). (pp. 43–76). New York: Routledge.

Index

Note: Page locators in **bold** refer to tables and page locators in *italic* refer to figures.

A-B-A-B designs 138, *139*, 140–141, **140**, 142–148; applied example 143, 173; combination designs 266, 267; design selection 270, 271, 272; formative analysis and phase change decisions 163–164, *163–164*; procedural steps 145–148; reversal variation 140, **140**, 143–145, 146, *146*, **147**, 174; studies using **144**; summative analysis and functional relation determination 168–169, 170; visual analysis protocols 170

A-B-A-C designs 141, *141*

A-B-BC-B-BC designs 148, 149, *150*, **151**, 175

A-B-C-B-C design 148, *150*, **151**

abscissa (x-axis) 120, 121, 124–126, *126*; blocking data 127; depicting time 123, *124*; labels 126; scale breaks 126–127; y-axis in proportion to 123

abstracts 319–320, 342, 347

adaptation threats 33, 40–41; in RIA designs **242**; in SIW designs **154**; in time-lagged designs **201**

adapted alternating treatments designs (AATD) 224, **225**, 226, 232–237, 244; applied example 237, 252; behavior sets, selecting and assigning 234–235, **236**, 241, 255; choosing between repeated acquisition designs and 273; combination designs 266, *269*; design selection 270, 273; functional relation decisions *257*; procedural steps 236–237; studies using **233–234**; supplemental analyses of data 259, *259*; terminology 224, 226; threats to internal validity 241–242, **242**

Addison, L. R. **151**

agreement: calculating 76; calculating interobserver 76–81; chance 77, 80–81; Kappa coefficient 80–81; percentage 37, 77–80; reporting 76

Ahearn, W. H. **144**

Allen, K.E. 145, **147**

Allen, M. **189**, **264**

American Psychological Association (APA) 7, 123, 242, 286, 289, 310, 317, 326, 330, 338, 347

ancestral searches 338

Anderson, C. M. **151**

Anderson, E. J. **303**

anonymity 281, 285

Anthony, L. **197**

applicability and generality in evaluating single case research 296–297

Applied Behavior Analysis (ABA) 311

applied research 4–6; integrating science into educational and clinical practice 4–6; participatory action research 6

arbitrarily applicable relational responding (AARRing) **97**, 104

Ardoin, S. P. **144**

assent to participate in a study 279; procedures 286

attrition 38

attrition threats 38–39; RIA designs 241, **242**; SIW designs 152–153, **153**; time-lagged designs 200, **201**

augmentative and alternative technology (AAC) 164–165, 228, 229, 243–244, 251

authorship status 289

automated recording devices 47

axes 121, 124–126, *126*; *see also* abscissa (x-axis); ordinate (y-axis)

axis labels (quantification of tic marks) 120, 121, 126

axis titles 120, 121

Ayres, K. M. 7, **144**, **197**, **233**

Bachmeyer, M. H. **151**

backward searching 338

Baer, D. M. 7, 10, 97, 98, 99, 104, 105, 106, 107, 109, 112, 119, 123, 129, 131, 145, **147**, 180

Bailey, K. M. **303**

Bak, M. S. **196**

Barry, C. T. **144**

Barton, E. E. 110, **147**, **151**, 162, 165, **230**, 301

baseline conditions 11, 30; RIA designs 229, 234, 244, 248; SIW designs 138, 139, 142; time-lagged designs 180, 187, 188, 191, 205; types and terminology 139–140; writing descriptions of 322

baseline logic 11

baseline phases 192, 205, 210–211

basic research 4

Bastiaenen, C. H. **303**

Bateman, K. J. 21, 22

B-C-B-C designs **140**, 148, *150*, **151**

Beckers, L. W. **303**

Behavior Analyst Certification Board (BACB) 7, 286, 289

behaviors: characterizing 46–47; choosing and defining target 44–45; coding definitions, examples and

non-examples 45, **45**, 72; non-reversible 46; reversible 46; short and long duration 46–47; trial-based vs. free-operant 47
behavior sets, selecting and assigning: AATDs 234–235, **236**, 241, 255; ME-ATDs 235
Behl, D. 5
Bell, D. **331**
Belmont Report 278, 283, 286
best alone phase 229
between-case standardized mean difference (BC-SMD) 171
between-groups research 10, 16, 29, 36
bias: observer 71, 73, 74, *75*, 294; risk of 294; risk of bias tools 299, 301; selection 38; social desirability bias 109
Birkan, B. 155
Blair, K. S. C. 56, 111, **265**
blind (naïve) observers 73, 74, 76, 294, 295
blocking data 127
Boolean operators 336, **337**
Bottema-Buetel, K. 280, 281
Boyle, M. A. 48, 105, **264**, 266
Bray, M. W. **231**
Brock, M.E. **303**
Brooks, M. C. **233**, 334
Bruhn, A. L. 149, 175, **264**, 334
Buckman, M. M. 329, **331**, 334
Buell, J. S. **147**
Burke, M. D. **189**
business-as-usual conditions vs. contrived baseline conditions 139–140

Caldwell, N, K. **197**
Camarata, S. 252, **265**
Campbell, A. 62, **151**, **189**, **264**
Capalbo, A. 189, 216, 217
Cardona-Betancourt, V. **189**
Cariveau, T. 234, 235, 241, 259
Carr, J. E. 32, **33**
carryover effects 39
cascading logic models 87, *88*, 91, 92
Castle, G. **265**
causality, attributions of 7–8
CEC (Council for Exceptional Children) Standards for Evidence-Based Practice 299–300
CEC-DR (Council for Exceptional Children Division for Research): Evidence-Based Practice Paper 298–299; Next Generation Guidelines 301–302
Cevher, Z. **197**
chance agreement 77, 80–81
changing criterion designs 154–158, *155*; applied example 156–157, 176–177; with behavior measurement across response topographies 155; combination designs 174, 266; demonstrating a functional relation using 169–170; distributed criterion design 155; internal validity 158; procedural steps 157–158; studies using **156**
Chazin, K. T. 22, 29, 41, **49**, 71, 73, 74, 111, 121, 140, **230**, 233, 281, 295, 302, **303**, 334
Check-In, Check-Out (CICO) 149
checklists 92–93
citationchaser 332, 338
citations 320, 321, 322, 326
Cividini-Motta, C. **265**

coding reports 339–342
Collins, T. A. **97**, **144**
combination designs 174, 262–270; SIW plus RIA combinations 267, *269*; SIW plus SIW combinations 266; studies using **264–265**; time-lagged plus RIA combinations 266, *267*, *268*, *269*; time-lagged plus SIW combinations 266; time-lagged plus time-lagged combinations 263
Common, E. A. 331, **331**, 334
Common Rule 278
Comparative Single Case Experimental Design Rating System (CSCEDARS) 301
comparison questions 312; designs appropriate for answering 270, **270**
component analysis questions 313
Comprehensive Integrated Three-Tiered Model of Prevention (Ci3T) 332
conclusion section in empirical reports 324
concurrence variations 185–187
concurrent multiple baseline (MB) designs 185
condition 30
condition, component of graphs 120
condition design: approaches to 84–87; evaluation of procedures vs. evaluation of processes 84–86, **86**; static vs. dynamic 86–87
condition labels 120, 121
condition modification lines 120, 121
conditions variation 192, *193*, *195*
confidentiality 281, 285–286; ethical scenarios **287**
conflicts of interest (COIs) 280–281
Conroy, M. A. **303**
consent to participate in a study 279, 286
consistency 127, 131–132
CONSORT (CONsolidated Standards Of Reporting Trials) 300
construct validity 23–25, 70; threats to 24–25, **24**
context-bound 63, 98
context characteristics 22
context-dependent 98
continuous recording 47, 48; duration and latency recording to measure time 50–51; event and timed event recording to measure count 48–50
continuous sampling 57
contrived baseline conditions vs. business-as-usual conditions 139–140
control condition 229, 234, 238, 241
control variables 89, 90; for common interventions **89**
convergent designs 11–12
Cook, B. G. 119, 302, 303, 310, 311, 325
Copeland, B. 111, 124, 175, **197**
Coping Power (CP) 149; and Check-In, Check-Out (CICO) 149
copyright protection 289
Cornish, F. 6
correlational research 9
Cosottile, D. **147**
Council for Exceptional Children (CEC) Standards for Evidence-Based Practice 299–300
Council for Exceptional Children Division for Research (CEC-DR): Evidence-Based Practice Paper 298–299; Next Generation Guidelines 301–302

count 48; estimating with interval-based systems 51–57; event and timed event recording to measure 48–50; examples in applied research **49**; transforming for data presentation 50

countertherapeutic contingency baselines vs. no treatment baselines 139

countertherapeutic trends 129

covariation 208, *208*

Covidence 332, 339

Crewdson, M. **144**

CSCEDARS (Comparative Single Case Experimental Design Rating System) 301

culturally responsive research 282

cumulative records 121, *122*

Curiel, E. S. **190**

Curtis, K. S. **264**

CW-FIT (class-wide function-related intervention teams) 149, 175, 176

cyclical variability 40

Dada, S. 233

D'Agostino, S. R. 109, 111, 112, 196, 219, **230**

Daniels, S. **144**

Dart, E. H. 56, 126, 127, **144**, 170, 186

data adequacy 296; RIA designs 255; RIA designs, examples of summative visual analysis 251, 252, 253; SIW designs 166–167, *167*, *168*; SIW designs, examples of summative visual analysis 173, 174, 175, 177; time-lagged designs 210–211; time-lagged designs, examples of summative visual analysis 216, 216–217, 218, 221

data analysis: interobserver agreement 74–76; RIA designs 247–261; section in empirical reports **319**, 323; SIW designs 161–178; time-lagged designs 204–222

data, blocking 127

data collection 63–64; ensuring reliability and validity of 71–76; on more than one behavior 65; piloting procedures 72, **73**; planning and conducting 64; using technology 64–65

data instability 39–40, *40*, 129, *130*

data instability threats 39; and choosing between MP and MB designs 199; RIA designs **242**; SIW designs 153, **154**; time-lagged designs 199, 200, **201**

data paths, graph 126

data recording procedures, selecting 47–48, **49**

data repositories, online 325

data representation 119–128; figures in single case design studies 119–127; tables in single case design studies 119, 128; transparency 119

data storage 285; ethical scenarios **287**

data sufficiency 210–211, 296

Davis, C. A. **144**

Davis, T. N. **147**

days variation 192, *194*; MP-Behaviors design example 193, 218–219; MP-Participants design example 196, 219–221

deductive research approaches 8, 311

demonstration questions 311–312; designs appropriate for answering 270, **270**

demonstrations of effect, potential 294–295; RIA designs 254, *254*, 255; SIW designs 140–141, *141*, 166, 168–169; time-lagged designs 187, 209, 211–212

Dennis, L **190**, **238**

dependent variables 4, 22, 44; coding form for *340*; primary 92, 166; reliability and validity of 69–82; secondary 92, 166; section in empirical reports **318**, 321; selection, characterization and measurement 43–68

descriptive research 9; questions **312**, 313–314

design adequacy: RIA designs 254, *254*; RIA designs, examples of summative visual analysis 251, 252, 253; SIW designs 166; SIW designs, examples of summative visual analysis 173, 174, 175, 177; time-lagged designs 209–210; time-lagged designs, examples of summative visual analysis 216, 218, 219–*220*

design appropriateness 294

design-comparable effect size (D-CES) 171

design-related confounds 41; RIA designs **242**; SIW designs 153, **154**; time-lagged designs 200, **201**

Dewey, A. **147**

Diekman, C. A. **265**

differentiation 90, 248, 249, 252, 258, 260

Dillon, M. B. M. **144**

direct consumers 107

direct observation measures, social validity 109–111

direct replication 16, 18, 19–20, 29

direct systematic observation 93

direct, systematic observation and recording (DSOR) 47, 63

discrepancy discussion 76

discrimination **97**, 98

discussion section: empirical reports 324–325; literature reviews 344–345

dissent to participate in a study 280, 286

doctoral dissertations 335–336; audiences 325–326; considerations for success 347–348; grey literature 335–336; technical/formatting requirements 326; *see also* empirical reports, writing

Doggett, C. G. **144**

dosage 22, 84, 89

Drabman, R. S. 99, 101, **102**

Drew, C. M. **49**

DSOR (direct, systematic observation and recording) 47, 63

Dueñas, A. D. 109, **196**, *220*, **238**, 253

Dufrene, B. A. **151**

duration, behavior 48; calculating IOA agreement 78, 79–80; estimating with interval-based systems 51–57; examples in applied research **49**; illustration of accuracy for behaviors with non-trivial 58–60, *59*; illustration of accuracy for behaviors with trivial 60–61, *61*; and latency recording to measure time 50–51; long and short 46–47; transforming into percentages 51

dynamic research approaches 8, 86, **86**

dynamic vs. static condition design 86–87

ecological validity 23; considerations relevant to 20–23

Education Resources Information Center (ERIC) 336

Edwards, M. **190**

effect size metrics 171, 213, 218, 258–259

Eiserman, W. D. 5

Elbourn, E. **303**

Eldridge, J. **190**

electronic: data collection applications 48–49, 64–65; searches 336–338, 339, 348

empirical reports, writing 308, 319–325; abstract 319–320; discussion section 324–325; introduction 320; method

section 320–323; results 323–324; supplemental material 321, 322, 323, 325; visualization *316*
endogenous implementers 23, 41, 107
equity of access to research participation 281–282
ERIC (Education Resources Information Center) 336
errors: checking your writing for 326; observer 71, 74, 76
Estrapala, S. **264**
ethical principles and practices in applied research 277–291; anonymity 281; assent 279; authorship status 289; confidentiality 281; conflicts of interest 280–281; consent 279; considerations for IRB applications 283–288; considerations in applied settings 279–282; culturally responsive research 282; dissent 280; equity 281–282; ethical scenarios **287**, **288**; formal approvals to conduct research 282–283; fully informed participants 279; history 278–279; outcomes that benefit participant vs. field 280; positionality statements 281; potential risk 284; publication ethics **288**, 289; reporting results **288**, 289; terminology 278
Ethical Principles of Psychologists and Code of Conduct (APA) 289
Ethics Code for Behavior Analysts (BACB) 289
ethnography 9
evaluating single case research 292–306; critical characteristics 294–296; data sufficiency 296; design appropriateness 294; fidelity 295–296; generality and applicability 296–297; internal validity, rigor and risk of bias 293–294; potential demonstrations of effect 294–295; potentially important characteristics 296–298; questionable research practices 302–303; randomization 297–298; reliability 295; resources, examples of syntheses using 302, **303**; resources for characterizing rigor 298–302
event recording 48; for free operant behaviors and total duration 79–80, *80*; within intervals 79; timed 48, 78–79, *78*; and timed event recording to measure count 48–50
evidence-based practice 6–7; CEC-DR Evidence-Based Practice Paper 298–299; CEC Standards for Evidence-Based Practice 299–300
Exline, E. **147**
experimental conditions, defining 89–90
experimental research: design description in empirical reports **318**, 322; differentiating non-experimental research from 7–8; questions 311–313, **312**
expert nominations of researchers and editors 339
explanatory sequential designs 11
exploratory sequential designs 11
extended community 107
external validity 16, 18, 19; considerations relevant to 20–23; and generalizable knowledge 15–27
Eyler, P. B. 22, 29, 106, 111, **303**
Ezell, H. 16, 21

facilitative testing effects 36, *37*
Fahmie, T. A. 23, 106, 334
Ferron, J. 170, 171, **239**
Fettig, A. 88, **144**
fidelity 295–296; defining experimental conditions 89–90; formative analysis 92–93; measurement of 87–90, 94; reporting 93–94; summative analysis 93; treatment fidelity 90; types 90–92, **91**; *see also* implementation fidelity; procedural fidelity

figure notes 120, 121
figure numbers 120, 121
figures: guidelines for constructing 123–127; in single case design studies 119–127; types 119–123; *see also* graphs
figure titles 120, 121
Fitton, L. **233**
Flood, W. A. **156**
Flowers, E. M. **144**
Foiret, J. **331**
font size and type, graphs 124
Forck, K. L. **264**
formal approvals to conduct research 282–283
formative analysis 92–93; including extra phases to establish non-effect 164–165; and phase change decisions in RIA designs 248–250, *249*, *250*; and phase change decisions in SIW designs 162–165, *162*, *163–164*; and phase change decisions in time-lagged designs 205–209, *206*, *207*, *208*, 214; planning frequency and rules for 172; section in empirical reports 323
formative triangulation 113
forward searching 338
Foster, R. J. **144**
Fournier, C. J. **264**
free-operant events 47, 50, 199; event recording for 79–80; transforming count 50; trial-bases vs. 47
fully informed participants 279
functional communication training (FCT) 20
functionally independent 183–184
functionally similar 183–184
functional relation determination, summative analysis and: RIA designs 250–259; RIA designs, examples 251–253; SIW designs 165–170; SIW designs, examples 173–177; time-lagged designs 209–213; time-lagged designs, examples 215–221
functional relations, defining 32
future research, writing about directions for: empirical reports 325; literature reviews 345

Gast, D. L. 5, 10, 18, 19, 25, 48, 77, 129, 142, 162, 180, 200, 248, 263, 266, 295, 334
Gast, H. A. **231**
Genc-Tosun, D. **197**, 272
generality 97–99; current state of field 111–112; domains of performance relevant to 99–101; and evaluation of single case research 296–297; labeling generalization and maintenance conditions 103–104; measurement of generalized behavior change 101–104, **101–102**, *103*, 188; mechanisms 104–105, *106*; mixed methods research 112–113; terminology 104; terms associated with **97–98**; theory of change and 104, 105
generalization: across contexts 99–100; to non-targeted behaviors 100; to non-targeted individuals 100–101
Gerow, S. **147**
Gersib, J. A. **303**
Gibson, J. **144**
Goad, M. S. **144**
Goetz, E. M. 145, **147**
Golden, A. K. 185, 188, **190**, 313
Goldstein, H. 84, **239**
Google Scholar 336, 338
Gorton, K. 192, *194*

graphic displays 119
graphs 119–127; components 120, *121*; guidelines for constructing 123–127; line 119–123, *121*; principles 119–120; proportions 123–124, *125*; purposes 119; reporting on graphed data 323–324; visual supports 127; when to graph data 127
Gregori, E. **196, 197**
Grey, L. **156**
grey literature 335–336
gross agreement (total agreement) 79–80
Gross, T. J. **234**
group research 10, 16, 29, 36
Gulboy, E. **303**

Haas, L. E. **144**
Hall, R. V. 154
Hall, S. S. **231**
Hammond, J. L. **231**
Hammons, N. C. **190**
Hancock, E. M. **151**
hand searches 338–339
Hanley, G. P. 109, 110, 121
Harbin, E. R. **231, 233**
Harbin, S. G. **144**
Hardy, J. K. 192, 193, 298
Harris, F. R. **147**
Hart, B. **147**
Hartman, D. P. 80, 154
Hawkins, R. O. **144**
Haws, R. A. **231**
Hawthorne effect **33**, 40–41
Hayes, D. **156**
Heal, N. A. 110, 121
Healy, O. **156**
Heider, A. E. 193, 218, 219
Hemmeter, M. L. 19, 88, **147, 190**, 192, 193, **197**
history effects 32–35, *34*
history threats **33**, *34*; RIA designs 251, 253; SIW designs 152, **153**; time-lagged designs 185, **201**, 207
history training 41
Hollahan, M. S. **49**
Holyfield, C. 228, 229, 251
Hopper, J. **144**
Hopton, M. **231**
Horner, R. H. 7, 129, 185, 298
Houchins-Juarez, N. J. 124, **147, 156**
Hua, Y. 209, **239**
Huffman, R. W. **190**
Hull, K. **239**

idiographic research approaches 8
immediacy of change 129–131, *131*
immediate community 107
implementation fidelity 91; vs. procedural fidelity 91–92, **91**, *92*
independent variables 4; coding form *341*; development and measurement 83–95
indirect consumers 107
indirect replication 18
individualization process, describing 317
inductive research approaches 8, 311

information, sharing of 286; ethical scenarios **287**
informed consent 279, 286
Ingersoll, B. **231**, 297
inhibitive testing effects 36, *37*
Institutional Review Boards (IRB) 278; confidentiality 285–286; considerations for applications 283–288; data storage 285; defining methods and procedures 284–285; ethical practice 288, **288**; formal approvals to conduct research 283; informed consent and assent procedures 286; potential risk 284; researcher expertise 287–288; sharing of information 286, **287**; special populations 283
instructive feedback 233
instrumentation threats **33**, 36–37; changing criterion designs 158; RIA designs **242**; SIW designs 152, **153**; time-lagged designs 200, **201**
interaction effect 267, *269*
inter-assessor agreement *see* interobserver agreement (IOA)
intermittent sampling 57
internal validity 31–32, 293; controls in nonconcurrent MB designs 185; establishing via within-study replication 28–42; evaluating 293–294; and mixed-methods research 112
internal validity, threats to 33–41; as categorized by other researchers **33**; changing criterion designs 158; RIA designs 241–242, **242**; RIA designs, control for likely threats 255; RIA designs, examples of visual analysis for control for likely threats 251, 252, 253; SIW designs 152–153, **153–154**; SIW designs, control for likely threats 167–168; SIW designs, examples of visual analysis for control for likely threats 173, 174, 175, 177; time-lagged designs 200, **201**; time-lagged designs, control for likely threats 211; time-lagged designs, examples of visual analysis for control for likely threats 216, 217, 218, 221
interobserver agreement (IOA): analyzing data 37, 74–76, *75*; calculating 76–81; collecting data 74; describing assessment methods 321; discrepancy discussions 76; reliability 295, 321
inter-participant replication 29, *31*, 138, 180; inconsistent 212–213
inter-rater reliability *see* interobserver agreement (IOA)
inter-response time 48
interval-based systems: collecting IOA data 74; comparisons among 57–62, *57*; continued use despite inaccuracies 58, 62; estimating count and duration with 51–57, *53*; flow chart for selecting *63*; illustration of accuracy for behaviors with non-trivial durations 58–60, *59*; illustration of accuracy for behaviors with trivial durations 60–62, *61*, *62*; with interspersed "record" intervals 56–57, **57**; momentary time sampling 55; partial interval recording 52–54; point-by-point agreement 77; Poisson correction 60; reporting use of 62; with rotating observations 56; variations in use of 55–57, **57**; whole interval recording 54
intervention conditions 11, 30, 90; RIA designs 224, 226, 228, 229, 248; SIW designs 138, 145, 146, 148; time-lagged designs 180, 187, 188, 201, 205; writing descriptions of 322
intervention features relevant to external validity 22–23
intervention removal 99, **100**, 101
intervention targets in time-lagged designs 182–185
interviews 109

intra-participant replication 29, *30*, 138, 180
introduction: empirical reports 320; literature reviews 329–330, 342; research proposals 315, **316**
IOA *see* interobserver agreement (IOA)

Jacobs, M. **144**
Johnson, A. H. 302, 303, 311
Johnston, J. M. 10, 16, **17**, 18, 19, 47, 48, 311
Joseph, J. D. 143, 173

Kaiser, A. P. 23, 29, 88, **190**, **303**
Kalra, H. D. **144**
Kang, V. Y. **49**, 185, **196**
Kappa coefficient 80–81
Kazdin, A. E. 10, 16, **17**, 18, 19, 58, 70, 76, 97, 99, 105, 109, 112, 129, 162, 248, 295
Keenan, G. **264**
Kehle, T. J. **231**
Kelley, M. E. **231**
Kennedy, C. H. 10, 84, 109, 110, 125, 127, 128, 129, 131, 311
Kim, H. **196**
Kim, S. 56, 185, **196**
Kirkpatrick, B. A **144**
Kodak, T. **231**
Koegel, L. K. 155
Koutsavalis, M. A. 110
Kurt, O. **197**

Laher, Z. 233
LaLonde, K. B. 238, 253
Lambert, J. M. 4, 38, 48, 86, 103, 105, 111, 113, 146, **147**, **156**, 174, 248, 266, 294, 295, 296, 301
Lane, J. D. 10, 45, 51, 52, 54, 55, 64, 103, 123, 129, *194*
Lane, K. L. 38, 93, 317, 322, 329, 331, 334, 336, 339
latency 48, 51; examples in applied research **49**
Leader, G. **156**
Leatherby, J. G. **49**
Ledford, J. R. 7, 19, 22, 23, 25, 29, 37, 38, 41, 44, 45, 47, 48, **49**, 51, 52, 54, 55, 58, 64, 65, 74, 76, 88, 89, 90, 93, 99, 106, 110, 111, 112, 121, 124, 142, 161, 162, 165, 180, 183, 185, 188, **190**, **197**, 200, 212, **230**, 243, 263, 271, 281, 294, 295, 296, 297, 301, 302, **303**, 311, 323, **331**, 333, 334, 339, 344
LeGray, M. W. **151**
Leitenberg, H. 138, 143, 145
LeJeune, L. M. 48, **303**
Lerman, D. C. **331**
Leslie, J, C. **233**
level 128, *130*
limitations, describing 324–325, 344
line graphs 119–123, *121*; cumulative records 121, *122*; standard celeration charts 121–123, *122*
literature reviews 328–351; approaches and procedures 330–345; considerations for success 347–348; data for 335–336; focusing topic 333–334; for informing proposals and reports vs. stand-alone studies 329–330; keeping records of procedures and decisions 348; locating relevant sources 335–339; number of studies to include 333; organizing findings and writing 342–345; PRISMA guidelines 345–347; process of conducting 332–342; reading and coding relevant reports 339–342; reliability checks 336–337, 339, 348; selecting topic 332–333; types 330–332, **331**; using 345
Lively, P. **147**
Lloyd, B. P. 52, 54, 55, **265**, 324, 344
logic models, cascading 87, *88*, 91, 92
log response ratio (LRR) 171, 173, 176, 258
Lopez, K. **147**
Luiselli, J. K. **156**
Luke, S. **49**
Lynch, A. **231**, 297

MacDonald, J. M. **197**
MacNaul, H. **265**
Madsen, K. **239**
Maggin, D. M. 171, 228, 300, 331, 332
magnitude estimates: AATDs 259; SIW designs 171, 173, 174, 176; time-lagged designs 213, 216, 218
maintenance 97, 99, 104; intervention removal classes relevant to 99, **100**; labeling generalization and maintenance conditions 103–104; MB designs 188; phase 192; or sustained use data 110; withdrawal designs 143
Majeika, C. E. **49**, **151**
markers, graph 126
Martinez, J. R. **303**
Martinez-Torres, K. A. **189**
masked analysis 165, 209
masked analysts 209
Mason, S. **303**
masters' theses 335–336; audiences 325–326; considerations for success 347–348; grey literature 335–336; technical/formatting requirements 326; *see also* empirical reports, writing
materials section, empirical reports 321
maturation effects 35, *35*
maturation threats 35–36, *35*; changing criterion designs 158; RIA designs **242**; SIW designs 152, **153**; time-lagged designs 185, 199, 200, **201**, 211, 213
McDaniel, J. 237, 252
McDougall, D. 155
McDowell, C. **233**
Meadan, H. 109
measurement occasions 30
Mechling, L. **197**, **233**
Mercer, S. **151**
meta-analyses 294, 330, 331–332, **331**; QUOROM Statement 345
methods and procedures, IRB applications 284–285
method section: empirical reports 320–323; literature reviews 342–343; questions to address for components of **318–319**; research proposals 315–319
Milam, M. E. 19, **147**, **156**
Milnes, S. M. **151**
mixed methods research 11–12, 112–113
MoBeGo 149, 175, 176
momentary time sampling (MTS) 53, 55; coding for more than one behavior 65; comparison with WIR and PIR 57–58, *57*; comparison with WIR and PIR, accuracy with non-trivial durations 58–60, *59*; comparison with WIR and PIR, accuracy with trivial durations 60–61, *61*; PLA-CHECK variation 56
Moore, T. **144**

Morales, V. A. **147, 156**
Morgante, J. D. **197**
Morris, K. A. **234**
multielement-alternating treatments design (ME-ATD) 224, **225**, 228–232, 244; applied example 229, 251; behavior sets 235; choosing between SIW design variations and 271; choosing between time-lagged design variations and 272; design adequacy 254, *254*; formative analysis decisions and phase change decisions 248–249, *249*, *250*; functional relation decisions *256*; phase variations 228–229, *230*; procedural steps 232; studies using **230–231**; supplemental analyses of data 258–259
multiple baseline (MB) designs 180, **181**, 188–**190**; across behaviors 183; across behaviors design, applied example 189, 216–218; across contexts 183; across participants 183; across participants design, applied example 188, 215–216; choosing between MP designs and 199; concurrent 185; data collection *181*, 182; difference between MP designs and 180–182; formative analysis across participants 205–206, *206*, 214; formative analysis with covariation 208, *208*, 214; inconsistent inter-participant replication 212–213; nonconcurrent 185–187, *186*; potential demonstrations of effect 294–295; procedural steps 198–199; selecting intervention targets 183–184, **184**; studies using **189–190**; threats to internal validity 200, **201**
multiple probe (MP) designs 180, **181**, 191–**197**; across behaviors 183, 192; across behaviors example (days variation) 193, 218–219; across contexts 183, 192; across participants 183, 185, 192; across participants design (days variation), applied example 196, 219–221; choosing between MB designs and 199; concurrent 185; conditions variation 192, *193*, *195*; data collection 182, *182*, 191, *191*; days variation 192, *194*; difference between MB designs and 180–182; formative analysis across behaviors 206–207, *207*, 214; naming conventions 192, *195*; probe conditions 192; probe sessions 192; procedural steps 198–199; selecting intervention targets 183–184, **184**; studies using **196–197**; threats to internal validity 200, **201**
multiple-treatment interference *see* multitreatment interference
multitreatment designs 138, **140**, 148–152, *150*; applied example 149, 175–176; to establish non-effects 164–165; evidence for functional relation 168–169; procedural steps 149–152; studies using **151**
multitreatment interference 39; RIA designs 229, **230**, 241; SIW designs 153, **153**; time-lagged designs 200, **201**

naïve observers 73, 74, 76, 294, 295
naïve ratings **108**, 110
narrative reviews 330, **331**
natural learning mechanisms (NLM) 105, *106*
Neil, N. **238**, 253
Nichols, H. **303**
Noel, C. R. **234**
Noe, S. **239**
nomothetic research approaches 8
nonconcurrent multiple baseline (MB) designs 186–187, *186*; rigor of 185
non-continuous recording 47–48, 51–52
non-effects, identifying 164–165

non-experimental research, differentiating experimental research from 7–8
non-occurrence agreement 77
non-overlap metrics 171–172
non-reversible behaviors 46, 191, 232, 235, 238; design selection 270, **270**
normative comparisons 109–110
Northup, J. **231**
no-treatment baselines vs. countertherapeutic baselines 139
number 48, *63*; *see also* count

observer: bias 71, 73, 74, *75*, 294; drift 71, 74, *75*; error 71, 74, 76; training 72
occurrence agreement 77
Oddo, J. **151**
Olmi, D. J. **151**
O'Neill, S. J. **233**
Onghena, P. 112, 180, 188, 263, **303**
onset/offset, behavior 48
onset variation of PIR 56
ordinate (y-axis) 120, 121, 124–126, *126*; consistency 127; labels 126; in proportion to x-axis 123; scale breaks 126–127
Osborne, K. 19, 165, 185, **230, 231**
outcome evaluation: RIA designs 255–258; SIW designs 168–170; time-lagged designs 211–213
overlap 131, *131*; estimates 171–172, 213

Pak, N. S. 272, **303**
parallel treatments design (PTD) 266, *267, 268, 269*
parametric questions 312
Paranczak, J. L. 98, 106, 111, **197**
Parikh, N. **147, 156**
partial interval recording (PIR) 52–54, *53*; comparison with WIR and MTS 57–58, *57*; comparison with WIR and MTS, accuracy with non-trivial durations 58–60, *59*; comparison with WIR and MTS, accuracy with -trivial durations 60–61, *61*; majority variation 56; onset variation 56
participant performance, describing 128–132; consistency 131–132; immediacy 129–131, *131*; level 128, *130*; overlap 131, *131*; trend 128–129; variability 129, *130*
participant preference 110–111, 243
participants: attrition 38–39; characteristics 20–22; coding form *340*; empirical reports 320–321; research proposals 317, *318*; selection bias 38; terminology 4
participatory action research 6
Patel, M. R. **151**
peer-review 335
Pennington, R. C. **97, 98, 144**
Pennypacker, H. S. 16, **17**, 18, 19, 47, 48
percentage agreement 37, 77–80
percentages: converting count measures into 50; converting duration measures into 51
Perdices, M. 299
Peredo, T. N. 29, 123, 185
Peters-Sanders, L. **239**, 244
Petursdottir, A. I. 32, **33**
phase change decisions and formative analysis: in RIA designs 248–249, *249, 250*; in SIW designs 162–165, *162, 163–164*; in time-lagged designs 205–209, *206, 207, 208*, 214

phase change lines 120, 121
phases 30, 120; comparing SIW and time-lagged design phases with RIA design 224, *225*; extending 129; including extra phases to establish non-effect 164–165; MB designs 188; ME-ATDs 228–229, *230*; MP designs 192; multitreatment designs 138; RIA designs 224, 228–229, *230*; SIW designs 138; time-lagged designs 180, 188, 192
phenomenology 9
Piazza, C. C. **151**
picture exchange communication system (PECS) 188, 215–216
pilot data collection procedures 72, **73**
PLA-CHECK 56
plagiarism 289, 310
Plavnick, J. B. **196**, *220*, **238**, 253
point-by-point agreement: event recording within intervals *78*, 79; timed event recording 78–79, *78*; trial-based behaviors and interval-based systems 77, *78*
Poisson correction 60
Pollack, M. S. **231**
positionality 281; statements 71, 281
potential risk 284
Powell, L. E. **144**
pre-registrations 346
pre-writing activities 326
PRISMA guidelines 345–347; PRISMA 2020 Statement, Checklist and Flow Diagram 337, *338*, 346; PRISMA extensions 347; PRISMA protocol 346–347
probe conditions 192
probe sessions 192
procedural fidelity 90; formative analysis 92–93; vs. implementation fidelity 91–92, **91**, *92*; reporting 93–94; section in empirical reports **319**, 322, 324; summative analysis 93; threats 38
procedural infidelity **33**, 38, 93; RIA designs 241, **242**; SIW designs 152, **153**; time-lagged designs 200, **201**
procedures: defining methods and procedures for IRB applications 284–285; section in empirical reports **318**, 322
procedure vs. process questions 8–9, 84–86; examples **86**
PsycINFO 336
publication ethics **288**, 289
published literature 335
Purrazzella, K **197**
Pustejovsky, J. E. 19, 171, 172, 173, 176, 183, 218, 258, **331**, 333

QualiCase (Quality Enhancement for Single Case Proposals) 302
qualitative case study 9
qualitative research 9
quality indicators 293; CEC-DR Evidence-Based Practice Paper 298–299; CEC Standards for Evidence-Based Practice 299–300
quantification of tic marks (axis labels) 120, 121, 126
questionable research practices 302–303
questionnaires 109
questions for scientist-practitioners 5–6
questions, research *see* research questions
Quinn, E. D. 4, 23, 90, **190**

QUOROM Statement (Quality of Reporting of Meta-analyses) 345

Radley, K. C. 10, 126, 127, **144**, 170, 186
Rakap, S. **303**
Ramirez, E. S. **189**
randomization 297–298
rapid iterative alternation (RIA) 223–246; adapted alternating treatments design 224, 226, 232–237, 244; assessing social validity using simultaneous treatment procedures 224, 243–244; choosing between AATD and repeated acquisition designs 273; choosing between ME-ATD designs and SIW design variations 271; choosing between ME-ATD designs and time-lagged design variations 272; comparison of condition ordering logic with time-lagged and SIW designs 224, *225*; design names associated with 226–227; features of studies using 224–*225*; multielement-alternating treatments design 224, 228–232, 244; names of designs associated with **225**; plus SIW combinations 267, *269*; plus time-lagged combinations 266, *267*, *268*, *269*; repeated acquisition design 224, 238–241, 244; strengths and benefits 227–228; threats to internal validity 241–242, **242**; weaknesses and drawbacks 228; when to use designs with 226–228
rapid iterative alternation (RIA), analyzing data from studies using 247–261; describing visual analysis 260; formative analysis and phase change decisions 248–249, *249*, *250*; summative analysis and functional relation determination 250–259; supplemental analyses 258–260
rapid reviews 330, **331**
rates, converting count measures into 50
rating frameworks: Comparative Single Case Experimental Design Rating System (CSCEDARS) 301; Single Case Analysis and Review Framework (SCARF) v 3.1 302
Rayyan 332
recording procedures, selecting 47–48, **49**
REDCap 332, 339
registered reports 346
regression to the mean **33**, 39–40, 129, **242**
Reichow, B. **49**, **234**, 301, **303**
reliability 71, 295; checks 336–337, 339, 348; data collection 71–76; documenting reliability of independent and control variables 89; section in empirical reports **318**, 321; of visual analysis 170
repeated acquisition designs 224, **225**, 238–241, *240*, 244; applied example 238, 253; choosing between AATD and 273; functional relation decisions *258*; studies using **238–239**; supplemental analyses of data 259–260
replication 16–18; across-literature 18; across-study 18; construct validity 23–25; direct 16, 18, 19–20, 29; ecological validity 23; failures 20, 29; indirect 18; inter-participant 29, *31*, 138, 180, 212–213; intra-participant 29, *30*, 138, 180; within-literature 18; making sense of 310; parsing critical from non-critical features via across-study 18–19; recommendations for across-study 25–26; within-study 18, 29–31; within-study replication, establishing internal validity via 28–42; systematic 18, 19, 310, 312; tactics for maximizing impact of across-study 19–20; types **17**
report agreement 76

reporting guideline in behavioral interventions, single case 300–301
report writing *see* empirical reports, writing
reproduction 16
research approaches 3–14; applied research 4–6; assumptions about generalizability 8; attributions of causality 7–8; characterizing designs 7–12; descriptive and correlational research 9; evidence-based practice 6–7; between-groups research 10; mixed methods 11–12; process vs. procedure questions 8–9; qualitative research 9; single case research 10–11; types 9–12
researcher expertise 287–288
research proposals 308, 314–319; introduction 315, **316**; method section 315–319
research questions: classifying and stating 311–314; classifying questions from single case literature 313–314; comparison questions 312; component analysis 313; demonstration questions 311–312; descriptive questions **312**, 313–314; design selection and appropriate 270, **270**; experimental questions 311–313, **312**; finding topics 309; moving from research topics to 309–310; parametric questions 312; process vs. procedure 8–9, 84–86, **86**; questions to consider when choosing **314**; RIA 250–251; writing 308–314
research topics: finding 309; moving to questions from 309–310
response generalization **98**, 100, 104
response-guided decision-making 162–163, *162*
results: describing visual analysis 172, 214, 260; empirical reports 323–324; ethical procedures for reporting **288**, 289; literature reviews 343–344
reversal design 140, **140**, 143–145; applied example 146, 174; difference between withdrawal design and 145, *146*; studies using **147**
reversible behaviors 46, 191, 235; design selection 270, **270**
review protocols 346–347
Richard, J. **144**
Riden, B. S. **331**
rigor: assessment prior to assessment of outcomes 293; critical elements in establishing 294–296; as a measure of internal validity 293–294; reasons to evaluate 293; resources for characterizing 298–302; syntheses using tools to assess 302, **303**
Rila, A. **264**
risk of bias 294; tools 299, 301
Risk of Bias in N-of-1 Trials (RoBiNT) Scale 299
risk, potential 284
Rivas, K. M. **151**
Robbins, A. **190**
RoBiNT (Risk of Bias in N-of-1 Trials) Scale 299
Rogers, L **197**
Ruiz, F. J. **189**

Sainato, D. M. **190**
Salazar, D. M. **189**
Sallese, M. R. **189**, **190**, 209, **264**
sampling bias 38
Samudre, M. D. **264**, 303
Sandall, S. **144**
Sartini, E. C. **264**
scale breaks 126–127

SCARF (Single Case Analysis and Review Framework) v 3.1 302
Schilling, D. **144**
Schimel, J. 315, *316*, 326
Schlosser, R. W. 10, 234, 241, 301
Schneider, N. **239**
Schulz, T. **265**
Schwartz, I. S. 103, 107, 109, 112, **144**
science, integration into educational and clinical practice 4–6
scientific writing 308; resources 326; *see also* empirical reports, writing; research proposals, writing
scientist-practitioners, questions for 5–6
scoping reviews 330, **331**
SCRIBE (Single Case Reporting Guideline in Behavioral Interventions) 300–301
search terms 336, 337, 343
secondary observers 295
selection bias 38
selection of designs 270–273, **270**; choosing among time-lagged variations 272; choosing between AATD and repeated acquisition designs 273; choosing between ME-ATD designs and SIW design variations 271; choosing between ME-ATD designs and time-lagged design variations 272
selection threats **153**, **201**
self-reports 93
sequential confounding (sequence effects) 39
sequential introduction and withdrawal (SIW) designs 138–160; A-B-A-B design 138, *139*, 140–141, 142–148; baseline, business-as-usual and treatment conditions 139–140; changing criterion designs 154–158; choosing between ME-ATD designs and 271; comparison of condition ordering logic with time-lagged and RIA designs 224, *225*; differences among designs **140**; features 138–141; multitreatment design 138, 148–152; plus RIA combinations 267, *269*; plus SIW combinations 266; plus time-lagged combinations 266; potential demonstrations of effect 140–141, *141*; reversal design 140, 143–145, 146, *146*, **147**; strengths and benefits 142; threats to internal validity 152–154; weaknesses and drawbacks 142; when to use 141
sequential introduction and withdrawal (SIW) designs, analyzing data from studies using 161–178; describing visual analysis 172–177; formative analysis and phase change decisions 162–165; summative analysis and functional relation determination 165–170; supplemental analyses 171–172
setting section, empirical reports 321
Seven, Y. **239**
Severini, K. E. 19, 164–165, 185, **231**, 312
Shadish, W. R. 16, 20, 24, 32, **33**, 38, 70, 171, 263
Shepley, C. 10, 45, **49**, 344
Shepley, S. B. **264**
Sherman, A. **239**
Sidman, M. 10, 11, 16, **17**, 18, 19, 20, 29, 104, 154
Simmons, C. A. **144**, 165
simultaneous treatments 224, **225**, **242**; applied example 243–244; assessing social validity using 243
Single Case Analysis and Review Framework (SCARF) v 3.1 302

Single Case Reporting Guideline in Behavioral Interventions (SCRIBE) 300–301
single case research approach 10–11
site-specific approvals 282
Skinner, B.F. 84, 112, 121, 242
Skinner, C. H. **144**, 248
Slocum, T. 170, 185, 210, 303
Smeets, R. J. **303**
Smith, K. A. 263
Snyder, E. D. **197**
social desirability bias 109
social validity 97, 105–107, **108**; difference between having and having evidence of 107–108; and generality, current state of field 111–112; measurement strategies and recommendations 108–111; mixed methods research 112–113; presentation of data 324; section in empirical reports **319**, 323; stakeholders 107–108; terms associated with **97–98**
Soto, X. **239**
special populations 283
Spencer, E. J. **239**
Spriggs, A. D. 4, **264**
stability 129, *130*
Stal, R. A. **303**
stand-alone studies, literature reviews for 329–330
standard celebration charts 121–123, *122*
standards: CEC-DR Next Generation Guidelines 301–302; CEC Standards for Evidence-Based Practice 299–300; CONSORT (CONsolidated Standards Of Reporting Trials) 300; Single Case Analysis and Review Framework (SCARF) v 3.1 300; WWC procedures and standards handbook 300
Stankiewicz, K. **147**, **156**
static research approaches 8, 86, **86**
static vs. dynamic condition design 86–87
status variables 21
Staubitz, J. E. 86, **231**
Staubitz, J. L. 86, **231**
Stay-Play-Talk 19, 84, 164–165, 183–185, **184**; coding forms 339–341, *340*, *341*, *342*, *343*; example research questions **312**
Steel, J. **303**
Steinhauser, H. M. 140, **144**
Stenhoff, D. **144**
Sterling, H. **151**
stimulus generalization **98**, 99, 104
summative analysis 162, 165; procedural fidelity 93; section in empirical reports 323
summative analysis and functional relation determination: RIA designs 250–259; RIA designs, examples 251–253; SIW designs 165–170; SIW designs, examples 173–177; time-lagged designs 209–213; time-lagged designs, examples 215–221
Su, P. L. **265**
supplemental materials, empirical reports 321, 322, 323, 325
surveys 109
Sutherland, K. S. **49**, 90
Sweeney, E. M. **147**, **156**, 266
Swensson, R. **147**
systematic: replication 18, 19, 310, 312; reviews 330, 331, **331**, 332

Tabbah, R. **239**
tables 119, 128, 344
tally-by-interval recording 49
target behaviors 44; characterizing 46–47; choosing and defining 44–45
Tate, R. L. 73, 295, 299, 300
Taylor, T. **231**
technical/formatting requirements 326
testing effects 36, *37*; controlling in nonconcurrent MB designs for 185
testing threats **33**, 36, *37*; choosing between MP and MB designs 199; RIA designs **242**; SIW designs **153**; time-lagged designs 185, 200, **201**, 210
Theodore, L. A. **231**
theory of change: generality and 104, 105; model 84, *85*; planning study conditions using 83–84
Thompson, J. L. **189**, **264**
tic marks 120, 124–126; quantification of 120, 121, 126
tiers 182, *182*, 205–206, 209, 210–211
time: duration and latency recording to measure 50–51; examples in applied research of measurement of **49**; measurement of 48, *63*; per occurrence 51; total 51; *see also* duration, behavior; latency
timed event recording 48, 78–79, *78*; to measure count 48–50
time-lagged designs 179–203; choosing among 272; choosing between ME-ATD designs and 272; comparison of condition ordering logic with SIW and RIA designs 224, *225*; concurrence variations 185–187; features 180–182; intervention targets 182–185; plus RIA combinations 266, *267*, *268*, *269*; plus SIW combinations 266; plus time-lagged combinations 263; procedural steps 198–199; strengths and benefits 187; threats to internal validity 200, **201**; weaknesses and drawbacks 187; when to use 187; *see also* multiple baseline (MB) designs; multiple probe (MP) designs
time-lagged designs, analyzing data from studies using 204–222; describing visual analysis 213–221; formative analysis and phase change decisions 205–209; summative analysis and functional relation determination 209–214; supplemental analyses 213
Tingstrom, D. H. **144**
Togher, L. **303**
Tönsing, K. M. 243
Torelli, J. N. 233, **234**, 244, **265**
Toste, J. R. 9, 10
total agreement (gross agreement) 79–80
total duration recording *78*, 79–80
total time recording 51
training: for human subject researchers 283; observers 72
treatment fidelity 90
trend 128–129, *130*; counterapeutic 129; direction 128–129; magnitude 129; stability 129
trial-based behaviors 47; collecting IOA data 74; vs. free-operant behaviors 47; point-by-point agreement 77, *78*
triangulation 112, 113
Trump, C. **303**
Tuck, K. N. 271; *see also* Zimmerman, K. N.

umbrella reviews 330, **331**
unaffiliated analysts 209

validity 70; construct 23–25, **24**, 70; ecological 23; ensuring validity and reliability of data collection 71–76; *see also* external validity; internal validity; internal validity, threats to; social validity
Van Camp, A. M. 149, 175
Vannest, K. J. **190**, 209
variability 39–40, *40*, 129, *130*
video recording 48–49, 64
Viotto, J. A. **303**
visual analysis 119, 162; components for describing participant performance 128–132; describing RIA 251–253, 260; describing SIW 172–177; describing time-lagged 213–221; descriptions in results section of empirical reports 323; and functional relations decisions 170; masked 209; protocols 170, 212; reliability 170
visual supports, graphs 127
Vorndran, C. M. **331**
vulnerable populations 283

Wade, T. **190**
Wang, J. **196**
Ward, S. E. **233**
Waters, C. L. **303**
Wawrzonek, A. **238**, 253
Wehby, J. H. **49**, **151**, 175, **265**
Werfel, K. L. **233**
Werts, M. G. 233
Whalon, K. J. **238**
What Works Clearinghouse (WWC) 76, 138, 166, 171, 280, 294, 296, 344; procedures and standards handbook 301
Wheatley, T. L. 156, 176
White, E. N. 188, 215
whole interval recording (WIR) 53, 54; comparison with MTS and PIR 57–58, *57*; comparison with PIR and MTS, accuracy with non-trivial durations 58–60, *59*; comparison with PIR and MTS, accuracy with trivial durations 60–61, *61*
Wicker, M. **147**
Wilder, D. A. **156**
Winchester, C. **151**, *162*, 163

Windsor, S. A. 22, 212, 303, **303**
withdrawal (A-B-A-B) design 138, *139*, 140–141, **140**, 142–148; applied example 143, 173; combination designs 266, 267; design selection 270, 271, 272; formative analysis and phase change decisions 163–164, *163–164*; procedural steps 145–148; reversal variation 140, **140**, 143–145, 146, *146*, **147**, 174; studies using **144**; summative analysis and functional relation determination 168–169, 170; visual analysis protocols 170
within-case SMD (WC-SMD) 171
within-literature replications **17**, 18
within-study replication 18, 29–31; establishing internal validity via 28–42
Wolery, M. 16, 18, 19, 21, 37, 38, 47, 48, 70, 73, 74, 88, 89, 90, 93, 172, **197**, 200, 233, **234**, 266, 294, 295, 297, 301, 333
Wolfe, K. 162, 166, 170, 171, 179, 212
Wolf, M. M. 97, **147**, 180
Wright, S. **144**
writing 307–327; considerations for success 325–326; empirical reports *316*, 319–325; literature reviews 342–345; research proposals 314–319; research questions 308–314; scientific writing 308
Wunderlich, K. **303**

x-axis (abscissa) 120, 121, 124–126, *126*; blocking data 127; depicting time 123, *124*; labels 126; scale breaks 126–127; y-axis in proportion to 123

y-axis (ordinate) 120, 121, 124–126, *126*; consistency 127; labels 126; in proportion to x-axis 123; scale breaks 126–127
Yoder, P. J. 46, 47, 48, 49, 57, 58, 60, 63, 74, 80, **97**
Yuan, C. **239**
Yucesoy-Ozkan, S. **303**

Zelaya, M. 29
Zhu, J. **239**
Zimmerman, K. N. 44, 46, **49**, 103, 171, 185, **231**, 298; *see also* Tuck, K. N.
Ziolkowski, R. **239**